Dante's *Vita nova*

THE WILLIAM AND KATHERINE DEVERS SERIES
IN DANTE AND MEDIEVAL ITALIAN LITERATURE

Zygmunt G. Barański, Theodore J. Cachey, Jr., and Christian Moevs, editors

RECENT TITLES

DANTE'S
VITA NOVA

A Collaborative Reading

Edited by
ZYGMUNT G. BARAŃSKI
and
HEATHER WEBB

University of Notre Dame Press
Notre Dame, Indiana

Published by the University of Notre Dame Press
Notre Dame, Indiana 46556
undpress.nd.edu

Published in the United States of America

Library of Congress Control Number: 2023942033

ISBN: 978-0-268-20739-7 (Hardback)
ISBN: 978-0-268-20740-3 (Paperback)
ISBN: 978-0-268-20743-4 (WebPDF)
ISBN: 978-0-268-20738-0 (Epub)

ABOUT THE WILLIAM AND KATHERINE DEVERS SERIES IN DANTE AND MEDIEVAL ITALIAN LITERATURE

The William and Katherine Devers Program in Dante Studies at the University of Notre Dame supports rare book acquisitions in the university's John A. Zahm Dante collections, funds a visiting professorship in Dante studies, and supports electronic and print publication of scholarly research in the field. In collaboration with the Medieval Institute at the university, the Devers program initiated a series dedicated to the publication of the most significant current scholarship in the field of Dante studies. In 2011 the scope of the series was expanded to encompass thirteenth- and fourteenth-century Italian literature.

In keeping with the spirit that inspired the creation of the Devers program, the series takes Dante and medieval Italian literature as focal points that draw together the many disciplines and lines of inquiry that constitute a cultural tradition without fixed boundaries. Accordingly, the series hopes to illuminate this cultural tradition within contemporary critical debates in the humanities by reflecting both the highest quality of scholarly achievement and the greatest diversity of critical perspectives.

The series publishes works from a wide variety of disciplinary viewpoints and in diverse scholarly genres, including critical studies, commentaries, editions, reception studies, translations, and conference proceedings of exceptional importance. The series enjoys the support of an international advisory board composed of distinguished scholars and is published regularly by the University of Notre Dame Press. The Dolphin and Anchor device that appears on publications of the Devers series was used by the great humanist, grammarian, editor, and typographer Aldus Manutius (1449–1515), in whose 1502 edition of Dante (second issue) and all subsequent editions it appeared. The device illustrates the ancient proverb Festina lente, "Hurry up slowly."

Zygmunt G. Barański, Theodore J. Cachey, Jr.,
and Christian Moevs, editors

DANTE

AL DVS

ADVISORY BOARD

CONTENTS

PREFACE

Zygmunt G. Barański and Heather Webb

This volume arises from many years of sustained conversation and dialogue between researchers at all points of their careers, across the United Kingdom and beyond. The productive potential of such collaboration had already become clear from the experience of the "Vertical Readings in Dante's *Comedy*," hosted in Cambridge from 2012 to 2016 and organized by George Corbett and Heather Webb. Over four years of lectures, recorded and archived online and now collected in three volumes, the "Vertical Readings" proposed a new model of Dante commentary and sparked vigorous and spirited debate. It was, in fact, at the last session of the series that we pondered how to continue to harness this energy as a group. In conversation with colleagues, including Kenneth Clarke, Tristan Kay, and Catherine Keen, we felt that the next text that demanded a new form of commentary was the *Vita nova*.[1]

The *Vita nova*, composed in Florence in the early to mid-1290s, has often been assessed and interpreted within relatively narrow parameters. As Dante's "youthful" work, it has been read as the quintessential stilnovist text, a work that focuses exclusively on love and love poetry from within a closed, elite circle. The poet's closing statements on his aspirations to speak of Beatrice in a new way have further served to encourage readers to consider the *prosimetrum* as a preamble to the *Commedia*.[2] Just as the "Vertical Readings" proposed looking at the *Commedia* from a different perspective—commenting three same-numbered cantos together with an open mind to what might emerge—we decided to read the *Vita nova* from a novel viewpoint, to see if we might not find fresh ways to do better justice to the multifaceted complexities of the *libello*, the "little book."

We wondered what might emerge if we systematically decoupled the *Vita nova* from the *Commedia* and read it in its own context, with careful attention to its situatedness in the landscape of the Florence of Dante's youth. We wondered, further, what might emerge from a slow reading, isolating small fragments of the text and exploring the contours of those textual moments in depth for what they might reveal as regards Dante's relationships with other poets, but also his social environment, his evolving vision of the scope of his poetry, and the development of his modes of exegesis, to give just a few examples. What if, we asked, we were to read the *Vita nova* the way that we are used to reading the *Commedia* in the great *lectura Dantis* tradition—just a small bit of the text at a time? So many sections of the *Vita nova* are considered to be merely placeholders. Some portions of the text that have at times been designated as chapters are only a few lines long. Could even those fragments prove productive under the lens of close scrutiny? The readers of this volume will come to their own conclusions, but we and our collaborators have found an immense richness in the experience of detailed, small-scale, and careful engagement with the *Vita nova*.

The project could never have come into existence without the generosity, trust, and shared enthusiasm of our collaborators. We settled on the idea of an itinerant series of seminars, in which each research center would take responsibility for hosting a meeting on a "section" of the *Vita nova*, inviting speakers, and putting forward an approach or approaches to their portion of the text. The research centers involved were chosen on the principle that most of us could travel there and back by train for a day. In addition to this, our trusted partners at Notre Dame London and Notre Dame Rome hosted the first and last sessions of the series, with Notre Dame Indiana connected by video for each session. We committed to attending all of the seminars where possible, so that our conversation could properly develop over the course of our readings.

The project, which spanned two years, formally began with a meeting at the London Global Gateway of the University of Notre Dame. The meeting served to frame our logistical and methodological approach to examining Dante's *Vita nova*. After this first encounter, we began our roving reading, gathering first at the University of Leeds before moving on to University College London and the Universities of Oxford, Bristol, Reading, Cambridge, and Warwick, and finally concluding our journey at the University of Notre Dame's Global Gateway in Rome. Even in the context of these peripatetic events, there was a foretaste of the virtual modes to come. Throughout the events, the majority of which were held in the United Kingdom, colleagues at Notre Dame and at the Rome Global Gateway, as well as other remote participants, joined us via video link, participating virtually in every meeting across great distances and time differences. The final event in Rome was not only an opportunity to bridge some of those distances; it was also a physical manifestation of our intent, as a group, to bring a collaboration between institutions in the anglophone world more explicitly into conversation with Italian scholars and scholarship. As will be clear from our bibliography, lively dialogue and deep engagement with the work of Italian colleagues was at the heart of our project from the very beginning. Despite being concentrated in anglophone countries, the project was never intended to be insular. Our commitment to international dialogue is reflected in this volume, which includes contributors from different parts of Europe, as well as from the United Kingdom and the United States.

Each center maintained its own identity throughout the project, and this was consolidated during the editorial process as each center collected and edited its contributions prior to the overall editing of the volume. The organization of the volume closely reflects the nature of the original meetings, with an overview prefacing the analyses of the individual chapters examined by a particular institution. In each case, those who authored the overviews coordinated and first edited the contributions making up their sections. The editors and section curators are Claire E. Honess, Catherine Keen, Manuele Gragnolati, Elena Lombardi, Francesca Southerden, Tristan Kay, Paola Nasti, Heather Webb, Simon Gilson, and Theodore J. Cachey Jr. Special thanks are due to David Bowe, who took on the task of coordinating the meetings, taking responsibility for the online materials relating to the meetings, and shouldering much of the work of eliciting contributions for the volume. His enthusiasm and energy fueled many stages of this project. All of our contributors were collaborators in the project, attending, participating, and often presenting at the original events. We are proud of the number of early career researchers who figure as contributors in the pages that follow, including PhD students and postdoctoral researchers.

In order to begin, it was necessary to wade into the fraught question of how to divide the text of the *Vita nova*. Our decision to follow the traditional organization into forty-two chapters canonized by Michele Barbi, which has recently been reaffirmed by Donato Pirovano in his excellent annotated edition, should not be taken as an expression of scholarly support for this particular division of the text over other schematizations (throughout citations are given both to Barbi's and Gorni's editions; at the same time, since we had based ourselves on Barbi's numbering, it seemed appropriate to use his 1932 edition as our textual point of reference).[3] Our choice was entirely pragmatic: we wanted to include as many contributors as possible in the project. And pragmatism, thanks to Claire Honess's clarity of vision and practical sensibilities, determined how chapters were organized into broader sections and assigned to different institutions. Thus we did not prioritize any existing ideas regarding the narrative, formal, and ideological structure of the *libello*. Each research center was asked only to consider how many chapters it could feasibly address, drawing not just on its own members but also on colleagues from other universities both in the United Kingdom and beyond, and on scholars from other disciplines. Initially, the aim was to assign one chapter per colleague; however, in a few instances, colleagues developed arguments that, of necessity, spanned two chapters. Once the order in which institutions would present had been confirmed, chapters were then distributed (it proved remarkably easy to share the chapters among the various centers). Thus we began with the University of Leeds "reading" chapters I–IV (1–2.5 in Guglielmo Gorni's edition). In general, it was felt that the "arbitrary" nature in which blocks of chapters were assigned allowed for considerable exegetical freedom and flexibility since contributors did not feel inhibited by existing critical orthodoxies. Our impression is that this approach has helped to highlight the *Vita nova*'s remarkably rich and complex "polysemy," as well as its structural fluidity.

The overviews for each section briefly summarize the central narrative events of their multichapter segment of the *Vita nova*. These introductory essays also seek to delineate the existing critical panorama, or the principal points of debate, on that portion of the text. The overviews thus free the short individual chapter essays of the burden of extensive bibliographical review so that they may pursue fresh interpretive directions.

Although each reading presents the personal views of its author, threads of communal discussions at the seminars and in other settings may also be discerned, as might be expected from a project as commitedly collaborative as this one. At the same time, we should like to stress that, despite the emphasis on collaboration, there has been no attempt to "homogenize" contributions either within a particular research center or across the volume. Thus a plurality of critical methodologies and exegetical perspectives has been employed, although one might note that many contributors have merged historicist with hermeneutic approaches. Such plurality means that readers can expect competing opinions to be aired and defended across the volume. The decision to encourage such multiplicities of readings has led to interesting results: for instance, there would seem to be rather more "pivotal" moments in the text than scholarship has hitherto acknowledged. Collaboration is for naught if it cannot accommodate and respect differing possibilities.

ACKNOWLEDGMENTS

Our project began when we were regularly able to meet in person; it was then brought to completion as we moved in and out of lockdown restrictions. Working in pandemic conditions has created numerous challenges, although people were able to support each other, as we have become used to doing, thanks to remote forms of communication. We are thus extremely grateful for the continuing commitment and enthusiasm of all our collaborators. The volume offers lasting testimony to their hard work, scholarly seriousness, and exemplary collegiality.

Our collaboration would not have been possible without the support and work of Vittorio Montemaggi (Kings College London), who organized the opening meeting at the University of Notre Dame Global Gateway in London; of Zyg Barański, Ted Cachey, and David Lummus, who arranged the final meeting at the Rome Global Gateway, which was funded by the Center for Italian Studies and the William and Katherine Devers Program in Dante Studies at the University of Notre Dame; and, of course, of the institutional leads (in chronological order of the events in the series): Claire Honess and Matthew Treherne at the University of Leeds; Catherine Keen at University College London; Manuele Gragnolati (Sorbonne), Elena Lombardi, and Francesca Southerden at the University of Oxford; Tristan Kay at the University of Bristol; Paola Nasti (Northwestern) at the University of Reading; Heather Webb at the University of Cambridge; and Simon Gilson (Oxford) at the University of Warwick. We are grateful for funding and support from all the host institutions.

Vita nova I–IV [1–2.5]

Things Never Said about Any Woman

CLAIRE E. HONESS

"Io spero di dicer di lei quello che mai non fue detto d'alcuna" (XLII.3 [31.3]) [I hope to say things about her that have never been said about any woman]. These words from the final chapter of Dante's *Vita nova*, often read proleptically (with, perhaps, just a touch of wish fulfillment) as a reference to the *Commedia*, might also stand as a sort of summative gloss on the *prosimetrum* as a whole, and, in particular, its first four chapters. Just as the end of the *Paradiso* anticipates the retelling of the protagonist's whole journey up to this climactic moment (*Par.* 31.43–45), so at the end of the *Vita nova* Dante's vision of Beatrice in heaven (which, like the pilgrim's final moment of communion with God in the *Commedia*, remains undescribed) is both the climax of and the pretext for the book that it concludes. Indeed, as the following chapters of the present volume will show, the *Vita nova* is, from its very beginning, aware of, and keen to highlight to its readers, its startling novelty in both form and content—a poetic novelty that is rooted in the nature of the work's subject, Beatrice, who is "uno miracolo" (XXIX.3 [19.6]) [a miracle]. Whatever Dante may have intended by his concluding promise to write about Beatrice in ever more innovative ways, it is clear that this resolution has already been fulfilled, at least in part, by the *Vita nova* itself, which deliberately sets out to shed new light on the writing of love poetry and to ask important moral and theological questions about the love that inspires it.

With this conclusion in mind, we should beware of taking at face value the apparently specific, subjective statement of the work's literary objectives with which the *Vita nova* opens:

In quella parte del libro de la mia memoria dinnanzi a la quale poco si potrebbe leggere, si trova una rubrica la quale dice: *Incipit vita nova*. Sotto la quale rubrica io trovo scritte le parole le quali è mio intendimento d'assemplare in questo libello; e se non tutte, almeno la loro sentenzia. (1 [1.1])

[In the book of my memory—the part of it before which not much is legible—there is the heading *Incipit vita nova*. Under this heading I find the words which I intend to copy down in this little book; if not all of them, at least their essential meaning.]

Here, the reference to the author's memory as the source of the text which is to follow—indeed, as Brian Richardson will demonstrate in detail in his contribution to this volume, as the source *text* from which the words contained in the *Vita nova* are copied—immediately identifies the story told in the *libello* as a personal one. Memories cannot be read, after all, by a "third party," but only by the individual to whom they belong; and, even when she or he chooses to share them with others, it is always the memories' owner who retains overall "editorial control" of what is, or is not, shared (just as Dante admits that he does not intend to copy down *all* the words that he finds in the "book" of his memory). The text is presented, then, as a personal story, shared by an author-protagonist who really experienced the events and emotions he describes: an autobiographical or even "confessional" text.[1] And yet the events that the author-protagonist rereads in the book of his memory and copies down in the *libello* do not concern him alone but have a significance that extends far beyond the events of his own life: indeed, it is precisely *because* the events described have this broader significance—because they have some deeper meaning or *sentenzia*—that they are considered to be worthy of sharing.

As we shall see, the deeper meaning that Dante extracts from the memories that he reads, edits, and writes down is multifaceted and wide-ranging, so that any attempt to pin down what the *libello* is "about" by limiting it to

just one area of significance seems doomed to fail: it is enough to think of
Barbara Reynolds's description of the *Vita nova* as "a treatise written by a
poet, for poets, on the art of poetry," a definition that unsatisfactorily re-
duces the poetic, religious, personal, and psychological depth of this work to
the stuff of a mere academic essay.[2] In contrast, as its first four chapters al-
ready clearly signal, the *Vita nova* is a text that is both personal and universal:
it is a human story that also sheds light on the broader story of God's rela-
tionship with humankind; it is a collection of poems that also offers a the-
oretical exposition of the composition and analysis of poetry; it is an account
of an entirely exceptional experience of love, but also an attempt to under-
stand the physical and psychological impact of love on human beings more
generally; and it is a work that carefully situates itself within a literary tra-
dition while simultaneously breaking new ground in its form, language, and
content.

Adding to these difficulties of definition and focus, moreover, it is
almost axiomatic to describe the *Vita nova* as a work almost entirely devoid of
context, cut off from time and place, unrealistic, oneiric, ethereal—this de-
spite the fact that, as we have seen, the focus on memory in the text's very
first words necessarily anchors it in the life of a particular individual. The
reader of the *Vita nova* is "insulated from spatial and historical specificity"
that would enable her to connect the text to a particular time and place,[3]
and the *libello* is seen as inward-looking, "closed" in terms of both its subject
matter and its audience.[4] Concerned only with the love story of its poet-
protagonist and with the poetry that the love story inspires, it is seen as being
characterized by an "assenza di esperienze extrapoetiche o sociali" [absence
of nonpoetic or social experiences],[5] as lacking any extraneous detail, char-
acter description, or scene setting. As evidence of the abstract and socially de-
tached nature of the text, commentators often cite the absence of proper
names in the text. The poet-protagonist remains unnamed, as do the women
to whom he addresses some of his compositions (the ladies who share his "in-
telletto d'amore," XIX.4 [10.15] [understanding of love]) and the other ver-
nacular poets with whom he engages; in chapter III, for example, these are re-
ferred to en masse as "li fedeli d'Amore" (III.9 [1.10]) [Love's faithful], while
the poet's primary interlocutor, Cavalcanti, is indicated as "primo de li miei
amici" (III.14 [2.1]) [my best friend].[6] Even in the case of the poet's beloved,
it is, in fact, entirely unclear whether the name, Beatrice, by which she is

known "da molti . . . li quali non sapeano che si chiamare" (II.1 [1.2]) [by
many without even knowing that was her name] is, in fact, intended to be
read as a proper name at all—let alone as a reference to the specific historical
Beatrice Portinari—or merely as a *senhal*, indicating her role, in the text and
in the author's life, as a bearer of blessing. Even the city in which the action of
the text takes place—hard as it is *not* to imagine it as late thirteenth-century
Florence—is never actually named but is only referred to as "la cittade"
[the city] or "la sopradetta cittade" [the aforementioned city],[7] giving the text
a universal quality that means the *libello* is not firmly "anchored" in time or
space. And yet, despite the abstraction achieved by the avoidance of proper
names, the *Vita nova* does seem to have been conceived as a broadly social
text, on a number of levels, which are already apparent in the work's first four
chapters, and which will be examined in more detail in the contributions
that follow.

In the first place, the fact that the *Vita nova* is written in the vernacu-
lar clearly helps to situate it in place and time (since variations in vernacular
languages, as the *De vulgari eloquentia* explains,[8] are both geographical and
diachronic). The city may not be named, in other words, but the language in
which it is described unavoidably places it in Tuscany, and probably even lo-
cates it precisely in Florence, since "omnia vulgaria in sese variantur, ut puta
in Tuscia Senenses et Aretini . . ., nec non in eadem civitate aliqualem varia-
tionem perpendimus" (*Dve* 1.10.7) [all these vernaculars also vary in them-
selves, so that the Tuscan of Siena is different from that of Arezzo . . ., and,
moreover, we can detect some variation even within a single city]. As will be
the case in the encounter with Farinata in hell, Dante's language gives him
away,[9] probably from the *libello*'s very first sentences; his reticence over the
specificity of the book's setting is only apparent. And the decision to write in
the vernacular also suggests that Dante has in mind a particular audience (or,
as we shall see, a particular series of audiences): one specifically associated
with the central Italian city-states, where Latin was associated primarily with
bureaucratic and legal writing, and where the use of the vernacular was not a
mere frivolous literary game, as it might have been in the courts of Provence
or Sicily, but a necessity, a marker not only of identity but also of active en-
gagement with the life of the city.[10] Indeed, it may not be fanciful to see in
the audience of the *Vita nova* an anticipation of that of the *Convivio*: cultur-
ally aware and politically engaged, though too taken up with "cura familiare

e civile" (*Conv.* 1.1.4) [domestic and civic responsibilities] for serious academic study.

It is clear that the decision to write in the vernacular belies the sense that this is an inward-looking, closed, perhaps even self-obsessed text. On the contrary, Dante's choice of language—and specifically of a language easily identified as Florentine—presupposes a specific set of *engaged* interlocutors, with potentially different approaches to the text and different understandings of its *sentenzia*. Indeed, it is clear from the text's first four chapters that these imagined interlocutors and their interests are many and varied. The *libello* cannot be read as a theoretical treatise addressing only poets (as Reynolds suggests), any more than it can be dismissed as nothing more than "cosette per rime" (V.4 [2.9]) [little rhymes], addressed, somewhat patronizingly, to those women for whom it is "malagevole d'intendere li versi latini" (XXV.6 [16.6]) [difficult to follow Latin verses], for all that Dante would later point to this group as the original and primary audience of poetry in the vernacular.

Already, then, these chapters introduce us to the "molti" (II.1 [1.2]) [many people] who recognize Beatrice as a blessing to her city. These are the citizens of Florence, taken as a whole, from whom the text's other audiences are drawn: they are the same citizens who will later find themselves miraculously ennobled by the mere sight of this miraculous woman,[11] and who will be left bereft, almost widowed,[12] by her passing. We might imagine these citizens as the recipients of the more "public" poems in the collection: those on the death of Beatrice's father (XXII [13]), for example, and that inspired by the visit of the two men of high social rank in the city (XXXIV [23]), as well as those on Beatrice's death and those in which her effects on all who see her are outlined. Within this broader collective, we also glimpse for the first time here the group of "gentili donne" (III.1 [1.12]) [gracious women] who will be Beatrice's constant companions in the text. These are the women who surround Beatrice at the wedding when she mocks the hapless poet (XIV.4 [7.4]) and who care for Dante when he is ill (XXIII.12 [14.12]); they are also, and most significantly, the women to whom he will address the turning-point poem, "Donne ch'avete intelletto d'amore" (XIX [10]) [Women who understand the truth of love]. A parallel male group—identified as the poet's friends—appears in chapter IV [2.3–2.5]. Here they express concern at his physical deterioration and peculiar behavior; later they will prompt him to write various poems, such as "Amor e il cor gentil" (XX [11]) [Love and the open heart], "Venite a intender li sospiri miei" (XXXII [21]) [Come and take notice of my every sigh], and "Quantunque volte, lasso!" (XXXIII [22]) [Whenever I, alas!]. Finally, from within or partially within this circle of friends, these chapters introduce the group of love poets—"li fedeli d'Amore" (III.9 [1.20]) [Love's faithful]—and among them "quelli cui io chiamo primo de li miei amici" (III.14 [2.1]) [somebody whom I consider my best friend], easily identified from the reference to the poem whose title is reported here as Guido Cavalcanti. This latter is also identified as the addressee of "Io mio senti' svegliar dentro a lo core" (XXIV [15]) [I felt awakening in my heart one day], while the group of love poets are the recipients of "Piangete amanti" (VIII [3]) [Cry, lovers].

The opening chapters of the *Vita nova*, then, set up the *libello* as a text that is only apparently personal, inward-looking, and private. In a similar way, the themes that these chapters start to address already point to the way in which the text as a whole will seek to reach beyond the individual story of one man and one woman to engage with deep questions about life and death, the creation and purpose of art, and love, both human and divine.

One of the primary themes of these early pages, highlighted immediately in the opening words of its first, very brief, chapter, is that of writing. Dante is always a self-conscious author, one keen to control and manage how his works should be read through careful metaliterary analysis and explicit direction of his readers.[13] Here, as Richardson's chapter will explore in more detail, he sets up what will become one of the main preoccupations of the text through a precise attention to the use of technical vocabulary about writing: from the source text or exemplar, the "libro de la . . . memoria" [book of memory], with its rubrics and paragraphs, to the "libello" selectively copied from it in order to clarify its meaning or "sentenzia." From the beginning, then, Dante assumes that his book's audience—or at least one of the audience groups identified above—will have an understanding of, and an interest in, these "technicalities," in the same way that he will later imagine their queries and objections in relation to his personification of Love: "Potrebbe già l'uomo opporre contra me e dire" (XII.17 [5.24]) [It is true that someone might object, saying], and "Potrebbe qui dubitare persona degna di dichiararle onne dubitazione" (XXV.1 [16.1]) [Here, a person worthy of having every doubt clarified might be doubtful].[14]

This imagined interest in writing takes on a specific flavor when it comes to the "fedeli d'Amore," experts in the field ("famosi trovatori in quello tempo," III.9 [1.20] [well-known poets of that time]), who are invited to interpret Dante's sonnet "A ciascun alma presa" [To all besotted souls] and to explain the meaning of the vision described there. Here Dante sets up poetry itself not as merely expository but—potentially, at least—as dialogic: his poem elicits many replies, with many suggested meanings, and allows him to establish what will become a long-lasting and influential poetic and personal relationship with the poet who would become his closest friend ("E questo fue quasi lo principio de l'amistà tra lui e me," III.14 [2.1] [This was, so to speak, the beginning of our friendship]). But at the same time, this episode also illustrates powerfully the need for a text such as the *Vita nova*, which is not just a collection of poems but also an attempt to convey their "sentenzia" in a more accessible and straightforward form. For none of these famous poets is able to grasp the "verace giudicio" (III.15 [2.2]) [correct interpretation] of the poet's dream; and if this correct interpretation is now "manifestissimo a li più semplici" (III.15 [2.2]) [clear to even the most simple-minded], this can only be because of the careful explanatory prose provided by the *Vita nova* itself, written with the benefit of hindsight and increased spiritual awareness, the acquisition of which constitutes one of the book's main themes. If the quasi-technical terms—that is to say, the terms used idiosyncratically by Dante himself to refer to the structures and techniques of his own writing—that will later come to be applied to them are not yet used explicitly here, chapter III of the *Vita nova* nonetheless demonstrates for the first time the importance and function both of the narrative prose that provides the poems' "backstory" (later referred to as their "ragione") and of that which breaks them down into their constituent parts in order to clarify how they should be read (the "divisione" that, Dante will later clarify, is intended to "aprire la sentenzia de la cosa divisa" (XIV.13 [7.13]) [open up the meaning of the thing divided]. The very first poem included in the *Vita nova* demonstrates clearly what its author would later turn into a statement of poetic intent: that is, that poetry is, by nature, a complex medium and that the writers of poetry owe it to their readers to provide the necessary interpretive tools to guide them toward a "verace giudicio" as to the "sentenzia" of what they have read: "Grande vergogna sarebbe a colui che rimasse cose sotto vesta di figura o di colore rettorico, e poscia, domandato, non sapesse denudare

le sue parole da cotale vesta, in guise che avessero verace intendimento"
(XXV.10 [16.10]) [It would be shameful for one who wrote poetry dressed
up with figures or rhetorical color not to know how to strip his words of such
dress, upon being asked to do so, showing their true sense].

It is surely no coincidence that the "verace intendimento" that Dante
claims, in chapter XXV [16], all poets should be able to point to in their verse
should pick up precisely the "verace giudicio" that all readers of "A ciascun
alma presa" so singularly fail to grasp. As Federica Pich will show in her
analysis of chapter III below, it is important to recognize that the inability
of readers to analyze the dream "correctly" at the time of the composition of
"A ciascun alma presa" is not so much a sign of the inadequate reading skills
of the "fedeli d'Amore" as a pointer to the inadequacy of Dante himself
as a poet at this early stage of his development. His original call for inter-
pretations of the dream-vision is a genuine one, not one designed to set up
his contemporaries to fail in order to reveal his own hermeneutic superiority.
He too, like his "primo amico," whose response to the poem ignores all hints
of fear or pain to provide an entirely positive reading of this dream of Love's
domination,[15] misunderstands this dream in an entirely romantic vein, to the
extent that there is nothing in the sonnet itself that might point to any other
possible reading.[16] This suggests that Dante himself initially misinterprets his
own vision and only later comes to recognize the real (but ultimately trans-
formative) pain—not just the sadness of waking from a lovely dream, as
Cavalcanti suggests—at the death of Beatrice to which it seems to point.[17]
Neither the narrative "ragione" nor the somewhat superficial "divisione"—
which merely divides the sonnet into the initial address to the reader and the
puzzle to be answered—makes this explicit, of course, and the vision retains
its darkly mysterious quality. However, the careful reader—and Dante always
demands care from his readers—cannot miss the reference to the "ineffabile
cortesia" [ineffable benevolence and grace] of Beatrice, "la quale è oggi meri-
tata nel grande secolo" (III.1 [1.12]) [which now is rewarded in eternal
life]—a reference that prefigures the text's closing words, in which the poet-
protagonist dreams of being reunited with "quella benedetta Beatrice, la
quale gloriosamente mira ne la faccia di colui *qui est per omnia secula benedic-
tus*" (XLII.3 [31.3]) [that blessed Beatrice, who gazes in glory into the face of
him *qui est per omnia secula benedictus*].

But if the dream-vision's subject is dead, then not only the vision itself
but also all that follows it needs to be read differently; it needs, that is, to be

read with an eye on that same "grande secolo" [eternal life] which is the goal of all the book's Christian readers. If the young Dante fails to grasp the vision's full import, it is because his understanding of love is, at this stage in his development, an excessively narrow one. It is, as Ruth Chester discusses more fully in her chapter below, an understanding that focuses on the physical impact of love on the lover, and specifically on the ways in which the proper functioning of the lover's body is negatively affected by the sight of the beloved, leaving him "di sì fraile e debole condizione" (IV.1 [2.3]) [so frail and weak] that his friends become concerned for his well-being. Chapter II of the *Vita nova* describes falling in love in terms of an invasion, as the "spirits" that control the lover's body—his heart, his mind, his eyes, and his digestive system—are, in turn, overtaken by the power of love, which exerts over him "tanta sicurtade e tanta signoria . . . che [gli] convenia fare tutti li suoi piaceri compiutamente" (II.7 [1.8]) [such confidence and power that there was no choice but to do whatever he wanted]. Here Dante is setting up the complete loss of control of his physical and mental faculties that will later bring him almost to the point of death,[18] and is illustrating the insidious nature of purely human love, which masquerades as something noble and reasonable,[19] only to reveal itself later as anything but. This almost forensic desire to apprehend and describe what love is and how it works is another theme that will be threaded throughout Dante's text, as it moves from this early physiological understanding, through the discovery of joy in purely altruistic love with the *stile della loda* (praise style), to the relapse into pain and confusion with the episode of the lady at the window, and finally to the sublimation of human love into the spiritualized love of Beatrice in heaven with which the *libello* ends.[20] Again, we see how the work's opening chapters serve to prepare the reader for what is to come: in this case, announcing that writing about love cannot be dismissed as nothing more than "parlare fabuloso" (II.10 [1.11]) [telling a tall tale], but rather that it is something to be considered "sotto maggiori paragrafi" (II.10 [1.11]) [under larger paragraphs], a term that, as Brian Richardson suggests, implies both the importance of the content that is to follow and the significance of the way in which it is to be presented.

In these early chapters, however, and as is appropriate for this stage in the development of both the poet and the protagonist, the religious significance that would later come to be attached to the figure of Beatrice and presented as the only "correct" approach to human love is not yet made explicit.

Rather, we find here mere hints of Christian meaning, whose sense will emerge clearly only on a second or subsequent reading. If, as I have suggested, the *Vita nova*, like the *Commedia*, has a "circular" structure, its end pointing back to its beginning, then it may be that only having glimpsed the Beatrice who contemplates, in eternity, the face of the one who is "*per omnia secula benedictus*" might we return to read these early chapters with greater insight. If the suggestion that Beatrice "non parea figliuola di uomo mortale, ma di deo" (II.8 [1.9]) [did not seem the daughter of a mortal man, but rather of a god] looks, at first reading, like rhetorical hyperbole, the later explanation that Beatrice is "uno miracolo, la cui radice . . . è solamente la mirabile Trinitade" (XXIX.3 [19.3]) [a miracle, whose root . . . is none other than the miraculous Trinity] implies, rather, that the poet's first impression was intended to be taken at face value. Likewise, as we have seen, her name—Beatrice—is no mere *senhal*: she literally blesses her lover, whose "salute"—his spiritual, moral, and physical well-being—depends on *her* "salute," her greeting.[21] Already, too, these early chapters point not only to classical and contemporary poets as sources of inspiration for the *libello*'s author,[22] but also to the Bible, which Barański identifies as "the *Vita nova*'s primary source."[23] The biblical echoes are particularly strong in chapter III's closing reference to the meaning of the dream-vision, which is now "manifestissimo a li più semplici" (III.14 [2.1]) [clear to even the most simpleminded]; this recalls, as Matthew Treherne also points out in his chapter below, the initial mystification and later comprehension of Christ's disciples concerning his triumphal entry to Jerusalem in John's Gospel,[24] as well as St. Paul's assertion that "quae stulta sunt mundi elegit Deus, ut confundat sapientes" (1 Corinthians 1.27) [the foolish things of the world hath God chosen, that he may confound the wise] and Jesus's own repeated assertions that the Kingdom of Heaven belongs not to the wise but to the "parvuli" [little ones].[25]

Even the book's designation as the story of its protagonist's "*vita nova*" (I [1.1]) cannot but recall that *novum testamentum* that tells the story of God's intervention in human history through the sending of that "verace luce" (XXIV.4 [15.4]) [true Light], which Beatrice herself will figure in the protagonist's vision in chapter XXIV, and who comes, precisely, "ut vitam habeant, et abundantius habeant" (John 10.10) [that they may have life, and that they may have it abundantly].[26] Dante's new life will ultimately be—

even if he fails to recognize this until much later—a new life *in Christ*, for which the new beginning marked by his first sight of his "beatrice" [the one who blesses him] prepares and equips him; and the words "*incipit vita nova*," as Alberto Casadei has shown,[27] have a long history of being used in reference to precisely this sort of Christian conversion, and, in particular, to the new life that begins with baptism and ends, as the *Vita nova* ends, in the light of the vision of God, "*qui est per omnia secula benedictus.*"

In this short introduction, I have attempted to show how the opening chapters of the *Vita nova* set up many of its key themes, as well as starting to define what kind of a text this is, its relationship with its immediate and broader social and cultural context, and its intended purpose and function. Above all, I have suggested that the *libello*'s conclusions—poetic, personal, and religious—are anticipated from its very beginning, revealing it to be anything but a simple "boy-meets-girl" story, but rather a tightly structured and highly novel text that, like the *Commedia*, begins in the streets of Florence but ends in the mind of God.[28] In the chapters that follow, my colleagues will explore each of these areas in more detail, outlining the importance of these opening chapters both in their own right and for the ways in which they anticipate the richness and depth of this text as a whole.

Vita nova I [1.1]

BRIAN RICHARDSON

To preface the narrative of the *Vita nova*, Dante makes a sustained use of the technical terminology of the manuscript book that is audacious for its combination of the metaphorical and the literal. He tells us that he is about to copy out a booklet whose source is an early section—with its own heading—of the book of his memory, although he will not transcribe it word for word: "In quella parte del libro de la mia memoria dinanzi alla quale poco si potrebbe leggere, si trova una rubrica la quale dice: *Incipit vita nova*. Sotto la quale rubrica io trovo scritte le parole le quali è mio intendimento d'assemplare in questo libello; e se non tutte, almeno la loro sentenzia" (I [1.1]) [In the book of my memory—the part of it before which not much is legible—there is the heading *Incipit vita nova*. Under this heading I find the words which I intend to copy down in this little book; if not all of them, at least their essential meaning]. After sketching an outline of his first encounters with Beatrice in the second chapter, Dante ends it by saying that he will omit much of the more youthful material in his source text and concentrate on the contents that the text itself marks as most significant: "Trapassando molte cose le quali si potrebbero trarre dello essemplo onde nascono queste, verrò a quelle parole le quali sono scritte ne la mia memoria sotto maggiori paragrafi" (II.10 [1.11]) [Passing over many things that could be copied from the same source, I come to words written in my memory under larger paragraphs]. What are the implications of Dante's bibliographical terminology, and how does he use it to set out the nature of his tasks as author?

Libro, Libello, Incipit, Rubrica

The metaphor of the "book of memory" is given exceptional prominence by Dante, but it was not new. From the classical period to the Middle Ages, there is a close association between the concept of perceptions recorded in locations of the memory and the wax tablet or the page on which something is recorded with signs. As Mary Carruthers observes in her great study of memory that takes its title from the *Vita nova*, Dante "was newly articulating a very old observation." She cites as an example the observation of Cicero in the *De partitione oratoria* (7.26) that "the structure of memory, like a wax tablet, employs places and in these gathers together images like letters."[1] Dante is recalling his own earlier use of the image of "the book of the mind" in his *canzone* "E' m'incresce di me," which was probably linked to his love for Beatrice but excluded from the *Vita nova*:

> Lo giorno che costei nel mondo venne,
> secondo che si trova
> nel libro de la mente che vien meno
>
> .   .   .   .
> e se 'l libro non erra
>   (*Rime* 20 [LXVII], lines 57–59, 66)

[The day when she came into the world, as is written in the book of my failing mind . . . and if the book does not err]

In this poem, Dante's memory fails or "faints" because of the effect of Beatrice. At the outset of the *Vita nova*, in contrast, Dante seems entirely confident in his power of recall, just as he is later in *Inferno* 2.6, when he writes of "la mente che non erra" [my unerring memory]. Carruthers notes the precision with which Dante conceives the layout of the *libro*: he "sees the work in visual form."[2]

Dante establishes a contrast between the remembered *libro* and the physical book that he is about to create, using *libello* to refer to the latter. This diminutive form is used three times later in the *Vita nova* (XII.17 [5.24], XXV.9 [16.9], and XXVIII.2 [19.2]), and three times in the *Convivio* (1.5.10, 2.2.2, 2.8.9), where it refers respectively to the *De vulgari eloquentia*, the *Vita nova*, and Cicero's *De senectute*. Dante avoids the option of the diminutive *libretto*, a term used by Brunetto Latini twice to describe his *Tesoretto*.[3] The Latin *libellus* was often used by classical authors to refer self-deprecatingly to a single work of theirs, for instance by Ovid in the first line of the *Remedia amoris*, which Dante instead respectfully calls a *libro* in the *Vita nova* when he quotes the second line of the poem (XXV.9 [16.9]). *Libellus* and *libello* could also refer to a subdivision of a work, as in Dante's reference in the *Paradiso* to the "dodici libelli" [twelve books] of Peter of Spain's *Summulae logicales* (12.134–35). In the *Vita nova*, Dante appears to use *libello* in the more specialized sense of a short unit that could form part of a larger *libro* but is textually complete, independent, and detachable. Such a *libello* could consist of one or more gatherings of parchment or paper.[4] Several *libelli* could be grouped together to create a larger composite manuscript that might then be bound. Dante refers to the practices of binding and detaching gatherings (*legare, squadernare*) in *Paradiso* 33.85–87.[5]

One of the contexts in which the *libello*, as an object, was used in the Middle Ages was the creation of liturgical booklets that could be used for a single occasion; they might contain, for instance, offices for a feast day, a funeral mass, or a sacrament such as baptism or extreme unction. But this practice declined after the eleventh century.[6] Another and more enduring context was hagiographical: a booklet containing a life of a saint, or a collection of lives of one saint, which could form part of a composite collection of saints' lives.[7] It is also worth noting that, at the start of these texts, whether or not they were transcribed in *libelli*, the term *incipit* was regularly followed by *vita*. As in all types of manuscript, section headings would often be written in red ink, creating a *rubrica*. An example (not Italian, but consultable online) is found in the third part of the Stuttgart Passionale (Württembergische Landesbibliothek, MS Bibl. fol. 58), dating from around 1130–35, in which the life of St. Alexis begins on folio 12r: "Incipit Vita sancti Alexii confessoris" [Here begins the life of St. Alexis, confessor].[8] Other examples come from Luzern, Zentral- und Hochschulbibliothek, MS P 33 4°, dating from around 1200, at the openings of the lives of St. Ulrich ("Incipit vita sancti Odalrici" [Here begins the life of St. Ulrich], fol. 1r) and of St. Gall ("Incipit vita beati Galli confessoris" [Here begins the life of the blessed Gall, confessor], fol. 32v).[9] The association between hagiographical manuscripts and the cluster of terms used in the *Vita nova* has significance for Dante's work, in view of his portrayal of the blessed nature of Beatrice.

Scrivere, assemplare, essemplo

Another subgroup of terms concerns the processes of locating a source text and then copying from it. Dante finds words written metaphorically in his book of memory, as he tells us in chapter I ("Io trovo scritte le parole" [I find written the words]) and again at the end of chapter II [1.11] ("quelle parole le quali sono scritte" [those words which are written]). His use of the past participle leaves open the possibility that the inspiration of the words was, at least in part, divine.[10] Taking this book as his *essemplo* or exemplar, he undertakes the task of *assemplare*, transcribing its words in order to make a material booklet with them. As commentators have noted, Dante is paying homage to Cavalcanti's *canzone* "Io non pensava che lo cor giammai" [I did not think my heart could ever be] in the *congedo* of which the poet writes that he has transcribed his poem from a longer set of *libri*: "Canzon, tu sai che de' libri d'Amore / io t'asemplai quando madonna vidi" [Song, you know that when I saw my lady I copied you from the books of Love].[11] Dante echoes the verb, and also the opening phrase of the *Vita nova*, in the *Commedia*, when he writes of the hoarfrost copying the image of snow with a pen that soon grows blunt:

> In quella parte del giovanetto anno
> . . . .
> quando la brina in su la terra assempra
> l'imagine di sua sorella bianca,
> ma poco dura a la sua penna tempra.
> (*Inf.* 24.1, 4–6)

[In that season of the youthful year when the hoarfrost copies out on the land the image of its snowy sister, although her nib does not stay sharp for long.]

Dante also tells us that, in creating the *libello*, he will act as an editor, "trapassando molte cose" (II.10 [1.11]) [passing over many things]. He is, after all, moving "from private to public,"[12] from what is written only in his mind to a text that is about to be circulated. (He signals another case of omission when he refers to his conversation with Virgil in the *Inferno*: "altro parlando / che la mia comedìa cantar non cura," 21.1–2 [speaking of other things, of which my comedy does not care to sing]).[13] Pamela Robinson has noted the "eclectic attitude" shown by scribes in the process of putting texts together for personal use: "Whatever he copied . . . , a scribe collecting for himself felt free to modify the text in the light of his own requirements and experience."[14]

Sentenzia, paragrafi

Dante's opening words identify another authorial function: he will give the *sentenzia* of some of the words written in the *libro*, that is, the interpretation and explanation of their meaning.[15] The term recurs with this exegetic implication in the *Vita nova*—"A questo sonetto fue risposto da molti e di diverse sentenzie" (III.14 [2.1]) [Many people responded to this sonnet and gave various interpretations of it]; "La divisione non si fa se non per aprire la sentenzia de la cosa divisa" (XIV.13 [7.13]) [Division is only for opening up the meaning of the thing divided]; "Non m'intrametto di narrare la sentenzia de le parti" (XXII.17 [13.16]) [I will not add anything to explain the meanings of their parts]; "la sentenzia di questa ragione" (XXXIX.6 [28.6]) [the meaning of this prose account]—and for instance in the *Convivio*: "Lo dono veramente di questo comento è la sentenza de le canzoni a le quali fatto è" (1.9.7) [The true gift of this commentary lies in the meaning of the canzoni for which it is made]. Singleton notes that Dante, as scribe, adds glosses to his text by explaining how the poems are to be divided, by commenting on his practice as poet (XXV [16]), and by reflecting further on the virtue of Beatrice's greeting (XI [5.4–5.7]) or on the significance of the number nine (XXIX [19.4–19.7]).[16]

As the phrase just cited from XIV.13 [7.13] shows, interpretation of a text was aided by its division into sections. Division was also associated with mnemonics. Carruthers cites the words of Fortunatianus in his *Artis rhetori-*

cae libri (3.13): "What assists memory the most? Division [*divisio*] and composition; for order serves memory powerfully." She links textual division with the classical and medieval distinction between recalling *res* [things] and *verba* [words]—between remembering a text according to its sense-units, *sententialiter* or *summatim*, and remembering it word for word, *verbaliter* or *verbatim*.[17] Dante is doing both: he is transcribing some *parole* exactly, but he is indicating the meaning of some sections.

The words to be transcribed are those written in the exemplar "sotto maggiori paragrafi" [under larger paragraphs]: that is, under certain of the critical signs that were used to divide texts into units. Among the shapes of these signs were one resembling a Greek capital gamma (Γ) and a "C" (for *capitulum*) struck through with a vertical abbreviation mark (hence also the sign "¶" with a tail), known in English as a paraph or, through a deformation, a pilcrow.[18] Dante is thus referring to signs indicating the *divisione* of the text. *Maggiori* may simply mean "more important" as regards their content. Dante himself mentions the possibility of subdividing parts of his *libello* into smaller but superfluous sections for the purpose of exegesis ("più minute divisioni," XIX.22 [10.33] [still subtler divisions]; "più divisioni," XXXVII.5 [26.5] [more divisions]). *Maggiori* might also have a more literal sense, in keeping with the visual connotations of Dante's terminology, referring to critical signs that have more significance than others within the book. Some *canzonieri* of Dante's period, for instance, employed a series of punctuation marks, including paragraph signs, to indicate sections of *canzoni* and sonnets.[19] Some manuscripts used the same paragraph sign in larger or smaller forms. This is seen, for example, in British Library, Royal MS 4 D III, containing St. John's Gospel with the *Glossa ordinaria*, copied in England or France in the last quarter of the twelfth century or the first quarter of the thirteenth. In the interlinear gloss to the main text, a small "¶" is found, while in the main glosses two larger sets of signs resembling "C" are used alternately to indicate new sections.[20] Two examples of legal texts from fourteenth-century Italy show hierarchies of paragraph signs in different sizes and shapes. Justinian's *Digestum novum* with the gloss by Accursius in Berkeley, Robbins Collection, Robbins MS 37, folio 27r, has three signs of apparently descending importance in the main text, "¶," "C," and the Greek capital gamma.[21] The *Summa super titulis decretalium* of Henricus de Segusia in MS 68 of the same collection is transcribed with two series of alternating red and blue paragraph signs in the form of "C," one series larger, the other smaller and less ornate. A few whole "paragraphs" are also marked with longer alternating red and blue signs in the margins.[22]

The authorial activities that Dante outlines in chapter I and in the concluding words of chapter II have three phases: the retrieval of words through his use of memory, the selective transcription of some of them, and their interpretation. The words of the *libello* are thus born ("nascono," II.10 [1.11]) from those of the *libro*. This birth is the result of a combination of practical steps—the use of mnemonic techniques, handwriting, exegesis—and of artistic creation. We can link Dante's insistence on his involvement in transcribing and elaborating the words that were in his mind with Armando Petrucci's observations on the rise of the "author's book" between the twelfth and the mid-fourteenth centuries. This period saw an increase in the direct participation of writers of prose and poetry, such as Salimbene de Adam, Francesco da Barberino, and Petrarch, in all phases of textual production, from making drafts to copying and correction, without the involvement of scribes to take dictation or to make a fair copy.[23] This participation is akin to the steps that Dante chooses to foreground at the start of the *Vita nova*.

Dante is also concerned with a fourth phase of the life of his text: its circulation beyond his desk. He refers later in the *Vita nova* to the oral publication of single poems: in "Con l'altre donne mia vista gabbate" [With other ladies you mock my distress] ("disiderando che [le parole] venissero per aventura nella sua audienza," XIV.10 [7.10] [in the hope [my words] might reach her ears by chance]), in "Donne ch'avete intelletto d'amore" [Women who understand the truth of love] ("Appresso che questa canzone fue alquanto divolgata tra le genti, con ciò fosse cosa che alcuno amico l'udisse . . . , avendo forse per l'udite parole speranza di me oltre che degna," XX.1 [11.1] [After this canzone was fairly well known, a friend of mine heard it, . . . having more faith in me because of that previous poem than perhaps I deserved]), and in "Donna pietosa e di novella etate" [A woman green in years, compassionate] ("Mi parea che fosse amorosa cosa da udire," XXIII.16 [14.6] [It seemed to me to be a love theme worthy of an audience]). Dante may well have drawn attention to his role as copyist of his *libello* as the first of his means of guiding its scribal publication. Wayne Storey has shown how, within the prose of the *Vita nova*, Dante "integrates instructions for copying his little book designed to guarantee its compilational

strategies of diverse and co-dependent genres and the ordering of its compo-
sitions."[24] Moreover, as Zygmunt Barański has pointed out, Dante appears to
have wished to synthesize prose and verse closely on the page, and he would
have wanted scribes to follow the *mise en page* of his autograph.[25] Dante may
be using the opening of the *Vita nova* not only to draw our attention to the
combination of mental and manual processes that is necessary if memory is
to be transformed into an author's text but also to invite those who were to
reproduce his work to note and respect the care with which he himself had
transcribed it.

Vita nova II [1.2–1.11]

RUTH CHESTER

The *Vita nova* has been extensively studied in temporal terms, with the focus on ideas and texts that went before and the ways in which the *libello* is the rebellious child of those texts and authors. Emphasis has been placed on situating the *Vita nova* within a historical narrative. What was Dante reading before he wrote the text? What would come after? And, even within the text itself, when did certain events happen? As a story of progression, of personal development, the *Vita nova* is inescapably temporal to some degree, and it would be redundant and skewed to claim otherwise or neglect its temporal components. However, in the focus upon *when* things happened, have we lost sight of *where* they happened?

In this brief offering, I consider some of the spaces of chapter II [1.2–1.11] of the *Vita nova* and suggest some ways of exploring them. However, I would like to start with some initial thoughts on the approach I am taking to the issue of space itself. Medieval space has often been conceived as hierarchical or as made up of contrasts—secular versus sacred, town versus country, earth versus heaven—but what we might emphasize further is that medieval space, and indeed all spaces, are not intrinsically fixed entities in themselves but are rather the manifestation of the practices that form them.[1] The anthropologist Alberto Corsín Jiménez has persuasively written that space "is what people do, not where they are. . . . The world happens with us and, in choosing what set of practices we will enact and engage in, we are also choosing what world we want to live in."[2] This is not to say that the physical characteristics of *place* are to be ignored, far from it; but focusing on activity, on lived experience as the constituent element of space that then builds those places, I suggest, is a particularly fruitful way to approach the *Vita nova*. The spaces of the *libello* are really only defined by the activities that take place within them: streets where people meet, a space where mourning is taking place, a room where ladies gather, a bedroom for sleep and dreams. By emphasizing activity, Dante is sketching out the significant elements of his experience that construct the world he both lives in and reproduces in the text—the world he "wants to live in," to take Jimenez's phrase above. Unlike the *Commedia*, with its detailed evocation of place and space, the *Vita nova*, with its paucity of physical description of these elements, is instead an intimate manifestation of one man's very personal and generally interior space.

As well as thinking about this nuanced idea of space as constructed within the *Vita nova*, we might gain much from thinking spatially in broader terms. To think spatially is not only to think about where things happened. To think spatially is to think of life and events as synchronous, interconnected, to see causality as continual, dialectic, fluid.[3] There is not one single cause of things, and (temporal) chains of events might rather be conceived of as nets. While the *Vita nova* is constructed as a series of events in time, it is also divorced from time and place. Time passing is indicated by change or development, but the self-referential nature of the text has us jumping back and forward from then to now, here to there, until we are caught in the text's open-ended net.

With these ideas in mind, let us turn to chapter II [1.2–1.11], starting, paradoxically, at its end, which references the text's first significant space, introduced in chapter I, the book itself, the "libro della mia memoria" (I [1.1]) [book of my memory]. The *Vita nova* evokes spaces but is also itself a constructed space, built by the act of writing. Moreover, from its very first line we know that it is a self-professed spatialization of the writer's interior self. Dante lays out his memory with rubric and paragraph ready for analysis. At the close of chapter II [1.2–1.11], the narrator states: "*verrò* a quelle parole le quali sono scritte ne la mia memoria sotto maggiori paragrafi" (II.10 [1.11]; my emphasis) [I come to words written in my memory under larger paragraphs]. Beginning with a verb of movement (*venire*), we travel through the text to the significant events of Dante's relationship with Beatrice. Dante exploits the physical structure of the text to emphasize the events that are important; he uses a book-shaped memory palace to undertake "the process of ethical valorizing," to use Mary Carruthers's terms.[4] The text provides a spatialized opportunity for self-editing: the bits that make it into the book are the bits Dante wants to be remembered. We are looking at a constructed space, a false space that nevertheless claims to be a space of sincerity.

In laying out his memory for all to see on the page, Dante initiates one of the text's main points of interest: the continual dialogue and blurring it enacts between external and internal space. A topographical conception of the psyche, such as I would suggest Dante is presenting metaphorically here, produced interesting questions in twentieth-century psychoanalysis, particularly in the work of Lacan, who coined the term *extimacy* to express the impulse by which humans seek to make their intimate selves visible to the external world in order to stimulate the world's response.[5] Dante's explicit laying out in book form of his interior space from the text's opening invites engagement, an engagement we know he also sought in practical terms by sending his poems on journeys out into the world to be read by other people.[6] We might think about how encountering the narrative through a spatialized self affects our engagement with both the text and the life of the person who wrote it. Do we feel closer to Dante's experience or further from it? Does his text-self engage or alienate us?

Vita nova II [1.2–1.11] introduces a further spatialization of the self that recurs throughout the text: that of the narrator's body transformed by love. While memory has been spatialized as a book, the narrator's body is mapped out as a house with rooms occupied by spirits who are overcome and ruled by the god of love:

> Lo spirito de la vita, lo quale dimora ne la secretissima camera de lo cuore, cominciò a tremare sì fortemente. . . . Lo spirito animale, lo quale dimora ne l'alta camera ne la quale tutti li spiriti sensitivi portano le loro percezioni si cominciò a maravigliare molto. . . . Lo spirito naturale, lo quale dimora in quella parte ove si ministra lo nutrimento nostro, cominciò a piangere, e piangendo disse queste parole: "Heu miser, quia frequenter impeditus ero deinceps!" (II.4–7) [1.5–1.8])

[The vital spirit, which dwells in the innermost chamber of the heart, started to tremble so powerfully. . . . The animal spirit, which dwells in the high chamber to which all the spirits of sensation carry their perceptions, began to marvel. . . . The natural spirit, which dwells where our food is digested, started to cry, and crying it spoke these words: "Heu miser, quia frequenter impeditus ero deinceps!"]

The narrator's body under the effects of love is one of the spaces in which we spend the most time in the early chapters of the *Vita nova*. Here in chapter II [1.2–1.11] the minute spatial dissection of the effects of the young Dante's first sight of Beatrice upon the spirits that dwell (*dimorare*) in the different "rooms" of the body makes us pause; events slow down as we watch and listen to these spirits worrying about what is going to happen to them. The syntactical structural repetition—the spirit's name, where it lives, its reaction, and its Latin tag—creates a kind of walking tour or map of the body where we stop and see the highlights. The systematic movement from heart to head to stomach emphasizes the total impact of this encounter, elevating a single brief vision into a transformative experience that takes over a whole being. The anthropologists Setha Low and Denise Lawrence-Zuniga, writing about embodied space, state: "The space occupied by the body, and the perception and experience of that space, contracts and expands in relationship to a person's emotions and state of mind, sense of self, social relations, and cultural predispositions."[7] In this encounter, the inside of the narrator's body expands to take over the whole page and becomes the whole space of the narrative, thus emphasizing the force of the experience of seeing Beatrice. As Heather Webb has so perceptively noted, the touchless, visual encounters of Beatrice and Dante nevertheless enact an invasion and transformation of the poet's internal bodily space.[8] We witness this invasion in detail, but I wonder whether we as readers truly engage with its willing victim. The systematic dissection of the spirits and their obscure Latin speeches create an odd, disjointed and artificial impression, a far cry from the evocative and engaging bodily experiences of the *Commedia*, which share more with the *Meditationes vitae Christi* than with the *Vita nova*'s studied descriptions. And yet the writer makes every effort to help us understand the dynamics of these invisible interactions. To help us conceive the impact of the intangible interchanges of gazes, words, and sighs that make up his encounters with Beatrice, they are described in spatial terms.

Following this invasion of the narrator's body, Love takes up permanent residence, commanding his new realm to pursue the beloved object: "Elli mi comandava molte volte che io cercasse per vedere questa angiola giovanissima; onde io ne la mia puerizia molte volte l'andai cercando" (II.8 [1.9]) [Time after time he ordered me to search for where I might glimpse this youthful angel, so that in my boyhood I went searching for her often]. While the first encounter of Dante and Beatrice occurs by chance, to progress their (one-sided) relationship, the narrator must embark on a sort of quest or hunt, setting out to search for the object of his love. It is interesting to consider the environment in which this quest would have taken place by thinking about the ultimate omnipresent yet absent space of the *Vita nova*, the city of Florence. Considering the city through which the young lover "went searching" raises some interesting historical questions. Walking through the streets of Florence in the 1280s meant walking through streets littered with the debris of buildings destroyed by internecine fighting; it meant walking through cramped thoroughfares with imposing fortified towers. It also meant staying in your own quarter for fear of violence. Yet Marco Santagata's detailed historical research suggests that Dante and Beatrice most likely lived on opposite sides of the Arno.[9] If this is the case, then for the young Dante to go searching for Beatrice would have been a dangerous undertaking, a quest indeed. The real situation in Dante's Florence, however, is not the writer's concern; indeed, the city of the *Vita nova* is nameless and almost entirely invisible. Might this be the case precisely because it was such a troubling space in which to live, thus transforming the *Vita nova*'s narrative into wishful escapism? Or is the city simply eclipsed by the intensity of the narrator's experience, his inner world expanding so far as to make the outer vanish or fade into irrelevance? The "sopradetta cittade" (VII.1 [2.12]; XXX.1 [19.8]) [abovenamed city] exists purely as an expression of the writer's experience in it, manifested only by the actions happening within it. The physical, historical space is rendered unimportant, nonexistent even, and instead what is there is an all-consuming manifestation of the central transformative events of the writer's early life. The only thing he notices on the battle-scarred, chaotic streets of Florence is the lovely Beatrice; when she is gone, the whole city mourns. The space of the city is the manifestation of the writer's experience.

If details of the earthly context of the *Vita nova*'s events are minimal, its heavenly context by contrast is very present. The moment of meeting between Dante and Beatrice at the very start of chapter II is framed by reference to the position of the heavens.

> Nove fiate già appresso lo mio nascimento era tornato lo cielo de la luce quasi a uno medesimo punto, quanto a la sua propria girazione, quando a li miei occhi apparve prima la gloriosa donna de la mia mente. . . . Ella era in questa vita già stata tanto, che ne lo suo tempo lo cielo stellato era mosso verso la parte d'oriente de le dodici parti l'una d'un grado. (II.1–2 [1.2–1.3])

> _____

> [Nine times, the heaven of the light had returned to where it was at my birth, almost to the very same point of its orbit, when the glorious lady of my mind first appeared before my eyes. . . . She had already been in this life long enough for the heaven of the fixed stars to have moved toward the east a twelfth of a degree since she was born.]

In a foretaste of the cosmic dynamics of the *Commedia*, the earthly events of the *Vita nova* are set firmly in relation to the workings of the heavens. By establishing the spatial relation between heaven and earth, Dante is dramatizing the invisible dynamics of divine grace that he seeks to emphasize as the cause behind the events of his early life, the dynamics that led that girl to appear at that moment in that place for him to fall in love with. However, it is significant that the position of the heavens is not external or objective here but is understood through and is a constitutive part of the ages of the protagonists. The heavens both give meaning to and take significance from this moment of meeting. The much-considered relevance of the number nine in the *Vita nova* begins here in the moment of meeting of these two nine-year-olds, which crystallizes a particular celestial formation that becomes important only because of these earthly happenings. Not only is the earthly realm a projection of the protagonist's internal self, but the position of the heavens themselves becomes interpretable and significant primarily through his own experience.

I would like to close with a brief excursus on a final "place," or rather "nonplace," in the above-quoted description of the heavens: "uno medesimo punto" (II.1 [1.2]) [the very same point]. Christian Moevs's gorgeous consideration of the "punto che mi vinse" (*Par.* 30.11) [point that overcame me] at the *Commedia*'s close, I suggest, can add depth to the *punto* that frames the first meeting of Dante and Beatrice. The *Commedia*'s *punto* is "a measure of space or time reduced to infinity, to the dimensionless," a subsuming of human categories in the oneness of pure existence, a point in time and space that reveals itself as beyond time and space.[10] It is also a moment of pure awareness, however—the point at which the human knows itself as divine. This complex significance of the *punto* might be more evident in the poet's later work, but what about this first *punto*, the *medesimo punto* that marks the moment of meeting? This is the *point* that links Dante's moment of birth to his (first) moment of rebirth that comes with the sight of Beatrice; the heavens have returned to the same point as when he was born, so this is a point that takes him back to the basis of his existence. It is a moment that is physically and historically grounded—the meeting happened at a discrete moment in a particular place—but in the *Vita nova* it is an event divorced from any space and time *that is not rendered through Dante's own experience.* Is Dante casting this first *punto* as a sudden flash of awareness, a point at which time and space are collapsed into a momentary revelation of the divine hand behind human experience?

Like any text, though perhaps more self-consciously than others, the *Vita nova* is a space formed by the practice of writing. The spaces within it— the body, the unnamed city, the heavens—are important as the sites in which Dante's new life is forged. They gain their import not because they are described in great physical or historical detail but because they are artfully molded to bring us back to one main point: the writer is and inhabits a space transformed by love.

Vita nova III [1.12–2.2]

FEDERICA PICH

In several interconnected ways, chapter III [1.12–2.2] of the *Vita nova* is an *inaugural* textual unity, hosting the very first instance of various structures and processes that will be repeated throughout the work: the first explicit selection made in transcribing from the book of memory (the "essemplo," II.10 [1.11] [source]); the first event in that same book to be placed "sotto maggiori paragrafi" (II.10 [1.11]) [under larger paragraphs], or so we must assume; the first vision to be reported; the first poem to be quoted; the first organization of the prose into *ragione* and *divisione*, although with no explicit identification of the former and only a fleeting mention of the latter: "Questo sonetto *si divide* in due parti" (III.13 [1.24]; my emphasis) [This sonnet is divided into two parts].[1] Despite the threshold status of the section, which sets up the core mechanism of the whole *libello*, at this stage Dante the author, editor, and commentator does not provide any overt declaration in order to introduce or explain such a mechanism, whereas metastructural statements of various kinds do occur in later chapters.[2] While two typically reductionist arguments might be adduced to make this absence unsurprising, both of them can be promptly undermined by counterarguments. First, the imperfect and possibly unfinished status of the work, which has been posited on the basis of a number of internal contradictions and underdeveloped sections,[3] cannot account for a prominent omission in the first part of the book,

27

which is the most controlled portion of the text. Second, the historical exis-
tence of several textual setups akin to the *libello* (prose *vidas* and *razos* inter-
spersed with *coblas*, prosimetrical works in Latin, classical texts with *accessus*
and commentaries) does not diminish the utter uniqueness of the *Vita nova*
as a new and idiosyncratic object, which cannot be pinned down to one
single genre and form, either in the 1290s or today.[4] Especially in an inaugu-
ral chapter, then, the possible deliberateness of Dante's silence—the silence
of a loquacious if selective self-commentator—might tell us something not
just about the specificity of this section but also about its place in the wider
project of the *Vita nova*.

In the absence of explicit metastructural comments, we must turn to
collateral signals, such as possible anomalies or distinctive features of the
chapter, in particular in the handling of the relationship between *ragione*,
poem, and *divisione*, which is here—implicitly—at play for the first time.
First of all, "A ciascun'alma presa e gentil core" [To all besotted souls] is
not just the first poem in the book; it is also presented as the first poem ever
to be circulated by Dante, albeit anonymously. Additionally, the sonnet ex-
pects replies and is part of a *tenzone*, hence belonging to a dialogic and col-
lective experience of poetry, which will resurface in later sections (XX.1
[11.1]; XXIV.6 [15.6]; XXXII–XXXIII [21–22]; XLI.1 [30.1]), but only in
this chapter is there mention or discussion of poetic responses.[5] Second, the
final part of the *ragione* and the concise *divisione* are unusually simple and
close to each other in content and are accurately echoed in the structure
of the sonnet.[6] Third, and most crucially, the *divisione* proper is followed
by a short prose section (III.14–15 [2.1–2.2]) that explains how, at the time
of the events, the meaning of the vision was misunderstood by all poet-
interpreters, including Dante himself, whereas in the present, from which
the retrospective narration is conducted ("ora" [now]) it is clear to everyone.
All these elements—the outward-looking, extroverted nature of the debut-
poem, the plain division matching the sentence that bridges the passage
from narration to poem, and the highly metainterpretive coda—emphasize
the exegetical net that surrounds the sonnet and point to the interpretive
process in which both the vision and the verse are immersed, making read-
ing, exegesis, and glossing a pivotal theme of the chapter.[7] More specifically,
the centrality of interpretation, and of *mis*interpretation, in the final part of
the section seems to make up for the absence of an early statement about the

nature and function of *ragioni* and *divisioni*, while casting a dubious light on them as technical tools for disclosing the *sententia*.

In order to develop this argument, it is essential to consider the contested structural boundaries of the section, whose final part (III.14–15 [2.1–2.2]) has been placed by editors either at the end of chapter III (Barbi, Pirovano) or at the beginning of chapter 2 (Gorni, Carrai). Even in the absence of any certainty about an authorial paragraph system, which might well never have existed, the issue remains relevant not only for the interpretation of the episode but also for a wider reflection on the nature of *ragioni* and *divisioni* and their interplay in the work. If read as a continuum, chapters III to VII [1–2] display a double tripartite structure, at whose center sits a short fragment of prose that retains a hybrid status (*ragione* + poem + *divisione* + [prose (?)] + *ragione* + poem + *divisione*), which can be solved or accounted for in various ways. The most straightforward solution is to consider it as part of the second *ragione*, as is suggested by the paragraph system adopted by Boccaccio in both his transcriptions (To and K²) and followed by Gorni; this is an economical solution, but one that requires an acknowledgment that the segment advances the narration but is not strictly part of the episode that explains the *Vita nova*'s second poem.[8] An alternative solution is to see III.14–15 [2.1–2.2] as a sort of follow-up to the first division, a digression including both a narrative aspect (a report on responses and the beginning of Dante's friendship with Cavalcanti) and an interpretive-theoretical one, deeply connected with the authorial discourse that, in the *libello*, is developed through self-commentary: the passage is precisely about incorrect interpretations (of Dante's vision), which will be overcome, after Beatrice's death, by a "verace giudicio" [correct interpretation]. A strong argument in favor of this solution lies in the mutual connection between the only two "proleptic" statements in the episode: the reference to the current condition of Beatrice as someone who has earned her place in heaven ("*oggi* meritata nel grande secolo," III.1 [1.12] [now rewarded in eternal life]), a condition that started with her death and continues in the present of narration), and the allusion to the fact that the true meaning of the vision escaped all readers at the time of events ("allora") but is now ("ora") "manifestissimo a li più sempici" (III.15 [2.2]) [clear even to the most simple-minded], with its biblical resonances further confirming the connection between the two chronological shifts.[9] This option has the further advantage of assimilating

III.14–15 with other prose sections that sit uneasily within the conventional distinction between *ragioni* and *divisioni*, some of which concern precisely a discussion of correct and incorrect interpretations of the poems, while others address poetics more generally. These sections have variously been described as "digressioni" [digressions], as "porzioni commentative" [commentary sections], and as part of the *libello*'s "self-commentary," invoking "the unspoken presence of . . . learned interlocutors."[10] Some of these passages are similarly located in the final parts of chapters and attached to divisions, such as XII.17 [5.24], which anticipates the theoretical digression of chapter XXV [16], in its turn placed after a division (XXIV.10–11 [15.10–11]), and XIV.13–14 [7.13–7.14], which explains the decision not to divide the sonnet and not to clarify the "dubbiose parole" [obscure words] in the relevant *ragione*; elsewhere, however, allusions to the fact that not all readers will be able to understand are inserted before the poems: "sì come appare a chi lo 'ntende" (VII.2, taken up in VII.7 [2.13 and 18]) [as is plain to anyone who understands it], "sì come appare manifestamente a chi lo 'ntende" (VIII.3 [3.3]) [as is quite clear to anyone who understands them], "chi sottilmente le mira vede bene che . . ." (XXXIII.2 [22.2]) [whoever subtly looks at them sees plainly], and "assai è manifesto a coloro a cui mi piace che ciò sia aperto" (XXXVIII.5 [27.5]) [and it is evident to those people for whom I like such things to be clear]. A similar metainterpretive dimension is at work also in the short passages that signal and explain the absence (XXXV.4 [24.4], XXXVI.3 [25.3], XXXIX.7 [28.7], XL.8 [29.8]) or position (XXXI.2 [20.2]) of divisions, their intentionally limited development (XIX.22 [10.33], XXXVII.5 [26.5], XLI.9 [30.9]), or their function of merely distinguishing different parts, whenever the *sententia* is made sufficiently clear in the *ragione* (XVI.11 [9.11] and XXII.17 [13.16]). If we exclude the preliminary section (chapters I and II in the Barbi edition) that precedes the "A ciascun'alma" episode, III.14–15 can be identified as the first of such passages, logically descending from the sonnet through its responses and inaugurating the meta-exegetical thread that will run throughout the *libello*, moving quite freely around *ragioni* and *divisioni* and thus attesting to the complex interweaving of narrative and glossorial prose.[11] In fact, a third explanation, more simplistic but ultimately acknowledging the unitary nature of the *Vita nova*, would be to see the main prose section, beginning at I.1 [1.1] and ending at XLII.3 [31.3], as a sort of all-encompassing frame into which the different specialized types of prose of the *ragioni* and *divisioni* are inserted alongside the poems. The poems would thus become the "centri gravitazionali" [gravitational centers] of each section, identifying "le unità microtestuali dentro la totalità macrotestuale" [the microtextual units within the macrotextual totality],[12] to some extent akin to the independent "mini-*prosimetrum*" formed by "a *vida* or a *razo* and an integrated *cobla*."[13] In this way, each prose segment that neither narrates the background story of a poem nor divides it—such as, precisely, III.14–15—could be simply considered as part of the overall narrative-commentative frame.

Whatever the option followed, the prose segment certainly does not fit into the distinction between narrative, lyric, and commentarial elements that has just been *silently* displayed for the first time: *Vita nova* III.14–15 could be described as a "digression," a *porzione commentativa* (commentary portion), or a "section of the prose frame," but probably not as a straightforward *ragione*, unless one were to adopt either the reconstruction of the episode that is implicit in Gorni's chapter system (where III.14 becomes the opening paragraph of chapter 2) or a wider notion of the meaning of *ragione*, as Picone and Ascoli seem to do.[14] More generally, it has been suggested that a conscious and definite use of *ragione* as a structural category should not be assumed for this early chapter, as the word is used consistently only from the episode of the *donna gentile* on, whereas in the absence of a specific term, the definition of the narrative prose centers on the notion of "causation" (XIV.13–14 [7.13–14], XVII.2 [10.2]).[15] In fact, *cagione* (reason) is the word that Boccaccio associates with the *ragioni* in his editorial note *Maraviglierannosi* ("dimostrazioni delle *cagioni* che a fare lo 'ndusse i sonetti e le canzoni" [explanations of the causes that led him to write the sonnets and canzoni]), as well as in the first redaction of his *Trattatello in laude di Dante* ("scrivendo le *cagioni* che a quelle [operette] fare l'avean mosso" [writing down the causes that had moved him to produce those works]).[16] Comparably, even though the words *divisione* and *dividere* are used from the early chapters of the *libello*, a proper definition of the term is not given until as late as chapter XIV, on the first instance when it is said to be unnecessary to divide the sonnet: "la divisione non si fa se non per aprire la sentenzia de la cosa divisa" (XIV.13 [7.13]) [division is only for opening up the meaning of the thing divided]. However, despite Dante's (assumedly) late and partial control of technical terminology or conscious laxity with it, the regularity of the tripartite structure *ragione*-poem-*divisione*, especially in the chapters that precede chapter XIV [7], is evident and cannot be overlooked. Boccaccio himself emphasizes this regularity in his *Trattatello*, to the extent of omitting macroscopic structural variations, most prominently the shifting of divisions from the space after the poems to that before them, and their intermittent absence: "Compose in uno volumetto . . . certe operette, sì come sonetti e canzoni, in diversi tempi davanti in rima fatte da lui . . .; *di sopra* da ciascuna *partitamente* e *ordinatamente* scrivendo le cagioni che a quelle fare l'avean mosso, e *di dietro* ponendo le divisioni delle precedenti opere" [He composed in a little volume . . . certain works, such as sonnets and canzoni which he had written earlier, at different times . . . ; before each one writing down, carefully and in detail, the causes that had moved him to produce them, and after each one setting out the divisions of the preceding works].[17] In chapter III, it is this very order that is both respected and undermined. As a rule, *ragioni* are set in time or more precisely suspended between two times, that of the events narrated and that of their narration, whereas divisions remain out of time in their glossorial, non-narrative quality. However, here interpretation is at stake *also* as a narrative core, as a fact *embedded in time*, all the more so because of the gap between the old (false) interpretations and the new (true) one.

Furthermore, the episode centers on a dream, the first of the *libello*, whose presence determines a stronger parallel between prose narrative and poem. First, "A ciascun'alma," a sonnet in the genre of *interpretatio somnii*, is more narrative than most other poems in the *Vita nova*;[18] significantly, out of six poems that are mainly built on a "singulative" narration, no less than four concern a vision or *ymaginatione* (those in chapters III [1.12–2.2], XII [5.8–5.24], XXIII [14], and XXIV [15]), and, of these four, the first and the last are addressed to Cavalcanti, with the last clearly anticipating chapter XXV [16] and establishing a "relay" back to chapter III.[19] Second, in retelling the vision, "A ciascun'alma" (5–14) establishes a distinctive interplay with the *ragione*, which includes a more detailed account of the same experience.[20] In comparing prose and sonnet, most scholars follow a genealogical route, focusing on the strategic control that the later prose exerts on the interpretation of a poetic *proposta* that had circulated autonomously (and possibly did not even concern Beatrice), a poem whose redirection is operated by expanding and enriching its narrative core in prose.[21] This critical perspective tends to hide a more basic point, which holds true within the *Vita nova*, regardless of the actual origin and circulation of the sonnet: "allora" [then] Dante himself did not see the dream's true *sententia*, even though he could count on extensive details that remained undisclosed to his addressees, and that are now described in detail in the *ragione*.[22] Therefore, *the poem itself* must have been flawed in the first place, because of its young author's own misunderstanding, on which that of his "risponditori" [respondents] is grounded. Strictly speaking, this seems to be Dante-character's only misunderstanding both *in re* and in poetry—that is, at the level of the facts narrated *and* of the poem originated by them—in the whole *libello*. According to Ascoli, by the stage represented by chapters XXIV and XXV [15 and 16], the aim of the commentary is "to reproduce the poet's intention at the point of composition, bridging the temporal gap between Dante reader and Dante author, *in sharp distinction from the situation in chapter III*."[23] Despite the unquestionable evolution of Dante-*agens*, this interpretation of chapter III of the *Vita nova* is challenged by the fact that, while the allusions to the present ("oggi," "ora" [today, now]) acknowledge—*post factum*—the gap between older reader and younger poet, they do not separate the younger reader from the younger author. Moreover, within the book (although not necessarily outside of it), "A ciascun'alma" and its narrative and glossorial counterparts do reflect the poet's experience and intention at the time of composition: what registers as misunderstood is not the meaning of the poem—quite obvious as a request preceded by a salutation and followed by a narration—but rather the meaning of the experience from which the poem sprang: that is, the dream. If we can logically assume, with Michelangelo Picone, that the awareness that Dante *agens* and *auctor* gained only over time must now inform *all* the *ragioni*,[24] what needs to be explained is not why Dante-character and his fellow poets were wrong about the dream but why Dante-*compilator* and commentator emphasizes the mistake without providing its correction: a textual omission that matches the metatextual one from which my reasoning began.

On a basic level, the combination of *ragione* and *divisione* opens up the *sententia* of the sonnet, which per se is all too clear, as confirmed by the almost tautological correspondence between the end of the *ragione*, the poem, and the brief division. However, the display of such a plain interpretive mechanism is immediately confronted with the metaexegetical prose that reveals the general misunderstanding concerning the dream narrated in the poem. This juxtaposition creates a strong anticlimax (from the straightforward and seemingly successful application of synchronic exegetical tools—*ragioni* and *divisioni*—to the absolute helplessness of past interpreters) and simultaneously a sudden shift of focus (from the sonnet to the dream), inextricably blending and confusing the past and present levels of discourse and interpretation: the poem by Dante-*agens* and the wrong "sentenzie" [meanings] attributed to it by his "risponditori" [respondents] (in the past); the narrative-commentarial *prosimetrum* and the right interpretation (or, more precisely, its announcement), *both* provided by Dante-author-commentator (in the present). The combination of what I described as an anticlimax and a shift of focus has a double effect: on the one hand, it sparks the sophisticated metaliterary discourse on reception that has been the object of Steinberg's analysis;[25] on the other, it enables Dante to postpone the revelation of the dream's true *sententia* as well as the explanation of the *libello*'s structural and exegetical mechanism, which is temporarily subdued by the gulf between poem and vision and by Dante's own initial misunderstanding.

In chapter III, the almost redundant correspondences established between *ragione*, sonnet, and *divisione* contrast all the more sharply with the absence of the vision's genuine *sententia*, which remains hidden from the readers' sight, even when it is said to be clear to everyone. The tools on which self-commentary will be based are clearly activated but neither named nor explained, as the empty shell of a process that in subsequent chapters will actually give meaning to poems and events, and will ultimately disclose an overall *sententia*, revealing the meaning of the first dream through the final vision.[26] The peak of Dante-character's misunderstanding is made to coincide with the reader's own helplessness when faced with a revelation whose content remained impervious to early skilled interpreters and is now clear to the simplest, but, crucially, is here still withheld from view, still unspoken: a most appropriate ending for a threshold section, which only announces the *sententia* that the whole book will serve to unfold.

Vita nova IV [2.3–2.5]

MATTHEW TREHERNE

At first sight, this very short chapter is quite straightforward, describing a set of conversations between Dante the protagonist and a group of acquaintances who are either concerned at his weak appearance or driven by less benign motives. The protagonist responds to their queries by responding that it is Love that has conquered him ("Amore era quelli che così m'avea governato," IV.2 [2.4] [Love was the one who had ruled me in that way]); but when they pursue the issue by asking him who has led Love to ruin him, he simply smiles at them and says nothing.

The chapter shifts the focus from the written to the spoken word, moving from the rarefied literary exchanges of the previous chapter to more everyday conversation. It serves a narrative function, preparing for the screen lady episode in the following chapter, as Dante the protagonist seeks a diversionary tactic to distract others from his love for Beatrice. It also links the literary and metaliterary reflections of chapter III [1.12–2.2] to the social dynamics of the protagonist's interactions in the city of Florence. Perhaps most critically, it develops tensions that shape some of the key themes that Dante is already introducing at this early stage of the *Vita nova*. These tensions concern the interpretation of language, and the relationship between linguistic expression and its reception. These linguistic issues also involve concerns about the connection between the named, particular person and a universal principle, Love—and, by extension, the link between embodied and spiritual experience. These themes will animate the whole of the *Vita nova*, and working through them will involve, among other things, the discovery of the praise style in chapters XVIII and XIX. Here in chapter IV [2.3–2.5], however, they appear as problems, manifested in the unresolved conversations between the protagonist and his interlocutors, and emblematized by the uncommunicative, smiling silence with which the chapter ends ("Io sorridendo li guardava, e nulla dicea loro," IV.3 [2.5] [I would look at them smiling and tell them nothing]).

These tensions connect with the end of the previous chapter, where Dante asserts that the true interpretation of the dream-sonnet, which at the time of its writing had not been clear to anyone, was now obvious even to the least sophisticated reader ("Lo verace guidicio del detto sogno non fue veduto allora per alcuno, ma ora è manifestissimo a li più semplici," III.14 [2.1] [The correct interpretation of my dream was not understood by anyone at first, but now it is clear to even the most simple-minded]). This formulation in chapter III itself raises questions: the meaning of the poem is far from straightforward, and it is unclear at this point in the text what might have changed to render its significance truly obvious to all. Nonetheless, and significantly, the idea that the meaning of the poem had been obscure, but would later become clear, echoes the way in which, in John's Gospel, the disciples failed to understand events and Christ's actions prior to the Crucifixion but were able to make sense of them after his Resurrection.[1] It anticipates, then, the death of Beatrice, as an event that will in some way offer revealed truth; and it suggests that language about Beatrice will need to be thought about in a manner that at least recalls the Incarnation.

The same parallels with Christ are present here in chapter IV: as Christ, in John's account, was taken into a multitude at Jerusalem, and misunderstood, Dante fears the misunderstanding of the crowd of his friends.[2] The identification of Dante himself, and Beatrice, with Christ picks up the complex reference to the Eucharist in the sonnet in the previous chapter. In chapter III [1.12–2.2], Beatrice's body is held aloft and a quasi-Eucharistic eating of flesh takes place; but it is not Beatrice's body but Dante's own heart that is eaten, as though his own body comes to be identified with the Eucharistic host. Here in chapter IV, it is Dante who fears misunderstanding, but he fears that it is any account of Beatrice, or her meaning, that would be misunderstood. Through these subtle allusions, identifying at turns both Beatrice and Dante himself with Christ, we can see that this chapter and the previous one wish to draw an association between questions of incarnation and of interpretation.

This helps us understand the tensions underlying the answers offered by Dante the protagonist to his questioners. When asked what has caused him to fall into such a state, he simply answers, "Amore" [Love]: an answer that is simultaneously truthful and obfuscating. While love is indeed the cause of the situation, the answer is offered, not in order to reveal, but to disguise the identity of his beloved, Beatrice; while being strictly true, the protagonist's response also serves the function of directing the questioners' attention away from the precise source of his condition. And the inadequacy of the answer lies in the fact that the identity of Beatrice, in her particularity, is critical to the event that has taken place in the protagonist's life. The revelation of the universal in the particular is at the heart of the *Vita nova*, of its concern to fuse sacred and earthly love in its particular form of incarnationalism; yet easy talk of this revelation, chapter IV shows, is impossible.

To speak truthfully of that revelation, of that presence of the sacred in the earthly, of the universal in the particular, would require a number of conditions. The first of these, and perhaps that which is most prominent over the course of the *Vita nova*, is the protagonist's development of a poetic style and idiom that might properly speak of Beatrice—a task that eventually leads, in chapters XVIII [10.3–10.11] and XIX [10.12–10.33], to the emergence of the praise style. In this chapter, we are very far from that point: the protagonist's love for Beatrice takes the form of a sort of absorption, a collapse in his functioning: "Da questa visione innanzi cominciò lo mio spirito naturale ad essere impedito ne la sua operazione" (IV.1 [2.3]) [From the time of this vision, my natural spirit started to be hindered in its functioning]. Indeed, in the light of the incarnational theme of the previous chapter, it is also striking how the bodily and the spiritual are seemingly at stark odds: the vision leads to the protagonist's emaciation and weakness ("Io divenni in picciolo tempo poi di sì fraile e debole condizione, che a molti amici pesava de la mia vista," IV.1 [2.3] [In no time at all I grew so frail and weak that the sight of me weighed on many of my friends]).

But in setting out how far the protagonist is from being able to speak of Beatrice, chapter IV also foregrounds the importance of an appropriately disposed audience as a condition for this speech. Many of the protagonist's friends are concerned for him, but others are motivated by envy ("pieni d'invidia," III.1 [1.12] [spitefully curious]), posing questions in malice ("malvagio domandare," III.1 [1.12] [malicious questions]); here then, the intention of the listener is presented as critical, alongside the ability of the speaker. Dante's questioners are establishing conditions into which the name of Beatrice would be received and interpreted, with motivations ranging from concern for Dante's welfare to envy and ill will. Unsatisfied with his generic answer, which conceals as much as it reveals, they push further, hoping to provoke a response. Seen in the light of the incarnational theme that was established in the previous chapter, part of the issue lies in the protagonist's suspicion that, should he reveal Beatrice's name, her true nature as revelatory of the universal in the particular would be misunderstood: the questioners seem to crave the particular detail of Beatrice's identity at the expense of, divorced from, the universal principle of love she manifests.

In this respect, the questioners can be seen to echo those readers described by Augustine in *De doctrina christiana* as motivated by *cupiditas*. *Cupiditas*—defined as a love for things in themselves, rather than in the context of love for God—is ruinous in the reading of scripture, as it leads to a confusion of the letter for the spirit, of the physical for its eternal meaning.[3] The naming of Beatrice would, in response to questions motivated by such *cupiditas*, lead to an interpretation of her as pure particularity. Indeed, Dante's acquaintances' questions seem motivated by a curiosity to distinguish her among particularities—as this particular person, as opposed to other particular persons—rather than to engage with, or recognize, her nature as a bearer of spiritual truth, as a revelation of the divine.

These issues all relate closely to the nature of the *Vita nova* as a *prosimetrum*: that is, to Dante's concern, manifested throughout, not only to present poetic works, but also to provide an appropriate framework for their interpretation. Even the most faithful expression of the deepest truths may be vulnerable to misunderstanding, as the text reminds us with its insistence on commentary and exegesis. This chapter reinforces that idea. But the shift of focus—from literary to ordinary discourse; from the written to the spoken word—also suggests something important about the project of the *Vita nova*. For it locates the search for meaning—and its risks—in embodied interaction, in time. This seems an important adjustment to the end of chapter

III; for there, Dante had suggested that the meaning of the sonnet and the vision had ultimately become clear and transparent to all. One might imagine, at this point in the text, that a perfect commentary or explanation had fixed the correct meaning. But chapter IV returns us to time-based, social interaction as a site where meaning, interpretation, and expression must be worked out. To put it another way: the reflection on meaning is taking place, not in exegesis, but in narrative. The relationship between the poems of the *Vita nova* and its prose *narrative*—as well as its directly exegetical passages—are beginning to emerge here.

The reflection on the risks of linguistic misinterpretation moves from written texts in chapter III—with the poem, circulating in writing, vulnerable to misunderstanding—to the spoken word here in chapter IV. The reflection is therefore concerned not only with the written text but with any sign. Spoken words, indeed, are critical to the *Vita nova*'s consideration of poetic practice. It is, after all, reflection on Beatrice's denied greeting in chapter XVIII [10.3–10.11] that will ultimately lead to Dante's discovery of the poetic praise style in chapter XIX [10.12–10.33], expressed in a poem ("Donne ch'avete") that is itself composed as a spontaneous act of speech. And the protagonist's reticence here in chapter IV to name the particular individual, Beatrice, anticipates the way in which he will be required to disentangle his fixation on the particular greeting, or *salute*, from the true salvation offered by Beatrice.

Chapter IV is therefore simultaneously simple and complex. After the dense symbolism of chapter III, and the rarefied exchange of poems between Dante and his friends, it offers a straightforward account of banter, chatter, and gossip. If it picks up key themes in the *Vita nova*, it does so primarily to model thematic tensions, in the form of the ultimately fruitless and frustrating conversations it describes. Yet it plays an important role in the *libello*'s progression. Most significantly, it shows that the *Vita nova*—for all the intensity of its literary and metaliterary considerations—does not consider poetry as an isolated realm, somehow divorced from ordinary life and discourse. Instead, it presents deep links between its reflections on the proper poetic mode in which to speak of love's truth, and everyday chatter. All language matters to the project of the *Vita nova*, this chapter shows; all language has a part to play in revealing or obscuring the truths that the text aims to disclose.

Vita nova V–XII [2.6–5.24]

A Lover's Trials

CATHERINE KEEN

This section gathers six essays covering eight chapters in the division numbering established by Michele Barbi's 1932 critical edition of the *Vita nuova*: chapters V to XII. In Guglielmo Gorni's renumbering, by contrast, this part of the book occupies slightly over three of his *paragrafi* (Barbi's chapters V, VI, and VII forming about two-thirds of Gorni's second *paragrafo* [2.6–2.18]; X, XI, and XII constituting his fifth). Our distribution of material between six contributors thus does not follow precisely either of the two great editors' solutions to textual division of the *Vita nova*, despite this volume's overall commitment to adopting Barbi's chapter scheme. Our pragmatic choice to make single entries for V and VI and for X and XI perhaps aptly highlights the challenges for philological scholarship in deciding how to edit the first of Dante's published works, in the absence of autograph manuscripts and in light of the variety of textual layouts adopted by the scribes of the earliest copies that do survive.[1] A six-part treatment thus provides another small variation within their editorial segmentation.

The question of textual editing is one that Dante as author also addresses within this part of the *Vita nova*. These chapters present the plot section dealing with the lover's early attempts to conceal his love for Beatrice behind apparent devotion to first one and then a second "screen woman," to whom he accordingly addressed a quantity of camouflaging lyrics. Readers learn that much, but not all, of this verse has been excluded from the *libello* (little book) but that some of the concealing poems in fact incorporate authentic praise addressed to Beatrice, thus meriting either mention or direct inclusion. Two sonnets mourning the death of a woman friend of Beatrice's also make their way into chapter VIII [3], though she is neither the beloved nor one of the screen women. Later, after the screen device has worked successfully for some time in disguising the protagonist's true affective situation and poetic intentions, his exaggerated performances toward the second screen woman cause public scandal. Beatrice withdraws into condemnatory silence, and after a period of intense perturbation and self-blame, the lover abandons the screening ploy and writes a new poem sending his excuses directly to his beloved.

Poetic Apprenticeship and Courtly Scenarios

Not only does the last poem in our chapter sequence, the *ballata* of chapter XII, resolve a plot issue concerning Beatrice's displeasure, but the analytical *divisione* (division) that follows it returns to the issues of selection, signification, and publication that have surrounded the explorations in these chapters of what it means to write poetry for women who are not Beatrice, or to have other people read a poet's verses without grasping the realities behind them. Dante's analytical comments on the *ballata*'s structure and content sum up several of the most fraught communicative issues confronted by the protagonist-poet in the narrative covering the period when he attempted to "screen" his attachment:

> Questa ballata in tre parti si divide: ne la prima dico a lei *ov'ella vada,* . . . e dico *ne la cui compagnia si metta* . . . ; ne la seconda dico quello che lei si pertiene di *fare intendere*; ne la terza la licenzio del gire quando vuole, *raccomandando lo suo movimento ne le braccia de la fortuna.* (XII.16 [5.23], emphasis mine)

> [This ballad is divided into three parts. In the first I tell it *where it may go,* . . . and I say *in whose company it may place itself.* In the second I specify

what it is supposed to *make known*. In the third I give it permission to go freely where it wants, *commending its movement to the hands of fortune*.]

The anxieties thus expressed about the circulation and interpretation of a single lyric text articulate a keen concern about authorship and authority, which itself is part of the motivation for enfolding lyrics into the *Vita nova*'s prosimetric structure.[2] The *libello*'s author removes his anthologized lyrics from "the hands of fortune" and attempts to determine how their meanings should be "made known." The screen women sequence of these chapters thus not only drives the narrative forward with a satisfying and recognizable literary formula of romantic estrangement and reconciliation but provides clues about the larger poetic and editorial ambitions underpinning the *Vita nova*'s preoccupation with its own formal structure and modes of communication, as it begins to rewrite components from Dante's lyric past, developing new modes of vernacular prose production in the process.[3]

As well as concealing the protagonist's amorous preoccupations, the women of these chapters provide him with opportunities for poetic experimentation. Scholars note how the lyrics in this section explore both form and theme within traditional confines, as appropriate to Dante's self-fashioning narrative of authorial evolution through the *libello*.[4] Although there is material evidence of alternative circulation datable before the *Vita nova* for only one of the poems, it is plausible that all five, with their rather conventional and imitative elements, might have been available in the early to mid-1280s, as the book's implied chronology suggests.[5] The five poems themselves show considerable metrical variety: two standard fourteen-line sonnets; two *sonetti rinterzati* combining short and long lines over twenty verses; and the *Vita nova*'s only *ballata* (ballad). With the *sonetti rinterzati* form's prominence in the corpus of Guittone d'Arezzo, and the *ballata*'s in Guido Cavalcanti's, these metrical choices seem designed to mark the screen woman phase as a period of technical apprenticeship. Given the fervent contemporary debate that surrounded both Guittone's and Cavalcanti's philosophies of love—the first opting for moralized rejection of courtly models through the complex palinodic structure of his *canzoniere*, the second for a complex negative psychology of love—the association of their preferred forms with youth, and with the failed screen experiment, implies judgment also on the love-doctrine of Dante's fellow poets.[6] It is no chance that these chapters fall early, and that these formal choices are not repeated, in a work that aims to establish the singularity of its author's understanding and poetic expression of love. The detailed analyses of the single lyrics that follow, in the contributions by Jennifer Rushworth, Daragh O'Connell, Sophie Fuller, and Emily Kate Price, highlight the individual targets of Dante's single lyric performances, and his framing editorial analysis.

Thematically, the poems present some stock scenes from an established courtly lyric tradition inherited from the Occitan troubadours as well from their Sicilian and Tuscan successors.[7] The whole sequence is dedicated to exploring the theme of *celar* [concealment], the troubadouric or romance trope that imposes absolute secrecy on lovers' relationships to protect them from intrusive gossip.[8] The single poems likewise adopt recognizable formulas from previous tradition. These include the funeral *planh* situation of chapter VIII [3]'s two poems. Chapter VII [2.12–2.18] draws partly on the same tradition, though lacking, when read in the context of the accompanying *ragione*, an explicit funeral occasion, making it also a *chanson d'absence*. Our sequence also includes a *chanson de change* (IX [4]), drawing heavily on *pastorela*, as well as an excusatory *escondit* (XII [5]). Chapter VI [2.10–2.11] mentions a *serventese*, though as well as briefly describing the poem it excludes it from the *libello*, and there is no such poem in Dante's *estravagante* (uncollected) corpus. Across this series of formal and thematic experiments, the protagonist negotiates a delicate pathway between exploring a gamut of conventional lyric scenarios for "placeholder" figures, and protestations of a single-minded devotion to the unique, sublime beloved.[9]

Self-Fashioning Prose and Narrative Time

The screen woman device and the overt conventionality of the scenes and songs related to them give prominence in these chapters to the narratological complexity of character and chronology so much discussed in criticism on the *Vita nova*. They cover a vague but lengthy period: involvement with the first screen woman lasts "alquanti anni e mesi" (V.4 [2.9]) [a number of years and months], though the excesses of simulated love for the second cause scandal "in poco tempo" (X.1 [5.1]) [in a short time]. Across this period, the naive intradiegetic protagonist is represented as taking on, inexpertly, some of the self-division fundamental to the *libello*'s whole conception. Among the young poet-protagonist's compositions, he already distinguishes, protoeditorially, between poems that are mere rhetorical exercises—the ones excluded from the *libello*—and those where he struggles to express himself effectively, albeit obliquely, about Beatrice. The traits of what Albert Ascoli calls an authorially "divided Dante" are thus already part of the protagonist's characterization, though in these chapters his performative duality becomes constricting, confusing, and ultimately self-destructive.[10] Producing and publishing his accomplished, if conventional, lyric material, he begins to gain recognition as an author and to face the challenges of managing his poetic reputation and guiding public interpretation of his production.[11] Yet whatever the poems' standing outside the *Vita nova*, in the judgment of the *libello*'s authorial voice their ethical duplicity and occasionality largely void their validity. By contrast the narrator, with his "book of memory" open and ordered under guiding rubrics or paragraphs (as explained in chapters I and II.10 [1.1 and 1.11]), can exploit the "division" between his past and present selves as a source of order and prioritization, building up his sequence of selected lyrics.

In this way, this section of the book casts a useful light on how the making of the *libello* transforms the poems selected for inclusion into "new poems which did not exist before and now exist alongside the originals," as Manuele Gragnolati puts it.[12] The screen women narrative insists that the poems must indeed have this dual life: however much Dante-author argues that inclusion in the *Vita nova* reveals a single true significance of constancy, the plot requires they should plausibly be readable also as articulating an unruly and mutable erotic drive; otherwise the whole episode cannot stand. Returning to the analytical *divisione* that follows the *ballata* of chapter XII [5], Dante-narrator can "specify what [his poems are] supposed to make known" as we read the full sequence of the *Vita nova* and enjoy its recuperation and rewriting of his lyric past, but we *also* have to believe that "fortune" has played a part in their more haphazard, individual dissemination and in diverse interpretations of their content.

Dante's authorial voice in the *libello* occupies a narrative temporality of retrospection, looking back to events experienced in the first person by himself as a youthful lover-poet, yet over which the authorial voice has gained greater analytical perspective. Teodolinda Barolini has stressed how the *Vita nova* also provides a sustained experiment on Dante's part in learning to "play narrative time and lyric time against each other" and to deploy extensive rhetorical prolepsis between the linear sequence of events and the circular processes of signification, beginning from a Beatrice who is always already dead and in glory, and a Dante forever reading backward through his "book of memory."[13] In chapters V to XII, the experiments with the screen women, and with poetry writing intended at least to occlude if not to remove the figure of Beatrice, complicate the book's self-reflexive presentation still further. Within the time frame of the narrative, the deficiencies of this apprentice phase of experience and of authorship will necessarily be discarded, and the repentant lover in chapters X–XII is already forced into a microretrospection. A new phase of temporal and poetic experience is promised in the solemn Latin declaration from Love personified that "tempus est ut pretermictantur simulacra nostra" (XII.3 [5.10]) [it is time for our false images to be put aside].

Settings, Spaces, and Companions

Critical discussion on this section of the *Vita nova* displays interest in the spatial and social environments against which its events take place. The screen woman device, for instance, draws heavily on literary tradition in its sense that prying onlookers, counterparts to the troubadours' *lauzengiers* in the feudal courts, surround the lover, though as Paolo Borsa notes, the external setting is updated and modified for an Italian context. While the atmosphere remains redolent of literary inspiration, it has been adapted to "una cortesia ormai tutta urbana, che si realizza in forma 'diffusa' nei luoghi frequentati dall'aristocrazia cittadina" [an entirely urban courtliness, manifested in a "diffused" manner within the locales frequented by a citizen aristocracy], and predominantly in settings linked to celebrating religious rituals. These include the celebration of a Marian liturgy (V [2.6–2.9]) and a mourning gathering around a young woman's funeral (VIII [3]).[14] In a more everyday scene, Beatrice, "passando per alcuna parte" (X.2 [5.2]) [passing by in a certain part], refuses to greet the protagonist in public: the episode mirrors in negative the blissful first greeting of chapter III [1.12], inviting the reader to imagine the same streetscape. Looking beyond the city, in chapter IX [4] the protagonist undertakes a longer journey on horseback. Although its parameters remain undefined, the scenario is given socio-spatial credibility by his mentioning that he travels in a largeish group ("la compagnia di molti," IX.2 [4.2]) and in the direction of the distant place to which the first screen woman has previously departed (VII.1 [2.12]). Though late nineteenth- and early twentieth-century positivist critics sometimes wished to pin down the topographical coordinates of these spaces and journeys, scholars now generally prefer to emphasize Dante's self-conscious occlusion of specifically Florentine detail and of identifying proper names throughout the narrative, however thinly veiled their presence sometimes seems to be.[15]

Another indication of avoidance of overtly Florentine referentiality in the carefully generic locations and the social interactions they afford is the extent to which, contrary to the considerable social segregation between men and women in thirteenth-century Florence, the lover's interactions within the *Vita nova*'s urban milieu are predominantly with women, albeit at a respectful distance.[16] For instance, the lover witnesses a mourning gathering of young women (VIII.1 [3.1]), providing a springboard for the poetry of *planh*, though later in the narrative we learn that men are debarred by custom from such gatherings (XXII.3 [13.3]). The "fedeli d'Amore" [Love's faithful] who make up audiences imagined for chapter VII's and VIII's lyrics constitute another cluster within the *libello*'s inscribed social world apparently grouped by literary more than civic criteria, as a masculine coterie who share an imaginative world defined by rarefied courtly lyric.[17]

Donato Pirovano notes that the *Vita nova*'s roadways pass between a deliberately undefined center and periphery, tracing centrifugal or centripetal lines across the book's spaces.[18] Within chapters V to XII, the author's spatially precise yet topographically undefined geometries delineate both real and metaphorical domains of action, from the church space crisscrossed by the dead-straight sightlines of visual geometry in chapter V, to the "centrum circuli" (XII.4 [5.11]) [circle's center] occupied by Love in the lover's dream of chapter XII.[19] Several of the prose and/or lyric settings blur the external and internal domains together. Thus the roadway of chapter IX [4] becomes the setting for a phantasmal encounter with the personified figure of Love, and its subsequent pseudotopographic description as the "cammino de li sospiri" (X.1 [5.1]) [road of sighs] makes the dreamscape more significant than its real-world counterpart. It recalls the "via d'Amor" (VII.3 [2.14], line 1) [Love's way] of the *libello*'s second sonnet, where the addition of the possessive *d'Amor* fuses the dolorous biblical landscape of the quote from Lamentations with the courtly or Ovidian allegorical landscapes of profane love literature.[20] In the episode closing the screen woman sequence, too, there is a rapid transition from outer to inner topographies. After Beatrice denies her greeting, the lover withdraws to weep in solitude, finally in a secluded bedroom where he falls asleep and dreams that Love joins him. The room becomes a more animated and interactive space in sleep than in waking life, and there are Boethian echoes in the setting as well as the dynamics of a consolatory and didactic conversation between the abject protagonist and the powerful allegorical figure who points the way out of an impasse (one moreover that proceeds prosimetrically, with the passage from prose dialogue into metrical diction).[21]

Amore: Personification and Poetry

The personified figure of *Amore* [Love] is perhaps the most memorable figure from the entire chapter sequence, and the one who most actively provides the lover with companionship and conversation. Beatrice and the screen women appear always at a distance, but Love is a constant presence both within the poems and in the accompanying prose. His allegorical personification forms part of a long-established poetic discourse, with its roots not only in vernacular courtly lyric but also in Ovidian love-lore, from the *Amores* and *Ars Amatoria* as well as the *Remedia Amoris* that Dante will cite in his excursus on the trope of personification in *Vita nova* XXV [16].[22] There he clarifies his understanding of the strictly fictive nature of the device that endows with *seeming* personhood what is, by Aristotelian definition, only "uno accidente in sustanzia" (XXV.1 [16.1]) [an accident in a substance], as well as establishing his ambitions to authoritative poetic status on a par with the classical authors cited.[23] In these early chapters, by contrast, Love's vividly imagined corporeality is not questioned: the exegetical effort is, rather, invested in showing how the protagonist responds in his actions and his poetry to Love's demanding, sometimes enigmatic or contradictory guidance.

Love appears in four out of the five lyrics from chapters V to XII. Only "Morte villana, di pietà nemica" (VIII.8 [3.8]) [Barbarous Death, compassion's enemy] dispenses with his personification, substituting a *prosopopeia* of

Death, while Death also appears in the previous sonnet, alongside Pity and the weeping figure of Love.[24] That weeping figure is sometimes interpreted as a quasi-figuration of Beatrice herself, anticipating the more explicit identification drawn between Love and the beloved in chapter XXIV [15]. Though the poem's double life (noted by Gragnolati) beyond and within the *libello* makes such an interpretation possible, this is also a conventional rhetorical figure and need not concretely link to Beatrice but simply amplify the funeral's pathos.[25] But more broadly, the funeral itself does anticipate the unavoidable future death of Beatrice, as Daragh O'Connell reminds us.[26] Similarly, when Love weeps in the vision of chapter XII, after the lover's breakdown at the loss of Beatrice's greeting, he is proleptically mourning the greater loss of the beloved herself, although the still-unknowing lover asks: "'Perché piangi tu?'" (XII.4 [5.11]) ["Why are you crying?"].[27]

The duality of the poems' histories thus permits creative prose exegesis of conventional poetic imagery on their reuse in the *libello*. This is evident also in the two visions that frame the brief but critical episode where the lover turns to the second screen woman. He first acts on instructions received from a wayfaring Love in chapter IX's "imaginazione" (IX.3, 7 [4.3, 7]) [imagining] and is then halted by Love's second intervention in the "sonno" [dream] or "visione" [vision] of chapter XII [5]. Critics note the interpretive importance of distinguishing between an "imagining," from which the lover falls into disgrace in overcomplicated concealments, and the "vision," occurring at the symbolic ninth hour, where Love speaks solemnly but obscurely of his own true nature before urging the protagonist to social, temporal, and poetic renewal in setting aside such *simulacra*. The first, deceptive imagining belongs to an experience where the protagonist takes the theatricality of courtly convention too far, peopling his interior world with the figures of interchangeable lyric *madonne* as well as of Love, who here for the first time speaks exclusively in vernacular. That Love, and the "simulato amore" (IX.6 [4.6]) [love fiction] strategy advocated in the dialogue, are self-projections seems confirmed by the narrator's comment that the image dissolves "per la grandissima parte che mi parve che Amore mi desse di sé" (IX.7 [4.7]) [through the fullness of himself which Love seemed to give me].[28] Chapter XII [5]'s revelatory dream-vision, by contrast, restores Love to a commanding external position. The scene acts as pendant to that introducing the *Vita nova*'s first sonnet, which also took place at a significant hour, and where Love also spoke commandingly and in part obscurely, using Latin. The two dream-visions of chapters III and XII bracket off the *libello*'s most explicitly "courtly" phase, as well as linking two moments where the lover's emotions are deeply swayed by the granting, and then the removal, of Beatrice's salvific greeting.[29]

The second of Love's Latin speeches in the vision has been the focus of much critical discussion, with his enigmatic self-declaration as center of a perfect circle while the lover remains geometrically defective: "Ego tanquam centrum circuli, cui simili modo se habent circumferentie partes; tu autem non sic" (XII.4 [5.11]). Roberto Rea sees Love's phraseology as echoing not so much the traditions of literary *eros* as those of Stoic and patristic self-governance.[30] By the end of the *libello*, love for Beatrice will indeed be shown as compatible with rational self-direction and the expression of faith, with all pretense and distraction set aside, and with perfect circularity positioning both lover and beloved within a system of celestial spheres.[31] Yet though proleptic, the poetic and moral implications of the dream's Latin utterances (like the meaning of Love's weeping) remain hidden from the lover within the linear narrative, and also therefore from the sequential reader. For the moment, Love returns to the vernacular and to a more conventional role as poetic preceptor. The protagonist begins to grasp the importance of writing authentically as part of his progress toward centering; yet he remains still some way from a proper understanding of love/Love and from the kind of scrupulous poetic clarity that will be needed to speak about Beatrice without mediation (embraced here in the *ballata*, as Emily Price stresses in her chapter on *Vita nova* XII), given the confusion and self-paralysis explored both immediately prior to the dream in chapter XI [5.4–5.7] and in the immediately following chapter XIII [6]'s conflicted reflections on his subjection to Love.

Prose and the Polyphony of Sources

Love's use of Latin in chapter XII is a striking instance of the interdiscursive and plurilingual dimensions of the *Vita nova*'s textuality. Latin already entered the *libello* in the opening "book of memory" image with its rubricated *incipit* (I.1 [1.1.]), directing attention to the text's relationship to models of authoritative literary and ethical discourse associated with the book-form transmission of classical culture.[32] As already noted, the personified Love of these chapters is immediately recognizable from the traditional *prosopopeia* of classical and courtly love literature, and his speeches likewise move fluently between the idioms of both.[33] But as well, the two Latin phrases of the closing dream-vision in chapter XII [5] pull in hints and tags from the scriptural and philosophical domain, providing an illuminating case study of the ambitious range of Dante's prose as well as lyric stylistic models. Thus, in "'Fili mi, tempus est ut pretermictantur simulacra nostra'" ["My son, it is time for our false images [or simulations] to be put aside"], critics see traces of Philosophy's reprimand to the imprisoned Boethius of the *Consolation*, already noted above as a possible source for the whole scene's dream setting; possible supplements or alternatives in both Thomistic and homiletic sources have also been suggested.[34] Love's vernacular reprimand against probing to clarify his obscure Latin speech additionally evokes a passage from Paul's letter to the Romans, before he shifts register and frame of reference back toward courtly sources in returning to the theme of Beatrice's displeasure.[35] And a directly Christological dimension is provided by Love's dazzling white robes, similar to those of the angel of the Resurrection guarding the Gospels' empty sepulcher; an allusion that again will signal to the perceptive reader that there are greater losses at stake here than the protagonist yet realizes.[36] From this one episode, it is thus evident that Dante's prose is wide-ranging and sometimes audacious in its allusivity. Framing poems that themselves provide evidence of considerable sophistication in his stylistic and thematic aims from an early point, the prose bears the hallmarks of a more ambitious sense of the seriousness and expressive potential of his vernacular literary culture.[37]

There is one direct quotation from the Latin scriptures in our chapter sequence, in which Dante-narrator again melds the solemnity of biblical discourse with the courtly fictions of love poetry: his translation and then direct quotation from Lamentations in the first screen lady sonnet, "O voi che per la via d'Amor passate," quoting "O vos omnes qui transitis per viam" (VII.3, 7 [2.14, 18]) [O all ye passing by along [Love's/the] way]. As Zygmunt Barański notes, the vernacular and Latin versions of the phrase are accorded equal footing, implying a "fluid, 'unproblematic' interchangeability between the two languages."[38] This underlines how closely and carefully Dante as author is establishing the pretensions of his self-editing and self-glossing *libello* to an authoritative status that his chosen descriptor—a *little book*—only partly elides.[39] Even that tag in fact echoes the Ovidian *Remedia amoris* (as well as *Amores accessus* texts), recalling how even profane love literature can be traced back to ancient, and moralizing, literary roots.[40] The prose passages of chapters V [2.6–2.9] and, especially, XI [5.4–5.7], with their survey of the physiology and psychology of sense perception, demonstrate Dante's confidence also in articulating in vernacular prose some of the scientific-philosophical innovations of contemporary avant-garde poets such as Guido Cavalcanti and Guido Guinizzelli, ably incorporating into his narrative the kind of technical concepts whose lyric borrowing from scientific fields had been condemned by other contemporary poets as both obscurantist and exclusive.[41] Like the Ovidian components, these allusions to a conspicuously learned, philosophically influenced strand of vernacular culture help support the ambitions to authority of the prose narrative as well as of the lyrics themselves.

If one of the ambitions of the *Vita nova*'s prose is to present the author's learned credentials, it nonetheless remains notably oriented toward the scriptural and ecclesiastical sources that were the resources most accessible to aspirant lay scholars in thirteenth-century Florence, which lacked a university.[42] In the essays of this section, our contributors note the wide range of biblical and Christian exegetical sources for scenes and sentences within the eight chapters under discussion, including the two Old Testament books that Ronald Martinez and Paola Nasti (among others) have suggested play a major intertextual role in shaping the entire narrative of the *Vita nova*: the book of Lamentations and the Song of Songs.[43] Besides the much-discussed direct quotation from Lamentations in chapter VII [2.12–2.18], the dejected, wayfaring figure of Love in chapter IX [4] recalls the same book's prophet mourning at the roadside; the countervailing joyful praise of the Song of Songs is recalled with the mention of a *serventese* praising sixty women in chapter VI; and the more disturbing moment of the loss of the beloved's greeting in chapters X and XI recalls the Song's anxious search for the lost spouse.[44] Alongside such reworkings of familiar biblical passages, Dante's prose draws on exegetical and homiletic resources, encountered from the pulpit or in the monastic *studia* that he probably began to frequent, as far as possible for a lay citizen, during the 1290s.[45] An illustration of how a single word in the *Vita nova*'s prose may provide clues about Dante's exposure to such sources is provided here by Giulia Gaimari's discussion of *redundare* in her study of chapter XI [5.4–5.7].[46] At the same time, Gaimari's discussion displays a broader sense of the sometimes-audacious hybridization Dante's prose maintains, as the same chapter on the lover's response to Beatrice's greeting melds Christian ethical *caritas* ("una fiamma di caritade," XI.1 [5.4]) with the Guinizzellian, lyric refinement of the troubadours' sublimated *fin'amors*.

Finally, no account of the sources for these chapters' prose could finish without mentioning the *divisioni* in which Dante provides the more technical commentary on his selected poems' structure, inscribed audiences, lexical choices, and often metaliterary ambitions. The *divisioni* themselves are much discussed in *Vita nova* criticism for their resemblance to various existing exegetical models, from the *divisio textus* apparatus used to gloss and analyze scriptural and classical texts, to vernacular prose models in *volgarizzamenti* [translations] and moral or rhetorical tracts.[47] Thomas Stillinger identifies them as the element providing "the most intimate contact of prose and verse" in the *Vita nova* and notes how during the screen women narrative the *divisioni* accordingly use a "rhetorical" approach to examine each separate part of the lyric utterance discretely, matching the thematic emphasis on the lover as subject and performer projecting elaborate screening fictions.[48] This is even made explicit: commenting on the middle part of "Cavalcando l'altrier per un cammino" (IX.9 [4.9]) [Riding along a road the other day], Dante's *divisione* notes that the sonnet omits part of the protagonist's conversation with Love as narrated in the *ragione*, "per tema ch'avea di discovrire lo mio secreto" (IX.13 [4.13]) [for fear of revealing my secret].

Yet although the approach is generally, as Stillinger suggests, discretely fragmented, the *divisioni*'s intimate relationship to the lyrics means that their analysis is never "merely" technical and rhetorical, while their very provision of structural and thematic commentary contributes to Dante's larger self-authorizing strategies. We have already seen how the *divisione* of chapter VII [2.12–2.18] introduces the Latin quotation from Lamentations that seeks to legitimate its translation and extension within the lyric and that also ostentatiously draws readers' attention to the mourning register of the same biblical text that, later, will climactically accompany the death of the beloved. Equally, in my opening remarks above the three-part division of chapter XII [5.8–5.24]'s *ballata* proved to point toward much larger anxieties concerning poetic communication, and lyric publication and editing. The same can also be said of its closing phrases:

> Potrebbe già l'uomo opporre contra me e dicere che non sapesse a cui fosse lo mio parlare in seconda persona, però che la ballata non è altro che queste parole . . . : questo dubbio io lo intendo solvere e dichiarare in questo libello ancora in parte più dubbiosa; e allora intenda qui chi qui dubita, o chi qui volesse opporre in questo modo. (XII.17 [5.24])

> [It is true that someone might object, saying he does not know whom my words are addressed to in the second person, since the ballad is none other than [these] words . . . : I still intend to resolve and clarify this ambiguity in an even obscurer section of this little book. And at that point may whoever has such doubts here, or wishes to object in this manner, understand what is said here.]

The gloss makes a specific technical point on the poem's self-apostrophe.[49] But it also looks ahead to chapter XXV [16], where the self-authorizing commentary on poetics resolves not only the kind of question about personifying Love already discussed above but also how structural *prosopopeia* of the poem itself is a permissible rhetorical figure for a vernacular poet. As these introductory notes have aimed to show, metaliterary ambitions on a grand scale are thus already a fundamental element within these early chapters, despite their preoccupation with exploring poetic, affective, and ethical failures. They can emerge even in those parts of the text—the *divisioni*—that seem to hold the least narrative appeal and that have been the most subject to slippage, neglect, and even omission in the contested editorial history of Dante's earliest work.[50]

Vita nova V and VI [2.6–2.11]

CATHERINE KEEN

These two chapters are both very brief, exclusively prose sections in the narrative of the *Vita nova*. Indeed Guglielmo Gorni's 1996 edition of the *Vita nova* does not create a separate space for Michele Barbi's two distinct chapters V and VI. In Gorni's reading, they fall within a sustained block of text that runs over eighteen *commi* (subsections), between the end of the prose *divisione* (division) following the first sonnet, "A ciascun'alma presa e gentil core" (III.15 [1.24]) [To all besotted souls, my counterparts], and the account of the events directly occasioning the second, the *sonetto rinterzato* of Barbi's chapter VII.3 [2.14], "O voi che per la via d'Amor passate" [O all ye passing by along Love's way].

Barbi's choice to assign the material to two separate narrative units marks how the prose deals with events not directly linked to the composition of a specific poem—or rather, not to poems that we can read within the text of Dante's finished *libello* [little book]. Chapter V describes how the protagonist, wishing to conceal the identity of the woman he truly loves, Beatrice, develops the ploy of pretending love for another woman as a "schermo de la veritade" (V.3 [2.8]) [screen for the truth]. He begins to write poems apparently expressing love for her, and chapter VI discusses one lyric in particular, a long *serventese*, in which the names of this screen woman and of Beatrice

55

are added into a composition centered on listing many women's names but not transcribed within the *libello*. Both chapters, therefore, are linked by their preoccupation with concealment, as the true identity of the protagonist's love object is hidden behind elaborate social and poetic "screens." Both also look beyond the boundaries of the book we are reading to present a wider and more varied portrait of the young protagonist-poet than the narrative has accommodated thus far. For the first time since the opening sonnet, we hear about the composition of new lyrics; but these are deliberately omitted from the *libello*, even though they cover the output of a substantial period of the protagonist's poetic career, lasting "alquanti anni e mesi" (V.4 [2.9]) [a number of years and months] and presumably at least up to the time of the *Vita nova*'s second sonnet.[1]

Concealment and omission are prominent and admittedly problematic topics, therefore, to which Dante as author insistently draws attention by underlining the gaps they create within the narrative. In accordance with what was claimed in chapters I and II, Dante may indeed be offering a selective anthology of his lyric production in the *Vita nova*, but far from disowning or erasing the traces of additional or alternative poetic experience, his narrative accommodates or even encourages his readers' possible encounter with it.[2] In this discussion of the two short chapters V and VI, I begin with some reflections covering both together, focusing on questions of structure and discussing how the themes of concealment and omission fit within the trajectory of the completed narrative. I then present a focused analysis of each chapter as a single unit. For chapter V, I explore how the "screening" device is presented both as a historical moment imagined in socially and spatially specific terms, and poetically as a precursor to the discovery that Beatricean poetics are characterized always by praise, which may color and valorize even a screening *exercice de style*. For chapter VI, I discuss how this connection with praise and epiphany underpins the *serventese*'s presentation, making the otherwise overelaborate commentary on an absent, occasional text serve more ambitious narratological purposes. In closing, I reflect on how both chapters' prose commentary on poems never included within the *libello* highlight the dissonance between its synchronic linear plot trajectory and the bi-temporal, circular, and prophetic ambitions that Dante develops for the *Vita nova*, as a "book of memory" that is on the way to becoming a "book of revelation."

Eloquent Absences: Screens and Poetic Omissions

The nature of the *Vita nova* as a prosimetric text, in which verse components are accompanied by a unifying narrative prose, is widely recognized as a key innovation in this first published work in Dante's authorial career. The introduction of prose auto-commentary expands both the temporalities of the book and its ambitions to literary authority and, as Domenico De Robertis notes, is its most distinctive formal novelty.[3] This stands out sharply in those sections of the text, like these two chapters, where prose alone carries forward the narrative and poems are cited without transcription. The chapters provide an acknowledgment of Dante's career as lyricist during the 1280s and his production of poetry in a variety of forms and registers and with diverse thematic scope. The prose takes account of his extradiegetic career as *rimatore* even as his new authorial project narrows the range of what is evidenced of his lyric achievements, and provides them with a manifestly selective teleology.[4] As Gianfranco Contini notes, the *Vita nova*'s lyric retrospection achieves only partial resolution or unification of Dante's early poetic career: "È dunque unificazione parziale, aneddotica, fatta con un presupposto di pluralità, e insieme unificazione trascendente, cercata in un sistema di *razos* e in uno schema narrativo" [It is thus a partial and anecdotal unification, achieved with a presumption of plurality, and simultaneously a transcendent unification pursued via a system of *razos* and within a narrative scheme].[5] The prose at once tells us that the *Vita nova* does not offer the *full* story of its protagonist's literary, social, and affective development, while also claiming to be the *true* story of its central moments.

Chapters V and VI cover a section of the narrative where for the first time Dante-narrator addresses his readers' knowledge of the experiences and poetry that apparently contradict the uniqueness of his devotion to Beatrice. The most significant prior nod to omission was explained on the grounds that it covered conduct and events consistently supporting this singular focus (II.7–10 [1.8–1.11]); now, it concerns the behavioral ruses and the Continian lyric plurality intended to misdirect observers from identifying his true love object. Chapter IV paves the way for this by introducing the motif of concealment so important to the conventions of courtly literary tradition. In chapter V, Dante-narrator declares how his younger self, with somewhat naive conventionality, follows a troubadouric script in creating performative and lyric smokescreens to divert envious or malicious observers away from guessing the true object of the love that renders him unmistakably weak and preoccupied.[6] The two short chapters V and VI become crowded with shadowy figures whose identities remain concealed to us as readers but who are recognizably part of the world of courtly lyric or romance: intrusive by-standers, gracious women, and the poetry-reading public seeking to follow the lyric record of the love story they think they have uncovered. Indeed, we are to imagine the screen woman herself as almost dangerously exposed to public scrutiny, both by the way that the lover behaves and by the poems that he purportedly addresses to her.

For the *libello*'s readers, the only woman named here is Beatrice (V.2 [2.7]), but the narrative stresses that in the temporal present of unfolding events, she would remain concealed while the screen woman, anonymous to us, would be identified by contemporaries.[7] They indeed read what we do not, both socially and textually. An emerging preoccupation with legibility underpins the complicated temporalities and geometries that Dante creates around the "screen" motif. We learn that the lover's face is an open book in-scribed with unmistakable signifiers of love ("Io portava nel viso tante de le sue insegne [*scil.* di amore], che questo non si potea ricovrire," IV.2 [2.4]). In chapter V, this apparent legibility in fact produces misreadings: the sight-line drawn by the lover's gaze toward Beatrice runs past a young woman who becomes its plausible alternative focus, disrupting bystanders' attempts to decode the visual evidence of young Dante's conduct. Shifting from sight- to script-based forms of communication, the protagonist dutifully writes the poems expected of so obvious a lover and addresses them to the screen woman. They are then published and become legible to the curious public surrounding the two; but these lyrics in turn are omitted from the finished anthology within the *Vita nova*, whose criterion for inclusion is the authen-ticity of both surface and deeper meanings of poems leading back to Be-atrice. Within the narrative, meanwhile, Beatrice's later denial of her greeting (X [5.1–5.3]) will offer a very public commentary or legible gloss on Dante's equally public misperformances, as the author of actions and poems that have caused offense by breaching the purported anonymity of the second screen woman.

The lyrics transcribed in the *Vita nova* are accorded ambitious literary status through the double framing provided by the prose narrative *ragioni*

and the analytical *divisioni* accompanying each one, as well as by the speci-
fying of their formal genre as *sonetto, ballata,* or *canzone*. As far as the omit-
ted, screening poems are concerned, chapter V simply classes them as "certe
cosette per rima" (V.4 [2.9]) [certain little rhymes]. There are no solid clues
to link them to other *rime* in Dante's corpus or to identify the screen woman
historically or poetically. Dante's suppression of any direct, identifiable in-
formation on these *cosette per rima* conveys a paradoxical commentary on his
own intradiegetic persona as poet, as he draws attention to his growing repu-
tation as a lyricist, and his production of works excluded from the *libello*. His
single proviso is that the *Vita nova* does have space to transcribe poems that
have a particular kind of double meaning, and whose subtext "facesse a
trattare di quella gentilissima Beatrice; e però le lascerò tutte, salvo che al-
cuna cosa ne scriverò che pare che sia loda di lei" (V.4 [2.9]) [relates in some
way to that most gracious lady, Beatrice. And so I will leave out all of them
other than something I will write down that plainly is in praise of her]. With
narrative prolepsis, Dante hints here at the praise style that will mark the
final collapse of courtly devices centered either on concealment or on re-
ward, since the condition for including any *cosetta* in the prosimetrum
should be its submerged involvement with praise for Beatrice (though as
other contributors in this section note, such connections are often ambigu-
ous or puzzling).[8]

Chapter VI continues by offering the sole concrete example of a poem
linked to the screen woman but omitted from the *Vita nova*, the *serventese*
written specifically to enable the young Dante to celebrate his true love
alongside her screen companion. There is no surviving historical trace of this
composition, in all likelihood a pure fiction confected in the prose. The *ser-*
ventese supposedly returned to the numerological preoccupations that held
such emphatic symbolic importance in chapters II and III [1.2–2.2], this
time by gathering Beatrice's and the screen woman's names among those of
"sessanta le più belle donne de la cittade ove la mia donna fue posta da
l'altissimo sire" (VI.2 [2.11]) [sixty of the most beautiful women of the city
where my lady was put by the supreme Lord].[9] Though a genuine poem ac-
cumulating such a vast catalog of women's names would risk extreme ba-
nality, by stressing its textual absence and merely evoking its sixty unuttered
names Dante underlines its laudatory purpose. Reduced from onomastic ex-
cess to a single phrase, the imagined poem moves from literary absurdity to

figural revelation, with its constellation of fifty-nine women surrounding the central figure of Beatrice recalling the handmaids who attend the bride in the Song of Songs (6:7–6.8).[10] And since "maravigliosamente" (VI.2 [2.11]) [wondrously] Beatrice's own name can occupy no other position than ninth, foreshadowing her later identification as "uno nove, cioè uno miracolo" (XXIX.3 [19.6]) [a nine, a miracle in other words], the poem's citation without transcription also anticipates revelations about Beatrice that will become fully manifest only later.[11] Ronald Martinez has argued that the *Vita nova*'s explorations of the themes of both the loss and the joyful (re)discovery of Beatrice follow a circular pattern drawing on traditional scriptural exegesis linking the bride of the Song of Songs and the widow of Lamentations.[12] Here, the absent bridal *serventese*, together with the Jeremian "lamentanza in uno sonetto" (VII.2 [2.13]) [lament . . . in a sonnet] that immediately follows, offers a first taste of how Dante's presentation of even the equivocal poems for the screen woman already proleptically articulates some of the stylistic and spiritual epiphanies to come.

Chapter V

Chapter V presents, in four short *commi*, an account of how and why the screen device came to play a part in the lover's experience. Its events begin with an elaborate yet abstract plotting of space and spatial geometries. We are in a church or a shrine, with seating, where the public can gather for a religious service dedicated to the Virgin but where social interaction can also take place. Thus the lover can seize the opportunity to look toward Beatrice; though with decorous terminology, eliding her name with the religious term *beatitudine*, the prose suggests that this is no erotic voyeurism but the expression of a controlled and respectful love, on the verge perhaps of realizing the spiritual transformation of later chapters: "Io era in luogo dal quale vedea la mia beatitudine" (V.1 [2.6]) [I was positioned in such a way that I saw my beatitude].[13] The metonymy of beatitude for Beatrice recalls how, at her first sighting in childhood, the lover's visual faculties and sensitive soul identified her (in Latin) as their sublime object, "beatitudo vestra" (II.5 [1.6]) [your beatitude]. The same emphasis on perceptual processes of sight, whose supreme object or focus point is Beatrice, links the two moments, with the opening phrases of chapter V filled with vocabulary from the domain of vision.[14]

While Beatrice remains (presumably) absorbed in her devotions, and the protagonist in his beatific contemplation of her, others are less single-minded, with the screen woman who sits in the lover's sightline disturbed by its intensity into gazing back toward him, and other congregants observing both the lover and the woman. The church space becomes a lesson in perspective and geometry, tracing the lines that link observers and observed, and the incidental intersections of subsidiary or nonfocalized objects. There is technical description of the linear rays that link the spectator and the beloved, with which the screen woman's seat is also aligned, and measurement of how they terminate, again repeating technical vocabulary (*retta linea* and *terminare* both occur twice): as Christine Gosselin observes, the scene is diagrammatic.[15] We should not, however, forget the further perspectives that link the place of worship on earth to the celestial realm, inhabited by the Virgin Mary, "la regina de la gloria" (V.1 [2.6]) [the Queen of Glory] alongside whom Beatrice will by the end of the book have taken up her place after death.[16] Within the sacred space where the Marian liturgy is being held, all thoughts of beatitude should properly serve this vertical perspective, though the young lover who still directs his gaze along horizontal trajectories has not yet fully grasped the miraculous quality of Beatrice and the way that she points him beyond herself toward the celestial realm. In corroboration, we may note how the vocabulary of vision, denoting ideal clarity, shifts to that of secrecy and screening: the lover in fact begins to congratulate himself on loss of legibility in both his actions and his texts. He enjoys baffling clear communication with the society around him, whether via visual signs ("lo mio secreto non era comunicato lo giorno altrui per mia vista," V.3 [2.8]) or by writing the *cosette* deliberately intended to support the mistaken identification.

Readers of the *Vita nova*'s prose, on the other hand, are in turn "screened" from any such delusion, in the narrator's retrospection over the events. The lover and his contemporaries directly use the name of the screen woman, "nominandola" (V.2 [2.7]), but readers of the finished *libello* never encounter it within Dante's pages. Instead, the singularity and persistence of love for Beatrice are underscored: here, by the sacred location of the opening scene and the wordplay on her name, which effectively appears three times in quick succession, first as *la mia beatitudine* (V.1 [2.6]) and then as *Beatrice* (V.2, 4 [2.7, 9]). The secret for us relates to the screen woman, not the true beloved. Thus the chapter's final statement stresses the deliberate omission of all the screen woman poems, "salvo che alcuna cosa ne scriverò che pare che sia loda di lei" (V.4 [2.9]) [something I will write down that plainly is in praise of her]. The verb *parere* (to show/to seem) underlines the *Vita nova*'s preoccupation with conversion and epiphany—*now*, the enlightened reader understands that praise in the poems selected for transcription must relate to Beatrice. Yet the careful exegesis of the transcription criterion, focused on true and false appearances—*parere*—accommodates the complexity of the figural discourse in this phase of the narrative, so dependent on retrospective authentication to demonstrate that all praise poetry, properly understood, serves the singular beloved and not her shadows or "screens."

Chapter VI

The next section of the narrative probes the questions of praise and of truth and concealment further, in imagining a long poem that could permit the lover to celebrate Beatrice's name publicly yet without scandal: "Sì mi venne una volontade di volere ricordare lo nome di quella gentilissima ed accompagnarlo di molti nomi di donne, e spezialmente del nome di questa gentile donna" (VI.1 [2.10]) [I was taken with a wish to record the name of that most gracious of women and to place it in the company of many women's names, especially this gracious woman's]. Dante tells us that the poem was successfully completed but has been excluded from the *libello*, and we learn little of substance about it: it celebrates the names of sixty women; poetic (but surely also providential) necessity places Beatrice's name immovably in ninth position; its metrical form is that of a verse letter, "una pistola sotto forma di serventese" (VI.2 [2.11]). Slight though they are, however, these indications provide food for further reflection about the evolution of the poetic and ethical ambitions of the *Vita nova*, which have been so carefully plotted into the prose narrative of Dante's ambitious little book.

The *libello*'s justification for mentioning the *serventese* is the marvelous necessity by which Beatrice's name occupies ninth position among the sixty women's names. But by the logic of the narrative, the lover's contemporaries would assume the desired name to be the screen woman's: this hypothetical poem has a hypothetical deception as well as a hypothetical truth embedded within it. (Incidentally, the prose *commi* presenting the lyric avoid names altogether, making Beatrice simply "la gentilissima" and "la mia donna" ["the most gracious" and "my lady"], as if the prose too momentarily must follow the same code of secrecy or misdirection as the putative, absent *serventese*.) Another effect of alluding to a poem of such length and onomastic overload is that it stresses the increasing confusion of the young poet-lover, protagonist within the narrative, after he engages with the distractions of screen devices.[17] Behind the safety of his misconceived courtly screen, the tyro poet uses an epistolary form to angle explicitly for public attention, but without yet fully understanding what his communicative ambitions ought to be. The only other epistle mentioned in the *libello* is the Latin prose letter, similarly mentioned but not copied, that Dante says he addressed to "li principi della terra" (XXX.1 [19.8]) [the rulers of the land] at the point of Beatrice's death.[18] Retrospectively, we can imagine how the two absent epistolary compositions might speak to one another in their reworkings of scriptural allusions to the dialectically paired Song of Songs and Lamentations; but the claims about their intended function and reception are more challenging to unpick. It is asserted that the Jeremian letter boldly proclaims the centrality of Beatrice to a whole community, whereas the *serventese*, however public, was designed to disguise which of its sixty women was the true subject for the other names to "accompagnare" (VI.1 [2.10]) [accompany]. As with the puzzling Jeremian quotation in the next sonnet included in the *prosimetrum*, "O voi che per la via d'Amor passate" (VII.3 [2.14]) [O all ye passing by along Love's way], the temporality and social contexts of the internal narrative prevent a full figural reading, which is blocked by the screen device even as the poet apparently strikes a prophetic, revelatory pose, here (chapter VI) with the symbolic number sixty.[19] And since both of the epistolary compositions are known to us only as phantom works absent from the text of the book we are reading, and from any other source (were they ever even written?), any final judgment about their putative intertextual strategies must remain permanently suspended.

In its immediate context of imagined production and circulation, the publicly oriented *serventese* is presented as a one-off stylistic experiment that celebrates an entirely feminine city. This marks one of the first indications of the importance given in the *Vita nova* to other women, as companions to Beatrice and interlocutors to her lover (though also as distractions, in the later screen woman episodes and the *donna gentile* encounter after Beatrice's death). The *serventese*'s proposed evocation of a city via the names of women would potentially challenge medieval male domination of the urban fabric and invite reflection on the networks that accumulate around women's lives in a city where marriages, funerals, and poetry all fall under women's spon-sorship within the narrative of the *Vita nova*.[20] Yet a poetic catalog of women would inevitably require recitation of either baptismal or familial names— which would remove the narrative from the abstract and universalizing space of "la cittade ove la mia donna fue posta da l'altissimo sire" (VI.2 [2.11]) [the city where my lady was put by the supreme Lord] into the concrete cityscape of Duecento Florence—or of poetic *senhals*, transforming this into a catalog of male love-poets, likewise emphatically Florentine, and destroy-ing the singularity of the poet-protagonist and his beloved.[21]

The virtual absence of proper names and precise historicizing detail is a striking characteristic of the *Vita nova*. Florence is never mentioned by name, and though Beatrice's name is ubiquitous in the prose it occurs very rarely in the lyrics, and only once before her death has been announced, in the sonnet of chapter XXIV [15]. There, names of the two women, Pri-mavera/(Gio)Vanna and Bice/Amore/Beatrice, which appear colloquially in the lyric, are carefully glossed in the prose as bearing biblical and transcen-dent, not historical meanings, indicating the relationship of springtime to beatitude, and of St. John the Baptist to Christ.[22] As in the case of the never-transcribed names of the *serventese*'s sixty women, the prose of chapter XXIV also takes care to ensure that Primavera should support Beatrice's most ab-stract and universal qualities, rather than draw attention toward the external Florentine world where Dante and his unnamed male friend (Guido Caval-canti) compose occasional poetry and address women with the quotidian local names of "monna Vanna e monna Bice" [Lady Joan and Lady Bea] (XXIV.8 [15.8]). In the context of what Dante claims about the *serventese*, it is perhaps worth noting that Beatrice's contracted-form name falls on the ninth line of this sonnet; as the only poem in the *Vita nova* that does give space to another named Florentine woman, there may be a playful echo be-tween the real poem and the phantom lyric where Beatrice's name insisted on ninth position. Indeed, the entire fiction of the *serventese* has elements of an elaborate literary joke, there is so clearly no place in the *prosimetrum* for a poem of this kind.[23]

Epiphanies of Omission: Behind the Screen

In the *Vita nova*, Dante experiments with the representation of a city that becomes universal, mythological, and sacred, thanks to the presence of a miraculous "Beatrice," whose real name can be simultaneously a courtly poetic *senhal* and a religious prayer or *beatitudine*. He almost completely eliminates any transcription of personal or topographical names, though he also provides just enough clues to remind us of the city of stone and of lived history that stands as a reference point behind the schematic version. A past lyric career that exceeds the parameters of the stylistic and affective consistency linked to the *Vita nova*'s version of the beloved is accommodated by the elusive references to missing texts—*cosette per rima* that include an improbable epistolary *serventese*. The screen woman narrative underscores the interpretive challenges in the story that Dante's prose presents to us, by insisting on failed interpretation, ambivalence, concealment, and omission on the part of a narrator whose unreliability is simultaneously highlighted and denied, thanks to the strategy of authorial and temporal division embedded within the "book of memory."[24]

In these two chapters, sacred realities endorse the seriousness of the mature prose narrator's intent, even if this phase of the story still points to its protagonist's lack of comprehension of how immanent spiritual truths lie all around him. In church, he can hear the name of the Virgin Mary and is ready to note the pairing of Beatrice-beatitude, but he is distracted into the screen game by the sound of another woman's name.[25] In the catalog of women mentioned in chapter VI his beloved could be a sturdily Florentine presence, a "monna Bice" whose ninth place in a list of sixty generates marvel, but not yet recognition. But with the plenitude of retrospection afforded to the readers of the *Vita nova*, even these early chapters already point toward later realities. The lover is finally brought to understand that names and numbers have little that is casual about them. If Beatrice were ninth in a list of sixty, this would transform a *catalogue galant* into a scriptural epithalamium. Beatrice is beginning to stand out from her handmaidens and manifest the qualities that express the fullness of her name. Her name, her Marian devotion in chapter V, and her symbolically unavoidable ninth place in the onomastic *serventese* of chapter VI all anticipate how she will later be imagined in paradise, "a gloriare sotto la insegna di quella regina benedetta virgo Maria, lo cui nome fue in grandissima reverenzia ne le parole di questa Beatrice beata" [glory[ing] under the banner of that blessed queen the Virgin Mary, whose name was held in utmost reverence in the words of this beatified Beatrice] (XXVIII.1 [19.1]).

Vita nova VII [2.12–2.18]

JENNIFER RUSHWORTH

Chapter VII [2.12–2.18] of Dante's *Vita nova* describes the protagonist-narrator's reaction to the departure of the first "screen lady," who had been elected earlier (see V [2.6–9]) as a way to hide his love for Beatrice. According to the narrative of the *libello* (little book), Dante writes a poem lamenting this departure, also included at this point in the text: the double sonnet "O voi che per la via d'Amor passate" (VII.3–6 [2.14–2.17]) [O all ye passing by along Love's way]. This sonnet begins with an obvious textual citation, whose origin the prose commentary also goes on to specify as "quelle parole di Geremia profeta: 'O vos omnes qui transitis per viam, attendite et videte si est dolor sicut dolor meus'" (VII.7 [2.18]) [those words of the prophet Jeremiah: "O is it nothing to you, all ye that pass by? behold, and see if there be any sorrow like unto my sorrow"]. These words—given first in Italian verse at the start of the sonnet and then in Latin prose thereafter—are those of a particular line from the book of Lamentations (1:12). There will be another explicit citation from this same biblical book in the *Vita nova*, namely the Latin interruption at the start of chapter XXVIII [19] announcing Beatrice's death, which borrows words from Lamentations 1:1. While the purpose of this short essay is to comment on chapter VII [2.12–2.18], awareness of this later quotation is vital for my analysis, since the question on which I will focus is, simply put, why Dante uses a text that he will later appropriate for the death of Beatrice so early in the *Vita nova* for a different woman, a woman who has not died but has gone away. This question concerns the use and reuse of a particular intertext, whose history I will first introduce. It also sheds new light on the still-thorny issue of the device of the screen lady, to which I turn in due course. Finally, it has quite broad implications for the relationships that we establish as readers between different texts, and between different moments within particular texts.

Lamentations: A Brief History

The book of Lamentations is known by a number of different names: *'êkâ/Eikhah* (from its first word in Hebrew, meaning "how" or "alas"); *Threni* (from the Greek "threnoi" or tears, in the Septuagint version); Lamentations (from the Vulgate gloss: "threni idest lamentationes ieremiae prophetae" [Threni, that is, the Lamentations of prophet Jeremiah]). Although it has traditionally been attributed to Jeremiah (including, as we have seen, by Dante in *Vn* VII), modern scholarship disputes this attribution, with some even suggesting different authors for the five poems that make up the book's five chapters.[1] Regardless of authorship, the book is certainly multifaceted thanks to its use in different contexts, both Jewish and Christian, and both scriptural and liturgical. In short, Lamentations proves to be very mobile already prior to its adoption by Dante.

In the Hebrew Bible/Tanakh, the five chapters of Eikhah are mostly structured around an alphabetical acrostic following the twenty-two letters of the Hebrew alphabet. The poems are usually considered to postdate and to mark the siege and destruction of Jerusalem in 587 BCE.[2] Thus what is being mourned is both the destruction of a city and the destruction of the Temple in that city. In Jewish liturgy, the book of Lamentations is read on Tish'ah be'av (the Ninth of Av), a day that commemorates not only the destruction of the First Temple by the Babylonians but also the destruction of the Second Temple by the Romans in 70 CE—and, as Daniel Grossberg notes, "around which the commemoration of other Jewish destructions and catastrophes have coalesced."[3] As Paul Joyce and Diana Lipton comment in their study *Lamentations through the Centuries*, the very language of Lamentations encourages broader comparisons between different forms of loss:

"The opening verse of the book of Lamentations powerfully brings together collective catastrophe in history ('How lonely sits the city that once was full of people!') with the deepest and most personal of individual human losses ('like a widow'). In this combination we find a key to the power of this small book to speak to numerous different human situations and conditions."[4] Similarly, in Shaye J. D. Cohen's summary of the rabbinic tradition, Lamentations transcends its original historical catalyst to become "the eternal lament for all Jewish catastrophes, past, present, and future."[5]

The "power of this small book" to refer to multiple catastrophes, after its own time, is also strikingly deployed by the appropriation of the book of Lamentations in the Christian tradition. In this new context, the book of Lamentations is interpreted as mourning, in anticipation, Christ's death on the cross. This reading is part of a broader Christian tradition that reads the Hebrew Bible, now understood and reworked as the Old Testament, as anticipating and prefiguring the events of the New Testament. In the case of Lamentations, that the book might mourn an individual is already implicit in the assumption—shared by the Jewish and Christian traditions alike— that Jeremiah is the author of these poems, mourning the death of Josiah (a reading based on 2 Chronicles 35:25). The shift from Jerusalem to Christ is partly enabled by the parallel, in the Gospels, between Christ's body and the Temple, both destined for destruction, but the former to be raised up in three days (see, for instance, John 2:19–22). Beyond the Christian commentary tradition, this shift is most evident liturgically, since readings from Lamentations feature prominently in the *Triduum Sacrum*, or three days of mourning and preparation preceding the Resurrection triumph of Easter Sunday. Quite clearly, in the Christian tradition the book of Lamentations is co-opted as a text of mourning for Christ's passion. The widowed city of Lamentations 1:1 may still refer to Jerusalem, but it is to a later Jerusalem that has witnessed the Crucifixion. In short, Lamentations proves to be "endlessly reusable."[6]

Dante's Lamentations

In the case of Dante, it is of course probable that he had in mind the Christian interpretation of the book of Lamentations and not its Jewish origins. I highlight the latter mainly to show that when Dante receives the book of

Lamentations, the process of the text's transformation and appropriation is already under way. Yet even given this background, Dante's own appropriation of the text remains highly daring. That Dante had a predilection for the book of Lamentations, as evidenced not only in the *Vita nova* but also in the *Commedia*, has been shown extensively by Ronald L. Martinez.[7] Commenting on the citation from Lamentations in "O voi che per la via d'Amor passate," a sonnet that is noted to preexist its integration into chapter VII of the *Vita nova*, Teodolinda Barolini has likewise remarked upon the "tenacità della memoria dantesca" [tenacity of Dante's memory] demonstrated by Dante's repeated return to Lamentations throughout his literary career.[8] In the case of chapter VII, nonetheless, what strikes me is not the consistency of Dante's citational tastes but rather the inconsistency that results from the same text being used in different ways, in different contexts, and at different times. To stay with the *Vita nova*, this inconsistency, as we have seen, leads to Lamentations being deployed with reference to both the screen lady and Beatrice, and to both departure and death. As a consequence, I have previously described the use of Lamentations in chapter VII as "awkward."[9] Martinez's view, faced with the same issue, is that the screen lady is "mourned exaggeratedly."[10] In both cases, Lamentations is felt to be excessive at this point in the *libello*.

The most frequent solution offered to this feeling of excess is a figural interpretation according to which, as Olivia Holmes writes, "the 'gentile donna' is a figure for which the 'gentilissima' is the fulfilment, and her departure is, in the context of the book as a whole, a presage or prophecy of Beatrice's death."[11] Such a reading borrows from Erich Auerbach's seminal essay "Figura," which studies the typological relationship established by Christian readers and commentators between the Old and the New Testaments, the latter being understood in this light as a fulfillment of the former.[12] As I have already noted, it is this technique of reading that allows for the Christian appropriation of the book of Lamentations as, literally, the lament for a city, and, allegorically, the lament for the death of Christ. Nonetheless, I think that there is a risk of erasing difference and tension by subscribing to this figural view of texts. With this caution in mind, let us turn to the citation of Lamentations in Italian verse in *Vita nova*'s chapter VII: "O voi che per la via d'Amor passate, / attendete e guardate / s'egli è dolor alcun, quanto 'l mio, grave" (VII.3 [2.14], lines 1–3) [O all ye passing by along Love's way, /

attend a while and see / if there be sorrow such as I sustain]. These lines are a very accurate translation of the Latin text that Dante then provides in the prose gloss on this sonnet, from the opening vocative to the paired impera-tives and even the identical noun *dolor* (shared by Italian and Latin). Notwithstanding, Dante does add two aspects to his translation: on the one hand, the specification that the "via" ("viam" in the Latin) is "d'Amor"; on the other hand, the qualification of the "dolor" as "grave" [serious, heavy, weighty].

Moreover, in both Latin and Italian the line is beautifully built around a series of finely wrought contrasts. First, there is the contrast between the movement of the passersby and the immobility of the grieving first-person speaker, with the former being invited to slow down to witness, and partici-pate in, the stasis of the latter. In this respect, the Latin verb *attendere* has a number of relevant senses: most obviously, "attend/pay (close) attention to, listen carefully," but also "turn/stretch toward."[13] In other words, attention calls for proximity, that is, for a conversion of the movement past (*transitis/ passate* [passing by]) into an affective movement toward the suffering first-person voice. Second, there is a further contrast between community and isolation, represented grammatically in the contrast between the opening plural ("vos omnes" / "voi" [all ye]) and the later singular (the "meus" that comes at the very end of the line in Latin, with "mio" instead the penulti-mate word in the Italian version). "Dolor" is strikingly singular and unique, as suggested by the invitation to the observers to consider "si est dolor sicut dolor meus" ("s'egli è dolor alcun, quanto 'l mio, grave") [if there be sorrow such as I sustain]. The question implicit here—Is sorrow comparable?— remains unanswered, although the speaker certainly implies that their grief is incomparable. And we might well concur with the speaker's view. After all, when all grief is necessarily experienced individually and in relation to a unique lost object, how could any grief be *like* another? The problematic pivot in this line is the conjunction *sicut* (in Dante's version, the contracted *si* of "s'egli"), for grief defies the logic of the similar and the simile (and, likely, all logic *tout court*).

How ironic, then, that it is this very line from Lamentations that should itself be so mobile: so prone to quotation, appropriation, and transforma-tion. I have already recalled in quite general terms the shift in import of Lam-entations between Judaism and Christianity. To return to that dissonance in greater detail, part of what is interesting about the first-person speaker of Lamentations 1:12 is its openness to different interpretations and uses. In the Jewish tradition, the "dolor" is that of a personified Jerusalem, but also, liturgically, that of the worshipping community. In the Christian tradition, the "dolor" may be read as that of Christ on the cross, crying for compassion, although Christians also appropriate this line for their own grief, transforming the "dolor" from Christ's unique physical suffering to their own experience both of "dying with Christ" and of mourning for Christ's death. In this sense, the first-person singular expresses a shared grief. Strangely, the "dolor" is, in turn, both that of the one who is mourned (Christ) and that of his mourners: truly a form of compassion, or "suffering together." In *Vita nova*'s chapter VII, in contrast, the first-person speaker invites the passersby to witness his grief, but his grief remains unique to his own situation. Daringly, Dante's sadness at the screen lady's departure is suggested to be comparable to the grief of both Christ on the cross and Christians for Christ's death. This comparison becomes even more daring if we consider the prose introduction that precedes the sonnet.

The Problem of the Screen Lady

Dante introduces the poem in chapter VII by telling us that he wrote it in order to feign grief at the departure of the screen lady. The adoption of Lamentations 1:12 to mark the departure of the screen lady is thereby rendered even more shocking. Not only does Dante instigate an implicit parallel either between himself and Christ (as the ones experiencing "dolor") or between Christ and the screen lady (as the love object being mourned), but the parallel is undermined from the outset by doubts about the sincerity of this "dolor." The poem is introduced as a rhetorical ruse, rather than as a record of emotions sincerely felt (not that any poem can ever straightforwardly be viewed in this last light). It is written so that "le persone" [people] do not discover Dante's "nascondere" (VII.2 [2.13]) [cover]. From this perspective, the quotation from Lamentations feels even stranger, since we witness a rift between the genuine experience of "dolor" and the decision to "parla[re] alquanto dolorosamente" (VII.2 [2.13]) [speak somewhat despondently] to maintain a fiction.

But are we so sure that Dante is faking this "dolor"? In the prose introduction, Dante's emotional state is suggested first by the Cavalcantian adjective *sbigottito* [disconcerted] and then by the admission of unconscious desires at work: "Assai me ne disconfortai, piú che io medesimo non avrei creduto dinanzi" (VII.1 [2.12]) [I felt utterly miserable—much more so than I would have believed possible], indeed "una frase rivelatrice" [a revealing phrase], as Domenico De Robertis has noted.[14] The fiction of the screen lady fractures, as Dante admits that he was not able either to anticipate or to control the emotions occasioned by her departure. These details make a figural reading of this episode difficult to sustain, since the departure of the screen lady is a separate event with its own emotional turmoil, quite apart from any foreshadowing of Beatrice's death. Instead, this prose introduction points to quite a different interpretation of the screen lady, according to which Dante used this device in order to bring preexisting poems about other women into the Beatrice-centered space of the *Vita nova*. Put starkly, the screen lady would then be a cover for emotional and poetic infidelity.

The interpretative clue that Dante himself offers of this episode does lean toward a figural reading, since Dante explains that he includes this sonnet in the *Vita nova* because "la mia donna fue immediata cagione di certe parole che nel sonetto sono, sí come appare a chi lo 'ntende" (VII.2 [2.13]) [my lady was the direct source for certain words in the sonnet, as is plain to anyone who understands it]. Yet I admit to not being one of those "chi lo 'ntende" [who understands it], considering both that Beatrice's death is still some way off (and therefore not immediate) and that the screen lady's purpose is precisely that of mediating Dante's love for Beatrice (see again chapter V [2.6–9]). A reading of one chapter in isolation cannot resolve these difficulties, especially since a second screen lady comes to complicate the picture even further (see chapter IX [4]). Nonetheless, my analysis of chapter VII does show that it raises crucial issues about citational practices, about the possibility of comparison, about the nature of grief, and about the sincerity of poetic expression.

In the end, I find it more productive to recognize the strange excessiveness of Dante's use of Lamentations for the screen lady than to attempt to explain this strangeness away through a figural sleight of hand. Thus my reading of the screen lady is ultimately anteleological and resistant to the Beatricean pull of the *libello*—not because I think that infidelity is necessarily at stake here (How could we know? And would it really matter?), but rather because I think that we ought to hold competing interpretations together, rather than attempting to resolve contradiction and tension into an overriding logic of figurality.

Manuele Gragnolati encourages us to see Dante's *rime* through a double lens, both outside and inside the *Vita nova*, without allowing the structure of the *libello* to take precedence or to erase alternative meanings.[15] The "screen lady" is, of course, a fiction of the *Vita nova*, and so the double sonnet of chapter VII proves to have not two but three different modes of existence: first, as a freestanding poem outside and prior to the *Vita nova*; second, as a poem about the "screen lady" (its claimed origin in the prose of chapter VII); third, as a poem actually about Beatrice (as also claimed by the prose of chapter VII). Following Gragnolati, I have argued that we should not allow the third mode to erase or overwrite the poem's earlier incarnations. From this perspective, beyond any potentially coexistent figural framework, Dante's reuse of Lamentations for two different women in the *Vita nova* suggests a bold, self-conscious challenge to the limits of comparability, the limits of textual appropriation, and the limits of interpretation. If we accept the additional limitation of reading only one fragment of the *Vita nova*, these limits become more visible, and we are encouraged to pursue an antiteleological reading of Dante's *libello*.

Vita nova VIII [3]

DARAGH O'CONNELL

In this section of the *libello* Dante moves from the preceding thematic areas
to the realm of death, loss, and praise. For the first time in the anthology, two
sonnets are placed side by side to interrogate these themes, and together con-
stitute the first articulations of what will form a neat triadic thematic cluster
centered on death: the death of Beatrice's father (XXIII [14]) and, in culmi-
nation, the death of Beatrice herself (XXVIII [19]). Indeed, the present chap-
ter announces the theme and intimates its growing importance, to the extent
that Death itself showed Dante the way that "leads from the vanity of *fin
amor* to that intellectual love of beauty, the ultimate object of which is God."[1]
Yet, oddly, it will be exactly in courtly terms that the chapter concludes. Here
he invests his explicatory prose with enhanced autobiographical and personal
content, which in itself differs from previous generic models of *prosimetrum*,
and does so in the full knowledge that in vernacular terms, what he is per-
forming is uncommon in that tradition, and seemingly at odds with the con-
tent of the *Vita nova* as a whole. A number of critics have viewed this section
of the work as slightly anomalous and have also questioned why Dante chose
to place so prominently two sonnets ostensibly written on the death of an
unnamed lady, whose relation to Beatrice was at best tenuous.[2] Marco Santa-
gata also notes that in the Italian vernacular tradition poems about death are
almost entirely absent, and therefore that Dante here innovatively promotes

the introduction of this thematic content into his anthology.[3] Here the concrete details of the *Vita nova* compete with contrived scenarios and allegorizing impulses gleaned from lived experience. However, in order to apprehend his motivation, we must also trust the literal meaning of the prose, as Dante later argues in the *Convivio*: "Sempre lo litterale dee andare innanzi" (2.1.8) [The literal must always go first].

Dante informs the reader that some time after the departure of the "gentile donna" [gracious woman] (the *donna-schermo* of VII), another lady, "una donna giovane" (VIII.1 [3.1]) [young lady], who was known throughout Florence for her charm, died unexpectedly. The poet sees her lifeless body being attended by other weeping women, "molte donne" [many women]. Remembering that he has seen her in the company of Beatrice, "quella gentilissima" [most gracious one], he too begins to weep, and resolves to write about her death by dint of her association with his lady—"la mia donna." The result is two sonnets, "Piangete, amanti, poi che piange Amore" (VIII.4–6 [3.4–6]) [Cry, lovers, since Lord Love is crying here] and "Morte villana, di pietà nemica" (VIII.8–11 [3.8–11]) [Barbarous Death, compassion's enemy].

Chapter VIII [3] opens with the first iteration in the *libello* of the adjectival conjunction *appresso* (after), which thereafter is the most commonly employed incipit for each division. Indeed, there are twelve other instances of chapters beginning with the term, though interestingly its usage is dramatically curtailed after the death of Beatrice to one single instance, the final chapter (XLII [31]). All the others (IX [4], X [5], XIII [6], XIV [7], XV [8], XVI [9], XX [11], XXII [13], XXIII [14], XXIV [15], and XXVII [18]) share with this one here in VIII the same function, that of marking sequentiality and propelling the narrative forward. In this Guglielmo Gorni sees the traces of a first ideation for the *Vita nova* that may have been initially structured along different lines.[4] Others have highlighted the wider semantic range of *appresso* in opposition to other variants such as *poi che* or *poscia che* in that it can refer "not only to temporal but also spatial relations," linking it to *appressare* (to approach or to draw close).[5] The proximal nature of the formulaic term neatly divides sections, enjoins the consequences of foregoing events, and points to the outcomes and different situations for the poet. It suggests both a movement from a concrete moment or event and a tending to a new situation to which the poet feels he must respond. In this sense, *appresso* itself tends toward something, and given its initial ubiquity and later scarcity, we can infer that that something is the death of Beatrice.

The introduction of the "donna giovane"—"Fu piacere del Signore delli angeli di chiamare a la sua gloria una donna giovane" (VIII.1 [3.1]) [It was the pleasure of the Lord of angels to call into her glory a young woman]— syntactically echoes the later prose of the *Convivio*: "Poi che fu piacere delli cittadini della bellissima e famosissima figlia di Roma, Fiorenza, di gittarmi fuori del suo dolce seno" (*Conv.* 1.3.4) [Because it was the pleasure of the citizens of that most beautiful and famous daughter of Rome, Florence, to banish me from her sweet breast]. Besides her youth, she was also "di gentile aspetto molto" (VIII.1 [3.1]) [so gracious in her appearance], a formulation Dante will refashion in his celebrated description of a noble, courtly Manfred in *Purgatorio* 3.107: "biondo era e bello e di gentile aspetto" [he was blond, handsome, and of noble aspect]. The unnamed deceased woman is being attended to by a chorus of women, who weep for her passing "assai pietosamente" (VIII.1 [3.1]) [pitifully]. This chorus assumes the role of a collective character according to Donato Pirovano, and one that is a staple of the *stil novo* tradition.[6] The deceased woman's function is that of having at one time been seen by the poet in the company of Beatrice, and as such she is a suitable vector for his sorrow. The scene anticipates the communal mourning for the death of Beatrice's father later in the *Vita nova* (XXII.3 [13.3]), and here as later Dante participates in the act of mourning, which provides the genesis for the two sonnets.

"Piangete, amanti, poi che piange Amore" marks the introduction of the *planctus* into the Italian vernacular tradition. Derived from the *planh* in the Occitan tradition, the lament serves the dual function of lament and praise. There are rich and varied examples in Europe of public poetic mourning for the death of a person of high social standing, and they usually involve a high quotient of praise for the deceased. One of the oldest forms of the genre is the Old Gaelic *Caíned* (or *caoineadh*, "to cry, to weep," from which the English *keening* derives). The link between death and praise is firmly established in the sonnet in what Teodolinda Barolini calls a "cause-effect relationship."[7] The poetics Dante strives to achieve will involve an overcoming of death *in* death through praise of Beatrice and culminates in the *canzone* "Li occhi dolente per pietà del core" (XXXI [20]) [My eyes, in sorrow for my heart's torment]. As intimated in this sonnet, the poet's happiness will not be in the object of his praise but is to be found rather in the words that praise his lady: "in quelle parole che lodano la donna mia" (XVIII.6–7 [10.8–10.9]) [in words that praise my lady]. This process begins in this sonnet and is underscored by the use of the verb *laudare* (to praise) prominently placed as the rhyming word in line 7 of the poem. Mario Pazzaglia reads the inclusion of this poem in the anthology, not as a moment in the poet's story of love for his lady, but rather as a moment in his developing poetics and representational concerns.[8] Indeed, many of the rhetorical features confirm this view, and stylistically the sonnet is certainly more evolved than the preceding ones.

The sonnet's lament begins with a threefold polyptoton—*Piangere, piange,* and *plorare* (also the technique of twinning the vernacular with its Provençal form—*piangere/plorare*—is a feature here, as with *onore* and *orranza* in lines 8–9). It is noteworthy that Dante adopts the polyptoton to great effect later in the *Commedia,* where again the accent of the poem is on the rhetorical manipulation of language, as in two examples from *Inferno* 13: "Cred'ïo ch'ei credette ch'io credesse" (*Inf.* 13.25) [I thought he thought that I thought]; "'infiammò contra me li animi tutti; / e li 'nfiammati infiammar sì Augusto'" (*Inf.* 13.67–68) ["inflamed all minds against me. / And they, inflamed, did so inflame Augustus"]. Moreover, the use of *plorare* establishes a link with the final line of the sonnet "O voi che per la via d'Amor passate" (VII.3–6 [2.14–17]) [O all ye passing by along Love's way] from chapter VII: "e dentro da lo core struggo e ploro" [while in my heart I wither and lament]. That poem is linked also to the poems of this section because of its form—*sonetto rinterzato,* or double sonnet—the other example of which is the second sonnet of chapter VIII. According to Stefano Carrai, terms linked to the semantic sphere of *pianto,* or lament, are a notable feature of the elegiac genre.[9] Equally, there is further wordplay through the use of *Amanti* (Lovers), *Amore, Amor* (Lord Love), and the paronomastic *amaro* (bitter). Kenelm Foster and Patrick Boyde comment that the opening lines of the poem actually "announce the theme of the whole poem" and function like a preview of its contents.[10] In the second quatrain the verses also contain the genesis of the next sonnet of the chapter through the formula "villana Morte" [base Death]. Rightly, Andrew Frisardi distinguishes between the different qualities of *villana* in this sonnet and the "Morte villana" [Barbarous Death] of the following one. Pirovano suggests that Giacomino Pugliese's *canzone* "Morte, perché m'ai fatta sí gran guerra" [Death, why have you waged such war on me] as a possible hypotext, given the occurrence of the syntagmatic "villana morte."[11]

"Piangete" is the plaintive address to the "amanti"—the *fedeli d'Amore*—with which the sonnet opens, and this announces its public dialogic nature, which is reinforced at the beginning of the sestet with "Udite" [Listen]. The poet entreats them to cry, since Love, personified here, cries and listens to the pleas of the women, witnessing the outward manifestation of their "amaro duol" [bitter pain], tears. What did this was death, cruel and unjust, laying waste to everything that is praiseworthy on earth ("laudare") in this "gentil donna" [gracious woman]. In the sestet Love pays homage to this lady, and the poet tells us he saw him there "in forma vera" [in a living body] weeping over the still-beautiful ("avvenente") body of the "la morte imagine" [dead and lovely image]. The soul of the woman is explicitly referred to as worthy of heaven (12–13). Barolini identifies this play on "vera forma" and "morta imagine" as an early signpost for Dante's long meditation on representation.[12] Indeed, there is something of a hermeneutical knot here that is not easily loosened, and it centers on the identification by some of "Amore" here "in forma vera" with the figure of Beatrice. In courtly love poetry and later in Dante, the figure of *Amore* and the woman who is loved often overlap and interchange. Marco Grimaldi states that in the *Vita nova* in general Beatrice both is and is not *Amore*.[13] However, in the context of the present sonnet there is nothing explicit to suggest such an identification, and Gorni rightly affirms that within the confines of the individual sonnet it is extremely unlikely that Dante encodes two distinctive identities within one figure.[14] Love, then, simply stated, in its "forma vera," views and laments the "morta imagine" of the lady. Some have seen an analogue to this *Amore* in Cino da Pistoia's sonnet "Vedete donne, bella creatura" [Ladies, see this fair creature], in which Love is made visible and is seen adoring the lady: "ch'io veggio Amor visibil che l'adora" (line 13) [I see Love, visible, adoring her]. Furthermore, Michelangelo Picone's analysis of Cino's presence in the *Vita nova* is apt in this regard in that it differs greatly from Cavalcanti's influence on Dante.[15]

The second sonnet of the chapter—"Morte villana, di pietà nemica"—constitutes a "vituperative apostrophe to death."[16] Like its counterpart, the narrator tells us it was occasioned by the death of the unnamed lady; however, here the similarities between the two end in what is a sustained attack on death set against a backdrop of courtly values. If in the first the space was public, populated by Love, keening women, and the poet himself, and the form addressed to a public (presumably for public recitation), here instead the poet is alone railing against the injustices perpetrated by Death, set against courtly ideals that the woman embodied in life. The first interrogated death through the eyes of Love; now Death itself is excoriated by the poet. Thus the theme of death and praise is continued, though without the developed sophistication of "Piangete, amanti, poi che piange Amore." Critics have rightly criticized it for being too heavily indebted to Guittone,[17] to the extent that Domenico De Robertis went so far as to claim that here Dante was even more Guittonian than Giuttone himself.[18] Notwithstanding these criticisms and others, the sonnet displays many features worthy of mention and taken together with the preceding two sonnets forms a cluster around notions of lamentation, death, and praise. Its form is the *improperium in Mortem.*

The invective against death occupies lines 1–12, and praise for the virtues of the lady destroyed by death takes up the remaining eight lines. The sonnet contains within itself a high degree of rhetorical flourish and a sophisticated courtly lexicon. Features such as the *amplificatio,* the apostrophe (sustained throughout the sonnet), *expolitio* (1–2, 7), accumulation of detail, and artificial inversions abound.[19] The subject of the first section is delayed until line 6: "di te blasmar la lingua s'affatica" [my tongue strains hard to blame you bitterly]. There is further wordplay with the etymological pun of line 9: "torto tortoso" [culprit, culpable], a feature not readily associated with later Dantean poetics, though there are some notable exceptions: "selva selvaggia" (*Inf.* 1.5) [wood, savage]; "più volte vòlto" (*Inf.* 1.36) [many times I turned]; "che 'l seguente canto canta" (*Par.* 5.139) [that the next song sings]. But Beatrice is absent both spiritually and stylistically from the sonnet. There is the same link as in the previous poem between lamentation and praise, yet here the lexical choices are drawn from the rarefied world of courtly love and its attendant traditions. The "donna giovane" [young woman] now becomes the embodiment of courtly ideals:

> Dal secol hai partita cortesia
> e ciò ch'è in donna da pregiar vertute:
> in gaia gioventute
> distrutta hai l'amorosa leggiadria
>   (VIII.10 [3.10], lines 13–16)

[Out of this world you've taken what is gracious / and everything we prize as woman's best. / You've crushed a lover's zest / in happy youth while it was most vivacious.]

The "gaia gioventute" recalls the final line—"gaia sembianza" [winsome grace]—of "Piangete, amanti, poi che piange amore." Moreover, that favored term of the courtly lexicon—*leggiadria/ leggiadro*—is present here and in the "O voi che per la via d'Amor passate" from the previous chapter: "cosí leggiadro questi lo core have?" (VII.4 [2.14], line 12)] [so weightless in his heart]. The later Dante of the *Commedia* writes with a longing for a bygone time of courtliness, in which "cortesia" had a special value, in the sense of munificence, generosity, liberality, and nobility. Paradoxically, this nostalgia for the "buon tempo antico" [good old times], ensures that it will be written out of any actual reality and be figured in the poem as either a lost ideal[20] or a perfected "corte del cielo" (*Inf.* 2.125) [Heaven's court] in the realm of paradise—that is, unattainable to the living, beyond mankind's grasp, and therefore impossible. And yet, this perfection is articulated in courtly terms, availing itself of the courtly semantic field.

It is true that courtly love is thematized throughout Dante's works, and the literary representation of it is never far behind his discussion of love. However, though the cultural milieu in which Dante mediated and wrote in his youth was one in which the whole system of *fin amor* was left behind by the newly intellectualizing and moralizing philosophical amatory systems of *stilnovismo* and its many immediate antecedents, certain remnants did survive into the poetry and thought of their day. Those courtly values—of love and the noble heart—both neatly enshrined in the concept of *cortesia* find in Dante's time their first transformation into idealized forms.

> Cortesia e onestade è tutt' uno: e però che nelle corti anticamente le vertudi e li belli costumi s'usavano, sí come oggi s'usa lo contrario, si tolse quello vocabulo dalle corti, e fu tanto a dire cortesia quanto uso di corte. Lo qual vocabulo se oggi si togliesse dalle corti, massimamente d'Italia, non sarebbe altro a dire che turpezza. (*Conv.* 2.10.8)

[Courtesy and honor are the same thing: and because in the courts of old, virtues and fine manners were the norm, as today the opposite is the norm, that word was taken from the courts and to say "courtesy" was to say "the norm of the court." This word, if it were taken from the courts now, especially in Italy, would mean nothing but degradation.]

In chapter VIII Dante's ceaseless self-reflection sees him develop exercises and experiments in the disparate literary traditions of poetry, most notably the *planh*. Here, however, his poetry is not anchored yet to the figure of Beatrice, and she is mostly absent from this chapter of the *Vita nova*, with only one clear reference to her role. These are not mere exercises in style and form, but rather adumbrations and articulations on death and lamentation that will open the path to the new poetics of internalized desire in praise of Beatrice. Lino Pertile comments that the transformation of Beatrice from courtly lady to saintly lady "represents the most mature literary fruit of this new humble tradition."[21] In chapter VIII Dante's lament and praise for the unnamed lady is grounded in death, a death that will be overcome poetically in praise of Beatrice.

Vita nova IX [4]

SOPHIE V. FULLER

Dante-protagonist-narrator's vision of Amore [Love] is central to *Vita nova* IX [4], both narratively and thematically. Consideration of both *Vita nova* IX's sonnet, "Cavalcando l'altr'ier," and the commentary Dante wrote later to accompany it renders this abundantly clear.[1] Yet this vision of Amore also contributes significantly to Dante's claim in the *Vita nova* to *auctoritas* both for himself and for the vernacular in which he writes.[2] As this study demonstrates, Dante's utilization of and challenge to his multiple intertexts form a fundamental aspect of this claim, as they do throughout Dante's oeuvre. Through analyzing Dante's positioning of the episode in the tradition of the *pastorelle*, his subversion of Cavalcanti's love poetry and use of screen ladies, and the possible echoes of Ovid's poetry about love, it argues that Dante undermines courtly love, its transience, and the artifices it employs.[3] This study also suggests that Dante uses the commentary to his sonnet and both scriptural and Virgilian precedents to undermine the fiction of the screen ladies and further his contrasting narrative of true love for Beatrice. It concludes that in *Vita nova* IX's vision of Amore, Dante successfully manipulates these various intertexts and his own poetry to further his narrative, thematic, and literary agendas.

The Importance of Textual Framing

Dante carefully establishes the narrative and thematic frame of reference for the forthcoming vision of Amore in the explanatory prose that textually precedes "Cavalcando l'altr'ier" but was written subsequently. He opens *Vita nova* IX [4] by reminding his readers both of the death of one of Beatrice's companions and of the first screen lady's departure from Florence (IX.1 [4.1]). Both separations constitute rehearsals for Beatrice's death in the *libello*'s second half, establishing separation and loss as key themes of this chapter.[4] Dante foreshadows the second screen lady's introduction by using the same formula to both open and close the matter of the first screen lady: "convenne partire" [a situation came up that forced [Dante-protagonist-narrator] to depart]. Dante also reminds us of the different narrative levels at play here—the fiction of the "difese" [defenses] or "screen ladies," a courtly device to divert spies and gossips, and the true love for Beatrice that it protects.

Similarly, Dante establishes the poetry of the man the protagonist-narrator calls "il primo de li miei amici" (III.14 [2.1]) [my best friend] and the *pastorelle* as literary frames of reference for "Cavalcando l'altr'ier" from its opening line. The sonnet's opening word, "Cavalcando" [riding], a hapax in the *Vita nova*, plays blatantly upon Cavalcanti's name. It is a fitting beginning for what Barolini calls the "manifestly Cavalcantian" section of the *Vita nova* (IX–XVI [4–17]).[5] Dante's use of a gerund here also recalls the *Fiore*, as five of its incipits commence with an initial gerund.[6] This presages Dante-protagonist-narrator's forthcoming dialogue with Amore, since the *Fiore*, which may also have been written by Dante, contains similar dialogues.[7] More significantly, the opening line of "Cavalcando l'altr'ier" recalls the *pastorelle*, with "l'altri'ier" [the other day] a convention to indicate an imprecise number of days.[8] "Un cammino" [a path] is similarly vague. In the *pastorelle*, a genre with which Cavalcanti had also experimented in "In un boschetto trovai pastorella" [In a wood I found a shepherdess] (my translation), a knight riding in the countryside would chance upon a comely shepherdess.[9] A dialogue would ensue in which the knight sought to seduce the shepherdess, and an amorous encounter would follow before the knight continued his journey.[10] Dante thus sets the scene for Dante-protagonist-narrator's forthcoming encounter with Amore. However, Dante will soon subvert our consequent expectations.

Dante strengthens the chapter's Cavalcantian ambience and recalls the traumatic alienation of Cavalcanti's lover as Dante-protagonist-narrator contrasts the multitude surrounding him with his anguish at leaving Florence ("Cavalcando l'altri'ier," IX.2 [4.2], line 2). Dante emphasizes the protagonist-narrator's suffering in the hyperbolic statement that "quasi li sospiri non poteano disfogare l'angoscia che lo cuore sentia" [even sighs could not release all the anguish [his] heart was feeling]. Dante recalls here the *sospiri* and *angoscia* that characterized Cavalcanti's lover, particularly the "angosciosi diletti i . . . sospiri" [anguished delights . . . the sighs] that Cavalcanti's protagonist-narrator emits in the sonnet "Se Mercé fosse amica a' miei disiri" (*Rime* 15.5) [If Mercy were the friend of my desires] (my translation). Cavalcanti also associates Amore, *sospiri*, and *angoscia* as his protagonist-narrator describes the "sospiri" and frequent closeness to "l'angosciosa Morte" [anguished death] that plagued him because of Amore in Cavalcanti's *ballata* "Vedete ch'i' son un che vo piangendo" (*Rime* 10.5 and 8) [See that I am one who goes along crying] (my translation).

Reading "Cavalcando l'altr'ier" alone, we might assume that Dante-protagonist-narrator's inability to reach the first screen lady causes his distress, since he fails to mention Beatrice. Instead, the accompanying commentary clarifies that this sorrow's true cause is the increasing distance from his *beatitudine* (IX.2 [4.2]) [beatitude], recalling Dante-protagonist-narrator's designation of Beatrice as his *beatitudo* in II.5 [1.6]. This discrepancy raises the possibility that the fiction of the screen ladies may in fact be a device to mask the young Dante's love for women who are not Beatrice.[11] Yet it also strengthens our sense of Dante-protagonist-narrator's true, salvific love for her. The recollection in Dante-protagonist-narrator's melancholy journey of Christ's two sorrowing disciples on the road to Emmaus (Luke 24:36–41) furthers this Christological agenda.

Love's Sudden Appearance

Dante's narrative, thematic, and literary agenda become more apparent in the vision of Amore that appears to the protagonist-narrator. The conception of *amor*/Amor as both an emotional force and a "god with human appearance and agency" seems to originate in Ovid, where Ovid vacillates between the amorphous abstraction and the human agent, and eventually conflates the two, along the model of Hesiod's Eros.[12] Dante renders apparent his Cavalcantian frame of reference and the link between "Cavalcando l'altr'ier" and the *pastorelle* tradition in his use of the keyword *trovai*. Cavalcanti had even used this word in the incipit of his own experiment in the genre, "In un boschetto trovai pastorella." However, Dante subverts the genre as Dante-protagonist chances upon not a shepherdess but Amore "in mezzo de la via" (line 3) [walking . . . on the way].

Dante-protagonist-narrator echoes Cavalcanti in Amore's domination of the lover, and perhaps Ovid's assertion that "uror et in uacuo pectore *regnat Amor*" [I burn and in my empty breast Love rules] (my italics and translation) in *Amores* 1.1.26, as Dante-protagonist-narrator reveals his own domination by love in his commentary to this vision. The repetition in "segnore" [lord] and "me segnoreggiava" [rules] emphasizes this subjugation. Yet Dante subverts both Ovid's burning love and the sense of Love's noxious dominion over the lover that permeates Cavalcanti's oeuvre, as Dante-protagonist-narrator calls Amore his "dolcissimo segnore" [sweet lord] and asserts that this love is inspired by "la vertù de la gentilissima donna" (IX.3 [4.3]) [by the power of that most gracious of women]. This is *fin amor*, not the *fol amor* that characterizes both the *pastorelle* and Cavalcanti's poetry. It recalls *Vita nova* II.7 [1.8], in which Dante-protagonist-narrator avers that after he saw Beatrice for the first time, "D'allora innanzi . . . Amore segnoreggiò la [sua] anima" [From then on, . . . Love dominated [his] soul]. Since Christ is also *segnore*, Dante's attribution of a Christological agenda to his love for Beatrice is also at play in *Vita nova* IX.3 [4.3]'s commentary.

Dante's complex interweaving of his various intertexts to further his own agenda is particularly apparent in the detailed description of Amore dressed "in abito leggier di peregrino" ("Cavalcando l'altr'ier," line 4), and "di vili drappi" (IX.3 [4.3]) [in the rough and tattered clothes of a wanderer]. Dante seems to recall the dialogues of the *Fiore* in his attention to scene setting in Amore's appearance and clothing.[13] Amore's clothing and his "capo chino" [head bent low] to avoid the gaze of others ("Cavalcando l'altr'ier," line 8) mirror Dante-narrator's own dejected exile from his beloved and alienation from his traveling companions. Yet they also figure Christ's appearance as *peregrinus* to two mournful female disciples on the road to Emmaus. They foreshadow the pilgrims passing through Florence in Holy Week shortly after Beatrice's death in *Vita nova* XL [29] and recall Amore's dressing "di novo d'un drappo nero" (*Rime* LXXII, line 9) [in a new black cloak] in one of the lyrics excluded from the *Vita nova*, "Un dì si venne a me Malinconia" ["One day Melancholy came to me"] (my translation). Amore's sudden appearance to a melancholy protagonist and his disheveled attire also recall the troubled Aeneas's vision among Troy's ruins of Hector, the dead hero beloved by the city's inhabitants and central to the Trojans' experience of the war, in *Aeneid* 2. Dante echoes this passage overtly when Amore later disappears (*Aeneid* 2.74; *Vn* IX.7 [4.7]). This vision therefore constitutes one of many anticipations of Beatrice's death that build through the *Vita nova*, from Beatrice's companion's death and the echoes of Jeremiah and his laments for another widowed city in *Vita nova* VII and VIII, through the episode of the *donna pietosa* in *Vita nova* XXIII, to *Vita nova* XXVIII–XXXI.[14] Accordingly, Dante's allusion to the Hector episode is not merely erudite or decorative but lays the foundations for Dante's ambitions to be a poet of stature in his focus on Beatrice's death and its transformative implications both for self and for society, just as Troy needed to fall so that Rome could be founded, and Christ had to sacrifice himself so that humanity could regain the lost Eden.

Dante subverts Cavalcanti's a/Amore as Dante-protagonist-narrator describes Amore as "disbigottito" (IX.4 [4.4]) [dejected]. This recalls Cavalcanti's address to "his" "voce sbigottita and deboletta" [dejected and weak little voice] that comes "piangendo d'un cor dolente" [crying from a pained heart], in the "ballatetta" "Perch'i' no spero di tornar giammai" [Because I never hope to return] (lines 37–38, my translation)].[15] Indeed, Cavalcanti's lover is "prey to an interior fragmentation that destines him to be forever in search of himself—forever a 'pilgrim.'"[16] Significantly, Dante even plays upon his own earlier echoes of Cavalcanti in his description of Amore "sospirando pensoso" ("Cavalcando l'altr'ier," line 13) [sighing in dismay] as he proceeds, just as Dante-protagonist-narrator was "pensoso" (line 2) [troubled]. In this depiction of Amore Dante perhaps also reflects Ovid's depiction of Amor in the *Ars amatoria*, who "engages the poet as an opponent" but is "aetas mollis et apta regi" [of vulnerable age and fit to be ruled].[17] Indeed, Dante's Amore is portrayed both as *segnore* and "come avesse perduto segnoria" ("Cavalcando l'altri'ier," line 5) [as though his mastery were gone]. However, much as Ovid's Amor in the end cannot be controlled, Amore's gaze first at the earth, symbol of endurance, and then at "ad uno fiume bello e corrente e chiarissimo" [a beautiful river of clear running water], symbol of transience and possibility, hints that he will soon regain *segnoria*.[18]

Amore's Vernacular Address

Amore's speech constitutes an important aspect of Dante's claim to *auctoritas*, as Amore speaks in the vernacular for the first time (IX.5 [4.5]). At his previous appearance in the *Vita nova*, he had addressed Dante-protagonist-narrator in Latin (III.3 [1.14]). Thus this shift seems to foreshadow Dante's defense of the vernacular poets and their ability to personify Love just as Ovid and the classical poets had done in XXV.9 [16.9].

In asserting this claim to *auctoritas*, Dante manipulates his scriptural sources freely in both Dante-protagonist-narrator's description of Amore's address and the address itself. Instead of merely translating the Latin text, Dante boldly rewrites Isaiah 45:4, "Et vocavi te in nomine tuo" [I have even called thee by thy name], in Dante-protagonist-narrator's statement "*mi* vide, *mi* chiamò per nome" ("Cavalcando l'altr'ier," line 9, emphasis mine) [he saw me, he called my name on cue]. This reversal of Isaiah and the repetition of the object in this poetic line and its accompanying explanatory commentary ("a me," "mi," "dicessemi," IX.5 [4.5]) emphasize Amore's dominion over Dante-protagonist-narrator. Dante subsequently both combines the Cavalcantian notion of the woman's unattainability and reverses Hebrews 10:37, "qui venturus est veniet et non tardabit" [he that shall come will come, and will not tarry], as Amore explains that the first screen lady will not return for a long time (IX.5 [4.5], line 10). Dante thus implicitly contrasts her with Beatrice, who like Christ will return.[19]

Dante further subverts Cavalcanti's poetry and the traditions of courtly love in Amore's introduction to Dante-protagonist-narrator of the second screen lady, or "difensione" [defense] (IX.5 [4.5]). Dante calls into question the authenticity of such "love" and undermines the agency of the lover, as Amore states that Dante-protagonist-narrator's heart was only with this lady through Amore's will ("Cavalcando l'altr'ier," line 11). This imagery of a heart taken to a woman appears in Cino da Pistoia, Lapo Gianni, and also *Fiore* 77.1.1–2, in which love similarly denies the lover control.[20] It perhaps also recalls the *uacuo pectore* over which Amor reigns in Ovid's *Amores* 1.1.26. Amore reasserts his dominion over Dante-protagonist-narrator as Amore avers that he has collected the heart only so it can "servir novo piacere" ("Cavalcando l'altr'ier," line 12) [serve a new delight], suggesting the ease with which this "love" can be transferred from one object to the next.

Dante recalls here Cavalcanti's "foresette nove" [young girls], whose wonder underscores tragically the lover's distance from the beloved. As such Dante looks ahead to the *Commedia*, when Beatrice scolds Dante-pilgrim for his desire for "o pargoletta / o novità di sì breve uso" (*Purg.* 31.59–60) [a green young girl or other novelty].[21] Dante therefore implicitly critiques the shallow, insincere love of conventional courtly poetry, which contrasts with his genuine love for Beatrice.

Dante continues this challenge to Cavalcanti and expressly highlights the artifice and fickleness of Dante-protagonist-narrator's love for this second screen lady, as Amore instructs Dante-protagonist-narrator not to reveal this "simulato amore" (IX.6 [4.6]) [fictional love], suggesting that by necessity there will be other screen ladies. Dante-protagonist-narrator thus continues the fiction that the "simulato amore" masks his genuine love for Beatrice, constituting a *difensione* for both him and his beloved. Dante-protagonist-narrator would have us believe that this is necessary because of the courtly world in which he and Beatrice live and in which spies and gossips are ready to ruin others' reputations. Yet Dante soon unmasks this "simulato amore" as another of the courtly world's "empty and artificial games."[22] Much as Cavalcanti's own use of screen ladies pushed the unknowable lady away, Dante-protagonist-narrator's "simulato amore" has an unfortunate, distressing result, leading Beatrice to deny Dante-protagonist-narrator her greeting (X [5]). Significantly, "Cavalcando l'altr'ier" contains no suggestion that Dante-protagonist-narrator's love for this second screen lady is anything other than genuine, even if it is fickle. Dante may well have been seeking to explain away love poetry that was not inspired by Beatrice—perhaps the real reason for Beatrice's denied greeting. However, Dante also seems deliberately to be undermining his own fiction, thus destabilizing the courtly trope of the screen lady and attacking the transient, transferable nature of courtly love.[23] By contrast, love for Beatrice is nontransferable and enduring, and its narrative will continue into *Convivio* and the *Commedia*.

Amore's Sudden Disappearance

Dante destabilizes his own narrative further as Dante-narrator takes of Amore "sì gran parte" [so much . . . in place] that Love vanishes from view

("Cavalcando l'altr'ier," lines 9–12). Dante subverts the *pastorelle* here for the final time, as Dante-protagonist-narrator, instead of taking pleasure with a comely shepherdess, is here taken charge of by Amore.[24] Dante also reverses here Amore's earlier sudden appearance, an antithesis highlighted in Dante-protagonist-narrator's commentary by the opposition of "disparve" (IX.7 [4.7]) [he disappeared] to the earlier "apparve" (IX.3 [4.3]) [he appeared]. This highlights the further reversal in the roles of Amore and Dante-protagonist-narrator, as Amore is once again *segnore* and Dante-protagonist-narrator again the "pensoso" [troubled] lover, sighing as he continues his journey (IX.7 [4.7]). While Amore's appearance earlier recalled Christ's appearance on the road to Emmaus, there is no such biblical echo here. This suggests the stark reality that the pursuit of this screen lady is futile and that Dante-protagonist-narrator's has been a "failed or false conversion."[25]

Dante hints at the tragic futility of the love for these screen ladies when, as mentioned earlier, he recalls Aeneas's vision of Hector during the fall of Troy in Dante-protagonist-narrator's assertion that he was "quasi cambiato" [somewhat changed] in appearance.[26] Dante subverts Virgil here, for while it was Hector's phantom who was "quantum mutatus" (*Aeneid* 2.274) [somewhat changed] from the Hector who had returned triumphant from battle, now Dante-protagonist-narrator applies this phrase to himself. This contributes to the reinstating of the original relationship between Amore and the lover, as Dante-protagonist is once more the tattered pilgrim, who continues on his "cammino de li sospiri" (X.1 [10.1]) [path of sighs]. Yet in recalling Aeneas's vision of Hector here, Dante seems to be implying that the protagonist-narrator who experienced the vision also figures Aeneas. This both enhances the sense of loss in this part of the *Vita nova*, since Aeneas must undergo many trials and tribulations even after Troy's fall, and also hints at future hope, as those trials ultimately lead to the founding of Rome. Similarly, by the *Vita nova*'s close, Beatrice has died but Dante-protagonist-narrator's *peregrinatio amorosa* leads him back to Beatrice, a presage of their reunion in *Purgatorio*, when she leads Dante-pilgrim to God.[27]

Accordingly, this study has demonstrated that *Vita nova* IX and in particular the vision of Amore fulfill an important role in both furthering and undermining the courtly fiction of the screen lady and challenging the poetry of

Dante's predecessors, particularly Cavalcanti. It has suggested that the commentary accompanying "Cavalcando l'altr'ier" should lead us to question whether this courtly fiction is really intended to explain Dante's love poetry for women other than Beatrice. It also argues that this commentary develops Dante's narrative of true love for Beatrice and the Christological agenda he attributes to it. Finally, this study has shown that in combining and subverting multiple classical, scriptural, and contemporary intertexts, *Vita nova* IX constitutes an important early claim to *auctoritas* both for vernacular literature in general and for Dante's oeuvre specifically.

Vita nova X and XI [5.1–5.7]

GIULIA GAIMARI

One of the most renowned love stories of Western literature begins with a greeting on the streets of late Duecento Florence. And one of the most significant innovations in the medieval tradition of love literature develops from the denial of that same greeting. The miraculous nature of Beatrice—pure manifestation of God's *caritas* (charity)—required a profound change in life and poetry. Dante's progressive discovery of her ontologically divine status blew away erotic and poetic clichés codified within the courtly world, as they proved deeply inadequate to grasp the true essence of the love that she could awaken. The *Vita nova* is precisely the account of the existential and artistic metamorphosis of its author, and, as a self-exegetical *prosimetrum* written in the Italian vernacular, it is itself a novelty that stands out within the literary panorama of late thirteenth-century Italy.[1] The ennobling power of *fin'amors* (courtly love) is a key feature of Occitan and Old French literature that was inherited and reworked by thirteenth-century Italian poets. It was Guido Guinizzelli who first explored uncharted territory by giving his poetry an unprecedented theoretical breadth rooted in scientific and philosophical doctrines and imbued with scriptural and liturgical motifs. With his lyric "Al cor gentil rempaira sempre amore" [Love returns always to a noble heart], which provoked puzzlement if not harsh criticism among his contemporaries,[2] Guinizzelli renewed the troubadour idea entailing the coexistence of love and nobility of the heart by drawing on natural philosophy, *scientia de anima* (knowledge of the soul), and metaphysical speculation.[3]

The Bolognese jurist paved the way for Guido Cavalcanti's and Dante's own poetic experiments.[4] Nevertheless, despite the undeniable presence of shared conceptual and stylistic patterns, the theory of love emerging from the *Vita nova* goes beyond any earlier or coeval literary model.[5] As early as *Vita nova* II.9 [1.10], Dante's *amore* (love) is conceived as always being governed by "the faithful counsel of reason," a conception remarkably close to the theology of *intellectus amoris* (intelligence of love) developed within the twelfth- and thirteenth-century current of affective mysticism.[6] As Roberto Rea notes, "Non può sfuggire come tale assunto, già in sé, costituisca un'evidente rottura rispetto alla concezione canonica, sorretta da un'amplissima tradizione culturale, letteraria e filosofica, che vuole invece amore e ragione come forze opposte e inconciliabili" [It is clear that this tenet, in itself, already marks a blatant rupture with respect to the prevailing conception envisaging love and reason as opposing and irreconcilable forces, a conception supported by a wide cultural, literary, and philosophical tradition].[7] The *libello* [little book] reveals Dante's gradual conquest of a rational and self-sufficient love that assumes the connotations of *caritas* and inspires the "parole che lodano la donna mia" (XVIII 6 [10.8]) [words that praise my lady], where the poet's ultimate happiness resides.[8] What is more, the psychological, spiritual, and poetic evolution recorded in the *Vita nova* lies at the heart of the fiction of the *Commedia*. Dante's disinterested love for Beatrice is the cornerstone of the poem's salvific itinerary.[9]

Vita nova chapters X and XI [5.1–5.7] offer a privileged point of view from which to look at the core of Dante's spiritual and literary conversion, as the loss of Beatrice's greeting is the first step toward understanding the true meaning of her presence on earth and thus conceiving, cultivating, and celebrating a new life filled with a transformed form of love. At the same time, these chapters may allow us to appreciate how the author uses and reworks doctrinal content probably available in late Duecento Florence. It is well known that Beatrice's refusal of her "dolcissimo salutare" (X 2 [5.2]) [wonderful greeting] arose as a result of the poet's indecorous attentions toward the second *donna schermo* (screen lady).[10] Dante's abuse of the courtly stratagem conventionally employed to hide the identity of the beloved provoked the rise of an uncurbed rumor depicting him as a dissolute lover, thereby eliciting the harsh reaction of the "distruggitrice di tutti li vizi e regina de le vertudi" (X.2 [5.2]) [enemy of depravity and queen of every virtue]. This shocking event—part of a series culminating in Beatrice's own death— prompts a digression where the *auctor* (author) reports the beatific effects that Beatrice's greeting had on him. Wherever she appeared, in the hope of her miraculous greeting, Dante was pervaded by a "fiamma di caritade" (XI.1 [5.4]) [flame of charity] that made him forgive whoever had offended him. When she was about to greet him, his eyes trembled with love as "uno spirito d'amore" (XI.2 [5.5]) [a spirit of love] would take the place of the spirits of sight; and when she finally greeted him, Love did not mitigate the unbearable bliss he felt but rather became so powerful so as to dominate and paralyze his body.[11]

As Donato Pirovano suggests in his commentary to these chapters, as long as the *agens* (protagonist) receives Beatrice's salutation, he cannot penetrate the mystery of her love. "Gli effetti non corrispondono alle premesse: se nell'attesa e nella speranza del saluto, Dante si sente pervaso da un ardente sentimento di carità, poi subentra in lui una passione dolce e paralizzante che ha i tratti di *eros*" [The effects do not meet the premises: in anticipation and in the hope of her greeting, Dante is first pervaded by a sense of ardent charity, which is then replaced by a sweet and paralyzing passion bearing the likeness of *eros*].[12] Beatrice's extraordinary benevolence is set out from the very beginning of the *libello*, when she first gives Dante her sweet salute (III 1–2 [1.12–1.13]). The exceptional, almost scandalous, nature of Beatrice's spontaneous acts rests on her possession of *caritas*, which allows for her break with contemporary social conventions codifying women's public behavior.[13] Beatrice's love transcends traditional codes. But the young Dante will understand this only when deprived of the gesture on which he mistakenly set his beatitude. The poems expressing the novel "stilo de la sua loda" (XXVI.4 [17.4]) [the style I had praised her with], as well as the prose sections framing them, visibly testify to his changed attitude: this is the case above all with the *canzone* "Donne ch'avete intelletto d'amore" [Women who understand the truth of love], and with the three praise sonnets "Ne li occhi porta la mia donna Amore" [My lady makes all gracious with her gaze], "Tanto gentile e tanto onesta pare" [So open and so self-possessed appears], and "Vede perfettamente onne salute" [To see my lady among other women].[14] Dante is finally observing, understanding and praising Beatrice as she truly is: a universal "miracolo" (XXI 4 [12.4] and XXIX 3 [19.6]) [miracle] inspiring love, virtue, honesty, and humility in whomever she meets. Dante now shares the salvific force proceeding from Beatrice with everyone in the city, he selflessly rejoices in people's moral reactions to her epiphany, and, as an evangelist he puts into writing her ecumenical significance.[15]

But let us return to chapters X–XI. At this stage of the story, Dante's psychological and physical responses to Beatrice's *saluto* (greeting) reveal that he is still unable to fully decipher her supernatural essence;[16] nevertheless, the biblical and theological substratum of chapter XI discloses the author's profound awareness of the spiritual and literary novelty he is offering to his readers, pointing to the self-fashioning strategies he is adopting to build up his reputation as a prominent lay poet and intellectual, one who attended the "scuole delli religiosi" and the "disputazioni delli filosofanti" (*Conv.* 2.12.7) [the schools of the religious and the disputations of the philosophers].[17] The awakening of charity prompting Dante to forgive his enemies in anticipation of Beatrice's greeting evokes Christ's famous precept "Diligite inimicos vestros, benefacite his qui oderunt vos et orate pro persequentibus et calumniantibus vos" (Matthew 5:44) [Love your enemies: do good to them that hate you: and pray for them that persecute and calumniate you],[18] which passed from the Bible into medieval discussions of *caritas* such as that present in Servasanto da Faenza's *Liber de virtutibus et vitiis*. The *Liber* is a *summa* of preaching material composed in Florence between 1277 and 1285 that may serve as a gauge of what theological views might have been available to the Florentine citizenry, and thus to Dante and his public, in the last decades of the Duecento.[19]

In the section of the *Liber* dedicated to "Qualis debeat esse dilectio proximi" [On how to love one's neighbor properly], the Franciscan friar argues that love for our neighbor must be "liberalis, sine cupiditate, ut non diligatur proximus pro mercede, ut non sit amor mercenarius, set puro corde exhibitus, non in se reciprocus, set libere transitivus. Unde in Lc [6, 32] sic dicitur: Si diligitis eos qui vos diligunt, [Mt 5, 46] quam mercedem habebitis? Ergo non solum amici, set amandi sunt inimici, iuxta illud Domini in Mt [5, 44–45]: Diligite inimicos vestros, scilicet corde, benefacite hiis qui oderunt vos, scilicet opere, et orate pro persequentibus et calumpniantibus vos, scilicet ore" [selfless, without greed, for one's neighbor must not be loved for a reward, for love must not be mercenary, but expressed with a pure heart, love must not be given in return, but it must flow freely. In Luke 6:32 it is said, "For if you love them that love you, what reward shall you have?" (Matthew 5:46). Therefore, not only friends but also enemies must be loved, as Christ himself urges in Matthew (5:44–45): "Love your enemies, that is with your heart, do good to them that hate you, that is with deeds, and pray for them that persecute and calumniate you, that is with your mouth"].[20]

Servasanto exhorts that one should love one's neighbor not "pro mercede" but unselfishly, thereby conceiving love of one's enemies as a pure expression of selfless *dilectione proximi*. However, the *agens* of *Vita nova*'s chapter XI does not fully comprehend the disinterested nature of Beatrice's *caritas*, or of the love she brings out in him. He is still trapped within the an- nihilating labyrinth of passion, and from initial good premises he slips back into trite erotic schemes. What follows in the digression on the effects of Beatrice's *saluto* is imbued with easily recognizable Guinizzellian and Caval- cantian motifs. The breakdown of the "spiriti sensitivi" (XI 2 [5.5]) [spirits of the sensitive soul] and especially the eviction of the "deboletti spiriti del viso" (XI 2 [5.5]) [weak spirits of sight] at the hands of the "spirito d'amore" [spirit of love] echo Cavalcanti's verses "E' [Amore] vèn tagliando di sì gran valore, / che' deboletti spiriti van via" (lines 5–6) [cut with such force / weak- ened spirits flee], from the sonnet "Voi che per li occhi mi passaste 'l core" [You who've pierced my eyes to my heart].[21] Likewise the final paralysis of Dante's body, which "si movea come cosa grave inanimata" (XI 3 [5.6]) [moved like a heavy, inanimate object], recalls Guinizzelli's lines 12–13, "re- magno como statüa d'ottono / ove vita né spirto non ricorre" [I stand quietly like a brass statue / With no life or spirit flowing], from the sonnet "Lo vostro bel saluto e 'l gentil sguardo" [Your lovely greeting and the gentle gaze], an image reworked by Cavalcanti himself in the sonnet "Tu m'hai sì piena di dolor la mente" [You've so filled my mind with pain]: "I' vo come colui ch'è fuor di vita, / che pare, á chi lo sguarda, ch'omo sia / fatto di rame o di pietra o di legno" (lines 9–11) [I walk as dead / appearing—to who will look—a man / made of bronze or stone or wood].[22]

Chapter XI ends with a sentence worth quoting in full, as the author's word choice may attest to his familiarity with contemporary theological vo- cabulary, possibly hinting at the shaping of his multifaceted self-portrait in a more learned direction, as well as at the diversification of the audience he aims to address: "Sì che appare manifestamente che ne le sue salute abitava la mia beatitudine, la quale molte volte passava e redundava la mia capacitade" (XI 4 [5.7]) [Clearly then my bliss depended on her salutation; it was a bliss that many times surpassed and overflowed my capacity to contain it].[23]

Let us especially focus on the verb *redundava*. *Redundare* is a Dantean hapax meaning "exceeding by superabundance," which exegetes commonly associate with Proverbs 3:10, "Et vino torcularia tua redundabunt" [And thy barns shall be filled with abundance, and thy presses shall run over with wine], a biblical passage dedicated to the benefits of acquiring wisdom.[24] The concept of *redundantia* [redundancy], however, surfaces frequently in scholastic texts, where it is often used to define a process of communication by superabundance between body and soul, or between the superior and inferior parts of human reason. For instance, in his commentary to Peter Lombard's *Sentences*, book III, distinction XV—a distinction dedicated to investigating the flaws of the body and of the soul that Christ took on because of his human nature—Thomas Aquinas explains that the joy Christ was experiencing in the superior part of his reason by fruition of God "non redundabat in inferiores," did not exceed so as to overflow into the inferior parts. That is why Christ could experience *laetitia* (joy) and pain at the same time.[25] In a passage on the resurrection of the bodies from the *Summa contra gentiles*, moreover, Aquinas clarifies that the glorified body will be clothed in splendor "per quandam redundantiam ex anima in corpus" [by a certain redundancy from the soul into the body], as the soul will be filled with spiritual brightness by virtue of the vision of God.[26]

In relation to *Vita nova* XI 4 [5.7], another passage from Bonaventure of Bagnoregio's commentary to the *Sentences* is of particular interest. In *Sentences*, book III, distinction XXVIII, Peter Lombard discusses whether we ought to love "totum proximum et nos totos" [all of our neighbor and all of ourselves, i.e., both the body and the soul];[27] the title of the conclusion of Bonaventure's *quaestio* "Utrum ex caritate sint diligenda corpora nostra" [Whether our bodies must be loved out of charity] avers: "Corpora nostra, cum capacia sint beatitudinis per quandam redundantiam, ex caritate sunt diligenda" [Our bodies, since they may be capacious of blessedness by a certain redundancy, must be loved out of charity].[28]

Dante's discourse is different from Bonaventure's, as he is saying that the bliss deriving from Beatrice's greeting was such that it surpassed the capacity of his body to contain it.[29] However, it is interesting to note that in

Bonaventure the concept of *redundantia* appears in relation to the *capacitas* of human bodies to contain *beatitudinem*.[30] The *Lectura* on *Sentences* II and III by the Franciscan Peter of Trabibus, probably held in Santa Croce between 1294 and 1295, testifies to the likely accessibility of this theme in Dante's Florence.[31] Peter, *lector theologiae* of the Florentine *studium* in the 1290s, specifies that charity is a "pondus inclinans ad summum bonum et beatitudinem perfectam" [force leading to the supreme good and to perfect bliss], that "omne illud est diligendum ex caritate quod beatum vel beatificabile est" [everything that is blessed or may be blessed must be loved out of charity], and that our body is "beatum" [blessed] because of redundancy, "per redundantiam."[32] It follows that we must love our body.

A more systematic study on the occurrences of the concept of *redundantia* in medieval theological texts, mystical writings, treatises, *summae*, *quaestiones*, and biblical exegesis is surely needed, so as to effectively evaluate their impact on Dante's choice of the verb *redundare*. However, this preliminary research shows that Dante's *redundava* may be a technical term deriving not by chance from specific discussions dedicated to the virtue of *caritas*, rather than a biblical Latinism of sapiential nuance. If this is the case, the author of the *Vita nova* is here re-elaborating a specific concept that he probably came to know during his attendance at the Florentine *studia* of Santa Croce, Santa Maria Novella, and Santo Spirito in the aftermath of Beatrice's death.[33] This, as suggested above, may be a sign of Dante's self-presenting tactics revolving around the exhibition of his rhetorical, philosophical, and medical as well as theological competencies,[34] just before or in the same years as his debut on Florence political scene as an advocate of peaceable cooperation between the Florentine elite and the popular movement.[35]

In this light, the ideal public of the *Vita nova* would thus include not only Guido Cavalcanti, dedicatee of the *libello* and model now overcome, not only other poets and enthusiasts of love poetry, not only women who possess intelligence of love, but also "un più indistinto pubblico, di estrazione tanto magnatizia quanto popolare, di individui *litterati* a diverso livello, costituito da un lato dal variegato gruppo dei professionisti della parola giuridica, retorica e politica e dall'altro dai *magistri artium* e dai loro 'seguaci.' Quest'ultimo gruppo comprende tutti coloro che, come Dante stesso dopo la morte di Beatrice, animavano o frequentavano le 'scuole delli religiosi' e le 'disputazioni delli filosofanti'" [a more indistinct public, composed of individuals belonging to both aristocratic and popular backgrounds, who understand Latin at different levels; these are experts in law, rhetoric, and politics, as well as *magistri artium* and their followers. This last group includes all those who, like Dante after Beatrice's death, attended the "schools of the religious" and the "disputations of the philosophers"].[36] As Paolo Borsa shows, Dante's literary production in the 1290s may reflect, as well as contribute to enhancing, his cultural, social, and political identity, and his theoretical and literary choices may well be revelatory of his political and public stances.[37]

Vita nova XII [5.8–5.24]

EMILY KATE PRICE

"Queste parole, fa che siano quasi un mezzo, sì che tu non parli a lei immediatamente, che non è degno." (*Vn* XII.8 [5.15])

[Make it so that your words are a kind of intermediary, so that you do not speak to her directly, which would not be proper.]

The *Vita nova* is a work fundamentally concerned with the medium of vernacular poetry, its nature and its capacities. Chapter XII, in which Love explicitly addresses the status of the chapter's inserted lyric—a *ballata*—as a "mezzo" and in which the protagonist famously addresses the *ballata* itself is, then, a key stage in the *Vita nova*'s metapoetical work. In his words to the protagonist, Love conceives of the *ballata* as a go-between that will address the lady, Beatrice, on Dante's behalf so that he will not have to address her directly, which is not considered acceptable behavior by the standards inculcated in the twelfth-century Occitan lyric and the courtly love tradition that grew out of it. This section of the *Vita nova* (chapters V to XII) is concerned with this anterior love poetics, brought into Italian by the *scuola siciliana* and developed later in different ways in the poetry of contemporaries of Dante's such as Cavalcanti, clearly referenced in this section of the *Vita nova*. The

term Love uses for the *ballata* in this chapter, *mezzo*, not only means interme-
diary but also is necessarily suggestive of the *ballata* as being between things.
In this rereading of chapter XII, I consider how the *ballata* as performable
song is presented not only as a means of (indirect) communication but as a
medium with an ambiguous and shifting ontology, constituted by a network
that spreads across space and time. To do this, I will consider the *ballata* not
just as a poem or even a song but also, as its form invites us to do, as a dance.

Our attention is drawn to the *ballata*'s tricky ontology by Dante himself
in the prose commentary that follows immediately after the lyric. In this
final section of the chapter, he anticipates objections to the fact that he ad-
dresses the *ballata* in the second person within the *ballata* itself, when, as he
puts it, "the ballad is none other than the words I speak": he promises to dis-
cuss this later, which he does in chapter XXV [16].[1] In his article on the *bal-
lata,* Martin Eisner begins with a page from an early twentieth-century edi-
tion of Dante Gabriel Rossetti's translation of the *Vita nova,* which presents
the lyric with musical staves and notation, despite the fact that Dante did
not set it to music.[2] Eisner argues that in this foregrounding of its musical
status, this modern iteration of the lyric is "a response to Dante's complex
presentation of the *ballata*" and answers Dante's implicit invitation to con-
sider the *ballata* not only as a poem but also as a song.[3] For Eisner, Dante's
poem serves to demonstrate the "crisis of authority" surrounding earlier sung
lyric and genres such as the *ballata* in contrast with the more self-sufficient
form of the *canzone,* as exemplified by "Donne ch'avete intelletto d'amore."[4]
It seems uncontroversial to read the chapter as a critique of a courtly poetics
that demands an indirect address and could be open to corruption in trans-
mission. Indeed, in bemoaning the miscommunications and misunderstand-
ings of a courtly love relationship, Dante's chapter here reproduces typical
tropes of troubadour lyrics. The denial of the lady's greeting that is the prem-
ise for this chapter is a central topos in Occitan love lyric. In its discussion of
the rumors circulating about Dante that Beatrice hears, and that cause her to
fear potential "noia" (XII.6 [5.13]) [unseemliness], the chapter reflect the
worries about reputation that permeate troubadour songs, in which singers
fret that their actions might be misinterpreted or that malicious *lauzengiers*
(slanderers) might spread gossip about them.

In the spirit of this volume, I will consider this chapter closely and in
relation to the chapters that precede it, reading the *ballata* backward into

earlier lyric traditions, rather than forward into the rest of the *Vita nova* and beyond. In its immediate context, the choice of the *ballata* form is significant. With the previous chapters all containing sonnets, chapter XII introduces a new poetic form, disrupting the reader's expectations. We are clearly invited, or indeed forced, to take notice. The use of this form, and the *ballata*'s self-referential address, as well as the emphasis on mediation in this lyric and chapter, all surely recall the lyrics of Dante's "primo amico" [first friend], Guido Cavalcanti, many of which are *ballate*. Yet the *ballata*'s *prosopopoeia* also clearly responds to the Occitan *tornada*, the final half stanza of a troubadour song, which often included an address to the song itself. Like these metapoetically rich Occitan endings that the *ballata* imitates and elaborates, the *ballata* offers a complex investigation of the ontology of sung poetry, which is only emphasized by the choice of a dance form. Dante thus prefigures modern medievalists such as Paul Zumthor and Seeta Chaganti in using dance as a way of thinking and demonstrating the workings of medieval poetry, its affordances and capabilities, its ontological nature. I will set out their principal ideas below before thinking through their relationship to Dante's lyric more specifically.

In the *De vulgari eloquentia,* Dante recognizes the *ballata* as a dance form and remarks that *ballate* "need dancers, for whom they were written in the first place" [indigent enim plausoribus, ad quos edite sunt].[5] It is because it is a collective as well as an embodied medium that Paul Zumthor suggests we use dance as a way of thinking about medieval poetry as voiced. For him, dance is a "paradoxical approach" to medieval oral poetry that can help us to retain the "community-like" nature of these works.[6] It also helps him to understand the form of oral poetry as a *Zielform,* one that comes into being, sometimes, in individual performances that are connected in networks of multiple performances, and that is constituted as much by its audience as by its creator(s).[7] Like Zumthor, Chaganti also conceives of form as something that comes into being as it is experienced, and that is constituted at least partially through the participation of an audience. Key to her arguments is the medieval notion of *ductus,* which "offers a term for an experience of participatory engagement with artistic objects. . . . [It] casts the viewer's experience of a work of art as a process through which one is led. . . . The condition of being led through an artistic object or spectacle allows the perceiver to deploy different perceptual faculties associated with multiple media simultaneously, so that the perceptual practices associated with one art can inflect the apprehension of another."[8] While for Zumthor dance is redolent of rhythmic regularity, Chaganti argues that by thinking of medieval poetic form "at its intersection with the virtual forces of dance," one can better get at its "ambiguous ontolog[ies], its 'strange footing.'"[9] A kinetic force at work between and amid the various agents of a dance, "virtuality is not simply synonymous with immateriality or artificiality; rather it participates in material and embodied realms even as it positions itself in a different ontological space and a different temporal structure."[10] As the dancers move to and fro, the dance bears the traces of its past movements and anticipates its next ones: this virtuality is, then, untimely, something that "disrupts ordinary structures of time and space."[11] Innovating a new kind of formalism, Chaganti is keen to show, using dance and its ambiguous ontology, rooted in movement, that the experience of form "does not entirely line up with what its attributes might appear to do."[12] Medieval form conducts "diverse perspectival trajectories," such that it is always an experience of what she calls "strange footing," a "reckoning with estrangement" that is a collective one, shared by the members of the audience.[13] Dante, as we have seen, foresees some sense of estrangement in response to the *ballata*, and the evidence suggests that in its earliest written forms scribes were most definitely wrong-footed by it.[14]

This sense of estrangement is provoked by its very first word, which announces the personification of the *ballata* itself. In troubadour song, such an address can mostly be found only at the end of the song, in a *tornada*, where the first person might send the song out into the world. Critics have noted the disruptive quality of this half stanza, which typically repeats the rhyme and melody from the second half of the last full stanza. During the song, the same melody and rhyme scheme, and often rhyme sounds, are repeated throughout the song with each stanza; but when the song reaches its *tornada*, that pattern is thrown off-kilter, and where an audience would expect to hear the beginning of the melody they are plunged into the middle of it: thus "the audience must struggle momentarily to reorient themselves within the melodic line as the poet reorients his own self-positioning."[15] The *tornada*'s disruption has been characterized as a moment when two worlds, the world of the song and the outside world, collide; where the main body of the song has often been unindexed in time and space, the *tornada* often contains the names of people and places.[16] In the case of the *ballata*, this jarring effect is intensified in that it comes not at the end of the lyric, where it might have been expected, but instead almost proleptically at the very beginning of the song.

Focusing on the *tornada* as the moment when the first person "turns" and hails another subject, musicologist Judith Peraino describes how the song at this point "takes a musical, even balletic form of call and response" as multiple agents interact.[17] The first four lines of the *ballata*, which constitute its refrain, represent a ductile experience in which the voice of the first person leads the *ballata*—and its audience—through the song. These lines introduce a network of subjects and agents whose relationships to each other shift and reconfigure like dancers. The first-person voice tells the *ballata* to find Love and then go, with him, to "madonna" [my lady], transmitting the apology ("scusa mia") of the singing voice, now sung by the *ballata* itself ("la qual tu cante" [which you sing]), so that afterwards, the first person's lord, Love ("lo mio segnore"), can speak with "madonna." In these opening lines, Dante perfectly captures the complex network of agents one finds not only in the *tornada* but in the Occitan love lyric more generally, where the first person's subjectivity is constituted in relation to a number of other agents, such as the song, the heart, the eye, the lady, the gaze, the court gossips, and so on.

The positioning of the first person in relation to his song is interesting here in that he appears to be inherent to but (temporally) distanced from it. His situation is summed up in Chaganti's description of how the virtual force of dance "always places the agent—who is himself often both observer and participant—a little out of time, anticipating and syncopated."[18] In the *ballata*, Dante's first person both participates in and observes himself as distinct from the song to which he gives voice. This out-of-joint positioning is suggested in the preceding prose narrative, when Love speaks "obscurely" to the protagonist in Latin ("oscuramente," XII.4 [5.12]). As Gorni reads it, Love says that he is like the center of a circle, to which all points on the circumference are equidistant; meanwhile the protagonist is "eccentrico . . . non al suo posto" [eccentric . . . out of place].[19] These lines suggest the quasi-divine relationship of Love to all things, characterized by uniformity and regularity. The protagonist, meanwhile, is doomed to a more earthly, contingent existence as part of a complex temporal network of irregular, various, and shifting relations, of which he is never properly the center. In the *ballata*, the singing voice plots out virtual trajectories that both precede and exceed the actual material form of the *ballata* as written and even as anticipated in performance. His singing prefigures the actions of the song itself ("Ballata, i'voi che tu ritrovi Amore" [Ballad, I wish you to find Love])[20] and also comprehends a time after the song, when it has finished and Love remains with the lady (line 4). This proleptic and retrospective effect, in which the song exceeds itself, its ontology poised between the virtual and the real, is intensified when one reads the lyric in relation to its inherently ductile prose frame. In a section preceding the *ballata* (XII.7 [5.14]), Love presents it as a solution to the protagonist's predicament following Beatrice's denial of her greeting. His description of the *ballata* and its multiple agents here is convoluted, making frequent use of the preposition *per* to plot the mediated trajectories of the *ballata* before the *ballata* proper—Is it the *ballata* proper?—begins. The protagonist later introduces the *ballata* itself using its first few words, beginning it before it begins, and indeed ending it before it begins, by virtue of a mix of tenses: "E feci poi questa ballata che comincia: *Ballata i'voi*" [And then I made this *ballata,* which begins . . .]).[21] Together these begin to form a transtemporal and virtual network of different versions of the *ballata* whose movements each haunt the "real" *ballata.*

In fact, the real *ballata* is hard to identify; it always seems to be just off where it appears to be, ahead of where it is, anticipated, promised. Within the *ballata,* it is told to go when it pleases (line 43). The existence of the performable lyric on what Zumthor calls the "desidereal plane" is then further spelled out explicitly in the prose that follows the *ballata,* where Dante describes how he permits the lyric "to go freely when it wants, commending its movement to the hands of Fortune" (XII.16).[22] That moment, then, is postponed to an indefinite, contingent futurity. Suggestions that the song could be performed in different ways, let alone in different times, also pepper the song. Dante recommends that it go with Love but acknowledges that it could travel unaccompanied, "sanza compagnia" (line 6). Love's suggestion in the prose that Dante "adorn" the lyric with a "sweet harmony" also raises the possibility of its traveling without musical accompaniment (XII.8 [5.15]). The *ballata* we have written down gestures to a different iteration of itself frequently: not only are we required to imagine a *ballata* containing only the *ballata*'s direct speech, rather than including the lover's instructions, but we must also imagine expanded verse instantiations of some of the instructions given more implicitly within the lyric. An example of this is in line 17, where, announcing what the *ballata* must say to his lady, he reminds it that first it must beg her forgiveness, but without explicitly saying *how*. In such a way, the lyric demands that we always imagine it to be otherwise than it is, which, perhaps, gestures to the heart of Dante's problem with the circulation of performed/sung lyric: the ways in which it can be altered or mediated. What we are experiencing here is reminiscent of Chaganti's description of medieval audiences' experience of dance, which involved "sensitizing oneself to forces and energies that anticipate or lag behind the dancer's body, that hover around it or off its center."[23]

Just as Zumthor hopes it might, reading the *ballata* as dance sensitizes us to the operation of voice in this medieval song. We have seen how the observation and activity of dance involve the perception of both the real and the virtual, anticipating and remembering. In this *ballata,* Dante dramatizes the strange work of the voice, which is emitted from a physical body but which then goes beyond that originary body and mediates between it and the world as part of an extensive network of people and things that stretches across space and time—even once it is over, the song's melody will remain with the lady (line 38). By refusing to let this *ballata* be *the ballata,* Dante's composition gestures not only at the fact that compositions might be altered in oral transmission but also at the way voice exceeds both language and its originary body.[24] In his prose commentary, Dante acknowledges the strange ontology of the *ballata,* but this goes beyond its use of *prosopopoeia* and resides rather in what this *prosopopoeia* allows the lyric to explore: the voice. In this *ballata,* voice stretches forward into a contingent future; it is, as Steven Connor says of what he calls the "vocalic body," "an impossible, imaginary body in the course of being found and formed," a body that might give multiple iterations of the song.[25]

At the beginning of this rereading, I suggested that if anything, I would be looking backwards, not forwards. Dante too, is looking backwards to a courtly poetics he hopes to move beyond. And yet in exaggerating the workings of these older songs, he creates a lyric that, while always retaining a trace of its origin, perpetually projects itself forward. Encouraging us to experience the *ballata* as the dance it should be, Dante's lyric reveals the "strange footing" of poetic form and particularly of performable song, whose ambiguous ontology is constituted by a network of the real and the virtual, the human and the nonhuman, past, present, and future. The chapter undoubtedly flags up the limitations—and mediations—of sung lyric. Yet even in leaving these previous lyric traditions in the past, Dante shows the persistent futurity of the courtly love song.

Vita nova XIII–XVIII [6–10.11]

Not Just a Passing Phase

MANUELE GRAGNOLATI,
ELENA LOMBARDI, AND
FRANCESCA SOUTHERDEN

Chapters XIII [6] to XVIII [10.3–10.11] of the *Vita nova* begin with the impasse following Beatrice's withdrawal of her greeting and record the utmost moment of desperation in Dante's "love story" with her, the so-called *gabbo*, where the beloved and her friends make fun of Dante-character at a gathering. But they also mark the beginning of a new era for Dante-the-apprentice poet, with the discovery of a "matera nuova e più nobile che la passata" (XVII.1 [10.1]) [a new and nobler subject matter than that of the past] that is emphatically presented as overcoming the limitations of past lyric modes and leading to a new way of writing and loving with the composition of the *canzone* "Donne ch'avete intelletto d'amore" [Women who understand the truth of love]. The central narrative action of these chapters is a panic attack followed by a seizure that affects the exhausted poet on the occasion of a sighting of the beloved during a social gathering (XIV [7]). The protagonist's reaction causes the women to laugh at him, inducing his consequent shame, reflection on his dire state, and subsequent change of erotic and poetic direction.

This section is often called the "Cavalcantian phase" of the *Vita nova*, since it features situations and poems that closely resemble (or even "mock") the notion of love of his "first friend" Guido Cavalcanti. For Guido, love was understood at once as ineluctable, painful, and death inducing. The essays in this section all reveal the nuanced and manifold ways in which Dante addresses the poetry of his "primo amico," how he embraces it and modifies it, making the departure from that poetry appear more radical and definitive than it has actually been.

The panic attack and seizure are together called a *trasfigurazione* (transfiguration) in the section, a term that is even attached to the key adjective of the *Vita nova*: "nova trasfigurazione" (XV.1 [8.1]). According to Natascia Tonelli, it indicates the corporeal *signa*, the symptoms, of love sickness, which Dante takes from Cavalcanti's poetry and which Dante, insofar as he shares an analogous medical expertise, is able to self-diagnose and, unlike his "first friend," even cure, thereby abandoning a negative condition of *amore doloroso* and turning toward a new, positive understanding.[1] *Trasfigurazione* (or *trasfiguramento*) is an unusual choice of word, which appears with this medical sense only in this section of the *libello*. In other occurrences, as for instance in *Convivio* 2.1.6 (but see also *Mon.* 3.9.11), it refers more ordinarily to the episode of the transfiguration of Christ, the moment in the Gospel when Jesus allows a few selected apostles to see him in his glory (as recounted in Matthew 17:1–8, Mark 9:2–8, Luke 9:28–36), which is referred to in *Epistola* 13.80, *Purgatorio* 32.76–81, and *Paradiso* 25.33. As noted in the *Enciclopedia dantesca*, transfiguration is, importantly, not a complete transformation but a change of figure or appearance: it is a change of external image, which does not involve the suppression of a previous state. In the case of Christ's glory, transfiguration is actually a "revelation" of an essence that is there, albeit not yet perceived by human eyes before.[2]

While usually critics place emphasis on the radical change, both erotic and poetic, that takes place in this section of the *libello*, we would like to propose the idea of transfiguration as the central strategy of these chapters: as well as Dante's physical transfiguration, we witness here a poetic change of image, which is not necessarily a change of substance, or not a complete one, mirroring the lines of "Con l'altre donne mia vista gabbate" [With other women you mock my distress], in which the poet writes, "ond'io mi cangio in figura d'altrui, / ma non ch'io non sente bene allore / li guai de li scacciati tormenti" (XIV.12 [7.12]) [Thus I am changed into the shape of another, but not so much that I cannot still hear the yells of anguish from those banished by the rout].[3]

Narratively, these chapters describe one of the many moments of crisis of the *libello*, which indeed could be understood as the account of a succession of crises, in both the ancient (choice), and modern (calamity) meaning of the word, a succession of many pathways that a poet-lover explores, and of many "roads not taken."[4] As Teodolinda Barolini has shown, there are many *cominciamenti* in this story, and not all of them are logically shaped.[5] Indeed, this particular crisis is narratively comparable in depth and scope to the two "jealousy" crises (the story of the "screen ladies" at the beginning and that of the *donna gentile* at the end), and to many moments of wavering and "vaneggiamento." The fact that this particular set of chapters is often singled out as the main crisis and, therefore, the main "new beginning" in the *Vita nova* is due perhaps to the weight that Dante himself gives to its closure (XVII [10.1–10.2]), which quasi-simultaneously implies the end of something, with the poet falling into silence ("credendomi tacere e non dire più") and the beginning of something new ("matera nuova e più nobile che la passata" (XVII.1 [10.1]). Moreover, the *canzone* that such a moment of "renewal" generates, "Donne ch'avete intelletto d'amore," has a crucial role, not only within the *Vita nova*, but also throughout Dante's work (in the *De vulgari eloquentia* and, especially, in the *Commedia*, where it is said to mark the beginning of "le nove rime" of the *dolce stil novo*).

Thematically, this series of chapters is articulated by doubt. Doubt is actually the key to the end of the previous section, which ends with a hypothetical reader expressing an objection (on the issue of personification) and the poet's resolution to discuss it later in the book, in a section that handles even more difficult, or "doubtful" problems: "E però dico che questo dubbio io lo intendo solvere e dichiarare in questo libello ancora in parte più dubbiosa; e allora intenda qui chi qui dubita, o chi qui volesse opporre in questo modo" (XII.17 [5.24]) [And so I say that I still intend to resolve and clarify this ambiguity in an even obscurer section of this little book. And at that point may whoever has such doubts here, or wishes to object in this manner, understand what is said here].

The doubt of chapter XII [5.8–5.24] is of a textual nature (the personification of the *ballata*), yet it connects to a place in the text where further doubts are raised (chapter XXV [16] and the personification of Amore), and it features Dante's audience as readers in doubt. That is, the previous section ends with a moment of suspension and uncertainty for both the writer and the audience, and yet it establishes both writer and public within the structure itself of the *libello*.

In the section under consideration, doubt, hesitation, and wavering are somewhat internalized by the poet and his narrative. Three chapters feature Dante at the center of conflicting thoughts. Chapter XIII [6] ponders four "pensamenti" in conflict on the subject of love (Love's lordship is good, Love's lordship is bad, Love's name is sweet, your woman is special). In a specular fashion, chapter XVI [9] describes the four ways in which Love affects the poet (the rhetoric is, likewise, one of war). And Chapter XV [8] features instead an actual argument between two opposing thoughts on the suitability of seeking to see the beloved.

Chapter XIV [7] stages the poet's wavering with regard to the powers of love and the sight of the woman precisely in the *trasfiguramento*, the seizure being an actual, physical vacillation that puts him in an almost out-of-self/out-of-body perspective, from which he watches the battles of his spirits and the women's *gabbo*. Chapter XVIII [10.3–10.11] stages instead a spectacular argument, a great back-and-forth/wavering between Dante and the group of women that is, in itself, a replaying in a choral and overtly poetic key of the internal debate that the protagonist had with himself in chapter XV [8] about why he should keep returning to what harms him. There is no "fixed" point in the whole section, if not, perhaps, the caesura between the old and the new states in the short passage that goes under the heading of chapter XVII in De Robertis's edition [10.1–10.2 in Gorni].

This section of the *libello* displays some interesting features in terms of place and character. It is set in three places: the main action begins at a wedding party, reflecting the custom of the bride and groom spending the feast of their wedding day with their relatives and friends. As well as rather vividly presenting this Florentine tradition, chapter XIV [7] gives us a rare snapshot of the architecture of medieval Florence, the elusive yet persistent setting of this love story. Here we catch the glimpse of a fresco on the outside wall of a building, against which the collapsing Dante leans: "Allora dico che io poggiai la mia persona simulatamente ad una pintura la quale circundava questa magione" (XIV.4 [7.4]) [Then I had to prop myself, surreptitiously, against one of the pictures that ran around the walls of this house]. From there, Dante withdraws into his "camera delle lagrime" (XIV.9 [7.9]; XIX.1 [10.2]) [room of tears], a place both in his house, supposedly, and within himself, which eventually he leaves for the momentous "cammino" [walk] that will bring him to change his writing.

In terms of characters, the swooning Dante is accompanied by an "ingannato amico di buona fede" (XIV.7 [7.7]) [well-meaning misguided friend], a brief but interesting appearance of a side character whom the narrator trusts and who miscalculates the effects that might derive from the exposure to Beatrice. More importantly, we witness a crucial shift in this section in the nature of female presence, from the single "donna" to the plural "donne." The previous chapters, although rich in female presence, nevertheless featured a series of women, one after the other: Beatrice, the first screen lady, the young dead woman, the second screen lady, all the way to the personified female text, the *ballata*, who goes in search of the beloved to give her the "true" message of the poet. Like the *ballata*, all previous female characters are very much set under the control of the demigod Amore (Amore holds Beatrice in the dream and shines in her eyes, Amore decides on the screen ladies, Amore suggest the writing of the *ballata* and goes with her to the beloved). In this section, Dante begins his productive engagement with multiple women, with groups of "donne." Initially featured as lethal, as they instigate the derision that destroys the poet, they are ultimately the agents of his new poetry.

Moreover, we witness here a change also in the choice of the internal interlocutor. After the "amici," then Amore, and the "public" who read with excessive prurience the fake texts for the screen ladies, here we see a brief, but important, spell in which Beatrice is set as the main interlocutor. The three sonnets that we read in this section are all presented as devised to explain to Beatrice the poet's status. Beatrice's stint is short-lived—and substituted by the famous "donne" who originate the writing of "Donne ch'avete intelletto d'amore."[6]

From the point of view of the poems, this section gathers four sonnets, two of which, "Con l'altre donne mia vista gabbate" [With other women you mock my distress] and "Ciò che m'incontra, nella mente more" [What meets me dies in memory]),[7] preserve traces of their pre–*Vita nova* existence. The major impact exerted on them by their insertion within the *Vita nova* occurs neither through their variants nor through the commentary, which at most makes them even more Cavalcantian than they are as free-standing poems, but through the order that they have within the new narrative of the *libello*:

poems, especially the final three of the section, which were originally written as homage to the *doloroso* mode of the first friend are now degraded to testi-fying to an erroneous phase to be overcome. The result is also that the figure of Cavalcanti is reduced to that of a poet uniquely *doloroso*, narcissistic, and irrational, whereas his poetry, like much of contemporary lyric poetry, was quite varied and even included "positive" poems centered on the attainment of happiness. In this way, the "stilo della loda," which consists in placing one's happiness not in encountering the lady's greeting (as before) but in praising the lady's beauty and virtue without expecting any reciprocation, can appear as a greater departure from Cavalcanti than it actually is.[8]

The ways in which these texts are handled in the prose is also evidence of a heightened engagement with the audience. In particular, chapters XIV [7] and (to a lesser extent) XVI [9] withdraw the persona of the commenta-tor, requiring the active presence of the audience.[9] The "ragione" (i.e., the narrativization of the poem that precedes it) is enough explanation, Dante tells his readers. Chapter XIV [7], however, resumes the rhetoric of textual doubt, which, again, joins author, book, and reader. There are, in the poem, some "doubtful words" that serve to polarize the audience, dividing it into those who are equipped to interpret them and those who are not: the com-mentary would, therefore, be either "indarno" [in vain], or "soperchio" [su-perfluous]. On the one hand, Dante seems to withdraw again into the magic circle of the "fedeli d'amore," the quintessential courtly/*stil novo* audience, the group of lovers/poets whom he had staged at the beginning of the *Vita nova* and had somewhat ridiculed as weak interpreters of dreams and poetry. On the other hand, he is clearly teasing his wider audience, challenging them to become expert readers:[10]

Questo sonetto non divido in parti, però che la divisione non si fa se non per aprire la sentenzia de la cosa divisa; onde con ciò sia cosa che per la sua ragionata cagione assai sia manifesto, non ha mestiere di divisione. Vero è che tra le parole dove si manifesta la cagione di questo sonetto, si scrivono dubbiose parole, cioè quando dico che Amore uccide tutti li miei spiriti, e li visivi rimangono in vita, salvo che fuori de li strumenti loro. E questo dub-bio è impossibile a solvere a chi non fosse in simile grado fedele d'Amore; e a coloro che vi sono è manifesto ciò che solverebbe le dubitose parole: e però non è bene a me di dichiarare cotale dubitazione, acciò che lo mio parlare dichiarando sarebbe indarno, o vero di soperchio. (XIV.13–14 [7.13–7.14])

[I do not divide this sonnet into parts: since division is only for opening up the meaning of the thing divided, and since the commentary on what occasioned the poem reveals enough, this sonnet does not require division. True, among the words that reveal the occasion for this sonnet some are obscure—for example when I say that Love kills all my spirits, while the visual ones remain alive although outside their organs. And this obscurity cannot be resolved by one who is not, to a similar degree, one of Love's faithful; and to those who are, it is clear enough how to resolve the obscurity of the words. Therefore it would do no good for me to explain such obscurity, since the explanation would be vain or superfluous.]

This is only the second time in the *libello* that Dante employs the word *sentenzia*, which beginning from the opening assertion—"In quella parte del libro de la mia memoria . . . si trova una rubrica la quale dice: *Incipit vita nova*. Sotto la quale . . . io trovo scritte le parole le quali è mio intendimento d'assemplare in questo libello; e se non tutte, almeno la loro sentenzia" (I.1 [1.1]) [In that part of the book of my memory there is a heading that states: *Incipit vita nova*. Under this heading I find written the words which I intend to copy in this little book; and if not all of them, at least their essential meaning]—punctuates the narrative of the *Vita nova*, tending to mark the moments in which the author seeks to exert the greatest control over his texts.[11] As we have suggested, however, and as the following essays on these chapters show, this episode of the *libello* is actually one of the most complex in its negotiation of the nature and the meaning of love, revealing continuities as well as differences with what has come before (both in the *Vita nova* itself and in the lyric tradition prior to it).

In fact, already with the episode of the *donna gentile* and up to *Inferno* 5 and 10, *Purgatorio* 16–18, and beyond, Dante never ceases to confront his "primo amico" in search of a way to integrate reason into the experience of love. Yet, as Contini famously stated, "Cavalcanti ha salato il sangue a Dante," has "salted his blood," leaving an indelible mark on him.[12] Elsewhere, he is said to be the "ghost" that haunts the author of the *Commedia* and is never laid to rest.[13] But his trace may even be more substantial if one considers how his poetry continues to resonate in the possibilities of lyric that Cavalcanti's poetry has shown and that Dante continues to actualize into the *Commedia* up to the end of the *Paradiso*: the receptivity of the subject, its capacity to be affected and moved by love, the sensuality of eros, and the potential that passion holds to open the self to the other.[14]

In a similar way, in the "Cavalcantian" section of the *Vita nova*, there are many elements of the lyrics of Dante's "first friend" that do not simply pass, to be replaced by something else; even the "matera nuova" is a reconfiguration of the previous matter, not a complete break from it.

Vita nova XIII [6]

REBECCA BOWEN

Placed between two longer narrative episodes, chapter XIII [6] displays a marked lack of plot-based action. The drama that unfolds is a battle between Dante's thoughts, an interior focus that is upheld in both the prose and the sonnet. As Teodolinda Barolini notes in her commentary to the sonnet "Tutti li miei penser" [All of my thoughts], Dante's "diversi pensamenti" (XIII.1 [6.1]) [different thoughts] in this chapter can be mapped quite neatly onto key developments in Italian poetic history, from the "Sicilian school" to the master of the externalized psychodrama, Guido Cavalcanti.[1] Read in the context of the surrounding chapters, this metapoetic discourse stands out as an indicative moment in the poetic autobiography of the *libello*, particularly as it is articulated in the prose, offering a critical reflection on literary influence and the construction of narrative in and around the poems contained by text.

The sonnet contained in chapter XIII, "Tutti li miei penser," clearly links Dante's warring thoughts to a metapoetic discourse on poetry and desire. At the start of the sestet, Dante uses the language of composition to express his confused mental state: "Ond'io non so da qual matera prenda / e vorrei dire, e non so ch'io mi dica" (XIII.9 [6.9]) [I know not from which I should take my material and I want to speak but I don't know what I should say].[2] If we read the "penser" [thoughts] described in this chapter through

117

the prism of literary *matera*, it seems that Dante uses his mental landscape to depict the major positions of the Duecento lyric tradition in which he was writing, their "gran varietate" (XIII.8 [6.8]) [great variety] reflecting the breadth of poetic positions available to readers and writers of the time.

The first two thoughts described in the prose encapsulate a central dialectic of the medieval courtly universe, the opposing effects of amorous servitude: "buona" / "non buona è la signoria d'Amore" (XIII.2–3 [6.2–6.3]) [good / bad is the rule of Love]. Articulated in terms common throughout the early lyric tradition, these first thoughts describe the lover as a "fedele" [faithful] to the feudal power of Love, who experiences servitude as a form of either protection or abuse: "però che trae lo intendimento del suo fedele da tutte le vili cose . . . quanto lo suo fedele più fede li porta, tanto più gravi e dolorosi punti li conviene passare" (XIII.2–3 [6.2–6.3]) [because he [Love] draws his faithful away from base concerns . . . the greater the faith of Love's devotees the more difficult and painful are the hoops through which they must jump]. This same binary battle is depicted in the description of the first two thoughts in the sonnet: "altro mi fa voler sua potestate, / altro folle ragiona il suo valore" (XIII.8 [6.8]) [one makes me want [Love's] reign, another reasons that his power is madness]. From the troubadours through the *poeti siciliani*, such dichotomized dynamics epitomize the struggle of the lover-poet in the grip of Love, whose feudal control over the love experience results in an emotional tussle between the virtues and vices of *amor*.

Instead of playing into this dynamic, however, the third thought stated in the prose cuts through the impasse, apparently resolving its tension in a reflection on the sweet sound of love's name: "Lo nome d'Amore è sì dolce a udire, che impossibile mi pare che la sua propria operazione sia ne le più cose altro che dolce" (XIII.4 [6.4]) [The name of Love is so sweet-sounding that it seems impossible to me that its effects could, on the whole, be anything other than sweet]. The simplicity of this statement works to offer a seemingly unassailable truth about the nature of love, its claim to sweetness stamped shut by the legalistic Latin at the end of the phrase: "con ciò sia cosa che li nomi seguitino le nominate cose, sì come è scritto: *Nomina sunt consequentia rerum*" (XIII.4 [6.4]) [whence it is that names follow the things they name, just as it is written: *Names are the result of things*]. This gnomic conclusion suggests a sense of self-assuredness, but a deeper complexity belies the natural simplicity of the terms in which it is posed.

As Maria Corti has noted, the phrase "nomina sunt consequentia rerum" comes from the *Institutes* of Justinian, but Dante makes a grammatical change to the original phrasing ("consequentia nomina rebus esse," II.8), switching the functional dative (*rebus*) for a more holistic genitive (*rerum*).[3] Replacing the dative, which can signal reference and purpose as well as possession, with a case that is more strongly focused on the interrelations of ownership intensifies his point, as the theoretical connotations of the Latin genitive, with its focus on possession and belonging, reinforce the reassuring sense of necessity that Dante wishes to establish between names and natures in this statement.[4] Through the very grammar of his phrasing, then, Dante sharpens the connection between *amore* and *dolcezza*, creating a reflection on the sound and meaning of love that seems to resolve into sweetness the debate between the "buona" and "non buona segnoria d'Amore."

The positive suggestiveness of the adjective *dolce* and the notion of love's natural sweetness does not actually engage with the ethical effect discussed in the first two thoughts. Authorized with a juridical Latin aphorism, the third thought shifts the field of reference posed by the moral contradiction, transposing the argument from the strictures of a feudal universe (the "segnoria d'Amore") to the more conjectural realm of words and meaning. As "lo nome d'Amore" unfolds as both the sound and sign of love, Dante homes in on one of the most performative aspects of language, that of sound, evoking a decisively poetic paradigm in the process. A mise-en-scène of the process of poetic reception can even be glimpsed in the movement from the aurality of Love's name ("sì dolce a *udire*") to the ontology of things expressed in the Latin statement ("sì come è *scritto*"), the shift from hearing to writing drawing attention to the role of reading as the true proof of the sweet sound of love, confirmed and performed by the sonority of the adjective *dolce* itself.

Differing from the prose, the description of the third thought in the sonnet distills the discussion, retaining only the idea of *dolcezza* in line 5: "altro sperando, m'apporta dolzore" (XIII.8. [6.8.]) [another, hoping, brings me sweetness]. The metapoetic connotations of *dolcezza* come to fruition in Dante's later works, eventually characterizing the poetic movement that he claims as heir to the early lyric tradition, the *dolce stil novo*.[5] As Barolini notes in her commentary, a reference to the *stil novo* can be identified in the line "altro sperando, m'apporta dolzore," since it is "optimistic in a way that recalls [Guido] Guinizzelli," the poet whom Dante terms the father of "rime

d'amor . . . dolci e leggiadre" (*Purg.* 26.99) [sweet and pleasant love poems]
during his definition of the *stil novo* in the *Commedia*.[6]

If the positive inflection in the sonnet's description of the third thought
can be said to recall Guinizzelli, the organic simplicity connected to love's
sweetness in the prose might also be seen to reflect a Guinizzellian focus, in-
voking an awareness of the naturalness of love that is exemplified in Guiniz-
zelli's programmatic *canzone* "Al cor gentil" [To the noble heart], in which
amore is shown to obey the laws of nature "come l'ausello in selva" (line 2)
[like a bird in a wood].[7] Reflecting on the nature of love ("la sua propria op-
erazione," XIII.4 [6.4]), Dante transposes the organic setting of Guinizzelli's
discussion, creating a juridical atmosphere in which language reflects both
names (*nomina*) and natures (*rerum*), turning the poet from an observer of
the natural world into cocreator of its eventual effects: "Impossibile mi pare
che la sua propria operazione sia no le più cose altro che dolce" (XIII.4 [6.4])
[It seems impossible that its effect on things could be anything other than
pleasant]. As the name of love, spoken by the poet, enacts its sweet effect ("sì
dolce a udire"; "m'apporta dolzore"), the polar experience of feudal love gives
way, in the prose, to a sophisticated, plurilinguistic reflection on the nature
of (love) language itself.

Identifying the metapoetic discourse of chapter XIII is key to interpret-
ing the fourth and final thought, which brings into play a central character
in the drama of love, so far absent from the scene: "La donna per cui Amore
ti stringe così, non è come l'altre donne, che leggeramente si muova dal suo
cuore" (XIII.5 [6.5]) [The lady through whom Love grips me thus is not like
other ladies, who have easy changes of heart]. The notion of privileging one's
own lady above all others is not an uncommon courtly theme, but the speci-
ficity and steadiness of Beatrice, in comparison to other love interests and
poetic addressees, plays a relatively revolutionary role in the poetic autobiog-
raphy constructed in the *libello*.

The realization of Beatrice's uniqueness is plotted throughout the *Vita
nova* but is particularly relevant to chapter XIII, as the metaphor of the *cam-
mino*, which directly follows the description of the four thoughts in the
prose, makes clear: "E ciascuno [dei pensieri] mi combattea tanto, che mi
facea stare quasi come colui che non sa per qual via pigli lo suo cammino"
(XIII.6 [6.6]) [And each of these [thoughts] battled within me so much, they
made me like someone who doesn't know which way to take for his journey],

a state described in the sonnet as "amorosa erranza" (XIII.9 [6.9]) [amorous wandering]. The metapoetic potential of the term *cammino* is most strongly established in the *Commedia*, where it forms the first metaphor for Dante's spiritual and poetic journey, which begins "nel mezzo del cammin" (*Inf.* 1.1). In the *Vita nova*, the image of the *cammino* occurs with more limited scope, appearing only within chapters IX to XIX [4 to 10.12–10.33]. These same chapters chart what is generally understood to be the *libello*'s main stylistic development, a narrative of poetic frustration and innovation commonly referred to as the "Cavalcantian arc."[8] The poems and prose in these chapters deliberately reflect the influence of the poet Dante terms his "primo amico" [first friend], Guido Cavalcanti, in order to establish an eventual liberation from his example and dramatize Dante's discovery of a new poetic mode.

The image of the *cammino* is intimately related to this narrative; the first and last appearances of the word *cammino* relate to the beginning (in IX [4]) and primary culmination (in XIX [10.12–10.33]) of this poetic journey. In chapter IX the term is used to describe the path ("cammino," IX.5; IX.9.1 [4.4; 4.9]) that takes Dante away from Florence and away from his beloved, inaugurating the Cavalcantian focus of the following sections. In chapters X [5] and XII [5.8–5.24] it is used in reference to this same episode, now dubbed the "cammino de le sospiri" (X.1 [5.1]; XII.6 [5.13]) [walk of sighs]; finally in chapter XIX it is used to describe Dante's whereabouts when he writes the first poem in his new, liberated style.[9] The connection between the *cammino* and Dante's poetic journey is further underlined by the fact that at the first and last instances of the term, a clear stream is described running alongside Dante's path, a common image for literary inspiration since classical antiquity.

The unique role of Beatrice in this metapoetic nexus is revealed toward the end of this journey, when Dante describes the resolution of his poetic crisis as the result of deciding to "prendere per matera de lo mio parlare sempre mai quello che fosse loda di questa gentilissima" (XVIIII.9 [10.11]) [take as material for my writing always that which praises this most noble woman]. The focus of the fourth thought in chapter XIII on Beatrice's uniqueness can be seen as a seedling for this later discovery, an advancement that solves the problem posed in chapter XIII ("qual matera prenda," XIII.9, line 1 [6.9, line 1] [which material to choose]). In dedicating himself to praising Beatrice, Dante (as poet-lover) also sidesteps the usual cause of sweetness and suffering in the courtly paradigm: the poet's longing for a response from the *donna*. By stating that his spiritual happiness ("beatitudine") rests in "quelle parole che lodano la donna mia" (XVIII.6 [10.8]) [those words which praise my lady], Dante highlights the self-sufficiency of his new poetics, solving the anxieties of poetic influence and physical recompense through a focus on his own poetic word.[10] In this sense, the resolution of Dante's poetic *cammino* resembles the reassuring specificity of the third and fourth thoughts in chapter XIII, where the sweet sound of love (occasioned by the poet's writing) transposes the courtly binary into a reflection on the language of love and the uniqueness of Beatrice, much as "quelle parole che lodano la donna mia" (XVIII.6 [10.8]) release the poet, metapoetically, from the state of "amorosa erranza" (XIII.9 [6.9]) [amorous wandering] into which his warring thoughts had cast him.

Although the courtly paradox gives way in the prose of chapter XIII to a focus on the poetic word and the uniqueness of Beatrice, this specific culmination is absent from the sonnet, in which the beloved *donna* is nowhere to be seen. Focusing on Dante's emotional distress, the third thought in the poem denies the promise of conclusion sown into the prose by focusing only on the poet's agitated emotional state: "altro pianger mi fa spesse fiate" (XIII.8 [6.8]) [another, often, makes me weep]. The metaphor of the *cammino* is also absent, replaced by the term *amorosa erranza*, which emphasizes pathlessness. The kernels of closure plotted into the prose are missing from the sonnet. In this divergence we can witness the author's attempt to contain the psychodrama of his original *rima* within the prose architecture of his new book, written after the poem, which would have circulated freely among readers until this point.[11] "Reperforming" the content of the sonnet through his gloss, Dante recasts the endless wandering described in the poem— which itself can move no further than the loop between its first and final lines—in a much more linear guise, constructing the conditions for a thematic development that will be mapped onto the teleological *cammino* of Dante's personal journey as both lover and poet.[12]

As an intermediate episode in this narrative, chapter XIII points to resolution rather than enacting it, as the final image, Dante's enmity toward Pity, makes clear. After describing his confused *cammino*, Dante states that the only solution to his warring thoughts is a "via molto inimica verso me, cioè di chiamare e di mettermi ne le braccia de la Pietà" (XIII.6 [6.6]) [route that is most undesirable to me, that is to invoke Pity and cast myself into her arms]. The inimical nature of this recourse is emphasized twice more before the end of the chapter, as Pity is called the poet's enemy in the sonnet (XIII.9 [6.9]) and its negative nature is underlined at the end of the *divisione* (XIII.10 [6.10]). The image of Pity, semipersonified and acting as the poet's enemy, is common in early lyric and is used to figure the disinterest of the *donna* in the plight of the lover-poet. Dante's deliberate distaste for *Pietà* may, however, have further resonances.

The figure of Pity is used with particular frequency in the poetry of Guido Cavalcanti, where it is also interchanged with the notion of *merzede*, a term used specifically for amorous reciprocation in early lyric.[13] By designating *Pietà* as his enemy, Dante displays a desire to reject two of the influences that will later be shown to stand in direct opposition to his achievement of a "nuova matera" [new material], a style that is not indebted to Cavalcanti and that does not focus on the need for *madonna* to pity the poet with recompense. Through the figure of *Pietà*, Dante thus instills a negative reaction to the notion of a particularly Cavalcantian poetics and frames this as the antithesis of his own stylistic innovation: the focus on "quelle parole che lodano la donna mia" that resolve poetic and amorous tension. The negative characterization of Pity in chapter XIII therefore creates conditions that emphasize the novelty and singularity of the literary achievements that will be revealed in later chapters, emphasizing the success of the teleological development when Dante finally reaches it at the end of his metapoetic *cammino*.

The psychodrama of chapter XIII thus mirrors key plot developments to come. The warring thoughts, which share so much with Guido Cavalcanti's frequently personified *spiriti*, build a wider discourse on poetic tradition and stylistic influence that, when understood in the context of the surrounding chapters, offers a strikingly self-aware statement on Dante's own authorial intent. In his drive to integrate the original *rima*, "Tutti li miei pensier," into the narrative architecture of his *libello*, Dante mitigates the state of "amorosa erranza" described in the sonnet through a series of narrative developments plotted into the prose, emphasizing the link between errant desire and literary mobility and pointing this poetic and psychological indecision toward its resolution in his own poetic advancements. By reconfiguring his sonnet as a necessary—but transient—stage in this narrative of stylistic progression, Dante's treatment of his "diversi pensamenti" (XIII.1 [6.1]) [diverse thoughts] in the prose of chapter XIII offers an insight into the construction of the *libello*'s poetic autobiography, as well as a statement on this early (but already self-aware) stage in the Dantean discourse on *parole rimate* and desire.

Vita nova XIV [7]

NICOLÒ CRISAFI

In the general economy of the *Vita nova*, chapter XIV [7] represents a moment of deep crisis.[1] The trigger, according to the prose narrative, is the so-called episode of the *gabbo* (mockery) when a group of Florentine ladies—the *gentilissima* Beatrice among them—derides the young protagonist for having what appears to modern readers as a panic attack at a wedding reception.[2] The ladies are seemingly unaware of the underlying cause of his reaction, which the narrator ascribes to the overwhelming effects of his secret love for Beatrice. Returning to the privacy of his chamber, the young Dante broods over the incident and remonstrates: "Se questa donna sapesse la mia condizione, io non credo che così gabbasse la mia persona, anzi credo che molta pietade le ne verrebbe" (XIV.9 [7.9]) [If this lady knew my state, I don't believe she would make fun of me like that; in fact I think she would feel mercy].[3] This fantasy of being able to explain his version of the events by addressing the lady directly is presented as the "original cue" for the sonnet "Con l'altre donne mia vista gabbate" [With other women you mock my distress].[4] The crisis then carries on in the following two chapters, XV [8] and XVI [9], and famously finds an existential and poetic resolution in the writing of the canzone "Donne ch'avete intelletto d'amore" (XVII–XX [10]) [Women who understand the truth of love].

The theme of the *gabbo* derives from an Occitan tradition.[5] By the time Dante appropriated it, it had been successfully adapted by poets writing in Italian vernaculars, from Giacomo da Lentini to Dante's friends Lapo Gianni and Cino da Pistoia.[6] The crisis it signals in the *Vita nova* hits several targets at the same time. It concerns "the relationship between the subject and the lady";[7] between Dante's search for a new poetic style and the poetic model of Guido Cavalcanti, the protagonist's so-called best friend (III.14 [2.1]) and main interlocutor of the *libello* (XXX.3 [19.10]);[8] and between the modes of love that underline the two poetics: one disinterested, theologized, and salvific, the other painful, destructive, and irrational.[9] These various facets are tightly interconnected. Indeed, fictionalized "life" and literature, especially, are inextricable in the *Vita nova*. Thus, if it is possible to argue that the episode of the *gabbo* "more than others could be read as an account of everyday life except that the situation it describes is exquisitely literary,"[10] one can equally argue that "the fact that the *gabbo* is a stock situation of courtly love poetry . . . does not necessarily indicate that Dante is inventing this entire scene."[11] This blurring of boundaries between fictionalized lived experience and literary inspiration is characteristic of the youthful *Vita nova* and plays an important role in all of Dante's later writings in the vernacular. In chapter XIV, the theme and significance of the *gabbo* lie in signaling an inadequacy on Dante's part that is at once portrayed as existential—having to do with his fictionalized experience of love for Beatrice—and literary—as its failure is a catalyst for articulating a new poetic style.

Chapter XIV displays significant intratextual links to the surrounding chapters. Its opening prose sets it in seamless continuity with the timeline of the previous chapter: "Appresso la battaglia de li diversi pensieri avvenne che" (XIV.1 [7.1]) [After the battle of various contending thoughts, it happened that . . .].[12] Equally, the poem "Con l'altre donne mia vista gabbate" shares the same rhyme scheme (ABBA ABBA CDE EDC) and two rhyme endings (in *-ate* and *-ore*) with its predecessor "Tutti li miei penser parlan d'Amore" [All of the voices vying in my brain].[13] Most notably, *Vita nova* XIV is intimately bound with the following chapters XV [8] and XVI [9], with which it forms a triad, joined thematically by the repeated insistence on a "Cavalcantian" experience of love that is divorced from reason, desperate, and self-destructive.[14] The imprint of Dante's first friend is unmistakable. It comes in the shape of specific allusions to Cavalcanti's poetry as well as a more general adherence to its model.[15] All but four words in the sonnet "Con l'altre donne" are found in some form or other in the Cavalcantian corpus.[16] Especially remarkable are Dante's references to the effects of an inner psychosomatic *battaglia* (battle) that fragments the subject (XIV.1 [7.1]);[17] the devastating *tremore* (trembling) that overwhelms him in the presence of the lady (XIV.4 [7.4]);[18] and the scene of Love striking, killing, or routing the poet's senses (described as *spiriti* and *spiritelli*). The latter dramatizes medieval medical theories but mediates them through Cavalcanti's "obsessive cultivation of 'spiriti' ('spirits') (Cavalcanti, *Rime* 28), from the repeated allusions to the lover's entire pneumatic system being routed (Cavalcanti, *Rime* 7.13; *Rime* 9.14) . . . to an allusion to visual spirit itself, 'quel sottile spirito che vede' ('and that delicate spirit of sight') (Cavalcanti, *Rime* 22.12)."[19] The esoteric nature of these references to medical theories is proudly declared at the end of the chapter, where Dante gives a nod to an implied readership that he calls "Love's faithful" (XIV.14 [7.1]). This elite circle of readers, he claims, needs no further explanation.

The question of Dante's readership, real or fictionalized, is important. It is not by chance that, according to the prose, chapters XIV–XVI are joined together "not as much by means of the *gabbo* motif, but by the fact that in these sonnets [Dante] does something he does not do elsewhere in the *Vita Nuova*: he directly addresses *Madonna* . . . to talk to her about himself."[20] The prose of the *Vita nova* explicitly draws attention to this fact when Dante refers to the three sonnets in which he addressed this lady directly (XVII.1 [10.1]); the direct addresses are also underlined in chapter XIV, where the prose relates how the protagonist "propuosi di dire parole . . . parlando *a lei*" [planned to say some words speaking *to her*] and wished that these words "venissero per avventura ne *la sua audienza*" (XIV.10 [7.10]) [might by chance reach *her*], translation modified, emphasis mine). The word *audienza* is particularly interesting, as it "stands for both 'hearing' and 'audience'" and is thus ambiguously poised between oral address (Andrew Frisardi translates it as "might reach her ear") and textual readership;[21] similarly, the phrase *dire parole* mixes connotations of orality with the textual meaning of "writing poetry."[22] This once again blurs the distinction between fictionalized everyday life and written textuality, while it also begins to chip away at the gendered distinction, in the *libello*'s fictionalized audience, between "published" male lover-poets ("Love's faithful," XIV.14 [7.14]) and a new readership of women associated "with orality and, therefore, with a less stable, more vulnerable, but possibly more productive kind of textuality."[23] Indeed, in the direct address "Se lo saveste, non poria Pietate / tener più contra me l'usata prova" (XIV.12 [7.12], lines 4–5) [If you knew, surely Mercy would be less entrenched with what she typically denies], the lady is cast not merely as a passive addressee but also in the potentially productive role of interpreter of the poet's experience.

This is an important "first" in the *Vita nova*. In her discussion of fictionalized women readers in the *libello*, Elena Lombardi has made an argument about the gradual emergence of a new gendered readership in the book.[24] In her view, this culminates in the writing of the *canzone* "Donne ch'avete intelletto d'amore," where the women described in the prose "act very much as critics of the poet as well as editors, if not censors, of his previous poetry, so much so that they could be taken as an image of the operation of the *Vita nova* itself," in which "the prose manipulates poetry and creates new meanings for it."[25] Chapter XIV marks an early stage in the making of this new gendered readership, a stage in which its depiction is emergent but still marked by a form of ambivalence that, as I will show shortly, is characteristic of the chapter as a whole. The ambivalence pits Dante's desire to communicate his experience against his anxiety that it may be misinterpreted. Thus, on the one hand, addressing the lady directly allows the poet to experiment with moving beyond the need of "a mediating figure between Beatrice and himself."[26] On the other hand, at this stage, his experimentation is held back by the fact that the lady is not yet conceived on a par with the closed circle of male lover-poets. In contrast with their ostensive ability to appreciate poetry's most esoteric meanings, she is represented as "only able to understand the message insofar as it is connected to her, without appreciating its universality and its depth."[27] A similar ambivalence on Dante's part between a new addressee and an old prejudice also manifests itself in the tone of the sonnet "Con l'altre donne mia vista gabbate," where "the poet talks to *madonna* without intermediaries but he does it in a particularly sharp way . . . that is not at all the deferential address of Dante to Beatrice in the *Commedia*."[28] Pointing out "the exceptional use of the present tense[s]" *gabbate* and *non pensate* in the sonnet's incipit (further emphasized by their *rima al mezzo*), Teodolinda Barolini even goes so far as to argue that it "amounts to an attack on *madonna*."[29] The sonnet is indeed imputing to the lady a lack: in the eyes of the narrator, she is guilty of mocking the secret causes of Dante's behavior ("gabbate," XIV.11 [7.11], line 1), not considering them ("non pensate," line 2), and not knowing them ("Se lo saveste," line 12). In other words, the lady is conceived as an interpreter but then accused of misinterpreting. Indeed, as Domenico De Robertis observed, "The reason of the sonnet is not the *gabbo* but the injustice that derives from ignorance of the reasons of the transfiguration that occasions it."[30] Thus, despite the innovation of the direct address to the lady that puts her in the role of the interpreter, she is not yet conceived as an adequate reader. Indeed, the *divisione* that follows the sonnet restricts this role once again to the closed circle of "Love's faithful" (XIV.14 [7.14]).

The *divisione* of chapter XIV is the occasion for a second important "first," as Dante, for the first time in the *Vita nova*, does not divide up the content of his sonnet. Paradoxically, this non-*divisione* is taken as an opportunity to explain the purpose of the *divisioni*. These hermeneutic sections of the *libello* are conceived as a means to "open up the meaning" of the text—an interpretive act that is said to be pointless here, "since the commentary on what occasioned the poem reveals enough" (XIV.13 [7.13]).[31] Dante qualifies this claim with a disclaimer, conceding that nevertheless some words might still remain *dubbiose* ("obscure," XIV.14 [7.14]). Yet instead of following through with his definition of the *divisione* as a place for "opening up the meaning," he unceremoniously shuts down further prodding of the poem's meaning with the assertion that "questo dubbio è impossibile a solvere a chi non fosse in simile grado fedele d'Amore" (XIV.14 [7.14]) [this obscurity cannot be resolved by one who is not to a similar degree, one of Love's faithful]. A similar reticence is not unique in the *Vita nova*.[32] In the context of chapter XIV, however, the conclusion appears to me to reproduce the same ambivalence that pervades the chapter. Thus, on the one hand, the young protagonist voices a desire for "opening up the meaning" of his experience—this desire is testified by the "publication" of the *Vita nova* as a whole and is expressed here both in the direct address to the lady and in the non-*divisione*'s claims about the sonnet's accessibility. On the other hand, however, Dante recoils from the vulnerability that this openness entails. In fact, first the protagonist hits back at the lady, reproaching her of misunderstanding him (XIV.12 [7.12], lines 4–5), and in the second instance he takes refuge in the closed circle of his elite interpreters (XIV.14 [7.14]). In both cases, something meaningful is tentatively offered up yet abruptly taken back. Initially, Dante appears to consider the possibility of sharing his secret with the lady ("Se lo saveste . . . ," XIV.12 [7.12] [If you knew . . .]) and even to admit to the wider readership of the *libello* that his writing may be a little too obscure ("Vero è che . . . si scrivono parole dubbiose," XIV.14 [7.14] [True, among the words some are obscure]). Yet these more generous concessions are immediately counterpointed by a more controlling attitude toward the interpretation of his text, as Dante dictates the affective response he wishes his readers to have ("non poria Pietate / tener più contra me l'usata prova," XIV.12 [7.12] [Mercy could not hold out against me any longer in the usual way]) and excludes them from the poem's implied readership, withdrawing any offer of help in interpreting it ("È impossibile a solvere . . . : e però non è bene a me dichiarare cotale dubitazione," XIV.14 [7.14] [this obscurity cannot be resolved . . . : therefore it would do no good for me to explain such obscurity]). The gap between the two impulses—openness and control, inclusivity and exclusivity—reflects the fundamental ambivalence that runs through the episode of the *gabbo*.

The Cavalcantian sequence ends in chapter XVII [10], with the protagonist's decision to give up the experiment of addressing the lady directly. In this new silence he will find an audience of women who do indeed interpret correctly "lo secreto del mio cuore" (XVIII.1 [X.3]) [the secret in my heart]. These women, who have an understanding of love, will declare the inadequacy of his previous poetry and become the new interlocutors of a new kind of writing. The episode of the *gabbo* makes first steps in this direction, but the turning point still lies ahead. In his desire to express but reluctance to share, in feeling misunderstood and fantasizing in private about correcting the misunderstanding, in longing for a wider public but retreating to a closed circle, the Dante of chapter XIV arguably displays "the self-mutilating narcissism of the lyrical culture that precedes him,"[33] yet perhaps, more simply, the anxieties and grandeur of a young man in search of a voice and a vocation. Over the space of three chapters, Cavalcanti's poetry briefly provides him with a model to follow. Yet that paradigm also feels very much like a dead end for the young protagonist. In fact, in "Con l'altre donne mia vista gabbate," writing *à la* Cavalcanti changes the poet into someone else, someone who is not quite himself ("mi cangio in figura d'altrui," XIV.12 [7.12], line 11 [I change into the appearance of another]). However, running against the Cavalcantian thread, where the self is fragmented and the passions fiercely strike, kill, and rout the subject's senses (XIV.12 [10.12]) in an irreversible trajectory without return (XIV.8 [10.8]), readers can find two delicate but irreducible trademark signs of Dante's oeuvre as a whole. The first sign is that, unlike Cavalcanti, Dante never claims here that his experience is ineffable and unknowable; quite the contrary, he is firmly optimistic about the fact that his experience can, and indeed should, be understood, but *in the way he intends*—where the protagonist's reaction is interpreted as love and the poem's obscurities as erudite allusions. Second, although he speaks the Cavalcantian idiom of self-destruction, the death he represents is not the last word but can be followed by a form of resurrection ("resurressiti," XIV.8 [10.8]).[34] As Barolini notes, renewal is a possibility "not considered in Cavalcanti's system: a death that is transfiguration, metamorphosis, and rebirth of the soul in a 'figura nova.'"[35] In select moments in Cavalcanti's poetry this change in appearance is indeed associated with the mark of death, an occurrence to be avoided ("che Morte non ti ponga 'n sua figura," Cavalcanti, *Rime* 33.8 [To show [Death's] pallid likeness in your stead]). But whereas Love itself appears to Cavalcanti as a "figura morta" [dead figure] in one of his sonnets (Cavalcanti, *Rime* 36.3), Dante's sonnet turns the adjective and rhyme-word into something else: "figura nova" (XIV.11, also line 3) [new figure]. The adjective *novo* is not an invention of Dante's—in the *canzone* "Quando di morte mi conven trar vita" [Since out of death I must indeed draw life], Cavalcanti talks about a Love that fleetingly renews, "formando di disio nova persona" (Cavalcanti, *Rime* 32.15) [shapes from desire a new form that lives] before its virtue degrades into vice—yet in Dante's hands its strategic significance is renewed. It is tempting to read into the adjective *nova* of this archaizing sonnet all the richness and significance it accrues over the course of Dante's *Vita nova*.[36] Set in their wider context, the phrases "figura morta" and "figura nova" chosen by Cavalcanti and Dante respectively could not appear more emblematic of the two poets and the crux of their disagreement. In the face of all his fascination with death, in this chapter and beyond, Dante is always irresistibly the poet of a new life.

Vita nova XV [8]

LACHLAN HUGHES

Chapter XV [8] comes at the center of a thematic cluster (chapters XIV–XVI [7–9]) that directly precedes—and, to a significant extent, also provokes—Dante's pivotal turn to the *stile della lode*, praise style, in chapters XVII–XXI [10–12]. This cluster is made up of three closely related sonnets that together offer an extended response to the *gabbo* incident of chapter XIV [7], Dante's humiliation at the hands of Beatrice and her companions. Significantly, these three sonnets, explicitly grouped together at the start of chapter XVII [10.1–10.2], are the only poems in the *Vita nova* that position the poet's beloved—identified as Beatrice only in the surrounding prose sections—as a direct, second-person addressee ("voi").[1]

The early chapters of the *Vita nova* have often been read in terms of a threefold itinerary of authorial influence and subsequent liberation: from a Guittonian phase (chapters VII–VIII [2.12–3], marked by the presence of *sonetti rinterzati*); to a Cavalcantian phase (chapters IX–XVI [4–9], containing the *Vita nova*'s only *ballata*, a poetic form favored by Cavalcanti); to Dante's turn to the *stile della lode* in chapters XVII–XXI [10–12], inspired in part by the poetry of Guido Guinizzelli.[2] In this reading, the influence of Cavalcanti's poetry, with its radical Aristotelian (and, as Natascia Tonelli has recently explored, medical) conception of love as an irrational and destructive passion, presents an impasse for Dante on his path to poetic maturity, an impasse that is then transcended by the "matera nuova e più nobile" (XVII.1 [10.1]) [new and nobler subject matter] of "Donne ch'avete intelletto d'amore" [Women who understand the truth of love], the turning point for Dante's conception of love as "a super-rational force that leads not to death but life."[3]

However, while there can be little doubt that Cavalcanti's poetry (or at least Dante's somewhat monochrome distillation of it) is strongly invoked in the three *gabbo* sonnets (XIV–XVI [7–9]), such a starkly teleological reading risks overlooking the subtle, yet significant ways in which Dante already distances himself from Cavalcanti in this early part of the *Vita nova*, not to mention the important role that Dante's "primo amico" [best friend] continues to occupy in later portions of the *libello* (especially chapters XXIV [15], XXV [16], and XXX [19.8–19.10]). In this chapter I will explore the precise nature and extent of Dante's Cavalcantianism in chapter XV [8] of the *Vita nova*.

While in the first sonnet of the *gabbo* episode—"Con l'altre donne mia vista gabbate" [With other women you mock my distress]—Dante's focus is principally on "la cagione del [suo] trasfiguramento" (XIV [7]) [the cause of [his] transfiguration], in "Ciò che m'incontra, ne la mente more" [And when I go to get a glimpse of you], the ninth poem of the *Vita nova*, focus shifts more intensely to the interior experience of the poetic subject undergoing such a transformation: to "quello che [gli] diviene presso di lei" (XV.3 [8.3]) [what happens to [him] when [he is] near her]. Cued by the two personified *pensamenti* of the introductory prose section (*sermocinatio*—a typical feature of Cavalcanti's poetry and of the early chapters of the *Vita nova*), this move toward interiority is accompanied by a pervasive contemplation of death, as the first line of the sonnet succinctly announces: "Ciò che m'incontra, ne la mente more" (XV.4 [8.4]) [What meets me dies in memory]. As Domenico De Robertis observed in his edition of the pre–*Vita nova* version of the sonnet, "more" [dies] is "the first link in a chain which, with its derivatives and synonyms, binds together the entire sonnet": "perir" (line 4), "tramortendo" (line 6), "moia, moia" (line 8), "ancide" (line 12), "morta" (line 13), and "morte" (line 14), not to mention the phonic presence of "more" in seemingly unrelated words such as "Amore" (line 3) and "tremore" (line 7).[4]

Alongside this dense lexical network, Dante evokes the destructive consequences of an encounter with the beloved in interesting syntactical ways, consistently unsettling any stable sense of subjective autonomy. In line 5, for example, the "color del core" in fact refers, through hypallage, to the poet's "viso." In turn, the poet's heart—the grammatical subject of the following clause ("che, tramortendo, ovunque pò s'appoia" [which, swooning deathlike, props itself nearby])—stands in for the poetic subject himself, suggestively re-evoking the prose narrative of the *gabbo* episode in chapter XIV [7]: "Allora dico che io poggiai la mia persona simulatamente ad una pintura la quale circundava questa magione" [Then I had to prop myself, surreptitiously, against one of the pictures that ran around the walls of this house]. Moving into the sestet, the poet's passivity, both grammatical and literal, is rendered absolute, with a series of concatenated relative clauses bringing the poem to its ultimate conclusion in a pairing of death ("morte") and desire ("voglia").

For Cavalcanti, Dante's "primo amico" and interlocutor, death and desire are inexorably linked. In several of Cavalcanti's poems amorous desire— a passion of the sensitive soul, and therefore ungoverned by reason—leads not only to the death of the poetic subject but to an incessant, masochistic desire for such a death. In the single-stanza *canzone* "Poi che di doglia cor conven ch'i' porti" [Since I have to bear a heart of pain], for example, Cavalcanti, in a fit of polysyndeton that conveys the poetic subject's expression of resigned passivity, writes:

> E dico che' miei spiriti son morti,
> e 'l cor, che tanto ha guerra e vita poco;
> e se non fosse che 'l morir m'è gioco,
> fare'ne di pietà pianger Amore.[5]
>
> (lines 5–8)

[And I say that my spirits are dead / and my heart is at war with itself; / and if dying weren't a joy for me, / I would make Love cry with pity.]

There is much in common here with "Ciò che m'incontra": the focus on the heart ("lo viso mostra lo color del core," line 5), a declared desire for death ("di lor morte voglia," line 14), an appeal for pity (lines 9–14). But there is one subtle, yet extremely important distinction: Dante informs us in the ensuing prose divisions that Love is "consigliato da la ragione" (XV.8 [8.8]) [advised by reason], a fact of which we are continually reminded at various stages throughout the *Vita nova* (though always in the prose sections, never in the poems themselves, where in fact Love does not appear always advised by reason). In chapter II [1.2–1.11], for example, in describing his first encounter with Beatrice, Dante informs the reader that Love thereafter never governed him without "lo fedele consiglio de la ragione in quelle cose là ove cotale consiglio fosse utile a udire" [the faithful counsel of reason, in those matters where such guidance was helpful]. So too, in chapter IV [2.3–2.5], immediately after describing the beginning of his friendship with Cavalcanti, Dante invokes "la volontade d'Amore, lo quale mi comandava secondo lo consiglio de la ragione" [the will of Love, who commanded me in keeping with reason's counsel].

In drawing on Cavalcanti's poetic toolbox in "Ciò che m'incontra," Dante in essence reprograms the elements of Cavalcanti's psychological theater of the self and frames the poet's *sbigottimento* as something that is caused, not directly by love, but—and this is the crucial point—by its absence. Love's warning—"'Fuggi, se 'l perir t'è noia'" (line 4) [If perishing disturbs you, flee!]—becomes, in light of Dante's autocommentary, not so much a threat (as it would seem to be in the freestanding, pre–*Vita nova* version of the poem), but rather a rationally motivated and well-intentioned (but clearly ignored) forewarning of the adverse effects of an encounter with the beloved, all of which is couched in a highly suggestive conditional: "*se* 'l perir t'è noia" [*if* perishing disturbs you]. Love, in Cavalcantian terms, isn't love at all, Dante seems to be suggesting.

This is already a significant shift from the previous *gabbo* sonnet, "Con l'altre donne mia vista gabbate" (XIV.11–12 [7.11–7.12]), in which, in a more straightforwardly Cavalcantian manner, Amore is in fact named as the direct cause of the bodily spirits' death, in no way "consigliato da la ragione":

> ché Amor, quando sì presso a voi mi trova,
> prende baldanza e tanta securtate,
> che fere tra' miei spiriti paurosi,
> e quale ancide, e qual pinge di fore,
> sì che solo remane a veder vui.
>
> (lines 7–11)

[since Love, when I am near you, fortifies, / taking on such nerve and brazenness, / he blasts my frightened spirits all about, / slaughtering some, while others he expels, / so he alone is left to look at you.]

Dante is all too aware of the ideological dissonance that his continual insistence on Love's appeal to reason causes within the context of the sequence of *gabbo* sonnets, not to mention the *Vita nova* as a whole; in the short prose section that follows "Con l'altre donne" he terms the above-quoted lines "dubbiose parole" [obscure words] and writes that "questo dubbio è impossibile a solvere a chi non fosse in simile grado fedele d'Amore" (XIV.14 [7.14]) [this obscurity cannot be resolved by one who is not, to a similar degree, one of Love's faithful]. By muddying the waters here, acknowledging but not resolving the obvious tension between the poetry and (aspects of) the prose in this early section of the *Vita nova*, Dante lays the groundwork for the radically altered phenomenology of love that emerges with the advent of the *stile della lode* in chapters XVII–XXI [10–12].

Returning to "Ciò che m'incontra," perhaps one of the most conspicuously un-Cavalcantian aspects of the sonnet comes in the description in line 7 of "la ebrietà del gran tremore" [the drunkenness my shakes impart], which occurs when the poet encounters his lady. *Ebrietà* is a hapax in the *Vita nova* and has no presence whatsoever in Cavalcanti's lyric vocabulary.[6] While many commentators have pointed to scriptural references (variously Ezekiel 23:33, Jeremiah 23:9, Isaiah 16:9, 29:9, Psalm 35:9, Song of Songs 2:4, 5:1), Manuela Colombo was the first critic to point to the term's widespread use in contemporary mystical poetry.[7] The Franciscan poet Jacopone da Todi (d. 1306), for instance, often invokes *ebbrezza divina* as a cipher for divine madness in his poetry, for a state of irrational love for Christ, where irrationality is framed in a positive light as a state of transcendence toward a more directly sensual encounter with the divine. In "All'Amor, ch'è vinuto" [To Love, which has become flesh], a *lauda* in praise of divine love, he writes:

Amor, or ne manteni
d'Amore ennibrïati,
teco stare abracciati
enn Amor trasformato![8]
    (lines 461–64)

_____

[Love, now keep us / drunk with love, / embracing you, / transformed in Love!].

This is the same *ebbrezza divina* that Dante evokes in the final cantos of *Paradiso*, as the pilgrim approaches the final vision of the Godhead; in canto 30, for instance, Dante describes the angels plunging in and out of the river of light as "come inebrïate da li odori" (67) [as though inebriated by the odors]. Teodolinda Barolini has also connected the term to the ecstatic visions of the purgatorial terrace of anger, where the pilgrim's walking is described as being "a guisa di cui vino o sonno piega" (*Purg.* 15.123) [like a person disoriented by wine or sleep].[9] In the context of "Ciò che m'incontra," the "ebrietà del gran tremore" links to the poet's internal experience, which, here in a negative light, transcends his external reality.

The result of Dante's "ebrietà," the stones that seem to cry out "'Die! Die!,'" finds a scriptural intertext in Christ's words to the Pharisees upon his entry into Jerusalem on Palm Sunday, as reported in the Gospel of Luke: "He answered, 'I tell you, if these were silent, the stones would shout out'" (19:40).[10] This is the very episode in which, in the Gospel of Mark, Jesus's disciples proclaim, "Benedictus qui venit" (11:9), the verse with which, save for a substitution of *venis* for *venit*, Beatrice's arrival in the Earthly Paradise is heralded in *Purgatorio* 30.19. Furthermore, in the following Gospel verse (11:10) Christ's disciples proclaim, "Hosanna in excelsis," a phrase that is later quoted in premonition of Beatrice's death in the *Vita nova*'s central *canzone*, "Donna pietosa e di novella etate" (XXIII.17 [14.17]) [A woman green in years, compassionate]. Given the well-documented Christological resonances throughout the *Vita nova* that position Beatrice as a *figura Christi*, and Dante's extensive recycling of this particular Gospel episode, it is hard not to see a nascent link to the Easter Week liturgy in the shouting stones of "Ciò che m'incontra."[11] But whereas the stones that are imagined as potentially crying out in Luke 19:40 would be praising God and proclaiming the authority of Christ to enter Jerusalem, the stones of Dante's sonnet seem merely to come to life as a psychomachic projection of the poet's masochistic desire for self-annihilation, crying, "'Moia, moia'" [Die! Die!]. If Dante is indeed drawing on a scriptural intertext here, it is nonetheless filtered through a Cavalcantian lens: while Christ's death on the cross is salvific, bringing about the redemption of mankind, the death invoked in "Ciò che m'incontra" is still very much "the erotic death of courtly lyric."[12] By mixing modes

in this way, planting a seed of salvific analogy in the fertile soil of Caval-
canti's irrational, destructive conception of love, Dante draws attention,
albeit in a veiled way, to the obstacles that lie dormant in such a concep-
tion, obstacles that he himself will ultimately attempt to overcome through
his move toward a theologizing poetics of disinterested praise, based solely
on "quelle parole che lodano la donna mia" (XVIII.6 [10.8]) [words that
praise my lady].

We see that "Ciò che m'incontra" is not merely a Cavalcantian imitation
or parody, not just an instance of Dante trying on a poetic garb before ulti-
mately opting for a different one; it is in fact already a multilayered, inter-
ventional critique of the Cavalcantian lyric mode, laying the groundwork for
Dante's later conception of love as a devotional force that is in no way anti-
thetical to reason. And yet, despite the performed subversion of Cavalcanti's
influence in the *gabbo* episode, the ghost of Guido clearly lives on in Dante's
poetic imagination, long into the *Commedia*. Chapter XV [8] is thus not
merely presenting a model to be superseded but is already a complex negoti-
ation, with far-reaching consequences, of what love is and can be.

Vita nova XVI [9]

FRANCO COSTANTINI

Chapter XVI [9] is the last chapter of the so-called Cavalcantian section of the *Vita nova*, and it precedes the fundamental chapters XVII–XIX [10], which will seal the process of Dante's poetic conversion. XVI [9] begins by establishing a connection to the previous chapter—"Appresso ciò ch'io dissi in questo sonetto" [After I composed this sonnet]—and it consists solely of the commentary on the sonnet "Spesse fiate vegnomi alla mente" [I often call to mind], also included in this chapter, which Dante presents as a further addition to the description of his desperate state: "parole, nella quali io dicesse quattro cose ancora sopra lo mio stato, le quali non mi parea che fossero manifestate ancora per me" (XVI.1 [9.1]) [to write something in which I would say four more things about my state, which, it seemed to me, I had not yet explained]. The sonnet itself is an iteration ("spesse fiate") of the obscure qualities ("le oscure qualità") of love (lines 1–4), describing the assault of Love on the subject (lines 5–8), its desolate and emptied state after the assault, the subject's attempt to heal itself with the sight of the woman ("credendo guerire," lines 9–11), and the subsequent "annihilation" of the subject (lines 12–14). The commentary is, rather traditionally, divided into four parts, and, in line with Dante's strategy in the *Vita nova*, it steers the poetry toward some specific meanings.

Chapter XVI [9] is crucial in many ways. From this moment on, many things will change: the way the lover considers his relationship with Beatrice, the way poetry conveys a certain temporality, and the way the author thinks about his own poetics. Focusing on the philosophical implications of this chapter, I aim to show that a transformation of lyrical subjectivity and of temporality is taking place here. In this chapter, I argue, Dante draws a caricature of the logical fallacy (and therefore failure) of a Cavalcantian subject in order to set the scene for his own new poetic beginning. Therefore, an apparent tribute to Guido Cavalcanti becomes an instrument for radical criticism.[1] While criticizing his first friend's "obscure" take on love, Dante offers a new possibility for the lover to exercise reason and also sets the stage for a revolutionary (in Walter Benjamin's terms) temporality for his *libello*: one that both explodes and fixates time and (personal) history. Between chapter XVI [9] and chapter XIX [10], the circular time of an errant desire is replaced by the ordered time of a converted subject.

It is important to notice at the outset that the love described by the sonnet "Spesse fiate" is marked by a "medical" aspect that is absent from the prose description. The prose oscillates, instead, between traditional military metaphors ("quando questa battaglia d'Amore mi pugnava," XVI. 4 [9.4] [when this battle of Love attacked me]),[2] and a more philosophical vocabulary ("la mia memoria movesse la fantasia ad imaginare quale Amore mi facea," XVI.2 [9.2] [my memory set my fantasy in motion to imagine what Love was turning me into]). In other words: while in the poem the focus is on the traditional physiological aspect of the harmful effects of the *amor hereos* (the "oscure qualità," XVI.7 [9.7] [obscure qualities] refer to the dark humor that characterizes the melancholic lover), the prose seems to try to reframe the sonnet from a more philosophical and less physiological perspective. While the prose makes use of a narrative imperfect past, the sonnet is written in a timeless simple present that fixes the action in an indeterminate repetition. The lover and the poet are, in this moment of the narration, locked up in the circular temporality of a dysphoric kind of love and poetry.

The act that initiates the whole movement of the sonnet is found in the first line, "Spesse fiate vegnomi alla mente" [I often call to mind]. This is made remarkably more profound and complicated by the prose, which affirms, in quite Aristotelian terms, that memory moves fantasy.[3] This movement, represented in the sonnet and described in the prose, is triggered by memory and seems to stop only in the last verse, with the departure of the soul from the poet's heart. A psychological movement, born in the sensitive soul (to which memory belongs), is communicated to fantasy (another faculty of the same sensitive soul) and ends up causing a physical action: the search for the lady. Nevertheless, the subject's hope of healing ("credendo guerire") is unjustified with respect to the memories of the most recent failures, narrated and analyzed in the previous chapters (XIV [7] and XV [8]).

Placed at the end of the "Cavalcantian" phase, chapter XVI [9] identifies a sticking point that Dante, or at least the new Dante that takes shape from chapter XVII [10] onward, may have found in Cavalcanti. Such a problem is linked to the notions of will and knowledge, and to the dissociation between these two components of the human rational soul. The chapter portrays an erroneous judgment as the result of a deviated desire, whereby everything is played out at the level of the sensitive soul (where memory, imagination, and the estimative faculty are located), without the contribution of the reason, which, according to what was announced since chapter II [1.2–11], should guide love. One of the questions that the text raises concerns this major error, which determines a bad and even dangerous action for the subject: How is it possible that, despite past experiences, the poet can believe in the thaumaturgical virtue of an image he should know to be completely destructive to him? How is the "credendo guerire" possible?

This lost and self-referential subject, unable to break the deadlock into which his self-pity throws him, is the lyric subject that Dante wants to replace. He is now mimicking his "first friend," exasperating certain aspects of Cavalcanti's poetry and highlighting the relationship between errancy and error. Indeed, errancy is the (logical) consequence and the (poetic) representation of error. The prose specifies that such error is due to a failure of memory: the subject is a sort of puppet wandering through the streets of Florence hoping to find the one who will lead him to death (the atmosphere recalls a passage from Cavalcanti's sonnet "Tu m'hai sì piena di dolor la mente" [You have filled my mind with such distress],[4] where the subject is described as a sort of bronze or stone creature acting mindlessly). However, whereas the "true" Cavalcantian lover always seems to be well aware of his condition, even if he cannot (and does not want to) change it, Dante in this chapter depicts what is almost a caricature of such a lover, choosing to emphasize his lack of reasoning and his self-destructive tendencies, in order to present the poetic conversion that will follow as necessary and redeeming.

What is lacking in the episode described in chapter XVI [9] is a true and rational deliberation in the practical reasoning that should direct human actions: between the major premise (the lady is beautiful) and the conclusion of seeking her or not, the minor premise (the vision of the lady is dangerous) is missing. The verb *credere*, a point of contact between prose and sonnet, indicates a deceptive knowledge, a belief based on an incomplete mental process. As Alain De Libera explains in his analysis of some medieval explanations of incontinence, "Desire erases and replaces the minor premise":[5] the intensity of the desire, the excess of concupiscence, and the narcissistic self-pity lead the practical reasoning to be cut short.

In chapter XVI [9], Dante is setting the stage for his own conversion, which is first and foremost a poetic renovation. As we shall see, the innovation of the *Vita nova* consists in converting without really "going back," without retracting his previous poetry (as frate Guittone did). The problem is not Beatrice, the object of the desire, but the attitude of the subject toward this object. One of the main problems that Dante faces is how to invalidate the traditional link between love and madness, pointed out by Guittone in his conversion *canzone*, "Ora parrà" [Now it will appear]: "ché'n tutte parte, ove distringe Amore, / regge follore—in loco di savere" (lines 10–11) [for wherever Love fixes his grip there reigns madness instead of wisdom].[6] Cavalcanti's poetry, at least through Dante's reinterpretation, only justifies this irreconcilable opposition: either love or intellect, either spirit or flesh, either desire or knowledge. By the filter of his rewriting in the *Vita nova*, helped by the performative value of the narrative format,[7] Dante tries to exonerate desire, which is not bad in itself, and to accuse the subject, who wrongly directs it.

Dante's presentation of the Cavalcantian subject is, however, rather biased for Dante's own purposes. While it can be considered a weak-willed subject,[8] deliberately acting against its own judgment, the lyric subject in Cavalcanti is not a self-deceiving one; it neither follows a deceptive belief nor is driven by an illusion. "Donna me prega" [A lady asks me] is quite explicit on this point when, speaking of Love, it affirms that "solo di costui nasce mercede" (line 70).[9] Love's discourse is a self-referential one: uncontrolled love is the cause of all the problems of the lover and at the same time the source of all his joys, and invoking the control of reason over desire is not only useless but also contrary to the very nature of love (and therefore of love poetry).

Dante's strategy consists in presenting the poetics of his first friend as insufficient, doomed to failure, marked by an inherent vice. In doing so, he can inaugurate his new poetics without renouncing the erotic language of lyric poetry and, instead, divert it in a theologized direction and create a morally, fully responsible subject. The lover should not be pleased with his own misery, and the figure of the beloved can no longer be destructive. Chapter XVI [9] helps Dante to show that suffering is due, not to the deadly nature of the woman, but to an error of the subject.

A new problem, however, arises: How to imagine a quest for bliss or happiness that coexists with a poetry that, like the courtly one, is based on a necessarily unfulfilled desire? A solution will be provisionally given in chapter XVIII [10.3–10.11] with the help of Augustinian philosophy: when, in the dialogue with the ladies, Dante affirms that Love has transferred his bliss "in quello che non mi puote venire meno" (XVIII.4 [10.6]) [to that which cannot fail me], he is maybe recalling the Augustinian bliss as it is presented in the treatise *On the Happy Life*, namely, as the possession of something "permanent, what no misfortune, however grave, can snatch away" (*De vita beata* 2.11).[10] The symbolical death of the subject staged in chapter XVI [9] is clearing the way for a rebirth; as in Augustine's *Confessions* and as in the first canto of the *Comedy*, one must hit rock bottom to be able to resurface.

The subject in chapter XVI [9] is not free and its action is not voluntary (in chapter XV.2 [8.2] we read, "S'io non perdessi le mie vertudi, e fossi libero" [If I had not lost my powers, and were free]), but it is determined by a process in which reason never takes part. The subject could not have done otherwise; he doesn't err willingly because, without reason, no free will can exist. In this scene, the subject is an impotent spectator of its own actions. It is, therefore, necessary to break the circle of desire and frustration that ties down a too self-indulgent and self-referential subject.

In the *Vita nova*, the gradual discovery of the nature of Love and the poetic apprenticeship that goes with it are part of a conversion process embedded in a linear autobiographical fiction. Only within this kind of historicized discourse of love can a new type of volitional subjectivity emerge. The narrative structure established by the prose serves the purpose of creating the conditions for the emergence of a disciplined will in a unitary subject. As Barolini points out, the opposition of temporalities is also an opposition of subjectivities.[11]

Chapter XVI [9] is an example of how the prose acts upon the poetry: by reframing in a more philosophical direction the sensual determinism conveyed by the sonnet, it fosters a more profound understanding of the psychological problem of the lover and represents a first step toward its solution. "Incipit vita nova": the declared beginning never ceases to return each time the lover-poet has an epiphany and reaches a further step in understanding the messianic character of the figure of Beatrice. Dante's strategy resembles the concept of "revolutionary" as expressed by Walter Benjamin in the "Theses on the Concept of History": "What characterizes revolutionary classes at their moment of action is the awareness that they are about to make the continuum of history explode."[12] Chapter XVI [9] is the border of a certain kind of poetry: the symbolic death of the lover ends one temporality and opens the doors to a new one. In this sense Dante is a revolutionary and the *Vita nova* functions as a "time-lapse mode of history":[13] the anniversaries of the meetings, of birth, and of death form a constellation of memories that reactivates time. This time is not the circular and repetitive time of clocks (and of lyrics), but the linear, oriented, messianic time of Christian calendars (and of teleological narrativity). When read as an isolated poem, "Spesse fiate" is the traditional narration of a circle of desire and frustration; in the *Vita nova*, it becomes a further step in a personal story of salvation and poetic conversion.

It is not surprising that the "dark qualities" of the lover reappear later in chapter XXXV [24], at the beginning of the so-called episode of the *donna gentile*. These chapters will stage a return to a desire conveyed by the body, to a passive subjectivity, and to the closed, agonizing temporality of repetition and error that characterized the Cavalcantian section of the book. Consequently, the expressions of this recurring temporality will largely come back: in chapter XXXVI [25] the subject is falling back again into a self-destructive and masochistic dynamic, and in the sonnet "Color d'amore" [Color of love], repetitiveness ("spesse fiate") and the opposition of will and desire return: "Io non posso tener gli occhi distructi / che non riguardin voi spesse fiate, / per disiderio di piangere ch'elli ànno" (lines 9–11) [For I cannot prevent my weary eyes from looking almost ceaselessly at you, because of their desire to shed more tears].

Moreover, the definitive recovery of Beatrice's worth will take place in chapter XXXIX.2 [28.2] by reconstructing the memories "secondo l'ordine del tempo passato" [*verbatim*: "according to the order of the past time"], which is almost a *mise en abyme* of the book itself: the acts of recovering Beatrice and transforming poetry coincide with the recollection and the selective rewriting as presented in the *libello*. In his commentary on Aristotle's *De memoria et reminiscentia,* Aquinas specifies the difference between memory and recollection, writing that "recollection bears a likeness to a sort of syllogism and . . . comes about only in those in whom there is a natural power for deliberating."[14] Recovering Beatrice "secondo l'ordine del tempo passato" is an act of *reminiscentia* and a rational operation of which the lover in "Spesse fiate" is not yet capable. What is needed by the lover to overcome the psychological impasse of chapter XVI [9], a rational will capable of controlling memory and desire, is also needed by the author to conceive the poetics of the entire *Vita nova.* The "book of memory" (I.1 [1.1]) is, indeed, the "book of recollection." The identification between love and reason (from which intentional will derives) is hence not only a profound anti-Cavalcantian assumption but also the theoretical premise for the entire operation of the *Vita nova.*

From a Benjaminian perspective, thus, Dante's "revolution" will consist, not in jumping forward, but in "activating the emergency brake"[15] of the train of his personal history, not overtaking Beatrice but dwelling in her and, in so doing, poetically freeing his desire from contingency once and for all (at least in the *libello*). In this sense, chapter XVI [9] is truly a turning point in the narrative plot of the *Vita nova,* both in its structure and in its philosophical and poetic implications. The self-control that is missing in this chapter and that the lyric subject must learn coincides with the control that Dante exercises over the text.

However, chapter XVI [9] is not a farewell to Cavalcanti's influence. It will take years for Dante to overcome the threat of a lyric subject partially emptied of its intellect and subdued, not without some pleasure, to the elusive phantasies of its desire[16]—years to be able to, as the young Joyce wrote, "recall the dark humour of Guido Cavalcanti and smile."[17]

Vita nova XVII and XVIII [10.1–10.11]

DAVID BOWE

Chapters XVII [10.1–10.2] and XVIII [10.3–10.11] together represent a pivotal episode in the subjective and poetic narrative of the *Vita nova*. In this part of the *libello*, Dante closes a series of frames and phases that have shaped his "little book" up to this point and opens a new chapter in his text. This transition marks the end of the "Cavalcantian" phase of Dante's poetic output; it brings the first explicit subcollection reported by Dante to a close; it mirrors and to some extent repairs the psychological damage of the *gabbo* (XIV [7]); and it prepares the way for the new mode of writing, the *stilo de la loda*, which will be introduced with the *canzone* "Donne ch'avete intelletto d'amore" [Women who have an understanding of love] in chapter XIX [10.12–10.33].

While Barbi divides this pivot across two chapters, XVII [10.1–10.2] and XVIII [10.3–10.11], Gorni incorporates them (along with Barbi's XIX) into one unit, his chapter 10. As noted in the introduction to this volume, these rereadings set out not to valorize one set of divisions or another but to examine Dante's text in manageable, recognizable sections, and this moment is a case in point. While Barbi's clean division of XVII and XVIII into separate units does not withstand the narrative and metaliterary impetus of the *Vita nova* at this point, neither does a straightforward elision of these passages into one flowing piece of text necessarily fit the dynamics of the *libello* here. Both division and continuity are complicated by the function of XVII [10.1–10.2] in relation to both XVIII [10.3–10.11] and the chapter that immediately precedes it.

What then is this function? XVII [10.1–10.2] is a transitional chapter. It offers us a new rubric or short proem to the new phase of Dante's tale of personal and poetic development marked by "Donne ch'avete":

> Poi che dissi questi tre sonetti, ne li quali parlai a questa donna però che fuoro narratori di tutto quasi lo mio stato, credendomi tacere e non dire più però che mi parea di me assai avere manifestato, avvegna che sempre poi tacesse di dire a lei, a me convenne ripigliare matera nuova e più nobile che la passata. E però che la cagione de la nuova matera è dilettevole a udire, la dicerò, quanto potrò più brievemente. (XVII.1–2 [10.1–10.2])

> [After I wrote these three sonnets in which I addressed this lady directly, since they told almost everything about my state, thinking it best to be silent and write no more since I felt I had explained enough about myself, although from then on I would refrain from addressing her directly, I needed to take up new and nobler subject matter than that of the past. And since the occasion for the new subject matter is delightful to hear, I will write it down, as briefly as I know how.]

This brief passage synthesizes what has happened and anticipates the following episode. It is one of many instances in the *libello* where Dante recalls something already written—the book of memory (I.1 [1.1]), these three sonnets, the "unfinished" *canzone* "Sì lungiamente" [So long a time] (XXVII.1–2 [18.3–18.5]), the final sonnet (XLII.1–3 [31.1–31.3])—and looks toward something to be (or not to be) written in the future—the *libello* (I.1 [1.1]), the promised account of Dante's new subject matter, the death of Beatrice (not to be discussed, XXVIII.1–2 [19.1–19.2]), "quello che mai non fue detto d'alcuna" (XLII.2 [31.2]) [to say things about her that have never been said about any woman]. These recollections and anticipations operate in relation to two categories of writing: things within the *Vita nova* and things outside it. The first and last chapters of the *libello* both refer to extra- as well as intratextual writing, things that came before and will come after the writing contained in Dante's little book. Chapter XVII [10.1–10.2], meanwhile, is entirely concerned with things that have been and will be written within the *Vita nova*.

Those things that have been written include his first direct addresses to Beatrice in the wake of Dante's disastrous strategies of concealment (the screen ladies) that led first to Beatrice's denial of her greeting and then to the mockery of Dante by Beatrice and the ladies present at the wedding (the *gabbo* episode of chapter XIV [7]) and the three woeful sonnets that follow it. In XVII [10.1–10.2], Dante officially "collects" these same sad sonnets into a three-text subsequence, "questi tre sonnetti," addressed to Beatrice and bemoaning the psychological and physiological fallout that Dante suffers from the *gabbo* in distinctly Cavalcantian terms.

The function of this short passage, then, is more paratextual than narrative. Given this essentially organizational role, it is not too much of a leap to identify this as marking the transition between two of the "maggiori paragrafi" anticipated in chapter I.

Before delving further into the passage, a brief definition of *paratext* will be useful. This term, coined by Gérard Genette, refers to the textual (and also often visual) material that accrues around a written work. Génette's concept falls into two main subcategories. The first is *peritext*, which comprises those materials making up a book that are not its "contents"—the cover, preface, titles, indexes, and the like. In a medieval manuscript context this could include rubrics, proems, paragraph punctuation, historiated initials, and so on. The second is *epitext*, which refers to materials produced about a book, such as reviews, interviews, and advertisements.[1]

With this definition in mind, it becomes clear that from the very beginning of the *libello*, the line between text and paratext has been blurred, as the narrator rejoices in the art of assembling the *Vita nova* from the archetype of the book of memory and recounts the intricacies of this process at various points in the text. This blurring is verifiable also in the early manuscript tradition of the *Vita nova*. While a number of witnesses preserve versions of Dante's text in broadly the shape we know it today, as a unified *prosimetrum*,[2] this is not by any means true of all texts circulating under the title *Vita nova*. Notably, Boccaccio shifted Dante's *divisioni* into the margins of his copies, presenting them as glosses to the "main" text,[3] while elsewhere collections of the lyric components alone, sometimes with excerpts of the accompanying prose, are recorded as the *Vita nova*.[4] This last example is the most extreme approach to Dante's text, effectively relegating the prose to the status of "optional extra," but it also serves as a reminder that all of the prose in the *Vita nova*, whether narrative, commentary, or "digression," is crucial to the *libello* as a whole.[5]

This particular short passage of prose plays a paratextual role, looking forward and backward to organize the text of the *libello*, but it also serves as a promise. It is a promise, much like Dante's promise at the close of the *Vita nova*, to silence one mode of writing, to write more and to write differently, to write more worthily about Beatrice. In both function and content, the *Vita nova*'s finale is foreshadowed at its turning point. Crucially, this passage is also a promise, not to write *to* Beatrice, but to write *about* Beatrice, for the dual reason that he has written enough about himself and that he must now write nobler verse, shifting away from the generic norms of courtly address (we need only recall Giacomo da Lentini's "Madonna vo voglio" as foundational and typical in the Italian vernacular tradition) to adopt an apparently less self-interested poetic project.

In keeping with the content of Dante's own brief declaration, I will refrain from further discussion of his new subject matter until the next section of this commentary and instead make a few concluding observations. This short passage is fundamentally an organizational moment: part of the *ordinatio* of Dante's little book, and a continuation of his tendency explicitly to narrate the structural elements of the *libello*. It makes the first pivotal gesture away from the recounting of his sorry state and toward the more pleasing discussion of his new subject. This brief indication of the forthcoming change of tone is carried across into chapter XVIII [10.3–10.11], with which it should perhaps form a single unit or to which it could even serve as rubric, as Dante narrates the events that follow the more public revelation of his love for Beatrice. This is also a movement away from disruptive polyphony and toward productive dialogue, a movement that we can also frame as the shift out from Dante's internal world to the realm of the piazza, which provides the scene for a group of attentive readers who will interrogate and thus alter the course of Dante's poetics in the course of their dialogue with him.

In chapter XVIII [10.3–10.11] Dante narrates a happier version of the *gabbo* scene that caused him so much suffering in chapter XIV [7]. This time he encounters another group of ladies, including some of those who had

been at the wedding narrated in that episode and therefore party to his disas-
trous display of lovesickness and complicit in mocking him. He is initially
cautious in approaching them, fearing a repeat of his earlier pain and hu-
miliation, which prompted the sonnet "Con altre donne mia vista gabbate"
[With the other women you mock my appearance]. Crucially, however, un-
like in the episode of the *gabbo*, Beatrice is not present. Moreover, it is par-
ticularly striking *how* it is that Dante realizes, in encountering these ladies
in chapter XIII [6], that Beatrice is not present in this new gathering: "La
donna che m'avea chiamato era donna di molto leggiadro parlare; sì che
quand'io fui giunto dinanzi da loro, e *vidi bene* che la mia gentilissima donna
non era con esse, rassicurandomi le salutai, e domandai che piacesse loro"
(XVIII.2 [10.4]) [I was called over by one of those lovely women—one
whose voice was especially charming. When I was right in front of them and
could see that that most gracious of women wasn't there, feeling more re-
laxed I greeted them and asked how I might be of service]. In the *gabbo* epi-
sode, Dante *felt* Beatrice's presence, as is the norm for his sensing of her
arrival, and descended into trembling, yet here he seems dependent on his
sight to confirm her absence. It's a small detail, but one that raises interesting
questions. Is this an anomalous moment in the treatment of the sensory and
porous poetic body and heart in the *Vita nova*?[6] Or is this a demonstration of
logical failure on Dante's part? In other words, if he is dependent on sight to
confirm Beatrice's absences, should he not already have ascertained the same?
This is, however, an encounter destined to go beyond seeing and to close the
distance between Dante and the *donne*, as is very quickly signaled by the *por-
tavoce* of the group calling Dante over:

> De le quali una, volgendo li suoi occhi verso me e chiamandomi per
> nome, disse queste parole: "A che fine ami tu questa tua donna, poi che tu
> non puoi sostenere la sua presenza? Dilloci, ché certo lo fine di cotale
> amore conviene che sia novissimo." E poi che m'ebbe dette queste parole,
> non solamente ella, ma tutte l'altre cominciaro ad attendere in vista la mia
> risponsione. (XVIII.3 [10.5])

> ———

> [One of whom looked directly at me and called me by name, saying,
> "What is the point of your love for this lady, considering that you can't
> endure her presence? We're curious, since the goal of such a love must be

unusual, to say the least." After these words, not only she but all the other women there were poised for my response.]

The opening of this examination explicitly situates this encounter as a direct response to the humiliation of chapter XIV [7], as well as preparing the way for the more readerly, analytical questioning of Dante's poetic mission and output to come in this exchange. At first, the focus is on Dante's symptoms, his evident lovesickness, the *amor hereos* that pervades Dante's more erotically and physiologically challenging moments in the *Vita nova*, but that also possibly permits its visionary finale.[7] Even this diagnostic questioning is not without its literary overtones, however. After all, did not Dante, following in the footsteps of his *primo amico*, give literary expression to his turmoil in the poems that precede this encounter in the *libello*'s narrative?

Diagnosis by both seeing and reading is available to the ladies gathered in the piazza. This latter readerly factor is part of an emerging phenomenon of imagining the woman reader,[8] in part the necessary logical conclusion of Dante's assertion, in chapter XXV [16], that "lo primo che cominciò a dire sì come poeta volgare, si mosse però che volle fare intendere le sue parole a donna" (XXV.6 [16.6]) [the first one who started to write poetry in the vernacular started to do so because he wanted to make his words comprehensible to women]. Dante, as vernacular poet, sets himself up for this fall through the evidence of his poetry. Thus these readers are also vocal literary critics who call into question Dante's claim that he has put his beatitude in something less transient than the greeting so recently denied to him, namely, "In quelle parole che lodano la donna mia" (XVIII.8 [10.10]) [In words that praise my lady]. Their questioning is couched in terms that refer to the lyric texts preceding this encounter, texts already in circulation among a lyric readership made up of women: "Allora mi rispuose questa che mi parlava: 'Se tu ne dicessi vero, quelle parole che tu n'hai dette in notificando la tua condizione, avrestù operate con altro intendimento'" (XVIII.7 [10.9]) [Then the woman added, "If what you're saying is true, those poems that you wrote about your condition must have been written with some other aim in mind"]. In responding to Dante's self-definition as a praise poet, the spokesperson clearly classifies the sonnets "Con l'altre donne mia vista gabbate," "Ciò che m'incontra, ne la mente more" [That which happens to me dies in my memory], and "Spesse fiate vegnonmi a la mente" [Often I remember], the three poems identified in XVII [10.1–10.2], as a corpus of work with which they are familiar. Again, the narrative serves to organize the text on a macro level, placing this subsequence of sonnets under one rubric, "le parole che n'hai dette in notificando la tua condizione."

Beyond the internal framing of these sonnets as contradictory to the protagonist's account of himself and his poetics at this point in the *Vita nova*, this scene also situates Dante's practice within an external lyric tradition according to which poets stage debates with their addressees, usually penning both parts of the exchange themselves. This tradition is a subform of *tenzoni* usually referred to as *tenzoni fittizie*. A brief digression on these modes of poetic exchange will provide a vital vernacular context for the ladies' critique of Dante in the piazza.[9]

Brunetto Latini provides us with a helpful working definition of the *tenzone* (a model with its earlier roots in the Occitan form of the *tenso*)[10] worked out against the context of Florentine communal politics and the exigencies of exile. In his *Rettorica*, a partial *volgarizzamento* and expansive gloss of Cicero's *De inventione* composed around 1260, Brunetto defines the *tenzone* through a discussion of letters and love poetry:

> Usatamente adviene che due persone si tramettono lettere l'uno all'altro o in latino o in proxa o in rima o in volgare o inn altro, nelle quali contendono d'alcuna cosa, e così fanno tencione. Altressì uno amante chiamando merzé alla sua donna dice parole e ragioni molte, et ella si difende in suo dire et inforza le sue ragioni et indebolisce quelle del pregatore. (*Rettorica* 76.14)

> [It is common for two people to send one another letters, in Latin, in prose, in verse, in vernacular, or in another form, in which they debate something, and thus they in engage in a dispute. Similarly, a lover, calling upon his lady for mercy, speaks and reasons at length, and she may defend herself with her own speech and establish her reasons and weaken her supplicant's.]

Brunetto expounds on and expands the scope of Cicero's treatise on oratory and civic debate, exploring its implications for dialogic, argumentative forms of writing, both letters and poetry.[11] In so doing, Brunetto devotes significant space to a treatment of the norms of erotic lyric verse together with the *ars dictaminis*. He then goes on to categorize the concept of *tenzone* as a mode of engagement rather than the mere fact of disagreement, citing the back and forth of the writer and the addressee, who maintains the right to reply using any of the techniques deployed by the appellant: "In questi modi puote quelli a cui vae la lettera o la canzone o negare o difendersi per alcuna scusa" (*Rettorica* 76.16) [In these ways the person to whom the letter or the *canzone* is sent either refuses, or defends themselves with any excuse].

Tenzoni, then, were a significant enough mode to be codified by Brunetto, among others, and to take up nineteen clearly demarcated folios, grouped under marginal rubrics describing each group as a *tenzone* and giving the number of component poems in the exchange, in the Vatican Canzoniere (Biblioteca Apostolica Vaticana, MS Vat. Lat. 3793).[12] It is, of course, also through a *tenzone* that Dante sets out his poetic stall, as narrated in the opening chapters of the *libello*, demonstrating his familiarity with the mechanics and expectations of this mode of literary exchange.

More specifically relevant to this episode in the *Vita nova* is the aforementioned phenomenon of the *tenzone fittizia*, the exchange between poet and imagined interlocutor, usually the lady addressed elsewhere in his verse. In these exchanges, the ladies often respond cautiously, suspiciously, or by unmasking the rhetoric directed at them. This sort of rhetorical questioning is to be found throughout the lyric history of the Italian peninsula in *tensos*, *contrasti*, and *tenzoni fittizie*, from the bodies of Occitan verse in Italian manuscripts to Dante's critical contemporary Cecco Angiolieri.[13] But, without straying too far from the *Vita nova*, it is useful to recall the ways in which some of its most striking and pivotal gestures are also entangled in the broader lyric fabric of the Duecento.[14] The parties, the subject matter, and the particular language of the exchange in XVIII [10.3–10.11] all suggest a reading of this encounter within the wider lyric coalition of ladies who read, understand, respond to, and critique poetic claims and rhetoric. A rather prolific exponent of this tradition, and one to whom Dante would not enjoy being compared, is Guittone d'Arezzo, a leading Tuscan poet of the Duecento and the target of Dante's jibes against stultified rhymers in chapter XXV [16]. In the "preconversion" collection of his sonnets as preserved in the manuscript Laurenziano Rediano 9, Guittone stages two exchanges with a suspicious lady, culminating in the poet's vicious attacks and the lady's

robust critiques articulated in a *tenzone fittizia* comprising six sonnets that alternate between Guittone and the "donna."[15] This exchange, sufficiently widely circulated as to be preserved in both the Laurenziano manuscript and the *Vatican Canzoniere,* features addresses to and rebuttals by a *donna* whom the poet derides as "villana," who in turn unpicks and exposes the disconnect between claim and truth, rhetoric and intention in the poet's writing. In the *donna*'s first response she declares:

> Non mi disdico, villan parladore,
> a quello *intendimento* che ditt'hai;
> or como crederia che 'n te valore
> di fine amante e amor fosse già mai?
> Ch'ogn'altra fina cosa è di te fore.
> (82.1–5)[16]
>
> ---
>
> [I don't deny, oh base speaker, that statement [lit. meaning/intent] you have uttered; now how could I believe that the worth of a fine lover and love was ever in you? As every other fine thing is lacking in you.]

The slippage between word and sense, between the poetic evidence and the poet's declarations that it countermands, is identified and excoriated in this exchange. In speaking about matters of love and poetry, *intendimento* becomes a loaded lyric term when uttered by a lady questioning a poet's motives and words.

Guittone's (anti)climactic *tenzone fittizia* is particularly resonant with *Vita nova* XVIII [10.3–10.11], as the *donna* in this exchange leaves the poet speechless, concluding her final response with a refusal to engage further in the exchange:

> Ben ti puoi tener ormai la lingu'acorta
> e dir ciò che ti piac'e star fidato,
> che' nn-alcun modo non responderaggio.
> (86.12–14)[17]
>
> ---
>
> [You could just as well keep your trap shut or say what you will and trust that I won't give you any sort of reply.]

There is no further response from Guittone, suggesting, according to Latini's rules of engagement for the *tenzone*, that the lady has won out and that the poet has nothing more to say. Indeed, this sonnet marks the end of Lino Leonardi's proposed "canzoniere," a group of eighty-six sonnets within the wider collection of the Laurenziano manuscript.[18]

Dante is left similarly silent in the face of a critical questioning of his "intendimento," having words only for himself as he departs: "Onde io, pensando a queste parole, quasi vergognoso mi partio da loro, e venia dicendo fra me medesimo: 'Poi che è tanta beatitudine in quelle parole che lodano la mia donna, perché altro parlare è stato lo mio?'" (XVIII.8 [10.10]) [At which point, reflecting on these words and feeling almost ashamed of myself, I left them; and as I went along I said to myself: "Since there is so much bliss in words that praise my lady, why have I spoken in any other way?"]. This is not the humiliation of the *gabbo*, but it is another instance of public shame, this time brought on by a weighing of Dante's literary output against his claims. In this scene, Dante echoes the burgeoning tradition of the *tenzone fittizia* while also, through the mise-en-scène of this episode, resituating the literary *tenzone* in the field of civic, or at least public, oratory and debate. Dante, poet of the city as well as poet of Beatrice, makes love lyric a matter for public discussion and dispute, elevating the genre even as it is criticized, or rather through that very criticism.

While Dante's return to introspection at the end of this exchange threatens to destabilize his new resolution further (Is not the whole *Vita nova*, on one level, a narrative of his *condizione*?), ultimately his poetic writing, the primary form of writing at stake in this exchange, does pivot, in the following chapter, to the *stilo de la loda*, inherited and adapted from Guinizzelli. Until that point, however, the *tenzone* in the piazza marks the end of a poetic phase and the threshold of another, daunting, mode of writing: "E così dimorai alquanti dì con disiderio di dire e con paura di cominciare" (XVIII.9 [10.11]) [And I lived that way for several days, wanting to write but afraid to start].

Vita nova XIX–XXIV [10.12–15.11]
A New and More Noble Theme

TRISTAN KAY

In chapter XIX [10.12–10.33] we reach not only a watershed in the poetic and narrative development of the *Vita nova* but also an episode of enduring significance in the history of Dante's poetic self-representation. Marking a decisive break from the turbulent *gabbo* phase of the *libello* (chapters XIV–XVI [7–9]), which unfolded under the manifest influence of Guido Cavalcanti, Dante now adopts what he introduced as a "matera nuova e più nobile che la passata" (XVII.1 [10.1]) [a new and nobler subject matter than that of the past]: a poetic theme that is morally superior and one he claims is his alone. The new theme, later defined as Dante's "stilo de la . . . loda" (XXVI.4 [17.4]) [praise style], is heralded by the first of the *Vita nova*'s three *canzoni*, "Donne ch'avete intelletto d'amore" [Women who understand the truth of love].[1] This poem will be cited with approval by Dante years later, first in his *De vulgari eloquentia* (2.8.8 and 2.12.3), where he twice commends its formal construction, and then in his *Commedia*. In a celebrated exchange between the pilgrim and Bonagiunta Orbicciani, on Purgatory's terrace of gluttony, the poet from Lucca cites "Donne ch'avete" as the lyric that heralded the "nove rime" (24.50) [new rhymes] and overcame the limitations, seemingly of both content and style, associated with the first generations of Italian poets. Their writing, by contrast, remained estranged from Love: its supposed creative source. Why, then, does this moment, still early in Dante's poetic career, retain such salience? What characterizes Dante's "new and more noble theme," and what is the true extent of its novelty?

Before arriving at "Donne ch'avete," we are left in no doubt as to its significance by the preceding prose. As in the exchange with Bonagiunta in *Purgatorio* 24 some twenty years later, Dante emphasizes his poem's innovation and its profound identification with a Love that resists straightforward categorization.[2] In chapter XVIII, he tells the ladies who serve as his interlocutors that his poetic attention is to move from his own experience of Beatrice's transient "greeting" ("lo saluto di questa donna" [the greeting of my lady]) to something that will not fail him ("quello che non mi puote venire meno," XVIII.4 [10.6]): namely, his words of praise for her, "quelle parole che lodano la donna mia" (XVIII.6 [10.8]). This transition signals Dante's abandonment of an essentially selfish conception of love, concerned with acquisition and possession, and his espousal of a charitable love that finds satisfaction in the act of praising Beatrice, irrespective of her physical presence. The prose of chapter XIX [10.12–10.33] depicts the genesis of this poem as an epiphany and a creative breakthrough. Dante finds himself alongside a clear river, carrying symbolic connotations of inspiration and eloquence, and is possessed by an urgent desire to compose a new lyric worthy of this theme.[3] His fivefold use of the verb *cominciare* and its cognates (*cominciai, cominciamento, cominciai, cominciamento, comincia*: XIX.1–3 [10.12–10.14]), later echoed in the recollection of the *canzone* in *Purgatorio* 24.50–51 ("*cominciando* / 'Donne ch'avete intelletto d'amore'"), stresses the poet's determination to present this poem as a radically new beginning.[4] Having been beholden in earlier chapters of the *Vita nova* to a model of love inherited from the Occitan and Sicilian poets, governed by arcane courtly conventions, as well as to the more contemporary Tuscan models of Guittone d'Arezzo and Guido Cavalcanti, Dante now insists upon the fresh and personal quality of his lyric expression. His poetic voice, he implies, is no longer one bequeathed by poetic tradition but rather issues from within, his tongue now moving of its own volition: "Allora dico che la mia lingua parlò quasi come per se stessa mossa, e disse: *Donne ch'avete intelletto d'amore*" (XIX.2 [10.13]) [my tongue uttered words almost as if it moved of its own accord]. From this point on, there is indeed a purging of the Occitan and Guittonian forms, linguistic features, and courtly formulae that were especially prevalent in the *Vita nova*'s first dozen chapters. At the level of style, one infers that Dante's less mediated relationship to his poetic theme informs the greater limpidity we witness in "Donne ch'avete," as courtly contrivance is replaced by a lyric spontaneity that brings him "grande letizia" (XIX.3 [10.14]) [great joy]. However, Dante maintains that this apparent lack of artifice does not detract from the intellectual rigor of "Donne ch'avete." On the contrary, in the *divisione* following the *canzone*, Dante is at pains to underline its subtlety of meaning compared to that of the poems that preceded it (XIX.15–22 [10.26–10.33]). Moreover, as we shall see, the appropriation of biblical language in the prose here points to a more profound and divine form of inspiration.

The *Vita nova*'s prose sometimes distorts our reading of its poetry, which can be more conventional than its framing in the *libello* would imply.[5] However, there can be no doubt that, irrespective of its aggrandizing preamble, "Donne ch'avete," which eulogizes Beatrice in a dramatically expanded cosmic setting, marks a substantial break from the poetry that precedes it in Dante's *prosimetrum*. The *gabbo* poems were characterized by melancholic introspection and unfolded in the claustrophobic space of Dante's "camera de le lagrime" (XIV.9 [7.9]) [room of tears]. They ultimately concerned Dante's own morbid condition (XVII.1 [10.1]), and this approach led him to a creative impasse and feelings of shame. "Donne ch'avete," by contrast, is the product of fruitful dialogue with intellectually astute ladies who possess "intelligence of love." Beatrice is now the exclusive object of Dante's attention and adulation, and his poetry opens up to the eternal realm. As Teodolinda Barolini notes in her commentary, the theological and metaphysical aspects of "Donne ch'avete" are intrinsic and are not conferred retrospectively by the *Vita nova*'s prose, as we see elsewhere.[6] An angel declares in heaven that Beatrice is a miracle incarnate (lines 15–18). Her absence is described as heaven's only defect (lines 19–20). Even God himself participates in her praise (lines 22–28). Yet while Dante's love poetry is "theologized" to a far greater extent than in any of the *Vita nova*'s previous poems, Beatrice's embodied beauty is not effaced but rather incorporated into her glorification (see especially lines 47–50), as loves human and divine are aligned. In contrast with the poetic example of Dante's dominant Tuscan precursor Guittone d'Arezzo, whose turning to God was predicated on a decisive rejection of love and love poetry, Dante's spiritual elevation comes *through* the figure of the beloved and is articulated in the language of

what he will term the "matera . . . amorosa" (XXV.6 [16.6]) [theme of love].[7]
Beatrice's beauty does not ensnare Dante but draws him closer to God, and
in exalting her Dante at once celebrates her creator. The compatibility of love
and probity, and love and intellection, is foregrounded. Indeed, it is here that
the *Vita nova*'s earlier assertion that Dante's love flourished in harmony with
reason (II.9 [1.10]) finds convincing poetic articulation for the first time. In
all of this, "Donne ch'avete" stands in opposition to Guido Cavalcanti's land-
mark *canzone* "Donna me prega" [A lady asks me] and its richly philosophical
disquisition on love as a turbulent force confined to the sensitive soul. The
ideological fissure between Dante and Guido that emerges in the *libello* is
here palpable in its poetry for the first time, and the relationship between
"Donne ch'avete" and "Donna me prega" has accordingly received much
critical attention.[8]

For all Dante's stress on the originality of his poetry, however, he re-
mains in dialogue with, and sometimes indebted to, the poetry of his con-
temporaries. Indeed, his putative "new theme," while signaling a break from
Cavalcanti, brings him into the orbit of his Bolognese precursor, Guido
Guinizzelli. A similar tension between Dante's poetic novelty and indebted-
ness to Guinizzelli can be identified in the *Purgatorio*, where Bonagiunta's
claim that "Donne ch'avete" heralded the "dolce stil novo" (24.57) [sweet
new style] is swiftly followed by the pilgrim's avowal of debt to the Bolo-
gnese, whom he describes as his "padre" [father] in using "rime d'amor . . .
dolci e leggiadre" (*Purg.* 26.97–99) [love's sweet and graceful rhymes]. In the
Vita nova, too, Dante acknowledges his debt to Guinizzelli. In chapter XX
[11], the sonnet "Amore e 'l cor gentil sono una cosa" [Love and the open
heart are always one], which expounds upon the genesis and phenome-
nology of love to an unnamed friend, describes the inextricable bond be-
tween love and the noble heart. In so doing, it rehearses the dominant theme
of Guinizzelli's *canzone* "Al cor gentil rempaira sempre Amore" [Love always
returns to the noble heart].[9] Guinizzelli, as Dante's new *maestro*, is invoked
as "il saggio" (line 2) [the sage]—an epithet used in the *Commedia* to address
the classical *auctores* Virgil and Statius. The sonnet's opening quatrain not
only cites Guido as a poetic authority but again points to the harmonization
of love and intellect, in comparing the bond between love and the noble
heart to that between reason and the rational soul (line 4). The poem thus
appears to stage a shifting of allegiance from one Guido to another, an en-

dorsement of the Guido from Bologna and a break from Cavalcanti's insistence on love's inherent irrationality and materialism. Nonetheless, as Simon Gilson explores in his chapter, lexical and tonal echoes of Cavalcanti's poetry remain apparent even at this ostensible moment of transition.

The extent to which Dante's *Vita nova* represents a Guinizzellian project requires a balanced appraisal. While neither stylistically nor thematically monolithic, Guido's poetry tends to be understood as distinct from that of his Italian predecessors on account of (1) its relative syntactic clarity and rejection of a rhetorical ornamentation associated, in particular, with Guittone; (2) its absorption of philosophical, scientific, and theological language and motifs, reflecting the intellectual refinement of Guido's Bologna; and (3) its formulation of an ethically and spiritually nourishing form of love, for a lady who takes on angelic qualities. The notion that there occurred in Guinizzelli's lyric production a radical break from previous Italian poets has been reinforced by his famous *tenzone* with Bonagiunta.[10] The Lucchese addressed Guido as "Voi ch'avete mutata la mainera" (line 1) [You who transformed the style], a poet who infused his poetry with the esoteric "senno . . . da Bologna" (line 13) [learning from Bologna].[11] This exchange of sonnets may tempt us to see Guido's poetry as a rupture from everything that preceded it, possessing a sophistication unfathomable to his more primitive contemporaries. Indeed, the schism implied by this *tenzone* feeds into Dante's literary historiography in the *Purgatorio*, where Guido is praised as the forefather of the "dolce stil novo" and placed in opposition to his hegemonic forerunner Guittone. We should, however, approach such dichotomies with caution. For example, Claudio Giunta has shown the stylistic affinities between Bonagiunta and Guinizzelli—poets who, in Dante's writing of lyric history, appear almost diametrically opposed.[12] Other intellectual and ideological features of Guinizzelli's verse also have deeper roots. As far back as the Sicilian school, Italian poets had drawn upon Aristotle and natural philosophy, while Guinizzelli's "signature" idea of the "donna angelicata" is foreshadowed throughout the early Italian lyric.[13] Thus, while incremental changes can and should be identified in his writing, Guinizzelli, whose influence on Dante is never more apparent than in these chapters, belonged to the same lexically and thematically restricted aulic tradition as poets to whom he is often today placed in opposition. His innovations are significant but occurred within this circumscribed literary framework and are arguably overdetermined in the *Commedia*'s highly influential account of early Italian poetic history.

Where Guinizzelli offered a template to Dante was as a "praise" poet, witnessed emblematically in his lyric "Io voglio del ver la mia donna laudare" [I want to truly praise my lady]. This sonnet, along with "Al cor gentil," is a touchstone for Dante in this part of the *libello*. Its octave sets out analogies and similes, comparing the lady not only to aspects of the natural world (lines 5–8) but even to the heavens themselves: "ciò ch'è lassù bello a lei somiglio" (line 4) [I compare her to everything beautiful on high].[14] That she is compared to the "rosa" [rose], "giglio" [lily], and "stella dïana" [dawn star] (lines 2–3) associates her with the Virgin Mary. Guinizzelli thus sacralizes his beloved and brings erotic and divine loves into rhetorical alignment. In so doing, he takes inspiration not only from other Romance poets and their glorification of their beloveds but also from mystical writings and the Song of Songs, where the language of earthly love became a productive means of conveying spiritual longing. But Guido's poetry is more audacious in the claims it makes for the human beloved herself. In the sestet, this lady extinguishes vice and even instills Christian faith in those whom she greets as she passes.[15] As in Dante's breakthrough "praise" poem, "Donne ch'avete," the flesh-and-blood lady becomes a vehicle of, and not an obstacle to, spiritual transcendence. The influence of this sonnet on "Donne ch'avete" is unquestionable. Lines 31–42 of Dante's *canzone*, in particular, draw heavily on the sestet of "Io vogli' del ver" and its description of the lady who "passa per via adorna e sì gentile" (line 9) [passes through the streets so elegant and noble].[16]

The same sonnet serves as a model for Dante in chapter XXI [12]. Here, the sonnet "Ne li occhi porta la mia donna Amore" [My lady brings Love into the eyes] encapsulates his deft negotiation of Guinizzelli and Cavalcanti alike. As noted by all commentators, this "praise" lyric strongly resembles not only "Io voglio del ver" but also Cavalcanti's "Chi è questa che vèn" (4) [Who is this [woman] that comes].[17] Dante invites direct comparison with Cavalcanti's sonnet by using four of the same words in rhyme (*mira / gira / sospira / ira*) and the same metrical scheme. While all three sonnets describe a lady of ineffable beauty and her powerful effects on those who behold her, their similarities and differences nonetheless suggest vital points of ideological alignment and divergence between their authors.[18] While Cavalcanti's sonnet begins in terms very similar to Dante's and Guinizzelli's, it ends with a more troubling sense of impasse and points to a tension between the lady's miraculous form and the lover's incapacity to respond to it positively. While first appearing to promise spiritual emancipation through love, Cavalcanti's poem—in the words of Robert Harrison—moves "from exterior to interior, from grace to disgrace, from liberation to confinement, from transcendence to finitude."[19] Such a description might similarly apply to the opening sixteen chapters of Dante's *Vita nova*, culminating in the Cavalcantian impasse of the *gabbo* episode. By contrast, Dante's sonnet here ends in hope and placation, the subject touched by an ineffable sweetness: "Quel ch'ella par quand'un poco sorride / non si può dire né tenere a mente / sí è novo miracolo e gentile" (lines 12–14) [How she appears when smiling: you're besotted, speech falters and your memory's too weak before this new and noble miracle]. While all three sonnets place an emphasis on unknowability and ineffability, on mortal faculties being pushed beyond their limits, it is the taste of transcendence associated with Guinizzelli's sonnet, and not the ominous confinement emerging in Cavalcanti's, that prevails in "Ne li occhi."[20]

Yet while the present sequence of chapters appears to signal Dante's adoption of Guinizzelli as his primary model and his abandonment of Cavalcanti, his relationship to both poets continues to be characterized by ambivalence. Even when ostensibly appropriating the poetics of his precursors, Dante sets out dividing lines as well as places of alignment. Take, for instance, Guinizzelli's landmark *canzone* "Al cor gentil." This poem can easily be seen as the archetype for the *Vita nova*'s theologized love poetry. Yet an important distinction can nonetheless be drawn. "Al cor gentil," in its closing stanza, confesses to the danger of its operation, as God rebukes the poet on account of his presumption in presenting his love for his lady (a love now abruptly cast in line 54 as a "vano amor") in terms that should apply only to divinity. Having challenged the opposition between erotic and divine love, the *congedo* reasserts the more conventional dichotomy between them. There is, however, no such climbdown in "Donne ch'avete," where God does not reprimand the poet but rather, as we have seen, *participates* in the praise of Beatrice. Thus, as Barolini writes in her commentary, "Dante makes more radical the already radical Guinizzellian mise-en-scène."[21] The model provided by Guinizzelli, Dante's boldest Italian precursor in terms of aligning erotic and divine loves, is hereby pushed still further. As we shall see, Dante's meditation on death in these chapters also sees him implicitly distance himself from Guinizzelli's example.

If Dante's treatment of Guinizzelli in these pivotal chapters is not passive imitation, neither is his stance with respect to Cavalcanti one of straightforward hostility. For all that chapters XIX–XXIV [10.12–15.11] mark a break from Cavalcanti's predominant philosophy of love, commentators have identified in them numerous echoes of the older Florentine poet, even in the anti-Cavalcantian "Donne ch'avete." Chapter XXIV [15] encapsulates Dante's conflicted attitude toward him, in one of the most dramatic examples of the *Vita nova*'s prose recasting a preexisting lyric and granting it a newly theologized meaning. The sonnet "Io mi senti' svegliar dentro a lo core" [I felt awakening in my heart] describes an encounter between Dante, the Lord of Love, and Dante and Guido's respective ladies: Beatrice and Giovanna/Primavera. This apparently innocuous sonnet is audaciously reframed by the prose as an epiphanic poem that decisively underlines both Beatrice's Christological status and the preeminence of Dante's new way of writing. Love tells Dante that not only does Giovanna's name link her to the figure of John the Baptist but her *senhal* Primavera can also be read as "prima verrà" [she who will come first], for she will appear *before* Beatrice on the occasion described in this sonnet. As such, she can be understood as a figure who paves the way for Beatrice as John the Baptist did for Christ: "Lo suo nome Giovanna è da quello Giovanni lo quale precedette la verace luce, dicendo: 'Ego vox clamantis in deserto . . .'" (XXIV.4 [15.4]) [Her name, Giovanna (or Joanna), is derived from that John who preceded the true Light, saying, "I am the voice of one crying in the wilderness . . ."]. The analogy doubtless pertains also to the poetry of Dante and Guido themselves and the provisional status of Guido's writing in relation to Dante's. As Manuele Gragnolati summarizes, the reframing of this sonnet "indicates that the author's Cavalcantian phase was merely a preparation for a new and correct way of writing that is superior to that of his 'first friend.'"[22] Yet the association of Cavalcanti and Giovanna with John the Baptist valorizes Guido as well as affirming his subordination. Cavalcanti emerges simultaneously as both lyric ally and ideological adversary in the *libello*. Indeed, Dante will again align himself with his fellow Florentine in disparaging "quelli che rimano stoltamente" (XXV.10 [16.10]) [poets who write in such a stupid manner], most likely Guittone and his followers, in the very next chapter.

While chapters XIX–XXI [10.12–12.8] and chapter XXIV [15] share an emphasis on love as praise and distance Dante from the ideology governing much of Cavalcanti's love poetry, chapters XXII–XXIII [13–14] are dominated instead by a meditation on death and transience. Praise for Beatrice is first interrupted by the death of her father in chapter XXII [13]. Dante writes two sonnets based on an imagined dialogue, one from the perspective of the ladies who are mourning with Beatrice (the text describes the Florentine custom whereby men and women mourned separately) and the other from Dante's own perspective in response.[23] The pain felt by Dante upon learning of Beatrice's grief at the loss of her father leads him in chapter XXIII [14] to a prophetic vision of Beatrice's death and ascension into heaven, described first in the prose and then in the *canzone* "Donna pietosa" [A woman compassionate]. Struck by an illness that restricts him to his bed for nine days, a psychosomatic ailment described with a notable technical precision, Dante becomes acutely conscious of mortality and afflicted by the knowledge that Beatrice herself must one day die. In his frenzied vision, he sees the faces of disheveled and weeping ladies, who remind him of his own mortal fragility, before he imagines a friend telling him of Beatrice's sudden passing. As I shall discuss later, Dante's account of his vision draws liberally upon biblical sources in a way that cements Beatrice's Christological status: the sun darkens, the earth shakes, birds fall from the sky, angels ascend into heaven singing "Osanna in excelsis." There is thus a stark tonal difference between the rather "gothic" and macabre vision described in chapter XXIII [14] and the joyful exaltation of Beatrice found in the previous chapters.[24]

Nonetheless, this thematic transition should not be understood as entirely abrupt, nor the governing themes of love/praise and death as isolated from one another, for the question of how love and death interrelate is one of the *Vita nova*'s central preoccupations. Indeed, while ostensibly a collection of love poetry, so integral is the *libello*'s meditation on death to its purposes that Stefano Carrai has argued that the work is best understood as an example of medieval elegy.[25] The death of Beatrice's father, which triggers Dante's meditations on mortality, is, after all, the second of three deaths that punctuate the *Vita nova*, preceded in chapter VIII [3] by the death of Beatrice's unnamed friend and followed in chapter XXVIII [19.1–19.3] by the passing of Beatrice herself. These episodes offer an unfolding reflection on mortality: the two earlier losses serve to prepare Dante for the death of his "gentilissima" and help him to reconfigure his understanding of mortality. In the present chapters, he is suspended between an understanding of death as a source of pain and fear and an appreciation of death as a second beginning, preparing him for an apparently more definitive reappraisal of the value of life on earth, and its essentially provisional nature, which emerges toward the end of the *libello*. Dante's invocation of death here as "dolcissima morte" (XXIII.9 [14.9]) [sweetest death] contrasts pointedly, for example, with his earlier description of "morte villana" (VIII.8 [3.8]) [Barbarous Death], following the death of Beatrice's friend. Having feared death as a terminal event, Dante now participates in a medieval Christian tradition of disparaging transient worldly pleasures and existence (*contemptus mundi*) and looks forward instead to the joys of eternal new life. Donato Pirovano suggests, for example, that the expression "dolcissima morte" calls to mind the words of St. Francis in Tommaso da Celano's *Legenda secunda S. Francisci*.[26] It is Beatrice's death—here envisioned and later experienced—that precipitates this shift in understanding. Her countenance in imagined death is notable for its hopeful serenity, seeming to say, "Io sono a vedere lo principio de la pace" (XXIII.8 [14.8]) [I am gazing upon the very source of peace].[27] The only peace that can bring the *Vita nova*'s tumultuous journey of "amorosa erranza" (XIII.9 [6.9]) [amorous confusion] to serene fulfillment resides with Beatrice in paradise.

We might consider that Dante's foregrounding of death in these chapters tacitly undermines the spiritual legitimacy of Guinizzelli as a model. After all, Dante's first "praise" poems, clearly informed by Guinizzelli, *precede* Beatrice's passing and the reorientation of Dante's desire toward heaven that it facilitates. As Elena Lombardi writes, Beatrice's death is what "allows for the stretching of desire-as-praise in a supernal direction, and for the completion and termination of desire/praise in a different eschatological dimension."[28] If the prospect of the beloved's death is absent from Guinizzelli's own lyric corpus, Dante's *canzone* "Donna pietosa," at the structural center of the *Vita nova*, features the word *morte* in all six of its stanzas. That the most conspicuously Guinizzellian phase of the *Vita nova* precedes Beatrice's death, just as its most overtly Cavalcantian phase precedes the "matera nuova," reflects Dante's endeavor carefully to present the influence of his erstwhile models as confined to earlier parts of his journey, as provisional steps toward a poetic destination that is his alone. Guinizzelli's later placement on Purgatory's terrace of the lustful underlines that Dante believes his predecessor's poetry, for all its spiritual intimations, does not offer a morally tenable solution in its negotiation of loves erotic and spiritual, and remains tainted by carnality.

The *Vita nova*, a text embedded in Florentine vernacular literary culture, is often seen as narrower in its cultural purview than Dante's later works. It is largely confined to an amatory subject matter and, at least in its poetry, restricted to an aulic register. Nonetheless, as Zygmunt Barański has argued, we witness in the *Vita nova*'s prose a foreshadowing of the mingling of styles and registers that will define his later *Commedia*.[29] While Dante's conception of love and his handling of other vernacular poets are of capital importance in the present chapters, it would be mistaken to read them exclusively in terms of Dante's dialogue with contemporary Italian poetry. In fact, we witness evidence of a careful engagement with a number of intellectual traditions that will assume ever-greater prominence in Dante's writing. Three discourses are especially pertinent here and warrant particular attention: (1) the use of the Bible to frame aspects of the *libello*, here in both epiphanic and elegiac registers; (2) the use of Aristotelian language in the *divisioni* of chapters XX–XXI [11–12]; and (3) the recourse to medical terminology in describing Dante's vision of Beatrice's death in chapter XXIII [14].

Two salient examples of Dante's appropriation of biblical language and imagery are his framing of the *canzone* "Donne ch'avete" in chapter XIX [10.12–10.33] and the account of his vision of Beatrice's death in chapter XXIII [14]. We have seen how Dante conveys the importance of "Donne ch'avete" through the prose's insistence on the poem's novelty and nobility and the rigorous *divisione* to which he subjects it. However, his foreword to the *canzone* is enriched by his use of biblical phrases to intimate the sacred quality of his love for Beatrice. Commentators have shown that the Psalms serve as an especially fertile part of the Bible here.[30] Dante may have had in mind Psalm 40:3, where we find references to these chapters' key concepts of novelty and praise: "Et immisit in os meum canticum novum, carmen Deo nostro" [He put a new song in my mouth, a hymn of praise to our God]. Psalm 50 offers a famous image of the mouth as an organ of praise (to which Dante will return in the *Purgatorio*), which resonates in Dante's image of his tongue moving autonomously in praising Beatrice: "Domine, labia mea aperies, et os meum annuntiabit laudem tuam" (50.17) [Lord, open my lips and my mouth will offer you praise]. Perhaps most strikingly, the image of

Dante's "inspired" tongue echoes the final words of David in 2 Samuel 23:2 and reinforces the idea of divine, Psalmic inspiration: "Spiritus Domini locutus est per me, et sermi eius per linguam meam" [The spirit of the Lord spoke through me; his word was on my tongue].[31] Still more infused with biblical allusions is the vision of Beatrice's death and ascension in chapter XXIII [14]. Dante draws especially on the Gospels' accounts of Jesus's death and thus buttresses Beatrice's Christological status. Her death in Dante's vision, like Jesus's death in Matthew's Gospel (27:45–52 and 28:2), is accompanied by the darkening of the sun and by an earthquake. She is surrounded by a multitude of angels that recalls that which heralds the birth of Jesus in Luke 2:13–14. The imagery of clouds and Beatrice's white garments have been associated with Acts 1:9–11, while De Robertis associates the weeping stars with prophetic passages in the Old Testament.[32] As such, chapter XXIII [14] not only prepares Dante for Beatrice's death several chapters later. It also, through its appropriation of biblical language, foreshadows her most definitive identification with Christ in the newly theologized "Io mi senti' svegliar dentro a lo core" in the following chapter.

In the *divisioni* of the sonnets compiled in chapters XX and XXI, meanwhile, as explored in detail in Gilson's chapter here, Dante draws on Aristotelian language to expound upon key concepts from these poems. In the prose following "Amore e 'l cor gentil," Dante describes the awakening of love described metaphorically in the sonnet by drawing upon a much more technical and manifestly philosophical lexis (expressions such as "di potenzia si reduce in atto," "produtti in essere," and "forma materia" are all of Aristotelian provenance). Following "Ne li occhi," meanwhile, we find reference to Beatrice's divine capacity to create love *ex nihilo* through the Aristotelian formulation "si riduce in atto questa potenzia secondo la nobilissima parte delli suoi occhi." While Aristotelian terminology had featured in the Italian lyric from as early as the Sicilian school, it is once again in the prose rather than in the poetry itself that the *Vita nova*'s full discursive breadth is most in evidence. In this case, Dante perhaps wishes to use the prose commentary to demonstrate that his preexisting lyrics possess robust philosophical underpinnings. As such, these philosophical borrowings serve to erode the barriers between vernacular and classical culture that might be seen to delimit the intellectual authority of his poetry in the mother tongue—an endeavor that will be elaborated upon more fully in chapter XXV.

Finally, chapter XXIII [14] is notable for its use of physiological language as well as its extensive use of scripture. Natascia Tonelli has shown Dante's use of terminology found in contemporary medical texts to describe his physical and increasingly hallucinatory condition.[33] The nature of Dante's relationship to these texts and indeed to Aristotelian philosophy circa 1295 should be treated with caution: he may well have accessed their ideas and language through Florentine compendia of philosophical sources rather than via a firsthand engagement with scholastic commentaries and translations.[34] Nevertheless, that the *libello*'s protagonist behaves here as a "farnetica persona" (XXIII.4 [14.4]) [delirious person] locates him within the symptomology of physiological treatises and associates him with a kind of melancholic delirium capable of yielding powers of prophecy (significant, of course, in view of Beatrice's death within several chapters). In his numerous references to *imaginazione* and *fantasia*, moreover, Dante shows a grasp of contemporary psychological theories of the imagination.

We therefore begin to witness, by the time of the composition of the *Vita nova*'s prose, a broadening of Dante's expressive range, his attempts to break down the barriers between Latin and vernacular (and between sacred and lay) cultural traditions, and signs of his growing intellectual dexterity. It should be underlined that Dante's engagement with these traditions is predominantly a feature of the prose. Indeed, there is arguably more innovation in Dante's prosaic engagement with these Latin traditions than in the content of the lyrics themselves, which—while here pushing Guinizzelli's ideas somewhat further—remain rooted in the evolution of Tuscan love poetry of the late Duecento. This likely reflects in part the passing of some years between the composition of the original lyrics and their later framing in the prose of the *Vita nova* (and the concurrent broadening of Dante's intellectual canvas), but also suggests the greater freedom of form and register available to an early Italian author of prose compared to a writer of poetry.

Vita nova XIX [10.12–10.33]

FILIPPO GIANFERRARI

Two ostensible paradoxes mark the intersection of "Donne ch'avete intelletto d'amore" [Women who have an understanding of love] with the prose of the *libello*. The first one lies in the tension between the novelty and complexity of this poem and its intended audience of women only. The author presents this *canzone* as a subtle and groundbreaking poem, which inaugurates a new poetic season centered on the praise of Beatrice. The sudden inception of the first line in the poet's mind suggests its divine inspiration, while the poem itself makes several striking—and seemingly absurd—theological claims about Beatrice's superhuman virtues. The following *divisioni* further the impression of the poem's exceptional difficulty—for the first time Dante provides a set of subdivisions. Notwithstanding its groundbreaking importance and complexity, Dante directs the *canzone* to a category of reader that was considered the least educated at the time—the woman reader. Whereas readers of this previously independent *canzone* could have interpreted the poem's appeal to such a peculiar audience as a mere rhetorical device, a poetic trope, the narrative frame of the *libello* insists on the reality of the poem's female audience.

The second paradox concerns the *divisioni*. To make the *canzone* more accessible, Dante explains, he has furnished it with an apparatus not only of divisions, as for the preceding poems, but also of subdivisions (XIX.15 [10.26]). While nineteen of the poems of the *Vita nova* are divided, the au-

thor provides subdivisions—a type of logical commentary typical of me-
dieval scholasticism—for only seven of them.[1] The subdivisions of "Donne
ch'avete," however, are only partial. As Dante points out, he could have fur-
ther subdivided the poem, but he did not do so. His reticence, the author ex-
plains, springs from a desire to limit full access to the poem to those readers
who can grasp the meaning of the undivided sections by means of their own
insightfulness (*ingegno*):

> Dico bene che, a più aprire lo intendimento di questa canzone, si conver-
> rebbe usare di più minute divisioni; ma tuttavia chi non è di tanto inge-
> gno che per queste che sono fatte la possa intendere, a me non dispiace se
> la mi lascia stare, ché certo io temo d'avere a troppi comunicato lo suo in-
> tendimento pur per queste divisioni che fatte sono, s'elli avvenisse che
> molti le potessero audire. (XIX.22 [10.33])

> [I will add, nevertheless, that to further clarify the sense of this canzone
> it would be necessary to use still subtler divisions. However, it does not
> bother me if anyone who is not insightful enough to understand the
> poem by using the divisions already provided leaves off trying, since in
> fact I fear I have already communicated its meaning to too many people
> simply by analyzing it as I have—assuming, that is, it should ever have
> a large audience.]

Scholars have noted that Dante's eagerness to control the poem's reception
apparently contradicts his initial desire to make it more broadly accessible.[2]
Less attention has been devoted to the evidence that Dante's final words ap-
pear to downplay the purpose and value of the extra subdivisions he has just
provided. His intended readers, in the end, are those who will be able to
grasp the full meaning of the poem *without* aid from his subdivisions. The
critical apparatus should offer them guidance, but the ultimate exegetical
success lies in their "ingegno." The divisions turn out to be accessorial rather
than instrumental to a correct and complete understanding of "Donne
ch'avete."

   If this is indeed the case, why does Dante provide extra subdivisions?
What kind of reader, already in possession of the intelligence necessary to
unravel the *canzone*'s hidden message, would nevertheless need more detailed

divisions? Perhaps Dante has two different categories of readers in mind: one, embodied by the ladies, whose limited education requires extra subdivisions to help them navigate such a complex text; the other, made up of well-educated readers who needed no divisions at all. The author, therefore, would dismiss the audience he begins to address through the poem and the additional subdivisions.

Most scholars agree that Dante wishes to narrow down the intended audience of the *canzone*. Some argue that this was likely even smaller than the coterie of poets that had made up the readership of the sonnet "A ciascun' alma presa e gentil core" (III.10–12 [1.21–1.23]) [To every in-love soul and noble heart]. The identity of such an exclusive audience remains an intriguing question. These insightful readers have generally been described as poets, or intellectuals more broadly, set apart by their exceptional learning and literary sophistication. Robert Durling and Ronald Martinez have proposed to see them as the members of "a small initiated elite" that would be able to appreciate the "esoteric meaning" of the text. The divisions, then, would guide the general readers through the basic, literal, interpretation of the poem, while inviting a select few "insightful" readers to unravel its hidden message.[3]

I would contend that the seemingly popularizing goal of the extra subdivisions may still be consistent with the poet's vision of an uncommonly insightful readership for this *canzone*, or, to put it another way, that its "exclusive" readership may be in fact a nonspecialist one, which would have appreciated the extra subdivisions. The answer to this apparent contradiction may be hidden in plain sight: "Women who understand the truth of love." Dante reiterates in both the *canzone* and the prose that women represent the intended—not the unique—readers of this poem, because they already own the key to its true meaning—they "understand the truth of love."[4] This evidence, I argue, explains why Dante wished to provide not only divisions but also subdivisions for this poem—dividing and subdividing was a didactic tool.[5]

Women's literacy was generally limited to the vernacular, and they were not expected to be advanced readers of complex poetic and philosophical texts. Women from wealthy families, like those from Beatrice's entourage—who question the protagonist in the previous chapter and become the addressees of "Donne ch'avete"—often possessed extensive literacy in the ver-

nacular. In most cases, the only formal education they received was ele-
mentary reading instruction. In the last stanza of the *canzone*, the poet also
includes noble men among his addressees: "solo con donne o con omo cor-
tese" (XIX.14 [10.25]) [only being seen by men and women versed in what
you mean], effectively broadening his intended audience beyond the gender
limitations implied by the first stanza. Hence, the "emphasis on the female
audience," as Justin Steinberg observes, "testifies to the expanded readership
afforded by composing in the vernacular. . . . The *donne* may stand for the
new vernacular audience."[6] If Dante wished to address "Donne ch'avete"
to this female-like public, he would have also been eager to offer an example
of close textual analysis for them to follow. The subdivisions of "Donne
ch'avete" would reflect a "spirit of cultural democratization," as Steinberg
puts it, which informs Dante's renewed poetics and, perhaps, the project of
the *Vita nova*.[7]

A closer look at the divisions, I believe, further clarifies why Dante
deemed the woman reader—and the lay, vernacular readership she repre-
sented—best equipped with the *ingegno* to understand "Donne ch'avete."
The author identifies three main sections of this *canzone* ("proemio," "in-
tento trattato," and "seviziale" [proem, exposition, handmaid]): he divides
the first one into four subsections and the second into a series of six progres-
sive subdivisions, whereas the third one, he claims, needs no subdivisions.
The second section of the *canzone* (lines 15–56) contains the heart of the
poet's claims about Beatrice and receives the most articulated subdivisions.
First, Dante splits it into two parts: Beatrice seen from heaven (lines 15–28)
and Beatrice seen from earth (lines 29–56). The first part is left undivided,
whereas the second one is subdivided into the discussion of Beatrice's two
nobilities: the nobility of her soul (lines 29–49), and the nobility of her body
(lines 50–56). The second term of the division is once again the only one to
be subdivided: the source of love is Beatrice's eyes (lines 50–54), and its end
is her mouth (lines 55–56). Although this second part does not allow for fur-
ther subdivisions, the poet provides a gloss to it. Following a regular pattern,
which is unique to the divisions of "Donne ch'avete," Dante subdivides only
the second lemma of each subdivision. Such symmetry reflects an order that
is already present in the *canzone* itself, as the author points out when intro-
ducing the poem: "*Ordinata* nel modo che si vedrà di sotto ne la sua divi-
sione" (XIX.3 [10.14]) [I constructed it in a way that will appear below in its

divisions].[8] This should not distract from the particular selection of passages that the poet leaves without subdivisions.

Leo Spitzer notes that the sections Dante subdivides are only those about the lady's earthly and bodily features. Spitzer dismisses the significance of this choice, arguing that this would simply reflect the practice of scholastic *divisiones* to isolate the narrowest particulars. Hence, Dante would leave without subdivisions the parts that are "more generic."[9] Yet the poet's choice to leave undivided precisely the poem's most striking theological claims—heaven's longing for Beatrice, her miraculous nature, and the nobility and virtues of her soul (lines 15–49)—seems counterintuitive. This decision can be neither coincidental nor a by-product of his scholastic approach to the divisions—especially since Dante himself draws the readers' attention to these voluntary omissions.[10] Rather, the missing subdivisions confirm that Dante sincerely believed that readers' *ingegno*, guided by the example of his subdivisions, would suffice for unlocking the *canzone*'s most groundbreaking claims.

Durling and Martinez argue that Dante's divisions are informed by the *canzone*'s hidden, Neoplatonic meaning and reflect a metaphysical scale from higher to lower being that is implied in the poem. Dante divides only the sections that pertain to the lower grades of this scale, thereby tracing the Neoplatonic procession of the world from God, while leaving it to the reader to discover the principle of return to God, which is described in the poem's undivided parts. Dante envisioned two categories of readers for this *canzone*, "the simple and the discerning"—the latter is equipped to recognize and reconstruct the Neoplatonic reading of the poem.[11] What I find unconvincing about this thesis is the implication that a reader endowed with the intellectual and cultural resources to carry out such a subtle reading would have needed extra subdivisions—or, for that matter, any division at all. This interpretation ignores the official audience of ladies to whom the poet addresses the *canzone*, who usually lacked the necessary philosophical training to carry out this reading. It also disregards Dante's claim that the poem should be "figliuola d'Amor *giovane e piana*" (XIX.13 [10.24], emphasis added) [Love's daughter young and mild]. How could Dante define this *canzone* as "young and plain," while also expecting his readers to reconstruct a Neoplatonic interpretation of such complexity? Either he openly contradicts himself here, or the "ingegno" that can unlock the undivided parts of the poem is not characterized by subtle philosophical learning.[12]

A relevant insight into the particular rationale of the subdivisions surfaces, I believe, when we reconsider them from the perspective of the *canzone*'s official audience. The ladies, who personally knew Beatrice, could have had direct experience of her visible virtues, which are discussed in the subdivided sections of the poem, but they would have been unaware of her supernatural ones, which are not the object of the subdivisions. Hence, the divisions would have guided readers in interpreting the parts of the *canzone* that discussed familiar notions about Beatrice, while, at the same time, teaching them how to unravel the rest of the poem. In order to understand and believe the radical claims contained in the undivided sections, readers needed to rely on their direct experience of Beatrice's extraordinary virtues. Ladies, in other words—as well as others who knew Beatrice without mediations—had the necessary *ingegno* to take the leap of faith required by the *canzone*'s theological claims. Given the Christ-like attributes that Dante confers on Beatrice in the *Vita nova* (especially at XXIX [19]), the progressive revelation of her divinity should not cause surprise.[13] As Christ's divinity reveals itself through his miraculous persona in the Gospels, so Beatrice's heavenly nature shines through her exceptional virtues in "Donne ch'avete."

From a cultural perspective, the subjects Dante discusses in the subdivided parts of the *canzone* would have been accessible to ladies and lay readers, who would have understood that the poet is reworking motifs and ideas previously developed by other vernacular poets, such as Guido Guinizzelli and Guido Cavalcanti.[14] Women and lay readers mostly read vernacular texts and were better acquainted with religious and love poems than with theological and philosophical works. Their limited education eventually led Dante to write the *Convivio*.[15] Hence, the poet designed the extra subdivisions of "Donne ch'avete" with these readers in mind. Dante's divisions first guided ladies through contents they already knew from their experience and their literary culture before offering an interpretive path to the theological core of the poem, thereby progressing from familiar to unfamiliar notions. The unique *ingegno* Dante expects from his intended readers is not defined by special learning or cleverness—it is a type of intelligence formed by experience and critical exercise.[16]

Earlier in the *Vita nova*, Dante had appealed to readers' poetic experience as as the key to some of his most ambiguous claims. Following the sonnet "Con altre donne mia vista gabbate" (XIV.11–12 [7.11]) [With other women you mock my distress], Dante chooses not to provide divisions. Although he raises concerns about certain "dubbiose parole" (XIV.14 [7.14]) [obscure words], which would require some *divisioni*, he dismisses the task as unnecessary on account of his intended readers, who would be able to grasp their meaning without his assistance. As the poet explains, the aim of the divisions in the *Vita nova* "is only for opening up the meaning of the thing divided" (XIV.13 [7.13]) [per aprire la sentenzia della cosa divisa]. The words of the sonnet that would require the divisions can be understood only in light of one's own poetic service to Love, without which no explanation would suffice: "E questo dubbio è impossibile a solvere a chi non fosse in simile grado fedele d'Amore; e a coloro che vi sono è manifesto ciò che solverebbe le dubitose parole: *e però non è bene a me di dichiarare cotale dubitazione*" (XIV.14 [7.14]; emphasis added) [And this obscurity cannot be resolved by one who is not, to a similar degree, one of Love's faithful; and to those who are, it is clear enough how to resolve the obscurity of the words. Therefore, it would do no good for me to explain such obscurity]. Dante's intended readers here are the coterie of love poets. Conversely, Dante may refuse to divide the most complex parts of "Donne ch'avete" because no explanation would suffice without the reader's "intelligence of love" and direct experience of Beatrice. It is worth noting that later in the *Vita nova*, Dante asserts that Beatrice and Love are one and the same (XXIV.5 [15.5]).

In chapter XXVI [17], Dante again reasserts the importance of experiencing Beatrice directly in order to believe his claims about her superhuman nature. As more and more people come to know her, the author narrates, many more experience her miraculous virtues, becoming "sì come *esperti*" (1) [as those with experience] who can proclaim what they have witnessed to those who are incredulous.[17] These witnesses, moreover, realize on their own the truth that Dante has revealed in the nonsubdivided parts of "Donne ch'avete," namely, that this lady "is no mere mortal woman, but she is one of the beautiful angels in heaven" and "a marvel" (XXVI.2 [17.2]) [Questa non è femmina, anzi è uno de li bellissimi angeli del cielo. . . . Questa è una maraviglia]. As a result, the poet decides "to resume the style" he "had praised her with" [lo stilo de la sua loda]. This time, he does not wish to write primarily for those "who could actually see her," as he did in "Donne ch'avete." Instead, he writes for those who cannot experience her directly and "would know of her to the extent that words can convey such things" (XXVI.4 [17.4]) [acciò che non pur coloro che la poteano sensibilemente vedere, ma li altri sappiano di lei quello che le parole ne possono fare intendere]. Dante refuses to divide the sonnet he wrote for this purpose, "Tanto gentile e tanto onesta pare" [My lady appears so gracious and dignified]. He states that divisions are unnecessary because the sonnet is "sì piano" (XXVI.8 [17.8]) [so simple]—the same attribute used for "Donne ch'avete"—thanks to the narrative introduction that precedes it. Hence, experiencing Beatrice directly is the key to unlocking the theological meanings of the poem, while the divisions are a didactic tool that helps readers navigate the complex form of the poetic text.

My proposed analysis sheds some further light on the role of the *divisioni* in the *Vita nova*. Dante claims that the role of the *divisioni* is to open up the poems' correct meaning (*sentenzia*) according to the author's *intentio*. In the case of "Con altre donne" and "Donne ch'avete," however, he entrusts his intended readers with the responsibility of assessing the most complex parts of the poem.[18] Dante's call for such a responsible and autonomous readership may be consistent with his desire to guide the reception of his poems through the *libello*'s rich apparatus of divisions. The purpose of the divisions is to assist his vernacular readership, which is embodied by the intended female audience of the *canzone*. On the one hand, he foresaw these readers' need for instructions in handling the difficult *forma tractatus* of the *libello*; on the other, he assumed that their experience of love and their direct knowledge of Beatrice prepared them to appreciate the *Vita nova*'s most revolutionary aspects. The principal aim of the divisions is didactic rather than prescriptive. They are meant primarily to assist the simple reader rather than to correct the mistaken interpretations of the learned. Given that the *divisiones* were an essential didactic tool of medieval education, it should not cause surprise that Dante conceived them with lay, vernacular readers in mind. Dante claims that the true meaning of his poems has now become "clear to even the most simple-minded" (III.15 [2.2]) [ora è manifestissimo a li più semplici]. The poet knew that his intended readers already had the right *ingegno* for the task, but he could now rest assured that the *divisioni* of the *Vita nova* would have taught them how to handle difficult poetic texts.

Vita nova XX [11]

SIMON GILSON

Readers and commentators have long recognized the central importance of "Donne ch'avete d'amore" [Women who have an understanding of love], the *canzone* that immediately precedes and so helps to color the present chapter or paragraph. That *canzone* inaugurates a new mode of writing, acts as a poetic and ideological pivot in the *libello*, and, in its language and style, offers a new poetical model, one closely connected with the Bolognese poet Guido Guinizzelli.[1] *Vita nova* XX [11] begins with what is by now a common and characteristically indeterminate temporal marker ("Appresso che . . ." [After . . .]), and its opening sentence emphasizes the circulation ("divulgare" may well harbor a biblical echo) of the *canzone* among Dante's first readers.[2] The imprecision in the chronological marker extends to the mention of a certain friend ("alcuno amico") who, on reading the composition, had asked Dante to speak about the nature of love. Dante resolves that the value both of any such exposition ("trattato," XX.2 [11.2]) and of his friend are such to justify the undertaking, with a prominent stress placed on his response as one in which he will seek to "trattare," that is, to expound scientifically, what Love is. The technical force of *trattare* is here notably accentuated by means of the emphatic triple polypton (*trattato, trattare, trattassi*, XX.2 [11.2]).[3] Dante's reply takes the form of a further Guinizzellian-inspired composition, the sonnet "Amore e 'l cor gentil sono una cosa" (XX.3–5 [11.3–11.5]) [Love and the open heart are always one] and its short accompanying prose explanation (XX.6–8 [11.6–11.8]).

The fact that this "amico" is said to "pregare" and that his superiority is stressed have led some to identify him with Guido Cavalcanti, but such a proposal is far from being universally supported.[4] At the same time, in setting out Dante's views on love, the sonnet clearly enters into dialogue with Cavalcanti and of course Guinizzelli. The present chapter has two main purposes. First, it explores some of the dynamics of the Dantean dialogue on love with both Cavalcanti and Guinizzelli. And second, it discusses the role of the prose and its doctrinal and philosophical content.

Dante elaborates his treatment of love in the sonnet in full awareness of the extensive contemporary debates on the origin, status, and meanings of love. The tradition was not only a poetic one: perhaps its most celebrated form is found in the *tenzone* between Iacopo Mostacci, Pier della Vigna, and Giacomo da Lentini, but it also extended to various prose treatises from Andreas Capellanus's celebrated *De amore* to the writings of medical writers at the Bolognese Studio.[5] In the first quatrain, Dante establishes an immediate link with Guinizzelli's philosophically elevated love lyric, through the subtle echoes of the Guinizzellian *canzone* "Al cor gentil rempaira sempre Amore" [Love always returns to the noble heart] (above all lines 1, 3–4; "the noble heart" is repeated at 1, 8, 11, 21, 28–29), the allusion to the rhetorically crafted nature of this composition ("dittare"), and the reference to Guinizzelli himself as "saggio," as a wise poet.[6] As critics have noted, Dante reformulates and adapts several prominent Guinizzellian motifs, with a shift onto the question of love's genesis and a greater stress on the identity between love and nobility rather than their reciprocal relationship. It is notable too what Dante both adds and removes. A simile, for example, is used in the sonnet, and this serves to indicate too a gesturing toward Guinizzelli's role. And yet, there are none of the intricate analogies found in Guinizzelli, who is of course never openly named either here or anywhere else in the *libello*. Nature, which is such a notable force in Guinizzelli's "Al cor gentil" in making both the heart and love (lines 4, 18), remains, but in Dante she becomes herself "amorosa" (line 5) [amorous]. At the same time—and with power and subtlety—Dante introduces the metaphor of sleeping in the second quatrain, a motif that continues to inform the final terzina. The Lord of Love dwells in the noble heart as in its home ("magione," line 6: it is more typical in scholastic sources for *mansio* to be used of memory), and it sleeps there until it is awakened by beauty. The phenomenology of love, familiar in part from Guinizzelli, Cavalcanti, and others, is then described in some detail.[7] The sight of beauty in the virtuous lady so delights the eyes that a desire for this pleasing sight is awakened in the lover's heart; the desire lasts so long in the heart that it wakes up the spirit of Love.[8] Capellanus's account of the role of sight in generating love is often cited here by commentators, though other phases in the description of love's genesis in the *De amore* are notably absent in Dante.

A strong undercurrent of dialogue with Cavalcanti is conspicous in the first quatrain with Dante's example of the bond between love and the noble heart being compared to that between rational soul and reason.[9] It is here difficult not to think of Cavalcanti, the supreme proponent of love's irrational sensualism. But other contrastive filiations with the "first friend" are possible, including the final line of Dante's sonnet, which, as Teodolinda Barolini has suggested, makes clear that the man may have the same effect on a woman whose role is that of a moral agent.[10] One thinks too of Cavalcanti's "Voi che per li occhi passaste" (13) [You who passed through the eyes], above all its opening quatrain where through the eyes the image of the lady enters and awakens "la mente che dormia" (line 2) [the mind that slept]. But tonally several other Cavalcantian compositions might be evoked, such as "Biltà di donna e di saccente core" (2.9) [Beauty of a woman and of a wise heart], "Un amoroso sguardo spiritale" (24.9–24.10) [A loving spiritual look], and "Veggio negli occhi de la donna mia" (26.3) [I see in the eyes of my lady], where a light brings "un piacere novo nel core" [a new joy in the heart]. Here, at least tonally and lexically, several elements in the phenomenology of love are common with Dante's account, even though contextually and ideologically Cavalcanti's presentation is one of Love's negative and destructive powers over the heart and spirits.

As for the prose *divisione*, probably written around five years later, this resolutely places the metaphor of sleeping in relation to the philosophical categories of potency (*potentia*) and act (*actus*) and links these with a further philosophical pairing, namely, form and matter. Commentators have long noted the philosophical language of the *Vita nova*'s prose at this point with its scholastic expressions, calquing both Latin technical terms such as *subiectum* and phrases such as "reducere ad actum . . . reduci habet de potentia in actu" [to bring to act . . . has the potential to bring to act].[11] Of course, it is beyond our scope and purposes here to explore the questions raised by Dante's interest in using philosophy, theology, and science in the *libello* and his appropriation of its concepts and language. However, it may be helpful to note at least three general points and three more specific ones. First—and most obviously—the *Vita nova* shows us a Dante capable of developing scientific prose and one clearly well informed on matters of astronomy, soul theory, medical lore, and some of the underlying categories and core concepts of medieval scholastic culture.[12] Second, the most sophisticated recent work has begun to explore carefully and closely how Dante might have acquired such knowledge, assaying his Florentine context—the environment of the schools and publicly accessible, orally diffused teachings to the laity available there—in the late 1280s and 1290s as one way of understanding his formation and access to theological, philosophical, and scientific materials.[13] Third, notwithstanding the value of such studies, research in this field is beset with all kinds of difficulty and complexity, from problems in reconstructing contemporary libraries, book collections, and conditions of access to them to the fraught issues with any attempt to construct Dante's own "library," and from the added complexities brought by the possibility of Dante's stay in Bologna (with the possible benefits and access to texts provided by that milieu) to Dante's characteristic freedom in the way he manipulates scientific and philosophical ideas.

Bearing in mind such issues, for our purposes and in relation to the *divisione* in this chapter of the *Vita nova*, one might note three further specific points. The first is that there may be a submerged Aristotelian context to the discussion. After all, several passages in Aristotle, above all the opening of *De somno et vigilia*, draw attention to sleep as a privation of waking. Other Aristotelian works, moreover, treat sleep as being explicitly in potency with respect to waking as act, above all in *De anima* 2.1.412a23–26 and *Metaphysics* 9.6.1048b1–2. Second, one should note that these passages and related ideas are refined and expanded in Arab and Latin translators and medieval commentators who make more explicit the language of act and potency.[14] A third point is that the core ideas and language of these translations and commentaries are also found in compendia, as well as in works with a pronounced oral diffusion such as disputed questions and philosophical florilegia designed for memorization. Thus, in a compendium such as the *Auctoritates*

Aristotelis, whose potential relevance for Dante has been recently studied by Andrea Robiglio, we find, alongside terms such as *in subiectum*, explicit reference to the opening of the *Somnia et vigilia* 1.454a8, for which the tag "cuius est potentia, eius est actum" [the subject of potency is the same as that of act] is recalled.[15] These notions are also found in other scholastic works, including late thirteenth-century collections of questions, such as those by Geoffrey of Aspel, a Regent Master active in the 1250s.[16] We cannot establish with any degree of certainty Dante's knowledge of any of these or related works, and to do so would probably be inappropriate given what we know of Dante's likely cultural and intellectual formation at this stage. However, building on Robiglio's work, the points of contact with the *Auctoritates Aristotelis* are noteworthy. And finally we should also note that related terminology can be found in contemporary vernacular works. Here, perhaps the best example is found in Brunetto Latini's *Trésor*, which, in Bono Giamboni's vernacular version, has the following comment: "Ogni cosa ch'è in noi per natura, si è in noi prima per Potenza e poi viene ad atto" [Every thing that is in us by nature is in us first by potency and then it comes to act].[17]

As we have seen, then, *Vita nova* XX [11] presents a striking example of how, by the time of its composition, we begin to see a Dante who reframes an earlier poetic composition in more intellectually robust and technical language, and one interested in fusing the vernacular and philosophical aspects of his developing intellectual inheritance. At the same time, too, we see how what might appear initially as a relatively slight chapter and a sonnet strongly indebted to Guinizzelli emerges, with regard to both its poetic and its prose components, as richly multifaceted in its engagement with different sources and traditions.

Vita nova XXI [12]

REBEKAH LOCKE

Like "Amore e 'l cor gentil sono una cosa" [Love and the open heart are always one] in the previous chapter, the sonnet we find in chapter XXI [12] appears strongly indebted to the poetry of Guido Guinizzelli. "Ne li occhi porta la mia donna Amore" [My lady's eyes bear Love] is written in praise of Beatrice and is one of several important examples of the *Vita nova*'s *stilo della loda*. It follows the example of Guinizzelli in depicting a lady who is able to bring the lover closer to God and who seems to bring earthly and divine loves into some form of alignment. The sonnet focuses on the ennobling power of Beatrice and the condition of those who behold her advent. In the prose, Dante goes one step further, declaring that the sonnet shows Beatrice to be divine in nature. While Dante's emphasis upon the salvific qualities of the *donna* may simply be dismissed as a stilnovist trope, a more detailed approach to lexis in this poem can provide a richer understanding of Beatrice's impact upon the condition of the lover. I will consider whether the transformative effect of the *donna* upon the lover can be better understood through a theological as well as a lyric prism. Specifically, the theological dimension of this chapter can be further interrogated through a focus on the notion of penitence, as well as Dante's treatment of vice and virtue. Indeed, this chapter is an early example of Dante exploring questions of vice and virtue that will prove so fundamental in his *Commedia*.

After the Fourth Lateran Council in 1215, it became obligatory to attend annual confession.[1] This regular introspective self-analysis meant that individuals were forced to take more personal responsibility for their fate in the afterlife. The sacrament of penance required individuals to recognize their sin, in a process known as contrition, before confessing this sin to a priest and finally undertaking an act of penance known as satisfaction. In his *Purgatorio*, Dante will identify satisfaction, not with the traditional outward performance of penance, but with the need to recognize Christ's love and focus on the inner renewal of the soul.[2] In this sonnet, those who behold Beatrice could be seen to undergo a similarly personal examination of conscience as part of the penitential process.

In the last line of the sonnet, Beatrice is described explicitly as a miracle—"sì è novo miracolo e gentile" (line 14) [this new and noble miracle]—thereby showing how Dante elevates her divine importance.[3] However, the association with the divine occurs most dramatically in the chapter's prose, where, rather than simply awakening Love, as in "Amore e 'l cor gentil," "che fa svegliar lo spirito d'Amore" (line 13) [gets Love himself to stir], here the lady is shown to bring Love into being where it did not previously exist: "e come non solamente si sveglia là ove dorme, ma là ove non è in potenzia, ella, mirabilemente operando, lo fa venire" (XXI.1 [12.1]) [and how it awakens not only where it is dormant but also where it is not even in potential: working miraculously, she brings it forth]. In describing this process, Dante's prose draws on the terminology of scholastic philosophy, as seen in the use of the technical term "in potenzia" (XXI.1 [12.1]) [in potential].[4] Love's miraculous creative power was an ability that scholastic philosophy recognized as being uniquely divine.[5] As the ability of the beloved to bring Love into being is not evident in "Ne li occhi porta la mia donna Amore," Dante uses the prose to revise the meaning of his sonnet and in this instance to equate Beatrice's role in his life to that of Christ. Beatrice's ability to create love for the divine where it was incomplete or nonexistent suggests that she has not only a Christological role but also a penitential one, as the process for repentance involved reshaping love for the earthly into love for the divine through a "change of direction of the inner will."[6] Dante does not simply emphasize the spiritually enriching qualities of the *donna*, as is seen in Guinizzelli's sonnet "Io voglio del ver la mia donna laudare" [I want to praise my lady truly], but rather claims that she *is* divine by her very nature. According to the prose, then, in "Ne li occhi porta la mia donna Amore," Beatrice embodies divine love as well as earthly love, and she can thus ultimately lead others to salvation, a concept that Dante develops further than any of his Italian lyric predecessors. Dante's glorification of Beatrice and the emphasis he places on her salvific role, especially in the prose, can therefore affect the way we view the condition of those who behold her.

Those who turn to see Beatrice as she passes, or are greeted by her, are powerfully affected physically: "e cui saluta fa tremar lo core, / sì che, bassando il viso, tutto smore" (lines 4–5) [she makes the heart of the man she greets tremble, / such that, lowering his gaze, he turns deathly pale]. Commentators have noted similarities here with Cavalcanti: "Chi è questa che vèn, ch'ogn'om la mira, / che fa tremar di chiaritate l'âre" (4.1–2) [Who is she that comes, attracting every man's gaze, who makes the air tremble with light].[7] Both authors use the verb *tremare* [to tremble] to signify weakness and powerlessness in the presence of the *donna*. Dante's use of "tremar lo core" (line 4) [trembling of the heart] and "tutto smore" (line 5) [deathly pale] demonstrates how the onlooker is completely overcome by Beatrice's greeting and is reminiscent of Cavalcanti's representation of love as a disruptive force. However, the sonnet's treatment of Beatrice also reveals that she can inspire a humble reaction in the beholder, who is shown "bassando il viso" (line 5) [lowering his gaze]. This unwillingness to meet Beatrice's gaze suggests that the lover recognizes that he is unworthy to enter her divine presence, and the act might thus suggest a contrite heart. Rather than reflecting the debilitating nature of earthly love, Dante's use of Cavalcantian language emphasizes the deep shame experienced by the lover when realizing his own sinful nature before Beatrice. The physical responses of those who observe Beatrice can therefore represent an outward manifestation of their contrition.

The presence of the divine not only imposes a physical reaction upon the lover but also initiates an active response from within him: "d'ogni suo difetto allor sospira" (line 6) [sighs for every one of his faults]. In her analysis of "Tanto gentile e tanto onesta pare" (XXVI [17]) [She seems so gentle and noble], Heather Webb considers the lover's sigh to be a "reciprocal movement," as it is directly provoked by a spirit that leaves Beatrice's lips and enters his heart.[8] When analyzing the word *sospira* (line 6) [sighs] in "Ne li occhi porta," which has also been linked to the notion of *amor doloroso* in

Cavalcanti's poetry, commentators stress the sense of remorse and repentance that it evokes.[9] This suggests that a penitential process is activated in the on-looker as a result of Beatrice's presence. The use of *sospira* hints that Beatrice prompts a physical reaction to sin from within the beholder, as any "difetto" (line 6) [fault] is forcibly expelled from the body in a sigh. This physical manifestation of regret and of ridding the body of sin returns in *Purgatorio*, where Belacqua describes repentance as 'i buon sospiri' (*Purg.* 4.132) [the good sighs]. In light of this, the lover's "sighing" can be considered almost to represent an oral rejection of sin—an act that can be identified with that of confession, the second stage of the sacrament of penance.

While the poet states that those who see Beatrice repent of *every* sin, "d'ogni suo difetto" (line 6), Dante nevertheless lists the specific sins that Beatrice removes from those who behold her in the line that follows: "fugge dinanzi a lei superbia ed ira" (line 7) [pride and anger flee before her]. In "Io voglio del ver," Guinizzelli likewise claimed that the *donna* reduces pride: "Passa per via adorna, e sì gentile / ch'abbassa orgoglio a cui dona salute" (lines 9–10) [Passing by, she is so beautiful and sweet that she reduces pride in those she greets], while Andreas Capellanus wrote in *De amore*: "super-bos quoque solet humilitate beare" (1.4) [[Love] blesses the proud with hu-mility]. In "Chi è questa che vèn," Cavalcanti contrasted the humility of the *donna* with anger: "cotanto d'umiltà donna mi pare, / ch'ogn'altra ver' di lei i' la chiam'ira" (lines 7–8) [The lady has so much humility / that, in com-parison to her, any other woman seems full of anger], and in "Assai v'ho detto e dico tuttavia" [Many times have I told you and I will continue to say], Chiaro Davanzati wrote, "Da sé diparte orgoglio e villania" (line 7) [Pride and villainy leave her].[10] Dante's decision to include the sins of pride and anger in his sonnet may therefore have been influenced by the trope of the humble *donna* found in these texts. Yet while the pairing of these two sins was relatively commonplace, it is worth further examining their use in Dante.

Hannah Skoda explains that anger "was often paired with pride and covetousness" in the thirteenth and fourteenth centuries, thereby suggesting that Dante's coupling of these sins was also a common religious practice.[11] In his *Moralia*, Gregory the Great considered pride to be the "root of all evil" (31.45.87), which lay at the base of the other vices. Anger was also consid-ered to be one of the most grievous sins, as it too "swiftly engendered further sins."[12] Moreover, in the Bible, both sins are shown to be the opposite of love: love "is not proud" and "it is not easily angered" (1 Corinthians 13:4). As the sins were considered to be the root of further sins, their inclusion in "Ne li occhi porta" underlines the necessity for the lover to repent of the deepest causes of sin in order to renew his soul completely.

The sins of "superbia ed ira" (line 7) [pride and anger], which have frequently been understood by commentators as the opposite of meekness and kindness, are consequently incompatible with Beatrice, who embodies divine love. Beatrice's presence instills humility in the beholder, as the act of "bassando il viso" (line 5) directly counteracts pride, revealing a physical opposition to the sin on the part of the lover. The complete rejection of sin is also underlined by the use of "fugge" (line 7) [to flee], which demonstrates that Beatrice cannot tolerate "superbia ed ira" as they flee before her. It has been suggested that Dante's personification of these sins may have been influenced by the book of Isaiah, where it is written that "gladness and joy will overtake them, and sorrow and sighing will flee away" (Isaiah 35:10).[13] The sins of pride and anger are thus physically expelled by the goodness of Beatrice. Dante therefore highlights Beatrice's divine role when describing how she removes the sins of those who meet her. Given that this powerful rejection of evil takes place within the lover, it points to the fact that this is a very personal process of transformation, like that undertaken in the sacrament of penance.

Although in "Ne li occhi porta la mia donna Amore" the removal of sin is portrayed as a physical and destructive process for the spectator, it is also shown to be one that leads to higher contemplation. While the lover's gaze was initially lowered in Beatrice's presence, it is now lifted up to see her smile: "Quel ch'ella par quando un poco sorride" (line 12) [How she appears when she smiles a little]. Moreover, pride and anger, which are driven away, are replaced by their opposing virtues, humility and gentleness: "Ogne dolcezza, ogne pensero umile / nasce nel core a chi parlar la sente" (lines 9–10) [All gentleness and every humble thought is born in the heart of him who hears her speak]. Both virtues belong to the so-called fruits of the Holy Spirit, as evidenced in the Letter to the Ephesians: "Be completely humble and gentle" (4:2). While the prose claims that Beatrice brings Love into being, the use of "nasce" (line 10) [is born] connotes a physical process, suggesting that she also brings into being "dolcezza" [gentleness] and "pensero umile" [humble thought] (line 9) in the lover *ex nihilo*. Beatrice is thus linked to the miracle of birth and life, hinting that she is returning the lover toward a state of innocence that is associated with virtue, not vice. While commentators have already noted that this exchange of vice for virtue indicates that Beatrice's presence is transformative and salvific, she also appears to have a purificatory role that transforms the lover so that he is fit to experience her divine presence. Beatrice does not simply encourage self-reflection and remorse as a means to remove sin from those who look at her but also produces virtue, enabling the beholder to partake in a more permanent transformation that permits access to the divine. This transformation can be linked to the inner renewal of the soul that Dante associates with the process of satisfaction.

Beatrice instills virtues into the lover through a sensual connection, whether that be seeing her pass by, "ov'ella passa, ogn'om ver lei si gira" (line 3) [wherever she passes, everyone turns to see her], or hearing her greeting, "a chi parlar la sente" (line 10) [him who hears her speak]. John Took underlines the spiritual impact of witnessing the divine presence in his analysis of the proud in *Purgatorio* who view divine engravings that depict exemplars of humility: "Standing now in the presence of piety, it [the soul] is, so to speak, possessed by that piety, re-shaped by it and, in its re-shaping, confirmed in the way of spiritual emancipation."[14] Beatrice's divine presence similarly appears to possess those who see her, freeing them from vice and reshaping their lives according to virtue: "ond'è laudato chi prima la vide" (line 11) [the first person to see her is praised]. Just as souls in Purgatorio are aided in their purgation by a physical encounter with divine virtue, so Beatrice represents a virtuous encounter for the beholder in "Ne li occhi porta la mia donna Amore." Moreover, like the purgation process, which constitutes spiritual transformation as both a physical and psychological process, Beatrice also provokes a physical and moral change in others. Beatrice thus inspires a penitential process in the onlooker, as the lover is shown not only to be remorseful and repentant of his sin but also to renew his soul, thereby following the three stages of the sacrament of penance.

It is thus possible to view Beatrice as an instigator of penance in "Ne li occhi porta la mia donna Amore." If, as the prose suggests, Beatrice is to be seen as a Christ figure, then the lover would need to go through the necessary penitential stages if he desired to turn to her as Christ. I have argued that this penitential process takes place in those who observe Beatrice, beginning with the act of "bassando il viso" (line 5), which can signify the humility required to recognize one's sin. This is followed by repentance, suggested by the use of *sospira* in line 6, which physically expels sin, and it ends with the inner renewal of satisfaction, which occurs when "ogne pensero umile / nasce nel core" (lines 9–10). Rather than viewing the salvific qualities of the *donna* in the sonnet solely as a stilnovist trope that transforms the lover, we can consider the condition of the lover in relation to the sacrament of penance. This religious perspective allows the lover to be viewed as penitent, while Beatrice can be seen as a Christ figure who activates this penitential transformation in those who behold her.

Vita nova XXII [13]

LUCA LOMBARDO

According to Fredi Chiappelli, chapter XXII [13], which describes the death of Beatrice's father and Dante's meeting with a group of women returning from her home, is a "paragraph on Beatrice's grief . . . arranged as syllogisms." These "syllogisms," dispersed throughout the opening prose paragraphs, form "a kind of gothic architecture" alongside the mournful lyric tone.[1] One structural peculiarity of chapter XXII [13] is the presence of two sonnets, which form a diptych so tightly connected to the prose as to be a faithful poetic transposition of the prose itself. Luca Carlo Rossi has traced the decision to organize the lyric component as a diptych to the theme of mourning, noting the parallelism between these sonnets and the pair of sonnets in chapter VIII [3] that describe the death of Beatrice's friend.[2] This event serves as the first hint of Beatrice's own death, which is further foreshadowed here by the death of her father. The thematic parallelism between chapters VIII [3] and XXII [13] is paralleled at the structural level via the duplication of the lyric element, which occurs only one other time in the *libello* (XXVI [17]). However, as Rossi also notes, the distinctive nature of chapter XXII [13]'s pair of mourning sonnets compared to those written following the death of Beatrice's friend depends on their different placement in the *libello*'s poetic evolution, as well as their relationship to the new "praise" style, which here

190

entails "the participation of the gracious women,"[3] alongside testimonies of mourning and active female interlocutors.

The death of Beatrice's father is therefore a narrative nucleus: the last omen of the *gentilissima*'s own death, the "second moment of approaching the *climax* of the *libello*'s central event."[4] The link between chapter XXII [13] and Beatrice's death is revealed not only through its account of the death of her father but also through its ties to the following chapter, which presents "the grand prose of Beatrice's death."[5] Chapter XXII [13] has the macro-structural function of introducing events that follow on from each other: specifically, the prophetic nightmare of Beatrice's death, the only explicit commemoration of the *libello*'s key event that is never actually described.

The Florentine backdrop of the story reemerges in chapter XXII [13] thanks both to Beatrice's father, the poet's illustrious fellow citizen, and the presentation of the funereal customs of the "cittade" (XXII.3 [13.3]) [city]. Dante does not reveal Beatrice's father's identity. The identification with Folco di Ricovero Portinari is normally based on Boccaccio's *Trattatello*. However, the earliest testimonies in this regard may be found in Andrea Lancia and Pietro Alighieri, who, glossing Beatrice in *Inferno* 2, discuss her historical identity and her Florentine lineage. Indeed, Lancia specifies the name of Beatrice's father, in addition to that of her husband.[6] In the second edition of Pietro's commentary, slightly later than Lancia's glosses, information on Beatrice's biography is vaguer, although he presents her as a member of the Portinari family while failing to name her father: "born into the family of certain Florentine citizens named Portinari."[7] The absence of Folco's name in chapter XXII [13] may be read as a rhetorical device tacitly to exalt Beatrice through the periphrasis referring to her genealogy.[8] At the same time, Dante's decision not to name Beatrice's father can also be explained in terms of the fact that, in the first instance, the *Vita nova* was written for a Florentine audience that almost certainly would have been familiar with the public figures and events presented in it.[9] This would have been especially the case as regards the Portinaris, a family of merchants and financiers with a high public profile. Folco had taken on public duties and had founded the hospital of Santa Maria Nuova, which was completed in 1288.[10] Dante confirms Beatrice's father's renown when he writes that it was widely recognized that he was "bono in alto grado" (XXII.2 [13.2]) [good to a high degree]. The phrase is the only marker that can be ascribed to Beatrice's father's social standing and relates to his well-known philanthropy. Boccaccio reaffirms Folco's standing in Florence. Perhaps influenced by the *Vita nova*, he calls Folco "uomo assai orrevole in que' tempi tra' cittadini" [a man of great honor among the citizens at that time]; "onorevole cittadino" [honorable citizen]; "antico cittadino di Firenze" [long-standing citizen of Florence].[11] Archival documents suggest that Folco died on December 31, 1289, a little less than six months before Beatrice's death on June 8, 1290, and therefore at a time consistent with the chronology of the *libello*'s narrative, which locates the death of the beloved shortly after that of her father.

It is striking that Dante should speak so positively about a banker, a profession that he would come to associate with usury. In addition to Folco's charitable activities, it is possible that Dante's friendship with Manetto Portinari influenced his opinion. Manetto, Folco's son, is termed Beatrice's "frate" [brother] at XXXIII.4 [22.4], and Dante also calls him "questo mio amico" [this friend of mine] (XXXII.3 [21.3]). It is thus apparent that Dante's poetic autobiography should also be considered in terms of his contemporary Florentine social context, since this provides some of the background to the events and relationships evoked in the *Vita nova*. The friendship with Manetto has been read by Silvia Diacciati as an association with "representatives of families doubtless more accomplished" than the Alighieris, a relationship from which it is not unlikely that Dante expected to gain social advantage.[12] The funeral elegy for a "banker and well-known politician" like Folco can therefore be interpreted, alongside its poetic function of exalting Beatrice, as an attempt to gain recognition among the most influential circles of the city as a friend of the wealthy Portinari family, which constituted the most important point of social and civic reference for an inhabitant of the district of Porta San Piero such as Dante.[13]

Chapter XXII [13]'s Florentine backdrop and its return to the public sphere are also highlighted thanks to the precision with which Dante describes Florentine funeral customs "secondo l'usanza de la sopradetta cittade" (XIII.3 [6.3]) [in keeping with the customs of the city mentioned earlier]. In the *Vita nova*, the syntagm "secondo l'usanza" [in keeping with the customs] refers to important communal religious and civic ceremonies, such as marriages and funerals. The public resonances of the funeral nevertheless establish a link between the love narrative and the urban landscape in which the latter is set. This landscape serves not just as a backdrop but also as a spatial counterpoint to the love story.[14] Chapter XXII [13] reveals that men and women were kept apart at funerals. Boccaccio mentions the same custom in the *Decameron* (1 Intr. 32); however, the *Vita nova* offers the oldest literary allusion to this socio-anthropological fact.[15] Further important information in this regard is found in the sonnet "Voi che portate la sembianza umile" (XXII.9–10 [13.9–13.10]) [You whose expressions are so meek and low], which, in line with the prose, stresses the key role that women played at funerals. As Marco Grimaldi observes, the social norms of Dante's time had women giving full expression to grief, while men were expected to practice restraint.[16] As such, the female voice of the chapter's second sonnet, "Se' tu colui c'hai trattato sovente" (XXII.13–16 [13.13–13.16]) [Are you that man who's often liked to write], which lays exclusive claim to weeping, restores the conventional order, which had been subverted by Dante mourning in the first sonnet. On the other hand, Dante's behavior demonstrates poetry's ability to disregard established social restrictions. On the narrative level, according to Donato Pirovano, the public nature of Dante's emotional crisis likens this event to that of the "gabbo" (XIV [7]): the two episodes share lexical and narrative elements despite the fact that Dante's emotional excess has different causes and consequences.[17]

On the structural level, chapter XXII [13]'s attention to formal detail is particularly striking. The first paragraph is characterized by the periphrasis to Beatrice's father, which, with mounting effect, announces the theme of death that is prefigured in the opening reference to Christ's demise. It also draws attention to Beatrice. The second paragraph hinges on a syllogism: the expression "con ciò sia cosa che" [inasmuch as] introduces three premises that lead to a conclusion, prefaced by the phrase "manifesto è che" [it is clear that], which, by assessing the bond between parent and child, demonstrates logically the extent of Beatrice's grief for her father's death. The function of the syllogism is rigorously to validate the elegiac character of Beatrice's grief, which acts as a premise for Dante's own, before this is granted poetic expression. The complexity of the formal architecture consists in the dependence of four causal prepositions on the final "manifesto è che." The prepositions, symmetrically placed in antonomastic phrases, move toward a climax.[18] Furthermore, Pirovano highlights the impact of the comparison, which chiastically emphasizes the relationship between father and daughter.[19] Indeed, Domenico De Robertis posits a connection with Matthew 11:27, where the mutual exclusivity of family bonds is expressed through chiasmus.[20] Commentators rightly underscore the Christological context in which Folco's death is located. The parallelism between the deaths of Christ and Folco established in paragraph 1 depends on the assured resurrection of the deceased—"a la gloria etternale sen gìo veracemente" [truly went to eternal glory]—as well on his being summoned by the "glorioso sire" [Lord of glory], a phrase that connects to "gloria etternale" [eternal glory], denoting death in a Christian sense, as in the "twin" chapter VIII [3].

As regards the love between father and child—"Nulla è sì intima amistade come da buon padre a buon figliuolo e da buon figliuolo a buon padre" (XXII.2 [13.2]) [No friendship is so intimate as that of a good father toward a good son or daughter and of a good son or daughter toward a good father])—De Robertis cites Cicero's *De amicitia* 27, a work that belongs to Dante's Florentine education, as the poet explains in *Convivio* 2.12.3.[21] Dante's reference can be equated to similar maxims on friendship based on Cicero found in Duecento Tuscan prose works written before the *Vita nova*. In Albertano da Brescia's *Liber de amore et dilectione Dei*, translated into Florentine vernacular in 1275, Cicero's moral teachings, introduced by formulations such as "Et Tulio nel libro de l'Amistade" [And Tully in his book on Friendship], are alluded to at least fifteen times.[22] Equally, in the Tuscan version of Brunetto Latini's *Trésor*, one finds "Tullio c'insegna" [Tullio teaches us] on the subject of friendship,[23] which points to the deep penetration of the Latin *auctoritas* in the Tuscan environment. The opening of chapter XXII [13] thus associates the *Vita nova* with contemporary moral and civic treatises.[24] For instance, the relationship between friendship (*amistà*) and family (*parentado*) had already been discussed in the *Trésor* and its vernacular translation, as well as in the 1268 vernacular translation of Albertano by Andrea da Grosseto.[25] The notion that *parentado* and *amistà* are naturally connected is also present in Edigio Romano's *De regimine principum*, translated into the vernacular in Siena in 1288, which clarifies the social functions of friendship in communal political and ethical terms while highlighting parental responsibilities, given that "intra il padre e 'l figliuolo si à naturale amistà" [between father and child there is a natural friendship],[26] a phrase that closely recalls Dante's later formulation.

In Duecento Tuscan prose, then, the ethical maxim on the friendship between fathers and children is charged with political and social significance.

Consequently, the same reference in chapter XXII [13] should be interpreted not only in a sentimental key but also in civic and social terms, as is confirmed by Orosius's *Storie contro i pagani*, translated into the vernacular by Bono Giamboni, where the *amistà-parentado* duality is presented in civic ideological terms as an instrument of political allegiance and social cohesion.[27] In addition to the filter of secular civic culture, through which echoes of the *De amicitia* may be heard in the *Vita nova*, it is noteworthy that Dante should have presented the Ciceronian reference in a syllogism,[28] a form that in its turn alludes to other types of philosophical discourse—those "traces of philosophy" that scholars have begun to identify in the *libello*.[29]

In the *Vita nova* in general and in chapter XXII [13] in particular, Dante formally elevates vernacular prose. His pursuit of stylistic and structural complexity accompanies the transition to the theme of mourning, with its corresponding elegiac register, which supplants the "praise style" inaugurated by "Donne ch'avete intelletto d'amore" (XIX.4–14 [10.15–10.25]) [Women who understand the truth of love], and which in chapter XXII [13] marks "a decisive break from the previous register."[30] Dante now has recourse, in both the prose and the two sonnets, to a lexicon of mourning, which belongs to the semantic field of "miseria" [misery].

"Voi che portate" and "Se' tu colui," respectively conceived as question and answer according to the dialectical structure of *sermoncinatio*, follow the rhetorical model of the *tenzone* or, as Grimaldi specifies, the subtype of the fictional *tenzone*, in which the poet pretends to have held a dialogue in verse with a real-life interlocutor. The periphrastic revelation of the author's identity in the "*tenzone* in the lady's voice" (XXII.13 [13.13]) constitutes an exception in the tradition of the genre.[31] The "sorrowful" stylistic register of the sonnets is anticipated in paragraphs 7 and 8, where Dante claims to have taken "matera di dire" [subject matter] from the words he had heard spoken by the women in mourning. As has been mentioned, the new "matera" cannot but be elegy. Poetry permits Dante to pose the questions that he would have liked to have asked the women but that went unasked owing to a fear of impropriety. The abortive dialogue is instead transferred from the diegesis to a poetic context, the imaginary *tenzone*. The genesis of "Voi che portate" is tied to meeting the women who were returning from the funeral of Beatrice's father. The sonnet records a dialogue that never in fact occurred. On the other hand, the response found in "Se' tu colui" is presented, not as a simple

fiction, but as a poetic version of the words that the poet heard the Floren-
tine women speak. By granting a poetic voice to women, whose engagement
with poetry was limited in late Duecento Florence, Dante made a significant
literary-social contribution.[32] He fashioned a genuine poetic conversation be-
tween the sexes, a feature already attested in elegy.[33] The poet's female inter-
locutors are those to whom he earlier addressed "Donne ch'avete"—a further
realistic element that provides an insight into the late Duecento Florentine
audience of Dante's poetry. Together with others who heard the news of the
death of Beatrice's father, the women are thus part of a relatively broad audi-
ence, which included notable members of the bourgeoisie like the Portinaris.

The opening of "Voi che portate la sembianza umile" is similar to the
incipit "Voi, donne, che pietoso atto mostrate" [Ladies who show pity in
your bearing] (*Rime* 71), while the phrase "la sembianza umile" [expressions
so meek and low] is already present in the so-called Amico di Dante.[34] In
contrast, the appearance and gestures of the women recall the Muses by
Boethius's bedside in *Consolatio philosophiae* 1.prose 1.12, a text that served
as an archetype of the *stylus miserorum*, and that, like *De amicitia*, Dante had
read following Beatrice's death, which, tellingly, is prefigured in this chapter.
The external details that reveal the women's affliction are concentrated in the
first quatrain (humble aspect, lowered eyes, paleness), and in the second ter-
zina (weeping). Line 6, "bagnar nel viso suo di pianto Amore" [Love soaking
our gracious lady's eyes with tears], describes Love being bathed in tears since
it resides in Beatrice's eyes, an allusion that connects it to the preceding chap-
ter's sonnet "Negli occhi porta la mia donna Amore" [My lady's eyes bear
Love]. The sonnets thus present two strikingly different ways in which Love
dwells in Beatrice: on the one hand, it is an indicator of sweetness, while on
the other it is elegiacally associated with words and tears.

In line 8, "perch'io vi veggio andar sanz'atto vile" [because I see you
going along with no base comportment], Dante deduces from their noble de-
meanor that the women have come from being with Beatrice (see lines 31–32
of "Donne ch'avete"). In keeping with the syllogism in the prose that demon-
strates Beatrice's grief, the lover of the lyric narrative also employs logical de-
ductive methods, so that the presentiment ("che mi 'l dice il core" (l. 6) [in
my heart it's plain])[35] recalls a logical deduction: it is evident that the women
have been with Beatrice, since they exhibit the same nobility of bearing
as her.

At line 9, "tanta pietate" [such a mournful scene] is a metonym indicating the death of Beatrice's father, which is not directly mentioned in the sonnet as it is in the prose. The *Vita nova*'s prose is able to linger on matters to which the lyrics, normally written earlier, only allude, given that they were immediate responses to specific events, such as Folco's passing, which would have been known to their Florentine readership. Stefano Carrai proposes an interpretation that projects the phrase into the Florentine urban space, giving it a physical dimension: "namely, the house where Beatrice mourns her father."[36]

Line 10, "piacciavi di restar" [please stay with me], returns in *Inferno* 10.24 ("piacciati di restare in questo loco"), but it also appears in the complementary sonnet, "Onde venite?" [Where do you come from?] (*Rime* 70.5–6), which equally describes the return of the grieving women. The connection with Farinata may well point to the strongly Florentine reverberations of the sonnet. Finally, the phrase recalls the typical formula of sepulchral epitaphs, whereby the deceased speak to the living.[37]

The chapter's second sonnet, "Se' tu colui c'hai trattato sovente," has more points of contact with the prose than the preceding sonnet, since it too presents the women's utterances, although arranging them in reverse order. At the same time, the sonnet depends on the prose, since it leaves vague the cause of the women's sorrow. Numerous lexical parallels also exist between the two sonnets that can be returned to the rhetorical norms of the *tenzone*. "Weeping" is the key term of the sonnet, with five occurrences of words belonging to this same semantic field, thereby emphasizing the elegiac register pervading the chapter. Moreover, De Robertis notes that the opening line, "Se' tu colui c'hai trattato sovente," anticipates Dante's famous reply to Bonagiunta in *Purgatorio* 24.49–51.[38] In both instances, Dante is recognized for being a poet, and specifically as the author of "Donne ch'avete." This fact confirms Dante's recognized status as a poet in Florence during the early 1290s. According to Pirovano, the expression "hai trattato" recalls line 11 of "Donne ch'avete": "tratterò" [I'll talk about], a technical term for writing poetry that once again distinguishes Dante as the poet of "praise" who addresses women who have intelligence of love.[39]

Line 3 ("tu risomigli a la boce ben lui" [your voice's tone suggests that he is you]) reveals that, given his changed appearance, the women recognize Dante from his voice. The form *boce*—with its occlusive bilabial—is "typically Florentine."[40] It functions as a linguistic marker of the Florentinity of the text. Indeed, the only occurrences of the form appear in Dante's Florentine works: *Fiore, Detto, Rime*, and *Vita nova*.[41] According to Pirovano, Dante is defined by his individual poetic voice that highlights his distinctive and personal style, which would again indicate his renown among his Florentine readers.

Line 10, "e fa peccato chi mai ne conforta" [he sins who ever tries to comfort us] reveals that the women's grief at having seen Beatrice's weeping is inconsolable. It anticipates the affliction felt by Dante at Beatrice's death in *Convivio* 2.12.2, from which he sought solace by reading Boethius and Cicero. However, the remedy for his grief is different: in the sonnet Dante cannot avail himself of literary consolation, which might suggest that, at the time of its composition, he had not yet read books of consolation. It is Beatrice's death that will trigger Dante's philosophical studies.

Finally, the elegiac mark is stamped on line 11, "nel suo pianto l'udimmo parlare" [we're the ones who heard her cry and talk]. Speech united with weeping recurs in *Inferno* (Francesca and Ugolino) but is also present in "Li occhi dolenti" (XXXI.9 (20.9)) [My eyes that grieve].[42] The link between "Se' tu colui c'hai trattato sovente" and the prose narrative is confirmed by the commentary, which limits itself to indicating the four divisions of the text, assuming that the introduction is enough to clarify "sentenzia de le parti" (XXII.17 [13.17]) [the meanings of their parts]. On the other hand, the telegraphic nature of the division of the poetic text may be explained in terms of the shared cultural horizon uniting the poet and his first readers, who were able to grasp without the need for detailed exegesis his implicit references to events and figures belonging to Florentine public life that are allusively placed at the center of this chapter.

Translated by J. C. Wiles

Vita nova XXIII [14]

PETER DENT

At some point during the papacy of Nicholas IV (1288–92) or soon after, the workshops responsible for the cycle of St. Francis in the Upper Church at Assisi painted the scene of the *Death of St. Francis*. In the lower foreground, the saint's body lies on a low bier surrounded by mourning friars. Behind these figures stands a bishop flanked by acolytes. Further members of the community crowd round. Above, in the upper third of the fresco, a flock of angels bears Francis's soul aloft in the whitest of clouds. At around the same date, perhaps just a year or two later, when Dante composed the section of the *Vita nova* (XXIII [14]) in which he witnesses the future death of Beatrice, he described a similar scene: "Io imaginava di guardare verso lo cielo, e pareami vedere moltitudine d'angeli li quali tornassero in suso, ed aveano dinanzi da loro una nebuletta bianchissima" (XXIII.7 [14.7]) [I imagined that I was looking towards the sky, and I seemed to see a multitude of angels ascending, and they had in front of them a little pure-white cloud]. This is immediately followed by a vision of "lo corpo ne lo quale era stata quella nobilissima e beata anima" (XXIII.8 [14.8]) [the body in which that most noble and beatified soul had been]. This too is a scene of lamentation. Women gather around the corpse and are about to veil Beatrice's head. Dante is afforded a brief glimpse of her features: "E pareami che la sua faccia avesse tanto aspetto d'umilitade, che parea che dicesse: 'Io sono a vedere lo principio de la pace'"

(XXIII.8 [14.8]) [And it seemed that her face had such a humble look that it seemed to be saying: "I am gazing upon the very source of peace"]. Her beatific vision also finds its parallel at Assisi—not in the scene of the *Death*, but later in the same bay, in the *Verification of the Stigmata*. The compositional outlines of the two frescoes are almost identical. Francis's body again lies in the foreground surrounded by members of the community. As the impression of Christ's wounds in his flesh is confirmed, establishing the perfection of Francis as an *imago Christi*, the *poverello*'s humble face gazes up at Christ's face depicted on a painted crucifix, which hangs at an angle above him from a rood beam. It is no accident that this image of Christ crucified, an image within an image, occupies the same space taken by Francis's soul in the scene of his death.

These deaths—of Beatrice and of Francis—are both framed with imagery that evokes Christ's death and resurrection. At Assisi, the *Death of St. Francis* lies at the heart of a major fresco cycle designed in part to flesh out the emerging discourse of Francis as *alter Christus*. Indeed, along with the *Stigmatisation* in the preceding bay and the *Crucifixion* and *Lamentation* in the sequence devoted to Christ in the tier above, the *Death of St. Francis* contributes to a particularly powerful visual intersection at this point where the narratives pass each other, unfolding in different directions along the nave. Likewise, allusions to Christ are threaded throughout Dante's account of Beatrice in the *Vita nova*.[1] In chapter XXIII [14], in particular, the nine days of suffering that preface the vision of Beatrice's death recall Christ's death on the cross at the ninth hour. Similarly, the darkening sun and the earthquake that accompany the procession of weeping ladies evoke the darkness that falls from the sixth to the ninth hour at the Crucifixion and the sudden shaking of the earth as Christ gives up the ghost. Although the effect serves a different purpose, Dante also employs countervailing narrative flows. The vision and awakening that he describes in sequential order in the prose section is subsequently reentered from its concluding episode in the *canzone*.

Although this shared Christological patterning has common roots in devotional culture, one detail suggests that Dante was also drawing on the example of Francis. The striking white cloud of the fresco is the visual analogue of "the little pure white cloud" in Dante's text. While there could be a common source (Revelation 14:14), the "nebuletta bianchissima" is very close to the "candida nubecula" that is a recurring feature in early descriptions of

Francis's death.[2] A Franciscan influence on the *Vita nova* would be under-standable. From the early 1290s, Dante was probably attending the Francis-can studium at Santa Croce.[3] No doubt he was familiar with Bonaventure's *Life* of the saint, but a visual source like the fresco may also have played a role. At Santa Croce, however, in the Bardi dossal (ca. 1245), which contains one of the few early surviving images of the scene from before the cycle at As-sisi, angels carry the soul of Francis aloft in a swag of white cloth rather than a cloud. Indeed, in medieval images of the *elevatio animae*, the swag of cloth is the most common way of representing the action described in the an-tiphon recited for the commendation of the soul: "Suscipiat te Christus qui vocavit te et in sinum Abrahae angeli deducant te" [May Christ who has called thee receive thee, and may angels carry thee into Abraham's bosom].[4] In fact, the fresco at Assisi was almost certainly the first time that the "can-dida nubecula" was realized as such a prominent visual element in a publicly accessible location.

There is uncertainty about Dante's whereabouts for several years in the first half of the 1290s, with some scholars suggesting a period in Bologna.[5] In the aftermath of Beatrice's death on June 8, 1290, as he reflected on mor-tality, a pilgrimage to Assisi might also have been a possibility. There is no evidence for such a journey, but the scenario is not improbable. Indeed, in 1291, another thirteenth-century Italian, Angela of Foligno, traveled to the Franciscan mother church on a pilgrimage that culminated in a profound mystical vision of the divine. Her *Memorial*, dictated to her Franciscan con-fessor over the next five years, reveals that the vision was prompted by an image seen inside the Upper Church: not a fresco, but a stained-glass win-dow in the south nave: "I saw there St. Francis represented in Christ's em-brace" [Vidi lì san Francesco raffigurato in braccio a Cristo].[6]

Given the long association of Giotto's name with the cycle at Assisi, and the apocryphal tradition that poet and painter were friends, it is tempting to imagine that the frescoes would have intrigued Dante.[7] In *Purgatorio* 10, when he names Cimabue and Giotto, the panel crucifixes by these Florentine painters at Santa Croce and Santa Maria Novella are a possible point of refer-ence in Dante's visual culture.[8] But the decoration of the Upper Church pro-vides another—more concentrated—context for such a comparison, given that Cimabue had already contributed frescoes in the transept. However, the purpose of this juxtaposition between Dante's vision of Beatrice's death and the *Death of St. Francis* is not to pursue the question of "what Dante saw." It has been introduced to frame the deeper relationships between images, image making, and imagination that are characteristic of Dante's world.⁹ These re-lationships underpin the dense layers of signification that run between text and image in this period, to which the cycle at Assisi and the *Vita nova* both testify. With this in mind, I want to focus on one particular element of Dante's imagined scene of Beatrice's death that leads back in an oblique but suggestive fashion to the fresco.

Dante's vision emerges piecemeal out of a delirium: "Che ne lo inco-minciamento de lo errare che fece la mia fantasia, apparvero a me certi visi di donne scapigliate, che mi diceano: 'Tu pur morrai'; e poi, dopo queste donne, m'apparvero certi visi diversi e orribili a vedere, li quali mi diceano: 'Tu se' morto'" (XXIII.4 [14.4]) [As my fantasy started to stray, faces of women appeared, their hair loose, telling me, "You too will die." Then, after these women, some grotesque faces appeared, horrible to look at, telling me: "You are dead"]. This fantasy then develops into the full-blown vision of the procession of mourning women and Beatrice's ascending soul and lifeless corpse. In other words, this imagined scene begins with a set of faces. It goes without saying that the face is an important—perhaps the most important—image-type in Dante's work. Beatrice's face, of course, is implicitly imprinted or painted in his heart. The Virgin's face in the *Paradiso* is "la faccia che a Cristo / più si somiglia" (32.85–86) ["the face that most resembles Christ"], an expression of how perfectly she conforms (like Francis) as an image and likeness. And most importantly of all, later in the *Vita nova*, and again in the *Commedia*, there is the face of Christ himself, which the pilgrim can en-counter in "quella imagine benedetta la quale Iesu Cristo lasciò a noi per essemplo de la sua bellissima figura" (XL.1 [29.1]) [the blessed image that Jesus Christ left us as an imprint of his beautiful visage]: the Veronica, at Rome, visited in anticipation of a final face-to-face in paradise. The *Vita nova* concludes with precisely that vision as enjoyed by Beatrice (like Francis on his bier).

But what are these faces here, conjured from Dante's imagination, that give rise to the vision? They are manifestly not the beautiful faces of Beatrice, Mary, or Christ. These disembodied faces seem to torment and mock him in his mortality. Unlike images of the isolated face of Christ derived from the Veronica, there is no obvious way of situating these heads—almost the anti-type of the face that promises eternal salvation—in thirteenth-century visual culture. However, in the following century a possible context does emerge. Disembodied heads mocking or mourning Christ increasingly appear as adjuncts to the *arma Christi* or gather around representations of the Man of Sorrows. In a midcentury panel of the *Man of Sorrows with Arma Christi* (Harvard Art Museums) attributed to Roberto Oderisi, for example, Christ appears upright in the tomb, flanked by mourning figures of Mary and John. His bowed head is bracketed by disembodied faces, spitting and blowing a horn. Further partial figures appear above, including Judas kissing Christ's face. The panel culminates—which is important—with Christ's own isolated face so that the viewer can move between his humanity in the tomb and his divinity in heaven, a composition structurally similar to the split between soul and body in Dante's vision and the Assisi fresco. The fragmentary images of heads function as mnemonic prompts for meditation. They open out the non-narrative image of the Man of Sorrows into the narrative context of the Passion. Moving around these visual prompts, the viewer is led backward and forward through the events leading up to Christ's death, like Dante navigating his vision twice over in prose and poem, or the viewer tracing the contrary motion of the cycles at Assisi. At the same time, along the vertical axis toward the vision of Christ's face at the apex, the viewer is also encouraged to traverse the path from material things to spiritual understanding, the goal of all such meditation. Although surviving examples of this iconography postdate the *Vita nova*, the devotional practices of visualizing such prompts and the texts from which these ideas and images derive were certainly in place by that date.

In other words, the faces that give rise to Dante's fevered vision of Beatrice's death are generically similar to the faces that populate this later type of image. The isolated faces give rise to the narrative of her mortality through which Dante moves, and subsequently this narrative takes us to Beatrice's face; it in turn points to "the very source of peace," which—almost inevitably—can be pictured as a vision of Christ's face, as in the panel. Like the earthquake and the eclipse, they are part of the patterning through which Beatrice is presented as Christ-like, as a figure who leads Dante toward Christ, like the Veronica that leads pilgrims toward Rome. But the way in which Dante deploys this material may rest on a slightly deeper foundation.

It seems important that Dante insists on a process involving the fantasy or imagination that generates the kind of mnemotechnical image that might be deployed as the opening visualization of a Passion mediation. As

Michelle Karnes has demonstrated, meditation on Christ as recommended by thirteenth-century theologians was underpinned by a thorough understanding of the processes of cognition largely indebted to Aristotle and the Arabic commentaries on his work.[10] Bonaventure, for example, granted imagination a particularly powerful role in generating images from sensory data that could be processed by the intellect in order to arrive at true knowledge. The passage from external object to intellectual understanding involved a series of steps in which the material particularity of the object of perception was dematerialized and departicularized in order to yield its universal truth—effectively equated with immaterial form. Christ himself through divine illumination facilitated the final transition from the imagination through the agent intellect to the potential intellect where understanding occurred. Bonaventure then employed this model for Passion meditation as a practice designed to move the devotee from Christ's humanity to his divinity. However, the process of cognition itself—regardless of the content—always involved Christ, because it engaged in various ways with human cognition as a manifestation of the divine image within humankind: in other words, all acts of understanding potentially led to him. Thinking about Beatrice's death is intrinsically an act through which Christ might be known, and implicitly it will lead from his material humanity to his uncircumscribed divinity.

We can perhaps see something of the result of this evolving process of understanding in the aftermath of Beatrice's actual death in chapter XXXIV [23] when Dante "draws" out the image of Beatrice from his memory and depicts her as an angel, externalizing the product of the cognitive processes operating over his year of mourning.[11] On his small panel, he represents her not as a particular individuated being but as something more generic and immaterial, an angel. It could be argued that this reflects precisely the process of understanding that leads from the object, through sensory perception, to the imagination, which delivers an almost dematerialized form to the agent intellect. Indeed, what could be more immaterial, in some respects, than an angel? But as an articulation of how he has come to understand Beatrice, her redescription as an angel, a messenger who brings good news, indicates how he has acquired an understanding of her fundamental significance in relation to Christ.

The power of visualization developed to a new pitch during the course of this period. Not only was it carefully theorized, but it became a fundamental and widespread aspect of devotional praxis. The masters of these techniques were the saints whose bodies or hearts came to bear the physical impress of their object of devotion after lengthy meditation on the Passion—Francis being the most well-known example. The close relationship between religious devotion and the conventions of love poetry meant that there was also a natural affinity with the image of the beloved's face inscribed on the heart.[12] The practice of visualizing faces in this way is perhaps described most powerfully in poem 129 of the *Rime sparse*, where Petrarch recounts what happens when, pausing in the landscape, he thinks of Laura:

> . . . nel primo sasso
> disegno co la mente il suo bel viso
>
> .   .   .   .
>
> I' l'ò più volte . . .
> ne l'acqua chiara et sopra l'erba verde
> veduto viva, et nel troncon d'un faggio
> e 'n bianca nube . . .
>
> .   .   .   .
>
> et quanto in più selvaggio
> loco mi trovo e 'n più deserto lido,
> tanto più bella il mio pensier l'adombra.

> ————

> [In the first stone I see I portray her lovely face with my mind. . . . I have many times . . . seen her alive in the clear water and on the green grass and in the trunk of a beech tree and in a white cloud . . . and in whatever wildest place and most deserted shore I find myself, so much the more beautiful does my thought shadow her forth.][13]

In other words, he encounters her features, like *vestigia Dei*, throughout the natural world.

This power of visualization—and of visualizing faces in particular—brings us back finally to the fresco of the *Death of St. Francis* at Assisi and the "candida nubecula" cushioning the saint's elevated soul. Emerging from among the formless wisps of white cloud is an unmistakable but enigmatic profile. The painter has conjured the features of a male face out of thin air. Published for the first time by Chiara Frugoni in 2011, its presence has prompted considerable debate.[14] It is potentially grotesque in appearance like the heads imagined by Dante, and there has been some suggestion that it possesses horns, although the visual evidence is ambiguous at best, as is its significance. Having entitled her article "Playing with Clouds," Frugoni concluded that it may be a visual joke, and in discussing it she made connections to the later discourse of Renaissance art in which artistic invention, imagination in particular, plays a central role. The question of its meaning, however, is complicated by the fact that the ghostly face would have been no easier to see from the nave below in the light conditions of a medieval basilica when it was first painted than it is now. It may yet prove to have some undiscovered iconographical source, but it may also testify to a simpler yet more profound characteristic of this period that also surfaces in chapter XXIII [14] of the *Vita nova*: the compulsion to make images, and to imagine faces, in meditating on the object of devotion.

Vita nova XXIV [15]

GEORGE FERZOCO

Of the *Vita nova*'s forty-two parts, the twenty-fourth can lay claim to having one of the oldest and probably best-known examples of misinterpreting, and thus misrepresenting, this *libello*. Of course, there were bound to be misreadings while the text circulated in manuscript copies.[1] The first printed edition, dating from 1576 in the midst of the Counter-Reformation, seems deliberately to have excised not only a phrase in Dante's vernacular but also a verse from the Vulgate. These words do not appear here: "Lo suo nome Giovanna è da quello Giovanni lo quale precedette la verace luce, dicendo: *Ego vox clamantis in deserto: parate viam Domini*" (XXIV.4 [15.4]) [Her name, Giovanna (or Joanna), is derived from that John who preceded the true Light, saying, *I am the voice of one crying in the wilderness; make straight the way of the Lord*].[2] These changes result in serious alterations in the way readers would follow the narrative.[3] Given such a history of misreadings based on outlooks colored by spiritual lenses, a focus on Dante's own religious milieu may assist in better understanding Dante's intentions here.

The *Vita nova* is rooted in its poetry, and there have long been considerations of Dante having deliberately arranged the poems symmetrically so as to bring greater meaning to the volume as a whole. The content and the order of the poems are weighted with significance; indeed, their order adds to their content. Most scholars have accepted the basic premises laid down by Charles Singleton, with ordinal Roman numerals representing the *canzoni* and Arabic numerals the other poetical works, Singleton presents the thirty-one poems as "1, 9; I; 4-II-4; III; 9, 1."[4] Chapter XXIV [15] follows immediately after the fulcral or central major poetic component of the work, its second *canzone* (in chapter XXIII [14]). This *canzone* is the sixteenth of the work's thirty-one poems, and establishes analogically the relationship between Beatrice and Christ, in foreshadowing Beatrice's death. Now with chapter XXIV [15] we have, according to the disposition of the metrical pieces, the start of the second half of the poetic production of the work.

Our chapter opens with the appearance of the god of Amor [Love], who suggests that Dante bless the day that Amor first took control of the poet— that is, the day that Dante was first smitten by Beatrice. That date was May 1—Calendimaggio, associated in Florence with the celebration of the season of spring.[5] After Amor speaks to Dante, the narrative presents two most beautiful ladies approaching Dante, mirroring a sonnet, of Dante's youth, not present in the *Vita nova*. The procession of that poem, "Di donne io vidi una gentile schiera" [I saw a lovely band of ladies][6]—similarly featuring ladies and Amor—occurs on November 1, the feast of All Saints. Calendimaggio and Ognissanti are exactly six months apart, a spacing not uncommonly found with thematically or onomastically related liturgical feasts. This helps explain why Dante receives not a gentle suggestion but a command: "Pensa di benedicere lo dì che io ti presi, però che tu lo dei fare" (XXIV.2 [15.2]) [Be sure to bless the day that I seized you, as you ought]. The use of *benedicere* is linked to religious devotion; it uplifts the memory of love and the birth of spring to a sacred level. Indeed, the command is emphasized: Dante is ordered "che tu lo dei fare" [literally, "for you must do this"]. Just as attending church on a major feast day is an obligation, so too is Dante's need to meditate upon the date of his first sighting of Beatrice.

The two ladies walking toward Dante have names rich in meaning. The first was the beloved of Dante's first friend, Guido Cavalcanti. Her name was Giovanna, but everyone knew her by a sobriquet, Primavera (Spring), recalling Calendimaggio on account of her spring-like appearance. Accompanying Giovanna/Primavera was Beatrice. As they passed Dante, it seemed to him that Amor spoke within his heart and explained the real reason for Primavera's name. In the spirit of the earlier statement in the *Vita nova* on the significance of names—"*Nomina sunt consequentia rerum*" (XIII.4 [6.4])

[Names are the consequences of things]—Amor tells Dante that Primavera's name exists as a sort of prophecy because "prima verrà" (XXIV.4 [15.4]) [she will come first] in the procession that Dante has at that very moment witnessed. But this woman's poetic etymology is overtaken by a biblical one, just as the poetic level of the *Vita nova* as a whole is gradually raised to a transcendent one. Not only does her alternate name declare she will precede another person, but her baptismal name does so as well. The name Giovanna (Joanna) is the feminine form of Giovanni (John), identified by Amor with Giovanni Battista, or John the Baptist.

Amor provides Dante a new name for Beatrice, and in place of an etymology he provides an analogy. This new name is that of the god of Love himself: Amor, "per molta simiglianza che ha meco" (XXIV.5 [15.5]) [because of the great resemblance she bears to me], for Beatrice is so very like him. This name does not, like the names of Giovanna/Primavera, mirror an action or a role; it reflects a greater reality, a theological virtue, encapsulated by the speaker's own name. If one is to take Amor's declaration here at face value, one has only to consult biblical passages such as 1 John 4:16[7] to see that charity, the highest form of love, is to be equated with God; it is difficult for the reader to escape connecting Beatrice with Christ.

Giovanna's given name mirrors her role, but Beatrice's name speaks of her essence and her effects: she is at once a *beata* (blessed) and a *beatrice* (bestower of joy and blessing). Just as the real name of Beatrice's companion comes from the one who cleared the path for Jesus, the name of Dante's beloved expresses the Love that is Christ, who is not named but referred to as "la verace luce" (XXIV.4 [15.4]) [the true light]. In this context, the medieval reader would likely recall the words of John 1:9 in describing Christ as the "lux vera" [true light]. And if the reader did not recall instantly the biblical source, then a liturgical one could not be missed: in the Nicene Creed, which was recited in every Mass, Christ is "lumen de lumine" [light from light]. In this way (and others), Dante aims to demonstrate to readers that his understanding and creation of poetry surpass that of his "primo amico" [first friend], Cavalcanti.[8] This demonstration of superiority occurs not in the sonnet of this chapter but in the explicit declarations and implicit allusions of its prose framework.[9]

Dante makes no effort to disguise the importance of Beatrice's name; indeed, he does the opposite. Although this is not a long chapter, there are no fewer than four occurrences of the name of Dante's beloved: in XXIV.3 [15.3] ("Vidi venire la mirabile Beatrice" [I saw coming the marvelous Beatrice]); XXIV.4 [15.4] ("Prima verrà lo die che Beatrice si mosterrà dopo la imaginazione del suo fedele" [She will come first the day that Beatrice appears, after the imaginings of her faithful one]); XXIV.5 [15.5] ("E chi volesse sottilmente considerare, quella Beatrice chiamerebbe Amore per molta simiglianza che ha meco" [And whoever wants to give the matter subtle consideration would call Beatrice "Love" because of the great resemblance she bears to me]); and XXIV.8 [15.8], in a line of this chapter's sonnet ("Io vidi monna Vanna e monna Bice" [I saw Lady Joan and Lady Bea]). Only one other chapter, XXXI [20], names Beatrice as often as does chapter XXIV [15], but in XXXI [20] two of the occurrences are in its poem, whereas the other two simply quote one of these passages again when the textual division of the poem is proffered.

We can achieve, however, a better idea of the particular weight of the four namings in chapter XXIV [15] with some observations. The name of Dante's beloved occurs twenty-four times in the *Vita nova*.[10] Of these twenty-four namings, the ones occurring in chapter XXIV [15] are, ordinally, the work's eleventh, twelfth, thirteenth, and fourteenth. These form a subgroup of four, on which the whole series of twenty-four occurrences seems to be centered: a first group of ten, then the central four, then a third and final group of ten. The groups of ten occurrences at each extreme that sandwich the central four can be further subdivided, given the symbolic and rhetorical importance of the first appearance in chapter II [1.2–1.11] and the final one in chapter XLII [31]. This creates a first group of ten that can be described as (1 + 9) and a final one that may be described in same manner (9 + 1). The very first sentence after the minuscule prologue famously mentions Beatrice's name (II.1 [1.2]): "A li miei occhi apparve prima la gloriosa donna de la mia mente, la quale fu chiamata da molti 'Beatrice' li quali non sapeano che si chiamare" [The glorious lady of my mind first appeared before my eyes— she whom many called Beatrice without even knowing that was her name]. This foreshadows Amor's parallels of both Giovanna/Primavera and Beatrice/Amor in chapter XXIV [15]. And reminiscent of the end of a prayer, the *Vita nova* concludes with Dante's supplication: "Piaccia a colui che è sire de la cortesia, che la mia anima se ne possa gire a vedere la gloria de la sua donna, cioè di quella benedetta Beatrice, la quale gloriosamente mira ne la faccia di colui *qui est per omnia saecula benedictus*" (XLII.3 [31.3]) [If it be pleasing to him who is the Lord of benevolence and grace, may my soul go to see the glory of its lady—that blessed Beatrice, who gazes in glory into the face of him *Who is blessed forever and ever*]. The end of the work is a hopeful fore-shadowing of the desired eternal aim of the poet: to be with the woman who will enjoy the beatific vision of her likeness, Christ. The *Vita nova* can be viewed, through its possible effects on the reader, like a book of hours, a contemplative guide, or a psalter, beginning and ending *in nomine Beatricis*.

In our chapter's sonnet, describing the two women's procession through the city, the names are given in ways that vary from the prose narrative: "monna Vanna" for Giovanna, and "monna Bice" for Beatrice. The poet may have used this form of his beloved's name because his immediate textual community would have known her (if not personally, then by reputation).[11] With the four uses of the beloved's name in this chapter, we have a lexico-graphical Trinitarian parallel: with the thrice-mentioned "Beatrice," we have also the simple "Bice" known more immediately to her intimates. And this Bice is seen for the last time by her contemporaries here in chapter XXIV [15], where the sonnet presents the name of Dante's beloved for the first time within a poetic composition included in the *Vita nova*. From here onward, her presence is in the memory or the spirit, not in the body; and from here onward, the god of Love disappears completely from the work as well. The soul of Beatrice assumes the god of Love.

In the *Vita nova*, Dante connects and even equates Beatrice with the number nine but also in a more veiled form with the number twenty-four. The Beatrice–twenty-four connection resonates even more loudly in the *Commedia*. In the Earthly Paradise at the summit of *Purgatorio* (29.82–87), while the procession of the Church Triumphant is in progress, Beatrice's imminent arrival is hailed by the twenty-four elders of the Apocalypse, crowned with flowers, marching in pairs and singing a hymn based on one of the biblical salutations of Mary (Luke 1:42). Then, in the Heaven of the Sun in *Paradiso* 10–14, two garlands of twelve luminous souls (for a total of twenty-four) shine with divine wisdom. They are associated with significant groups of twelve and twenty-four in the Bible and in nature: the apostles, the tribes of Israel, the signs of the zodiac, the stars in the crown of the woman in Apocalypse 12:1, the hours of the day, and the elders surrounding the throne of God in the Apocalypse.[12]

Another important element of the Dantean vocabulary has a central role in this chapter. The heart—*cor, core, cuore*—is mentioned eleven times here: XXIV.1 [15.1], XXIV.2 [15.2] (three times), XXIV.3 [15.3], XXIV.4 [15.4], XXIV.6 [15.6], XXIV.7 [15.7], and XXIV.10 [15.10] (three times). This is by far the most concentrated usage of this term in the work as a whole. Apart from chapter XXXVIII [27] (eight appearances, twice in its poem) and XXXI [20] (seven appearances, with all but one in its *canzone*), the greatest number of times *cuore* appears in a chapter is five; almost all the other chapters that include the word do so an average of two times. The term, as used in the *Vita nova*, is probably most memorably used in chapter III [1.12–2.2], when Amor holds Dante's heart aflame and gives it to Beatrice, who with some hesitation eats it. There is no one usage of *cuore* in chapter XXIV [15] that remains in the mind of the reader so strikingly, but unlike the term's usage in chapter III [1.12–2.2], where it is clearly a physical object, here it is rather the deepest core of Dante's being, the seat of his innermost thoughts and emotions. The narrator aims for the reader of chapter XXIV [15] to consider, even to meditate, upon the name of Beatrice and on the seat of consideration, the heart. Perhaps this explains why the only two appearances of *considerare*, meaning "to meditate" or "to ponder," are to be found precisely in this chapter and nowhere else.

Cuore and "Beatrice" reach their quantitative apex together here in a chapter whose number mirrors the number of years lived to this point by both Dante and Beatrice. The poet was to turn twenty-five in late May 1290, while his beloved died very shortly after Dante's silver birthday but before she herself reached that age. Dante was to reach maturity by the time he wrote the *Vita nova* in the early 1290s, but Beatrice would remain forever young. In *Purgatorio* 30.124–26, Beatrice says that she died on the threshold of her second age; in other words, she left this world when she was ending her youth but had not yet entered maturity, which—according to Dante's own division of the ages of life as given in *Convivio* 4.24.2—begins at the age of twenty-five. Beatrice's last physical appearance in the *Vita nova*, at age twenty-four, is witnessed by Dante, also age twenty-four, in a chapter that is well known as the twenty-fourth division of this book—a book containing twenty-four mentions of the name of Dante's beloved.

The *libello*'s series of twenty-four namings begins precisely with a passage (II.1 [1.2]) that states the ages of Dante and Beatrice: when they first met, Dante was nine and Beatrice still in her ninth year. From this first post-prologue sentence onward, the name and person of Beatrice may be associated with specific and general considerations of "age." Initially this association is seen with the number nine. The meaningfulness of the number twenty-four reveals itself only later, albeit through a darker veil, at the time of their last encounter and of her death.

Chapter XXIV [15], in the heart of the *Vita nova*, brings together the name of Dante's beloved, the heart, and meditation. But one other term is often overlooked or confused in the context of this chapter: laughter. There is often a tendency to glide over *ridere* (to laugh) or *riso* (the noun "laugh"), eliding them with *sorridere* (to smile) or *sorriso* (a person's smile). The first of three appearances of *ridere* in the *Vita nova* is in XVIII.3 [10.5], where Dante is among a large group of ladies, some of them chatting with each other, others watching Dante for anything he might say, and a third group laughing among themselves ("che si rideano tra loro"). The context and word choice, given this is a group of ladies and not common people, lead one readily to picture them, not in a raucous cackle but in an enjoyable and even uplifting conversation. The second usage is in our chapter's sonnet, in which Amor orders Dante—"'Or pensa pur di farmi onore'" ["Now think on how to render homage to me"]—and in which the poet while so doing says of the god, "e 'n ciascuna parola sua ridia" (XXIV.7 [15.7]). Commentators have not too much to say with regard to the concept transmitted here by the word *ridia* (or, in some editions that use the Sicilian rhyme, *ridea*),[13] so it is revealing, and more immediate, to see how this term is rendered into another language (in this case, English). In his translation of the *Vita nova*, Andrew Frisardi translates literally these words as follows: "'Now think only of honoring/thanking me'; and he smiled in each of his words."[14] Dino Cervigni and Edward Vasta translate the second of the chapter's two mentions of the term as "and with each word he smiled";[15] Mark Musa, "and each word was a smile";[16] and Barbara Reynolds, "smiling with joy at every word."[17] Each of these translations favors some form of "to smile" here. But very shortly after chapter XXIV [15], the final of the three appearances of *ridere* is to be found (XXV.2 [16.2]). This follows immediately upon the portrayal of chapter XXIV [15]'s god of Love, as part of a short discussion on the qualities of being a human person, and it is interesting to see that of the four aforementioned translations, three of them translate the term as "to laugh." It seems these translators—and by extension, their readers—feel most comfortable in reading the term in Dante's poems and his prose commentaries as "to smile" but permit themselves to use "to laugh" when looking from a greater distance at the elements of humanity in a more clinical view. We should be led by Dante himself, who explains in *Convivio* 3.8.11 that laughter is "una coruscazione della dilettazione dell'anima, cioè uno lume apparente di fuori secondo sta dentro" [a coruscation of the soul's delight, that is, a light appearing externally which corresponds to the state of being within]. He proceeds to say that Beatrice's wondrous laughter was silent: "Ahi mirabile riso della mia donna, di cu'io parlo, che mai non si sentia se non dell'occhio" [Ah, wonderful laughter of my lady, of whom I speak: it never made itself known except through her eyes]. Given the identification between the god of Love and Beatrice in *Vita nova* XXIV [15], nothing stops the reader from accepting that Amor himself could give a command to Dante, not simply with a smile, but while laughing—if not audibly, then at least in this interior manner.

Historical and literary research on medieval laughter has increasingly shown that despite earlier monastic prohibitions or early scholastic condemnations, a shift toward accepting laughter is visible in early writings by and about the early Franciscans.[18] Thomas Aquinas, asking whether a lack of mirth is sinful, answers in the affirmative.[19] Vernacular theologians and mystics were known to have laughed; Julian of Norwich, for example (albeit from a later period: b. c. 1342, d. *post* 1415), laughed in front of Jesus, who did not reprimand her.[20] Indeed, in the case of Meister Eckhart (d. 1327), laughter was the expression of the persons of the Godhead between themselves.[21] Peter Hawkins opines that Dante's use of smiling and laughing may be "his most original and indeed useful contribution to medieval theology."[22] Dante's god of Love and Beatrice herself laughed, even if many readers—like the first publisher of the *Vita nuova* in 1576—may have misread, misrepresented, or misunderstood Dante.

Vita nova XXV–XXVII [16–18]

Literature as Truth

PAOLA NASTI

The section of the *libello* analyzed in these pages includes two chapters, XXV [16] and XXVII [18], that, by actually and metaphorically breaking the narrative flow of the book, have been considered as metaliterary digressions, interruptions, or pauses.[1] Chapters XXV–XXVII [16–18] are in fact central to the definition of the *Vita nova* as a *libello* that reconfigures the traditional understanding of love and love poetry, since they provide the means to understand the revolution that Dante is carrying out in his own writing as well as in the love lyric tradition.[2]

To appreciate how these three chapters contribute to the radical novelty of the *libello*, we must look back and forward to the two momentous chapters that frame them. In chapter XXIV [15], Dante establishes the figural correlation between Cavalcanti's lady, Giovanna, and John the Baptist to hint at the Christological nature of Beatrice, presented as the true light announced in John's Gospel (8:12).[3] In chapter XXVIII [19] Dante will announce Beatrice's death and, more "shockingly," her association with the number of the Trinity.[4] In other words, chapters XXV–XXVII [16–18] develop in the "space" between the two most daring revelations concerning Beatrice's sacredness.[5] Their position in the structure of the *libello* is therefore crucial.

Timing, namely, when something ought to be introduced into the text, is central to chapter XXV [16], a lengthy discussion on the technique of personification and an excursus on its uses in classical authors.[6] Given that the poet has been using the personification of Love for twenty-four chapters, the technical "digression" seems long overdue. Nothing, however, is arbitrary in the *libello*. Dante had already raised concerns about his use of personification in chapter XII [5.8–5.24], which includes the book's most sustained dialogue with the lord of Love (I shall return to the latter's representation).[7] Here the poet had clearly stated his intention to postpone the theoretical discussion to a later stage, giving us a rare insight into how he constructed his work:

> Potrebbe già l'uomo opporre contra me e dicere che non sapesse a cui fosse lo mio parlare in seconda persona, però che la ballata non è altro che queste parole ched io parlo: e però dico che questo dubbio io lo intendo solvere e dichiarare in questo libello ancora in parte più dubbiosa; e allora intenda qui chi qui dubita, o chi qui volesse opporre in questo modo.[8] (XII.17 [5.24])

> [It is true that someone might object, saying he does not know whom my words are addressed to in the second person, since the ballad is none other than the words I speak. And so I say that I still intend to resolve and clarify this ambiguity in an even obscurer section of this little book. And at that point may whoever has such doubts here, or wishes to object in this manner, understand what is said here.]

As chapter XII [5.8–5.24] reveals, chapter XXV [16] is an explicatory digression that Dante had planned to delay, since, until this juncture, he deemed it inappropriate. This is the "parte più dubbiosa" [even obscurer section of this little book] that requires an epistemological pause to reflect on the ways in which we read and understand both texts and reality. Significantly, as in the *Commedia*, the word *dubbio* (doubt) is indicative here of an epistemological hiatus, a cognitive hurdle that requires effort to be properly surmounted. The hurdle that has triggered chapter XXV [16] is, in my view, Dante's declaration in chapter XXIV [15] that Beatrice is the "verace luce" [true Light] that comes after Cavalcanti's Giovanna in a manner that recalls Christ, who came after John the Baptist:

Queste donne andaro presso di me così l'una appresso l'altra, e parve che
Amore mi parlasse nel cuore, e dicesse: "Quella prima è nominata Prima-
vera solo per questa venuta d'oggi; ché io mossi lo imponitore del nome a
chiamarla così Primavera, cioè prima verrà lo die che Beatrice si mosterrà
dopo la imaginazione del suo fedele. E se anche vogli considerare lo primo
nome suo, tanto è quanto dire 'prima verrà,' però che lo suo nome Gio-
vanna è da quello Giovanni lo quale precedette la verace luce, dicendo:
'Ego vox clamantis in deserto: parate viam Domini.'" (XXIV.4 [15.4])

———

[These women passed near me, one after the other, and it seemed that
Love spoke to me in my heart, saying: "That first woman is named Prima-
vera only in honor of today's coming. I moved the one who gave her
that name to call her Primavera, that is, *prima verrà*, she will come first
the day that Beatrice appears, after the imaginings of her faithful one.
And if you also consider her given name, you will see that it is practically
the same as saying *prima verrà*, since her name, Giovanna (or Joanna), is
derived from that John who preceded the true Light, saying, 'I am the
voice of one crying in the wilderness. Make straight the way of the
Lord.'"]

Dante's claim is clear and yet daring: Beatrice is the true likeness of
Christ,[9] and, as Love-the-character declares to the lover in the exegetical
prose, she has such a strong *somiglianza* with Love that she can be identified
with it by those who are able to assess her true nature: "Ed anche mi parve
che mi dicesse, dopo, queste parole: 'E chi volesse sottilmente considerare,
quella Beatrice chiamerebbe Amore, per molta simiglianza che ha meco'"
(XXIV.5 [15.5]) [And it also seemed that he said: "And whoever wants to
give the matter subtle consideration would call Beatrice 'Love' because of
the great resemblance she bears to me"]. The scriptural references in chapter
XXIV [15] are so strong that the reader, called to interpret *sottilmente*, can-
not but acknowledge Love as *caritas*, the divine essence announced by Jesus
in the Gospel of John (4:7–8). Beatrice's likeness ("somiglianza") to *caritas* is
thus revealed as the medium through which Dante learns about love as an
intelligible concept. The epistemological process by which one can know
charity through its species was defined by Aquinas in his *Quodlibet* 8.2.2: a
likeness of charity ("similitudo caritatis") can be perceived by the senses and

the imagination through sensible objects ("species"). From this, the power of the active intellect abstracts the true likeness of the real essence of charity, which allows even those who do not have charity to know what charity really is: a gift of grace uniting human affections to God.

Clearly, by identifying the lady who gives him "salute" [salvation] with Christ and *caritas*, the poet-commentator is transforming the lyric tradition into a discourse on revelation and salvation. In this new discourse there is no room for the personification of Love, a traditional technique belonging to the realm of literary fiction, which Dante has deployed even in this momentous chapter by attributing to Love a human body and behavior (XXIX.2 [15.2].[10] True *caritas*, as Augustine wrote, does not walk or talk, but is known inwardly:

> If you know love, God is love [*caritas*]. . . . So if you love, how do you love? It comes to you, and you know and see it. And it is not seen in a place nor is it sought with the eyes of the body, to love it more intensely. Nor is it heard speaking and when he comes to you it is not heard walking. Have you felt the soles of Love's feet walking in your heart? What is it then? Whose is this thing that is already in you and is not grasped by you? Thus, learn to love God.[11]

In the *Vita nova*, the revelation that love is the true divine essence, which is made manifest to Dante through Beatrice, must therefore coincide, and does indeed coincide, with the disappearance of Love as a personification. Once the powerful lord of Love has been assessed in chapter XXV [16], he does not speak again to Dante-character but disappears from the *libello*.

The decision to include a digression on personification at the very moment in the story when Dante eliminates the obsolete figure of the Ovidian and medieval lord of Love should therefore be seen as an apologetic explanation for the modes of signification that Dante has used up to this point, as well as a signpost of the transition to a new poetics of *caritas*. To alert his readers in this regard, the author provides the epistemological tools that they need to understand the difference between the traditional poetic discourse on love as a passion and his *libello*. From this perspective, it is no accident that chapter XXV [16] is Dante's most sustained technical piece of writing before the philosophical arguments of the *Convivio*.

Commentators have noted how the chapter's prose is structured on the model of syllogistic reasoning. More specifically, the register and style are dictated by Dante's focus on a philosophical consideration of the attribution of a body to an abstract idea or concept like love, namely, personification. The terminology used is technical: *sustanzia* (substance) and *accidente* (accident) are common scholastic terms employed to discuss beings, forms, and matter. Aristotle, "lo Filosofo" (XXV.2 [16.2]) [the Philosopher], is cited to hint at Dante's authority and competence in the subject. On the basis of his brief but effective philosophical analysis, Dante establishes that, in line with Cavalcanti's ideas, love is a "sostanzia intelligente" [intelligent substance] as well as "uno accidente in sustanzia" [accident in a substance], an entity that cannot exist in itself but only as a subject's quality. He then considers what a bodily substance ("sustantia corporale") is according to philosophy so as to explain the human attributes he has given to the personification of Love (love moves, speaks, and smiles) (XXV.1–2 [16.1–16.2]).[12] Considered in the context of the rhetorical and poetic literature of the period, Dante's theoretical reflection on personification is unique and unexpected. This is one of the first times, if not actually the first, in the history of Italian vernacular love poetry that the nature or ontology of love is openly investigated and examined from a philosophical perspective within a broader technical framework. If one accepts the *Vita nova*'s chronological priority, Cavalcanti would reply to the *Vita nova* in general and to this digression in particular with the most sophisticated philosophical *canzone* of the Italian vernacular tradition.[13] At the same time, chapter XXV [16] would place Dante first in the race to claim that poetry and philosophy are inseparable.[14]

By "demonstrating" the philosophical quality of his poetry, the poet also silently establishes his credentials as a learned writer who can share the stage with the great Latin *auctores*. An *auctor*, as Barański clearly notes, was an "'authoritative' author . . . worthy of trust and obedience' (*Conv.* IV, vi, 5)" who could teach essential truths "thanks to the distinction and usefulness of what *he* had written."[15] It is no coincidence, therefore, that after remarking how personification had been used for centuries by ancient "litterati" [lettered poets] and "dicitori d'amore" (XXV.3 [16.3]) [vernacular rhymers], Dante boldly moves to proclaim the equivalence between classical authors and modern vernacular writers (XXV.4 [16.4]). For the first time in his writings, Dante sets his work within a genealogy of literary *auctores* and draws attention to this fact. However, it would be wrong to believe that these philosophical and metaliterary remarks on personification are simply a means to elevate Dante and his art. They are also an essential introduction to the rhetorical definition of prosopopoeia provided by the poet to illuminate his work, its paradigms, and its true meaning.

Like the rest of chapter XXV [16], Dante's approach to matters rhetorical is ambitious and original. Thus his discussion of personification is more extensive and differs from the explanations normally found in the most common medieval manuals of rhetoric, *ars poetriae*, and *ars dictaminis*. Medieval texts normally provided succinct definitions of personification: the influential *Poetria nova* by Geoffrey of Vinsauf, for example, dedicates "no more than a single, scholium-styled line to *conformatio* [the most common Latin term used for prosopopoeia]."[16] Dante, on the other hand, offers a careful description that, focusing on the vocabulary of the ontology of being introduced at the start of the digression, reflects on personification's "degree of truthfulness":[17]

> Dunque, se noi vedemo che li poete hanno parlato a le cose inanimate, sì come se avessero senso e ragione, e fattele parlare insieme; e non solamente cose vere, ma cose non vere, cioè che detto hanno, di cose le quali non sono, che parlano, e detto che molti accidenti parlano, sì come se fossero sustanzie e uomini; degno è lo dicitore per rima di fare lo somigliante, ma non sanza ragione alcuna, ma con ragione la quale poi sia possibile d'aprire per prosa. (XXV.8 [16.8])

> [Therefore, if we see that poets have addressed inanimate things as if they had sense and reason, and also have made them talk—and not only real things but imaginary things as well—that is, they have written that things which do not exist, speak, and that many accidents speak as if they were substances and men, it is right that the vernacular rhymer would do the same, though not without some rational intention, but with a rational intention which then would be possible to open up by means of prose.]

Having brought poetry into the realm of ethics, Dante now looks at rhetoric as a toolkit, or a set of devices that must be assessed not just for their ability to make speech artful but also for their power to manipulate truth and the real.[18]

Yet even this explanation does not seem to suffice. In keeping with the rhetoricians' manner, the poet also adds a series of examples taken from the *auctores* (Virgil, Lucan, Horace, and Ovid) that both showcase his expertise and consolidate his position within the literary tradition. It would appear that none of the examples he provides derive from well-known manuals available at the time. The *sententiae* in chapter XXV [16] are, according to some scholars, unlikely to be the product of Dante's firsthand reading of the classics. It is not impossible, however, that the poet encountered these citations in the context of his training (whether preprofessional or nonprofessional) in the art of verse and prose writing (*ars poetriae* and *ars dictaminis*).[19] The theory and practice of personification, for example, was one of the topics included in the *ars dictaminis* curriculum specifically to train students in letter writing. Although not a fixed feature of the texts used to teach prose composition, examples of prosopopoeia (perhaps in the ancient shape of *progymnasmata*, preliminary rhetorical exercises) were introduced by teachers to illustrate how to write letters impersonating a famous ruler or historical character.[20] Regardless of their "origin," however, and considering that the poets cited are the same masters of the *bello stile* whom Dante-character will meet in Limbo, the examples of personification in chapter XXV [16] provide insights into Dante's engagement with a canon of classical authors studied as models of style and form.[21] In this sense, the last of the examples, a quotation from Ovid's *Remedia amoris*, offers a useful vantage point from which to make some observations on the question. Of all the examples, in keeping with Ovid's medieval reputation as the *magister amoris*, this is the only passage to concentrate specifically on the personification of Love, and therefore on Dante's own practice in the book: "Per Ovidio parla Amore, sì come se fosse persona umana, ne lo principio de lo libro c'ha nome *Libro di Remedio d'Amore*, quivi: *Bella michi, video, bella parantur, ait*. E per questo puote essere manifesto a chi dubita in alcuna parte di questo mio libello" (XXV.9 [16.9]) [Through Ovid, Love speaks as if he were a human being, at the beginning of his book called *The Cure for Love*: "It's war, you declare against me, I see, it's war." And this should clarify things to whoever is in doubt over a certain part of this little book].

There can be little doubt that, in the *Vita nova*, like most love poets of the period, Dante loosely modeled his personification of Love on the young and unpredictable character created by Ovid in the *Amores* and reinterpreted by countless medieval writers. Yet Dante also repeatedly distanced his "lord" from the capricious Ovidian figure by attributing to his figure of Love biblical overtones, as in chapter XII [5.8–5.24], where Love appears dressed in white like the transfigured Christ (Matthew 17:3).[22] Equally, Dante's representation of Love never calls into question the opening declaration of the *libello*: "E avvegna che la sua imagine, la quale continuatamente meco stava, fosse baldanza d'Amore a segnoreggiare me, tuttavia era di sì nobilissima vertù, che nulla volta sofferse ch'Amore mi reggesse sanza 'l fedel consiglio de la ragione in quelle cose là ove cotal consiglio fosse utile a udire" (II.9 [1.10) [And even though her image, which was constantly with me, was the means by which Love ruled me, it was so dignified in its power that it never allowed Love to govern me without the faithful counsel of reason, in those matters where such guidance was helpful]. The claim that love and reason are interdependent, as Dante scholars have often noted, not only is original but polemically distances the poet from the classical conceptualization of love as a passion "divorced from the intellect,"[23] which his friend Guido Cavalcanti inherited and developed. From this perspective, it is not difficult to understand why Dante should cite Ovid's *Remedia amoris* and not the influential *Amores*: the *Remedia*, a work allegedly focused on condemning physical love, was considered morally sound in the Middle Ages. Like all the other examples included in Dante's list, the Ovidian quotation is evidence of Dante's rhetorical training and not of his profound knowledge and approval of the Ovidian representation of love. This is even more likely if we consider that most of the examples offered by the poet (with the exception of that from Lucan) relate to pagan deities (Aeolus, the sons of Dardanus, the Muses), which are dismissed by Dante as mythological fictions (XXV.9 [16.9]).[24]

In sum, the long and sustained digression on prosopopoeia helps Dante elevate his standing as a poet familiar with the literary and rhetorical tradition. In addition, it asserts his role as a thinker who strives to reflect on the relationship between literature and the philosophical categories of truth and reality to establish the ontological and epistemological value of what he writes. The chapter clarifies that up to this point Dante has followed a fictitious mode of writing that he now finds uncomfortable, so much so that he needs to justify it to defend himself from the shame of writing verses with no deeper meaning. As the last paragraph of chapter XXV [16] confirms, rhetorical "coverings" or figures are acceptable in the epistemological universe of the *Vita nova* only if they are a veil covering a greater truth ("verace intendimento"):²⁵ "E acciò che non ne pigli alcuna baldanza persona grossa, dico che né li poete parlavano così sanza ragione, né quelli che rimano deono parlare così non avendo alcuno ragionamento in loro di quello che dicono; però che grande vergogna sarebbe a colui che rimasse cose sotto vesta di figura o di colore rettorico, e poscia, domandato, non sapesse denudare le sue parole da cotale vesta, in guisa che avessero verace intendimento" (XXV.10 [16.10]) [And in order that some coarse person does not get presumptuous about these things, I will add that the ancient poets did not write in this manner without reason, nor should vernacular poets write like this without having some understanding of what they are saying. For it would be shameful for one who wrote poetry dressed up with figures or rhetorical color not to know how to strip his words of such dress, upon being asked to do so, showing their true sense].

The language of this closing passage adds a further dimension to Dante's idea of prosopopoeia: the use of expressions such as "clothing and undressing the truth" point to the medieval concept of *integumentum*, "a kind of teaching which wraps up the true meaning inside a fictitious narrative (*fabulosa narratio*), and so it is also called 'a veil' (*involucrum*)."²⁶ As an interpretive tool, *integumentum* was particularly useful to appropriate classical literary fictions so that they would be accepted by Christian readers as valuable if they could be shown to reveal higher moral and spiritual truths. By employing the technical terms usually associated with this exegetical category, the last section of chapter XXV [16] would seem to shift attention from the classical rhetorical tradition to the Christian way of reading texts. Dante appears to move almost seamlessly from personification to "veil" and from fiction to true meaning in order to call for a moralizing reading of the fictional elements that he has so far used in the *libello*, thereby distancing himself from the practice of poetry seen as literary imitation and aristocratic divertissement.

Having considered different approaches to personification and exposed its limitations, Dante abandons it in the name of a poetics that focuses not on fictitious beings but on Beatrice as the source of true *caritas*. The digression, as I said at the start, marks a point of fracture and change. As such, chapter XXV [16] also provides clues regarding another of its structural concerns: its implied readers. There is no doubt that this section speaks to poets such as Guido Cavalcanti, the main addressees and readers of the *libello*, to underscore Dante's departure from the Romance tradition of love poetry. Yet the digression seems rather long and detailed to be just aimed at fellow poets. Poets of the standing of Cavalcanti had access to the same kind of knowledge about theories of poetry and prosopopoeia that Dante showcases here. In fact, this strategic discourse on poetry, truth, and authority has a precise didactic aim: the poet seems to be instructing readers who have no access to precise knowledge on rhetoric, philosophy, and exegesis. The *Vita nova* is also a book about poetry, but not an exclusively elitist poetry. It also speaks to the less educated in order to teach a "verace intedimento." The truth the poet wishes to teach to a universal public concerns the order (*ordo amoris*) to follow in experiencing and understanding love, from its earthly manifestations to the revelation of its spiritual and divine nature. As in the Gospels and in the sermons of preachers, this truth is taught through parables and examples drawn from Dante's own progressive discovery of Beatrice as a miracle, a manifestation of the divine, a *similitudo caritatis*.[27]

Once fiction is abandoned in chapter XXV [16], in chapter XXVI [17] the poet celebrates the attributes and the qualities that, as announced in chapter XXIV [15], make of Beatrice the very likeness of love and reveal her presence in the world as a true theophany. Even though the language and images of the two sonnets included in the chapter, "Tanto gentile e tanto onesta pare" [So open and so self-possessed appears] and "Vede perfettamente" [He sees completely], are reminiscent of Calvalcanti's poetry, the narrative prose, as Grimaldi demonstrates in his chapter, moves away from Guido's agnosticism to allow the reader to appreciate Beatrice's Christological traits as a source of salvation. Like Christ, Beatrice attracts crowds to witness her presence (Mark 3:8); her effects are greeted by people with the same words used to celebrate God's miracles (Psalm 71:18); she has learned from Christ to be "gentle and humble in heart" (Matthew 11 29), so much so that, in her presence, as in Christ's, people experience sweetness (Matthew 11:30) and find virtue. Of course, Beatrice is not Christ but a woman who perfectly imitates Christ in his perfection. In this sense, she resembles the perfection of the Virgin Mary. Mary is in fact the exemplary "figure" looming behind Beatrice's actions, faith, beauty, and above all humility. Yet of all the attributes that Dante perceives in Beatrice, one is arguably the most Marian: "honesta." The adjective belongs to the semantic field of *decorum* that is associated with women's honor in Christian culture. St. Paul, in particular, had used the term *honest* to describe women's behavior in conjugal relationships. The attribute of "honesty" in this sense is also ascribed to the Virgin Mary. As Jacobus de Voragine notes in his *Liber Mariale*, her "honesty" is evident above all in her very few and controlled "relationships" with honest people:

> Ista dilectio pulchra in quatuor consistit: in diligendo Deum, in Deo diligendo et habendo Dei sapientiam, in amando et seruando precepta et consilia Dei, quarto consistit in puritate mentis et corporis et honestate conuersationis. . . . Tertio eius conuersatio fuit ualde honesta, quia semper cum honestis personis fuit conuersata, scilicet aut cum filio, aut cum angelo, aut cum cetu Apostolico, aut cum Ioseph sponso suo, aut cum Ioanne sibi in custodem deputato.[28]

> [This beautiful love is made up of four things: the love of God, in loving God and having his wisdom, in loving and observing his precepts and counsel, the fourth depends on physical and mental integrity as well as on honest behavior. . . . Third, her way of life was that of a very good woman, because she always dealt with honest people, with her son, or with the angel, or with the congregation of the apostles, or with Joseph, her spouse, and, with John, who was appointed to be her keeper.]

Given that Beatrice is described in her act of greeting or interacting with those who meet her, the honesty of her behavior is related to how she is seen behaving. Like Mary's, Beatrice's interactions with others are modest; unlike other ladies in the *libello*, she is never presented as speaking directly. In other words, Beatrice is not silent but her speech is portrayed as reserved, her communications with others are "honest" because they are pure and virtuous, and as such they are expressions of her perfect adherence to the divine charity that she testifies and infuses through her presence.

Presence, as David Lummus explains in his chapter, is the thematic core of chapters XXVI [17] and XXVII [18]. However, while the former focuses on the effects of Beatrice's presence on others, the latter concentrates on Dante's metamorphoses in the presence of love—"Questo m'avvene ovunque ella mi vede" (XXVII.5 [18.5]) [Each time she sees me this takes place anew]—when Beatrice looks at him and transforms him into living proof of her miraculous operations. The poetics of presence is marked by the

recurrent use of words belonging to the semantic field of vision and revela-
tion (*pare*, appears; *occhi*, eyes; *guardare*, to look; *mostrare*, to appear; *mirare*,
to gaze; *vedere*, to see; *vista*, sight), as well as to that of testimony and belief
(*provare*, to try; *credere*, to believe). In other words, Dante insists on seeing
and witnessing Beatrice just as the presence of the apostles emphasizes the
experience of seeing Christ as a source of revelatory grace, truth, and mira-
cles. Similarly, the effects of Beatrice's presence on those who are touched by
it are, much like Christ's impact on his followers, sweetness and spiritual
well-being.

In "Sì lungiamente m'ha tenuto Amore" [Since Love took hold of me it's
been so long], the identification between love and *caritas* and the revelation
of Beatrice's presence as the source of spiritual sweetness allow Dante to
transform further the traditional representation of the service and sickness
of love. The lover feels faint, his "viso . . . smore" (line 8) [his face becomes
pale], and his soul is "frale" (line 7) [fragile], yet these expressions of pain,[29]
generally associated with the Cavalcantian creed of love as death, have now
been resemanticized. Causing sweetness, the malady affecting Dante comes
from the salvific wounds of *caritas*. The paradox of the healing power of the
pain caused by love was central to the medieval understanding of the rela-
tionship between God and humanity: Christ himself had died on the cross
for the love of humanity. In medieval religious and spiritual literature, the
miraculous wounds of *caritas* were famously celebrated through references to
the Song of Songs, the Old Testament poem about earthly love between a
bride and her bridegroom that was (and still is) read as a way to demonstrate
and understand divine love.[30] In this erotic and yet sacred poem, the pain of
the bride (seen as an allegory of the soul) longing for God's love is described
as a wound and as a malady through memorable exclamations. Having met
the divine groom, the soul announces that she is wounded by *caritas* ("vul-
nerate caritatis ego sum") and turned pale by her ardent love ("amore lan-
gueo"),[31] and that her soul is melted by love's sweet fire: "Anima mea lique-
facta est" (5:6). Nonetheless, as Gregory the Great commented, as did other
exegetes of these verses, this sickness was the necessary "violence" that brings
the soul back to God: "[Corda nostra] vulneratur ut sanentur, quia amoris
sui spiculis mentes Deus insensibiles percutit, moxque has sensibiles per ar-
dorem caritatis reddit. Vnde hic sponsa dicit: Vulnerata caritate ego sum"
[[Our hearts] are wounded that they may be healed because God strikes un-

feeling minds with the darts of love for him and soon makes them full of feeling through the burning heat of charity. Hence here the Bride says: I have been wounded by love].[32]

Yet as medieval exegetes of the Song of Songs noted, a lover's joy cannot be anchored to bodily presence. The sudden fleeing of the divine groom in the last verses of the epithalamium was seen as evidence of the fact that spiritual love is not to be found in the earthly joy of each other's presence.[33] Likewise, in the *Vita nova*, the poet understands that the presence of Beatrice's *caritas*, intended as a divine gift, is to be sought, not in the circumscriptive mode of bodily appearances, but in the repletive (omnipresent) mode of spiritual beings that fill a place without being contained in any place.[34] As the Gospel of John recounts, Christ himself had constantly reminded his followers of the temporary nature of his presence among them: God's love exists outside the boundaries and limitations of body, time, and space (John 16:16). Christ's departure from earth, the theologians argued, was necessary to stimulate the ascending movement of the faithful soul from the material and transient manifestations of its love to the spiritual and unchanging divine essence of *caritas*. Like the Savior, at the height of her earthly glory, Beatrice must die for her salvific mission to continue.[35]

Having already eliminated the ghost of Love, Dante must now eliminate the last impediment to his education in the order of *caritas*: Beatrice's body. So far Dante-character has learned to renounce any earthly contact with Beatrice, even a simple greeting; now he must relinquish the sweetness of her presence. The *canzone* "Sì lungiamente" is interrupted as abruptly as Beatrice's life because the poetics of earthly presence must slowly give way to the understanding that *caritas* is a gift that transcends the material and the mutable.

Vita nova XXV [16]

REBECCA BOWEN

As a pause at the level of narration, the digressive nature of *Vita nova* chapter XXV [16] opens out as a space for critical reflection. Formally, the chapter resembles the prose *divisioni* that accompany most of the poems in the text. Unlike those earlier authorial interventions, however, the critical discourse of chapter XXV [16] is not anchored to a specific poem. As such, it can float more freely to the surface of the *libello*, its focus on poetic figures and literary history and culmination in a discussion of textual interpretation presenting tantalizingly appropriate paradigms for analyzing broader aspects of the literary/poetic enterprise of the *Vita nova*.[1]

The notion that this chapter contains potentially self-referential, metapoetic discourse is suggested by the opening phrases, which offer an invitation to the reader to engage in the critical practice of "doubting." The first words—"Potrebbe qui dubitare persona degna di dichiararle onne dubitazione" (XXV.1 [16.1]) [Any person worthy of declaring their doubts could raise them here][2]—recall the technical discussion of personification deferred at the end of chapter XII [5.8–5.24]: "Potrebbe già l'uomo opporre contra me e dicere che non sapesse a cui fosse lo mio parlare in seconda persona . . . e però dico che questo dubbio io lo intendo solvere e dichiarare in questo libello ancora in parte più dubbiosa" (XII.17 [5.24]) [Someone could already oppose me saying that it is not clear who I am addressing in the second person . . . and so I say that I intend to resolve and clarify this doubt in an even more doubtful part of this little book]. Chapter XXV [16] is the "parte più dubbiosa," now is the time to doubt and discuss: "qui dubitare" (XXV.1 [16.1]).

That the promised discussion of personification centers on the figure of Amore is no accident. As both a character in the text and the name of the abstract concept that summarizes two of the *libello*'s central, if at times antagonistic, themes (eroticism and spirituality), the word/figure *a/Amore* is a privileged and slippery signifier in Dante's little book. This volatility is the target of the strong truth claims that follow the opening section of chapter XXV [16]. Focusing the readers' doubts on the fictionality of his own literary creation—"che io dico d'Amore come se fosse una cosa per sé" (XXV.1 [16.1]) [that I speak of Love as if it were a thing in and of itself]—Dante forces the poles of truth and fiction to collide—"la quale cosa, secondo la veritate, è falsa" (XXV.1 [16.1]) [which is, according to the truth, false]—as his characterization of Love is found wanting in comparison to a field of philosophical veracity established with specific reference to Aristotle, "secondo lo Filosofo" (XXV.2 [16.2]). Whether or not we read a reference to Cavalcanti's programmatic *canzone* "Donna me prega" [A lady asks me] in the mention of Love's "accidental substantiality," the discussion of "lo Filosofo" and his tenets for personhood sets a clear marker for "la veritate," turning Love's two roles in the text—personification ("sustanzia corporale") and abstract noun ("sustanzia intelligente") (XXV.1 [16.1])—into the keystones in a debate between fiction and truth.[3]

To borrow a term from Teodolinda Barolini, we might say that the personified figure of Amore becomes, at this point, a "lightning rod" for the veracity of the discourse of love in the *Vita nova* more broadly.[4] Dante's dismissal of Love's personified body is undoubtedly a way of distancing the figuration of Amore in the *libello* from the courtly/romance tradition that generated and popularized the personification of love as a powerful young lord—from which the presentations of Love in chapters III [1.12–1.18], IX [4], and XII [5.8–5.24] clearly descend. Critics in the past have been quick to identify a moral intent to this distancing of love from its literary lineage, reading the move away from embodiment as a dismissal of the more earthly and erotic elements bound up in the secular traditions in which personifications of Love were particularly prevalent.[5] While the rejection of Love's personified form clearly bolsters the truth claims of Dante's amorous narrative, chapter XXV [16] does not contain a direct discourse on the moral nature of the love under discussion, nor does it offer to realign *amore* with a more spiritualized notion of Christian *caritas*—a noun that appears only once in the *libello*, where its symbolic importance is overshadowed by that of the word *amore*.[6] Rather than necessitating the rejection of one meaning (erotic love) in favor of another (Christian love), removing the figural constraint of love's physical body (the aspect of its presentation that most directly connects it to fictional discourse) simply enables *amore* in the abstract to range more freely at a deeper semantic level.

By defracting critical attention onto the (courtly) personification of Amore through this negotiation between truth and fiction, Dante does not necessarily construct and uphold a binary distinction between courtly/erotic and Christianized love, but creates the very conditions for diffusing the more radical implications of their co-presence, allowing the noun *amore* to move between the poles of multiple meanings unimpeded by the connotations of any one fixed physical form as it slides on a spectrum from spiritual to secular concerns.[7] This is a particularly relevant development given the stunning collision of biblical and courtly references witnessed in the preceding chapter, where Dante's beloved Beatrice is presented as a figure for Christ, whose name is love, in the words of the (now-discredited) courtly personification whose name is also Amore.

That such deep semantic and figural negotiation is at play in chapter XXV [16] is upheld by the fact that a dispensing with the body of Love in favor of a focus on the hermeneutical complexities of the word *amore* is embedded in the ensuing discussion. Although the opening section promises a debate on love's personified body, the body of chapter XXV [16] moves from Dante's Amore to a *corpora* of other poetic texts. Constructing a clever genealogy for the vernacular tradition that claims Latinate *auctoritas* for lyric poets who write well, and who write about love, Dante insists that vernacular love poetry can be analyzed according to the hermeneutical standards applied to Latin *auctores*: "Se noi vedemo che li poete hanno parlato a le cose inanimate . . . degno è lo dicitore per rima di fare lo somigliante, ma non sanza ragione alcuna, ma con ragione la quale poi sia possibile d'aprire per prosa" (XXV.8 [16.8]) [If we see that the Latin poets have talked to inanimate things . . . the vernacular poet is allowed to do the same, but not without a good reason, but with a reason that could then be laid out in prose]. As critics have noted, the *ragione* behind the personification under discussion in this chapter is not entirely forthcoming, since, as the above phrase demonstrates, Dante has shifted his focus from love to "alcuna figura o colore rettorico" (XXV.7 [16.7]) [any figure or rhetorical coloring]. Rather than an explanation for the specific case of Love, the *prosa* in this chapter seems to present a lesson in interpreting poetic figures more generally.

This despecification from Love to poetry continues as the argument builds and Dante cites examples of personification from the works of four classical poets: Virgil, Lucan, Horace, and Ovid. As Zygmunt Barański in particular has shown, these classical quotations are carefully and inventively chosen to display Dante's firsthand knowledge of classical literature and to negotiate the position of his own vernacular writing.[8] Love, once again, is missing from all but one of them; only the Ovidian quotation contains a personification of *amor*. The line that Dante chooses comes from the opening of the *Remedia amoris*, the first words spoken by Love in reaction to the title of the book: "'Bella michi, video, bella parantur,' ait" (XXV.9 [16.9]) ["Wars I see, you are readying wars against me," he says]. As critics have reasoned, the choice of Ovid's *Remedia* can be read as a rejection of carnal or erotic love on the part of Dante, quoting from Ovid's manual on healing lovers.[9] Indeed, the absence of Cupid from the classical examples more broadly might even be seen as a tactic for avoiding the introduction of any potentially pagan (and therefore spiritually dubious) resonances to Dante's discussion of love. But the specific choice of the Ovidian quote might also reference a different task at hand in this chapter, the interrogation of, and eventual dispensation with, Love's personified form.

The notion that what is under attack in this passage is the personified body of love, rather than its specifically erotic connotations, is sustained at a linguistic level as the focus of Dante's argument comes to rest on voices and words rather than on Love's body. This begins with the mention of the "*dicitori* d'amore," is sustained in the section on vernacular verse, "trovato per *dire* d'amore" (XXV.6 [16.6]) [created to *speak* of love], and comes to bear in the classical examples, where the verbs *parlare* and *dire* proliferate and the noun *corpo* is nowhere to be seen. Our attention is drawn to the fact that "li poete hanno *parlato* a le cose inanimate . . . e fattele *parlare* insieme . . . che *detto* hanno, di cose le quali non sono, che *parlano*, e *detto* che molti accidenti *parlano*, sì come se fossero sustanzie e uomini" (XXV.9 [16.9]) [poets have *spoken* to inanimate things . . . and had them *speak* to each other . . . they have *said*, that things which do not exist *speak*, and they have *said* that many abstracts *speak*, as if they were substances and humans]. It is the speech acts of the poets and their poetic creations that concretize the personifications, not their bodily presence. Such focus on speech was an important facet in the definition of personification in rhetorical handbooks from as early as the classical *Rhetorica ad Herennium* and, in particular, Quintilian's *Institutio oratoria*.[10] The focus on voice in chapter XXV [16] of the *Vita nova* has a particularly potent emphasis, however, as it fits into the wider avoidance of the personified body already identified in the shifting topics of Dante's argument from love's *corpo* to the *corpora* of poetic tradition.

The avoidance of specifically figural traditions is also evident in the evocation of contemporary poets with which the chapter closes: "Grande vergogna sarebbe a colui che rimasse cose sotto vesta di figura, e poscia domandato non sapesse denudare le sue parole da cotale vesta, in guisa che avessero verace intendimento. E questo mio primo amico e io ne sapemo bene di quelli che così rimano stoltamente" (XXV.10 [16.10]) [Great shame it would be to anyone who composed things under the cover of a figure and, when asked, did not know how to strip their words of that garment, so that the truth of them might be properly understood. And this my first friend and I know well about those who write such stolid rhymes]. One "stolid rhymer" who could be under fire here is Guittone d'Arezzo. Several critics have identified Guittone as an antagonistic presence in this chapter, partly due to the fact that Dante's "first friend," Guido Cavalcanti, wrote a sonnet specifically castigating Guittone's ability to construct successful poetic figures, and partly due to Dante's earlier injunction against writing "sopra altra matera che amorosa" (XXV.6 [16.6]) [on any other matter than love], as Guittone wrote many poems on other topics.[11] Indeed, Guittone spent the second half of his poetic career castigating the lyric tradition as a definitive route to sin, a project that Tristan Kay has shown to be in direct opposition to the syncretic approach to courtly and divine resonances displayed by Dante in the *Vita nova* and elsewhere.[12]

During this second poetic phase, Guittone composed the *Trattatto d'Amore*, a *corona* of sonnets that work in the tradition of the moralizing mythographies to deconstruct a personification of Love as a demon and to condemn Amor as a presentation of carnal sin.[13] The *Trattato* is heavily focused on a figural representation of Love, the sonnets insist on the figural reality of the personification they discuss, and their pictorial focus is emphasized through references to a miniature that should have been painted alongside the poems.[14] The first sonnet opens with an invocation to look at the picture: "caro amico, guarda la figura / 'n esta pintura del carnale amore" (1.1–1.2) [dear friend, look at the figure in this painting of carnal love].[15]

Where Dante eschews closure in his presentation of Love, focusing on its voice, its role as a "figura rettorica" and complex figure of speech, Guittone focuses solely on Love's appearance, as the first line of his *Trattato* underlines: "guarda la figura / 'n esta pintura" [look at the figure in this painting]. When placed in relation to this Guittonian work, Dante's parting attack on those poets who create personifications "sotto vesta di figura" seems to focus its crosshairs on that "stolto rimatore" whose discussion of love personified centered on its "figura," bringing its "colore rettorico" to life as a "pintura" of a very specific type of love: "carnale amore."

By calling into question the use of personification as a stand-alone device, I believe that Dante encourages the reader to reject the specificity implied in most uses of personification, not only in the figuration of Love in the moralizing traditions, but also in the courtly/lyric literature to which the presentation of Amore in the first half of the *libello* is clearly indebted. Denuded of its figural dress and stripped of a personified body, Dante's Amore becomes a flexible abstract noun. Clothed in nothing more than the letters of its name, love is able to navigate between multiple meanings and cultural agendas, rather than being stuck in the dead letter of a single painted image. This lack of corporeality and focus on flexibility is reflected in the sustained discussion of poetry and interpretation—"quelli che rimano deono parlare [. . . con] ragionamento in loro di quello che dicono" (XXV.10 [16.10]) [poets must write [with] a reasoned understanding of what they are writing] and in the absence of Love's body from the main digression of chapter XXV [16]. It is also suggested in the language of dressing and undressing employed in the final lines, a trope commonly used in medieval discourse to describe processes of rhetorical embellishment and textual exegesis.[16]

The very words with which Dante "denudes" his presentation of love thus endorse the importance of careful reading and subtle interpretation when approaching textual figures. Rather than a simple indication that the "courtly" aspects of Love will be set aside for the remainder of the text, although Amore does not appear again in the prose of the *libello*, the lack of a clearly stated "ragionamento" to this effect means that the meaning behind Dante's presentation of love is never really concluded. The lesson in interpretation given by this chapter, and its focus on the hermeneutical complexities of poetic representation, provide a suggestion that the meaning of *amore* is to be gained, not from the finality of a single interpretation, but from the very exegetical processes through which many interpretations might be formed. Lacking the sure anchorage of a specific *figura*, Dante's *amore* is left open to many traditions, capable of representing many figures—from the lordly *Amor* of courtly literature, to the Christian God of Love, via likeness to the beloved (Christ-like) Beatrice. Read in this way, chapter XXV [16] and its digression on poetry, personification, and the truth of love present, not a judgment on the courtly figure of Amore, but a lesson in reading, a blueprint, perhaps, for decoding the dizzying signifying potential that will be awarded to that same noun in Dante's later works.

Vita nova XXVI [17]

MARCO GRIMALDI

Chapter XXVI [17] is very much the climax of the book. After three sonnets centered on the representation of love's effects on the lover—"Con l'altre donne mia vista gabbate" (XIV.11–12 [7.11–7.12]) [With other women you mock my distress], "Ciò che m'incontra ne la mente more" (XV.4–6 [8.4–8.6]) [And when I go to get a glimpse of you], and "Spesse fiate vegnonmi a la mente" (XVI.7–10 [9.7–9.10]) [Over and over in my mind preside]—in chapters XVII [10.1–2] and XVIII [10.3–10.11] Dante explains the rationale behind his decision to "prendere per matera" for his poetry "sempre mai quello che fosse loda di questa gentilissima" (XVIII 9 [10.11]) [to take as the subject matter from then on what would be praise for this most gracious of women].[1] In chapter XIX [10.12–10.33], therefore, he introduces his first *canzone* entirely dedicated to praising Beatrice, "Donne ch'avete intelletto d'amore" [Ladies who have understanding of love]. The subsequent progression toward praise poetry is not linear, however. Rather, it is interspersed with a theoretical sonnet on the nature of love—"Amore e 'l cor gentil sono una cosa" (XX.3–5 [11.3–11.5]) [Love and the open heart are always one]—and, above all, compositions on the death of Beatrice's father: "Voi che portate la sembianza umile" [You whose expressions are so meek and low] and "Sè tu colui c'hai trattato sovente" [Are you that man who's often liked to write] (XXII.9–10 and 13–16 [13.9–13.10 and 13–16]). It is also marked by the *canzone*

235

"Donna pietosa e di novella etate" (XXIII.17–28 [14.17–14.28]) [A woman green in years, compassionate], which stages presentiments of the death of the *gentilissima*. In this way, praise and death, to which he has already referred in "Donne ch'avete," are increasingly intertwined in the narrative of the *Vita nova*. The sonnet "Io mi senti' svegliar" (XXIV.7–9 [15.7–15.9]) [I felt, awakening in my heart one day] is also, at bottom, a prophecy of the death of Beatrice: one that the prose invites to interpret allegorically according to the complex network of correspondences between Giovanna and Beatrice, and between John the Baptist and Christ (as well as between Guido and Dante). After the theoretical chapter (XXV [16]), in which Dante demonstrates the legitimacy of using, in vernacular poetry, a personified form of Love and, more generally, allegorical writing—"sotto veste di figura o di colore rettorico" (XXV.10 [16.10]) [dressed up with figures or rhetorical color]—and interpretation—"il *saper* denudare le *proprie* parole da cotale vesta" (XXV.10 [16.10]) [to know how to strip his words of such dress])—Dante proposes, in chapter XXVI [17], to "ripigliare lo stilo" (4) [resume the style] of praising Beatrice. It is the climax of the story in the sense that beyond the sonnets "Tanto gentile e tanto onesta pare" [So open and so self-possessed appears] and "Vede perfettamente onne salute" [To see my lady among other women] (XXVI.5–7 and 10–13 [17.5–17.7 and 10–13]), the praise of a mortal woman is no longer possible. Subsequently, there will be only the *canzone* that is interrupted by news of the death of the *gentilissima*—"Sì lungiamente m'ha tenuto Amore" (XXVII.3–5 [18.3–18.5]) [Since Love took hold of me it's been so long]— with which the first part of the book, treating of Beatrice in life, concludes.

In the prose, Dante clearly describes the events that precede the composition of two sonnets. The "gentilissima" Beatrice "venne in tanta grazia de le genti" [the most gracious of women came to be much admired and sought after by people],[2] and as she passed by, all who were near rushed irresistibly to see her, despite not having the ability to "rispondere al suo saluto" (XXVI.1 [17.1]) [respond to her greeting]. They even compared her to the angels, considering her to be a divine miracle (2). Nobody, however, could express the "dolcezza onesta e soave" (3) [pure and gentle sweetness] that they felt on seeing her, and nobody was able to suppress their "sospirare" (3) [having to sigh at once]. Nor was it only Beatrice who was "onorata e laudata" (8) [honored and praised]: by means of her, many other women came to be praised as well (8–9). Faced with such a marvel, the poet thus decided once again to take up "lo stilo de la sua loda" (4) [the style I had praised her with], which had been inaugurated by "Donne ch'avete," and he wrote the sonnets "Tanto gentile" and "Vede perfettamente." The first of these is dedicated to praising Beatrice, in order that everyone, and not only those who have been able to admire her in person, may know of the "mirabili ed eccellenti operazioni" (4) [the wondrous and excellent effects she brought about]. The second concerns the women who "per lei erano onorate e laudate" (8) [were honored and praised on her account]. To all intents and purposes, then, these two sonnets form a diptych.

Let us consider the first part of this diptych. The sonnet "Tanto gentile" is composed entirely of motifs, images, and structures that are widespread in the medieval tradition, and particularly in the Italian poetry of the second half of the thirteenth century. Dante also deploys these same elements elsewhere, for instance in "Donne ch'avete," "Negli occhi porta," "Vede perfettamente," and then, to different effect, in "Amor, che ne la mente mi ragiona" [Love, that speaks to me within my mind].[3] "Tanto gentile," perhaps Dante's best-known sonnet, is a good exemplar of the ways in which aesthetic canons are transformed, and of how a poem (which is not absolutely original on the level of content) became emblematic of an entire poetic era. As regards the choice of themes, and the overall conception of love, Dante is still very much in keeping with courtly tradition when he writes "Tanto gentile." The sonnet's most important themes are already articulated, for example, in Andreas Capellanus's *De amore*, which draws together themes and motifs that were widespread in medieval Latin literature and romances and promotes their use in medieval literary spaces.[4] In both the treatise and the sonnet, for instance, love has an ennobling effect and inspires humility in those who are proud:[5] "Effectus autem amoris hic est, quia verus amator nulla posset avaritia offuscari; amor horridum et incultum omni facit formositate pollere, infimos natu etiam morum novit nobilitate ditare, superbos quoque solet humilitate beare; obsequia cunctis amorosus multa consuevit decenter parare. O, quam mira res est amor, qui tantis facit hominem fulgere virtutibus, tantisque docet quemlibet bonis moribus abundare!" (1.4.1) [The effect of love is that no greed can cheapen the true lover. Love makes the hirsute barbarian as handsome as can be: it can even enrich the lowest-born with nobility of manners: usually it even endows with humility the arrogant. A person in love grows to the practice of performing numerous services becomingly to all.

What a remarkable thing is love, for it invests a man with such shining virtues, and there is no-one whom it does not instruct to have these great and good habits in plenty!].[6]

In "Tanto gentile," Dante gives form and substance to this idea of love, and in order to achieve this, he could draw on numerous eminent models.[7] In this regard, first among his immediate predecessors was Guido Guinizzelli, who in "Io voglio del ver la mia donna laudare" (5) [I wish to praise my lady][8] stages a scene similar to that recounted in the *Vita nova*.[9] Here, in fact, we find the same primary motifs as in "Tanto gentile": (i) the praise of the beloved woman, which is in the incipit of Guinizzelli's poem, while in "Tanto gentile" she is praised in line 5 by the "genti," as mentioned in the prose; (ii) the passing through the street ("Io voglio," line 9: "Passa per via adorna" [The beautiful woman passes along the road]), which is likely alluded to in line 2 of "Tanto gentile" but which is explicitly referred to in the opening prose paragraph; (iii) the capacity to humble the arrogant behavior of those whom the lady meets in the street when she greets them, thanks to her "inner nobility": "Io voglio," lines 9–10: "e sí gentile / ch'abassa orgoglio a cui dona salute" [so gracious / that pride is quelled in whomsoever she greets], a motif that reappears in lines 3–4 of "Tanto gentile"; (iv) the "conversion of the faithful," a theme that Guinizzelli emphasizes when he affirms that the lady is able to make a man "de nostra fé se non la crede" (line 11) [of our faith, even if he does not believe it], the ability to convert a nonbeliever to Christianity. However, there are also substantial differences between Guido and Dante. Indeed, Guinizzelli lists in his quatrains a series of natural similes by means of which he means to reestablish the idea of the beloved's beauty, using a form typical of medieval Latin praise poems and romances. Only in his tercets does Guido focus on elements that connect his poem to "Tanto gentile."

The structure of Dante's sonnet is also very similar to that of Guido Cavalcanti's "Chi è questa che vèn":

> Chi è questa che vèn, ch'ogn'om la mira,
> che fa tremar di chiaritate l'âre
> e mena seco Amor, sí che parlare
> null'omo pote, ma ciascun sospira?
> O Deo, che sembra quando li occhi gira!

dical'Amor, ch'i' nol savría contare:
cotanto d'umiltà donna mi pare,
ch'ogn'altra ver' di lei i' la chiam'ira.
Non si poria contar la sua piagenza,
ch'a le' s'inchin' ogni gentil vertute,
e la beltate per sua dea la mostra.
Non fu sí alta già la mente nostra
e non si pose 'n noi tanta salute,
che propriamente n'aviàn canoscenza.[10]

———————

[Who comes this way, that all men stand and gaze, / Who gives a trembling brightness to the air, / And leads Love with her so that no one there / Can speak a word, but all must melt in sighs? / O god, the radiance of those glancing eyes, / Beyond what I can say, let Love declare: / All other women seem but fretful care / Before this lady's modest gracious ways. / There is no tongue that can describe her grace, Before her all the noble virtues bend, / Beauty's divinity made manifest. But we were never granted such great bliss, / Nor was our mind so raised as to pretend / To knowledge of her as she truly is.][11]

Guido's opening recalls the incipits of several verses from the Song of Songs: "Quae est ista quae progreditur quasi aurora consurgens pulchra ut luna electa ut sol terribilis ut acies ordinata" (6:9) [Who is she that looketh forth as the morning, fair as the moon, clear as the sun, and terrible as an army with banners] and "quae est ista quae ascendit de deserto" (8:5) [Who is this that cometh up from the wilderness]. The redeployment of scriptural stylemes and expressions was common in secular lyrics, and the Song of Songs in particular was frequently used in romance literature as a repertoire of imagery and expressions to use in love poetry.[12] The opposite was also possible: texts whose content was religious, but that were composed using forms and stylemes characteristic of courtly poetry. The French *trouveurs*, for instance, often used opening lines from secular poems in their religious lyrics.[13] In the same way, Dante's poetry and that of the *stilnovisti* are run through with motifs, images, and vocabulary from sacred texts. To name just one example, in his description of Beatrice's movement—"Ella si va, sentendosi laudare" (line 5) [She senses all the praising of her worth, and passes by]—Dante appears to alluding to Christ, who, in Acts 10:38, "pertransiit benefaciendo" [went about doing good].[14]

Furthermore, all of the principal motifs of "Tanto gentile" appear in the first quatrain of "Chi è questa che vèn": trembling (a typical Cavalcantian verb), the inability to speak, and, above all, the need to sigh, which will of course be a sigh of love.[15] In the lines that follow we once again find the exaltation of the power of the lady's gaze, the topos of the inexpressibility of the beloved's qualities, and the emphasis given to her modesty. In line 11 it is beauty itself (perhaps to be understood as a personification) that recognizes the lady as a goddess. Even the image of "Tanto gentile"'s final tercet (lines 12–14) has a parallel in Cavalcanti. If *labbia* is understood as "appearance,"[16] it is quite possible that Dante is describing a phenomenon similar to that seen in "Veggio negli occhi" (26, lines 5–12), [I see in those eyes], where Cavalcanti transposes into verse the process of the apprehension and abstraction in the imagination (from which, according to Aristotelian philosophy, the intellect extracts cognitive material) of the lady's visible form—or rather, her form as perceived by the mind, which is represented by her beauty, thereby achieving an "eccezionale messa in scena dell'intellezione finale del fantasma amoroso" [an exceptional staging of the final intellection of the amorous spirit].[17] At the heart of lines 12–14 of "Tanto gentile" there seems to be an analogous philosophical reasoning. Dante, however, skips several logical steps and concentrates on the spirit that detaches itself from the lady's face and that tells the soul to sigh.

More generally, the dominant motifs of "Tanto gentile" are also present in compositions by the poets of the so-called "Sweet New Style," although it is reasonable to assume that, in many of these cases, the poets were imitating Dante. This is the case as regards the idea of comparing the beloved lady to a divine miracle, which we find several times in Cino da Pistoia: "Li vostri occhi gentili e pien' d'amore" (92, lines 9–14) [Your eyes so gracious and filled with love] and "Guardando a voi" (10, lines 1–6) [Looking upon you].[18]

Starting with a traditional assortment of themes and motifs, therefore, Dante composed a sonnet that illustrates several developments, in terms of both the literary tradition and his own poetic output. This evolution is essentially founded on the decision to push the intention to take the subject matter of his poetry, "quello che fosse loda di questa gentilissima" (XVIII.9

[10.11]) [praise for this most gracious of women], to its logical extreme. In Guinizzelli and Cavalcanti, the motif of "praise" was already present, but it was treated from the poet's perspective. In "Tanto gentile," Dante eliminates all subjective elements, and it is presented from an objective, universal, and collective point of view. The lens is no longer directed toward the effects of love on the poet, but rather toward the visible manifestation (the "miracle" of line 8) of a creature gifted with unique qualities. One element alone connects the phenomena described in the sonnet back to the poet: significantly, it is the traditional expression "my lady," which also reappears in "Vede perfettamente" (line 2) and is stripped of any reference to a concrete subject. Furthermore, the lexicon is chosen to attain an effect that becomes particularly evident when compared to Dante's models. To give an example: in "Chi è questa che vèn," Cavalcanti resembles Dante in terms of his desire to praise a lady from a more generalizing perspective (the reference to "our mind" should, in all probability, be interpreted in this way); however, in Guido's poem, references to the subject's perceptions are present ("ch'i' nol savría contare," line 6) that in "Tanto gentile" are entirely moved on to an objective, impersonal plane: "Mostrasi sí piacente a chi la mira" (line 9) [She shows herself so pleasing to the one who sees her]; "che 'ntender no la pò chi no la prova" (line 11) [as he who's missed it never knows]). Equally, to elucidate a concept that recurs in Dante, Cavalcanti had written: "cotanto d'umiltà donna mi pare" ("Chi è questa che vèn," line 7), while in Dante's sonnet, the lady "pare" [appears] without a pronoun, "gentile e . . . onesta."[19] The difference is subtle but profound. The verb *parere*, in older forms of Italian, fluctuates in meaning between "appearing" and "seeming," "a seconda che il contesto alluda a cosa che si presenti alla vista del soggetto con i connotati di una realtà obiettiva, ovvero a cosa che costituisca di per sé materia opinabile, e che del soggetto impegni le facoltà razionali" [depending on whether the context is one of alluding to something present to the subject's view, and with characteristics based in objective reality, or to something that is less tangible, and requires the engagement of the subject's rational faculties].[20] Frequently, the only distinction between the two meanings is conveyed through the presence or absence of a pronoun. Dante, however, eliminates any possible ambiguity. The appearance of Beatrice is represented as a universal phenomenon and not as a subjective perception. We owe the precise definition of this particular aspect of the sonnet to Contini: "Il problema espressivo di Dante non è affatto quello di rappresentare uno spettacolo, bensì di enunciare, quasi teoreticamente, un'incarnazione di cose celesti e di descrivere l'effetto necessario sullo spettatore. A Dante, qui, non interessa punto un visibile, ma, ch'è tutt'altra cosa, una visibilità. Non si preoccupa di sensazioni, ma di metafisica amorosa e di psicologia generale" [The issue of Dante's expression is not one of representing a spectacle, but rather of articulating, quite theoretically, the incarnation of heavenly things, and describing the necessary effect on the spectator. Dante is not interested in a visible thing, but in visibility, which is another thing entirely. He does not occupy himself with sensations, but with the metaphysics of love, and psychology in general].[21] This expressive choice signals the apex of the poetry written in praise of Beatrice in life.

The sonnet's manuscript history confirms its development relative to its models. "Tanto gentile" is one of a group of poems in the *Vita nova* for which De Robertis, examining their independent circulation, identified authorial "first versions" that predate the writing of the *libello*.[22] There are two especially significant differences relative to the text in the *Vita nova*. Lines 7–8 in the first draft, "credo che sia una cosa venuta / di cielo in terra a miracol mostrare" [I think she came from heaven to show a miracle on earth], become "e par che sia una cosa venuta / da cielo in terra a miracol mostrare" [appearing manifest from heaven to show a miracle on earth] in the version included in the *libello*. Line 10, "che fier per gli occhi una dolcezza al core" [a sweetness hurts through the eye to the heart], is also altered, by the repositioning of object and subject, so that it becomes "che dà per li occhi una dolcezza al core" [she gives a sweetness through the eye to the heart].[23] In the former case, given the semantic ambiguity of *parere*, it may be a question of a copyist's error, and therefore an unauthorized variation.[24] However, if both changes are accepted as being Dante's own, one can clearly see, in the transition from one version to the other, a search for greater objectivity in describing phenomena: from *credere* to *parere*. In the second case, the first draft has "fier per gli occhi," which is to say, *ferisce* [wounds]. Here as well, accepting the hypothesis that this is an authorial variant, one can see an evolution from a phenomenology that is subjective to one that is more objective (the verb *ferire* has a meaning that is far more concrete than *dare*).[25]

Let us now turn to the second half of the diptych, "Vede perfettamente onne salute." A first draft is also hypothesized for this sonnet, but the differences between that text and the *Vita nova* are minimal and less significant.[26] From a reading in parallel with "Tanto gentile" there emerge both the formalism and tension toward variety that are typical of Dante and of the medieval lyric.[27] The theme and lexicon can, in fact, be almost entirely superimposed onto those of "Tanto gentile" and other compositions, for example "Ne li occhi porta" (XXI.2–4 [12.2–12.4]). Even disregarding the prose narrative, there are nevertheless small but significant formal variations. The metrical structure of "Vede perfettamente," with alternating rhymes in the *fronte*, is deemed to be more archaic than that of "Tanto gentile." Consequently, it has been suggested that it may have been written first, despite the fact that Dante claims to have written it at a later date.[28]

As has been noted, the motif of the lady who gives honor to all who follow her is already present in *De amore*. In "Vede perfettamente," Dante specifies that, in this way, jealousy is eliminated: "che nulla invidia all'altre ne procede" (line 6) [it doesn't rouse their jealousy]. Jealousy, after all, is the opposite of love, of *caritas*, as Thomas Aquinas explained: "invidia misericordiae opponitur et caritati" (*Summa theologiae* 2.2.36, art. 3 ad 3) [jealousy is opposed to pity and charity]).[29] These and other elements are amply attested, for example, in Cino da Pistoia and help to delineate the stylistic and thematic unity of the Sweet New Style. The motif of the feminine "brigade," which recurs in the *stilnovisti*, and here is invoked in the first quatrain, is only partially realistic.[30] The daily lives of women were frequently collective and rarely individualistic. However, it is also a traditional element, since, in general, the lady in the medieval love lyric is represented chiefly in public situations (the court, festivals, liturgical rites) and only occasionally caught in solitude. The relationship that connects Beatrice to other women highlights the transition from the poetry to the prose. If the sonnet originally described a group of women connected by a common habit "di gentilezza, d'amore e di fede" (line 8) [of faith, and love, and dignity], in the prose, by contrast, the devotion to Beatrice needs to be read in a sacred key, framed by the gradual process of the identification between Beatrice and Christ.

The diptych, therefore, is perfect: "Tanto gentile" describes the earthly manifestation of the miracle that is Beatrice and the effect that she has on all who see her; "Vede perfettamente" follows that miracle as it radiates over all the women who are around her. Between the two poems, however, there is a further substantial difference. Indeed, having transcribed "Tanto gentile,"

Dante explains in the prose that it is "sì piano a intendere" [so simple] to understand in light of what has already been narrated that there is no need "d'alcuna divisione" (XXVI.8 [17.8]) [to divide it up]. So the absence of any "division" of "Tanto gentile" seems to allude to the second part of the book, "after the death of Beatrice," in which the divisions, that in the first part had followed the compositions, are placed after the poems, so that each one, beginning with the canzone "Li occhi dolenti" [My grieving eyes], might "paia rimanere più vedova dopo lo suo fine" (XXX.2 [19.9]) [appear more widowed when it is done]. The zenith of the praise for Beatrice contains its own negation: the description of the miracle that is manifested on earth is the prelude to the disappearance of that selfsame marvel.

Translated by J. C. Wiles

Vita nova XXVII [18]

DAVID G. LUMMUS

Chapter XXVII [18] in the Barbi divisions of the *Vita nova* is composed of
two prose sentences and the first stanza of a *canzone*, "Sì lungiamente" [So
long a time], which is interrupted by the start of the following chapter. It
builds on Dante's effort in the previous chapter to foster understanding of
Beatrice's "mirabili ed eccellenti operazioni" (XXVI.4 [17.4]) [marvelous and
extraordinary workings] for those who are not physically present to see them.[1]
Dissatisfied with what he wrote, or perhaps merely wanting his poetic en-
gagement with Beatrice's miraculous work to be complete, Dante decides to
compose a *canzone* that focuses on the workings of Beatrice's influence and
power over him personally.

The complexity of the reflection calls for a *canzone*, Dante writes, be-
cause it cannot be treated in the short form of the sonnet. The partial *can-
zone* resembles a sonnet in length, although the single *settenario* in line 11
and the rhyme scheme of the tercets mark it as a stanza of a *canzone*.[2] The
composition of the poem is interrupted by the Latin insertion from the
Lamentations of Jeremiah that opens the following chapter, announcing the
death of Beatrice and marking the start of the final narrative section of the
work. In this way, as Teodolinda Barolini has observed, Beatrice's death takes
place "not so much *in mediis rebus* as *in mediis verbis*."[3] The *canzone* itself
again takes up the poetic language of the Sicilian school and the theme of

love's power typical of the poetry of Guido Cavalcanti, both of which were prominent in the early chapters of the *Vita nova*. Together with the prose, the poetic composition employs a well-known terminology to speak about the effects of love and of Beatrice's presence on Dante's body and mind, with a view to explaining the production of poetry.

In the prose, for example, terms such as *disposto* (XXVII.2 [18.2]), *operazione, operava* (2), *adoperava* (1), and *vertude* (2) are translations of the language of scholastic-Aristotelian philosophy.[4] The term *disposizione* is the vernacular version of the Latin word for διάθεσις as *dispositio*, which denotes a condition or state of being of the body or soul toward another entity— in this case, Beatrice and her *virtù*. Similarly, *operazione* (*operatio/ἐργασία*) indicates the function or process of work that Beatrice's *vertude* (*potentia/δύναμις*), or power, enacts on Dante's soul, while the verb *adoperare*, also used by Guido Guinizzelli and Chiaro Davanzati, indicates the productive action that results from that work.[5] The power and grace of Beatrice had been the subject of the two sonnets in the previous chapter, where the latter three of these terms were also employed in the praise of Beatrice's effects on others. In XXVII [18], Dante is writing about the potential of his own soul to receive Beatrice's grace and the productive effect of that grace on his soul. The inward-looking perspective that these terms demonstrate is precisely that of the first third of the *Vita nova*, where Dante initially endeavors to explain the effect of love on his body and mind. While at the beginning of the book Dante is concerned with understanding what has happened upon the appearance of Beatrice, here he has finally arrived at describing the quality of that presence by praising its effects. It is astonishing that it takes Dante so long to try to examine Beatrice's effects on himself. Up until this point, he has examined the work of love and of Beatrice's *virtù* only mimetically, through third persons.

This mimetic distancing of himself from Beatrice, which is inherent in the poetry of praise that characterizes the middle section of the *Vita nova*, is the defect that makes his treatment of love incomplete. Critics differ slightly in their interpretation of the adverb *defettivamente* (XXVII.1 [18.1]), a hapax in Dante's works, in the first prose sentence of the chapter. Domenico De Robertis leaves open the interpretation, providing three not-quite synonyms as potential translations: "difettosamente, imperfettamente, non compiutamente" [defectively, imperfectly, not completely].[6] Fernando Salsano glosses the term as "in modo inadeguato" [inadequately], while Guglielmo Gorni chooses "non compiutamente" [not completely].[7] Donato Pirovano has recently implied that it indicates a lack of perfection, writing that Dante did not want to leave his "'vangelo' lirico imperfetto" [lyric "gospel" imperfect].[8] It is difficult not to juxtapose this admission of incompleteness of speech with the perfect manifestation of Beatrice's effects in the previous chapter's sonnets. The second sonnet employs the opposite adverb, *perfettamente* (line 1) [completely or perfectly], to describe how those who look at Beatrice perceive joy ("salute"). In the opening lines of this chapter, Dante comes to realize that his representation of the effects of Beatrice's grace has been only indirect up until this point. De Robertis noticed the peculiarity of Dante's inward turn here, suggesting that it was superfluous to the praise style that reached its culmination in XXVI [17]. De Robertis's hypothesis, which he saw confirmed in the communal grief of XXVIII (19), was that the general effects of Beatrice on everyone who saw her were enough to redeem the individual experience of love as well.[9] In my view, however, with the inward turn Dante seeks to address what cannot be accounted for via praise of outward effects. If, as De Robertis suggested, the sonnets of the preceding chapter are indicative of both Dante's own experience and that of others, then in "Sì lungiamente," Dante's inner experience would also be indicative of that of others. Indeed, for his discourse of praise to be complete, Dante needs to address the readiness ("disposizione") of the soul to receive the workings of her grace.[10] How else could he do this other than by speaking of himself?

The fourteen lines of the *canzone* itself retell the story of the *Vita nova*. Critics have noticed how the lexicon used in the sonnet links it to Dante's earlier experience of love, noting that it is the product of a young Dante.[11] For example, the opening line echoes Guido delle Colonne's opening "Amor, che lungiamente m'ai menato" [Love, you who have led me for so long a time], while the imagery of love's mastery over the lover is linked to the influence of Cavalcanti, which is dominant in the first third of the book's narrative. From this beginning, Dante follows Cavalcanti in the first four lines, describing how his habituation to the power of love changes his experience from harshness into tenderness. The next eight lines contain the stanza's principal ideas, explaining how Love drains his strength and makes him pale and noting first how Love makes his spirits ("spiriti") flee from his frail soul and then how it leads them to seek out his lady in speech, asking her for

more sweet joy. He concludes the stanza with a reminder that this opera-
tion is passive on his part. It occurs, he says, every time she looks at him, not,
as in "Vede perfettamente" (XXVI.10–13 [17.10–17.13]) [He sees com-
pletely], when others look at her. Reading the poem as a complete and inten-
tionally monostrophic canzone, Barolini has noted that in it Dante unites
the "tragic Guido" to the "tender Guido" and shows his control over Caval-
canti as a source to be overcome through imitation.[12] Yet the stanza does
much more than this. It describes the process through which poetry is
formed thanks to Beatrice's grace joined with Love's domination of Dante's
heart. Indeed, Dante's discussion of the readiness of his own soul to receive
Beatrice's power—experienced by him as a passion or potentiality—is linked
to a product—an action or actuality—that is poetic in nature.

   In the poem, Dante's *spiriti*, or spirits, are synonymous with his po-
etic speech—his *dir* or *parlar*—in what Giorgio Agamben has called the
"pneumo-phantastic" circle of thirteenth-century love lyric, in which poetic
speech is an expression of *joi d'amor* in all its plenitude.[13] For Agamben, this
closed circle leads from the phantasm of the beloved imprinted on the heart
of the lover, through the lover's desire, to the lover's speech. It represents
the spiritual movement of love that is synonymous with the poetic sign, the
plenitude of which heals "the fracture between desire and its unattainable ob-
ject."[14] At the very moment when Dante turns to describe the poetic pleni-
tude brought on by the experience of Beatrice's grace—the physiological
workings of the production of the poet's sighs or spirits (*sospiri, spiriti*)[15]—he
performs the most dramatic rupture imaginable between desire and its ob-
ject. The importance of the fracture here suggests that, within the economy
of the *Vita nova*, the interruption and incompleteness of the poem are central
to its meaning. The poem's incompleteness embodies the breaking of the
perfect enclosure of *joi d'amor* that the poetic word ought to be. Its lack of
perfection coincides with the abrupt absence of Beatrice, just as much as per-
fection and presence were linked in the sonnets of the previous chapter.

   The narrative effect of this interruption serves to highlight the differ-
ence in quality between Beatrice and the other beloveds of the *dolce stil novo*.
For the *stil novo* poets, the production of poetic speech was linked to a phan-
tasm of the beloved in the heart of the poet, ruled over by Love, and to the
subsequent disturbance of the flow of spirits that govern imagination,
thought, and life itself. As Robert Harrison has argued, however, this para-

digm is not entirely applicable to Dante and Beatrice.[16] In his poems of praise, and especially in the sonnets of XXVI [17], Dante implies that Beatrice's effects emerge directly from her presence and from the mere sight of her. Her grace is external and accessible by all. It is not limited to Dante alone.

The death of Beatrice, her irrevocable absence, highlights the necessity of her physical presence to her graceful effects, especially with regard to the production of poetry. Following on "Tanto gentile" and "Vede perfettamente," "Sì lungiamente" promised to be Dante's programmatic response to Cavalcanti's doctrine of pneumo-phantastic love poetry in "Donna me prega" [A lady asks me]: a poetry of miraculous presence, not of phantasms that indicate absence. The challenge that Dante faces because of Beatrice's death can be described in terms of poetics and desire. First, Dante must come to terms with how to speak of Beatrice now that she is not there. Is the memory of her presence enough to elicit the same wondrous effects? Second, Dante can still desire the phantasm of Beatrice even when she is just a memory. When the phantasm has no embodied referent, Dante is unsure where this desire will lead him. The plenitude of love, the *joi d'amor* that was guaranteed by Beatrice's presence, is no longer possible—it is subsumed by memory. As Giuseppe Mazzotta has noticed, Beatrice's death causes Dante to confront "the issue of images voided of any concrete referents" and to make sense of them so that they do not become "cadavers of a past."[17] Her death presents the ultimate challenge to his poetics of presence and forces him to find a new way to conceive of love that loosens the knot created by the *dolce stil novo*.

Vita nova XXVIII–XXXIV [19–23]
The Poetics of a New Affective Community

HEATHER WEBB

When, in chapter XXX [19.8–19.10], Dante comes to gloss the startling opening of *Vita nova* XXVIII [19.1–19.3], he refers to that opening as the "entrata della nuova materia" (XXX.1 [19.8]) [a preamble to the new material that follows].[1] For Guglielmo Gorni, this is the single division in the work that matters most: "*Incipit vita nova*" (I [1.1]) [Here begins the new life] opens the section "in vita" [in life] of Beatrice, and "*Quomodo sedet sola civitas plena populo! facta est quasi vidua domina gentium*" (XXX.1 [19.8]) [How doth the city sit solitary that was full of people! How is she become a widow, she that was great among the nations!] opens the section "in morte" [in death].[2] What then, is new in this "nuova materia" within the book of the already new, the "vita nova"? Chapters XXVIII–XXXIV [19–23] achingly show forth absence in an unabashed multiplicity of ways, tying together multiple responses at the boundaries of that absence, each already forestalled by their confessions of insufficiency. Here, borrowed words are borrowed again, endings are truncated, conclusions denied. Existing formulas are revisited in visibly deflated ways. In other arenas of Dante studies, scholars have spoken of a palinodic Dante, one who revisits earlier formulations to revise them and to show triumphal overcomings of past attempts in the light of new revelation.[3] But here, in these chapters in the wake of Beatrice's unspeakable death, revisitings of earlier formulations have nothing of that triumphal tone.

In what follows, I will very briefly set out some of the ways in which the borrowings and revisitings in these chapters establish a lacuna that draws the reader's attention to the missing body of Beatrice, to take up Robert Harrison's title.[4] But where Harrison turns to what he terms the "Petrarchan alternative" to think through absence in the wake of Beatrice's death, I will propose thinking though this absence as a call for a new readerly engagement with the text as a space in which reading communities are collected. In the essays in this section we have all sought to pay attention, in diverse ways, to the techniques the text employs to engage readers. This "nuova materia," I will suggest, is a new poetics in the absence of Beatrice's physical presence that seeks explicitly to create an affective community of readers. This community of readers is formed around the discriminating factor of those who have the greatest capacity to be affected.[5]

Dante says at the opening of chapter XXVIII [19.1–19.3] that this is not the place in which to "trattare alquanto della sua partita da noi" (XXVIII.2 [19.2]) [say something about her departure from us]. A number of scholars have suggested that Dante's extensive drawing of our attention to the silence around Beatrice's death, with three enigmatic reasons, points to a mystical experience on Dante's part. In various ways, and to various degrees, they have proposed that Dante has a vision of Beatrice assumed into heaven.[6] The key to these readings is the interpretation of "Trattando, converebbe essere me laudatore di me medesimo" (XXVIII.2 [19.2]) [Such writing would put me in the position of singing my own praises] as an allusion to Paul's Second Letter to the Corinthians, in which he troubles the issue of seeming to glorify himself by recounting his experience.

While the absence of Beatrice's bodily presence is clearly at issue here, and Dante is noticeably at pains to point to this absence and keen to avoid filling that gap with words as poor substitutions for that particular bodily presence, I would offer that, more than indicating a Marian Assumption, this gap is visibly staged to push readers to new agency and to new collective experience.

This agency takes multiple forms. An early example comes immediately in chapters XXXVIII–XXIX [19.1–19.7], when, as Donato Pirovano notes, this central event, the death of Beatrice, is the departure point from which Dante invites the reader to reread the *Vita nova* in a new light, offering the number nine as the interpretative key for this rereading.[7] A number of other semantic keys will be offered in the following chapters for enhanced readerly engagement. Only through such engagement, we will suggest, can readers face the new challenge of experiencing Beatrice's salvific powers entirely through Dante's visionary poetry and without the possibility of direct contact with the lady herself.

The *canzone* "Li occhi dolenti" (XXXI.8–17 [20.8–20.17]) [The grieving eyes], posited as a "sorella" [sister] or "gemella" [twin] of "Donne ch'avete intelletto d'amore," (XIX.4–14 [10.15–10.25]) [Ladies who have understanding of love][8] and sharing the same macrostructure, points to Beatrice's soul departing her body: "Partissi de la sua bella persona / piena di grazia l'anima gentile" (lines 29–30) [That noble soul left behind her beautiful earthly body, so full of grace].[9] The reference to the soul's departure would seem to me to work against the notion of a fully Marian Assumption into heaven. What the *canzone* does clearly seek to do, if not establish the notion of Beatrice's assumption and Dante as witness for such, is instead to define an existing readership anew. The *canzone* sets out its purpose to convince the "donne gentili," Dante's readers of the *poesia della lode*, to stay with him as readers in a community of mourning:

> Ora, s'i' voglio sfogar lo dolore,
> che poco a poco a la morte mi mena,
> convenemi parlar traendo guai,
> E perché mi ricorda che io parlai
> de la mia donna, mentre che vivia,
> donne gentili, volontier con vui,
> non voi parlare altrui,
> se no a cor gentil che in donna sia:
> e dicerò di lei piangendo.
> (XXXI.8–9, lines 4–12 [20.8–20.9])

[Now, if I want to let my sorrow vent, / by which, a little at a time, death nears, / I am constrained to speak in words and wails. / And since I well remember the details / I spoke about my lady while she lived, / my gracious women, willingly to you, / I'll speak to no one new, / save to the open heart that women give. / And as I talk of her I'll weep.]

Dante stresses here that he wishes to speak to the same "donne gentili" that he spoke to "mentre che vivia," while Beatrice was alive. In "Donne ch'avete," he described a need to "isfogar la mente" (XIX.4, line 4 [10.15]) [to ease my mind]. Here, he has centered on a specific affect that must be shared and is described as accompanied by bodily manifestation: "s'i' voglio sfogar lo dolore . . . convenemi parlar traendo guai . . . dicerò di lei piangendo."[10] This affect begs reciprocal response in his carefully selected audience, a response that is codified later in the *canzone*, as we will see.

Despite what comes across here as a sort of urgency to bring readers along in mourning who were previous listeners to verses of praise, Stefano Carrai has shown how the *Vita nova* as a whole has a kind of circularity around the theme of "pianto," reaching from "O voi che per la via" [O you who along the way] in chapter VII [2.12–2.18] to its specular pair in "Deh peregrini" (XL [29]) [Oh, pilgrims]. While Beatrice's death constitutes a definitive shift into a tone of pain and mourning, this mood has been prepared throughout the *Vita nova* with a sequence of elegiac poems that mourn the death of Beatrice's friend, then Beatrice's father, then Beatrice herself in an imagined death before we face the event of Beatrice's death itself in chapter XXVIII [19.1–19.3]. As Carrai notes, a key elegiac trait of the text is "l'invito a partecipare al dolore del poeta" [the invitation to participate in the poet's pain].[11] Carrai discusses the stylistic and lexical elements of the text that insist upon pain and suffering and must be read in an elegiac mode. In our contributions on chapters XXVIII–XXXIV [19–23], we seek to investigate a sort of typology of these invitations to participate in the poet's pain, even as we inquire into the implications of such a program of invitations to participation and indeed agency within a defined affective community of interpreters.

De Robertis has called "Li occhi dolenti" "la canzone delle manifestazioni del dolore" [the *canzone* of the manifestations of pain],[12] but perhaps what we find here are not only manifestations but manifestations visibly targeted to trigger response. In many ways, we can see that while we might say that it is "Donne ch'avete" that prepares the way for "Li occhi dolenti," we could equally assert that "Li occhi dolenti" revisits, in the key of loss, the tenets of "Donne ch'avete." "Donne ch'avete" warns us that "Madonna è disiata in sommo cielo" (line 29) [My lady is desired in the highest heaven], a statement that finds its accomplishment in "Li occhi dolenti":

Fé maravigliar l'etterno sire,
sí che dolce disire

lo giunse di chiamar tanta salute;
e fella di qua giù a sé venire
        (XXXI.10, lines 23–26 [20.10])

————

[that it astonished our eternal Sire, / so that a sweet desire / to call such wholeness came to Him at length; / and from down here He raised her to His choir.]

If, in "Donne ch'avete," bystanders were either ennobled or killed by Beatrice's presence, according to their nobility of heart—

Quando va per via
gitta nei cor villani Amore un gelo,
per che onne lor pensero agghiaccia e pere;
e qual soffrisse di starla a vedere
diverria nobil cosa, o si morria
        (XIX.9, lines 32–36 [10.20])

————

[Love casts into vulgar hearts an ice / that makes their thoughts drop dead from shocking cold. / As for the one who manages to hold / his gaze: he's either killed or dignified]

in "Li occhi dolenti" it is the act of *ragionare*, of speaking of Beatrice's death, that provokes the discernment between those of noble heart and those who are "vili":

Chi no la piange, quando ne ragiona,
core ha di pietra sí malvagio e vile,
ch'entrar no i puote spirito benegno.
Non è di cor villan sí alto ingegno,
che possa imaginar di lei alquanto,
e però no gli vèn di pianger doglia:
ma ven tristizia e voglia
di sospirare e morir di pianto,
e d'onne consolar l'anima spoglia
chi vede nel pensero alcuna volta

quale ella fue, e com'ella n'è tolta.
  (XXXI.11–12, lines 32–42 [20.11–20.12])

[Whoever speaks of her without laments / has granite for a heart, so mean and foul / no spirit of goodwill can find a space. / For want of subtlety, no heart that's base / has mind enough to picture her in thought, / and so it never suffers pain to cry. / But endlessly to sigh, / to mourn, to die of weeping is what's sought, / stripping the soul of what might pacify, / by him who sees in thought the nucleus / of what she was and how she's torn from us.]

We may note Dante's emphasis on the individual's capacity to be affected.[13] In some ways, we may see this as a broadening of the potential affective public for the reception of Beatrice's *sentenzia*. While "Donne ch'avete" suggests that in life the processes of ennoblement through Beatrice were available to those who were able to be physically in her presence, "Dico, qual vuol gentil donna parere / vada con lei" (XIX.9, lines 31–32 [10.20] [to be more noble, all you have to do is be with her], here it is enough to "ragiona*re*," or "imaginar di lei alquanto," or "vede*re* nel pensero."

As will become increasingly clear over the course of the *Vita nova*, and certainly by the time Dante is appealing to the pilgrims passing through Florence in chapter XL [29], it is not only a memory of the living body of Beatrice that can activate these effects but Dante's own words that hold something of her spiritually potent presence. In "Li occhi dolenti," it becomes clear that the spiritual worth of those listening to Dante's words can be distinguished by the affective response or lack of affective response to those words, what Colombo calls "un'aristocrazia del dolore" [an aristocracy of pain].[14] The heart of stone evoked here is one that would be impenetrable to the presence of benign spirits, in this case spirits in the shape of Dante's poetic voice, a voice that bears shadowy traces of Beatrice's presence. And it is those traces that serve to show forth the lack of Beatrice's presence among us. As the spirits enter into the *cor gentile*, tears spill forth. The inability to weep shows that the spirits have not managed to enter. Emotional response is thus a test of discernment for readers. The *congedo*—

Pietosa mia canzone, or va piangendo;
e ritruova le donne e le donzelle

a cui le tue sorelle
erano usate di portar letizia;
e tu, che se' figliuola di tristizia,
vatten disconsolata a star con elle
    (XXXI.17, lines 71–76 [20.17])

————

[My sad canzone, go your way and weep: / search out those women
and those girls again / to whom your sister-kin / would once upon a time
bring happiness: / while you, who are the daughter of distress, / go off
disconsolate to be with them]

—insists again upon the continuity of readership in joy and in sadness.
And yet, we may note the seeds of possibilities for a broadening of readership
if the potential discernment mechanism between readers is now located di-
rectly in the poem itself, rather than in the experience of Beatrice's physical
presence. The *canzoni* are presented as affective vehicles here, capable of
carrying joy or sorrow to cohabit with the listener.

It is in the prefatory comments to this *canzone* that Dante announces his
structural shift in the work, moving his *divisioni* from the end of the poems
to their new opening position, "acciò che questa canzone paia rimanere
più vedova dopo lo suo fine" (XXXI.2 [20.2]) [so that this canzone may ap-
pear more widowed after the end].[15] Ronald Martinez refers us to William
Durand and a liturgical model for this conception of widowing, noting that
matins including reading from Lamentations are "widowed" when specific
opening and closing psalms and prayers are suspended during the triduum:
"And thus this office, which lacks a beginning and end, will appear as if dead
and widowed, as our fathers were bereft after the death of Christ."[16] This
liturgical connection gives the structural shift here a distinctly Christological
significance, in which poems treating the mourning of Beatrice's death are
framed—or rather unframed—in the way that the readings from the Lamen-
tations of Jeremiah are unframed to emphasize the mourning at the death of
Christ. We might ask here as well how this unframing, this lack of comment
in the wake of a poem of mourning, makes different demands on readers,
who can no longer expect a rationalization of what they have just read and
must, as the *congedo* suggests, simply dwell with the sorrow that has been
transported into their midst.

The lack of framing conclusions seems, in fact, to foster greater continuity between these poems of mourning, as if they each attempt, with self-conscious declarations of their own insufficiency, to convey sorrow on behalf of, but also toward, a variety of audiences. Chapter XXXII [21] begins with the request, on the part of a close relative of Beatrice's (we can most likely assume it is her brother), to write a poem for a woman who has recently died.[17] "Simulava sue parole," Dante tells us, "acciò che paresse che dicesse d'un'altra" (XXXII.2 [21.2]) [He disguised his words so that it seemed that he was speaking of another]. But Dante recognizes that Beatrice is the woman his friend mourns. The simulations and dissimulations continue, however, throughout chapters XXXII–XXXIV [21–23]. Dante goes on to explain that, on this commission, he writes "Venite a 'ntender li sospiri miei" (XXXII.5–6 [21.5–21.6]) [Come and listen to my sighs] from his own suffering "nel quale mi lamentassi alquanto" [in which I would mourn a little], but that in giving it to his friend "paresse che per lui l'avessi fatto" (XXXII.3 [21.3]) [it seemed that I had composed it for him].

"Venite a 'ntender li sospiri miei" picks up with a recall of "Li occhi dolenti" and introduces tight textual links between the two.[18] Teodolinda Barolini points out that the first version that predates the *libello* is less tightly connected to "Li occhi dolenti,"[19] and so this continuous period of mourning is very much emphasized for the purposes of the *libello*. The fact that "Venite a 'ntender li sospiri miei" is commissioned by a particular person as set out in the prose does not fundamentally alter the fabric of the poetry, which maintains a consistent affective atmosphere through the *canzone* and the sonnet.

These games of seeming accelerate in XXXIII [22], when Dante writes two stanzas of a *canzone*, "Quantunque volte, lasso!" (XXXIII.5–6 [22.5–22.6]) [Whenever I, alas], to accompany the sonnet for Beatrice's brother. Dante notes that only those who look "sottilmente" [subtly] will see that the first stanza is written in the voice of the brother and the second stanza is written in the voice of Dante himself. As Katherine Powlesland points out in her contribution here, Dante moves from a sonnet that could be read in either voice to an explicit division with one stanza for each mourning voice. Dante stresses the "veracemente" (XXXIII.2 [22.2]); unlike the sonnet, one stanza was truly written for the brother in "Quantunque volte, lasso!" And yet this difference is made visible to the reader of the *Vita nova*, not to the brother himself. These games, centered on the availability of semantic keys, establish the multiple possibilities of audiences for Dante's work and invite the reader to play with the notion of the temporalities of revelation. Such a chain of expanding frames of reference for a succession of audiences suggests a progressive opening out of the readership.

Ultimately, all the glossing and self-commentary provided in the prose here does not in fact subdue the reader into accepting a set, controlled, authoritative reading, but rather empowers the reader to take agency within the text. Powlesland suggests that the reader might be prompted by this exposition to move back and forth within the text, going back from XXXIII [22] to XXXII [21] to compare the subtle differences in the voice of lament.

To pick up on the point that Helena Phillips-Robins makes with her interrogation of the possibility of taking up the voice of the Lamentations for personal, private sorrow, I would suggest that the chapters from XXVIII [19.1–19.3] on investigate the reader's or listener's capacity to inhabit the affective space of another's suffering. Beatrice's brother's lack of awareness of the voicing shifts that the reader of the prose frame of the *libello* is privy to signifies that the brother can indeed mourn his sister from within Dante's voice in "Venite a 'ntender li sospiri miei." He can, furthermore, although unaware, slip back and forth from Dante's ventriloquizing of his voice to Dante's own voice of suffering in "Quantunque volte, lasso!, mi rimembra," and in that way not only share Dante's pain but also fulfill his own fraternal mourning.

The questions of the transposabilities of affect between subjects and voices are presented in another way in chapter XXXIV [23]. The chapter takes place on the day of the anniversary of Beatrice's death. An anniversary of the beloved's death was a novel subject for poetry, and this new poetic choice of subject presents itself in contrast to the more conventional celebration of the anniversary of the date in which the poet fell in love.[20] Here Dante remembers Beatrice precisely one year after her death and, while remembering her, draws an angel. He is so absorbed in this activity that he does not notice the arrival of certain unnamed gentlemen, who watch him for some time before the poet-artist realizes they are there and finally greets them. Dante explains to them that while drawing, he was, in his thoughts, in the presence of someone else. When they leave, he carries on his drawing, and this activity induces him to continue his explanation of this presence

that he experienced while drawing. The explanation takes the form of a son-
net, but an unusual "double-headed" one.

Like the two stanzas of "Quantunque volte, lasso!, mi rimembra," the
double opening of "Era venuta ne la mente mia" [She had just come into
my memory] offers two alternative spaces to enter an atmosphere of mourn-
ing (XXXIV.7–8 [23.7–23.8]). The two openings seem to pose explicitly
the problem of multiple audiences for Dante's poetry. Gorni has suggested
that the two openings correspond to a private need and to a narrative drive.[21]
What sort of audience do the two men who pass by constitute? They are
not defined by bonds of family relation or by the designs of the god of Love,
as many other characters in the *Vita nova* are. They are simply "uomini a li
quali si convenia di fare onore" (XXXIV.1 [23.1]) [men whose rank required
that one greet them respectfully].

There has been significant debate on the genesis and chronology of the
two beginnings of "Era venuta." A number of scholars have suggested that
the poem, with the second beginning, predates the *libello*. As Barolini under-
stands it, for instance, Dante composed a new first beginning to highlight
Beatrice's ascension to paradise.[22] Marco Grimaldi argues instead that the
two beginnings are chronologically consecutive, with the second beginning
more closely tied to the prose frame.[23]

The first beginning connects Beatrice's apparition in Dante's mind with
her presence in Empyrean and the company of the Virgin Mary. The second
connects Beatrice's apparition to Dante with the terrestrial and chronologi-
cally fixed presence of the men who came to look over Dante's shoulder as
he drew. As Federica Pich has observed, the doubleness of the sonnet ren-
ders visible the multiplication of levels of communication.[24] This process of
accumulation of levels not only of communication but also of interpretation
has effectively accelerated at every step since the new beginning of chapter
XXVIII [19.1–19.3].

The first beginning outlines, among other things, the subject of Dante's
intense focus before he recognizes the presence of his observers, while the
second correlates Dante's vision, or sense of Beatrice's otherworldly presence,
with a specific time and place marker and with clear narrative coordinates.
For Gorni, Dante's lack of awareness that he is being observed shows that the
experience is a mystical one, as when Dante is abstracted from his immediate
context by the visions that rain into his mind in *Purgatorio* 17.[25]

There is a marked shift from the discussion of such abstraction in "Li occhi dolenti," in which Dante explains that

quando 'l maginar mi ven ben fiso,
giugnemi tanta pena d'ogne parte,
ch'io mi riscuoto per dolor ch'i' sento;
e sí fatto divento,
che da le genti vergogna mi parte.
     (XXXI.14, lines 49–53 [20.14])

[And once her image in me is arranged, / such pain comes over me in every part, / I shudder suddenly awake with woe: / and I am altered so, / shame cuts me off from people; I depart.]

When Dante comes to himself, he flees the company of others. By the time we reach the anniversary, he seeks out instead something communicable about the image in his mind.

No matter how we classify the experience recounted in "Era venuta ne la mente mia," the two openings of the sonnet weigh up the shareability of the experience. If Dante feels Beatrice's presence in his mind, what can a passerby observe? Will traces of that presence communicate themselves to the *tavolette*? To the poem that follows? Can an observer experience something of that salvific presence in the form of words that dwell on Beatrice's heavenly status, or words that seek to create a crossroads between Beatrice's heavenly removal from earth and the encounters that might occur in the streets or *botteghe* of Florence?

Vita nova XXVIII [19.1–19.3]

HELENA PHILLIPS-ROBINS

Vita nova XXVIII [19.1–19.3] opens with a cry of lament: "*Quomodo sedet sola civitas plena populo! facta est quasi vidua domina gentium*" [How doth the city sit solitary that was full of people! How is she become a widow, she that was great among the nations!]. It is a cry used in the liturgy on Maundy Thursday to grieve the death of Christ. Dante is not simply quoting another text, but rather drawing on and refashioning a lived experience, available to medieval readers, of using that text to express grief. In this chapter I investigate how grief is articulated and lived out through the "Quomodo sedet," and focus particularly on the type of engagement that I suggest Dante invites from readers here. In chapter XXVIII [19.1–19.3] Dante draws on liturgical practices and liturgically informed modes of thought to reflect on Beatrice's death, to live out his relationship with her, and to invite readers to themselves indwell the words of the "Quomodo." It is also through liturgy that Dante presents Beatrice's eternal life in heaven and the unfolding of her relationship with Mary and with God.

The desolation and loss articulated in the cry "Quomodo sedet sola civitas" is personal. The cry articulates something of Dante's pain and shock at the death of "la donna mia" (XXVII.4 [18.4]) [my lady], as she is celebrated in the *canzone* that the lament interrupts, grief for one who grants *me* "salute" (XXVII.4 [18.4]) [bliss], who looks at *me* (XXVII.5 [18.5]). But at the same time the cry attributes grief to the whole city; not only Dante, but Florence and all in her are widowed, made desolate by Beatrice's death: "sedet sola civitas . . . facta est quasi vidua." Citizens of Florence are cast as already involved in the grief articulated in the *Vita nova*, raising at least the possibility that Dante is here addressing the *libello* to any literate inhabitant of Florence, or, if read in the light of chapter XL [29], also to anyone who passes through the city.

As Ronald Martinez has discussed, the words "Quomodo sedet sola civitas" had a prominent place in the liturgy of Maundy Thursday, specifically in the office of matins, the service sung in the early hours of the morning.[1] Maundy Thursday matins was made up of three nocturns, and each nocturn consisted of a series of psalms, followed by a series of readings. The first reading of the first nocturn was the opening of Lamentations 1. For information as to how matins was to be carried out, we can turn to medieval ordinals, texts that give minutely detailed instructions on how to perform the Mass and office in a specific cathedral or church throughout the year. Two ordinals survive from the cathedral of Santa Reparata in Florence, and one of them prescribes the following for Maundy Thursday matins:

> In nocte Cene domini ad matutinas sonetur unum signum tantum, quoadusque populus conveniat. . . . In primo nocturno . . . tres lect[iones] leguntur ex Lamentatione Jeremie prophete ab eo loco ubi ait *Quomodo sedet sola civitas plena populo* [Lam. 1:1] usque *Cogitavit dominus dissipare murum* [Lam. 2:8].

> [In the night [i.e., the early hours of the morning] of Maundy Thursday let one bell only be rung until the people gather for Matins. . . . During the first nocturn . . . three lessons are sung from the Lamentations of the prophet Jeremiah, beginning in the place where he says *Quomodo sedet sola civitas plena populo* up to *Cogitavit dominus dissipare murum*.][2]

One of the cathedral bells was to be rung in order to call the citizens of Florence to church. The ordinal expresses the aim of having at least some of the laity attend matins on one of the holiest days of the year, though being an instruction manual, it does not document to what extent they actually did. The ordinal continues with instructions for the first nocturn, and Santa

Reparata, in having readings from Lamentations, follows the liturgical prac-
tice shared across the medieval West.

"Quomodo sedet sola civitas" are thus words of lament that a medieval
reader of the *Vita nova* may well have heard performed many times. It would
have been a cleric who sang the text on Maundy Thursday, but this does not
mean that the laity in the congregation were not involved in its performance.
As Benjamin Brand puts it in his work on medieval liturgy more generally,
"Congregants were to be neither passive listeners to [the] music nor unre-
sponsive observers to the ritual."[3] Various medieval liturgical texts and trea-
tises advise that the laity should pay attention to what was sung in church,
and they cast attentive listening as a mode of turning toward God.[4] Depend-
ing on his or her level of literacy, a lay person may have followed the words of
the "Quomodo sedet" silently as he or she listened to them, and participated
in the emotion the words express.

In the context of the Holy Week liturgy, Jeremiah's words were used
to grieve for Christ. In his *Rationale divinorum officiorum*—the most exten-
sive and widely circulated liturgical treatise of the Middle Ages (circulating
from ca. 1292)—William Durand, following earlier medieval commenta-
tors, writes:

> Tres prime lectiones, uel in quibusdam ecclesiis sex, sunt de Trenis Ieremie
> deflentis captiuitatem populi sui. . . . Sicut enim ille deplorauit mortem
> Iosue regis occisi in futuram destructionem gentis, ita et nos deploramus
> mortem et passionem Christi regis nostri. (*Rationale divinorum officiorum*
> 6.72.11)
>
> ———
>
> [The first three, or in some churches six, lessons are from the Lamen-
> tations of Jeremiah as he weeps over the captivity of his people. . . . For
> as he wept and lamented for the death of Joshua, the king who would be
> killed during the destruction of his people, so we weep and lament for
> the death and passion of Christ, our king.]

In using the "Quomodo" cry to mourn a Christ-bearing figure, one in whom
divinity is made incarnate—for Beatrice has earlier in the *Vita nova* been
presented as, miraculously, this—Dante echoes its use in the Maundy Thurs-
day matins. Martinez argues that the book of Lamentations and its uses in

the liturgy inform aspects of the structure of the *Vita nova*.[5] The point I would like to stress is that in inserting the words "Quomodo sedet sola civitas" into the *Vita nova*, Dante puts the *libello* in dialogue not only with another text but also with the practice of using that text to express and live out grief. Dante evokes, and fashions a new version of, a lived experience that would have been available to medieval readers.

Jennifer Rushworth observes that in quoting Lamentations, Dante "involves the reader in the protagonist's grief by an appeal to a common mournful text."[6] What sort of engagement does Dante invite from the reader here? The "Quomodo"—like any liturgical prayer, song, or lament—is a text whose words can be spoken, taken up, indwelt, by different people in different ways. As David Ford writes, "It is a feature of good liturgical texts that they allow large numbers of diverse people to identify themselves through them."[7] Durand indicates as much in his comparison of how the words were used before and now after the Incarnation.[8] More generally, people scattered across time and space have used Jeremiah's words to articulate their own experiences of grief at Christ's death. Dante, through his act of using the "Quomodo" to express his grief for Beatrice, illustrates precisely the availability of these words to be inhabited in different ways by different people. The "Quomodo" is a cry that is open to be taken up and inhabited by anyone who reads or hears it. It is not limited, either in medieval liturgy or in the *Vita nova*, to being spoken by only one particular person. Might Dante, then, be inviting readers to indwell these words? One can, of course, read the "Quomodo" with emotional detachment, solely as a record of and means of communicating Dante's pain. But as readers voice these words, whether silently or aloud, they also have the opportunity for a more active response; they have the opportunity to take up as their own the grief that the words express.

In the sonnet "Deh peregrini" (XL.9–10 [29.9–29.10]) Dante, again echoing Lamentations 1, reflects that if pilgrims passing through the desolate, abandoned Florence knew of the city's widowing—of the city's loss of that which is both human and divine—they would weep. In the accompanying prose Dante declares his desire to write poetry "that would make anyone who heard [it] cry"—"io direi parole le quali farebbero piangere chiunque le intendesse" (XL.4 [29.4])—and he ends the sonnet with the claim that words spoken of Beatrice "hanno vertù di far piangere altrui" (XL.10 [29.10]) [have force enough to make a stranger grieve]. Not only pilgrims on their way to

Rome but everyone is invited to weep, and this includes readers of the *Vita nova*. With the "Quomodo" of chapter XXVIII [19.1–19.3] Dante gives us the opportunity, as he will again more explicitly in chapter XL [29], to share his sorrow. By indwelling the words of the "Quomodo," readers can to some measure participate in the event of Beatrice's death; they can participate in acknowledging that divinity can be, and is, made incarnate in particular human beings. Beatrice's death cannot be recounted (XXVIII.2 [19.2]), but what Dante—and, if they choose, readers—can do is, through grief, in some degree to share in it. Throughout the *Vita nova* words fall short in describing Beatrice. The "Quomodo," and chapter XXVIII [19.1–19.3] as a whole, suggest, in a different mode, what the poetry of praise also does: one cannot fully describe another person, but one can enter into relation with her.

What I have suggested regarding the "Quomodo sedet" as words open to be indwelt by readers is potentially troubled, however, by Dante's commentary on the "Quomodo" in chapter XXX [19.8–19.10]. There Dante states that after Beatrice's death he wrote a letter to the "principi de la terra" (XXX.1 [19.8]) [rulers of the land] that began "Quomodo sedet sola civitas." Read in the light of chapter XXX [19.8–19.10], the "Quomodo" of chapter XXVIII [19.1–19.3] is a respeaking of the beginning of Jeremiah's Lamentations, and a respeaking of the beginning of Dante's letter to the *principi*. While Jeremiah's lament, in its biblical and liturgical contexts, is open to being indwelt by anyone, Dante's letter is a text that we are not allowed even to read. Dante rather pointedly excludes the rest of the letter from the *libello* (XXX.2 [19.9]). Chapter XXVIII [19.1–19.3], like much of the *Vita nova*, offers the possibility for multiple modes of reading. If read as a liturgical text, the "Quomodo" is a lament that any reader can indwell. If read as an extract from Dante's letter, then this is a text that is fully accessible only to a certain group of readers.

Let us return to the liturgical dynamics of chapter XXVIII [19.1–19.3]. One of the functions of liturgy in the Middle Ages was to enable worshippers to understand and experience their own lives as part of the unfolding of salvation history. To quote Margot Fassler, "The liturgical framework was understood to underlie lives from the distant past, from the immediate past, and in the present. All these lives were believed to unfold according to a commonly held sense of progression and motivation." Taking part in the daily, weekly, and yearly cycles of liturgy allowed worshippers to learn to recognize how their lives participated in, responded to, and were dependent on the events—past, present, and to come—of universal salvation history.[9]

This liturgical mode of thinking informs *Vita nova* XXVIII [19.1–19.3]. In the liturgy of Maundy Thursday, Good Friday, and Holy Saturday, participants witness Christ's suffering, death, and resurrection and learn to see and live their lives as unfolding in the light of those events. In using words that in the liturgy are used to mourn Christ, Dante not only reiterates the identity, proclaimed in chapter XXIV [15], between Beatrice and Christ but invites us to consider what it might mean for Beatrice to be Christ-bearing. In using those words Dante also invites us to set Beatrice's death in the context of the Maundy Thursday liturgy and so to consider her death from the perspective of Christ's death. Furthermore, Dante asks us to hold together reflection on Beatrice's absence with reflection on Beatrice as participating in the communal life and liturgy of heaven.[10] Beatrice now glories— she rejoices and praises God: "Lo segnore de la giustizia chiamoe questa gentilissima a gloriare sotto la insegna di . . . Maria" (XXVIII.1 [19.1]) [The Lord of Justice called this most gracious of women to glory under the banner of . . . Mary]. Beatrice is repeatedly described as *gloriosa*, but this is the only use of the verb *gloriare* in the *Vita nova*, and its rarity gives particular emphasis to Beatrice's ongoing activity. Viewing Beatrice's death and her life in heaven from the perspective of Christ's death offers multiple avenues for reflection. Among them is the truth, in Dante's worldview, that Beatrice's participation in eternal life is made possible only because of Christ's death, mourned in the Maundy Thursday "Quomodo sedet." Beatrice is both Christ-bearing and utterly dependent on Christ.

Beatrice glorifies God "sotto la insegna di quella regina benedetta virgo Maria, lo cui nome fue in grandissima reverenzia ne le parole di questa Beatrice beata" (XXVIII.1 [19.1]) [under the banner of that blessed queen the Virgin Mary, whose name was held in utmost reverence in the words of this beatified Beatrice]. Beatrice's devotion to Mary is cast as a continuation, in a transformed, heavenly mode, of her living out of a relationship with Mary and with God on earth. *Parole* is a designation sufficiently general that it could refer to communal practices of Marian prayer, as it does in chapter V [2]—"Un giorno avvenne che questa gentilissima sedea in parte ove s'udiano parole de la regina de la gloria" (V.1 [2.1]) [It happened one day that this most gracious of women was sitting in a place where words about the Queen of Glory were being listened to]—and also to prayers offered when no one else is physically present. That, when Dante invites us to imagine Beatrice glorifying God and celebrating Mary in heaven, he gives as much attention to Beatrice's acts of prayer on earth suggests the importance, in Dante's worldview, of lived practices of prayer in the unfolding of relationships between humans and God.

The Marian titles—"regina benedetta virgo Maria"—are standard ones that would have been deeply familiar to a medieval reader from, among other contexts, any number of Marian prayers. Mary is addressed by name in the most popular Marian prayer of the later Middle Ages, the Ave Maria; she is addressed as "virgo Maria" and "Regina" in the widely used Salve Regina and Regina Caeli, and as "virgo" in the other two highly popular Marian antiphons, the Alma Redemptoris Mater and the Ave Regina Caelorum; and these titles are also used in *laude* and numerous other prayers.[11] The Latinism *virgo* further strengthens the association with Marian prayer.[12] This passage is one of only two uses of Mary's name in the *Vita nova* (the other is at XXXIV.7 [23.7]), and Mary is one of the few figures to be named in the book.[13] The word *Maria* thus has particular resonance. Dante's use of Mary's name and other titles is not a direct address to Mary; this is neither a salutation like the Ave Maria nor an extended direct address like the Vergine Madre of *Paradiso* 33. But proclaiming Mary's name with a list of titles is itself a way of celebrating Mary. Naming her as the "regina benedetta virgo Maria" is a way of praising her. As such, we might consider the act of writing this part of chapter XXVIII [19.1–19.3] as an act of prayer, as Dante too holding the Virgin "in grandissima reverenzia," as one small living-out of Dante's own relationship with Mary.

Vita nova XXIX [19.4–19.7]

AISTĖ KILTINAVIČIŪTĖ

If, in Guglielmo Gorni's appraisal, the *Vita nova* generally lacks memorable elements, such as poetic lines and character portrayals that will come to define the *Commedia*, chapter XXIX [19.4–19.7] proves to be an exception: "La connessione tra Beatrice e il 'nove' . . . è forse l'invenzione di più comune notorietà" [The connection between Beatrice and the number nine . . . is perhaps [Dante's] most famous invention (in the *Vita nova*)].[1] In *Vita nova* XXIX [19.4–19.7], Dante creates a numerical identity for his beloved through the most counterintuitive of statements: Beatrice truly *is* the number nine ("Questo numero fue ella medesima" [She herself was this number]).[2] As I will show in this chapter, the extended meditation upon Beatrice's "nineness" allows Dante not only to articulate Beatrice's Christological significance but also to reflect on the intertwined principles of intellectual subtlety and pleasure involved in explaining it.

The paronomastic play on the words *nove* and *novo* that the *libello* encourages indicates that the number nine must express the extreme novelty that Beatrice's miraculous nature represents for Dante; yet this novelty is born out of reliance on the ancient traditions of numerical interpretation and the established metrics of measuring time.[3] This dependence is best visible in Dante's examination of the novenary elements in the date of Beatrice's death, June 8, 1290, which leads to the recognition that Beatrice's "nineness" is truly universal: it is observable "secondo l'usanza d'Arabia," "secondo l'usanza di Siria," and "secondo l'usanza nostra" [according to the custom of Arabia, according to the custom of Syria, and according to our custom].[4] The rhetorical ease with which Dante joins these methods of measuring time obscures the difficulty that one would have had in integrating the diverse systems of temporal logic that otherwise share little common ground. If medieval chroniclers writing cross-cultural history have something to teach us, it is that the variety of lunar, solar, and lunisolar calendars used across the world never synchronized with each other, making the writers extremely conscious of the coexistence of a "plurality of times."[5] For Dante, Beatrice has the power to bring local conventions into harmony with each other, acting as a kind of universal standard. The most unlikely correspondence of asynchronous metrics signals the extraordinary nature of the event: Beatrice's "nineness" is not the author's narrative whim but rather is truly inscribed in the stars, in an improbable alignment of systems normally out of sync.

In *Vita nova* XXIX [19.4–19.7], Dante tells us that all nine motioning heavens were perfectly harmonized at the moment of Beatrice's conception: "Tutti e nove li mobili cieli perfettissimamente s'aveano insieme" (XXIX.2 [19.5]) [All nine motioning heavens utterly, perfectly harmonized with one another]. For this alignment to occur, Beatrice must be a creature of perfection attainable only to the likes of Christ: "Se tutte le precedenti vertudi s'accordassero sovra la produzione d'un'anima ne la loro ottima disposizione, che tanto discenderebbe in quella de la deitade, che *quasi sarebbe un altro Iddio incarnato*" (*Conv.* 4.21.10) [If all of the preceding virtues in their best disposition were brought into agreement in the creation of a soul, so much of the Deity would descend into it that it would *almost become another God incarnate*].[6] Beatrice's death, just like her conception, is a moment of *plenitudo temporis* (fullness of time), observable in various cultures and from diverse latitudes, just like the promise of salvation represented by Christ.[7] In suggesting that the perfect human individual resembles "Iddio incarnato" [God incarnate], Dante is careful to retain the analogy aspect of "quasi": Dante's beloved cannot possibly be another Christ, but insofar as it is possible for a human being to be Christ-like, Beatrice embodies human perfection in a way that could potentially be appreciated anywhere and everywhere. The deliberation upon the meaning of nine in Beatrice's life at the moment of her passing thus allows Dante to articulate the greatness of the loss: what she was ("fue," "era")—and what she might continue to be—not just for Dante, but for a much broader possible audience, namely, the entire world.

Even as Dante attempts to establish Beatrice's universal significance, he articulates it from an emphatically personal perspective: Dante's "formula asseverativa" [asseverative formula]—"Io dico che" (XXIX.1 [19.4]) [I tell you that]—suggests that the writer's mediation of the beloved's presence remains at the center of the presentation.[8] Although Beatrice's miraculousness is inscribed in the fabric of the cosmos, it has been waiting for an appreciative audience and a suitable form of expression that *Vita nova* provides: "Questo numero fue amico di lei *per dare ad intendere* che ne la sua generazione tutti e nove li mobili cieli perfettissimamente s'aveano insieme" (XXIX.2 [19.5]) [This number was her friend *in order to make it understood* that all nine motioning heavens utterly, perfectly harmonized with one another]; "Questa donna fue accompagnata da questo numero del nove *a dare ad intendere* ch'ella era uno nove, cioè uno miracolo" (XXIX.3 [19.6]) [This woman was accompanied by this number nine *to make it understood* that she was a nine, a miracle in other words]. Beatrice's uniqueness in turn implies the exceptional status of the poet-lover who is chosen to communicate this as part of the novenary logic linking him to Beatrice from an early age: "Io la vidi quasi da la fine del mio nono [anno]" (II.2 [1.3]) [I saw her when I was almost at the end of my ninth year]. If, by reading chapter XXIX [19.4–19.7], readers realize how the mathematical and the numerological can also be personal and intimate, it is precisely this effect that Beatrice's "nineness" has on Dante. For Dante, Beatrice's death becomes a point of breakthrough in interpreting his own life: just as Beatrice was a mediator between "la mirabile Trinitade" (XXIX.3 [19.6]) [the miraculous Trinity] and Dante, so Dante himself can become a mediator of her significance to those able to peruse his works.

If Dante sees mathematical logic not as distant and abstract but as acting in the here and now, it should not surprise us that the numerical rules discovered in Beatrice's life also inform Dante's own art. In chapter XXIX [19.4–19.7], Dante develops his literary version of "manifest" logic insofar as he attempts to convince his readers of the importance of ternary principles not only through intellectual persuasion but also through the integration of Trinitarian structures in the rhythms of his prose. The very first sentence of the chapter is structured as a tricolon ("secondo l'usanza d'Arabia," "secondo l'usanza di Siria," "secondo l'usanza nostra"), bringing together the triple system of thought that explicates Dante's reasoning. Numerous words and their forms appear thrice: *nono/nove* (nine), *usanza* (custom), *primo* (first), *anno* (year). The word *partita* (departure), repeated three times in the previous chapter, is echoed in the triple repetition of "si partìo" [departed]. Insofar as the prose mirrors the ternary qualities of Dante's beloved, Beatrice's absent presence informs both the structure and meaning of the chapter. Writing in a ternary way is not simply a literary choice but also Dante's way of maintaining the connection with the departed beloved by channeling Beatrice's presence in his writings. If *Vita nova* XXIX [19.4–19.7] amounts to Dante's experiment in how his words can bear shadowy traces of Beatrice, this makes the chapter one of the most positively inflected episodes in this section of the *libello*. The loss of Beatrice is reason not only for grief but also for a broadening of the audience that can appreciate her miraculousness, since, even though the direct contact with the lady herself can no longer happen, it becomes possible to experience Beatrice's salvific powers indirectly, through Dante's Beatricean writing.

Dante's treatment of Beatrice's "nineness" is also indebted to the understanding of numbers as mediators between the sublunary and the eternal in Christian philosophy. Perhaps the most concise summary of this idea can be found in the *Convivio*, where, as in *Vita nova* XXIX [19.4–19.7], Dante associates the deciphering of numerical logic with subtlety ("chi ben considera sottilmente"), even if it is ultimately in the nature of numbers to exceed human minds ("questo non potemo noi intendere"): "Non solamente in tutti insieme, ma ancora *in ciascuno è numero*, chi ben considera sottilmente; per che Pittagora, secondo che dice Aristotile nel primo de la Fisica, poneva li principii de le cose naturali lo pari e lo dispari, considerando *tutte le cose esser numero. . . . 'l numero, quant'è in sé considerato, è infinito, e questo non potemo noi intendere*" (2.13.15–19) [*Number exists* not only in all of them [the principles of natural things] together, but also, upon careful reflection, *in each one individually*; for this reason Pythagoras, as Aristotle says in the first book of the Physics, laid down even and odd as the principles of natural things, considering *all things to have numerical aspect. . . . Number insofar as it is considered in itself is infinite, and this we cannot comprehend*].

The idea of numbers as present in all things ("in ciascuno è numero") bears a close affinity to Augustine's examination of numbers as mediator figures, indebted to a long tradition of Christian exegesis.[9] For Augustine, numbers present a language a step further away from mutability and human error, because their laws come to minds and bodies from a Truth independent of both: "Through eternal Form, every temporal thing . . . can manifest and embody number in space and time."[10] Of particular interest to the interpretation of *Vita nova* XXIX [19.4–19.7] is Augustine's idea of corporeal numbers (*numeri corporales*), connecting mutable things to the realm of the eternal and unchanging: "From corporeal . . . numbers we arrive at immutable numbers, . . so that 'the invisible things of God are seen through the things that have been made.'"[11] If Beatrice as a nine is just such a corporeal number, revealing the numerical language of the creator in lived time and humanizing the cosmic dimension, the outlines of the ambassador of heaven she is to become in the *Commedia* are already visible in *Vita nova* XXIX [19.4–19.7]. At the moment when Beatrice's physical absence from this world is most keenly felt, the meditation upon "nineness" amounts to a strategy of processing pain, insofar as it allows Dante firmly to establish Beatrice as his enduring connection to "immutable numbers."

Dante's choice to treat the number nine as an enabler of relationality with a positive Augustinian inflection is far from conventional. As Carlo Vecce points out, "Il lettore contemporaneo che avesse avuto una qualche familiarità con l'esegesi biblica sarebbe rimasto a ragione meravigliato" [The contemporary reader who had any familiarity with biblical exegesis would have rightly been amazed].[12] In many expositions of biblical passages, nine is interpreted negatively: according to St. Jerome, it is a number of pain and punishment, primarily because associated with the hour of Christ's death.[13] Amazement, as Vecce points out, may well be an appropriate response to the parallel set up by Dante. However, Dante's unorthodox response to the Christological significance of the number is also a logical extension of the traditional association, allowing Dante to embrace the more optimistic possibilities of Beatrice's death. If one decides to focus not on the pain and sorrow that Christ's death brings but rather on its salvific potential for all humankind, one might begin to understand how the death of Beatrice, which, as we have seen, is an equally potent moment of *plenitudo temporis*, might also be personally salvific for Dante. While it might be true that the meanings assigned to individual numbers and numeric proportions in the Middle Ages gradually became relatively stable,[14] what *Vita nova* XXIX [19.4–19.7] shows is that they are far from incontestable. In recuperating the negative potential of nine *in bono* and converting it from a sign of pain to the number of possibility, *Vita nova* XXIX [19.4–19.7] is a prime example of Dante's reading the numerical tradition "subtly," that is, testing the applicability of conventional interpretations to the story of his life.

The very meaning of subtlety is up for debate in the chapter. As *TLIO* documents, subtlety in this period was primarily understood as intellectual and interpretive complexity or the capacity to process it: "sottile: difficile, complesso; che richiede attenzione e capacità di distinzione e interpretazione per essere correttamente compreso."[15] At first, Dante seems to suggest that even if numbers are excessive in relation to human subtlety, they encourage a proliferation of subtle interpretations. His interpretation in *Vita nova* is simply one of many possible ones, and perhaps not even the most sophisticated one: "Forse ancora per più sottile persona si vederebbe in ciò più sottile ragione" (XXIX.4 [19.7]) [Perhaps a still subtler person would see a subtler reason in this]. While critics have traditionally viewed Dante's admission to analytical crudeness as lacking in sincerity,[16] I believe that the originality of Dante's treatment of subtlety emerges particularly clearly when placed in the context of the ongoing medieval debate about *sottigliezza*.

Dante's choice of vernacular prose to explore subtle relationships between the macro- and microcosm is striking at a time when it was still not self-evident that *sottigliezza* was something that the vernacular, or those who wrote and read in the vernacular, were capable of achieving. As Bono Giamboni puts it in his *Fiore di rettorica* (1260s): "La materia è molto sottile, e le sottili cose non si possono bene aprire in volgare, sì che se n'abbia pieno intendimento" (5) [The matter is very subtle, and subtle things cannot be explained well in the vernacular so that one can achieve a complete understanding of them].[17] According to Francesco Bruni, subtlety was initially ascribed to university-style philosophical arguments conducted in Latin.[18] Even when subtlety came to describe vernacular writing, it was a mark of Latinate poetry: *De vulgari eloquentia* suggests that Dante and Cino da Pistoia compose poetry "more sweetly and subtly" (*dulcius . . . subtiliusque*) than other vernacular poets because their poems are more firmly grounded in the Latinate "grammatica" (1.10.4). In stilnovist poetry, subtlety continues to carry the risk of the abuse of philosophical inspiration, as when the accusation of *sottiglianza* is brought against Guido Guinizzelli by Bonagiunta in "Voi, ch'avete mutata la mainera": "Così passate voi di sottigliansa, / e non si può trovar chi ben ispogna, / cotant' è iscura vostra parlatura" (lines 9–11) [So completely you outdo everyone with your subtlety that none can explain the obscurity of what you say], or when Guido Orlandi warns Cavalcanti: "Per troppa sottiglianza il fil si rompe" (line 1) [the bowstring breaks from excessive subtlety]. The novelty of *Vita nova* XXIX [19.4–19.7] is that subtlety, which characterized primarily, if not exclusively, Latin disputation and the stilnovist lyric in the Italian tradition, is now applied to theological and philosophical inquiry conducted in vernacular prose. In the chapter, vernacular prose becomes a medium subtle enough to negotiate the very meaning of subtlety.

However, the inflection of Dante's subtlety in *Vita nova* XXIX [19.4–19.7] is very different from the finesse of thought normally indicated by *sottile* in the early Italian lyric. While within the parameters of the stilnovist poetic debate, the language of subtlety is often paired with obscurity, willful or otherwise ("campo semantico di *escur*"),[19] Dante's language in the chapter is aimed at achieving maximum clarity. Dante is hardly ever as explicit in expounding any event in the *libello*: "dunque" [therefore] begins a further explication of reasoning already clearly expressed, with "cioè" [that is] appearing thrice in the very same sentence. The intention to leave no crucial element incomprehensible, to reveal all relationships as openly as possible, is evident in Dante's use of the syllogistic method ("e ciò intendo così" [by which I mean the following]), and the reliance on accepted astronomical and calendrical knowledge.

At the same time, Dante's explication stresses the writer's intellectual humility in producing an explanation that is knowingly limited: "questa potrebbe essere *una* ragione" (XXIX.2 [19.5]) [*one* reason . . . could be this]; "Questa è *una* ragione di ciò" (XXIX.3 [19.6]) [This is *one* reason]. The role of reason in deciphering Beatrice's "nineness" remains deliberately ambiguous, not least because *sottile* in *Vita nova* often signals an interpretation of events that is indebted to visions and revelations and not logic, as in the vision of chapter XXIV [15]: "Chi volesse sottilmente considerare, quella Beatrice chiamerebbe Amore" (XXIV.5 [15.5]) [Whoever wants to give the matter subtle consideration would call Beatrice "Love"].

In her contribution to this volume on chapter XXXIII [22], Katherine Powlesland rightly points out that *sottile* in *Vita nova* signals the cognitive lacunae deliberately left by the author to encourage readers' engagement. When Dante invites the reader, "più sottile persona" [subtler person], to guess the other possible meanings of Beatrice's "nineness"—"più sottile ra-gione" (XXIX.4 [19.7]) [subtler reasons])—evoked but unexplained, the fi-nality of Beatrice's death is contrasted with the openness of interpretation, the ongoing questioning of her significance for Dante and the world. Yet this invitation is also a provocation: if Dante's explanation is authorized by "la in-fallibile veritade" (XXIX.3 [19.6]), which has been identified with theol-ogy,[20] it is hard to see how the readers' intellectual subtlety, no matter how great, can see further than "infallible truth." If initially Dante seems to en-courage the plurality of interpretive possibilities, at the end of the chapter he enacts a seemingly arbitrary countermove. Ever-subtler intellectualization is not the way to proceed; the right explanation is the one that pleases *me*, says Dante: "Ma questa [ragione] è quella . . . che più mi piace" (XXIX.4 [19.7]) [This is the [reason] that I like the most].

In *Paradiso*, it is scripture that sets the limits of intellectual questioning:

> Certo a colui che *meco s'assottiglia*,
> se la Scrittura sovra voi non fosse,
> da dubitar sarebbe a maraviglia.
>   Oh terreni animali! Oh menti grosse!
>   (*Par.* 19.82–85)

[Certainly the one *who matches wits with / me*, if the Scriptures were not over you, there would be wondrous cause for doubt. / Oh earth-bound animals! Oh gross minds!][21]

In *Vita nova* XXIX [19.4–19.7], perhaps more interestingly, what signals the end of interpretation for Dante is a perceptible sense of fittingness. The im-pulse to end the chapter after having discovered the most auspicious words is fueled by a realization that Dante's understanding of Beatrice's "nineness" simply does not benefit from further intellectual investigation. "[W]hen somebody says that . . . seven and three are ten, nobody says that they *ought to be*, but recognizing simply that they *are* so, he does not correct them as an examiner, but simply rejoices as a discoverer," says Augustine.[22] In represent-ing Dante as just such a discoverer, rejoicing in the newly unearthed sense of

Beatrice's place in the divine order, the passage warns against the kind of intellectual calisthenics that only results in increased bafflement, summarized in a still-recognizable proverb that appears in Petrarch's *Canzoniere*: "Chi troppo assottiglia si scavezza" (105.48) [He who is too subtle breaks his own neck].[23]

If *Vita nova* XXIX [19.4–19.7] highlights a certain futility in looking for ever-subtler interpretations, this does not mean that the new authorizing principle of pleasure is expendable on intellectual terms. Because of the semantic range of *piacere*, which encompasses both the purely physical-sensory and the rational-intellective,[24] the explanation "che più mi piace" [that I like the most] can combine both the intellectual joy associated with finding a rationalization that best fits the available data, and the satisfaction experienced on the level of repetition and sound, which, as we have seen, is achieved through Dante's incorporation of ternary structures into his writing. The logic of *piacere* governing the chapter amounts to Dante's acknowledgment that true conviction comes from words as bearers not only of meaning but also of feeling, combining intellectual fittingness and subjective conviction that exceeds discursive knowledge.

Sottile may be a profoundly aspirational term, insofar as it is an angelic attribute, as Dante suggests in *Vita nova* XXXIII.8 [22.8]: "lo intelletto loro alto, sottile / face maravigliar" (lines 25–26) [their high, subtle intellect / amazes]. For a living being, it is impossible to be perfectly subtle and completely free of "grossezza di materia" (*Conv.* 3.7.5) [the material dimension]; nor is it necessary. Accepting that some degree of "grossezza" is only human, Dante explores how earthly "gross minds" (*Par.* 19.85), through their connection with Beatrice, "angiola giovanissima" (II.8 [1.9]) [youthful angel], may approach the angelic condition and experience this connection as a source of intellectual and aesthetic pleasure. The miracle of Beatrice's "nineness" as explored in *Vita nova* XXIX [19.4–19.7] is that, by embodying the Trinitarian principles in her life, a mortal person can assist the angelization of another fully material man's mind.

Vita nova XXX [19.8–19.10]

ALESSIA CARRAI

At the beginning of chapter XXVIII [19.1–19.3], the quotation from Jeremiah's Lamentations—"Quomodo sedet sola civitas plena populo! facta est quasi vidua domina gentium" [How doth the city sit solitary that was full of people! How is she become a widow, she that was great among the nations!][1]—marks a turning point in Dante's life, opening a new section of the *Vita nova*.[2] In chapters XXVIII–XXIX [19.1–19.7], the author chooses not to talk about Beatrice's death and to offer instead a retrospective reflection on the relationship between his beloved and the number nine, thus showing his readers the signs of Beatrice's connection to God. After this suspension of the narrative, chapter XXX [19.8–19.10] returns to the events that immediately follow the death of the "gentilissima" [the most gracious lady].

The very first words of the chapter—"Poi che fue partita da questo secolo" [because she had departed from this world]—recall Dante's hallucination of Beatrice's death, as described in chapter XXIII [14]: "La tua mirabile donna è partita di questo secolo" (XXIII.6 [14.5]) [Your miraculous lady has left this world]. They immediately bring the reader into an atmosphere of loss and mourning. The first thing that Dante says he does—as a character—after the death of Beatrice is to write a letter to the most powerful citizens of Florence, "li principi de la terra" [the rulers of the land], to talk about the state of desolation and misery of the whole city. As Marco Santagata points out, the letter Dante is referring to was probably actually written and is not an element that was invented for the purposes of the narrative. In June 1290, Cino dei Bardi (cousin of Simone dei Bardi, Beatrice's widower) became one of the priors of the city of Florence. It is likely that Dante wrote a letter of condolence to a close relative of Beatrice and that this letter was written in Latin in order to show his learning and to prove his rhetorical ability.[3]

However, in the carefully planned structure of the *Vita nova*, Dante's mention of this episode serves a purpose that goes far beyond the mere factual account. In what follows, I will analyze two main features of this missing letter and I will show how the reference to this omitted text fosters reflection on the function of poetry and the role of readership in the *Vita nova*. This short and yet very dense chapter of the *libello* constitutes a fundamental step for the understanding of Dante's poetic choices in the last part of the book and sets some essential coordinates for the interpretation of the prosimetrum as a whole.

The letter starts with the same quotation from the book of Lamentations that opened chapter XXVIII [19.1–19.3]. The intense dialogue between Dante's *Vita nova* and Jeremiah's Lamentations has been thoroughly analyzed by scholars, especially (but not only) as regards the section *in morte* of the *libello*.[4] As Ronald Martinez has pointed out, the presence of this intertext in the *Vita nova* works on multiple levels. First of all, it provides a rhetorical model of grieving, with some specific tropes and words that Dante reuses and adapts to his own needs.[5] Second, the book of Lamentations was closely connected to medieval liturgy and was used, in particular, to mourn Christ's death during the matins of Holy Week.[6] This means that, for a medieval reader, Dante's references to Jeremiah's book would immediately create (or rather reinforce) a parallel between Beatrice and Christ. Moreover, as Helena Phillips-Robins suggests in this volume, the connection to medieval liturgy works as an invitation to Dante's readers actively to participate in this grief, indwelling Jeremiah's words in different and personal ways.[7]

Martinez has also shed light on the dialectic between the private and the public spheres contained in Lamentations. Analyzing the commentary tradition on Jeremiah's book, Martinez has shown that the public lament for the state of Jerusalem was interpreted as an echo of Jeremiah's personal lament for the death of King Josiah, killed several years before the destruction of the city. The cry for a person and the cry for a city are closely intertwined in the book of Lamentations as part of a rhetorical strategy aimed at moving the public to pity or anger.[8] This crucial point of intersection between private and public becomes a fundamental model for Dante's *Vita nova* and comes particularly to the fore in chapter XXX [19.8–19.10]. Here Dante uses the same language as Lamentations, creating an implicit comparison between himself and Jeremiah, who both cry and write at the same time,[9] and the two cities of Florence and Jerusalem. As many commentators have noticed, the description of Florence as widowed ("vedova"), deprived ("dispogliata da ogni dignitade"), and desolate ("desolata") (XXX.1 [19.8]) derives both from the text of Lamentations and from its commentary tradition.[10] The atmosphere of grief involves the whole city, and the death of Beatrice cannot be regarded as a private event.

This leads us to the first key point of chapter XXX [19.8–19.10]. It is clear that, after Beatrice's passing, the *Vita nova* openly addresses a broader public.[11] In the section *in vita* of his *libello*, Dante presents his work as a conversation with a selected aristocracy of "fedeli d'amore" (III.9 [1.20]) [Love's faithful]. After Beatrice's death, Dante's relationship with his readers seems to change. The letter to the most influential citizens of Florence, followed by Dante's interaction with some Florentine "uomini a li quali si convenia di fare onore" (XXXIV.1 [23.1]) [men whose rank required that one greet them respectfully] reveals that the whole city has now become the interlocutor of Dante's discourse on poetry and love. When, in chapter LX [29], Dante will address his sonnet "Deh peregrini" [Oh, pilgrims] to pilgrims walking through Florence on their way to Rome, the process of broadening the work's audience will cross the city limits and reach its apex. The reason for this poetic choice lies in Dante's new idea of love, which is developed throughout the *libello*. If Beatrice, as commentators suggest, embodies the concept of *caritas*,[12] the kind of love she represents and inspires is not tied to her physical presence and is not restricted to a cultural elite. After her death, her salvific powers survive in Dante's words, which must therefore reach a broader public. And this shift from a private to a collective dimension is so important in the *Vita nova* that the first text that Dante writes after the death of the "gentilissima" [the most gracious lady] is not a poem but a letter addressed to the rulers of Florence.

The first signs of the *Vita nova*'s universal scope can be found in its very first chapters. The strong presence of scriptural references in the opening pages of the *Vita nova*, as well as Beatrice's early and ongoing association with Christ, had already suggested that this book tells a story that is only apparently private.[13] After the death of the woman, however, Dante's aspiration for universality finally becomes evident. If the reference to Lamentations in chapter XXVIII [19.1–19.3], followed by the meditation on Beatrice's relationship with the number nine (XXIX [19.4–19.7]),[14] already gave the idea of a grief that needed to involve the whole community, in chapter XXX [19.8–19.10] the letter addressed to "li principi della terra" explicitly gives Beatrice's death a public—almost civic—resonance, opening a new phase in Dante's dialogue with his readers.

The second piece of information that Dante gives us about the letter is that it is written in Latin and that, for this precise reason, it has not been included in the *libello*. In the second part of the chapter, the author's voice intervenes to discuss and explain his choices. The metapoetic content of this passage is immediately clear if we look at the terms that Dante uses. The verb *scrivere* (to write) is used six times in the same short paragraph, while the term *parole* (words) appears twice. Moreover, the presence of the word *intendimento* (intention, purpose), which occurs twice in this form and once as *intenzione*, draws the reader's attention to the programmatic nature of chapter XXX [19.8–19.10].

A similar combination of words can be found in other passages of the *Vita nova* that involve the author's active role in selecting the material that should or should not enter the *libello*. In the very first chapter, in the well-known metaphor of the book of memory that opens the *prosimetrum*, Dante claims that, under the rubric "incipit vita nova," he found "scritte le parole le quali è mio intendimento d'assemprare in questo libello" (I.1 [1.1]) [the words which I intend to copy down in this little book]. The opening lines of the *Vita nova* contain the exact same combination of words that we find in chapter XXX [19.8–19.10], at the beginning of a new section of the *libello* written after Beatrice's death.

However, a similar vocabulary is also connected to the author's choices in chapter V [2.6–2.9], when Dante states that he does not want to include poems written for the first "donna dello schermo" [screen woman]: "Feci per lei certe cosette per rima, le quali non è mio intendimento di scrivere qui" (V.3 [2.9]) [I wrote certain little rhymes for her which I do not intend to write down here]. And the word *intendimento* also occurs in chapter XVIII

[10.3–10.11], where Dante introduces the concept of the "poesia della lode" [poetry of praise] and discusses his new poetic ideas with some "gentili donne" [lovely women]. Here, one of the women denounces Dante's inconsistency regarding his poetry: "Se tu ne dicessi vero, quelle parole che tu n'hai dette in notificando la tua condizione, avrestù operate con altro intendimento" (XVIII.7 [10.9]) [If what you're saying is true, those poems that you wrote about your condition must have been written with some other aim in mind]. Finally, Dante the author talks about his "intendimento" in chapter XXVIII [19.1–19.3], when he declares that he is not going to talk about Beatrice's death directly: "E avvegna che forse piacerebbe a presente trattare alquanto de la sua dipartita da noi, non è lo mio intendimento di trattarne qui per tre ragioni" (XXVIII.2 [19.2]) [And though it might be desirable at this point to say something about her departure from us, it is not my intention to write about it here, for three reasons].

As Barański has noted, Dante is very keen to guide his readers and orient the reception and interpretation of his book.[15] And the word *intendimento* (combined with the semantic area of writing and words) seems to mark some pivotal moments in Dante's reflection on his own poetry in the *Vita nova*, especially as regards the selection of the material to be included in his *libello*. In chapter XXX [19.8–19.10], this metapoetic reflection revolves around the language to be used in the *Vita nova*.

Dante has already discussed the status of the vernacular in chapter XXV [16], where he states the equivalence between "dire per rima in volgare" [to write rhymes in the vernacular] and "dire per versi in latino" (XXV.4 [16.4]) [to write verses in Latin].[16] Here, for the first time, he refers to the vernacular as another discriminating criterion for the words that can or cannot enter his *libello*. So far, the only selecting criterion that he explicitly declared was connected to the subject matter of his poems. In chapter I [1.1], Dante warned his readers that he was going to make a selection of his memories in composing and organizing his book. At V.3 [2.9], he added that the words contained in the *Vita nova* must all be written to praise Beatrice.[17] Now the reader is once again invited to reread the previous parts of the *libello* keeping in mind that these words must be spoken in the vernacular.[18]

At the beginning of the last section of the *Vita nova*, before he starts mourning Beatrice by means of his poetry, Dante opens a space to interact with his readers and to discuss a poetic project aimed at redefining the potential and the value of the vernacular. And in so doing, he also inserts himself into a broader context, demonstrating his self-awareness as a poet in the literary scene of thirteenth-century Italy.[19] At the end of chapter XXX [19.8–19.10], Dante refers to Guido Cavalcanti, "questo mio primo amico" [my best friend], as the official dedicatee of the *libello*, who shares with him a similar idea of poetry, the same poetic "intenzione" [idea].[20]

The relationship between Dante and Guido is complex and fascinating. On the one hand, the early poetic correspondence between them testifies to a period of intellectual affinity and friendship.[21] On the other hand, it is equally evident that there is a moment of ideological and personal rupture in the relationship between the two poets, whose respective ideas of love and poetry became at some point irreconcilable. The chronology and dynamics of this crisis continue to inform the critical debate on Dante's and Guido's works,[22] although, in the absence of reliable philological evidence, the problem seems to date unresolvable.[23]

Some scholars have noted that the *Vita nova* itself, while stating an intellectual agreement with Guido Cavalcanti, also presents some passages that seem to suggest Dante's overcoming of his "primo amico" [best friend].[24] Despite this ambiguity, however, the author of the *Vita nova* is very clear in casting his *libello* in terms of a poetic project shared and approved by the older Guido, at least as far as the linguistic choices are concerned. And in the context of the reflection about language proposed in chapter XXX [19.8–19.10], the dedication to Guido Cavalcanti is particularly significant, given his *auctoritas* as one of (if not the) most important vernacular poet in late thirteenth-century Florence.[25] The reference to Guido allows Dante to legitimate his *libello* as part of a broader movement aimed at renovating the language of literature and establishing the vernacular's authoritativeness. On this matter, Dante and Guido cannot but share the same poetic "intenzione" [idea]. The subject matter of this new vernacular poetry is a completely different matter, and the presentation of arguments that are incompatible with Cavalcanti's ideas finds its place in other passages of the *Vita nova*.

To summarize, chapter XXX [19.8–19.10] is a space where the voice of the author emerges to reflect on his own poetic program. Paradoxically, the letter written to "li principi de la terra" [the rulers of the land], which we are not allowed to read because it is excluded from the *libello*, gives us some fundamental information about Dante's poetic project. First of all, it makes clear that Beatrice's death is not a private event and that the novelty of the love she represents and of the poetry she inspires concerns a public broader than the elite of "fedeli d'Amore" [Love's faithful]. It is not by chance that Dante defines this new section of the book, written after the death of Beatrice, as "nova materia" [new subject matter]. The author of the *libello* traces here a clear distinction between old and new topics, inviting his (new) readers to engage with his loss and to reflect on the poetry that came before the death of Beatrice and on the one that will come after.

Second, the absence of the letter from Dante's book informs us about the linguistic choices of the author. After Beatrice's death, Dante's "stilo de la sua loda" (XXVI.4 [17.4]) [the style I had praised her with] acquires a universal significance, and he makes clear that this salvific message must be entrusted to the vernacular. With striking concision, Dante gives this short chapter a programmatic relevance that helps us to understand not only the last part of the *libello* but the poetics that lies behind the whole project of his *Vita nova*.

Vita nova XXXI [20]

RYAN PEPIN

In the "Introduzione" to his 1939 commentary on the *Rime*, Contini wrote that Dante's style involves a "perpetuo sopraggiungere della riflessione tecnica accanto alla poesia" [perpetual superaddition of technical reflection alongside the poetry].[1] This idea sits behind the "metaliterary" Dante dear to Anglo-American critics,[2] but in prewar Italy the poet's "technical reflection" on style had another ring to it too. In 1940, Arnaldo Bocelli summed up the critical innovations of the new generation of Italian poets, to which Contini belonged, as "una sorta di poetica empirica, sperimentale, che fa largo posto ai problemi particolari, ai singoli fatti o elementi tecnici, stilistici, espressivi, al valore formale della parola e della pagina" [a sort of experimental, empirical poetics that gives considerable space to particular problems, to individual facts or technical, stylistic, and expressive elements—to the formal value of the word and the page].[3] Dante's poetry, in Contini's eyes, was not of a piece with the stylistic modes of his contemporaries but was motivated by a "technical" criticism of those modes, a manner of making that could be a resource for the new, minute, "experimental" criticism developed by the twentieth-century interwar generation. Innovating "technical reflection" on style was quickly becoming an important desideratum for philology in the twentieth century. Paul Maas, in his famous *Textkritik* of 1927, wrote that "the core of practically every problem in textual criticism is a problem of *style*, and the categories of stylistics are still far less settled than those of textual criticism."[4]

Understanding Dante's style is particularly important in this section of the *libello*. Fifteen years ago Stefano Carrai wrote that the style of chapter XXXI [20] was a "key" to the whole of the *Vita nova*—the most explicit rendering of the *plaint* or *elegy* genre to which the whole work belongs.[5] So here I would like to ask again how the poem embraces a *style*, tracing the poet's "riflessione tecnica" on the elements that make it up.

The *canzoni* in the *Vita nova* are distinct from the other poems. Scribes lavished colored initials on the *canzoni*, often one for each strophe,[6] and this codicological distinctiveness gives them an architectonic distinctiveness in the overall work. So it is particularly significant that, in a poem that acts as a lodestar, Dante refers to a stylistic genre. He calls "Li occhi dolenti" "mio lamento" (line 54) [my lament].[7] But how does he reflect on the prior techniques of mournful song?

In one significant sense, the genre is reflected as if in a mirror. Medieval Latin love-laments or *planctus* are often sung in a female voice, be it in the person of Dido, or, particularly, Mary.[8] Not only is "Li occhi dolenti" addressed to women, "le donne e le donzelle / a cui le tue sorelle / erano usate di portar letizia" (lines 72–74) [the women and girls to whom your sisters [other canzoni] used to bring happiness], but it keeps exclusively female company: "non voi parlare altrui" (line 10) [I do not want to talk to others]. Early *planctus* are shot through with passionate cries of women's pain: in the tenth-century *Augsburger Passionslied*, Mary breaks off—"Si greu est a pærlær!" [How difficult it is to speak!].[9] Centuries later Dante still cries, "Lingua non è che dicer lo sapesse" (line 62) [There is no tongue that knows how to say it]. So to begin, Dante's *canzone* is a male "reflection"—in the sense of a seeing backward—of a preceding stylistic genre. And it has an effect on the future of lament too. In Chaucer's Dido-lament in the *Legend of Good Women*, we find the lines:

if that God, that hevene and erthe made,
Wolde han a love, for beaute and goodnesse,
And womanhod, and trouthe, and semelynesse,
Whom shulde he loven but this lady swete?[10]

This bold metaphysical conceit, which Dronke sees as new to the genre with Chaucer, seems like a borrowing from the range of "Li occhi dolenti,"[11] in particular from lines like "ché luce de la sua umilitate / passò li cieli con tanta vertute / che fé maravigliar l'etterno sire" (lines 21–23) [a [ray of] light of her humility / passed [through] the [nine] heavens with such force, / that it made the Eternal Sire marvel].[12]

At least one reader, then, returned Dante's innovations to the tradition of female lament. Distinct from female love-lament, however, there was a tradition of Occitan political lament—a genre of men weeping over famous men. In Gaucelm Faidit's *planh* for Richard Lionheart, "Fortz chausa es que tot lo major dan" [It is a terrible thing, that the greatest loss], the poet admonishes his audience: "Ben a dur cor totz hom c'o pot suffrir" (line 9) [Whoever can stand it truly has a hard heart]. Dante similarly admonishes: "Chi no la piange, quando ne ragiona, / core ha di pietra sì malvagio e vile, / ch'entrar non i puote spirito benegno" (lines 32–34) [Whoever does not cry over her, when he discusses her, has a heart of stone so wicked and low, that a benign spirit cannot enter there]. If hard-heartedness is perhaps a broader commonplace, Occitan lament for the death of a political leader offers a precedent for Dante's particular mix of praise with sorrow in funerary song. Giraut de Borneil sings, in his *sirventes* on the death of Aimar V of Limoges, "Plaing e sospir / E plor e chan, / Mas no m'adu mos chantz solatz" (62.1–3) [I lament and sigh / and weep and sing, / but my song brings me no pleasure]. This weeping-singing characterizes "Li occhi dolenti" too: "*piangendo* ragionassi" (31.1 [20.1]), "convenemi parlar *traendo guai*" (line 6), "Poscia *piangendo*, sol nel mio lamento / chiamo Beatrice . . . / e mentre ch'io la chiamo, me conforta" (lines 54–56) [Then crying, alone in my lament / I call on Beatrice . . . / and while I call on her, I am comforted] (compare Giraut's lack of "solatz"). Giraut continues:

> Non puesc trobar
> Cui li met'en eganza,
> Ni de man bel enseignamen,
> Per que iois fail e genz gabars
> Merm'ar e desenanza.
>   (62.40–44)

———

[And I can find / no one to equal him / in pleasing conversation and in the many fair accomplishments that were his / so that joy fails and gracious jesting / is now lost and in decline.]

"Li occhi dolenti" is often seen as a mournful reprocessing of the praise style of "Donne ch'avete" ["Women who have"], but praise and lament have a long history together in *planctus*. It is right to say that "Li occhi dolenti," as a lament, reworks the earlier praise style of "Donne ch'avete." But it is also true that lament and praise have a history bound up with each other, and mourning has perhaps always been a reflection on the meaning of praise.

"Technical reflection" on style, for the new critics as well as for Dante, can also be more than a question of genre. Style can be the "singoli fatti" of a poem's language. De Robertis notes in his commentary that the beginning of the regular strophes in "Li occhi dolenti" have something in common: "Ita n'è Beatrice" (line 10) [Beatrice has gone], "Partissi" (line 29) [It parted], "Dannomi" (line 43) [They give me], "Pianger" (line 57) [Crying]. Each strophe begins emphatically with a verb.[13] Each, save the last, also happens to emphasize a sound law of old Italian—the Tobler-Mussafia law. According to this rule, a clitic pronoun cannot be placed first in the sentence (so "Partissi" cannot be "Si partì"). Analogously, a weak auxiliary verb will not be placed in the first position, and will often follow the participle in old syntax: line 10, "Ita n'è Beatrice," is in fact Rohlfs's own example of this phenomenon (§985).

Stylistic critics often think of style as the exception: the *clic*, as Spitzer calls it, that lifts off the particular voice from the norms of grammar—the solecism involved in Proust's reference to "mon moi." But observing an old sound rule might also help focus in on facts of style. I sense in these regular stanza openings this canzone's particular absorption in questions of verbal voice. We might ask: Is "Ita n'è Beatrice" really a *passato prossimo*, where "Ita" is equivalent to the participle *andata*, or does this resemblance to a deponent form (*ita est*) instead convey a middle voice—as again in line 13, "si n'è gita" [she [+ *si ne*] has gone]?[14] A similar question arises for "èssi gloriosa" (line 31) [is [+ *si*] glorious] and indeed for the perfect form in 'Partissi . . . l'anima gentile' (lines 29–30) [The noble soul [+ *si*] parted]. Verbs in the middle voice and perfects, like these, have a very ancient connection in Indo-European languages.[15] The middle was formed on the perfect at a time when the perfect expressed, not a temporal fact, but a "way of being for the subject" or a *habitus*.[16] The middle "Ita n'è Beatrice" can, of course, be simplified to the passive-voiced "tolta ne fue"—she was taken—as it is in the prose (XXXI.5 [20.5]).[17] But given, in the poem, Dante's attempts to express a state—"quale ella fue" (line 42) [what she was], "quale è stata la mia vita" (line 60) [what my life was], "qual ch'io sia" (line 69) [what I am]—an experiment with *stative* aspect, a glimmer of which perhaps still attaches to these middles and perfects in emphatic positions, is worth raising. Here grammar may speak to style after all: something particular about a poet's voice emerges through his probing of the richness of verbal voice in old syntax.

A special issue in the *Vita nova*, when it comes to style, is the technical difference between prose and poetry. This relationship is still for the most part framed as a question of models for the use of both together: Menippean satire, *prosimetra,* scriptural commentary, the *vidas* and *razos* prefacing *chansonniers.* But to take a step back, we might simply ask: How did the Middle Ages understand the stylistic difference between poetry and prose? There are a range of ways this distinction was framed, from "no difference at all,"[18] to ideas, especially in the High Middle Ages, of poetry's conciseness relative to prose—such that it could supply memory and better organize knowledge.[19] Chapter XXXI [20] offers a unique example in the *Vita nova* of a common practice in the Middle Ages where the prose/poetry distinction is a matter of not just theoretical concern: the practice of "translation" from verse to prose.[20] The first sentence of prose renders lines 1–6 of the accompanying *canzone.* "Lagrimato" [having cried] in the prose renders the poem's "lagrimar" (line 2) [crying], "disfogare" in the prose the poem's "sfogar" (line 4) [venting], but the rest of the prose rendering is not so simple. There is both an effort at simpler explication in the prose—eyes that are "vinti" [overcome] in the poem (line 3) become "affaticati" (XXXI.1 [20.1]) [worn out]—but also at more complex rhetorical periphrasis: the poem's "dolore, / che a poco a poco a la morte mi mena" (lines 4–5) [suffering, / which bit by bit leads me to death] becomes, in the prose, pain that "era fatto distruggitore de l'anima mia" (XXXI.1 [20.1]) [had become destroyer of my soul]. The stylistic relationship of poetry to prose is not one way: both can compete to render a rhetorically ornamented artifact of the other.[21]

The opening lines of the *canzone* have seemed to many to be particularly syntactically complex[22]—something this poem shares with "E' m'incresce a me" [It causes me compassion], a poem that it points to at line 59 and that also begins in "doglia" and "pietà" [suffering and pity]. Syntactical wroughtness, surprisingly, is an accomplishment of Dante *poeta*, not Dante *prosatore*. Some of this impression of wroughtness has to do with syntax that was normal in the Middle Ages but that no longer is: line 2, "hanno di lagrimar sofferta pena" [have, from crying, suffered pain], sounds wrought now but involves a separation of auxiliary verb and participle quite common at the time.[23] But we can still ask: Is "per pietà del core" [because of /for pity of the heart] in line 1 a "per" of *cause* ("Bewegrundes") or *interest* ("Interesses")?[24] Is it the heart's or the eyes' "pietà"? The extended coordination in the opening lines of the poem has a counterpart in the prose. In the prose "version," we see all this rendered in well-executed periodic structure, with relative isocola and clearly distinguished connectors: "Poi che . . . e . . . pensai . . . ; e però . . ." [After . . . and . . . I thought . . . ; but . . .]. Prose and poetry are distinct techniques, and their stylistic accomplishments can even be reflected in one another: the prose can simplify or ornament the lexis of the poem, and poetry and prose can even compete against another to render complex syntax through rhythmical partitions.

Contini's sense of Dante's "technical reflection" involves casting the poet as a critic—of his contemporaries, and also of his own work. In one particular sense, this is especially true of the present *canzone*. The medieval critical form of *accessus ad auctores* demonstrated to readers of a text how to reflect on what they read. It asked readers to bear in mind the *W*'s, as we say now: the *quis, quid, cur, quando,* and *ubi*.[25] The regular strophes of "Li occhi dolenti" are structured this way: stanza 2 asks "perché" (line 27) [why]; stanza 3 asks "chi" [who]; stanza 4 asks "quando" [when]; stanza 5 asks "quale" [which]. In addition to the *divisio* in the prose section, which for the first time here is moved up to preface the poem—"La dividerò prima che io la scriva; e cotale modo terrò da qui innanzi" (XXXI.2 [20.2]) [I will divide it up before I write it down; and I will maintain this method from this point on]—another means of "technical reflection" lends shape to the poem.

These notes begin, and hardly exhaust, an analysis of what makes up Dante's style. But I hope they are enough to suggest that when we refer to Dante's style, we cannot use givens. Male and female voices, mourning and praise genres, standard and marked syntax, poetic and prose ornament, even poetic composition and critical reflection—all of these have a stake in the other. By pursuing "singoli fatti," we quickly discover we are following a "dialectical torment,"[26] to use Contini's phrase, which is perhaps as close to the poet's style as we can come.

Vita nova XXXII [21]

VALENTINA MELE

That the *Vita nova* is a book composed of poetic occasions, of *causae scribendi*, is an aspect so obvious that it often goes unobserved.[1] It is Dante himself who first made this clear in the work's very incipit, announcing his intention to transcribe "le parole" [the words] from "the book of [his] memory" (I.1 [1.1]). Here "le parole," as Guglielmo Gorni suggests, might perhaps be understood as verses, in what is a typically Dantean use of the term,[2] qualifying Domenico De Robertis's more generic interpretation of the term as instead referring to "i ricordi" [the memories].[3]

Chapter XXXII [21] constitutes a particularly relevant example of occasional poetry, as it includes a sonnet that the author himself notes in the prose as having been commissioned. As De Robertis proposes, there is no reason not to believe the author, and not to accept his explanation,[4] given that we have a pre–*Vita nova* version of the lyric, which has been reconstructed by De Robertis on the basis of the manuscript tradition of Dante's *Rime*.[5] The purpose of this chapter is to analyze aspects relating to the content, language, and style of the verses included in the chapter, with a particular emphasis on the choice of vocabulary. The declared occasional nature of the lyric and its two *redazioni* (drafts) will be discussed in light of the poems' intertextual connections to the lyric tradition and specifically to the poetry of Guido Cavalcanti.[6] The analysis will be set within the framework of spiritual and poetic refinement that can be observed throughout the narrative development of the *prosimetrum*.[7]

As the reader learns in chapter XXXII [21], the sonnet "Venite a intender li sospiri miei" [Come listen to my sighs] was composed in the context of a very specific social dynamic (the public expression of mourning), whose composition in verses expresses pain and sorrow at the loss of a woman. The link between the text and the occasion can be deduced only from the prose that both precedes and introduces the lyric, providing details that do not come to light in the verses themselves.

The prose makes it clear that the commissioner of the sonnet is a friend of the autobiographical subject of the *Vita nova*, one categorized as "immediatamente dopo lo primo" (XXXII.1 [21.1]) [the friend of mine right after the first]. This friend has been identified as Manetto Portinari,[8] the brother of Beatrice. The prose informs the reader that the request to write "alcuna cosa per una donna che s'era morta" (XXXII.2 [21.2]) [something for him about a woman who had died] is made without specifying that the woman at issue is Beatrice. Dante, however, infers that the object of this request is indeed the *gentilissima*—"accorgendomi che questi dicea solamente per questa benedetta" (XXXII.2 [21.2]) [realizing that he was simply talking about the blessed one], a close relative of the commissioner of the piece: "E questi fu tanto distretto di sanguinitade con questa gloriosa che nullo più presso lo era" (XXXII.1 [21.1]) [And he was such a close blood relation of the glorious one that nobody was closer to her]. The poet thus decides to acquiesce to his friend's request, taking the opportunity to voice his own suffering and grief at the loss of Beatrice, and, in so doing, composes a lyric that gives voice to the anguish of another.

The theme of the sonnet is the lyric I's outpouring of his suffering and his plea for compassion. The quatrains open with an invocation to the "cor gentili" (line 2) [noble hearts], with particular reference to the "donne gentili" [gracious women] apostrophized in "Li occhi dolenti" (XXXI.8–17 [20.8–20.17]) [My eyes suffering] in the preceding chapter. The addressees are implored to listen to the sighs of the subject. Having abandoned the *Io*, the "sospiri" have now become the interpreters and advocates of his mourning. The emphatic apostrophe, reiterated at the beginning of the tercets, is further intensified by the use of a *registro pietoso* (plaintive register).[9] These formal traits create a system with strong thematic implications, including the interjection "oi" (line 2)—and its courtly counterpart "lasso" (line 7)—whose semantic connotation, linked to the expression of sorrow, has recently been discussed by Lucia Bertolini.[10]

While commenting on "il linguaggio del sonetto" [the language of the sonnet], De Robertis notes its "estrema semplicità" [extreme simplicity], attributing the cause of this to the occasional nature of the composition.[11] In fact, at first glance, the conventional choice of vocabulary is striking. This is especially the case when reading the sonnet in the context of the Duecento love lyric and considering it in light of the medieval physiology of love.[12] In particular, a number of elements in the sonnet appear to be markedly Cavalcantian.

To clarify further this observation, it is important to pay special attention to the apostrophe that opens Dante's sonnet. As Gorni observes, the plea to listen implies, in fact, "l'invito a condividere un lutto" [an invitation to share in a sorrow], to pity the suffering of the subject.[13] Such a request, and its very specific articulation, appears to be modeled on the biblical text that, in Dante's time, was the example par excellence for introducing the theme of sorrow and invoking the reader's attention and compassion, namely Jeremiah's Lamentations. This intertextual influence and reference are so clear as to lead Stefano Carrai to refer to "Venite a intender" as a brief Jeremiad, making an overt connection to the biblical text.[14]

Although justified by the quotation that introduces the "nova materia" (XXX.1 [19.1]) [new material], and although it has been widely demonstrated that Lamentations acts as "a model and intertext that illuminates the *Vita Nuova* in depth, breadth, and detail,"[15] it is noteworthy that the reuse of the allocutive model of the Lamentations as one that invites the reader to share in the subject's pain is a trait that is markedly Cavalcantian in origin and inspiration.[16] Scholars who have commented on "Venite a intender" have drawn attention to this intertextual connection, at times suggesting parallels with Cavalcanti's well-known ballad, "I' prego voi che di dolor parlate" (XIX.1–3) [I ask you who speak of grief].[17] The verses in question are in fact representative of Cavalcanti's interiorization of the same Jeremian source used by Dante in "Venite a intender"—in particular verse 12, "O vos omnes qui transitis per viam adtentide et videte si est dolor sicut dolor meus" [Look well, you that pass by, and say if there was ever grief like this grief of mine].[18] In both Cavalcanti and Dante the verse has a similar objective, namely an invocation of attention and compassion, as is also evident in the *ripresa* of Cavalcanti's *ballata*: "I' prego voi che di dolor parlate / che, per vertute di nova pietate / non disdegniate—la mia pena udire" (XIX.1–3) [I pray you who speak of grief / That, out of unprecedented compassion / You disdain not to listen to my sorrow].

The comparison with the biblical model emphasizes Cavalcanti's reuse of the distinctive traits of the Jeremian plea. In these opening lines we can note the original structure of the intertext by observing the illocutive pronoun *voi* followed by the relative determiner and the word *dolor* (line 1), later repeated through the *variatio* of *pena* (line 3).[19]

Establishing the nature of the intertextual relationship between the two lyrics is problematic. In part, this is due to the fact that it is not possible to establish an accurate and reliable chronology for the *Vita nova* and for Cavalcanti's lyric production. The situation is further complicated when we recognize that Lamentations was widely used as a literary model as in the *consolatio*.[20]

Manuele Gragnolati observes that the imagery of the personified grieving sighs that leave the body in Dante's sonnet—"li qual disconsolati vanno via" (line 3) [My sighs, disconsolate, arise and go]) bear a resemblance to Cavalcanti's "piange ne [l]i sospir' che nel cor trova, / sì che bagnati di pianto escon fòre" (XVII.1–11) [[my soul] weeps among the sighs it finds in the heart / so that they emerge wet with weeping].[21] The parallelism with the "first friend" would be even more evident in the "first redaction" of "Venite a intender," where we find "sconsolati" rather than "disconsolati."[22] In Cavalcanti's "Io non pensava che lo cor giammai" (IX) [I never thought that the heart], we find "la mia virtù si partìo sconsolata" (line 9) [my vital force departed disconsolate], where the subject's predicative complement, referring to "partìo," alludes to a semantics of affliction. It is relevant to note that "sconsolato" is found only once in Cavalcanti's *Rime* and does not seem to occur in the lyric before Cavalcanti.

Equally significant is the occurrence of the notion of the "anima dolente," or grieving soul, in line 13, identified by many scholars as having a Cavalcantian cadence.[23] It is worth noting that words and expressions relating to *dolore* (pain, sorrow) are frequently used in the Duecento love lyric. In keeping with this usage, as Roberto Rea observes, we find thirty-nine occurrences of such words in Cavalcanti's corpus. The majority of these, following the lyric tradition, are used to qualify the condition of the suffering lover or, as is often the case in Cavalcanti's poetry, to characterize its dismembered hypostasis.[24] Moreover, it is particularly significant that the term *anima dolente*, which Rea highlights as scriptural in character, is found in the preceding lyric production only in Chiaro Davanzati.[25] According to Gragnolati, another interesting link can be established between Dante's "in persona dell'anima dolente" (line 13) [in place of the suffering soul] and Cavalcanti's sonnet XX.4: "ti raccomanda l'anima dolente" [recommends to you the suffering soul].[26]

The tercets of "Venite a intender" redeem, from a perspective that we might term as ideological, the situation just described. It is worth noting that the "first redaction" of line 11 read "al loco degno" [the place deserving]; this was later replaced by "al secol degno" [to the otherworld deserving] in the version of the sonnet included in the *libello*. As De Robertis has observed, commenting on this variant, "secol" resonates with the lyrics of the *Vita nova* that are adjacent to "Venite a intender" ("Li occhi dolenti," line 61; "Quantunque volte" (XXXIII.5 [22.5]], line 8), as well as in the prose of chapter XXX [19.8–19.10], thereby establishing a formal coherence in this section of the *libello*.[27] If we contextualize "secol" within the broader project of moral and poetic refinement that Dante undertakes during the course of the book's narrative, it is clear that the variant "secol," characterized by its markedly religious stamp, in replacing the more generic "loco," defines the celestial, eternal dimension to which the *io*'s sighs are directed, adding an important element to the exegesis of the sonnet. The opposition between the celestial kingdom in which the woman resides and mortal life is further emphasized in line 12 and is achieved through a parallelism between "chiamar" (line 9) [calling] and "dispregiar" (line 12) [despising], both of which are dependent on "udirete" (line 9) [you will hear], and through the use of the deictic "questa" (line 12) [this [life]], which adds a negative nuance when referring to the earthly realm.

The final lines, in mitigating the doleful outpouring of the sonnet and contextualizing the suffering of the *io* within a Christian framework, acquire further significance when considered in light of the Cavalcantism discussed above, as well as in light of the precise information offered by the prose. The periphrasis that identifies the commissioner of the poetic *planctus* in fact contains the last allusion to Cavalcanti in the *Vita nova*. Here, the "primo amico" is alluded to as a friend of a higher grade only in comparison to Manetto, precisely at the point at which the partial rewriting of the "prima redazione" appears to temper the work's Cavalcantism by emphasizing (at least in the tercets) the orthodox reading of the Christian lament. This aspect corroborates De Robertis's observation whereby the mention of Manetto places the occasion within a system of literary relations.[28] Dante's series of dissimulations, therefore, as well as his precise stylistic choices, serve to unfetter him from the work of his "first friend." Vincent Moleta argues that Dante, using the pretext of friendship, was distinguishing himself among the other Florentine poets: "Dante, nella ricostruzione retrospettiva del primo decennio della sua carriera, si voleva vedere matricolato e indipendente, prima dell'autunno del 1290, dal suo mentore non solo come scrittore di un'epistola 'a li prìncipi de la terra,' ma anche come poeta civico, e proprio nel cerchio letterario più ricercato di Firenze" [Dante, in attempting to reconstruct retrospectively the first decade of his career, before the autumn of 1290, wanted to see himself as independent and emancipated from his mentor, not only as the writer of an epistle "to the Princes of the Earth," but also as a civic poet belonging to Florence's most distinguished literary circle.][29]

The dissimulation in the chapter that follows (XXXIII [22]) further confirms this interpretation. As we learn, Dante, deeming "Venite a intender" rather "povero" [paltry] and inadequate—"nudo" [bare] (XXXIII.1 [22.1])—when considered from the point of view of the hierarchy of metrical forms, decides to compose a new lyric that more appropriately laments the death of Beatrice. In the *ragione* introducing the two-stanza canzone "Quantunque volte," the *io* clarifies that "ne la prima stanzia, si lamenta questo mio caro e distretto a lei" [in the first stanza, this dear friend of mine and close relative of hers is grieving], namely, Manetto; and "nella seconda mi lamento io" [in the second part I am grieving] (XXXIII.4 [22.4]), namely, Dante. The significance of these distinctions is amplified with the knowledge that the first stanza, corresponding to the voice of Manetto, is rich in Cavalcantian motifs (among which at least "dolorosa mente" [sorrowful mind] needs to be mentioned), whereas the second stanza, written in the voice of the autobiographical subject of the *libello*, is directed entirely at celebrating the dead beloved in paradise. This seems to be a further and more pronounced step toward the "de-Cavalcantization" that we have observed in the process of Dante's rewriting of "Venite a intender." In the *libello* this occurs precisely when the "primo amico" is mentioned for the last time, thereby constituting an indirect and, as ever, cursory overcoming of Guido.

Vita nova XXXIII [22]

KATHERINE POWLESLAND

Chapter XXXIII [22] foregrounds the questions of narrative order and voice, and explicitly identifies a particular "key" for the reader of the *libello* to unlock understanding of the *canzone* "Quantunque volte, lasso!, mi rimembra" [Whenever I, alas! recall], through the use of a possessive determiner ("la donna mia" (line 18) [my lady]). In this chapter I shall suggest that the key contained within the *Vita nova*'s thirty-third chapter in fact reveals a substantially more radical gateway to reader interaction with the *libello* than that explicitly identified in the text by the poet, one that marries a foundational development in lyrical voice with an innovation in what I am calling an "invited" mode of reading.

The chapter opens with a reference to the sonnet that has just closed chapter XXXII [21], "Venite a intender li sospiri miei" [Come listen to my sighs]. After writing the poem at the request of a close relation of Beatrice, the *libello*'s narrator recalls that he saw, "vidi," that something was manifestly not right with it: "Vidi che povero mi parea lo servigio e nudo a così distretta persona di questa gloriosa" (XXXI.1 [22.1]) [I saw how poor and bare a service it seemed for such a close relation of this glorious woman].[1] Without explicitly setting out for the reader precisely what constituted this "poor and bare service," his immediate sequitur—"e però" [and so]—is a conclusion that the corrective lay in using two voices within one poem: one voice truly

297

for ("per") the close relation, one for himself, "l'una per costui veracemente, e l'altra per me" (XXXIII.2 [22.2]) [one actually for this man, and the other for me]. As a result of this reflection, he continues, he elected not to give the sonnet to the close relation for whom it had been written until he could also give him the *canzone* that follows in chapter XXXIII [22]: "Questa canzone e questo soprascritto sonetto li diedi" (XXXIII.3 [22.3]) [I gave him this canzone and the sonnet transcribed above]. Not all readers of this new *canzone* with its corrective of articulation, he comments, will perceive the distinction of the two voices; indeed, only those who read the verses with a particular attentiveness will do so, "Chi sottilmente le mira vede bene che diverse persone parlano" (XXXIII.2 [22.2]) [Whoever subtly looks at them sees plainly that different people are speaking]. But to the reader of the *libello* he offers a simple and manifest key relating to technical deployment of a part of speech: one voice does not call the lady his own, using the possessive determiner, while the other does: "L'una non chiama sua donna costei, e l'altra sì, come appare manifestamente" (XXXIII.2 [22.2]) [One doesn't call on this woman as his lady and the other does, as is clear].

All this information is contained within just the first three sentences of the prose gloss, placing a relatively heavy load on the reader in terms of cognitive processing of information. But its essence in terms of local coherence, or plot, is relatively simple: something is wrong with one poem that is corrected in the next. Since this appears to be a matter primarily for the poet— one of poetic technique, that is—it is noteworthy that he chooses to be so detailed in his description of the processes of production and reception involved in the correction, actively drawing the reader's attention to the order of writing, giving, and reading the sonnet and the *canzone*. The reader may also observe that her reading experience, staged by the linear framework of the *libello*, here diverges from that self-consciously curated by the poet for the close relation: the close relation will see the two poems together, while the reader has already read the sonnet and at this point is still separated from the *canzone* by the current gloss. The intense retrospective focus on a deficiency in the previous sonnet at no point actually identifies the nature of the deficiency, additionally separating the reader's experience from the poet's own, but also raising a question: Did the reader see this deficiency for herself as she read "Venite a intender"? If not, will she take the poet's word for it? Or will she go back and reexamine the sonnet in the light of this new information? In this short analysis, I shall seek to demonstrate the strategic nature of the invitation to consider questions such as these, both in the sense that a sustained and consistent narrative technique is at work and in the sense that the reader is actively being *invited* to engage in a relationship of heightened interaction with the poems, one privileged by the device of the *libello*.

The chapter begins with an analepsis, a brief doubling-back in the narrative to the sonnet the reader has just read in the previous chapter. The narration of the order of events is explicit. After ("poi che") writing the sonnet, the poet identified a problem, and so before ("anzi ch[e]") giving the sonnet to the close relation, he wrote two stanzas of a *canzone*. Here the narration points to the opening of a gap between the reading experience of the reader of the *libello* and the reading experience of the close relation. We know from earlier chapters that narration of order is important to the narrator of the *libello*: the ordering of Giovanna and Beatrice was reinforced six times in chapter XXIV [15]; in chapter XXXI [20], the ordering of the prose gloss and poem was permanently reversed so as to construct a gap, a "widowing," immediately after the poem: "E acciò che questa canzone paia rimanere più vedova dopo lo suo fine, la dividerò prima che io la scriva e cotale modo terrò da qui innanzi" (XXXI.2 [20.2]) [And in order to make this canzone appear more widowed when it is done, I will divide it up before I write it down; and I will maintain this method from this point on]. It seems unlikely, then, that the detailed description of the sequencing of events in chapter XXXIII [22] is inconsequential.

The ordering under discussion is that of the writing sequence (sonnet–*canzone*) and the giving sequence (*canzone* + sonnet, with an implicit simultaneity). The probable initial reading order for the reader of the *libello*, however, given the conventions of reading narrative texts, is sonnet–*canzone*, controlled by the frame of the linear narrative. The close relation, of course, is free to read his two poems in any order he chooses, particularly in the event that they were offered as two unbound artifacts: he might shuffle them out of the order in which they were delivered; he might read or compare them side by side. Of course, if the reader of the *libello* is so minded, she too may read in any way and in any order that she chooses, as was commonplace in many medieval reading practices.[2] She is of course free to disrupt the implicit imperative of the linear narrative frame, choosing instead to pause, to go back, to cross-reference, to follow intertextual references. The analepsis here, I suggest, functions as a reminder or invitation to even the habitually interactive reader to not allow the linearity of the narrative frame to seduce her into a mode of epistemic immersion but instead to engage in a dynamic, multidirectional mode of reading, reading analytically, comparatively, and critically.

Suppose the reader does not feel confident that she has observed the defect in "Venite a intender" and so chooses at this point to reread the sonnet. The sonnet is inadequate, the narrator has said, its service "povero e nudo" (XXXIII.1 [22.1]) [poor and bare] for one so closely related to Beatrice. By contrast with "Quantunque volte," however, there is no key to unlock the sonnet, so the reader is left to identify for herself the particular elements that rendered the poem so perceptibly "poor and bare" for the poet. The reader's only potential clue is that since the corrective relates to writing a poem truly "for" someone, "l'una per costui veracemente, e l'altra per me" (XXXIII.2 [22.2]) [one truly for this man, and the other for me], the defect in "Venite a intender" is probably one of voice.

At this point, matters become more complex since, the reader may recall, multiple players have been alluded to in the prose gloss of chapter XXXII [21] in relation to the commissioning of the poem, with its dissembled object and dissembled voice. In response to the close relation's brief to the poet to write, for him, about another woman who had died, "Mi pregoe ch'io li dovessi dire alcuna cosa per una donna che s'era morta" (XXXII.2 [21.2]) [He pleaded with me to write something for him about a woman who had died], the poet voiced his own lament in response to the death of Beatrice, giving it to the close relation *as if* it were "per lui': "Onde poi, pensando a ciò, propuosi di fare uno sonetto, nel quale mi lamentasse alquanto, e di darlo a questo mio amico, *acciò che paresse che per lui l'avessi fatto*" (XXXII.3 [21.3]; my emphasis) [so that, thinking it over, I planned to compose a sonnet in which I would mourn a little, and give it to this friend of mine, *in such a way that it seemed that I had composed it for him*]. The poet has written a sonnet that voices his own truthful response to Beatrice's death, but the sonnet is *not* truthful in the sense that it does not express the close relation's voice: it expresses the poet's, "*mi* lamentasse alquanto" (XXXII.3 [21.3]; my emphasis) [*I* would lament somewhat]. This is another matter of poetic technique. In which specific ways might one voice in a poem be differentiated from another when both issue from the same author? Is this the corrective the reader will find in the *canzone* to follow in chapter XXXIII [22]? (In that case, the reader may want to read ahead and compare the two poems side by side.) But there is nothing in the gloss to "Venite a intender" to confirm whether this is indeed the defect and its correction. I suggest that, in fact, the specific technical nature of the defect, while certainly instructive in itself, is secondary at this stage: the reader has been invited to go back, and it is that habit of going back, of being curious and agile in readership even of a linear narrative text, that is important. There is no gamification here, no prize for proof of knowledge: the challenge instead is to hone a mode of engaging with a text.

Returning to the remainder of the prose gloss in chapter XXXIII [22], the reader next encounters a prolepsis, a preview, of the poem to come. As well as the newly standard prefatory gloss of the divisions of the *canzone* that will follow, the prose section sets out a key that will identify two different voices in the poem. "Quantunque volte" is a *canzone* of two stanzas, writes the narrator, "l'una per costui veracemente, e l'altra per me" (XXXIII.2 [22.2]): one truly "for" the close relation—perhaps as opposed to merely "appearing" to be for him, as with "Venite a intender," "accio che paresse che per lui l'avessi fatto" (XXXII.2 [21.2])—and one for the poet. This means that each stanza is voiced by a different *io*: in the first, the close relation laments, "Si lamenta questo mio caro e distretto a lei" [This dear friend of mine and close relative of hers is grieving]; in the second, the poet laments: "Mi lamento io" [I am grieving] (XXXIII.4 [22.4]). This fact of a doubling of voice in one poem is confirmed twice more in the gloss: the first laments "come frate" [as a brother] and the second "come servo" [as a servant-lover] (XXXIII.4 [22.4]). That is, two people manifestly lament in this *canzone*: "E così appare che in questa canzone si lamentano due persone" (XXXIII.4 [22.4]) [And thus it seems that two people are grieving in this canzone]. The reinforcement is explicit.

However, the two discrete voices will not be apparent to all. Those who do not look attentively, "sottilmente," will perceive the stanzas to be voiced or spoken, "detta," by the same person: "avvegna che paia l'una e l'altra [stanza] per una persona detta, a chi non guarda sottilmente" (XXXIII.2 [22.2]) [although to one who doesn't consider things subtly both may seem voiced by one person]. Those who do look with care and finesse will see clearly that different people speak: "Ma chi sottilmente le mira vede bene che diverse persone parlano" (XXXIII.2 [22.2]) [But whoever subtly looks at them sees plainly that different people are speaking]. Here the invitation to reader engagement is rather more direct than was the case with noticing (or not) the defect in "Venite a intender": Are you, reader, in that group that engages with subtleties in the text, that reads *sottilmente*? But again, there is no gamification, no test: instead, the prose gloss is collaborative in mode, offering a key to what it means to read *sottilmente*. In this instance, it is simply to be alert to a technical detail: to observe that one voice does not use a possessive determiner in relation to the *donna*, while the other does: "L'una non chiama sua donna costei, e l'altra sì, come appare manifestamente" (XXXIII.2 [22.2]) [One doesn't call on this woman as his lady and the other does, as is clear]. The reader is equipped with a concrete lexical anchor to look for in the poem.

The first stanza of "Quantunque volte" is that of the close relation. It narrates, in the first person, the *dolore* [grief] in his body, heart, and mind each time he remembers that he will never again see the lady he mourns, and he welcomes death to escape his torments. It is a report: a feeling mediated through language, and a report characterized by repetition—both a repeated event, "quantunque volte" (line 1), and cognates of a repeated feeling, "dolente," "dolore," "doloroso" (lines 3–5). The report is allusive and conceptual, unanchored in time and place, but is nonetheless profoundly earthbound, the discourses with his soul and with Death both framed in the mortal realm: "li tormenti che tu porterai / nel secol" (lines 7–8) [the torments that you'll bear to stay / in this world]; "Ond'io chiamo la Morte . . . e dico "Vieni a me"" (lines 10, 12) [And so I call to Death: "come to me"]. For this *io*, seemingly, the lady's presence is a binary: she is either here or there; these are absolutes, not relatives. Never again will he see her here, "non debbo già mai / veder la donna ond'io vo sì dolente" (lines 2–3) [I will never lay / my eyes on her I grieve for sans relief], and so he wants to die: "ond'io chiamo la Morte, / come soave e dolce mio riposo; / e dico "Vieni a me"" (lines 10–12) [and then I call for Death, / so mild and sweet a moratorium: / "Now, come," I beg]. And in line 3, as previewed, he invokes Beatrice as not *his* lady but *the* lady: "*la* donna ond'io vo sì dolente" (my emphasis).

In the second stanza, the poet's own *io*, lamenting "come servo [d'Amore]" (XXXIII.4 [22.4]), begins with an echo of the notion of calling, "chiamando," upon Death, "un sono di pietate, / che va chiamando Morte tuttavia" (lines 15–16) [a sound of pity / starts to press, calling on Death without a pause]. However, the style of narration changes at the point when the possessive determiner is used, at the invocation of "la donna mia," when death took her, "quando la donna mia / fu giunta da la sua crudelitate" (lines 18–19) [when my lady was / snatched away by Death's vindictiveness]. This second *io* mourns the loss of the pleasure of Beatrice's beauty on earth but is simultaneously able to identify the presence of her beauty in heaven and, in so doing, revises the perception of her beauty as contingent on human capacity for a certain sort of sight, "partendo sé da la nostra veduta [here on earth]" (line 21) [taking itself from our sight], and becoming instead a beauty perceptible in heaven, one that disseminates light of love, "divenne spirital bellezza grande / che per lo cielo spande / luce d'amor" (lines 22–24) [became great spiritual beauty then, / which through the heavens extends / the light of love]. This is a metaphor of visibility, certainly, but also one of taking up space, a physical expansion, a metaphor rooted in bodily experience. This second stanza is rich in evocation of body states, viscerality, and physicality, with verbs of action, relationality, and dynamic directional movement. There are sighs, "sospiri" (line 14), and pity vocalized, "un sono di pietate" (line 15). These are direct, nonlinguistic, embodied expressions of feeling, different from the mediated reported speech of the first stanza, "io dico: 'Anima mia, che non ten vai?'" (line 6) [I say, "My soul, why don't you go away?"]. Not only is Death now called, *chiamata*; this *io*'s desires *turn*, in a metaphor of embodiment, to Death, "si volser tutti i miei disiri" (line 17) [to her my every least desire turned]. In a metaphor of physical proximalization, his lady is taken; she is coupled or joined, "giunta" (lines 18–19), with the cruelties of Death. She departs from physical sight, "partendo sé de la nostra veduta" (line 21); and her mortal beauty is finally transformed, in a metaphor of perceptible generative expansion, into a ceaselessly extensive light of love through heaven, "spirital bellezza grande / che per lo cielo spande / luce d'amor" (lines 22–24); his lady, at last, is located in heaven, "sì *v'è* gentile" (line 26; my emphasis) [so gentle is she *there*]. The first *io*, then, mediates his feelings through conceptual language and affective abstraction, speaking of *dolore, tormenti, paura, astiosità* (grief, torments, fear, envy). The second expresses them through embodied metaphor, through narration of *doing*: *si raccoglie, si volser, giunta, partendo sé, spande, face maravigliar* (gathers, turns, joined, departs, expands, astonishes).

Teodolinda Barolini has called the *canzone* "Cavalcantian," suggesting that "*Quantunque volte* seems to mark a step backward with respect to *Li occhi dolenti* and *Venite a 'ntender*, as indicated by the use of the verb *chiamare*. Instead of calling on his dead lady and bringing her to life so that she comforts him . . . , *Quantunque volte*, more traditionally, calls on Death."[3] But she goes on to acknowledge the shift in narrative mode made manifest in the metaphor of expansive light of love in heaven, writing that "the meditation on the moment of death of *madonna* [line 19] . . . seems to lend wings to the imaginative capacity of the lover. . . . A canzone of Cavalcantian stamp here shows itself capable of reaching a linguistic register that recalls *Paradiso*; "luce d'amor" in line 24 consistently elicits comparison to "luce intelletüal, piena d'amore (*Par.*, 30.40) [intellectual light, full of love]."[4]

My reading is that this shift in voice, from one we might recognize as Cavalcantian in the first stanza to one we might retrospectively define as paradisiacal in the second, is strategic on the poet's part. In juxtaposing the two voices, the poet not only invites the reader to experience for herself the contrast between them but in addition actively calls attention to it, inviting the reader to attend closely to the mode of interaction cued by each voice and the point of view or apperceptual frame through which each voice perceives the world, to observe its technicalities, and to respond with *sottilezza* to the different effects each invites. The contrast marks a change in Dante's mode of technical lyrical narration that differentiates him from *stilnovismo*, and he is at pains to make this shift perceptible to the interested reader. The earlier revised ordering of the prose gloss and poem means there is an instant payoff for the reader in engaging with this new lyrical narrative mode: the reader having been transported to heaven by the second stanza, the *libello* leaves her there in the widowed space, free to dwell.

Under this analysis, the notion of the possessive determiner as key to the poem is revealed as the tip of an iceberg of invitations to the reader to read actively, attentively, and with *sottilezza*, even to cultivate a mode of reading that is constantly sensitive or alert to other keys in the text—a mode constantly repaid by the text. A reader newly sensitized to echoes in the *libello* may notice that "Venite a intender" is not the only occasion in the *libello* when the narrator recalls having spoken "defectively." In chapter XXVII [18], shortly before the poet will hear of Beatrice's death, he narrates that he reflected on how he had spoken of his lady, "Cominciai a pensare uno giorno sopra quello che detto avea de la mia donna" (XXVII.1 [18.1]) [One day I started to consider what I had said about my lady], in the two sonnets just set out in chapter XXVI [17]. He recalls that he saw (*vedere* again) that he had not spoken of what she "worked" [adoperava] in him; and as a consequence he saw that he seemed to have spoken "defectively": "E veggendo nel mio pensero che *io non avea detto di quello che al presente tempo adoperava in me, pareami defettivamente avere parlato*" (XXVII.1 [18.1]; my emphasis) [And seeing, as I reflected, that I had not spoken of what at that time she worked in me, it seemed that I had spoken defectively]. In this instance, then, to speak defectively of Beatrice was to fail to speak of the present effects she wrought in him, "di quello che al presente tempo adoperava in me" (XXVII.1 [18.1]). A reexamination of the two sonnets reveals that both are characterized by external description of Beatrice's effects on others. After all, this is their point: her effect is universal. In "Tanto gentile" [So gracious], for example, every tongue falls mute, "ogne lingua deven ... muta" (l. 3); all eyes dare not look, "li occhi no l'ardiscon di guardare" (line 4); and the sight of her initiates a chain reaction from the eye to the heart, "dà per li occhi una dolcezza al core" (line 10) [sweetness passes through the eye to the heart]. But, the poet qualifies, this is only the case for those who experience it themselves: those who do not recognize this feeling will not understand, "che 'ntender no la può chi no la prova" (line 11) [which no one understands who does not feel it]. Here the poet points to a limitation in his poetry: such a feeling must be *experienced* to be felt; it cannot be understood by report alone. This, I suggest, is the poet's challenge, one he identifies for himself at this point in the *Vita nova*: How can he make this feeling available to all of us, including those who will never physically experience Beatrice's presence? Is there a way of writing that can invite the reader to experience what he experiences?

He sets out an answer immediately in chapter XXVII [18]. He will write verses, the poet pledges, that say how he seems to be available to her influence, "Propuosi di dire parole, ne le quali io dicesse come me parea *essere disposto a la sua operazione*" [I planned to write a poem in which I would say how *I seemed to be susceptible to her influence*], and how her power, her *vertude*, worked in him, "e *come operava in me la sua vertude*" (XXVII.2 [18.2]) [and *how her power influenced me*] (my emphasis). He will deploy his own body to mediate the experience for the reader, speaking of the effects love realizes in him, not through the diegesis of conceptual language or of affective abstraction, but instead through a concretized narration of the internal and external body states he experiences in response to Beatrice's physical presence or—as he sets out in chapter XXXI [20] in "Li occhi dolenti" [Grieving eyes]—when she is conjured in thought, "chi vede nel pensero" (line 41) [one who sees in thought]. And if the reader compares the two "defective" sonnets of chapter XXVI [17] with the unfinished *canzone* of chapter XXVII [18], "Sì lungiamente m'ha tenuto Amore" [So long a time has Love had hold on me] in which the alleged defect has been corrected, this different mode of narration is indeed manifest. In "Sì lungiamente," the first-person point of view is interior and intimate, describing a sequence of body states as love "operates" on the poet: the sense of gentle love in his heart, "così mi sta soave ora nel core" (line 4) [now he is gentle in my heart]; an embodied metaphor of a sense of weakening, "mi tolle sì 'l valore" (line 5) [he so drains [my] strength]; a sweetness in the soul that makes him grow pale, "allor sente la frale anima mia / tanta dolcezza, che 'l viso ne smore" (lines 7–8) [then my fragile soul feels / so much sweetness that my face pales from it]. The consequence of these body states is an urge to call upon his lady for further beatitude, "più salute" (line 12), a generative effect that is refreshed—in a form of grace over which he is not in control—wherever *she* sees *him*, "ovunque ella mi vede" (line 13). He no longer reports abstracted affect in relation to Beatrice's presence; instead, he evokes the body states he experiences in relation to her presence, material or virtual.

Beatrice's death interrupts this exploration of a new mode of lyrical narration, but Dante returns to it in chapter XXXIII [22], in which the juxtaposition of the two voices explicitly indexes the contrast and invites attention to this new, more cognitively participatory model of narration—one in which the reader not only listens to a report of another person's feeling but through evocation of the associated body states is invited to imaginatively experience for herself how that person feels. "Quantunque volte" constitutes an explicit invitation to the reader to engage with Dante's poetry in a new way: with curiosity and a highly active, hermeneutic approach to linear narrative, and with a sensitivity to the type of imaginative or cognitive work in which the reader is being invited to participate. In this way, I suggest, in chapter XXXIII [22] the poet actively draws attention to his innovative new model of narration and challenges the reader to respond.

Vita nova XXXIV [23]

KATHERINE POWLESLAND

Chapter XXXIV [23] introduces the sonnet with two beginnings, "Era venuta nella mente mia" [She had come into my mind]. Each beginning is presented to the reader with apparently equal weight: neither is described as having greater merit than the other, nor is one preferred or recommended over the other by the poet. However, a matter of order made explicit in the poem's paratext indicates a numerical first and a second in the sequencing of the two beginnings: a "Primo cominciamento" and a "Secondo cominciamento." The paratext calls attention to itself for two reasons: it is mentioned in the gloss—"E dissi allora questo sonetto . . . lo quale ha due cominciamenti" (XXXIV.3 [23.3]) [And then I composed this sonnet . . . which has two beginnings][1]—suggesting that the two paratextual insertions are intrinsic to the text of the poem; and this is the only time a poem bears a paratext in the *libello*. As with "Quantunque volte" [Whenever] in the preceding chapter, the prose gloss offers an apparently simple key to understanding the difference between the two beginnings (notwithstanding Dante's use of the same enumeration system for the divisions as for the beginnings): in the second beginning, the poet is specific about *when* the lady had come into his mind, recording a particular temporal trigger, but not so in the first: "Ne la prima parte [of the second beginning] dico quando questa donna era così venuta ne la mia memoria, e ciò non dico ne l'altro [the first beginning]"

(XXXIV.6 [23.6]) [In the first part [of the second beginning] I say when this woman had come into my memory, something I do not mention in the first beginning]. But if she is reading *sottilmente* (XXXIII.2 [22.2]), then the reader of the *libello* knows that comparison and review can lead to new understanding. What, then, might the curious reader learn in chapter XXXIV [23] from attending closely to the operations of the two beginnings?

The chapter opens with a mechanic of narrative time, an ellipsis: a year has passed since Beatrice's death. The reader, having been invited at the end of the last chapter to contemplate a notion of heaven, where Beatrice's spiritual beauty is perceptible as expansive light of love, must make a rapid adjustment to her mental model of the poet's own situation. She has only just left that space to which he transported her, but he, by contrast, has continued his earthly life, and indeed it is already a year later. The prose narrative is notably concrete: the *libello*'s *io* recalls being materially situated and immersed in a bodily activity, drawing an angel on panels that are described with a degree of particularity: "Mi sedea in parte ne la quale . . . disegnava uno angelo sopra certe tavolette" (XXXIV.1 [23.1]) [I was sitting in a place where . . . I was sketching an angel on some boards]. Mentally, though, this *io* is elsewhere, occupied with thoughts of Beatrice, with whom he experiences himself as virtually copresent: "Altri era testé meco, però pensava" (XXXIV.3 [23.3]) [Someone else was just with me; that is why I was absorbed in thought], he later explains to interlocutors. (This notion of copresence is common in the *libello*: "meco" [with me] is used fifteen times in the *libello* and designates both virtual and physical copresence, with no differentiation made between the two.) In this opening sentence, then, the prose gloss models an experience of feeling present in two spaces simultaneously, the material and the virtual.

Despite his immersion, the poet senses that he is being observed and turns his eyes, "volsi li occhi" (XXXIV.1 [23.1]). From the external viewpoint from which the reader has observed the poet's actuality, at work in time and space, she is now invited mentally to share his line of sight to turn to look at a group of estimable men who are watching him, "uomini a li quali si convenia di fare onore" (XXXIV.1 [23.1]) [men whose rank required that one greet them respectfully]. Depending on her personal mental model, the reader may find she looks *with* him, through his eyes, at the men, or in a gesture of joint attention, that is, switching her line of sight away from him and instead toward the men to whom she knows he himself attends: either is possible within Dante's narrative construction of point of view here.

The narrating *io* of the *libello* is scrupulous at this juncture in his explanation of point of view: "E secondo che me fu detto poi, elli erano stati già alquanto anzi che io me ne acorgesse" (XXXIV.2 [23.2]) [And to judge by what was said to me, they had already been there for a while before I realized it]. Importantly, both "già" [already] and "anzi che" [before] indicate a reversal of narrative order, an unexpected time inversion: the men had been watching him for some time before he noticed them. A telescope of attention has been set up: its vanishing point, its *punto*, Beatrice, attended to by the drawing Dante, who in turn is observed by the honorable men, who themselves in turn are observed by the others who later report it to the narrating *io*. The reader of the *libello* may find herself curious as to where she herself is located in this coaxial line of sight given this new information. She has been looking at the poet before turning with Dante to see the estimable men; but she discovers, via the *già*, that they too have been watching Dante in the last few moments. That is, she discovers that she and the men have been jointly attending Dante, observing him as he is immersed in his inner memorializing of Beatrice (and arguably outer memorializing too, if we choose to read the drawing of the angel as symbolic). The time inversion set up by the *già* functions as an invitation to the reader to penetrate the narrative frame, finding herself virtually copresent with the estimable men.

The narrator of the *libello* then describes how he went to greet the men, telling them his mind had been elsewhere. The men are reported to leave, with no further documented interaction. However, the event serves to inspire the notion of an anniversary poem, one that will be written in response to his visitors, "scrivere a costoro li quali erano venuti a me" (XXXIV.3 [23.3]) [addressed to those men who had visited me]. Next, in the prose gloss, the poet offers the reader a series of divisions that, as set out earlier in the *libello* in chapter XIX [10], serve to open the meaning of his poetry: "A più aprire lo intendimento di questa canzone, si converrebbe usare di più minute divisioni" (XIX.22 [10.33]) [For this canzone to be better understood, it is appropriate to use finer divisions]. It is significant at this point that the meaning of the poem is deemed not wholly self-evident, since from the next chapter onward the poet will largely stop offering such divisions, as he expresses, for example, in identical terms in chapters XXXIX

[28] and XL [29]: "Questo sonetto non divido, però che assai lo manifesta la sua ragione" (XXXIX.7 [28.7]; XL.8 [29.8]) [I do not divide up this sonnet, since its account makes it sufficiently clear]. For now, there remains a need for guidance. In addition to the two beginnings, there are four divisions in total: the poem has three parts, and the second part is further subdivided into two.

The two beginnings show consistency in voice ("who speaks," in the terms of narratologist Gérard Genette), but they diverge in focalization, setting up two different virtual spaces or standpoints for the reader to inhabit: one transcendent and internal (the *io*'s own cognitive space); the other, external observation of an earthly event (the sonnet's *io* being watched at his work).

The first beginning sets out an inner experience, a mental event:

Primo cominciamento
Era venuta ne la mente mia
la gentil donna che per suo valore
fu posta da l'altissimo signore
nel ciel de l'umiltate, ov'è Maria.

(lines 1–4)

[*First beginning* / She had just come into my memory, / that gracious one whose virtue's true reward / was to be stationed by the highest Lord / with Mary, in the heaven of humility.]

There are no observers, no outer world; this is the narration of an individual finding a connection, through his beloved, to the divine.

The second beginning, in contrast, evokes an earthly situated event:

Secondo cominciamento
Era venuta ne la mente mia
quella donna gentil cui piange Amore
entro 'n quel punto che lo suo valore
vi trasse a riguardar quel ch'eo facia.

(lines 1–4)

[*Second beginning* / She had just come into my memory, / that gracious lady Love is weeping for, / the moment that her virtue's great allure, / led you to watch what I was doing.]

It is located in time—"'n quel punto che" (line 3) [the moment that]—and describes a materially situated historical event—"vi trasse a riguardar quel ch'eo facia" (line 4) [led you to watch what I was doing]. Crucially, the invitation to reader copresence with the estimable men that was set up in the prose narrative imbues this "vi" [you (plural)] with the possibility of participation: the reader was there too—just now—at that very event, jointly attending, with the men, the occasion of the poet's immersion in thought of Beatrice as he worked at his drawing. The first beginning invites the reader to listen to a reported inner experience. The second offers the reader the possibility not only to listen but also, through finding herself imaginatively copresent with the poet, to witness directly for herself the effects worked on the poet as he is imaginatively copresent with Beatrice.

The body of the poem then describes precisely these effects; specifically, in the second division, what Love did to or worked in him, "quello che Amore però mi facea" (XXXIV.4 [23.4]) [I say therefore what Love was doing to me]—that is, the poet's inner body states; and, in the third, the effects of Love, "gli effetti d'Amore" (XXXIV.4 [23.4])—his outer, manifest body states. Internally, then, Love is awakened in his ravaged heart, "s'era svegliato nel distrutto core" (line 6) [[Love] awoke within my heart's demolished core]: the poet reexperiences, re-*cognizes*, perhaps, the complexity of his response to his experience of Beatrice, both the sweetness of loving her and the pain of her loss. Love then commands his sadness, his sighs, to manifest physically: "Andate fore" (line 7) [Go forth]. Consequently, he weeps, his sorrow now perceptible: "piangendo uscivan [i sospiri] fuor de lo mio petto" (line 9) [they went out of my chest, weeping]. This is new information not revealed in the prose gloss. But if his sorrow is externalized in perceptible body states, then anyone who perceives these body states may have compassion, may *feel with* him, as those who saw Beatrice weep for her father in chapter XXII [13] may have done, as her friends then commented: "Certo ella piange sì, che quale la mirasse doverebbe morire di pietade" (XXII.3 [13.4]) [The way she is crying surely would be enough to make anyone who watched her die of pity]. By making manifest the effects of Beatrice's operation on him, the poet invites the copresent reader to empathize, to feel *with* him, to experience what he experiences, in this telescope of attention on the virtual Beatrice.

The first beginning of the sonnet, then, prepares the way: a singular voice, a personal witness, that testifies to Beatrice's place in heaven, as Giovanna preceded Beatrice in chapter XXIV [15], as John the Baptist preceded Christ. The second beginning opens the way to participation: the Beatrice to the first beginning's Giovanna; Christ, the "verace luce" (XXIV.4 [15.4]), to John the Baptist. It invites the reader to witness Beatrice's working, the operation of love, mediated through the poet's body in such a way that, copresent with the poet as he brings to mind Beatrice, the reader may feel what he feels as it is made manifest in his body states. From this second beginning, the sonnet continues in the same mode, seeking to make present to the reader the effects that Beatrice has on his visceral and affective body states. This is a form of memorializing that is not merely a seeing again but one that involves reconstructing feelings and body states: a cognitive reexperiencing through memory and imagination, a re-*cognition*. Through the device of the reconstruction and transcribing of memory, and the model of prose narrative frame + auto-gloss + poem, the *libello*'s *io* offers his reader a framework for beginning to model this process of active recognition herself, through skilled and attentive deployment of her compassionate imagination. In this way, the reader will manifestly understand; truly one of the "fedeli d'Amore" (III.9 [1.20]) [Love's faithful], not because she has been persuaded by a singular account, but because, responding to invitations to imaginative copresence, she has directly witnessed the operation of Beatrice for herself, mediated through the poet's body states.

Vita nova XXXV–XXXIX [24–28]

The Donna Gentile *Episode*

SIMON GILSON

This section of the *Vita nova* presents a pivotal episode in the *libello*, one focused on a turbulent conflict aroused by Dante turning his affections from the memory of the dead Beatrice to a living *donna gentile* (gracious lady). The crisis ends when, after a tumultuous vision of the young Beatrice, he turns back to his beloved, a return marked by the final sonnet of the sequence, "Lasso, per forza di molti sospiri" [Alas, by force of all my sighs]. The episode of the *donna gentile*, or *donna pietosa* (compassionate lady) as it is also known, includes five sonnets in all, and at least three of these predate the *Vita nova*. The sonnets for which we have earlier redactions are the first two, "Videro gli occhi miei quanta pietate" [My eyes saw mercy that was fathomless], "Color d'amore e di pietà sembiante" [Color of love and true compassion's guise], and the final one. The remaining two sonnets "L'amaro lagrimar che voi faceste" [Your bitter weeping when you were bereaved] and "Gentil pensero che parla di voi" [A gentle, gracious thought that speaks of you] might also have existed in earlier forms preceding the *libello*, although we lack any documentary evidence for such preexistence. The *donna gentile* episode is—as is well known—one of the most discussed and most controversial in Dante's "small book." As such, it has elicited a rich array of interpretations and much controversy. This introduction has two main aims. It will first provide a discursive running commentary on the relevant chapters of prose and the poems, setting out some of their major thematic features and discussing the literary and other models implicated. The chapter will also provide a coda related to some of the major critical discussions regarding the *donna gentile* episode.[1]

Characteristically indeterminate use of temporal and topographical markers is made in the very opening part of the prose explanation or *ragione*, a term that is related to the provençal *razos* and is first used explicitly in this very opening chapter (XXXV.4 [24.4] and then used repeatedly in this section: XXXVI.3 [25.3]; XXXIX.6, 7 [28.5, 6]; XL.8 [29.8]). We are in a period that is at least a year after the anniversary or "annovale" (XXIV.3 [23.3]) of Beatrice's death. Dante's interiorized grief is such that he takes on a most distressing, turbulent external appearance, "una vista di terribile sbigottimento" (XXV.1 [24.1]) [an outward appearance of horrible turmoil]. The unusual noun *sbigottimento* is one of a number of lexical, thematic, and tonal markers in this group of chapters that are reminiscent of Guido Cavalcanti's poetry and are to be found in both Dante's prose and verse.[2] At the same time, the heightened interiority of this section is a pronounced thematic feature throughout the chapters, and this again recalls the complex interior landscape evoked by Cavalcanti—that intense and divided psychic realm where warring spirits, phantasms, and sighs make up the landscape of the self. Aware of his own inner turmoil and its outward manifestations, Dante looks up to see if anyone might have seen him. He espies "una gentile donna giovane e bella molto" [a gracious woman, young and very beautiful], who gazes at him "sì pietosamente, quanto a la vista, che tutta la pietà parea in lei accolta" (XXXV.2 [24.2]) [so compassionately, to judge by her look, that all compassion seemed gathered in her]. The prominence of sight and visual motifs here is notable, and it continues throughout the entire episode. However, unlike the trajectories of sight and the relative positions of viewers highlighted in earlier encounters (V.1 [2.6]; XI.1–4 [5.1–5.4]; XIV.4 [7.4]; XXII.3 [13.3]), the gaze is now from a high vantage point, and crucially it takes place across a window. This is a feature that is not mentioned anywhere in the poems within the episode. Of course, the window is a richly polyvalent device in earlier contexts and literatures, often closely bound up with how boundaries and hierarchies—social, gender, ethnic—are represented. The "lady at the window" and its models are multiple, biblical, classical, and romance. There may well be suggestions, though these remain to be explored fully, from French romance, where the appearance of the lover at a high window or aperture is a recurrent topos and has a decisive role in amorous encounters, often at major narrative turning points.[3] In classical sources, too, some notable modulations include Ovid's treatment of female viewers staring down on male figures from high towers, such as Scylla's gaze on Minos at the opening of *Metamorphoses* 8 and, above all, the tale of Anaxarete and Iphis in book 14. In this account, Iphis is unable to subdue his passion by reason (14.701–2) and commits suicide at her door in despair. His funeral procession and its weeping crowd ("funera . . . lacrimosa" [14.746]) passes Anaxarete's house, and she ascends on high in order to observe it, only to be transformed into stone as her gaze fixes on Iphis's corpse.[4] The Bible remains the most important model, however, and fittingly so, in keeping with the tendency for Dante's language to take on an ever more prominent biblical patina as the *libello* progresses. There are several scriptural passages dealing with gazing from a window on high, involving both male and female protagonists (Genesis 26:8; Proverbs 7:6) and often with associations of betrayal, adultery, and prostitution.[5] We should also note the scornful gaze that Michal directs from on high at the whirling dancing jigs of King David (2 Samuel 6:12–23; and see *Purg.* 10.67–69). However, the precedent that is most noteworthy is a passage in 2 Kings 9:30 related to Jezabel, the idol-worshipping Phoenician queen, wife of Ahab, the king of Israel. Jezabel is presented as painting her eyes and dressing her hair before being defenestrated after taunting the warrior Jehu on his entrance into Ahab's capital: "Venitque Jehu in Jezrahel. Porro Jezabel, introitu ejus audito, depinxit oculos suos stibio, et ornavit caput suum, et respexit per fenestram" (2 Kings 9:30; and see 30–37) [And when Jehu came to Jezreel, Jezabel heard of it, and she painted her eyes and adorned her hair and looked out of the window]. As with Ovid's Anaxarete, the portrait is entirely negative. Particularly notable given the narrator's subsequent and increasingly negative characterization of the *donna gentile* is the attention paid in the biblical account to Jezabel's imperious gaze from on high and her role in promoting the worship of idols. Finally, following the recent discussion of Luca Lombardo, we should also signal some likely traces of the prologue scene in Boethius's *Consolatio philosophiae*. Lombardo draws particular attention to the gaze aloft, the appearance of the woman, and the shame of the protagonist—all of which are common both to Dante and to Boethius.[6]

The pity generated by the lady's response is such that Dante is moved to tears and then feels both shame and the need to flee. Fearing that the lady might be shown Dante's "vile vita" (XXXV.3 [24.3]) [base condition], he removes himself from her eyes: "Mi partio dinanzi da li occhi di questa gentile" (XXXV.3 [24.3] [I took myself away from the eyes of this gracious lady]). The prose is here stronger still than the sonnet, which nonetheless refers to "viltade" (line 8) [wretchedness]. The phrase "vile vita" in particular seems to echo Cavalcanti's celebrated yet enigmatically allusive sonnet to Dante "I' vegno 'l giorno a te 'nfinite volte" [I come to you countless times], where his first friend speaks repeatedly of Dante's vile life (line 2: "vilmente;" line 9: "la vil tua vita;" line 14: "anima invilata") and the inferior company he keeps.[7] Thrown into a state of deep recollection, Dante dialogues with himself on the eminently noble nature of the love that the "donna pietosa" (XXXV.4 [24.4]) [compassionate woman] must feel for him, and proposes to put into a sonnet all the events occasioned by these circumstances: "tutto ciò che narrato è in questa ragione" (XXXV.4 [24.4]) [all that is told in this prose account]. The sonnet itself (XXXV.5–8 [24.5–24.8]) is rich in imagery and language relating to vision and pity. As we have noted, the prose makes the role of pity and compassion even more prominent and places a greater stress on the "vita vile," but there remain strong elements of continuity between prose and poetry. The sonnet also reveals some further Cavalcantian elements, with its emphasis on "dolor" (line 4) [distress], the "anima trista" (line 11) [sad soul], and "lagrime" (line 14) [tears].[8]

The next chapter (XXXVI [25]) charts how the lady continues to see Dante and show pity for him. The effect of her gaze on Dante's mien brings a pallor to her own face. Commentators frequently cite here Ovid's own Book of Love, the *Ars amatoria*, though the theme is more prominent and developed in an elegiac poet such as Propertius. Rather than classical sources (it is most unlikely that Dante knew Propertius), however, the topical theme may well owe more to contemporary lyric and to works such as Andreas Capellanus's *De amore*.[9] The pallor of the "donna pietosa" reminds Dante of his own most noble lady, the dead Beatrice—this is an element, we should note, introduced by the prose alone. The narrator relates how he repeatedly visited the new lady and how she drew tears from his eyes. The emphasis on sight, and on a reciprocity of gazing, remains strong, and it permeates both the prose *ragione* (XXXVI.1–2 [25.1–25.2]): "ovunque questa donna mi vedea . . . io andava per vedere" [wherever this woman saw me . . . and I went to see] and the sonnet "Color d'amor" [Color of love]. In this poem, the "donna" gazes (line 3: "per veder sovente," and line 6: "vedetevi") on Dante's tearful eyes and grieving face ("labbia dolente," line 6). The lady's visual act elicits within Dante's own "mente" (line 7) [perceptive powers/ memory] the fear that his heart will break apart. As a result, the poet remains unable to look on the lady, and his interiorized pain is manifested in his eyes, which are "distrutti" (line 9) [worn sore] and then "consumano tutti" (line 13) [waste away]. Once again, we find here a pronounced Cavalcantian imprint, especially in the interiority evoked with the image entering the heart and the eyes, which are said to be destroyed and consumed.[10] Dante declares that the poem is easily understood and needs no division because of the preceding "ragione." However, what the prose account provides that is nowhere in the sonnet is the connection with Beatrice and the explanation that Dante's interest is aroused by the new lady's similarity to her.[11]

In chapter XXXVII [26] the emphasis on sight remains a dominant thematic feature, but a notable shift takes place. If, at one level, we return to the language of an experience that is "vile" (XXXVI.1 [26.1]) [loathsome], this term now assumes a different valence; as Dante's eyes are said to take excessive delight in seeing the lady, his visual power starts to "dilettare troppo di vederla" (XXXVI.1 [26.1]) [relish the sight of seeing her too much]. Turning ever more within himself to dialogue with his own thoughts, Dante feels shame and curses the "vanitade de li occhi" (XXXVII.2 [26.2]) [the inconstancy of my eyes], a markedly moralizing term and one that thematically recalls biblical admonitions to guard against the dangers of improper sight.[12] Dante speaks to his eyes and remonstrates with them for forgetting "la gloriosa donna" (XXXVII.2 [26.2]) [the glorious lady]. The effects of this scenario become ever more Cavalcantian in tone as the narrator describes how his sighs assail him as in a "battaglia" (XXXVII.3 [26.3]) [battle], and this situation prompts the writing of the sonnet "L'amaro lagrimar che voi faceste" [Your bitter weeping when you were bereaved]. The prose divides the sonnet into two parts, with the first part concerned with how the eyes speak to his heart and the second setting out the identities of the respective "speakers." Teodolinda Barolini has judiciously noted the major ideological operation that Dante performs in the final lines of the sonnet, with its stress on the question of fidelity to the dead lady and the movement—decidedly un-Cavalcantian in spite of the tonal similarities—from the existential domain to the ethical one.[13]

In chapter XXXVIII [27] the focus remains with the *donna gentile* and the excessive pleasure she provokes in the protagonist ("Ne pensava sì come di persona troppo mi piacesse," XXXVIII.1 [27.1]), as well as his own internal dialogue. The prose presents the competing thoughts as rhetorical questions that begin to battle with one another. The first thought is that the woman has appeared by the will of Love in order to allow his life some repose. After deep amorous pondering, his heart assents to this line of reasoning. Yet almost immediately, and spurred by reason, Dante thinks again and asks god why the lady "in così vile modo vuole consolare me e non mi lascia quasi altro pensare" (XXXVIII.2 [27.2]) [in such a base manner wants to console me and leaves me thinking about almost nothing else]. The verb *consolare* prompts reflection on likely traces of Boethian influence, and recently Lombardo has confirmed the value of the *Consolatio* in providing structuring and imaginative elements at this point in the *donna gentile* episode. Lombardo again draws attention to the prologue scene in which the Muses, soon to be chased out of the protagonist's chamber by Lady Philosophy, are unable to assuage his pain and indeed only provide further succour for his suffering with the thorns of intemperate passion.[14]

Another thought then arises, suggesting once more that the lady provides respite from Dante's great tribulation and bitterness—one notes here the scriptural patina, where not only "tribulazione" [tribulation] and "amaritudine" [bitterness] calque biblical terms, but this may be the case too for the unusual noun *spiramento* (XXXVIII.3 [27.3]), referring to a spirit-like emanation from the lady's eyes.[15] In what are again strongly Cavalcantian terms, the narrator likens the to-and-fro of opposing thoughts to a "battaglia de' pensieri" (XXXVIII.4 [27.4]) [battle of thoughts]. It is this "battle," or so the prose tells us, that leads to Dante to write the sonnet "Gentil pensero." And yet, as commentators and critics have repeatedly noted, the sonnet itself has little of the intense psychological drama presented in the prose. The discontinuities between prose and poetry put into relief the role of the narrator's prose in casting a moralizing and negative interpretation over the verse, one that stresses how base the experience is: "vile" is now transposed to the entire experience of the *donna gentile* episode. This kind of operation is conspicuous in the way Dante reinterprets the sonnet's opening adjective:

"E dico 'gentile' in quanto ragionava di gentile donna, ché per altro era vilissimo" (XXXVIII.4 [27.4]) [And I say "gracious" in so far as it involved a gracious lady, for in all other respects it was most base]. The narrator's exegetical acrobatics continue as the prose introduces further new elements not found in the sonnet regarding the dialogue between the soul and reason (XXXVIII.5 [27.5]). The narrator explains that the heart stands for the appetite and the soul for reason, a contraposition that introduces more philosophical and moralizing categories for the physical ones.[16] The role of the prose in controlling and redirecting meaning is also apparent in the following section, in which Dante attempts to reconcile contrary interpretations of the earlier sonnet.

The final chapter (XXXIX [28]) is the most powerful and dramatic of all. It now casts the *donna gentile* in the role of the adversary of reason. The opening of the chapter returns us to the very first vision and to a language of mystified visionary experience as a powerful imagined vision rises up in Dante—"Si levoe . . . una forte imaginazione in me" (XXXIX.1 [28.1]) [There arose in me . . . an intense imagining]—at the hour of nones, that is, at three in the afternoon.[17] Dante appears to see Beatrice as she first appeared to him in the blood-red crimson vestiments of the first vision, "con quelle vestimenta sanguigne co le quali apparve prima a li occhi miei" (XXXIX.1 [28.1]) [wearing the same crimson clothes in which she first appeared to my eyes]. Several important studies have probed the role of the imagination in the *Vita nova*, its likely backgrounds and models and its significance within the work overall.[18] This passage may be the most radical. Dante is in a waking state, and a strong imagination rises up in him. The best precedent known to me, though much more work needs to be done to understand whether Dante knew this text, related ones, or contemporary discussions, is an account in Albert the Great's remarkable treatise on dreaming and wakefulness, *De somno et vigilia*.[19] In his third book, when discussing at great length prophetic dreams, Albert outlines a form of prophecy that involves a powerful celestial form entering the human imagination and prompting a withdrawal from exterior sense perception: "quando forma coelestis est adeo fortis, quod movet in vigilia aversum a sensibus et retrahentem sensus intra se" [when the celestial form is sufficiently strong that it moves a waking person to abstraction from the senses and moves their senses within].[20] Drawing on Avicenna, al-Kindi, and others, Albert explains that this heavenly form so powerfully moves the human imagination that it not only results in humans being detached from their external senses but also allows the mind to receive higher forms into the imagination.[21]

The power of this experience is such that Dante's heart repents of the desire that has overtaken him against the constancy of reason, and all his thoughts return to Beatrice, now "gentilissima" (XXXIX.2 [28.2]) [most gracious]. We remain within an interiorized landscape with Dante's sighs calling her name, and he forgets all else, including his thoughts and even where he is. Dante's unrestrained effusion of tears is such that around his eyes "si facea uno colore purpureo" [a reddish color formed], that is, like the appearance of a "martirio" (XXXIX.4 [28.4]) [martyring agony]. These signs of suffering act—Dante tells us—as just rewards for his "vanitade" (XXXIX.5 [28.5]) [inconstancy]. The prose "ragione" stresses once more how the composition of the final sonnet in our sequence arose from his desire to obliterate the "desiderio malvagio e vana tentazione" (XXXIX.6 [28.6]) [wicked desire and vain temptation] of the *donna gentile*.

The sonnet provides little of this starkly moralizing final estimate of the *donna gentile* or indeed of the conversion to Beatrice: this is all the work of the prose. Once more, the control exercised on the reader by the narrator's glosses is notable in the explanation provided for the sonnet's opening exclamation, "lasso" (XXXIX.6 [28.6]) [alas]. Rather than marking his emotions at the loss of the lady, this word, the narrator avers, reveals the shame he felt for the transgressions of his eyes. The sonnet itself—as commentators have widely noted—speaks of spirits arising from the heart and overpowering the eyes. The effects of prolonged crying and the signs of martyrdom ("corona di martìri") are retained. Anguish is prominent, and the Cavalcantian echoes remain significant,[22] but this is not a battle in Cavalcantian terms—the emphasis remains on the dead lady, not on the existential destruction of the lover—nor is there anything in the verse of the *cri di coeur* and the tone of repudiation and humiliation found throughout the final prose chapter in our episode.

Throughout this chapter we have purposefully refrained from bringing into the discussion Dante's later treatment of the *donna gentile* in the *Convivio* (2.2 and 12) and possibly a still later allusion within the *Commedia* (*Purg.* 30.124–28). Of course, Dante himself encourages his readers to make this connection and to trouble over it when, in the *Convivio*, he presents again the *donna gentile*, explicitly referring to her as the woman of the *Vita nova*. Debate has long raged, at times furiously, over the tensions and contradictions between the account in the *Vita nova* and the radical rewriting in the *Convivio*, where Dante provides a complex set of new information regarding the dating of the episode (*Conv.* 2.2.1–2) and a new "story" of her influence on him (2.12.7–9). The new "story" emphasizes her status as an allegory of his own passionate and apparently autobiographical immersion in philosophy.[23] Such are the contradictions that some critics have engaged in attempts to explain away the episode with the hypothesis that a first redaction of the *Vita nova* ended with the *donna gentile* episode and that the small book was then refashioned in a later redaction to provide an ending consistent with a return to Beatrice.[24] Three points bear stressing here by way of a concluding coda. First, there is no documentary evidence for a first redaction of the *Vita nova*. Second, the handling of the *donna gentile* episode in the *libello* remains consistent with other episodes in the *libello* that deal with the theme of constancy toward the dead beloved and its interruptions. More significantly still, one should note that the *donna gentile* episode is consistent with Dante's richly complex interest in narratives of conversion, in questions of seeing and nonseeing, in modes of worship, in the status and attention to be paid to the living and the dead, and in the relationships between ethics and eros.[25] Third, rather than attempting to resolve the issues raised by the different accounts, it may be more helpful to note how Dante in fact thrives on such tensions and how constant and keen his interest is in resemanticizing certain figures and themes throughout his oeuvre, as well as in maintaining a remarkably tight control over his narrative and his readers' responses to, and interpretations of, his works.

Vita nova XXXV [24]

FEDERICA COLUZZI

Chapter XXXV [24] marks the opening of the last of the three narrative sequences forming what John C. Hirsch referred to as "the prose structure" of Dante's *libello* to stress its "contrapunctual relationship to the poetic" traditionally privileged by commentators.[1] Following the tragic *acme* of Beatrice's death, chapters XXXV–XLII [24–31] recount the final stage of the lover's sentimental journey. Connected to one another like tiles of a mosaic, each chapter frames a precise moment in the retelling of Dante's history of emotional (and erotic) deviation and his ultimate wholesale return to Beatrice (XLII [31]).

Self-contained and yet deeply significant in its poetic and spiritual implications, the episode (XXXV–XXIX [24–28]) of the "gentile donna giovane e bella molto" (XXXV.2 [24.2]) [gracious woman, young and very beautiful] is one of most explored passages of the *Vita nova*. Nevertheless, its critical reception suffers the weight of later auto-exegetical interventions through which Dante-*auctor* redirects the readers' fruition and "perception of [his] poetic production" along specific (mostly, corrective) paths of interpretation.[2] The influence exerted by the author "as the best possible *lector* of his own verse" has been such as to produce a distorting effect for which we have come to evaluate the episode and its functional segments through the lenses of later palinodic rereadings[3]—first, in *Convivio* (2.2), where the "revaluation of the *donna gentile* sequence" becomes the very "pretext" for the composition of the work, and then in *Purgatorio* 30.127–38, where both figures are definitively re-mediated.[4] Adhering to Dante's own later interventions, commentators have sidelined the experience of the lyric poet, preferring the allegorical recantation of Dante-philosopher or the conclusive condemnation uttered by Beatrice's own voice.

My rereading of *Vita nova* XXXV [24] is a deliberate act of hermeneutical insubordination. It is one that not only rejects the *auctor*'s resignification of this erotic and intellectual impasse but applies the theoretical discourse of affective narratology to reassert the textual and structural significance of the episode as a purely emotional experience. I adopt Patrick Colm Hogan's taxonomy to dissect the narrative and poetic units into four distinct phases of the lover's encounter with the lady of the window: the representation of the emotional preconditions (XXXV.1 [24.1]); the "incident" as the key generative moment of emotional response triggering the existential (and narratological) deviation (XXXV.2 [24.2]); the "situational response" intended as "the immediate actional outcome" following the incident (XXXV.3 [24.3]); and the self-conscious reaction with the "causal attribution of the event and its ultimate sublimation in poetic form" (XXXV.4 [24.4]).[5]

Applied to the *fabula* of the episode, the division reads as follows: a certain time after the first anniversary of Beatrice's death, the lover languishes in a state of harrowing melancholy caused by the painful memory of his long-lost beloved (XXXV.1 [24.1]). Aware of the skewing effect that such inner sorrow has on his outer appearance, he raises his eyes to canvass his surroundings. Here his gaze is immediately arrested by the sight of a gentle, young, and beautiful woman at a window who gazes upon him with a look of deep and sincere compassion (XXXV.2 [24.2]). Bewildered and feeling tears welling up, Dante withdraws from her sight but senses nevertheless that these feelings are signs of an elevated spiritual nobility and of the presence of Love (XXXV.3 [24.3]). Comforted by this realization, the poet addresses the *donna pietosa* in a sonnet serving at once as a justification of his behavior and a sublimation of their emotional experience (XXXV.4 [24.4]).

The introduction of the *donna pietosa* as the functional element of temporary destabilization and final reorientation of Dante's path toward Beatrice is prepared by a layered and evocative portrayal of the lover's aggrieved condition of emotional fragility. Despite its brevity, the description is densely charged with semantic and thematic echoes that inscribe this particular moment within the longer period of grief and sorrow begun in chapter XXII [12] and culminating in XXIII [13].

Dante says that "le lagrime m'avevano assalito" [tears had assailed me] after he had heard women talking about Beatrice, who, "amarissimamente piena di dolore" [most bitterly full of grief], "piangea pietosamente" [wept pitifully] after the death of her beloved father, Folco Portinari (XXII.2–3 [13.2–13.3]). Word of her lament causes him an immediate sense of "tristizia," sadness, that lingers and weighs on him for a certain time until its psychosomatic elaboration into a "dolorosa infermitade" (XXIII.1 [14.1]) [grievous infirmity]. From a physical illness, a quasi-hallucinatory event unfolds in which the invalid is hunted by sounds and apocalyptic visions of darkness, death, and suffering, culminating in the prefiguration of Beatrice's death. This "vana imaginazione" (XXIV.1 [15.1]) [powerful fantasy] throws him in an emotional turmoil so strong that his "singulto di pianto" (XXIII.11 [14.11]) [agonized tearful sob] transcends the oneiric dimension and grows stronger in its wake, generating a chain of "expression-triggered emotions."[6] The sight of the lover as ailing man stirs the sympathetic weeping of a "donna giovane e gentile" (XXIII.11 [14.11]) [young and gentle woman] sitting by his bed; she, in turn, draws a crowd of "altre donne" (XXIII.12 [14.12]) [other women], who shake Dante from his dream, comforting him with their enlightened understanding of his strife. Despite their temporal and structural displacement, the two chapters shape the emotional context from which chapter XXXV derives, bound to them by a thick "lexical network made of words such as *dolore, doloroso, dolente, lagrimare, lagrime, lamentare, lamento, piangere, pianto, singulto, tristizia* and the like."[7] In particular, the chapter functions as the closing element of a dramatic triptych exploring the manifold manifestations and effects of grief on the lover, as well as of the consolatory role of the *donne pietose.*

At the opening of chapter XXXV [24], the lover lies in a state of deep emotional introspection in which the temporal and spatial landscapes are blurred. An indefinite duration of hours, days, or even months has passed from the last secure time reference as "quello giorno nel quale si compie l'anno che questa donna era fatta de li cittadini di vita eterna" (XXXIV.1 [23.1]) [on the first anniversary of the day that this woman was made one of the citizens of eternal life]. On the day of the anniversary of Beatrice's death, Dante sketches the portrait of an angel on "certe tavolette" (XXXIV.1 [23.1]) [certain tablets]. This detail leads the reader to imagine—and reproduce, as Dante Gabriel Rossetti did in his 1853 eponymous painting—the presence of a desk within the room perimeter. Now the physical space becomes an intangible and internalized "parte" (XXXIV.1 [23.1]) [a place] of Dante's psyche, consecrated to the remembrance of the "passato tempo" (XXXV.1 [24.1]) [the past], and within which "the emotional memory" acts as a perpetually controlling force that consumes the lover's mind.[8] Triggered by the activation of the emotional memory, a harrowing sense of anguish ravages the depths of the inner self and erupts onto the surface, projecting a distraught image of the lover into the public world. Deformed by a "terribile sbigottimento" (XXXV.1 [24.1]) [outward appearance of horrible turmoil], the lover's lineaments are horribly subverted by grief to the point that he is almost unrecognizable: once again he "non pare esso, tal e' divenuto" (XXII.6 [13.6]) [is so changed that he doesn't seem himself!]. Against these effects, the lover's exercise of emotional memory—striving to re-create and preserve the mental image of Beatrice as ever present—becomes a predictive form of infernal punishment binding him to an eternal state of psychological and physical vexation. Prefiguring what will be portrayed in *Inferno,* Dante-lover is the victim of what Chiarantini calls "a reversed kind of *damnatio memoriae* which is not condemnation of memory, but rather condemnation to memory."[9] Although the lover does not seek "forgetfulness" as "a craved respite," his outer behavior mimics that of damned souls of the first *cantica* for the way he strives to shelter his figure and private suffering from the sight of others.

Notably, the dread of being seen by "altri" [others] prompts the simple but salient gesture that initiates the "first incident" of the overall episode of the *sviamento erotico.*[10] The lifting of the gaze ("levai li occhi," XXXV.2 [24.2] [I raised my eyes]) is a moment of utmost vulnerability for the lover, who emerges from his mournful solipsism in order to inspect his surroundings and ensure his intimacy before sinking back into the depths of his intimate sorrows. The coveted descent into the oneiric space of memory is disrupted by the startling sight of a woman standing, in all her carnal youth and earthly beauty, by a nearby window and gazing at him. The spatial detail of the window reinforces the realism of her figure but also frames her in a physical posture that mirrors the lover's psychological condition of immobility: at the *seuil* between private and public sphere, intimate and shared experience.

The initial epithet with which Dante presents her as a "gentile donna giovane e bella molto" [a gracious woman, young and very beautiful] is an interesting recombination of the appellatives used for the many women encountered in the *libello* (Beatrice included). In particular, the epithet establishes a veiled continuity with the young and gentle women that rushed to console him at the peak of his oneiric delirium. This becomes more evident when she is referred to as "questa pietosa donna" [that compassionate woman]: a phrase that echoes the first verse of the *canzone* "Donna pietosa e di novella etate" (XXIII.17–28 [14.17–14.28]) [A woman green in years, compassionate]. Compared to them, however, the lady at the window is a superior *other* in whom "pietà" [compassion] is not simply expressed but powerfully sublimated and conveyed through her entire being: "tutta la pietà parea in lei accolta" (XXXV.2 [24.2]) [all compassion seemed gathered in her]. While the "pietà" of the women in chapter XXIII [14] was a form of static comparticipation in his sufferings, the sentiment powerfully embodied by this new lady offers the glimpse of promise of spiritual consolation and sentimental regeneration.

The compassionate gaze of the woman deprives the lover of his agency as a gazer, turning him into an object of contemplation and forcing him to reflect upon his deep-rooted condition of unhappiness ("come li miseri" [people in misery]). Despite his being brought to tears by the piercing force of her gaze, this incident does not unfold as a traumatic experience for the lover, differently from chapter XIV [7] where his emotional "trasfigurazione" (7) [transfiguration] caused by the sight of the *gentilissima* at a wedding is ridiculed in front of her by a group of women. Where the display of his "distrutti . . . spiriti" (5) [overcome spirits] was met with derision, the *donna pietosa* contemplates them with sincere understanding and compassion, demonstrating an unparalleled degree of emotional intelligence. Arguably, this affective behavior traces a sentimental and intellectual continuity between this woman and the "Donne ch' avete intelletto d'amore" [Women who understand the truth of love] of chapter XIX [10]. Like them, she produces in Dante a sort of revelation regarding "a new conception of human love" as "full actualization of the nobility that lies in the spirit, and hence as exaltation of the individual and achievement of his inner harmony."[11] This configures a form of self-consciousness through which the lover comes to realize that "li miseri" [people in misery] can gain a better understanding of their own emotional responses when confronted with the compassion engendered in others by their miserable condition.

The move from intellectual cogitation to factual realization of the emotional response is immediate as the lover "sentì allora cominciare li miei occhi a volere piangere" [I felt my eyes starting to want to cry]. Once again, the *pianto* overcomes him as a bodily instinct that he counteracts through two distinct yet interrelated actions. First is physical withdrawal "da li occhi di questa gentile" (XXXV.3 [24.3]) [I took myself away from the eyes of this gracious woman], which Hogan's taxonomy classifies as a "situational" and "actional response" through which the subject attempts to shield his emotional condition.[12] In this particular case, the abrupt departure is due to the dread of revealing his dismay further. At this point in the narrative, the concept of "vile vita" (XXXV.3 [24.3]) [my base condition] and "viltate" [wretchedness] holds an "exclusively affective meaning," but it will acquire moral significance later in the episode (XXXVII [26]) as the lover will become more aware of his *deviamento*.

The retreat into a more private, hence safer, space gives way to a moment of intellectual metabolization of the incident through what Hogan describes as a "simplifying" act of "automatic and immediate causal attribution."[13] The intimate rereading of the lived experience marks a crucial turning point within the narrative of the overall episode for the way it initiates the "mechanism of self-illusion" that stands at the basis of the broader, erotic transgression.[14] The double negation in the self-directed discourse "E' non puote essere che con quella pietosa donna non sia nobilissimo amore" (XXXV.3 [24.3]) [It cannot be that in this compassionate woman there is anything but a sublimely noble love][15] marks the moment in which the lover's hermeneutic and sentimental *deviation* begins. It signals not the earthly erotic impulse but rather the presence of "nobilissimo amore" (XXXV.3 [24.3]) [sublimely noble love] in her. The epithet used up to that point for Beatrice elevates this lady to the status of an earthly and living replacement of her.[16] As such, the *donna pietosa* is interpreted as an earthly savior that relieves the suffering lover from his infernal condition of perpetual mourning, reviving him with new emotional impulses. However, as Tristan Kay noted, "What begins as a non-erotic esteem soon escalates into a treacherous physical attraction" in a quick turnaround of the narrative.[17]

The sudden *anagnorisis* is followed by the decision to address his new interlocutor ("ne la quale io parlasse a lei" [in which I would talk to her]) and sublimate ("conchiudesse" [put into]) in a higher, poetic form ("uno sonetto") (XXXV.4 [24.4] the emotional experience recounted in the narrative prose, here denominated by the Occitan technical term of *ragione* (prov. *razos*). Employed here for the first time in the *libello,* this designation recurs throughout the episode of the *donna pietosa* to denote the passages of contextualization of Dante's poetic compositions. Despite its brevity, the declaration of intent signals the lover's recovery of poetic agency after his momentary annihilation as an object of gaze. On a formal level, the choice of the sonnet as the poetic form taken as the first predictive sign of the true nature of the episode will unfold over the course of the four ensuing chapters (all characterized by the same type of poem).

The sonnet rereads the incident with what Mario Pazzaglia describes as "a more discursive tone" and "a more hushed and subtle emotional participation."[18] Where the prose is the affective record of the incident and its shocking impact on the lover, the poetry displays a sort of synthetic rereading in which actions, thoughts, and emotions are transfigured by the lyrical vocabulary. Exercising editorial authority, the poet omits any prefatory description to prioritize the exchange of gazes between the lover and the *donna pietosa.* Here the reciprocity is emphasized by the juxtaposition of the Cavalcantian "Videro" (line 1) [my eyes saw] and her "guardaste" (line 3) [you had seen]. Such alternation of their perspective is carried onto the second quatrain, where his "m'accorsi" (line 5) [I perceived] is mirrored by her "pensavate" (line 5) [you were about to guess], thus conveying a dynamic reproduction of the character's *actions* in the scene that closes with the lover's hurried return to a safe but lonesome space ("tolsimi dinanzi a voi," line 9 [I shrank back from you]), where he can then talk to himself, here described in Cavalcantian terms as an "anima trista" (line 12) [sad soul].

Particularly noteworthy is the poet's rewriting of the overall emotional experience through the workings of his new poetic memory. While the visibly deforming effects of the lover's mourning of Beatrice are largely downplayed, subsumed in the vague reference to "gli atti e la statura" (line 3) [old gesticulations and the mien], the poet gives voice to the thoughts underlying the lady's expression of *pietate.* Taking a leap in imaginative hermeneutics, he interprets her interest in vaguely philosophical terms, given the use of the term *qualità* to describe the "qualità de la mia vita oscura" (line 6) [the state of darkness that my life had been]. In this sense, the figurative "darkness" could indirectly emphasize the strength of the woman's interpretive effort as much as it directly characterizes the nature of the lover's affective condition.

The lyric transition from narrative to poetic recounting is evident in the repeated phraseological use of *cor* and *core* throughout the sonnet, through which the poet refers to the heart as the source of all emotional responses, not just amorous passion: first, as the place in which the fear ("paura," line 7) of revealing the depths of his afflictions to the *donna pietosa* supervenes ("giunse," line 7) and grows strong, provoking the instinctual response: "tolsimi dinanzi a voi" (line 9) [I pulled myself away from your presence], and second, as the originating place ("dal core," line 10) of tears ("le lagrime," line 10) that overcome him following her disrupting exchange of sights. The lyrical elevation of the narrative discourse continues with the rewriting of the reflective response to the incident as a moment of profound introspection. The representation of the self is replaced by "anima" [soul], almost synonymously intended as the spiritual source of his affections. The insertion of the adjective *trista* adds a layer of melancholy and gloom to this final description of the poet's affective condition following the encounter. Sublimating the whole poetic rereading is the capitalization of the word "Amore" (line 13) [Love], thus marking the definitive acknowledgment of the presence of the divinity with whom Dante has been dialoguing over the course of *libello* in the figure of the *donna pietosa*.

Reread in literary and historical isolation and through the lenses of Hogan's affective narratology, chapter XXXV [24] of the *libello* reveals its greater significance as a painfully vivid and sincere portrait of Dante-lover in his most fragile emotional state. Staging the germinal moment of a longer period of erotic deflection toward an earthly figure, it reveals the lover in all his sentimental prostration and intellectual fallibility that caused embarrassment to the mature poet. The palinodic recantations in the *Convivio* and *Purgatorio* can be interpreted as the way in which Dante sought to preserve his status of *auctor*—"at once a writer and an authority, someone not merely to be read but also to be respected and believed"—in the eyes of present and future generations of readers.[19]

Vita nova XXXVI and XXXVII [25–26]

K. P. CLARKE

> *A successful poem . . . is "a machine for rereading."*
> —Michael Hofmann

The *Vita nova* is a "machine for rereading." The sequence of prose and verse pivots on the read and reread, a dynamic of before and after where the prose exerts a narrative force on the verse, and the poetry exerts a lyric force on the prose, each pushing the other to its generic limits and beyond. The outer edges of the work are marked at one end by the already written (I.1 [1.1]) and at the other by that which has not yet been written (XLII.2 [31.2]), so that rereading becomes a creative act, its results unpredictable.

Chapters XXXVI [25] and XXXVII [26] form part of the so-called *donna gentile* episode (XXXV [24]–XXXIX [28]), an episode that Dante himself reads and rereads in his subsequent work: first in the *Convivio* (2.2.1–2), where the *donna* is interpreted allegorically as Philosophy, and again in *Purgatorio*, where in the earthly paradise Dante is finally reunited with Beatrice, who refers to a "pargoletta / o altra novità con sì breve uso" (*Purg.* 31.59–60) [young woman, or other fleeting novelty].[1] The episode prompts a series of rereadings within the *Vita nova* itself, where the *donna gentile* is recognized as a self-deception. The sonnet "Color d'amore e di pietà sembianti" (XXXVI.4–5 [25.4–25.5]) [Color of love and true compassion's guise] has many traditional love-lyric aspects, with a narrator declaring the comfort he takes in his beloved. But within the poem there is already a signaling of a crisis, which escalates in "L'amaro lagrimar che voi faceste" (XXXVII.6–8 [26.6–26.8]) [Your bitter weeping when you were bereaved], with its fierce debate between the heart and the eyes on the danger of forgetting Beatrice.

The first three sonnets of the *donna gentile* episode are marked by the repetition of key themes and motifs. So for example, "amore" in the final line of "Videro li occhi miei quanta pietate" (XXXV.5–8 [24.5–24.8]) [My eyes saw mercy that was fathomless] is reprised in the opening line of the following sonnet, "Color d'amore," while "lagrimar" in its final line is reprised in the first line of the next sonnet, "L'amaro lagrimar."[2] A further repetition of *pietate/pietà* may be observed in the first lines of "Videro li occhi miei" and "Color d'amore." These formal techniques of repetition are reminiscent (respectively) of *coblas capfinidas* and *coblas capdenals*, which in Occitan lyrics link stanzas, but which here link whole compositions, emphasizing not just the highly wrought surface of the text but especially the forward and backward movement between poems and the continual rereadings prompted by such repetition.

In "Color d'amore" Dante also signals a break with what has gone before. The poem intensifies the engagement with the beloved by addressing her directly, in striking contrast to the *stilo de la lode*, the praise style, where the lady is praised in the third person and nothing is sought from her. In terms of the coordination of narrative and style in the *Vita nova*, this direct address represents a regression, a return to a mode that had been overcome. "Color d'amore" signals a further shift in deploying a metrical scheme (ABBA, ABBA, CDE DCE) that was not previously used in the *Vita nova* and that is repeated in all of its remaining poems. Thematically the crisis of this episode unfolds in the context of metrical stability and sameness.[3] While the scheme is not rare, its use is mainly associated with Guido Cavalcanti, Dante, and Cino—including a number of correspondence poems between them: associated, that is, with the *dolce stil novo*.[4] The tone and atmosphere of "Color d'amore" resonate with stilnovist elements, and Mario Pazzaglia has noted how these *donna gentile* poems come close to the sweetness of Cino's work.[5] Indeed, Cino himself writes a sequence of sonnets that evoke this *donna gentile* episode in the *Vita nova*, and his sonnet "Occhi mïei, fuggite ogni persona" [Eyes of mine flee every person] is a free imitation of "L'amaro lagrimar."[6]

The attention Dante affords the lyric contours of the language of the *Vita nova* is precise, fierce, and unrelenting. At this point in the *Vita nova* Dante looks back to an earlier moment in the *libello*, in particular to the sequence of sonnets in chapters XIII [6]–XVI [9], which includes the so-called episode of the *gabbo*, of the women making fun of the lover. These poems are marked by a strong Cavalcantian influence, emphasizing the destructive powers of love. The debate between the heart and the eyes in XXXVII [26] is described as a "battaglia," a battle, a word that occurs three times in the episode of the *gabbo* (XIV.1 [7.1] and XVI.4 [9.4]). The prose section of XXXVII [26] is marked by an emotional heightening with words such as *vile* (loathsome), *vanitate* (inconstancy), *maladetti occhi* (cursed eyes), and *morte* (death), including terms that appear only once in the *libello*: *crucciare* (to torment) and *bestemmiare* (to curse), for example. The Latinism *disturbare* (used in the sense of "to remove"), which appears in line 7 of "L'amaro lagrimar," is a hapax in Dante, and rather rare in early Italian. If "L'amaro lagrimar" takes the form of an *insectatio in oculos*, we have already in "Color d'amore" a focus on the eyes, with a violent escalation from the "occhi gentili" [gentle eyes] of line 4 to the "occhi distrutti" [destroyed eyes] of line 9. The two component parts of the sonnet, the octet (*fronte*) and the sestet (*sirma*), are not just connected in the repetition of the phrases "temo . . . non" and "non posso" [I cannot] in lines 8 and 9 but also bound by the two words in rhyme position: *schianti* (break) and *distrutti*.[7] This structural poetic threshold holds in play the possible and the impossible, a fear that something *might* happen ("temo . . . non" is a Latinate construction, *timeo ne*, "I fear that," followed by the subjunctive) which then gives way to a declaration of what cannot happen. In that verb *schiantare* Dante rereads a lyric tradition as well as signaling a departure from it.

Commentators typically observe that the verb *schiantare* is associated with a popular register, adding a note of what might be called "local color," and frequently cite examples (including of the derivative noun *schianto*) in the work of Rustico Filippi, as well as the thirteenth-century *contrasti* (dialogue or debate poems, usually on love) "Mamma lo temp'è venuto" [Mother, the time has come], where the daughter, impatient to be married, declares to her mother: "'Matre, lo cor te· se· sclanti, / s' tu me· lo· vòi contrariare'" (*CLPIO* B 4, lines 11–12) [Mother, let my heart break if you propose to refuse it], and Cielo d'Alcamo's "Rosa fresca aulentissima" [Fresh and most fragrant rose], where the narrator declares "'Donne, quante sono le schiàntora che m' à' mise alo core'" (*CLPIO* V 54, line 41) [Ladies, how many are the breaks that she has placed on my heart].[8] If the verb in line 8 of "Color d'amore" is read filtered through this register, it takes on a quality of exaggeration, of overstatement. It is this comic tone of exaggeration that may be heard in the use of *schianto* in an extensive *tenzone* between two thirteenth-century Florentine poets, Schiatta Pallavillani and Monte Andrea, where the former offers a sustained critique of the intensity of the latter's experience of love.[9] Schiatta suggest this love will bring Monte suffering and heartbreak, "di ciò averete al core dolgli' e schianti" (*CLPIO* V 663, line 7) [of this you will have pains and breaks on your heart], while Monte accords the noun an emphatic focus in his reply, drawing it into the incipit: "Sento ·mi al core dolorosi schianti" (*CLPIO* V 664, line 1) [I feel in my heart painful breaks].[10]

The earliest occurrence of the verb *schiantare* in vernacular Italian is found in the *canzone* "D'amoroso paese" [From a loving country] by Tommaso di Sasso, a poet active in the so-called Sicilian School, and probably in its earliest phase.[11] The narrator laments not being able to find anyone who knows what love is, and so he dies of suffering, "non trovo chi lo· saccia, ond' io mi· schianto" (*CLPIO* L[b] 115, line 18; cfr. *CLPIO* V 21).[12] It is notable, however, that this is also the *only* occurrence of the verb in the Sicilian corpus, while the noun *schianto* has a relatively limited diffusion.[13] As a term to describe the suffering experienced by the lover, it appears not to have been widely adopted. But it is precisely this restraint in the use of *schiantare* that renders it possible to trace its discrete but discernible presence among a group of poets in the circle of Dante in the decade of the 1290s, casting its appearance in "Color d'amore" in a sharper light.

A pre-stilnovist atmosphere may be felt in the image of the heart breaking in "La gioven donna cui appello Amore' [The young woman whom I call love], a *canzone* by the so-called Amico di Dante, where the lover holds an image of the lady in his heart and if he hears word of her (or perhaps her voice?), his heart seems to break: "ma, ss' à udita anchora la parladura, | ben pare allora- che 'l chore gli· si· schianti | -chéd e' si· parte."[14] A certain strain or overstatement may be felt in the poet's use of *schiantare* and *partire* as synonyms. This *canzone* has been described as a "little dictionary of Sicilian and prestilnovist topoi," which suggests that the use of the verb *schiantare* in respect of the lover's heart has become a commonplace, perhaps a kind of cliché.[15] The anonymous poet responsible for this remarkable cycle of sonnets and *canzoni* is certainly a reader of the work of Cavalcanti and Dante, but as Contini observed, he is a follower of the old style and not someone who has embraced the *stil novo*.[16] In "Pegli occhi miei una donna e Amore" [Through my eyes a woman and Love], a sonnet attributed to a certain Jacopo Cavalcanti, related to (but not, as often declared, the brother of) Guido, a dialogue describes the emotional, internal torments of love.[17] In a theme of internal turmoil familiar from the work of Guido, the "sospiro," or sigh, addresses the heart, observing the extreme effects upon it of the beloved: "e di tue pene poco le ne caglia; / anzi ha le tue vertù pres' e schiantate" (lines 12–13) [and of your suffering she cares little; rather, she has taken your strength and destroyed it]. The force evoked in the verb *prendere* is considerably intensified when combined with *schiantare*, resulting in an extreme expressiveness that Domenico De Robertis characterized as an "excess of 'incarnation' of the virtues." At stake, then, in Jacopo's use of *schiantare* is a failure to sufficiently balance the spiritual and the physical, the abstract and the concrete.

In a *tenzone* sonnet, "Sì m' è fatta nemica la Mercede" [Thus Mercy has become my enemy] by Onesto da Bologna, the narrator laments that even though he has not done anything wrong ("non fallai") he seems to be treated particularly harshly by his lady, and he concludes by declaring that his desire is crushing his heart, "ch' esto disio tutto lo cor mi schianta" (line 14).[18] Cino da Pistoia's reply asserts that there is not much to be done, since Love is the domain of the lady, to whom the beloved remains utterly subject. The highly unusual metrical form and rhyme scheme of this *tenzone* highlight a lexical resistance to *schiantare* in Cino's reply. The form is known as a "sonetto continuo," where only two rhymes are used across the *fronte* and *sirma* (in this case –*anta* and –*ede*), and the scheme, ABBA ABBA ABA BAB, is used only once again by Cino, in "Omo smarruto che pensoso vai" [Lost man who pensively goes].[19] In an acknowledgment of the relative difficulty of rhymes in –*anta*, Cino reuses two of Onesto's rhyme-words, "pianta" (line 2) and "vanta" (line 14), and the others he includes in this poem constitute the sum total of examples of such a rhyme in his entire poetic corpus.[20] Thus the exclusion of *schianta* can be read as a polemical nod to Onesto's poetics of the past and a restatement of his own stilnovist poetics of the present.

Dante's use of the verb *schiantare* can be read as signaling a poetic acknowledgment of pre-stilnovism, intended to evoke a moment of regression in the narrative, with Dante describing his "self-deception" in words that belong to a lyric now surpassed. The lyric dessication of the term reaches completion by *Inferno*, when Dante meets the Sicilian poet and imperial *logotheta* Pier delle Vigne, who declares that his position of trust and intimacy was such that he held both keys to the heart of Frederick II. But when Pier uses the verb *schiantare* he is referring, not to his broken heart, but rather to the broken branch that is now his infernal form, and when he asks in anguish, "Perché mi schiante?" (*Inf.* 13.33, in rhyme with *piante* : *avante*) [Why do you break me?], the verb fully embraces the real, the physical, the literal.

Vita nova XXXVIII and XXXIX [27–28]

NICOLÒ MALDINA

In chapters XXXVIII–XXXIX [27–28] of the *Vita nova*, the episode of the so-called *donna gentile* (or, more precisely, the episode in which Dante falls in love with another woman after Beatrice's death) comes to an end.[1] Albeit relatively short in its development (chapters XXXV–XXXIX [24–28]), this episode is nonetheless of crucial importance not only in the narrative context of the *libello* but also with reference to the continuing autobiographical feature of Dante's works in the vernacular (*Vita nova, Convivio, Commedia*). However, I shall not try to offer here a comprehensive discussion of the relationship between chapters XXXVIII–XXXIX [27–28] of the *Vita nova* and the responses to this narrative present in the philosophical *prosimetrum* or in the *Commedia*.[2] On the contrary, I shall limit myself to offering a brief discussion of some of the key features of these chapters with reference to the narrative context of the *Vita nova* by focusing on two words that play a key role in better defining the importance of these two chapters within the *libello* as a whole: *tribulazione* (tribulation) and *pentére* (to repent). While the importance of these expressions has been so far underestimated in this context, I believe that a better understanding of their precise meaning will offer new ground to define more precisely the expression that is traditionally perceived as the semantic center of the chapters, namely the "costanzia della Ragione" [constancy of Reason] (XXXIX.2 [28.2]).[3]

In *Vita nova* XL.1 [29.1] the conclusion of Dante's infatuation for the *donna gentile* is defined as a "tribulazione"—"Dopo questa tribulazione avvenne, in quel tempo che molta gente va per vedere quella immagine benedetta" [After this tribulation, at that time when many people go to see the blessed image]—with a word that echoes the definition of the prostration of the protagonist after Beatrice's death in XXXVIII.3 [27.3]: "Or tu se' stato in tanta tribulazione" [You have been in such a state of tribulation]. These are the only two passages of the *libello* in which the word *tribulazione* occurs, and this recurrence is hardly accidental considering the biblical nuance that distinguishes the word on both those occasions.[4] Before moving on to consider this nuance in more detail, it is important to appreciate that this highly connoted parallel is intended to invite the reader to compare the two paragraphs. However, the recurrence of the same term is conceived here not to stress a similarity between the situations described in each of the aforementioned passages but rather to highlight a substantial difference between the forms of suffering described in *Vita nova* XXXVIII.3 [27.3] and XL.1 [29.1].

In the first of these paragraphs, the word *tribulazione* is pronounced within the fictional dramatization of Dante's indecisions by one of his thoughts as part of a sentence that aims to exhort him to surrender to the new feelings for the *donna gentile* by presenting this new love as a solution to recover from the prostration for Beatrice's death: "Poi si rilevava un altro pensero e diceame: 'Or tu se' stato in tanta tribulazione, perché non ti vuoli tu ritrare da tanta amaritudine?'" [Then another thought arose saying to me: "You have been in such a state of suffering, why don't you withdraw from such bitterness?"]. The words *tribulazione* and *amaritudine* are a synonymic repetition reinforced by the anaphora of the adjective *tanta* ("tanta tribulazione . . . tanta amaritudine") that refers to Dante's mourning for Beatrice's death with the deliberate purpose to shed a negative light on Dante's sorrow, being (as it is) primarily intended to convince Dante that he has suffered enough and thus can be allowed to forget Beatrice. As a matter of fact, the *altro pensero* that uses the word *tribulazione* for the first time agrees with the first thought made by Dante after having seen the *donna gentile* for the second time—"E pensava di lei così: 'Questa è una donna gentile, bella, giovane e savia, e apparita forse per volontà d'Amore acciò che la mia vita si riposi'" (XXXVIII.1 [27.1]) [I thought about her as follows: "This is a woman who is gracious, beautiful, young and wise, and perhaps she appeared by Love's will so that my life might find rest"]—and is opposed to the different thought that, moved by reason, invites Dante not to consider the love for the *donna gentile* as a form of consolation for his sorrow: "E io mi ripensava sì come da la ragione mosso e dicea fra me medesimo: 'Deo, che pensero è questo, che in così vil modo vuol consolar me e non mi lascia quasi altro pensare?'" (XXXVIII.2 [27.2]) [And when I had consented in this way, I returned to the sort of thinking that springs from reason itself, telling myself: "God, what thought is this, which in such a base manner wants to console me and leaves me thinking about almost nothing else?"].

This latter definition—"sì come da la ragione mosso" [that springs from reason itself]—invites us to consider the aforementioned *altro pensero* as contrary to reason, which means that the thought that exhorts Dante to recover from his *tribulazione* and *amaritudine* is the adversary of reason that, in chapter XXXIX, will be overwhelmed by a strong vision of Beatrice: "Contra questo avversario della Ragione si levòe un die, quasi nell'ora della nona, una forte immaginazione in me, che mi parve vedere questa gloriosa Beatrice" (XXXIX.1 [28.1]) [Against this adversary of reason there arose in me one day, at about the hour of nones, an intense imagining that seemed to see this glorious Beatrice].[5] It is therefore significant that in chapter XL.1 [29.1] the second occurrence of the word *tribulazione* refers precisely to the rising of this vision of Beatrice against the thought, adversary of reason, that in chapter XXXVIII [27] first used this expression to negatively define the mourning for Beatrice. The incipit of chapter XL [29] "Dopo questa tribulazione" [after this tribulation] cannot but refer to the event described in the proceeding chapter, and paradoxically enough, what is defined a *tribulazione* here is the conflict between the thought that prompted Dante to consider his sorrow for Beatrice a *tribulazione* and Beatrice herself. It concludes with the victory of Reason over the *altro pensero*, or, in other words, of the memory of Beatrice over the infatuation for the *donna gentile*: "Allora cominciai a pensare di lei e, ricordandomi secondo l'ordine del tempo passato, lo mio cuore cominciò dolorosamente a pentére de lo desiderio a cui sì vilmente s'avea lasciato possedere alquanti die contra la costanzia della Ragione; e, discacciato questo cotale malvagio desiderio, sì si rivolsero tutti li miei pensamenti a la loro gentilissima Beatrice" (XXXIX.2 [28.2]) [Then I started to think about her; and remembering her as she was in the past, my heart painfully started to repent the desire by which it so basely had let itself be seized for a number of days against the constancy of reason: and after casting out this malicious desire, all my thoughts began to revert to the most noble Beatrice].

This marks a substantial difference in the semantics of the two, apparently identical, occurrences of the word *tribulazione* in XXXVIII.3 [27.3] and XL.1 [29.1]. The negative meaning of the term is the same on both occasions, and in both cases the word is used to describe one of the greatest novelties of Dante's approach to love poetry: the act of mourning for the death of the poet's beloved;[6] however, while in XXXVIII.1 [27.1] it is the memory of Beatrice to be defined in such a negative way, in XL.1 [29.1] it is the trouble generated by the temptation to forget Beatrice that comes to be qualified as a tribulation. Such a divergence of perspectives needs to be considered alongside the differing identities of the characters who speak the word *tribulazione* in each of the aforementioned paragraphs: in the first, this is a thought defined as contrary to reason, and in the second, it is Dante who, as the author of the *Vita nova* (i.e., writing after the strong vision narrated in chapter XXXIX [28]), is fully aware that this thought was in actuality a "malvagio desiderio" (XXXIX.2 [28.2]) [wicked desire]. It would therefore be difficult to deny that the negative meaning of the word *tribulazione* is rightly attributed to the temptation to surrender to the *donna gentile* and only superficially to the sorrow for Beatrice's death.

However, what is important to stress is that both in chapter XXXVIII [27] and in chapter XL [29] the word *tribulazione* is used with reference to the articulated conflict between the old and the new love generated by Dante's infatuation for the *donna gentile*. In other words, the advent of the *donna gentile* generates a tension that in the *Vita nova* is described twice with reference to the word *tribulazione*: chapters XXXVIII [27] and XXXIX [28] narrate, respectively, the climax and the solution of a *pugna intellectualis* initiated with the "battaglia ched io avea meco" [battle which I had with myself] narrated in chapter XXXVII.3 [26.3] and continued in the "battaglia de' pensieri" [battle of thoughts] described in chapter XXXVIII.4 [27.4]—a battle that might logically be defined as a *tribulazione*, with reference to the aforementioned twofold meaning that this term holds in the lexicon of the *Vita nova*. To better understand the topic of these chapters it is thus important to fully understand the implications of Dante's use of the term *tribulazione*, with special reference to its possible sources. Let us begin by saying that both the words used in chapter XXXVIII.3 [27.3] (*tribulazione* and *amaritudine*) are likely to hold a biblical meaning: in particular, while the word *amaritudine* should be read alongside Isaiah 38:15 ("in amaritudine animae meae" [in the bitterness of my soul]),[7] the entire opening of chapter XL [29] translates Matthew 24:29 ("post tribulationem dierum illorum" [after the tribulation of those days]).[8]

This latter evangelical intertext is of great importance, especially considering the narrative context of this biblical verse.[9] Matthew is narrating the events that will occur as the second advent of Christ approaches, and the tribulation he mentions refers to the conflict generated by the contrast between the advent of false prophets that will precede the second coming of the true Christ and his actual Parousia. Before the second coming of Christ many false Christs will rise to seduce man ("multi pseudoprophetae surgent et seducent multos," Matthew 24:11 [many false prophets will arise and seduce many people]); they will do so with false miracles: "Surgent enim pseudochristi et pseudoprophetae et dabunt signa magna et prodigia ita ut in errorem inducatur" (Matthew 24:23–24) [there will arise many false Christs and false prophets and they will show great signs and prodigies so that they lead people into error]. The main effect of those false miracles will be that among those who believe in them, love for the true Christ will abate—"et quoniam abundavit iniquitas, refrigescet caritas multorum" (Matthew 24:12) [and since iniquity will abound the love of the many will become cold]—until the Parousia reveals the falseness of those pseudoprophets, inspiring thus a penitential impulse in those who have been misled by them for the true Christ: "et tunc planget omnes tribus terrae" (Matthew 24:30) [and then shall all the tribes of earth mourn].

The context described by Matthew seems particularly close to the events narrated in the chapters about Dante's infatuation for the *donna gentile* in the *Vita nova*.[10] Reduced to its essentials, in this episode Dante is tempted by a woman whose attributes are comparable with those peculiar to Beatrice: "Questa è una donna gentile, bella, giovane e savia" (XXXVIII.1 [27.1]) [This is a woman who is gracious, beautiful, young and wise] and "gentile donna" (XXXVIII.4 [27.4]) [noble woman]. And it seems sensible to conclude that Dante decides to surrender to this temptation, so that "ne la battaglia de' pensieri vinceano coloro che per lei parlavano" (XXXVIII.4 [27.4]) [the battle of the thoughts was won by those thoughts speaking about her], because he believes that the *donna gentile* can become a sort of new Beatrice for him: "Molte fiate mi ricordava de la mia nobilissima donna" (XXXVI.1 [25.1]) [Many times I was reminded of my most noble lady].[11] This might be the reason why in chapter XXXVIII [27] the "disiri" [desires] brought by the "spiritel novo d'amore" (10) [new spirit of love] win over the "desiderio ... di ricordarmi de la gentilissima donna mia" (XXXVIII.6 [27.6]) [desire ... to remember my most gracious lady]. In this respect, the relevance of Matthew 24:11–30 can be fully appreciated only if one bears in mind the Christological representation of Beatrice in the *Vita nova* and, more precisely, the Christological nature of Dante's mourning for her death:[12] the *donna gentile* looks like Beatrice, and Dante believes in her as in a new Beatrice before the vision of the true *gentilissima* narrated in chapter XXXIX [28] reveals to him the misunderstanding and reorients his love to Beatrice.

Given the equivalence between Beatrice and Christ, this "forte imaginazione" (XXXIX.1 [28.1]) [powerful imagining] can be compared to the Parousia—a parallel reinforced by the fact that in this vision Beatrice appears "con quelle vestimenta sanguigne colle quali apparve prima a li occhi miei" (XXXIX.1 [28.1]) [wearing those same crimson clothes with which she first appeared to my eyes]: indeed, Beatrice first appears to Dante in a Christological manner, as is clearly evident, for instance, in the borrowings from the Gospels discernible in the expressions "Ecce deus fortior me qui veniens dominabitur michi" [Here is a god stronger than I that comes to rule me] and "Apparuit iam beatitudo vestra" [Your beatitude has now appeared] (II.4–5 [1.5–1.6]).[13] What needs to be stressed, moreover, is that, just as in the Gospel of Matthew, this second coming after death is preceded by the advent of false images of the true Beatrice-Christ (i.e., the *donna gentile*); while at first Dante believes in the goodness of the love he feels for the *donna gentile* and thus his love for Beatrice diminishes, he is just like the faithful in the Gospel of Matthew in that he is induced to repent by Beatrice's Parousia: "Lo mio cuore cominciò dolorosamente a pentére de lo desiderio cui sì vilmente s'avea lasciato possedere alquanti die contra la costanzia della Ragione" (XXXIX.2 [28.2]) [My heart painfully started to repent the desire by which it so basely had let itself be possessed for some days against the constancy of Reason].

It is clear that a closer consideration of the relevance of the biblical source alluded to (almost by chance) in the expression "Dopo questa tribulazione" not only contributes to a more precise understanding of Dante's use of the term *tribulazione* but also better locates the translation of Matthew 24:29 in *Vita nova* XL.1 [29.1] within the complex narration of Dante's love for Beatrice in the *libello*. The second occurrence of the word *tribulazione* in XL.1 [29.1] corrects the nuance attributed to the word by the "spiritel novo d'amore" [little spirit of new love] in XXXVIII.3 [27.3]: it is the tormented defeat of the desire for the *donna gentile* that is a tribulation, not the sorrow for Beatrice's death. It is also because he misunderstands what tribulation means in a love affair that the *altro pensero* that exhorts Dante to surrender to his desire for the *donna gentile* can be defined as an "avversario della Ragione" [adversary of Reason] that inspires in Dante thoughts "contra la costanzia della Ragione" [against the constancy of Reason] (XXXIX.1 [28.1]) and thus proves to be a "desiderio malvagio e vana intenzione" (XXXIX.6 [28.6]) [wicked desire and vain intention]. Analogously, it is because Dante at first trusts the *spiritel novo d'amore* in believing that he has suffered enough for Beatrice that he needs to recognize this mistake and repent for it. This is the condition for overcoming the tribulation generated by the advent of the *donna gentile* and returning to his mourning for Beatrice, which is no longer a form of sorrow for her death (i.e., a *tribulazione* in the sense given to the word by the "spiritel novo d'amore") but a positive consideration of "quella benedetta Beatrice, la quale gloriosamente mira la faccia di Colui *qui est per omnia secula benedictus*" (XLII.3 [31.3]) [that blessed Beatrice who gazes gloriously at the face of he who is blessed for ever and ever].

In short, then, one can read chapters XXXVIII–XXXIX as the story of the *tribulazione* (I am using here the term in its evangelical sense) that leads to a renewed conception of the possibility of remaining faithful to Beatrice after her death, to maintain the poet's thought on "quello che nel cuore si ragionava, cioè lo nome di quella gentilissima, e come si partio da noi" (XXXIX.3 [29.3]) [that which was being spoken about in my heart, that is, the name of that most noble one and how she departed from us]. As mentioned, the resolution of this tribulation coincides with Dante's repentance for his infatuation with the *donna gentile*: "Lo mio cuore cominciò dolorosamente a pentére" (XXXIX.2 [28.2]) [My heart painfully started to repent], which brings us to the second key word of chapters XXXVIII–XXXIX [27–28]: *pentére*. Despite the evangelical context in which the term is used, the verb *to repent* does not seem to have in XXXIX.2 [29.2] the same technical sense that it had in late medieval religious culture. It would be hard to deny that, after having repented for his infatuation, Dante feels ashamed, as is evident in the following passages: "lo desiderio a cui sì vilmente s'avea lasciato possedere alquanti die contra la costanzia della Ragione" (XXXIX.2 [28.2]) [the desire by which it so basely had let itself be possessed for some days against the constancy of Reason] and "vergognoso cuore" (XXXIX.3 [28.3]) [shameful heart]). Equally, after Dante's repentance, the desire for the *donna gentile* is characterized in a morally negative way: "desiderio malvagio e vana intenzione" (XXXIX.6 [28.6]) [wicked desire and vain intention]. Furthermore, the poet's eyes are punished for their vanity: "Dintorno a loro si facea un colore porporeo . . ., onde appare che de la loro vanitade fuoro degnamente guiderdonati" (XXXIX.4–5 [28.4–28.5]) [Around them there appeared a reddish color and so it appeared that they were fittingly repaid for their vanity],[14] to the extent that they can no longer make a mistake when looking on another woman—"sì che d'allora innanzi non potéro mirare persona che li guardasse sì che loro potesse trarre a simile intendimento" (XXXIX.5 [28.5])—as occurred when Dante saw the *donna gentile* the first time: "Levai li occhi per vedere se altre mi vedesse. Allora vidi una gentile donna giovane e bella molto" (XXXIV.2 [23.2]) [I raised my eyes to see if other women could see me. Then I saw a noble woman who was young and very beautiful]. However, it would be problematic to define the outcome of his repentance as strictly speaking religious, since it coincides rather with the total destruction of the lover's desire for the *donna gentile*: "volendo che cotale desiderio malvagio e vana intenzione paresse distrutto" (XXXIX.6 [28.6]) [wanting to ensure that such wicked desire and vain temptation appeared completely wiped out] and with the return of Dante's thoughts exclusively to Beatrice: "sì si rivolsero tutti li miei pensamenti a la loro gentilissima Beatrice" (XXXIX.2 [28.2]). The outcome, in other words, is that Dante's "pensieri" and "sospiri" are definitively reoriented to Beatrice and they will only bring "quel dolce nome di Madonna scritto / e de la morte sua" (XXXIX.2 [28.2]) [that sweet name of my Lady written, and of her death].

What is important to stress is that the *tribulazione* from which Dante repents coincides with a battle whose field is exclusively Dante's mind: the *donna gentile* does not take any action to tempt him. On the contrary, the *donna gentile* "non mira voi se non in quanto le pesa de la gloriosa donna di cui piangere solete" (XXXVII.2 [26.2]) [looks at you for no other reason than that the thought of the glorious lady, whom you usually cry for, weighs on her], and it is Dante who, baselessly, confuses her grief for Beatrice's death with a compassionate attention for his own sorrow.[15] This misinterpretation leads Dante to "dilettare troppo di vederla" (XXXVII.1 [26.1]) [enjoy the sight of her too much], and this pleasure tempts him to forget Beatrice: "Ora pare che vogliate dimenticarlo per questa donna che vi mira" (XXXVII.2 [26.2]) [Now it seems that you want to forget it in favor of this woman who looks at you]. This forgetfulness is precisely what the "spiritel novo d'amore" presents to Dante as the way to overcome the "tanta tribulazione" [so much tribulation] and "tanta amaritudine" [so much bitterness] (XXXVIII.3 [27.3]) caused by Beatrice's death. A battle, in essence, takes place between the desire for a new love for the *donna gentile* and the memory of the old one for Beatrice, whose outcome is likely to be, in the acme of Dante's temptation, the defeat of Beatrice and the erasure of the memory of her: "però che la battaglia de' pensieri vinceano coloro che per lei parlavano" (XXXVIII.4 [27.4]) [since the battle of thoughts was won by the thoughts that were talking about her].[16] It is not by chance, then, that, once the "forte imaginazione" [powerful imagination] of Beatrice eventually wins over the thought that is "avversario della Ragione" [adversary of Reason], Dante should return his thoughts to Beatrice "ricordandomi di lei secondo l'ordine del tempo passato" (XXXIX.2 [28.2]) [remembering her as she was in the past].

What lies at the core of the infatuation for the *donna gentile* is the risk of forgetting Beatrice, that is, of jeopardizing the memory of her upon which the entire *Vita nova* is based as Dante's "libro de la mia memoria" (I.1 [1.1]) [book of my memory]. In this regard, Dante's repentance for the infatuation for the *donna gentile* results in a reorientation of his memory of Beatrice, which after this episode is no longer an *amaritudine* but the natural condition of the poet who continues to love his beloved after her death. Such a reorientation coincides with a return to weeping: "Per questo raccendimento de' sospiri si raccese lo sollenato lagrimare" (XXXIX.4 [28.4]) [Through this rekindling of sights the diminished weeping rekindled]. However, this weeping, albeit painful, is no longer something Dante needs to overcome: this weeping becomes the essence of his poetry for Beatrice, whose aim now is to share his sorrow with the citizens of the "dolorosa cittade" (XL.3 [29.3]) [suffering city] as well as with those who are not aware of Beatrice's life and death (like the pilgrims to whom Dante addresses the sonnet introduced in chapter XL [29]: "Deh peregrini, che pensosi andate" [Oh pilgrims that pass by deep in thought].

After having recognized the "spiritel novo d'amore" as it truly is, as a "desiderio malvagio e vana intenzione" (XXXIX.6 [28.6]) [wicked desire and vain intention], Dante is able positively to share with others the grief for the loss of Beatrice. On the other hand, the episode of the *donna gentile* begins because he misinterprets the *pietà* felt by this woman, not recognizing that this feeling was for Beatrice and not for him: "Le pesa de la gloriosa donna di cui piangere solete" (XXXVII.2 [26.2]) [The thought of the glorious lady, whom you usually cry for, weighs on her]. Because of this, Dante is not capable of sharing his sorrow with that of the *donna gentile*, and he regards this woman not as at a fellow griever but rather as a new love that can help him to stop crying for Beatrice's death: "Che mai, se non dopo la morte, non dovrebbero le vostre lagrime avere restate" ([XXXVII.2 [26.2]) [For never, except after death, should your tears have stopped]; "acciò che la mia vita si riposi" [so that my life might find rest] and "Perché non ti vuoli ti ritrarre da tanta amaritudine?" [Why don't you want to withdraw from such bitterness?] (XXXVIII.1 and 3 [27.1 and 3]). On the contrary, after repenting for his mistake, not only does Dante share his sorrow with that of the entire city of Florence, "dolorosa cittade" (XL.3 [29.3]) [suffering city], but he also uses his poetry to inspire in others the same grief that he feels for Beatrice, as he affirms in lines 9–14 of "Deh peregrini, che pensosi andate" [Oh, pilgrims who go absorbed iin thought]: "che lagrimando n'uscireste poi" (line 11) [your eyes will fill with tears before you leave]; "ànno vertù di far piangere altrui" (line 14) [words have force enough to make a stranger grieve]. In other words, Dante no longer wants to end his weeping by forgetting Beatrice; on the contrary, he wants to make other people cry as well by sharing his memory of Beatrice.

To sum up, the repentance for his infatuation allows Dante properly to understand that the attempt to overcome his sorrow by forgetting Beatrice in favor of another woman is a "vil modo di consolar" [a base manner of consolation] suggested by a thought that is "vilissimo" [most base] (XXXVIII.2 and 4 [27.2 and 4]), as it is inspired by an "evil desire and vain intention" (XXXIX.6 [28.6]). In this regard, it is important to stress that the *tribolazione* described in chapters XXXVIII–XXXIX [27–28] also coincides with a battle between Dante's "desiderio . . . di ricordarmi de la gentilissima donna mia" [desire . . . to remember my most noble lady] and his desire "di vedere costei" [to see her] (XXXVIII.6 [27.6]). That said, one might suggest that the infatuation for the *donna gentile* is morally wrong first and foremost because it pushes Dante to behave in a way contrary to the ethics of friendship described in a book, Cicero's *De amicitia*, whose influence on the final chapters of the *Vita nova* is certified by Dante himself in the *Convivio* (2.13).[17] It would not be hard to identify different aspects in Dante's behavior during the episode of the *donna gentile* that qualify him as a bad friend of Beatrice according to Cicero's definition of virtuous friendship.

For the sake of brevity, I shall focus exclusively on the feature of Cicero's dialogue that most fits the development of chapters XXXVIII–XXXIX [27–28], and more precisely on the importance of memory in his definition of the behavior that virtuous friends should keep once their friend dies. From the beginning of the dialogue, Laelius makes clear that, albeit pained because he is "tali amico oblatus," "non egeo medicina: me ipse consolor" (3.10) [deprived of such a friend, I want no medicine; I comfort myself]. Such a self-consolation is described in detail in the following paragraphs and ultimately pivots around the pleasure derived from what Laelius defines "recordatione nostrae amicitiae" [memory of our friendship], combined with the hope that "amicitiae nostrae memoriam . . . sempiternam fore" [the memory of friendship may be everlasting] (4.15). This idea is echoed at the end of the dialogue, when Laelius states that "quarum rerum recordatio et memoria si una cum illo occidisset, desiderium coniunctissimi atque amantissimi viri ferre nullo modo possem" (27.104) [if the recollection and memory of these things had perished with the man, I could not possibly have endured the longing for one so closely united with me in life and affection]. These words are of capital importance to appreciate the episode of the *donna gentile*, the conclusion of which coincides with the recovery of a memory of Beatrice—"ricordandomi di lei secondo l'ordine del tempo passato" (XXXIX.2 [28.2]) [remembering her as she was in the past]—that is opposed to the (apparently similar) memory that triggers the episode: "mi ricordava del passato tempo" (XXXV.1 [24.1]) [I remembered time gone by]. While this latter form of memory generates "dolorosi pensamenti" [painful thoughts] and coincides with a "sbigottimento" [turmoil] (XXXV.1 [24.1]), the memory that Dante recovers after having repented his infatuation is still painful—"molte volte avenia che tanto dolore avea in sé alcuno pensero" (XXXIX.3 [28.3]) [and frequently my thought had so much pain in it]—yet seems to be different inasmuch as the pain it generates does not need to be overcome and Dante is able not only positively to fulfill his "desiderio . . . di ricordarmi de la gentilissima donna mia" (XXXVIII.6 [27.6]) [desire to remember my most noble lady] but also to keep this memory alive by sharing his painful memories with others (starting with the pilgrims in chapter XL[29]).

One might say, in sum, that, by repenting for his infatuation with the *donna gentile*, Dante finds a way positively to console himself for Beatrice's death according to the Ciceronian ethic outlined above and to abandon the "pensero" [thought] that suggested that he ought "consolar" [console himself] in a "vil modo" [vile manner] (XXXVIII.2 [27.2]). This positive consolation allows Dante to remain a faithful friend-lover to Beatrice also beyond her death. In other terms, he overcomes the "avversario della Ragione" [adversary of Reason] and adheres to the "costanzia della Ragione" [the constancy of reason] (XXXIX.1–2 [28.1–28.2]).

Vita nova XL–XLII [29–31]

A Portrait of the Artist as a Young Man

THEODORE J. CACHEY, JR.

To "reread" Dante's first book inevitably involves comparing and contrasting today's reading to those of the past, to when one first encountered the *libello* at university, and to those occasions over the years when one has reread it for research or in preparation for teaching Dante, as I have done countless times. Since I first read it more than thirty years ago, the text has itself evolved over time. Indeed, the *Vita nova* has proved to be perhaps the most mobile of Dante's works, shifting back and forth in its editorial appearance over the last generation, even changing its title, as new editions and commentaries have appeared. As is well known, this instability is a characteristic that goes back to its earliest manuscript tradition. Even before Boccaccio's interventions, copyists seem to have been uncertain about what to make of the text.[1] A first thing to reflect upon, therefore, before considering the final three chapters, is how the text has evolved, just as we as readers have evolved, both collectively and individually over time. How is the ending of the *Vita nova* different from the ending we thought we knew?

What's new about the *Vita nova*, now that we seem to have come to some kind of provisional *traguardo* or finish line, at least in terms of the currently available texts and commentaries? I say provisional because as far as the contemporary editorial presentation of the *libello* is concerned, the present state of the question of the text and its division into chapters is as mobile and unstable as it ever was. Stefano Carrai, in fact, adopts Guglielmo Gorni's ordering and the title *Vita nova* in his edition and commentary, while Donato Pirovano has returned to Michele Barbi's chaptering and title. In light of the fact that "the manuscript tradition does not support in any way the hypothesis of an original paragraphing of the *Vita nuova*,"[2] it is hard to dissent from Richard Lansing's judicious review of the question of the formal structure of the text and his conclusion that the genuine structure of the work "is created by its events, the experiences that the poet relates sequentially, the nature, tenor, and symbolic significance of its episodes."[3] Perhaps for this reason toggling back and forth between the Gorni and Pirovano editions can be very stimulating from an interpretive point of view. It leads one to reflect, for example, on the nature of the transition between the last movement of the episode of the *donna gentile* and chapters XL–XLII [29–31], the final section of the work under discussion in the triptych of readings that follows. To what extent does chapter XXXIX [28] mark the end of the *donna gentile* episode, and to what extent does it mark the beginning of the final resolution of the book, as Gorni suggested ("La porzione di testo definito dai paragrafi 28–31 è quasi una 'vita nova' della vita nova" [The portion of the text demarcated by chapters 28–31 is virtually a "new life" of the new life])?[4] In any event, the final chapters are ideal for fostering retrospective and anticipatory reflections—retrospective to the extent that the discussion of these final chapters can illuminate major episodes, images, and themes that have come before; anticipatory to the extent that these same episodes, images, and themes can be projected into the future and can have implications for Dante's works to come, representing a new beginning, "a *vita nova* of the *vita nova*."

Can our "Rereading the *Vita nova*" project mark the point of departure for a new life for the *Vita nova* from a critical and hermeneutic point of view? The diversity of viewpoints and perspectives that emerged from the discussions and analyses of single chapters or microsequences of chapters over the course of two years of meetings, including this final triptych of readings, was truly remarkable. Beyond demonstrating an enduring collective fascination with Dante's enigmatic first book, the seminars revealed that currently there does not appear to be any shared understanding of what the main interpretive challenges facing readers of the *Vita nova* might actually be. By the time we arrived at the last seminar dedicated to the final chapters of the *libello*, held in Rome in May of 2019, it had become clear that the critical heterogeneity of our conversations constituted a rationale for bringing them together in the volume that you are reading. It is in this spirit of critical heterogeneousness that my personal reflections on rereading the *Vita nova* are offered here by way of introduction to the final readings. Two things in particular stood out for me: first, the extent to which the *libello* represents a point of departure, Dante's own "portrait of the artist as a young man," if you will;[5] and second, the way the *libello* establishes a signature cosmological framework for the subsequent development of Dante's literary project as an essential part of the artist's apprenticeship. Both features achieve a culminating flourish in the last three chapters.

   To begin with the ending, just as *Portrait* ends with Stephen Dedalus, Joyce's alter ego, announcing his future intention to forge the consciousness of his race, the final chapter of the *Vita nova* (XLII [31]) paradoxically announces, as Anne Leone incisively illustrates in her chapter, a new beginning. Like Leone, I find it difficult to agree with those who view the ending as marking a failure of the *libello*.[6] Instead, as Toby Levers demonstrated in an important contribution, the end of the *Vita nova* presents a kind of birth of the artist Dante. Having explored in the narrative prose during the course of the work all forms of medieval authorship, according to Bonaventure's typology, from scribe to compiler to commentator to author, Dante *auctor* emerges free and clear for the first time in the last chapter. In the four sentences that make up chapter LXII [31], the fundamental separation between Dante the narrator and Dante the poet abruptly vanishes. "With these sentences," Levers writes, "Dante binds together the *Vita Nuova*'s divided images of authorship, and for a crucial moment, he presents himself with a unified 'io.' . . . A central image of Dante is created at the close of the *libello*: Dante the active poet, working at the present moment to revise his poetic project—an image that is realized in the present-tense statement of the sentence that . . . 'E di venire a ciò io studio quanto posso' [To achieve this I am studying all that I can]."[7]

   One cannot help but notice similarities between the ending of the *Vita nova* that is a new beginning and the ending of the *Commedia* that features a substantially revised and fully elaborated version of the poet's earlier encounter with the "mirabile visione" [marvelous vision] of *Vita nova* XLII [31]. Moreover, at the end of both works the final vision represents a beginning insofar as it precedes and establishes the premises for the writing of a work.[8] Beyond the question of the emergence of Dante *auctor*, however, the problem of beginnings and endings can also be considered under the heading of the spatial parameters of Dante's project, that is, in terms of the works themselves as constituting textual territories, both singly and collectively insofar as they come to constitute an oeuvre. From this perspective, both deferrals at the end of the *Vita nova* and of the *Commedia* are noteworthy for their spatial implications, that is, for the way in which they both offer textual solutions to the problem of the inevitably alienated relationship of the pilgrim-exile and of the language of the exile to truth. Both endings ultimately come up against the limitations of human language and intellect, albeit from different perspectives and at different points along the trajectory of Dante's career, limitations that Lorenzo Dell'Oso, in his intervention on chapter XLI [30], explores in relation to the history of Dante's Florentine intellectual formation.

I want to take a step back from the metaliterary gesture of the final chapter that establishes and at the same time transcends the farthest limit of Dante's literary project as a textual territory at the time of the *Vita nova*, in order to consider the cosmological parameters of the project that are similarly established and transcended along their vertical axis in the prose and poetry of the previous chapter. Domenico De Robertis noted in his commentary that chapter XLI [30] features the first appearance in Dante's oeuvre of the Empyrean heaven in the physical sense.[9] Gorni, on the other hand, avers that despite its generous, cosmically ambitious impulse, "Oltre la spera" [Beyond the sphere] "è di ardua esegesi, anche perchè di accidentata scrittura e di affliggente ripetitività: il Dante del *Paradiso* è ancora lontano" [is of arduous exegesis, also due to uneven writing and troubling repetitions: the Dante of the *Paradiso* is still far off].[10] This is, after all, a portrait of the artist as still a young man. In fact, the commentators pick up on both of the features of the *Vita nova* that I find worth highlighting. The verticality Dante achieves in the chapter is noteworthy, even if we are left to wonder how Dante would have defined at this early stage in his intellectual formation the tenth heaven whose characteristics will evolve in the passage from the *Vita nova* to the *Convivio* and then to the *Commedia*.[11] What could the Empyrean have meant to Dante at this point in his intellectual development in the 1290s?

Anna Chisena has recently offered a fundamental scholarly reconnaissance regarding the question of Dante's intellectual formation at the time of the *Vita nova* under the heading of cosmology. She has found that Dante was considerably more philosophically advanced than he is usually given credit for before the exile, for example in his description of a Christianized "Ptolemaic" cosmos made of nine heavens.[12] Yet there is little to go on with regard to the question of what the Empyrean might have meant to him at this time. The cosmological elucubrations and developments of the *Convivio* were still in the future. Nevertheless, as De Robertis noted, Dante's Empyrean in the *Vita nova* clearly relates to a physical mapping of the cosmos, a feature of the *Vita nova* that much later Cecco d'Ascoli would take the trouble to ridicule: How could Dante's *sospiro* arrive where there is no there?[13]

Moreover, we can only appreciate in retrospect that the journey of the "sigh" to the Empyrean to contemplate Beatrice in her glory arrives as the culminating gesture of the *libello*. In fact, its transcendence of the cosmos has been prepared since the very beginning of the *Vita nova* in the narrator's account of the turnings of the eighth and ninth heavens in chapter II.1–2 [1.2–1.3] that serve to attribute to the start of the poet's love story nothing less than the "formative" intentionality of a Christianized cosmos. The cosmological parameters of the narrative are reaffirmed and further developed during the course of the *prosimetrum*, for example, in the verticality of "Donne ch'avete intelletto d'amore" (XIX.4–14 [10.14–10.25]) [Women who understand the truth of love], which ranges from the heights of God's Empyrean heaven down to the depths of hell, where even the damned are said to appreciate the beatific power of the poet's lady. There is, admittedly, some difference of opinion regarding the maturity of the metaphysical and cosmological poetics of "Donne ch'avete." Aspects of the poem struck Foster and Boyde (and to some extent, Barolini) as "theologically absurd," while Durling and Martinez attribute to the *canzone* something approaching full Neoplatonic self-awareness.[14] Yet we should probably bear in mind that this is, after all, still a portrait of the artist as a young man.

Then there is the disquisition on the providential arrangement of the nine heavens of the Christianized cosmos at Beatrice's conception in chapter XXIX [19.4–19.7] (not her birth, pace Gorni): "Ne la sua generazione tutti e nove li mobili cieli perfettissimamente s'aveano insieme" [XXIX.2 [19.5] [All nine motioning heavens utterly, perfectly harmonized with one another at the moment of her conception]. It perhaps bears emphasizing, since the commentators generally do not underscore this point, that Dante's birth is thereby made to coincide with the perfect disposition of the heavens that superintended Beatrice's "generazione." By bringing together what we learn in chapter XXIX [19.4–19.7] with what we learn in chapter II [1.2–1.11], namely, that Dante was born eight to nine months before Beatrice, it becomes apparent that the situation of the heavens at Dante's birth and Beatrice's conception corresponded to an optimal celestial state. As Dante later writes in the *Convivio*, if the disposition of heaven "la quale si varia [per] le costellazioni, che continuamente si trasmutano" (4.21.7) [that varies with the constellations, which are continually changing], were brought into perfect harmony, and "se tutte le precedenti vertudi s'accordassero sovra la produzione d'un'anima nella loro ottima disposizione, . . . tanto discenderebbe in quella della deitade, che quasi sarebbe un altro Dio incarnato" (4.21.10) [if all the above powers involved in creating a soul were harmonized in their optimal disposition, so much of the deity would descend into it, that it would be almost like an incarnate God]. In any event, the cosmic foundations of Dante's subsequent project are established along their vertical axis for the first time in the *Vita nova*, including a hyperbolic (in the literal sense) aspirational journey beyond the ninth heaven and therefore beyond space and time, as recounted in chapter XLI [30]. The emergent "physical" sense of Dante's Empyrean is what strikes me as key. Dante's cosmos in the *Vita nova* is more than a poetic trope: it is on its way to becoming a full-blown cosmology that will eventually be capable of supporting the project of the *Commedia*. When Dante says that he is "studying" to become capable of writing about Beatrice what has never been said about any other woman, he is talking about, among other things, developing the intellectual infrastructure to provide a cosmology that will underwrite his future poetic project. In the *libello* the artist as a young man has laid out the basic cosmological parameters that, going forward, will require further study and elaboration.

But in speaking of cosmology and of the spatial parameters that Dante establishes for the first time in the *Vita nova*, albeit in a preliminary manner, we need also to address the horizontal or terrestrial spatial dimension, as Dante does in chapter XL [29]. As with the extension of the vertical axis of the cosmos of the *libello* in chapters XLI [30] and XLII [31], during the course of the work, Dante prepares for the geographical expansion of the work's parameters effected in chapter XL [29]. If one accepts De Robertis's understanding of the addressees of the letter that Dante wrote in Latin to the "princes of the earth" about the widowed state of Florence following Beatrice's death ("Scrissi a li principi de la terra alquanto de la sua condizione [di Firenze]," XXX.1 [19.8] [I wrote to the rulers of the land something about its condition), then Dante was seeking to spread the news of Beatrice's death beyond the walls of the city.[15] Similarly, the prose discourse on the identification of Beatrice as the number nine in chapter XXIX [19], which interprets her death date according to three different calendric systems (the Arabic, Syrian, and Christian), locates the miracle of Beatrice in a global framework. The mapping impulse of chapter XL [29] that Chiara Sbordoni explicates in her reading serves to establish essential geographical parameters that will inform Dante's later writings, including the pilgrimage itinerary of the *Commedia* that will feature Rome as its destination.[16]

To continue and to conclude with our cosmological conceit: if we were to create a map of the last three chapters of the *Vita nova*, it might resemble a medieval T-O map of the world, which, oriented to the East, represented the inhabited world of the three continents in the figure of a T, surrounded by Ocean in the figure of an O. The vertical stem of the T represented the Mediterranean separating Europe on the left and Africa to the right, while the crossbar, representing the Don and the Nile, separated Asia from Europe and Africa. If we project this pattern on the final chapters of the *Vita nova*, a map of the cosmos emerges, with the horizontal axis of chapter XL [29] intersecting the vertical axis of chapter XLI [30] that ascends as far as the Empyrean. The final chapter XLII [31] would correspond to Ocean, the figure of the enclosing circle, insofar as it presents an ending that is a beginning, and closes the circle of the book of memory by bringing us back to the author and his literary project *in fieri*. The circle cosmologically and metaphysically would mark the boundary between the physical cosmos and the Empyrean: the nine heavens of time and space enclosed by the Empyrean, the mind of God that contains them. This was the Christian metaphysical solution to the classical problem of the place of the world that Dante implicitly endorses here.[17] The final chapter accordingly closes the circle of the literary artifact, which can be said to contain the world and to grant it place according to Aristotelian physics. In terms of literary space, the mind and the memory of the author, like God in the Empyrean, lies beyond the final containing surface, "oltre la spera." The *Vita nova* and its final chapters map the cosmo-logical and metaphysical parameters of Dante's world according to its hori-zontal and vertical axes, and ultimately, in relation to a trajectory of exile-pil-grimage. No less importantly, the circle marks the boundary of the literary artifact, suggestive of the textual means by which the author will continue to seek to overcome the alienated condition of being outside his home.

Vita nova XL [29]

CHIARA SBORDONI

In the final chapters of the *Vita nova*, Dante recapitulates the central themes of the *libello*, from both narrative and poetic perspectives, and projects them into the future, together with the promise that, in time, he will deliver a new kind of literature. The narrative trajectory of the work and the progress of the poetic apprenticeship of the poet-narrator are summarized, reconfigured, and given new meaning; in particular, the author refocuses the relationship between the first-person narrator and lyric subject and the space in which the story of his love, his soul, and his poetic work unfolds. Dante expands the geographical range within which he recognizes the addressees of his poetry to encompass the Christian world, returns one last time to correlate earth and heaven as the cosmic setting of the work, and writes a (provisional) final word on his poetics. While reconfiguring the earthly boundaries of the story and locating it within a cosmic framework, Dante also evokes explicitly for the first time at the narrative level the theme of pilgrimage in the encounter with the "peregrini" directed to Rome, a theme that will subsequently play a vital structural role in the *Commedia*. Moreover, he presents the city of Rome for the first time in a figural connotation that will also be valid for the poem, both as a threshold between earth and heaven and as a figure of paradise.[1]

The subject matter of chapter XL [29], which comes after the episode of the *donna gentile*, can be summarized as follows: the first prose sequence has

357

a narrative function and presents in *medias res* a group of pilgrims passing through the center of the unnamed city of Florence directed to Rome, where the pilgrims will gaze upon the sacred image of Christ's face known as the Veronica. This is followed by the reaction of the narrator at the sight of the pilgrims, who are unaware of the grief of the city for the death of Beatrice. The narrator then affirms that he would be able to move the pilgrims to tears with his words and resolves to write a sonnet addressed to them. The next prose sequence has a metalinguistic and encyclopedic rather than a narrative function. The term *peregrini* is explained according to its various meanings, and it is announced that the sonnet that follows will not receive any commentary. The sonnet "Deh peregrini" [Oh, pilgrims] that concludes the chapter is an appeal addressed to the pilgrims, which recapitulates the reflections already presented in the narrative prose, emphasizing the pilgrims' lack of awareness of Florence's grief and the power of Dante's poetry to express that grief. The sonnet's elegiac language and style, which will subsequently return to inspire the treatment of the theme of pilgrimage in famous passages of the *Purgatorio* (8.1–6 and 23.16–18), is amplified here by the same quotation from Jeremiah's Lamentations that was earlier evoked at the beginning of chapter XXVIII [19.1–19.3] to announce the death of Beatrice.

The theme of *peregrinatio*, pilgrimage, has actually been present implicitly as one of the supporting structures of the *Vita nova* from the very beginning. Indeed, one of the dominant images of the book is that of the journey, whose storyline, or *affabulazione*, to use Michelangelo Picone's term, began when the narrator first saw Beatrice walk down the street in chapter III [1.12–2.2].[2] The symbolic values of both the street and the city it traverses, respectively the *via d'Amore*, the road of Love, as an individual path of the *peregrinus amoris*, the pilgrim of love, following in the footsteps of Beatrice, and the *civitas terrena*, the earthly city, contrasted with Augustine's *civitas coelestis*, heavenly city, are reactivated and reach their figurative destination in the final chapters of the *libello*. Along this itinerary, the earthly exile corresponding to the passionate lover described at the beginning of the book undertakes a *peregrinatio* that is tantamount to the progress of the narrative through its different stages of the narration until the vision of Beatrice is finally granted to the "peregrino spirito" [pilgrim spirit] "Oltre la spera che più larga gira" [Beyond the sphere that turns the widest gyre] (XLI.10–11 [30.10–30.11]).

In chapter XL [29] the theme of pilgrimage is explicitly evoked in the description of a group of pilgrims coming from afar, walking through the center of the city along the road that cuts it into two halves. For the first time in the book, a spatial relation between an urban feature, the road, and the city that it divides is presented in exact detail. In fact, while in the case of the departure of the narrator from Florence in chapter IX [4] the destination is left totally vague, in chapter XL [29] the pilgrims' final destination is immediately revealed. They are headed to Rome, where they will venerate, probably during the Holy Week of 1292, the true image of the face of Christ called the Veronica (derived from the false etymology *vera icona* [true icon]). Neither a painting nor an actual relic, but a specular image made by the direct impression of the face of Christ on a cloth, the Veronica was kept in the basilica of Saint Peter. While the *libello* has emphasized from the beginning the cosmic space-time dimension in which the life of the two protagonists has been inscribed according to the revolutions of the heavens of the Ptolemaic universe, and has left earthly geography largely indefinite until this point, the episode of the pilgrims presents a surprising breakthrough of realistic geographical space, albeit still charged with highly symbolic meaning. What is the specific meaning of this explicit reference to an itinerary that leads to the center of Christian Rome from the center of the *città dolorosa* or *dolente* [suffering city], as Florence is defined in both the prose and the sonnet, using the same two adjectives that Dante will use to define hell in *Inferno* 3.1 and 9.32?

What does the emphasis on the last stretch of a pilgrimage started far away, "di lontana parte" (XL.2 [29.2]), which spatially links for the first time the two principal cities featured in Dante's work, signify? How is the relationship between Florence and Rome defined here? And how is this new attention to earthly geography connected with the cosmic dimension that frames the *libello*? The reader will find the answers to these questions in the metalinguistic prose section, where it becomes clear that the new interest in space is not limited to the explicit declaration of the destination of the pilgrims' journey to Rome. Indeed, the overall meaning of the image of the *romei* emerges only when this image is projected onto a much wider geographical background in the subsequent metalinguistic sequence. I use the verb *to project* in its cartographical connotation because in chapter XL [29], as we will see, Dante engages in a capital example of cartographic writing.[3] In the metalinguistic prose sequence, the poet-narrator first analyzes and explains the term *peregrini*. To elucidate the meaning of the word, the author proposes two definitions, one more general and connected to scripture and one more specific that requires the consultation of the map of the Christian world with Rome at its center. The first and more general definition of the term *peregrini* is a *volgarizzamento*, or translation into the Florentine vernacular, of Isidore of Seville's definition of the word in Latin: "Peregrinus, longe a patria positus, sicut alienigena" (*Etymologiae* 10.215) [Pilgrim, someone who is far away from his homeland, like a foreigner].[4] In his turn, Dante writes: "E dissi 'peregrini' secondo la larga definizione del vocabulo; ché peregrini si possono intendere in due modi, in uno largo e in uno stretto: in largo, in quanto *è peregrino chiunque è fuori de la sua patria*" (XL.6 [29.6], my emphasis) [I wrote *pilgrims* in the broader sense of the term, for the word *pilgrims* can be understood in two ways, one broad and one narrow: in the broad sense, a *pilgrim* is anyone who is outside his homeland]. Dante then continues by discussing the more specific meaning of the word:

> In modo stretto non s'intende peregrino se non chi va verso la casa di sa' Iacopo o riede. E però è da sapere che in tre modi si chiamano propriamente le genti che vanno al servigio dell'Altissimo: chiamansi palmieri in quanto vanno oltremare, là onde molte volte recano la palma; chiamansi peregrini in quanto vanno a la casa di Galizia, però che la sepultura di sa' Iacopo fue più lontana de la sua patria che d'alcuno altro apostolo; chiamansi romei in quanto vanno a Roma, là ove questi cu' io chiamo peregrini andavano. (XL.6–7 [29.6–29.7])

> _____

> [In the narrow sense *pilgrim* is used only for one who travels toward the home of St. James or returns from it. And it is worth noting that there are three separate terms for people who travel to honor the Supreme Being: they are called *palmers* if they travel to the Holy Land, where they often carry the palm; they are called *pilgrims* if they travel to the home of Galicia, since the tomb of St. James was farther from his homeland than that of any other apostle; they are called *romers* if they travel to Rome— the place where those I am calling *pilgrims* were headed.]

Dante uses *peregrini* in its more general meaning: *peregrini* are those who find themselves outside their own country. This definition denotes the condition of the Christian exile, and, most importantly, it corresponds to the way in which both Paul and Peter characterize those who live according to God's will: "peregrini et hospites" (Hebrews 11:13) [foreigners and strangers]; "advenas et peregrinos" (1 Peter 2:11) [visitors and foreigners]. The first and fundamental meaning of the word *peregrini* is thus "foreigners." Why then does Dante further elucidate the meaning of the term? In the more specific definition, the word *peregrini* designates those wayfarers who travel to the tomb of St. James. The saint whose mortal remains are kept in the farthest place (Compostela in Galicia) from his original birthplace (Jerusalem),[5] St. James is a sort of proto-pilgrim or Ur-pilgrim *post mortem*. Thus *peregrini* refers properly speaking only to those who serve God by going to venerate St. James's body in Galicia. Others, who cross the sea headed to the Holy Land, where they visit the empty sepulcher of Christ and bring back "il bordon di palma cinto" (*Purg.* 33.78) [the staff wreathed with palm], are called "palmers," while those who go to Rome are called "romers."[6] All these wayfarers share two fundamental conditions that determine their status as pilgrims: first, they are pilgrims insofar as they are all foreigners and exiles from their homelands (especially their heavenly homeland), and second, they are pilgrims insofar as they are all headed on the route of salvation to the same destination beyond the earthly one (whether Santiago, Jerusalem, or Rome). The tension between the two meanings of the word *peregrini* is located at the threshold between earth and heaven, between the map of Christendom that includes all the earth in chapter XL [29] and the moment when the spirit of the poet becomes itself a pilgrim and ascends to heaven in chapter XLI [30]. Indeed, bringing to the reader's attention the polysemous value of the term *peregrini*, Dante aims at presenting a map of the contemporary Christian world along the main pilgrimage routes, with the city of Rome at its center. In placing his account within the geography of Christendom, the poet provides the reader with a new key for interpreting this. The map of the Christian world with Rome and not Jerusalem at its center revealed by Dante's quest in chapter XL [29] serves to reorient the erotic content of his book. From an initial courtly and municipal inspiration addressed to a small circle of elect faithful of Love, who are wayfarers on the road of Love, through the transition represented in the middle of the book by the turn to the poetry of praise, the idea of love is completely freed at the end of the book from its erotic connotation. It is spiritualized and projected onto a universal dimension as *caritas* and is directed toward Christian humanity on its way to salvation.

Where does this image of the map of the Christian world come from, and how does Dante turn the individual (Florentine) perspective of the *libello* into a universal ("Roman") message? As De Robertis noted, the transition from the episode of the *donna gentile* to Dante's return to Beatrice ("Dopo questa tribulazione avvenne che . . . ," XL.1 [29.1] [After this tribulation it happened that . . .]) is marked by a key allusion to Matthew 24:29— "post tribulationem dierum illorum" [after the tribulation of those days]— part of the *sermo eschatologicus*, eschatological sermon, addressed by Christ to the disciples on the Mount of Olives.[7] The "detour" of the "gracious lady" is defined as a "tribulazione," and the *donna gentile* is revealed to have been a misleading consolation after Beatrice's death. The poet's grief and repentance deriving from this experience are interwoven with the evangelic prediction contained in Matthew's Gospel. In the sermon on the Mount of Olives, Christ evoked an apocalyptic Jerusalem at the end of times, deserted and infested by false Christ-like figures and false prophets to whom the gracious lady is implicitly compared in contrast to Beatrice. In the Jerusalem evoked in the eschatological sermon, Christ will appear like lightning at his second coming in front of all the tribes of the earth amid the cataclysm of heavenly forces, while his angels will bring together the elect with the sound of their trumpets. The allusion to the "tribulazione" at the start of the chapter thus recalls these apocalyptic events. Dante accomplishes the transition from the deceptive experience of the "gracious woman" to the new advent of Beatrice, *figura* Christi, image of Christ, against a backcloth that embraces the whole earth, before this setting is projected in the next chapter "Oltre la spera che più larga gira" (XLI.10 [30.10]) [Beyond the sphere that turns the widest gyre].

In addition, Dante's doubt that the "peregrini" walking through Florence know about Beatrice's death evokes the Gospel of Luke (24:13–18) when the two disciples encounter the resurrected Christ on the way to Emmaus. The disciples do not recognize Christ because their eyes are kept from seeing him ("cum oculi autem illorum tenebantur"). In Luke, Christ is addressed as "peregrinus," foreigner: "Tu solus peregrinus es in Ierusalem et non cognovisti, quae facta sunt in illa his diebus?" [Are you the only foreigner in Jerusalem who didn't learn what happened there in these days?]. Only after patiently listening to the disciples' account of his passion and death and the discovery of his empty sepulcher on the third day after his death does Christ reproach the disciples for being slow to believe the prophets who in the Old Testament predicted the death of Christ and his resurrection within three days. In other words, the disciples' blindness is an inability to interpret the present according to the scriptures: they are bad readers. The evocation of Emmaus offers a hermeneutic cue to the readers of the *Vita nova*, an invitation to open their eyes and recognize the hidden layers of meaning embedded in chapter XL [29] by aligning it with a tradition of sacred texts.[8] The Gospel episode ends with Christ breaking bread at dinner. Only when they see the reenactment of the Eucharist are the disciples' eyes opened, and they finally recognize Christ, who then ascends to heaven, thereby concluding his historical presence on earth with his glorification in a metahistorical dimension that will lead to the salvation of humanity. The next appearance of Christ on earth will be at the second Parousia at the end of time, as evoked at the start of chapter XL [29]. Just before presenting the ascension of the poet's spirit to the vision of Beatrice contemplating Christ in paradise, Christ's entire mission is recapitulated through the intertextual evocation of its culminating moments. The death, the Resurrection, and the Second Coming are all evoked against the backdrop of Christian geography, which serves as the premise for the cosmological-metaphysical vision of chapter XLI [30].

Similarly, Dante uses the pilgrims to connect heaven and earth at the narrative level. They may be ignorant of what happened in Florence, but they are enlightened by a clear vision of their proper path to salvation. In fact, they are on their way to their destination, Rome, which recalls Christ-the pilgrim on the road to Emmaus. Once in Rome, the pilgrims will contemplate the historical trace of Christ's face in the Veronica. At the same time, Dante describes Beatrice contemplating the face of Christ in the glory of paradise, thereby offering a key for interpreting the significance of the Veronica and of Rome in the *Vita nova*. The Veronica, in fact, besides being the true historical image of Christ, is an analogy on earth for Beatrice in heaven. The Veronica functions as the means that allows the pilgrims to encounter Christ on earth, just as the contemplation of Beatrice in Dante's poetry serves as a means of accessing Christ in heaven. It will be to Beatrice that Dante's pilgrim spirit will ascend in the next chapter. Indeed, Beatrice is also a figure for Dante's poetry, which declares its own function as a means of experiencing Christ. In choosing the icon Veronica rather than the sepulcher (whether the empty tomb of Christ in the Holy Land or St. James's tomb in Galicia) as a medium to experiencing the divine, Dante suggests that his poetry represents an *itinerarium mentis*, a journey of the mind, as the means of achieving a transcendent vision of God.[9] The city of Rome for the first time, here in the *Vita nova*, is thus presented as a threshold to the divine, namely, the "Rome where Christ Himself is Roman" (*Purg.* 32.102) [Roma onde Cristo è romano],[10] and where the pilgrim spirit will arrive virtually in the next chapter. For the first time in his work Dante presents the eternal city as a metahistorical place beyond time and space, thereby authorizing a figural reading of the *Vita nova*.[11] The pilgrimage to the Veronica will accordingly be evoked at the end of the *Commedia*, when Dante the pilgrim finds himself at the threshold of the Empyrean (*Par.* 31.43–48 and 103–11). The comparison between Rome and Florence is also subsequently developed when they are juxtaposed one last time a few tercets from each other, as if to summarize in one last image the whole arc of the journey to salvation. The amazement of the barbarians who contemplate the magnificence of the Lateran from Monte Mario is compared to Dante the pilgrim's wonder on arriving at the Empyrean: "io, che al divino da l'umano, / a l'etterno dal tempo era venuto, / e di Fiorenza in popol giusto e sano" (*Par.* 31.37–39) [I, who had come to things divine from man's estate, to eternity from time, from Florence to a people just and sane].

But returning to earth and to the *Vita nova*, it is worth noting that the *mappa mundi* that Dante constructs around the word *peregrini* testifies to his incipient quest for a literary vernacular that could express all contents and styles, a project that Dante will further develop in the *De vulgari eloquentia* and later fully achieve in the plurilingualism of the *Commedia*. In chapter XL [29], Dante joins Matthew's Gospel to Isidore of Seville's encyclopedia, drawing from Latin sources that he translates into the vernacular, which he weaves together in the linguistic and cultural system of the *Vita nova*. Dante demonstrates that he is capable of appropriating and rendering into his vernacular a range of suggestions beyond those normally current in lyric poetry, incorporating experiences, images, and texts of different genres that permeated the culture of his time, including sacred icons, contemporary representations of the world, such as road maps and T-O maps in which Jerusalem and Rome are represented as centers of Christianity, scripture, hagiographic literature like the *Legenda aurea*, chronicles, and itineraries to places of worship such as the *Mirabilia*. In other words, chapter XL [29], while still deeply characterized by an elegiac content and style,[12] already reveals Dante's predisposition for cultural synthesis. Indeed, Dante's vernacular functions in the *Vita nova* as a threshold between Latin and vernacular culture, and between the culture of images (whether the Veronica, a map of the world, or the visions sought by means of contemplation) and literature. Dante seems to be testing the capacity of the vernacular to mediate between different cultural realms. The prose in particular coherently organizes a range of elements and approaches to the subject matter of the *libello*, investigating and refining the vernacular as a vehicle for literature. At the same time, the subject matter of the book has itself evolved in terms of its content and its audience. Ceasing to be personal and elitist, Florentine and local, it becomes autobiographical in an exemplary perspective, and universal in terms of its resonance. Consequently, the invitation for the reader to consider the pilgrims' route to Rome in a figural sense explicitly inaugurates an allegorical poetics that the poet will later deploy in the *Commedia*. Through the use of his source materials in chapter XL [29], Dante foregrounds hermeneutic instructions for reading the *libello*, which needs to be interpreted in a figural and eschatological sense, as a pilgrimage projected horizontally on the *mappa mundi* of Christianity in anticipation of the vertical universal projection that will be the subject of the following chapter. The construction of his complex persona as author starts here: Dante, now prophet and evangelist, now exegete, now lexicographer, now poet, develops a form of vernacular prose writing capable of translating the contemporary cultural system, including the forms and contents of Latin culture, thereby suggesting the future promise and potential of a vernacular literature that will be able to say about Beatrice what has never been said about any other woman.

Vita nova XLI [30]

LORENZO DELL'OSO

From its first sentence, chapter XLI [30] of the *Vita nova* brings something innovative to the *libello*. Dante explains his intention to send two sonnets he has already composed—"Deh peregrini" [Oh, pilgrims] and "Venite a 'nten-der" [Come listen]—and a new one "Oltre la spera" [Beyond the sphere] to two "donne gentili" [two lovely women].[1] In describing his intention, the poet explicitly notes his desire to make a new thing: "Propuosi di mandare loro e di fare una cosa nuova . . . acciò che più onorevolmente adempiessi li loro prieghi" (XLI.1 [30.1]) [I decided to send some poems to them and to compose something new to more worthily satisfy their request], where "cosa nuova" [something new], can refer to a newly written poem as well as to the novelty of its substance, making it unlike any work that the poet had previously produced. Indeed, the resulting sonnet has five parts, the highest number of divisions of any sonnet in the *Vita nova*, and Dante specifies that the poem might be divided even further (XLI.9 [31.9]). In "Oltre la spera," Dante recounts the journey that a sigh ("pensero," XLI.6 [30.6]) took from his heart to the Empyrean, where it saw Beatrice. The sigh ascended so high into Beatrice's divine nature that Dante's mind could not grasp what the sigh was telling his grieving heart, "cor dolente" (line 11), given that the human intellect functions in the presence of the blessed souls ("benedette anime") as the weak eye does in the presence of the sun ("sí come l'occhio debole al

366

sole," XLI.6 [30.6]). However, despite this failure, Dante does manage to discern the name of Beatrice. The entire chapter ultimately celebrates her triumph in the Empyrean.

The central motif of the sonnet, the "intelligenza nova" (line 3) [new awareness] that Love has placed in the heart and that draws the sigh toward the Empyrean, can plausibly be read both as inherited from the courtly tradition and as the starting point of a contemplative perspective.[2] Donato Pirovano, who opts for the second reading, points out that, at this point in the *libello*, Amore cannot any longer be the *eros* of the courtly tradition but coincides with *caritas* (a divinely inspired love) and that "Oltre la spera" represents the beginning of Dante's period of "approfondimento teoretico" [theoretical study].[3] Indeed, it has been suggested that the last pages of the *libello* appear to provide evidence of Dante's attendance at the Florentine "schools of the religious orders" and at the "disputations of the philosophizers" (*Conv.* 2.12.7).[4] Here I would like to further support this suggestion by highlighting how, in explaining two elements in the sonnet—the "sigh"'s contemplation of the beloved in the Empyrean and the author's inability fully to grasp her essence—Dante was appropriating a gnoseological motif characteristic of contemporary theological discussions. This motif is the Aristotelian quotation from the second book of the *Metaphysics* that treats the relationship between "our intellect" and the "blessed souls": "Ne la quarta dico come elli la vede tale, cioè in tal qualitate, che io nol posso intendere, cioè a dire che 'l mio pensero sale ne la qualità di costei in grado che 'l mio intelletto nol puote comprendere; con ciò sia cosa che 'l nostro intelletto s'abbia a quelle benedette anime sí come l'occhio debole al sole: e ciò dice lo Filosofo nel secondo de la *Metafisica*" (XLI.6 [30.6]) [In the fourth part I tell how my thought sees her in such a way—that is, so essentially—that I cannot comprehend it; in other words, that my thought ascends so far into her essence that my intellect cannot comprehend it; for, as the Philosopher says in the second book of his *Metaphysics*, our intellect is to those blessed souls as a weak eye is to the sun].

This Aristotelian *sententia*, which Dante cites again in *Convivio* 2.4.17, was very well known in thirteenth-century scholasticism.[5] Given its diffusion, it comes as no surprise to find this *sententia* also quoted in a public theological debate in Florence in the 1290s. Indeed, the same quotation from the second book of Aristotle's *Metaphysics* was used by the Franciscan theologian Peter of Trabibus in 1295, while Dante was writing or had recently completed the *libello*.[6] In a "school of the religious orders" such as the Franciscan convent of Santa Croce, Trabibus held a *Quodlibet,* probably one of the "disputations of the philosophizers" Dante talks about in the *Convivio,* that were open to both religious and seculars.[7] The friar answers a *quaestio quodlibetalis* on whether it is possible to know a "veritas fidei" [truth of faith], through "scientia litterarum humanarum" [knowledge of the humane letters], which broadly may refer to pagan poetry and philosophy, as is evident from the previous *quaestio.*[8] After having explained that the knowledge of what pertains to faith can be attained only through a supernatural light ("lumen supernaturale"), the *lector theologiae* argues that "bene tamen animus multus peritus potest scire quid Deus, quid mundus, quid creaturae, quid virgo, quid parere, quid pati et quid resurgere. Sed quod haec simul conveniant non potest nisi adiutus et elevatus Deo munere, *sicut oculus noctue nisi adiutus potest videre lucem solis licet sit magis visibilis quam lumen candelae*" (BNC, Florence, *Conv Soppr.*, D.6.359, 110ra; emphasis added) [however, a very expert soul may well know what God is, what the world is, what creatures are, what a virgin is, what giving birth is, what suffering is, and what the resurrection is. But he cannot know how these things can be together, if he is not helped and raised by the gift of God, *just as the owl's eye, if not helped, cannot see the light of the sun, although this is more visible than the candle light*].

An investigation into possible intertextual connections between Peter and Dante's texts would probably be fruitless, not least given their very different purposes and forms. However, we can compare some aspects of Peter's *quaestio* and chapter XLI [30] in order to determine how two different texts (one orally discussed in Latin, the other written in the vernacular) dealt with a similar theological topic at the same time (1294–95) in Florence. First of all, Peter and Dante's texts use the same Aristotelian quotation in different contexts. Dante's intellect cannot know what the "pensero" tells the heart about its vision of Beatrice, just as a weak eye in front of the sun cannot discern what it sees. Conversely, the "animus multus peritus" [very expert soul] of Peter's *quaestio* cannot fully know how the terms used in the formulation of dogmas are compatible without the support of faith, just as the eye of an owl, unless it is aided, cannot look at the light of the sun. While a formal similarity between the texts can be identified, it would be difficult to argue that Beatrice—even as a celestial being in the Empyrean—is merely a literary representation of a truth of faith, or that the "animus multus peritus" of Peter's *quaestio* might be a scholastic version of Dante's "pensero." Each text is also different in its focus. The purpose of chapter XLI [30] is to depict the triumph of Beatrice in the Empyrean, while the purpose of Peter's *quaestio* is to address the possibility of knowing the truth of faith through humane letters. Still, despite these differences, the texts do have at least two points in common. First, both texts quote from Aristotle's *Metaphysics* in order to illustrate the process of human knowledge, as was typically the case in scholasticism. Second, Peter claims in another passage of the *quaestio* that, in the science of faith, reason is moved, not by its own force, but by the higher, infused movement of divine inspiration.[9] Similarly, Dante writes that his "pensero" can see Beatrice in the Empyrean thanks to an "intelligenza nova" that "pur su lo tira":[10] it is a divinely inspired love that inspires the sigh with a new awareness. *Amore* thus propels the sigh toward Beatrice in the Empyrean and inspires Dante to write "una cosa nuova," a new sonnet in which he reaches an incomplete awareness of this celestial creature.[11]

A further point of contact between Peter's *quaestio* and chapter XLI [30] may concern the key question of the conception of poetry as this emerges from Peter of Trabibus, from Dante, and, more generally, from 1290s Florence. In his *quodlibetales* (including *quaestio* 19), Trabibus determines that poetry and philosophy are useless for the sanctity of the soul.[12] Given the presence in Florence of individuals like Guido Cavalcanti and Dante, who had a shared interest in both poetry and philosophy, it is not unlikely that a Franciscan such as Trabibus would have also been indirectly criticizing these poets. Dante of course does reflect on poetry in the *Vita nova*. In chapter XXV [16], he starts with a digression addressing a rhetorical problem—the literary justification for the personification of Love—which he explains using a quotation, again, from Aristotle, "lo Filosofo" (XXV.2 [16.2]). He then goes on to reflect on recent poetry in the vernacular. He considers "certi poeti in lingua latina" to be "dicitori d'amore" (XXV.3 [16.3]) [certain poets who wrote in Latin versified on love]; he then focuses on the "poete volgari" [vernacular poets]—an unprecedented phrase in the thirteenth century— and states that "dire per rima in volgare tanto è quanto dire per versi in latino, secondo alcuna proporzione" (XXV.4 [16.4]) [to write rhymes in the vernacular is as valid, mutatis mutandis, as writing verses in Latin].[13] As examples of poets "che hanno parlato a le cose inanimate" [have addressed inanimate things] Dante cites some of the most authoritative classical poets (Virgil, Lucan, Horace, Homer, and Ovid) and concludes by saying that, just as the Latin poets "*non* parlavano così sanza ragione, né quelli che rimano deono parlare cosí, non avendo alcuno ragionamento in loro di quello che dicono" (XXV.10 [16.10]) [did not write in this manner without reason, nor should vernacular poets write like this without having some understanding of what they are saying]. Given that Dante considered Guido and himself to be "poete volgari" indirectly linked to the classical poets, one can further speculate that, if Dante were actually present at Peter's *Quodlibet*, he would undoubtedly have noticed that the *lector theologiae*'s views on poetry did not align with his own. In fact, one can hypothesize that chapter XLI [30] of the *Vita nova* aimed to demonstrate that it was indeed possible, in an erotic literary text, to deal with a "veritas fidei" through poetry and to conceive of love as *caritas*, a divinely inspired love.

The differences between the theologian and the poet may help explain an aspect of Dante's conception of poetry, as articulated in chapter XLI [30]. On the one hand, Peter of Trabibus defines humane letters as useless for the acquisition of the sanctity of the soul and for knowledge of a truth of faith. On the other, in chapter XLI [30] Dante employs a vocabulary normally used in theological discussions (and by Peter himself) to discuss that which pertains to faith (the Empyrean, the "benedette anime," the impossibility of fully grasping what the "pensero" says about Beatrice as a celestial creature, the salvific role of a mortal woman), but he does this in an erotic literary work in the vernacular that combines poetry and prose. Thus, according to Dante, poetry may indeed lead to salvation.[14]

Besides contextualizing Dante's conception of poetry, the differences between Peter of Trabibus's *quaestio* 19 and *Vita nova*'s chapter XLI [30] can thus shed light on other relevant aspects of the *libello*. For instance, they lend greater credibility to the hypothesis that the *Vita nova* was the cause for the start (or the exacerbation) of Dante's antithetical relationship with some of the "religiosi," the members of religious orders, that would emerge more forcefully a few years later in the *Convivio* and in the *Comedy*.[15] In addition to this, they raise the question of why Dante wrote his *prosimetrum*. As I discuss elsewhere,[16] Dante's decision may in part have been the result of his intention to distinguish himself from Florentine secular intellectuals, such as his "first friend" Guido Cavalcanti, as well as from the theologians of the local "schools of the religious orders," Florence's most influential religious thinkers. A sonnet such as "Oltre la spera," along with the prose part of chapter XLI [30], likely contributed to medieval readers' perception of the *Vita nova* as an "outsider" text, an unprecedented text in the Italian and medieval literary tradition.[17]

Vita nova XLII [31]

ANNE C. LEONE

The final chapter of the *Vita nova* closes the work with an emphasis on new-ness and beginnings, which of course are also themes of the work as a whole. As Zygmunt Barański writes, chapter XLII [31] is a "final and crowning dec-laration of the *prosimetrum*'s *novitas*."[1] In a related way, Giuseppe Ledda characterizes the chapter as "proemiale" since it includes several elements that are traditionally associated with the exordium.[2] In his words: "Secondo la dottrina retorica degli *officia* esordiali, la dichiarazione della novità degli argomenti da trattare era uno degli elementi principali per la ricerca dell'*at-tentio* del pubblico" [According to the rhetorical doctrine of exordial conven-tions, the declaration of newness of the themes to be addressed was one of the principal elements for capturing the public's attention].[3] Ledda considers the chapter to be "a reinterpretation and dramatization" of the rhetorical schema "protasi con dichiarazione negativa—dichiarazione positiva limi-tante" [protasis with negative declaration—positive limiting declaration].[4] The negative declaration—"Io vidi cose che mi fecero proporre di non dire più di questa benedetta infino a tanto che io potessi più degnamente tractare di lei" (XLII.1 [31.1]) [I saw things that made me decide not to say anything more about this blessed lady until I was capable of writing about her more worthily]—is overcome by the positive claim: "Io spero di dire di lei quello che mai non fue detto d'alcuna" (XLII.2 [31.2]) [I hope to say things about her that have never been said about any woman].[5]

The point I would like to make about this chapter is related to what Barański and Ledda claim: the last chapter of the *Vita nova* is also a beginning. Of course, in the most basic and functional sense, by declaring the hope to write of his beloved what has never been said of "alcuna," the final chapter of the *libello* announces the beginning of a new work. Yet the issue of what that new work is (or will be) has divided critics. Mark Musa and Robert Pogue Harrison have each referred to the final chapter as an admission of the work's failure: if Dante had spoken of his lady in a worthy enough way during the course of the *Vita nova*, why would he need to write another work?[6] But others, including Barański and Ledda, argue that this is instead a huge boast: after a period of self-imposed silence, the poet is confident that he will be able to speak of his lady in a way that is entirely new.[7]

I incline toward the latter argument. Though the chapter points toward many other ineffability topoi in the *Vita nova* and in the *Paradiso*—the opening of *Paradiso* 1 is particularly resonant: "Nel ciel che più de la sua luce prende / fu'io, e vidi cose che ridire / né sa né può chi di là su discende" (*Par.* 1.4–6) [I was in that heaven which receives / more of His light. He who comes down from there / can neither know nor tell what he has seen][8]— these particular lines in XLII [31] claim only a temporary inexpressibility topos: if it is one at all, it is only partial and can be overcome. Furthermore, the arguments of Musa and of Harrison make less sense when one remembers that Dante has transcribed the *Vita nova* from his book of memory (I.1 [1.1]). Why would he bother to "copy" this *libello* from his memory if it were a failure? In considering the final chapter's claims of newness, and its concern with beginnings, it is important to remember the complexities of temporality raised by the work's description of its genesis. Since the work was "copied" from a book that already existed in Dante's memory, and since many of the poems in the work had been written and arguably disseminated before Dante compiled them into the *libello*, the task of distinguishing between when each element of the work (poems and commentary, etc.) was composed and/or copied for a first, second, or even third time is complicated.

Regardless of these complexities, one cannot overlook the chapter's movement toward the future (in Guglielmo Gorni's words, the chapter is a "profezia di una profezia" [prophecy of a prophecy[9]])—a future that many scholars have tried to identify, albeit without arriving at a consensus. Does Dante fulfill his promise to write of his lady what no one has ever written

before? He could have begun a work and not finished it or destroyed it—
questions to which we can never really know the answer (as Donato Pirovano
rightly notes in his commentary).[10]

On the other hand, as many scholars have maintained, the *Commedia*
may fulfill the promise declared in the *Vita nova*'s last chapter (see, for in-
stance, Francesco Flamini, who argues that "la *Vita Nuova* è, dunque, come
il preludio o il preambolo della *Commedia*" [the *Vita Nuova* is, therefore, like
the prelude or preamble of the *Commedia*]).[11] Other scholars claim that only
Paradiso fulfills the promise. At least one critic maintains that neither the
Paradiso nor the *Commedia* answers the challenge of the final chapter. For in-
stance, Colin Hardie argues that the answer lies in the poem "Amor tu vedi
ben che questa donna" (*Rime* CII).[12] Without being able to delve further
into this tangled question, we can at least acknowledge that the end of the
Vita nova also marks the beginning of a new text—regardless of whether that
text is ideal or actualized.

I also wish to raise another question: What if the *libello*'s final chapter—
an end that is also a beginning—looks toward its *own* beginning, rather than
(or in addition to) the beginning of another text? Several scholars hint at this
idea. In Barański's words: "The powerful forward thrust of the [final] chapter
has largely prevented critics from appreciating its yet more powerful retro-
spective force."[13] For Gorni, the final chapter's emphasis on wonder or mar-
vel brings us back to the third (but what he considers the first) chapter of the
libello: "*Mirabile*, uno degli epiteti caratteristici di Beatrice, rinvia, chiu-
dendo il cerchio, alla 'maravigliosa visione' di I.14 [III.3]" [*Miraculous*, one
of the characteristic epithets of Beatrice, brings us back, closing the circle, to
the "marvelous vision" of I.14].[14] Gorni also highlights the structural sym-
metry of the work via its use of Latin: "Il libro si apre con la rubrica latina
'incipit vita nova,' e con una frase latina si chiude: in perfetta simmetria
anche con l'esordio della seconda parte, 'quomodo sedet sola civitas'" [The
book opens with the Latin rubric "incipit vita nova" and ends with a Latin
phrase: in perfect symmetry also with the exordium of the second part, "quo-
modo sedet sola civitas"] (which is chapter XXVIII in Barbi's numbering,
and 19 in Gorni's).[15]

In Singleton's opinion, the reader knows from the first phrase of Chap-
ter II [1.2] (what he calls the first real chapter, since it is not the proem)—"la
gloriosa donna della mia mente"—that Beatrice has already passed on, which

has implications for the shape of the work as a whole.[16] He writes: "We ought now to recall what we have seen to be the nature of the form of the *Vita Nuova*, how it ends where it begins, with Beatrice dead and now in the glory of eternal life."[17] Thus, by the time we read about her death in chapter XXVIII [19], in Singleton's words, "a circle is complete. At the end we know again what we knew at the beginning." In this sense, the *Vita nova* invites us to read in a circular way: sending us back not only to the first chapters but also to some of the middle chapters. Indeed, for Singleton, Beatrice's death marks a beginning and an end, which, "when they are the same, constitute an 'ideal center.'"[18]

I would like to suggest that chapter XVII [10] might also been read as a "center" of the text, inasmuch as it marks a beginning and an end: "Poi che dissi questi tre sonetti, nelli quali parlai a questa donna, però che fuoro narratori di tutto quasi lo mio stato credendomi tacere e non dire più, però che mi parea di me assai avere manifestato, avegna che sempre poi tacesse di dire a lei, a me convenne ripigliare materia nuova e più nobile che la passata. E però che la cagione de la nuova materia è dilettevole a udire, la dicerò, quanto potrò più brievemente" (XVII.1–2 [10.1–10.2]) [After I wrote these three sonnets in which I addressed this lady directly, since they told almost everything about my state, thinking it best to be silent and write no more since I felt I had explained enough about myself, although from then on I would refrain from addressing her directly, I needed to take up new and nobler subject matter than that of the past. And since the occasion for the new subject matter is delightful to hear, I will write it down, as briefly as I know how]. At a fundamental level, both chapters XLII [31] and XVII [10] emphasize the need for authorial silence followed by the promise of a new kind of text. In XVII [10], the "materia"—speaking in praise of his lady—is new, whereas in XLII [31], the way of talking about her must change: "infino a tanto che io potesse più degnamente trattare di lei." Toby Levers also contrasts chapter XVII [10] with XLII [31], arguing that the comparison reveals a shift in the narratorial voice: "The control of the narrative itself is transferred from Dante the commentator (recounting the story in a retrospective voice [in XVII [10]]), to Dante the author, who is *simultaneously* a working poet and the narrator of chapter XLII [31]."[19]

Thus we might say that the final chapter asks us to look backward at several other key points—the beginning of the work (I [1.1]), the death of

Beatrice (XXVIII [19]), and the beginning of the phase of praise (XVII [10])—each of which, as we have seen, has been characterized as a center that marks endings and beginnings. Reading chapter XLII [31], one is prompted to look toward the future but also to return to XVII [10], which in turn causes one to look again toward the future. In other words, when we reach an end, we are also invited to start again at a beginning. This is perhaps not surprising in light of Barański's claim that the *Vita nova* is "obsessed with beginnings," which mirrors, in Augustinian terms, the Christian's duty to reflect and then strive for spiritual renewal.[20]

Indeed, while the last chapter of the *Vita nova* is an ending that is also a beginning, the first chapter of the *libello*, in a fitting reversal, describes itself as copied from the book of memory. As Barański suggests, this may be an allusion to Augustine's gloss on Malachi 3:13–16 in the *City of God*: "'*Haec oblocuti sunt qui timebant Dominum, unusquisque ad proximum suum; et animadvertit Dominus et audivit: et scripsit librum memoriae in conspectu suo eis qui timent Dominum et reverentur nomen eius*' [Mal. 3:16]. Isto libro significatum est testamentum novum" (*De civitate Dei* 18.35) ["Those who feared the Lord spoke these scornful words, each one to his neighbor; and the Lord marked it and listened; and he wrote a book of remembrance in his sight for those who fear the Lord and reverence his name." By that book he means the New Testament].[21] If Barański's suggestion is correct (as I believe it is), the allusion reveals an important point that would support my argument further: for Augustine glossing Malachi, the book of remembrance *is* the new text. The old text, as it prophesies the coming of Christ, looks toward the new, and the new looks back at the old. In other words, the reference to Malachi (via Augustine) reinforces an association between chapter XLII [31] and chapter I [1.1], as well as Dante's project of associating memory, perhaps somewhat counterintuitively, with newness.

In this way, the emphasis on God's name in Malachi might also shed light on the sonnet in the penultimate chapter of the *libello*, "Oltre la spera" [Beyond the sphere], in which the sigh's vision of the divine is incomprehensible to Dante's mind, except that he knows it speaks of Beatrice: "So io che parla di quella gentile, / però che spesso ricorda Beatrice" (XLI.13 [30.13]) [I know he's speaking of that lovely one, / Beatrice, since he often mentions her]. In one sense, recording a name and the act of remembering or memorializing Beatrice are central aspects of the project of the *Vita nova*, which look retrospectively at her life; and yet, its retrospective concerns are also inextricably linked to the work's obsession with *novitas*.

While we have considered the final chapter's connections with the other chapters in the work, and how these relate to issues of circularity, *novitas*, and memory, I would now like to turn to the issue of looking itself. In the final chapter, the act of looking is emphasized through repetition: *vedere* is used twice, *visione* once, and *mirare* once: "E poi piaccia a colui che è sire della cortesia che la mia anima sen possa gire a vedere la gloria della sua donna, cioè di quella benedetta Beatrice, la quale gloriosamente mira nella faccia di Colui *qui est per omnia secula benedictus*" (XLII.3 [31.3]) [Then, if it be pleasing to Him who is the Lord of benevolence and grace, may my soul go to contemplate the glory of its lady—that blessed Beatrice, who gazes in glory into the face of Him *qui est per omnia secula benedictus*]. As Stefano Carrai has argued, Dante may be alluding to poem 12 of the third book of Boethius's *Consolation of Philosophy*, which concerns Orpheus's attempt to win Eurydice back from death. Contrastive parallels abound: Boethius's poem is preceded in the prose by reference to a sphere, while in the *Vita nova* the poem "Oltre la spera" precedes the prose. Orpheus looks back to the underworld, while Dante looks up to Beatrice, who is herself looking at God.[22] Both passages emphasize circularity, but in Boethius the circularity highlights futility. Orpheus loses again what he had already lost: ("Orpheus Erydicen suam / Vidit, perdidit, occidit," 3.12, lines 50–51 [Orpheus his Eurydice / Saw, lost, and killed]).[23] Eurydice "dies" for a second time, whereas the glory of Beatrice in everlasting life is affirmed twice, in the final and first chapters of the *libello*. One might say that Orpheus and Eurydice provide a model of a kind of circular futility, while Dante's love for Beatrice provides a model of the circularity of Christian salvation: Beatrice returns to God, where she has always belonged.

To conclude, I return to Singleton's view: that the beginning of the *Vita nova* may be seen as the end of the text. It reveals Beatrice's death before it happens, and it colors the way we read the rest of the work: knowing what we know at the beginning of our reading, perhaps we read mournfully before she has even died in the text. But is there a sense in which the end of the *libello* could also announce its own beginning? Keeping in mind the circular ways in which the text encourages us to read, and keeping in mind the complex temporal and authorial issues that are emphasized throughout the work (as

Toby Levers, Edoardo Sanguineti, and others argue, there are several authoial voices, narrator/author/*agens*/scribe, who speak or write from different temporal perspectives),[24] could there not be room for this (albeit highly speculative) suggestion? Here at the end of the *Vita nova*, which "Dante" is speaking? From which point in the composition of which text does his voice come?

As Barański argues, by alluding to a line in Augustine's *Enarrationes*, Dante emphasizes the newness and inventiveness of the *libello* as a whole: "Si habemus novam vitam, cantemus canticum novum, hymnum Deo nostro" [If we have new life, let us sing a new song, a hymn to our God].[25] In the next line, Augustine refers to the "heading" of the book that is written about the author: "In capite libri scriptum est de me, ut faciam voluntatem tuam: Deus meus, volui, et legem tuam in medio cordis mei" [At the foremost place in the book it is written of me that I should do your will; O my God, this I have wanted, your law in the midst of my heart]. Barański compares this heading to the "rubrica" to which Dante twice refers in the opening lines of the *libello*: "In quella parte del libro de la mia memoria dinanzi a la quale poco si potrebbe leggere, si trova una rubrica la quale dice: *Incipit vita nova*. Sotto la quale rubrica io trovo scritte le parole le quali è mio intendimento d'assemplare in questo libello; e se non tutte, almeno la loro sentenzia" (I.1 [1.1]) [In the book of my memory—the part of it before which not much is legible—there is the heading *Incipit vita nova*. Under this heading I find the words which I intend to copy down in this little book; if not all of them, at least their essential meaning].

Barański's assertion is convincing and strongly suggestive, especially since in the next lines, Augustine claims that the book of Psalms turns to itself for authority:

> Ecce ad membra respexit, ecce et ipse fecit voluntatem Patris. Sed in quo capite libri scriptum est de illo? Fortasse in capite libri huius Psalmorum. Quid enim longe petamus, aut alios libros inquiramus? Ecce in capite libri huius Psalmorum, scriptum est: *Beatus vir qui non abiit in consilio impiorum, et in via peccatorum non stetit, et in cathedra pestilentiarum non sedit, sed in lege Domini voluntas eius fuit: hoc est: Deus meus, volui, et legem tuam in medio cordis mei: hoc est, et in lege eius meditabitur die ac nocte* (Ps 1:1–2).

[See how he now turns to his members, and how he himself did the will of his Father. But what book does he mean, where this is written of him at its foremost place? Perhaps it is written at the opening of this very Book of Psalms. What need is there for a more extensive search? Why should we investigate other books? Look where it is written on the opening page of this Book of Psalms, *Blessed is the person who has not gone astray in the council of the ungodly, and has not stood in the way of sinners, and has not sat in the seat of pestilence, but in the law of the Lord was his will.* This is the same thing as in our psalm here: *O my God, this I have wanted, and your law is in the midst of my heart*; and this again means the same thing as *on his law will he reflect day and night* (Ps 1:1–2).]

The book of Psalms has a reciprocal and circular structure: its author's destiny, to write the book, is written by God: "At the foremost place in the book it is written of *me* that I should do your will" (emphasis mine.) But the book is also about God. And, according to Augustine, the book of Psalms turns to its own beginning for justification of its origin, asking: What other books are needed?

Dante's *libello* imitates this circular and self-reflective structure, and it also turns to itself for authority.[26] Many scholars have attributed to its last line an allusion to First Corinthians 13:12: "Videmus nunc per speculum in enigmate, tunc autem facie ad faciem. Nunc cognosco ex parte, tunc autem cognoscam sicut et cognitus sum" [We see now through a glass in a dark manner, but then face to face. Now I know in part, but then I shall know even as I am known].[27] However I would like to call attention to Paul's next verse as well (13:13): "Nunc autem manent fides, spes, caritas, tria haec; maior autem horum est caritas" [And now there remain faith, hope *and* charity, these three; but the greatest of these is charity]. By the end of the work, the *Vita nova* claims to be about the kind of love that is reciprocated, reciprocal, inclusive, and everlasting: a love of which Dante, Beatrice, and all Christians can be a part.

Many critics also point to the resemblance of the last line of chapter XLII [31] to the last line of Epistle 13, in which Dante dedicates the *Paradiso* to Can Grande della Scala: "Et quia, invento principio seu primo, videlicet Deo, nichil est quod ulterius queratur, cum sit Alfa et O, idest principium et finis, ut visio Iohannis designat, in ipso Deo terminatur tractatus, qui est benedictus in secula seculorum" (13.90) [And since, when the Beginning or First, which is God, has been reached, there is nought to be sought for beyond, inasmuch as He is Alpha and Omega, that is, the Beginning and the End, as the *Vision* of John tells us, the work ends in God Himself, who is blessed for evermore, world without end].[28] For the author of the letter, the work will end in God, but God himself is the end and the beginning.

NOTES

Preface

1. We prefer the form *nova*, rather than *nuova*, since this title is given in the text itself and is repeated in the *Convivio* 1.1.16, 2.2.1, and 12.4.

2. No volume in Dante studies can ever stand on its own, and this one, in its deliberate push to pursue fresh readings, is certainly no exception. We will thus not take, here, the extensive space necessary to rehearse information about the *Vita nova*'s textual transmission, reception history, and interpretive history that is available elsewhere. We refer interested readers to Zygmunt G. Barański, "*Vita nova*," in *Dante's "Other Works": Assessments and Interpretations*, edited by Zygmunt Barański and Theodore Cachey (Notre Dame, IN: University of Notre Dame Press, 2022), 71–124.

3. Unless otherwise indicated, translations of the *Vita nova* into English are taken from Andrew Frisardi's 2012 highly readable and energetic version.

Vita nova I–IV [1–2.5]: Things Never Said about Any Woman

1. See, for example, Picone, "*Vita Nuova* fra autobiografia"; Took, "Dante and the *Confessions*"; Pacioni, "Autobiografia."

2. B. Reynolds, "Introduction," 11.

3. Barolini, "'Cominciandomi dal principio'" [1994], 122.

4. De Robertis, *Libro della "Vita Nuova"* [1970], 9.

5. Vallone, *Prosa della "Vita Nuova,"* 38.

6. Compare also *Vita nova* XXIV.3 and 6 [15.3 and 6], XXV.10 [16.10], and XXX.3 [19.10].

7. See, for example, VI.2 [2.11], VII.1 [2.12], VIII.1 [3.1], IX.1 [4.1], XIV.3 [7.3], XIX.3 [10.14], and XXX.1 [19.8].

8. See *Dve* 1.9.10 and 1.10.7.

9. See *Inf.* 10.25–27.

10. Ciacci, *Realismo della "Vita nuova,"* 24.

11. Beatrice "fa gentil ciò ch'ella mira; / ov'ella passa, ogn'om ver lei si gira" (XXI.2 [12.2]) [ennobles all she looks upon; / wherever she passes all turn to look at her].

12. "Rimase tutta la sopradetta cittade quasi vedova" (XXX.1 [19.8]) [the entire above-named city was like a widow], where "the city" clearly refers not to its physical structures or bureaucratic organizations but to its citizens.

13. See, for example, Ascoli, *Dante and the Making*; Barański, "Dante Alighieri."

14. See Cristaldi, *"Vita Nuova" e la restituzione*, 73.

15. "Vedeste, al mio parere, onne valore / e tutto gioco e quanto bene om sente" [You saw, I believe, all worth, all the joy and good that a man can feel].

16. On the discrepancies between the poetic and the prose accounts of the dream-vision in *Vita nova* III [1.12–2.2], see Gragnolati, "Trasformazioni e assenze."

17. Cavalcanti writes that "Quando v'apparve che se 'n gia dolendo, / fu 'l dolce sonno ch'allor si compiea" [When it seemed to you that he left with such sadness, it was because the sweet dream was coming to an end]. "Vedeste, al mio parere, onne valore," lines 12–13, in *Poeti del Duecento*, Contini ed., 2:544.

18. "Io tenni li piedi in quella parte de la vita di là da la quale non si puote ire più per intendimento di ritornare" (XIV.8 [7.8]) [I have set my feet in that place in life beyond which one cannot go with the intention of returning].

19. "di sì nobilissima vertù, che nulla volta sofferse che Amore mi reggesse sanza lo fedele consiglio de la ragione" (II.9 [1.10]) [so dignified in its power that it never allowed Love to govern me without the faithful counsel of reason].

20. For a reading of this ethical development according to Bonaventure's *Itinerarium mentis in Deum*, see Crudale, "Love and *Civitas.*"

21. See, for example, chapter XI [5].

22. Homer is identified, in chapter II, as the source of the comparison of Beatrice to the daughter of a god, while the role of the "chorus" of contemporary poets, the "fedeli d'Amore," has been explored above.

23. Barański, "'Lascio cotale trattato,'" 31n15.

24. "Haec non cognoverunt discipuli ejus primum: sed quando glorificatus est Jesus, tunc recordati sunt quia haec erant scripta de eo" (John 12.16) [These things his disciples did not know at the first; but when Jesus was glorified, then they remembered that these things were written of him].

25. See, for example, Matthew 11.25; Luke 10.21.

26. See Barański, "'Lascio cotale trattato,'" 20–21.

27. See Casadei, "Incipit vita nova," 180–81.

28. Compare *Par.* 31.39, where the Dante character is described as having traveled "di Fiorenza in popol giusto e sano" [from Florence to a people just and whole]. Dante, *Paradiso*, Durling trans.

Vita nova I [1.1]

I am very grateful to Zyg Barański for his comments on an earlier version of this chapter.

1. Carruthers, *Book of Memory*, 18. On medieval antecedents, see also Singleton, *Essay*, 127–29; Branca, "Poetica del rinnovamento," 123; Barański, "'Lascio cotale trattato,'" 17–23.

2. Carruthers, *Book of Memory*, 279.

3. In *Poeti del Duecento*, Contini ed., 2:223 (line 1347), 259 (line 2407).

4. Robinson, "'Booklet'"; Hanna, *Pursuing History*, 21–34; Todorović, *Dante and the Dynamics*, 147–51. On some uses of *libello* with reference to vernacular works in Dante's time, see Storey, "Following Instructions," 118–21.

5. Ahern, "Binding the Book."

6. Palazzo, "Rôle des *libelli*," 12–13.

7. Philippart, *Légendiers latins* [1977], 99–101, and [1985], 22–23; Poulin, "*Libelli* dans l'édition hagiographique."

8. Boeckler, *Stuttgarter Passionale*, 5, 14, plate 129, and *Passionale, pars tertia*, http://digital.wlb-stuttgart.de/purl/bsz332502295.

9. Walahfrid Strabo, Ulrichs-Vita des Bern von Reichenau und der Hl. Gallus und Othmar, ca. 1200, e-codices, www.e-codices.unifr.ch/de/list/one/zhl/P0033-4.

10. On St. Bonaventure's conception of divine inspiration of the human *auctor*, see Minnis, *Medieval Theory of Authorship*, 95.

11. In *Poeti del Duecento*, Contini ed., 2:501 (lines 43–44).

12. Steinberg, *Accounting for Dante*, 91.

13. On Dante's use of omissions, see Curtius, *European Literature*, 328–29, and Gardini, *Lacuna*, 17–19, 41, 46–55.

14. Robinson, "'Booklet,'" 61.

15. As Gorni writes, "L'autore . . . si atteggia a copista, breviatore ed esegeta della propria opera" [The author . . . plays the part of scribe, editor, and interpreter of his own work]. Dante, *Vita Nova*, Gorni ed. [2011], x.

16. Singleton, *Essay*, 53.

17. Carruthers, *Book of Memory*, 110–11 (quotation from 110), 113–15, and see 279 on Dante's procedure.

18. Parkes, *Pause and Effect*, 305. On paragraph signs in manuscripts of the *Vita nova*, see Cervigni, "Segni paragrafali," esp. 291–94, and Gorni, "'Paragrafi' e titolo."

19. Coluccia, "Teorie e pratiche interpuntive," 77–80.

20. Parkes, *Pause and Effect*, 203 and plate 25. A similar distinction of size is found in Milan, Biblioteca Ambrosiana, MS H 69 sup., containing St. Paul's Epistles with glosses, datable to the twelfth century: Gengaro and Villa Gugliel-metti, *Inventario*, 121 and plate 105.

21. Justinian, *Digestum novum*, Robbins Collection, UC Berkeley Library, http://ds.lib.berkeley.edu/RobbinsMS037_11.

22. Henricus de Segusia, *Summa super titulis decretalium*, Robbins Collection, UC Berkeley Library, http://ds.lib.berkeley.edu/RobbinsMS068_11, for instance fol. 27v.

23. Petrucci, "Minute, Autograph, Author's Book."

24. Storey, "Following Instructions," 118.

25. Barański, "'Lascio cotale trattato,'" 7–11.

Vita nova II [1.2–1.11]

1. Foucault, "Of Other Spaces," 22.

2. Jimenez, "On Space as Capacity," 140–41.

3. For the theoretical background to this idea, see, for example, Massey, *For Space*; Bachelard, *Poetics of Space*; Lefebvre, *Production of Space*.

4. Carruthers, *Book of Memory*, 226.

5. Tisseron, "Intimité et extimité."

6. See *Vita nova* III.9 [1.20].

7. Low and Lawrence-Zuniga, *Space and Place*, 1.

8. Webb, *Medieval Heart*, 69.

9. Santagata, *Dante*, 39–40.

10. Moevs, "'Punto che mi vinse,'" 267.

Vita nova III [1.12–2.2]

1. On the introductory and demarcatory status of chapter III, see Picone, "*Vita Nova* come romanzo," 250; Barański, "Roots of Dante's Plurilingualism," 121; Steinberg, "Dante's First Dream," 95; Ascoli, *Dante and the Making*, 185.

2. Botterill, "'Però che la divisione,'" 66; Ascoli, *Dante and the Making*, 187.

3. Santagata, *Io e il mondo*, 114–24.

4. Botterill, however, suggests that it is only the *absence* of *divisione* that seems to require justification in the *libello* ("'Però che la divisione,'" 74).

5. Pirovano, "Nota introduttiva," 29; Steinberg, "Dante's First Dream," 101. The fictional *tenzone* of *Vita nova* XXII [13] can be excluded because its response is penned by the poet himself.

6. Larson, "A ciascun'alma presa," 90–96.

7. On the centrality of interpretation in this chapter, see Steinberg, "Dante's First Dream," 93–94.

8. Banella, *"Vita nuova" del Boccaccio*, 46.

9. *Vita nuova*, Pirovano ed., 94; Steinberg, "Dante's First Dream," 98; Barański, "'Lascio cotale trattato,'" 6.

10. Picone, *"Vita Nova* come *prosimetrum,"* 245; Banella, *"Vita nuova" del Boccaccio*, 37; Steinberg, "Dante's First Dream," 112.

11. Storey, "Following Instructions," 123–26.

12. Picone, *"Vita Nova* come macrotesto," 227–28.

13. Todorović, *Dante and the Dynamics*, 114.

14. Picone, *"Vita Nova* come macrotesto," 244n13. Ascoli, *Dante and the Making*, 187.

15. Santagata, *Io e il mondo*, 122; Todorović, *Dante and the Dynamics*, 127.

16. Boccaccio, To, c. 29r; Id. *Trattatello in laude di Dante*, I red., par. 175 (my emphasis), Ricci ed.

17. Boccaccio, *Trattatello in laude di Dante*, I red., par. 175 (my emphasis), Ricci ed.

18. Giunta, *Due saggi sulla tenzone*, 28; Meneghetti, "Beatrice al chiar di luna"; Picone, *"Vita Nova* come romanzo," 252; Kruger, *Dreaming in the Middle Ages*, 134.

19. Ascoli, *Dante and the Making*, 201n54. On the importance of Cavalcanti to the authorial "performance" of the *Vita nova*, see Gragnolati, "Trasformazioni e assenze."

20. Dronke, *Verse with Prose*, 109. Pirovano notes the "attacco narrativo" of line 5 (*Vita nuova*, Pirovano ed., 92).

21. See, in particular, Gragnolati, "Trasformazioni e assenze."

22. Candido argues that the sonnet misleads its recipients through an excess of (incorrect) details rather than through reticence, as more commonly suggested ("Per una rilettura").

23. Ascoli, *Dante and the Making*, 223 (emphasis mine). Ascoli argues that chapter XXV accounts for the otherwise unexplained tripartite structure (poems, *ragioni*, *divisioni*) of the *libello*.

24. Picone, *"Vita Nova* come romanzo," 254.

25. Steinberg, "Dante's First Dream," 112–13.

26. Picone, "*Vita Nova* come romanzo," 250.

Vita nova IV [2.3–2.5]

1. "Haec non cognoverunt discipuli ejus primum: sed quando glorificatus est Jesus, tunc recordati sunt quia haec erant scripta de eo, et haec fecerunt ei" (John 12.16) [These things his disciples did not know at the first; but when Jesus was glorified, then they remembered that these things were written of him, and that they had done these things to him].

2. "Cum autem tanta signa fecisset coram eis, non credebant in eum" (John 12.37) [And whereas he had done so many miracles before them, they believed not in him].

3. See, for instance: "Ea demum est miserabilis animi seruitus, signa pro rebus accipere; et supra creaturam corpoream, oculum mentis ad hauriendum aeternum lumen leuare non posse" (*De doctrina christiana* 3.5.9, ed. Martin) [It is, then, a miserable kind of spiritual slavery to interpret signs as things, and to be incapable of raising the mind's eye above the physical creation so as to absorb the eternal light]. On Augustine, *cupiditas*, and hermeneutics, see Sellgren, "Reading Dante's *Commedia*," 53–70.

Vita nova V–XII [2.6–5.24]: A Lover's Trials

Three of the papers in this section are based on presentations from the *Vita nova* workshop held at University College London on November 10, 2017, dedicated to chapters V–XII. I would like to thank my UCL colleagues Giulia Gaimari, Jennifer Rushworth, and John Took for having joined me as speakers at the event, though John was not in the end able to contribute to this volume. Alexandra Lee gave invaluable support in organizing the workshop and the associated exhibition of copies of the *Vita nova* from UCL Library's Special Collections, which was curated in collaboration with rare books librarian and Dante collections expert Tabitha Tuckett.

1. Barbi's and Gorni's two editions provide ample notes on the criteria used for establishing their chosen textual forms. For further thorough, recent discussion of key points in the debate, see Pirovano, "Per una nuova edizione," presenting the criteria for his edition of the *Vita nova* in vol. 1 of the Nuova Edizione Commentata delle Opere di Dante (NECOD), directed by Enrico Malato, as well as Pirovano's "Nota introduttiva" and "Nota al testo" within that volume.

2. Ascoli, *Dante and the Making*, esp. chap. 4, "Auto-Commentary," 175–226; De Robertis, *Libro della "Vita Nuova"*; Picone, "*Vita Nova* come macrotesto"; Pirovano, "Nota introduttiva," 3–9, 29–33; Storey, "Following Instructions."

3. See Barański, "Roots of Dante's Plurilingalism"; Borsa, "Identità sociale," 286–94; De Robertis, *Libro della "Vita Nuova"*; Gragnolati, "Trasformazioni e assenze," and "(In-)Corporeality."

4. Ascoli, *Dante and the Making*, 188–99, 223–25; Picone, *"Vita Nuova" e tradizione romanza*.

5. See the notes situating the poems within a plausible chronological sequence in the main editions of the *Vita nova* and *Rime* I have been able to consult: *Vita Nuova*, Barbi ed. [1932]; *Rime giovanili*, Barolini ed.; *Dante's Lyric Poetry*, Foster and Boyde ed.; *Vita Nova*, Gorni ed. [1996/2011]; *Vita nuova*, Pirovano ed.; *Rime*, Grimaldi ed.; *Rime*, De Robertis ed. [2002]. De Robertis gives a note on the "redazione pre-*VN*" of "O voi che per la via d'Amor passate" (VII.3 [2.14]) [O all ye passing by along Love's way], attested in three manuscripts (3:298–300). See also Barolini, "Editing Dante's *Rime*," 255–56, 265–71; Gragnolati, "Trasformazioni e assenze," 79–81.

6. See Borsa, "Identità sociale"; Gragnolati, "Trasformazioni e assenze"; Kay, *Dante's Lyric Redemption*, 93–127; Picone, *Vita Nuova e tradizione romanza*; Pirovano, "Nota introduttiva," 26–35.

7. See Picone on the *Vita nova*'s lyric genres, in "*Vita Nova* come macrotesto," 231–35. On lyric "genre," especially in Occitan, see Paden, *Medieval Lyric*. For the Italian tradition, see the useful *variorum* of D'Arco Silvio Avalle's essays, *Forme del canto*; Decaria and Lagomarsini, *Confini della lirica*.

8. Mainini, "Schermi e specchi"; Pirovano, "Nota introduttiva," 23.

9. See Holmes, "Dante's *Vita nova*," 129–34; also Mainini, "Schermi e specchi," 154–60; Picone, '*Vita Nuova*' e *tradizione romanza*, and "*Vita Nova* come macrotesto," 233–34.

10. See Ascoli, *Dante and the Making*, esp. "Auto-Commentary," 175–226. Rea notes how "si è perduto dietro le fragili dinamiche della sua storia cortese" [he has become lost behind the fragile dynamics of the courtly storyline], in "Amore e ragione," 175.

11. Borsa, "Identità sociale"; Santagata, *Io e il mondo*, 119–24, 141–44, 153–61.

12. Gragnolati, "(In-)Corporeality," 216, and "Trasformazioni e assenze." See also Banella, *"Vita nuova" del Boccaccio*, 90–91; Moleta, "*Vita Nuova*"; Picone, "Teoria dell'*auctoritas*."

13. Barolini, *"Cominciandomi dal principio"* [2006], 177. See also Carrai, *Dante elegiaco*, 55–58; Moleta, "*Vita Nuova*." Temporality is also treated in detail

here by Rushworth (on chapter VII), O'Connell (on chapter VIII), and Price (on chapter XII).

14. Borsa, "Identità sociale," 288; see also Rea, "Amore e ragione," 172.

15. Pirovano, "Nota introduttiva," 16–17; Viegnes, "Space as Love."

16. See Gosselin, "Shape of Things"; McLain, "Screening the Past"; Pirovano, "Nota introduttiva," 16–20; Santagata, *Io e il mondo*, 173–78.

17. These *fedeli* are mentioned in the *divisioni* at VII.7 [2.18] and VIII.7 [3.7]. The expression probably indicates a circle of poets linked by shared literary tastes, perhaps the nucleus of the so-called *stilnovisti* (on which, see Pirovano's *Dolce stil novo*), though some critics (notably Gabriele Rossetti in the nineteenth century and Lorenzo Valli in the twentieth) have taken these and other passages from the *Vita nova* and elsewhere as referencing a circle dedicated to esoteric studies and a program of radical religious and political reform.

18. Pirovano, "Nota introduttiva," 16.

19. Viegnes, "Space as Love."

20. Turco, "Restaging Sin," draws out the scriptural aspects of Dante's spatial representations, including those of "O voi che per la via," which are also a focus in Rushworth's chapter here.

21. On Boethius's *Consolation of Philosophy* as genre model/antimodel, see Picone, "*Vita Nova* come *prosimetrum*," esp. 238–41; Todorović, *Dante and the Dynamics*, 18–66. On chapter XII [5], see Carrai, *Dante elegiaco*, 28 (but Boethian relationships are a substantial focus throughout the study); Lombardo, *Boezio in Dante*, 431–35; Rea, "'Ego tanquam centrum circuli,'" 753–55.

22. See Agamben, *Stanze*; Picone, *Vita Nuova e tradizione romanza* and "Teoria dell'*auctoritas*," 181–87; Roglieri, "Per Ovidio parla Amore."

23. Ascoli, *Dante and the Making*, 189–200; Barański, "Roots of Dante's Plurilingualism," 107–14; Hooper, "Exile and Rhetorical Order," 20–21; Van Peteghem, *Italian Readers of Ovid*, 125–33.

24. On chapter VIII [3]'s poems, see Brugnolo, "'Sovra la morta imagine avvenente.'"

25. See Brugnolo, "'Sovra la morta imagine avvenente,'" 121–22; *Rime*, ed. Grimaldi, *ad loc.*

26. See O'Connell and Rushworth in this volume.

27. Carrai, *Dante elegiaco*, 27–31, 36–38; Rea, "'Ego tanquam centrum circuli,'" 744–49.

28. *Vita nuova*, Pirovano ed., *ad loc.*

29. *Vita nuova*, Pirovano ed., *ad loc.*; Rea, "'Ego tanquam centrum circuli.'"

30. Rea, "'Ego tanquam centrum circuli'" and "Amore e ragione."

31. Gosselin, "Shape of Things," 5–7; Picone, "Teoria dell'*auctoritas*," 180–81; Rea, "'Ego tanquam centrum circuli,'" 754–56.

32. Ascoli, *Dante and the Making*, 178–201; Barański, "Roots of Dante's Plurilingualism"; Picone, "Teoria dell'*auctoritas*."

33. Barolini's commentary highlights Cavalcantian influence in the prose's discussion of mediated vs. direct approaches to the beloved, as well as in chapter XI [5.4–7]'s focus on the *spiriti*; *Rime giovanili*, 224–25.

34. Lombardo, *Boezio in Dante*, 432–33; Rea, "'Ego tanquam centrum circuli,'" 749–56.

35. Romans 12:3: "Dico enim per gratiam quae data est mihi, omnibus qui sunt inter vos, non plus sapere quam oportet sapere" [For I say, by the grace that is given me, to all that are among you, not to be more wise than it behoveth to be wise]; *Vita nuova*, Pirovano ed., *ad loc.*

36. Rea, "'Ego tanquam centrum circuli,'" 745–46.

37. Barański, "Roots of Dante's Plurilingualism"; Borsa, "Identità sociale," 286–94.

38. Barański, "Roots of Dante's Plurilingualism," 113.

39. On *libello* as material form, see Todorović, *Dante and the Dynamics*, 147–51.

40. Picone, "*Vita Nova* come *prosimetrum*," 244–48, and "Teoria dell'*auctoritas*," 176; Van Peteghem, *Italian Readers of Ovid*, 129–33.

41. Akbari, *Seeing through the Veil*, 117–24; Borsa, "Immagine e immaginazione," 141–43; S. Gilson, "Dante and the Science," 189–90; Pirovano, *Dolce stil novo*, 105–57, 196–207.

42. Barański, "Sulla formazione intellettuale" and "On Dante's Trail"; Pegoretti, "Filosofanti."

43. Martinez, "Mourning Beatrice"; Nasti, "Nozze e vedovanza," and *Favole d'amore*.

44. Hooper, "Exile and Rhetorical Order," 12; Martinez, "Mourning Beatrice," 8–13, 28; Nasti, "Memoria del *Canticum*," 19.

45. Barański, "On Dante's Trail," 7–14.

46. See Gaimari's chapter in this volume.

47. Stillinger, *Song of Troilus*, 57–72, 84–88, 94–109; Todorović, *Dante and the Dynamics*, 95–101, 127–29. The recent volume edited by Barański, Cachey, and Lombardo, *Dante e la cultura fiorentina*, provides extensive new reflections on such resources.

48. Stillinger, *Song of Troilus*, 59 and 84 (quotations), and 84–88.

49. See Price's notes on the *prosopopoeia* and its relationship to *tornada* or *congedo* forms in her chapter in this volume; see also Keen, "'Va', mia canzone.'"

50. It has been welcome to see a renewal of interest in precisely the *divisioni* and their editorial fortunes in recent scholarship; see, for instance, Banella, *"Vita nuova" del Boccaccio*; Eisner, *Boccaccio and the Invention.*

Vita nova V and VI [2.6–2.11]

An earlier draft of this paper was presented at the *Vita nova* workshop held at University College London on November 10, 2017, dedicated to chapters V–XII, and has benefited from audience feedback during the workshop and from additional discussion with Giulia Gaimari and Jennifer Rushworth.

1. Gorni, "Saggio di lettura," 247.

2. Santagata, "Introduzione," liv.

3. De Robertis, *Libro della "Vita Nuova."* 5–7. Of the numerous studies of the innovative intentions and effects of the prose, see also Ascoli, *Dante and the Making*, 179–81; Barański, "Roots of Dante's Plurilingualism"; Todorović, *Dante and the Dynamics.*

4. Pirovano, "Nota introduttiva," 4–7. The intentional suppressions within the prose comments remain prominent whether they form single Barbian chapters or Gornian *commi* within a longer narrative unit.

5. Contini, *Idea di Dante*, 3. See also Barolini, "*Cominciandomi dal principio*" [2006]; Gragnolati, "(In-)Corporeality," 214–18.

6. Rea, "Amore e ragione," 171–73; McLain, "Screening the Past"; Pirovano, "Nota introduttiva," 8, 10–11, 23.

7. On the *Vita nova*'s complex double temporality, see Barolini, "*Cominciandomi dal principio*" [2006]; Giusti, "Recitation."

8. See especially, in this volume, Jennifer Rushworth on chapter VII [2.12–18], and Emily Kate Price on chapter XII [5.8–24].

9. For an extended study of number symbolism in Dante, including detailed reflections on the *serventese*'s numerology and potential relationship to other Dantean and stilnovist lyrics, see Gorni, *Lettera nome numero*, 76–81; also Carrai, *Dante elegiaco*, 46–49.

10. Gosselin, "Shape of Things," 12; Martinez, "Mourning Beatrice," 28–29; Nasti, "Nozze e vedovanza," 72–73, 87.

11. Gorni, "Saggio di lettura," 247; Barolini, "*Cominciandomi dal principio*" [2006], 184–85.

12. Martinez, "Mourning Beatrice."

13. Rea, "Amore e ragione"; Borsa, "Immagine e immaginazione," 156–57.

14. In the first two *commi*, we find the terms *vedea, aspetto, s'accorsero, vedi, mirava, sguardare, mirare, gli occhi miei* [saw, appearance, noticed, see, looked,

gaze, look, my eyes]. See also Akbari, *Seeing through the Veil*, 116–19; Borsa, "Immagine e immaginazione," 141–43.

15. Gosselin, "Shape of Things," 14. See also Mainini, "Schermi e specchi," 160–69; McLain, "Screening the Past," 6–7.

16. Mainini, "Schermi e specchi," 160. Beatrice is placed beside the Virgin after death at its first announcement, with the Jeremian quotation, in XXVIII.1 [19.1] and in the "primo cominciamento" [first beginning] to "Era venuta ne la mente mia" (XXXIV.7 [23.7]) [She had just come into my memory]. In the book's last sonnet, the poet's vital spirit follows an upward path of contemplation, "Oltre la spera che più larga gira" (XLI.10 [30.10]) [Beyond the sphere that turns the widest gyre], into the heavenly space, where it gazes on Beatrice (*vede, mira*). See also Carrai, *Dante elegiaco*, 70–73; Barański, "Roots of Dante's Plurilingualism," 114; Stillinger, *Song of Troilus*, 56–57.

17. McClain, "Screening the Past," 7. Ascoli's notion of the "divided Dante" is foregrounded strongly in the screen woman episodes (*Dante and the Making*, 178–201, 218–26).

18. Many of the lyrics in fact seek to address destinatees, whether fellow-poets or the women who become the book's principal inscribed poetic audience, but these are the only two mentions of—absent—epistolary compositions. See Ascoli, *Dante and the Making*, 186–89; Pirovano, "Nota introduttiva," 25–26; Todorović, *Dante and the Dynamics*, 94–95, 160–62.

19. See *Vita nuova*, Pirovano ed., *ad loc.*; also Barański, "Roots of Dante's Plurlingualism," 111–15; Martinez, "Mourning Beatrice," 28–29.

20. Gosselin, "Shape of Things."

21. The apparatus to *Vita Nova*, Gorni ed. [2011], and *Vita nuova*, Pirovano ed. (*ad loc.*), provide examples of onomastic courtly *serventesi*, both from the troubadour and trouvère traditions prior to Dante and in Antonio Pucci's slightly later Florentine "Leggiadro sirmentese," listing twenty-eight women's names.

22. Gorni, *Lettera nome numero*, 28–31; Gragnolati, "(In-)Corporeality," 218.

23. I'd like to thank Jennifer Rushworth for helping with this insight, in a comment at the University College London seminar where I presented an earlier version of this paper.

24. Ascoli, *Dante and the Making*; Barolini, "*Cominciandomi dal principio*" [2006].

25. As well as vision, oral and aural sense perception is underscored in chapter V by a lexis of sound: "s'udiano parole de la regina de la gloria" [words about the Queen of Glory were being listened to]; "mi sentio dire" [I heard people saying];

"nominandola" [hearing her name]; "dicea di colei" [they were talking about the woman]; "persone che di me ragionavano" [people who talked about me].

Vita nova VII [2.12–2.18]

A first version of this essay was delivered at the *Vita nova* day in University College London on November 10, 2017. I would like to express my thanks to all those present at that day who responded to my presentation, with particular thanks to Catherine Keen for the invitation to speak and, subsequently, to participate in this volume.

1. Bier, *"Perhaps There Is Hope,"* although the thesis of multiple authors is treated skeptically by Dobbs-Allsopp, *Lamentations*, 5.

2. Joyce, "Lamentations"; Dobbs-Allsopp, *Lamentations*, 4.

3. Grossberg, "Lamentations," 1589.

4. Joyce and Lipton, *Lamentations through the Centuries*, 27.

5. Cohen, "Destruction," 20, also cited in Grossberg, "Lamentations," 1587.

6. Barbour, *Story of Israel*, 139.

7. Martinez, "Mourning Beatrice," "Lament and Lamentations," and "Dante between Hope and Despair." See also, most recently, Kempshall, "Dante's Lamentations."

8. *Rime giovanili*, Barolini ed., 106; *Dante's Lyric Poetry*, Barolini ed., 72.

9. Rushworth, *Discourses of Mourning*, 119.

10. Martinez, "Mourning Beatrice," 16.

11. Holmes, *Assembling the Lyric Self*, 129.

12. Auerbach, "Figura."

13. Citing from William Whitaker's Words, http://archives.nd.edu/words .html.

14. De Robertis, *Libro della "Vita Nuova,"* 56.

15. Gragnolati, "Without Hierarchy."

Vita nova VIII [3]

1. Valency, *In Praise of Love*, 267.

2. Santagata, *Amate e amanti*, 96.

3. Ibid., 69.

4. Gorni, "*Vita Nova* dalla Donna Gentile," 13.

5. Kleiner, "Finding the Center," 89.

6. *Vita nuova*, Pirovano ed., 106.

7. *Dante's Lyric Poetry*, Barolini ed., 76.

8. Pazzaglia, "Piangete, amanti," 477.

9. Carrai, *Dante elegiaco*, 22–23.

10. *Dante's Lyric Poetry*, Foster and Boyde ed., 42.

11. *Vita nuova*, Pirovano ed., 108.

12. *Dante's Lyric Poetry*, Barolini ed., 75.

13. *Rime*, Grimaldi ed., 361.

14. *Vita Nova*, Gorni ed. [2011], 838.

15. Picone, "Cino nella *Vita Nova*," 110.

16. *Dante's Lyric Poetry*, Foster and Boyde ed., 45.

17. Pazzaglia, "Morte villana, di pietà nemica," 3:1042; *Vita nuova*, Pirovano ed., 110; *Rime*, Grimaldi ed., 363–64; *Vita Nova*, Gorni ed. [2011], 841.

18. *Vita Nuova*, De Robertis ed. [1980], 60.

19. Ibid., 58–59.

20. Curtius, *European Literature*, 195–200.

21. Pertile, "Works," 481.

Vita nova IX [4]

1. On the time lag between the *Vita nova*'s lyric poems and their explanatory prose, and the opportunity this gives Dante to both edit and interpret his poetry, see McLain, "Screening the Past," 1–2.

2. On Dante's claim to *auctoritas* more broadly, see Ascoli, *Dante and the Making*, passim.

3. On the fiction of the screen ladies, their disguising of Dante's love for other women and illustration of "who and what Beatrice is," see McLain, "Screening the Past."

4. On the *Vita nova* as "a series of separations and losses," see Martinez, "Mourning Beatrice," 16.

5. *Dante's Lyric Poetry*, Barolini ed., 134–35.

6. Notes in *Vita Nova*, Gorni ed. [2011], 848.

7. Ibid., 849. The question of Dante's authorship of the *Fiore* is rehearsed, with full recent bibliography, in Allegretti, "Autore."

8. Notes in *Vita Nova*, Gorni ed. [2011], 845.

9. Cavalcanti, *Rime* 46, De Robertis ed.

10. On the tradition of the *pastorelle* (pastourelles) in general, see W. Jones, *Pastourelle*.

11. On the fiction of the screen ladies, their disguising of Dante's love for other women and illustration of "who and what Beatrice is," see McLain, "Screening the Past."

12. On Ovid's *amor*/Amor in the *Amores* and *Ars amatoria*, see A. Park, "Two Types."

13. Notes in *Vita Nova*, Gorni ed. [2011], 849.

14. On the series of separations and losses in the *Vita nova* and Beatrice's death, see Martinez, "Mourning Beatrice."

15. Cavalcanti, *Rime* 35, De Robertis ed.

16. *Dante's Lyric Poetry*, Barolini ed., 136.

17. *Ars amatoria* 1.9–10. On the tension in Ovid's presentation of Amor in *Ars amatoria*, see A. Park, "Two Types," 231.

18. On the futility of the notion that Amor can be controlled in Ovid, see A. Park, "Two Types," 237.

19. Notes in *Vita Nova*, Gorni ed. [2011], 847.

20. Ibid., 849.

21. *Dante's Lyric Poetry*, Barolini ed., 134.

22. On Dante's use of the *Vita nova* to unmask these "courtly imports," see *Dante's Lyric Poetry*, Barolini ed., especially 136.

23. On Dante's telling of "a story full of contradiction and confusion . . . that almost begs us to doubt its veracity" and his undermining in this part of the *Vita nova* of the fiction of the screen lady, see McLain, "Screening the Past."

24. Borsa, "Identità sociale," 23.

25. On *Vita nova* IX and its narrative of "failed or false conversion," see McLain, "Screening the Past," 14.

26. Notes in *Vita Nova*, Gorni ed. [2011], 848.

27. On the *Vita nova* as a *quête* like those of Chrétien de Troyes, see Picone, "Presenze romanzesche," 2.

Vita nova X and XI [5.1–5.7]

1. For an overview of the genesis of the *Vita nova*, its models, and its intrinsic novelty compared to the thirteenth-century literary scene, see Pirovano, "Nota introduttiva," 3–36; on the key role that the exegetical tradition of the Song of Songs played on the structural, thematic, and narrative levels of the *Vita nova*, see Nasti, *Favole d'amore*, 53–85; on the *Vita nova* as an elegy, and on its

formal and stylistic relation to Boethius's *De consolatione philosophiae*, see Carrai, *Dante elegiaco*; on the *Vita nova* and Brunetto's *Tesoretto*, see Lombardo, "'Ed imaginava lei," 42–51, 55–59; on the relation of the prose sections of the *Vita nova* to vernacular texts in prose conceived in late Duecento Florence, see Lombardo, "Primi appunti"; on the reactions of the first readers of the *Vita nova*, especially on the *tenzone* between Bernardo da Bologna, Onesto da Bologna, and Cino da Pistoia, see Azzetta, "Fece molte canzoni," 59–63.

2. On the poetic, ideological, and political contrasts between Guinizzelli and Guittone d'Arezzo, and on the *tenzone* between Guinizzelli and Bonagiunta Orbicciani, see Steinberg, *Accounting for Dante*, 36–46; Borsa, *Nuova poesia*, 13–145; Pirovano, *Dolce stil novo*, 105–11. English translations of Guinizzelli's poems are from *Poetry of Guido Guinizelli*, Edwards ed. and trans.

3. See Pirovano, *Dolce stil novo*, 111–28; 268–80; Borsa, *Nuova poesia*, 161–80; on the interactions between Occitan love poetry and mystical writings, and on the role of this early dialogue in relation to Dante's own reception of religious mysticism, see Mocan, "'Intelletto d'amore,'" 89–94; on the female figure in the *stilnovisti*, and on her biblical and liturgical attributes, see Pirovano, "'Chi è questa che vèn?,'" 95–106.

4. On Cavalcanti's use of the Bible, see Nasti, "Nozze e vedovanza."

5. See Ardissino, "*Vita nova*"; Brugnolo, "Conservare per trasformare"; Borsa, "Immagine nel cuore." On the complex, polemical relationship between Dante and Guido Cavalcanti, as well as on Cavalcanti's poetic reactions to the *Vita nova*, see at least Malato, *Dante e Guido Cavalcanti*, 11–73. For a different perspective, see Rea, "*Vita nuova* e le *Rime*"; Rea, "Cavalcanti nella *Vita nuova*."

6. On the profound affinity between Dante's theory of love and the theology of *intellectus amoris* as especially present in William of St. Thierry's, Richard of St. Victor's, and Bernard of Clairvaux's writings, see Mocan, "'Intelletto d'amore.'"

7. Rea, "Amore e ragione," 166. Rea goes on to associate Dante's conception of rational love to writings belonging to the current of Cistercian mysticism, especially William of St. Thierry's *Tractatus de natura et dignitate Amoris* and Bernard of Clairvaux's *Sermones in Cantica Canticorum* (168–69).

8. On Dante's conquest of a self-sufficient form of love, see Rea, "'Ego tanquam centrum circuli.'"

9. See Picone, "Beatrice personaggio," 125–28.

10. On the theme of concealment, see Keen in this volume.

11. On the influence of Christian mysticism on this passage, see Ledda, "Ineffabilità nella *Vita nova*," 92–94.

12. Commentary to *Vita nuova*, Pirovano ed., 122–23.

13. See Santagata, "Saluto di Beatrice." As Santagata notes, moreover, the motif of the *saluto* appears in other Duecento poets, but without taking on the profound meaning that Dante gives to it in the *Vita nova*. For instance, on the salvific power of the beloved, and especially of her greeting, see Guinizzelli's sonnet "Io voglio del ver la mia donna laudare" [I want to praise my lady truly]; instead, in his "Lo vostro bel saluto e 'l gentil sguardo" [Your lovely greeting and the gentle gaze] *madonna*'s greeting "ancide" [kills] the poet.

14. On Dante's inclusion and framing of "Donne ch'avete" in the *Vita nova* as a response to its early reception, e.g., the *canzone* "Ben aggia" [Blessed be] in the manuscript Vaticano Latino 3793, see Steinberg, *Accounting for Dante*, 61–92.

15. Not by chance, in the sonnet "Bernardo, quel gentil che porta l'arco" [Bernardo, that noble one who carries the bow], Cino da Pistoia compares Dante to Mark the Evangelist. On Beatrice's Christological features, see at least *Vita nova* XXIV [15].

16. See commentary to *Vita nuova*, Pirovano ed., 123.

17. See Pegoretti, "Filosofanti"; on Dante's intellectual formation, see Barański, "Sulla formazione intellettuale"; Barański, "On Dante's Trail"; Dell' Oso, "Per la formazione intellettuale"; and Lombardo, "'Ed imaginava lei.'" See also Barański, Cachey, and Lombardo, *Dante e la cultura fiorentina*, and Dell'Oso, *How Dante Became Dante*; I am very grateful to Lorenzo Dell'Oso, who kindly shared his thesis with me.

18. See commentary to *Vita nuova*, Pirovano ed., 121.

19. On Servasanto's homiletic practices in relation to the theme of friendship and, in particular, to Dante and Beatrice's friendship (*Inf.* 2.61–63), see Maldina, "Classicising Friar."

20. Servasanto da Faenza, *Liber de virtutibus et vitiis* 4.24.8–10, Del Castello ed., *Tradizione*, 195. See also 4.34.1–5, Del Castello ed., *Tradizione*, 219.

21. See Pirovano, commentary to *Vita nuova*, 121–22; English translations of Cavalcanti's poems are from Cavalcanti, *Complete Poems*, Cirigliano trans.

22. See commentary to *Vita nuova*, Pirovano ed., 121–22.

23. See Borsa, "Identità sociale," 21.

24. See "Redundare," in *Enciclopedia dantesca*; commentary to *Vita Nova*, Gorni ed. [2011], 855; commentary to *Vita nuova*, Pirovano ed., 122.

25. Thomas Aquinas, *Super Sent.*, lib. 3, d. 15, q. 2, a. 2, qc. 1 co., Alarcón ed., *Opera omnia S. Thomae*. See also Gaimari, "Letizia di Cristo," 165–81.

26. Thomas Aquinas, *Summa contra gentiles*, lib. 4, c. 86, n. 2, Alarcón ed., *Opera omnia S. Thomae*. On the redundancy of bliss related to the glorification of the bodies at the end of times, see Augustine, *Epistle* 118.3.14 [PL 33], a passage condemning the Epicurean doctrine: "Sanitas autem perfecta corporis, illa ex-

trema totius hominis immortalitas erit. Tam potenti enim natura Deus fecit ani-
mam, ut ex eius plenissima beatitudine quae in fine temporum sanctis promitti-
tur, redundet etiam in inferiorem naturam, quod est corpus, non beatitudo quae
fruentis et intellegentis est propria, sed plenitudo sanitatis, id est incorruptionis
vigor" [The perfect health of the body shall be that final immortality of the whole
individual. For God made the soul with such a powerful nature that from its
full bliss, which is promised to the saints in the end of times, there will overflow
also into the lower part of our nature, the body, not the bliss that is proper to the
part that enjoys and understands, but the plenitude of health, that is, the vigor of
incorruptibility].

27. See Peter Lombard, *Sententiarum libri quatuor*, lib. 3, d. 28; the topic of
dilectio corporis [love of the body] appears in Augustine, *De doctrina christiana*
1.25–27 [PL 34].

28. See Bonaventure of Bagnoregio, *Comm. in quatuor lib. Sent.*, lib. 3,
d. 28, q. 4 (conclusion), in *S. Bonaventuarae opera omnia*, Collegium S. Bonaven-
turae ed. The text proceeds as follows: "Cum caritas sit pondus inclinans ad sum-
mum Bonum et perfectam beatitudinem, omne illud facit diligere, quod est bea-
tum, vel beatificabile . . .Beatum denique per quandam redundantiam est corpus
humanum, in quod gaudium gloriae redundat per coniunctionem sui ad animam
beatam" [Since charity is a force leading to the supreme Good and to perfect bliss,
it makes us love everything that is blessed or may be blessed. . . . The human body
is blessed thanks to a certain redundancy, as the joy of glory overflows into it
because of its union with the blessed soul].

29. See Ledda, "Ineffabilità," 93–94, who stresses that the idea of over-
whelming bliss pertains to the sphere of Christian mysticism.

30. See also Thomas Aquinas, *Super Sent.*, lib. 3, d. 28, q. 1, a. 7 co., *Super
Sent.*, lib. 3, d. 28, q. 1, a. 7, ad 1, and *Super Sent.*, lib. 3, d. 28, q. 1, a. 7, ad 3, all
in *Opera omnia S. Thomae*, Alarcón ed.; *Summa theologiae* II-II, q. 25, a. 12, ad 2,
Ediciones Paulinae ed.: "Subiectum caritatis est mens rationalis quae potest bea-
titudinis esse capax, ad quam corpus directe non attingit, sed solum per quan-
dam redundantiam. Et ideo homo secundum rationalem mentem, quae est prin-
cipalis in homine, alio modo se diligit secundum caritatem, et alio modo corpus
proprium" [The subject of charity is the rational mind that can be capable of
containing bliss, to which the body does not reach directly, but only by a kind
of redundancy. Hence, by his reasonable mind which holds the first place in
him, man, out of charity, loves himself in one way, and his own body in another].

31. On Peter of Trabibus's activity in Santa Croce and for further bibliogra-
phy, see Dell'Oso, *How Dante Became Dante*, 27–37. The teaching and study of
Peter Lombard's *Sentences* were at the center of Santa Croce's didactic activity; see

Pegoretti, "'Nelle scuole delli religiosi,'" 14–15, and Dell'Oso, *How Dante Became Dante*, 25–29, 64–65.

32. I am deeply grateful to Lorenzo Dell'Oso, who generously gave me the transcription of this section of Trabibus's *Lectura* on *Sentences*, book III, distinction XXVIII, present in the MS Florence, Biblioteca Nazionale Centrale, Conv. Soppr. D.6.359. Trabibus likely bases his discussion on Bonaventure's own gloss; see above, note 28.

33. On the impact of Peter of Trabibus's *Quodlibet I* on Dante's *Vita nova*, and especially on Dante's disagreement with some of Trabibus's doctrinal stances, see Dell'Oso, *How Dante Became Dante*.

34. See Borsa, "Identità sociale," 18–20, 27.

35. On Dante's political affiliations and career, especially in 1295–96, see Diacciati, "Dante," and Milani, "Dante politico fiorentino."

36. See Borsa, "Identità sociale," 21.

37. In this view, Dante's dispute with Cavalcanti would occur not only on an ideological level but also in relation to their different social and political identities; see Borsa, "Identità sociale," 21–24, 27–29. Some critics, e.g., Malato, *Dante e Guido Cavalcanti*, suggest that in the sonnet "I' vegno 'l giorno a te 'nfinite volte" [Each day I come to you an infinity of times], Cavalcanti condemns Dante's attendance at Florence religious *studia*. On the strong relationship between literary preferences, social affiliations, and political stances in Duecento Bologna, as testified by the selection of vernacular poetry copied in the *Memoriali bolognesi*, see Steinberg, *Accounting for Dante*, 17–60.

Vita nova XII [5.8–5.24]

1. All English translations are Frisardi's, except where noted otherwise.

2. Eisner, "Dante's *Ballata*," 299.

3. Ibid., 301.

4. Ibid., 311–12.

5. Dante Alighieri, *De vulgari eloquentia* 2.3.5, Botterill ed. I am using Botterill's translation from the same edition.

6. Zumthor, "Text and the Voice," 90.

7. Ibid., 77.

8. Chaganti, *Strange Footing*, 43.

9. Ibid., 283.

10. Ibid., 49.

11. Ibid., 13.

12. Ibid., 21.

13. Ibid., 283.

14. Eisner, "Dante's *Ballata*," 305; Storey, "Early Editorial Forms."

15. Levitsky, "Song Personified," 32.

16. Phan, "Tornada et l'envoi," 57.

17. Peraino, *Giving Voice to Love*, 35.

18. Chaganti, *Strange Footing*, 52.

19. *Vita Nova*, Gorni ed. [2011], 857, note to [5.11]. Translation my own.

20. Translation my own.

21. Translation my own.

22. Zumthor, "Text," 77.

23. Chaganti, *Strange Footing*, 13.

24. Cavarero, *For More Than One Voice*, 12.

25. Connor, *Dumbstruck*, 36.

Vita nova XIII–XVIII [6–10.11]: Not Just a Passing Phase

1. Tonelli, *Fisiologia della passione*, 82–86. See also Tonelli, "Medicine."

2. See Mariani, "Trasfiguramento" and "Trasfigurazione."

3. *Vita nova*, Frisardi's translation amended.

4. On the concept of the paths not taken in Dante, see Crisafi, "Master Narrative."

5. See Barolini, "*Cominciandomi dal principio*," esp. 178–84.

6. See XVII.1 [10.1]: "Poi che dissi questi tre sonetti, ne li quali parlai a questa donna però che fuoro narratori di tutto quasi lo mio stato, credendomi tacere e non dire più però che mi parea di me assai avere manifestato, avvegna che sempre poi tacesse di dire a lei" [After I wrote these three sonnets in which I addressed this lady directly, since they told almost everything about my state, thinking it best to be silent and write no more since I felt I had explained enough about myself, although from then on I would refrain from addressing her directly]. For the implied and imagined readership of the *libello*, see Lombardi, *Imagining the Woman Reader*, 60–77.

7. In the case of "Ciò che m'incontra," we cite part of the second line of Frisardi's translation, which corresponds to the Italian incipit.

8. See Gragnolati, "Authorship and Performance."

9. For the undivided poems in this section and elsewhere in the *Vita nova*, see Botterill, "'Però che la divisione,'" 61–76, esp. 74–75. For Dante's search for an active reader in the *libello*, see Amtower, *Engaging Words*, 90–105.

10. Dante will apply the same strategy of "reverse psychology," as we would call it today, to stimulate his readers in the famous "O voi che siete in piccioletta barca" [Oh you who are in the small boat] of *Par.* 2.1–6.

11. See in particular XXXIX.6 [28.6], where Dante expresses the desire to exonerate himself from the faithlessness to Beatrice manifest in the poems addressed to the *donna gentile*: "Onde io, volendo che cotale desiderio malvagio e vana tentazione paresse distrutto, sì che alcuno dubbio non potessero inducere le rimate parole ch'io avea dette innanzi, propuosi di fare uno sonetto ne lo quale io comprendesse la sentenzia di questa ragione" [So that, wanting to ensure that such wicked desire and vain temptation appeared completely wiped out, in order that the poems I had written earlier could not lead to any doubt, I planned to compose a sonnet in which I would include the gist of this prose account].

12. Contini, "Cavalcanti in Dante," 157.

13. Harrison, *Body of Beatrice*, 69. See also F. Sanguineti, "Ombra di Miseno," and Gorni, *Dante*, 85.

14. See Lombardi, *Wings of the Doves* and "Identità lirica"; Southerden, "Lyric Mode"; Gragnolati and Southerden, *Possibilities of Lyric*.

Vita nova XIII [6]

1. Dante, *Dante's Lyric Poetry*, Barolini ed., 143–45.

2. On metaliterary discourse in the *libello*, see Barański, "Lascio cotale trattato."

3. Bruno Nardi was the first to note this correspondence ("Linguaggio," 218–25). For discussion of its significance in Dante's theory of language, see Lombardi, *Syntax of Desire*, 140, and "Pensiero linguistico," 129–30.

4. Corti, *Dante a un nuovo crocevia*, 73.

5. *Purg.* 24.57; see also *Dve* 1.10.4.

6. *Dante's Lyric Poetry*, Barolini ed., 143.

7. *Poeti del Duecento*, Contini ed., 2:460–64.

8. Dante, *Dante's Lyric Poetry*, Foster and Boyde ed., 71–72; Barolini, *Dante's Poets*, 136–39; Gragnolati, "Trasformazioni e assenze," 15–17; Lombardi, *Wings of the Doves*, 129; and Kay, *Dante's Lyric Redemption*, 112–17.

9. The word *cammino* appears only at *Vita nova* IX.4 [4.4]; IX.9 [4.9]; X.1 [5.1]; XII.6 [5.13]; XIII.6 [6.6]; and XIX.1 [10.12]. It does not occur in other forms.

10. Steinberg, *Accounting for Dante*, 61; Lombardi, *Wings of the Doves*, 128–31; Kay, *Dante's Lyric Redemption*, 29–37.

11. Gragnolati, "Trasformazioni e assenze."

12. Gragnolati, "Performance senza gerarchia."

13. Rea, *Cavalcanti poeta*, 393–402; Cropp, *Vocabulaire courtois*, 174–77.

Vita nova XIV [7]

1. Picone, "Modelli e struttura," 74; *Vita Nova,* Rossi ed., 62; *Vita nuova,* Pirovano ed., 139.

2. Pirovano calls it a "panic attack"; *Vita nuova,* Pirovano ed., 138. Bartoli, "Traccia scientifica," 18, speaks of "syncope" and refers to the medical theories of Galen.

3. Translations from the *Vita nova* are taken from *Vita nova,* Frisardi ed.

4. *Vita nuova,* Pirovano ed., 142.

5. *Vita Nova,* Gorni ed. [1996], 254. Sbacchi, "Sull'episodio del gabbo," discusses the *gabbo* in the Oitanic tradition.

6. *Vita nuova,* Pirovano ed., 142.

7. Picone, "Modelli e struttura," 74.

8. See, most recently, Rea, "Cavalcanti nella *Vita nuova.*"

9. See, famously, Singleton, *Essay on the "Vita Nuova."*

10. *Vita Nova,* Gorni ed. [1996], 254, translation mine.

11. *Vita nova,* Frisardi ed., 164.

12. Barolini, "'Cominciandomi dal principio,'" 134.

13. *Vita Nuova,* De Robertis ed. [1984], 90; *Vita Nova,* Gorni ed. [1996], 79; *Vita nuova,* Pirovano ed., 142–43.

14. *Dante's Lyric Poetry,* Barolini ed., 144, stretches the beginning of the sequence as far back as the punning sonnet "Cavalcando l'altr' ier" (IX [4]) [Riding the other day].

15. *Vita nuova,* Pirovano ed., 140.

16. The terms absent in Cavalcanti are *gabbare, baldanza, securtate,* and *pingere.*

17. See, for instance, Cavalcanti, *Rime* 7.2 and 9.11.

18. See, for instance, Cavalcanti, *Rime* 13.13–14.

19. S. Gilson, "Visual Theory," 248. Translations are taken from *Poetry of Guido Cavalcanti,* trans. Nelson.

20. *Dante's Lyric Poetry,* Barolini ed., 154.

21. Lombardi, *Imagining the Woman Reader,* 65.

22. The connotation of *dire* as "writing poetry" is "more frequent in the *Vita nova* than in the *Convivio,* and absent in the *Commedia*" (Ambrosini, "Dire"). See also Lombardi, *Imagining the Woman Reader,* 39.

23. Lombardi, *Imagining the Woman Reader,* 95.

24. Ibid., 61.

25. Ibid., 70. On the performative relationship between prose and poetry, see Gragnolati, "Authorship and Performance": "The *libello* does not discover or describe the true meaning of the poems originally written as free-standing *rime*, but rather creates new poems which did not exist before and now exist alongside the originals" (129).

26. Holmes, *Assembling the Lyric Self*, 133.

27. Lombardi, *Imagining the Woman Reader*, 65.

28. *Dante's Lyric Poetry*, Barolini ed., 146.

29. Ibid., 146.

30. *Vita Nuova*, De Robertis ed. [1984], 94, translation mine. See also *Vita Nova*, Rossi ed., 62.

31. See Botterill, "Però che la divisione," 75.

32. Ibid., 73, on XIX.22 [10.33]. See also Steinberg, "Dante's First Dream," 112–13.

33. *Dante's Lyric Poetry*, Barolini ed., 154.

34. Ibid., 147.

35. Ibid.

36. On the significance of the adjective *nova*, see most recently Gragnolati and Lombardi, "Autobiografia d'autore," 146.

Vita nova XV [8]

1. *Vita nova* XVII.1 [10.1]: "Poi che dissi questi tre sonetti, ne li quali parlai a questa donna però che fuoro narratori di tutto quasi lo mio stato" [After I wrote these three sonnets in which I addressed this lady directly, since they told almost everything about my state]. While "Ballata, i' voi che tu ritrovi Amore" (XII [5.8–24]) [Ballad, I wish you'd find where Love has gone] might also plausibly be included in the group of *Vita nova* poems addressed to Beatrice, it is important to make a distinction between the narrative conceit of the text (i.e., that the *ballata* should present itself before the poet's lady) and the actual second-person addressee (the imagined *ballata* itself). All English translations of the *Vita nova* are taken from Frisardi's translation. All other translations are my own.

2. Moleta, "*Vita Nuova* as a Lyric Narrative," 378: "It is clear that by the early 1290s Dante saw himself as having passed through first a Guittonian and then a Cavalcantian phase before forging his own 'new style.' And the sequence of poems in the early chapters of the *VN* is a faithful witness to this development

of theme and style." While Moleta places the start of the Cavalcantian phase at chapter XII [5.8–5.24], many critics see the *Vita nova*'s Cavalcantian phase as beginning with the sonnet "Cavalcando l'altr'ier per un cammino" [Riding along a road the other day] in chapter IX [4]; see, for example, Barolini, *Dante's Poets*, 136–37; Gragnolati, "Trasformazioni e assenze," 79–80.

   3. Barolini, "Dante and the Lyric Past," 22. On the influence of Averroist philosophy on Cavalcanti, and on "Donna me prega" in particular, see Inglese, *L'intelletto e l'amore*, 3–55; on the influence of medical texts, see Tonelli, *Fisiologia della passione*, 3–70.

   4. *Rime*, De Robertis ed. [2005], 359.

   5. Cavalcanti, *Rime*, Rea and Inglese ed., 90.

   6. Although see also Dante's description in chapter III [1.12–2.2] of being "come inebriato" [as if . . . drunk] after first receiving Beatrice's greeting.

   7. *Vita Nuova*, Colombo ed., 88.

   8. Iacopone da Todi, *Laude*, Leonardi ed., 191.

   9. Dante, *Rime giovanili*, Barolini ed., with notes by Gragnolati, 245.

   10. New Revised Standard Version. As Gragnolati has noted, Dante's change from "par che dican" to "par che gridin" in the *Vita nova* version of the sonnet renders the possible reference to Luke 19:40 more explicit; see Dante, *Rime giovanili*, Barolini ed., 249n.

   11. See, chiefly, Singleton, *Essay on the "Vita Nuova,"* 6–24; Martinez, "Mourning Beatrice."

   12. Dante, *Rime giovanili*, Barolini ed., 242.

Vita nova XVI [9]

   1. In the *Vita nova* the boundary between homage to and accusation of Guido Cavalcanti is blurred, but in this chapter, especially if read in the light of the subsequent ones, tribute becomes an instrument for radical criticism. For a recent reading of Cavalcanti's presence in the *Vita nova* from a different perspective, see Rea, "Cavalcanti nella 'Vita nuova.'"

   2. I cite, for the poetry, Richard Lansing's translation and, for the commentary, Andrew Frisardi's; both are found in Dante, *Dante's Lyric Poetry*, Barolini ed.

   3. On medieval theories of memory, see Carruthers, *Book of Memory.*

   4. Cavalcanti, *Rime*, Rea and Inglese ed., 72–75.

   5. De Libera, *Volonté et l'action*, 220. My translation.

   6. Moleta, *Early Poetry of Guittone d'Arezzo*, 27.

7. On the concept of performance in the *Vita nova*, see Gragnolati, "Trasformazioni e assenze" and "Without Hierarchy."

8. Holton, "How Is Strength of Will Possible?," 39: "Weak-willed agents . . . are those who intentionally do other than that which they judge to be best." On this topic, see also Saarinen, *Weakness of the Will.*

9. "From him alone mercy proceedeth"; I borrow the poetic translation from Pound, *Cantos,* 179.

10. Augustine, *Selected Writings,* 176. The original extended Latin quotation reads: "Ergo nullo modo dubitamus, si beatus esse statuit, id eum sibi comparare debere quod semper manet, nec ulla saeviente fortuna eripi potest." As far as I know, this passage has never been considered a direct possible source of the dialogue in *Vita nova* XVIII.

11. Barolini, "'*Cominciandomi dal principio*'" [2006].

12. Benjamin, "On the Concept of History," 395.

13. Ibid.

14. Aquinas, *Commentaries on Aristotle's "On Memory and Recollection,"* 230. On melancholic temperament and recollecting, see Aristotle, *De memoria* 453a14–20.

15. "Marx says that revolutions are the locomotive of world history. But perhaps it is quite otherwise. Perhaps revolutions are an attempt by the passengers on this train—namely, the human race—to activate the emergency brake." Benjamin, "On the Concept of History," 402.

16. The *canzone* "Amor, da che convien pur ch'io mi doglia" [Love, since after all I am forced to grieve], composed after the exile, shows, among other texts, the persistent fruitfulness of this alternative lyric subjectivity.

17. Joyce, *Portrait of the Artist,* 148.

Vita nova XVII and XVIII [10.1–10.11]

1. Genette, *Paratexts,* 1–3. See also Cooper, "What Is a Medieval Paratext?," 37–50.

2. See, for example, Biblioteca Apostolica Vaticana, MS Chigiano L VIII 305, or Florence, Biblioteca Nazionale Centrale, MS Magliabechiano VI 143.

3. Toledo, Archivo y Biblioteca Capitulares, MS Zelada 104.6 and Vatican, Biblioteca Apostolica Vaticana, MS Chigiano L.V.176.

4. Keen, "New Lives."

5. See, for example, Botterill, "Però che la divisione," 61–76.

6. See Webb, *Medieval Heart.*

7. Tonelli, "Medicine," 227–41.

8. Lombardi, *Imagining the Woman Reader*.

9. For more extensive treatments of the *tenzone* and its uses in Duecento verse, see Coggeshall, "Jousting with Verse," 99–118; Bowe, *Poetry in Dialogue*, especially 3–9; Giunta, *Due saggi sulla tenzone* and *Versi ad un destinatario*; Gorni, "Forme primarie," 439–518.

10. For texts and bibliography, see *Troubadour Tensos and Partimens*, Harvey et al. ed.

11. Steinberg, "Brunetto Latini," 745–46. See also Keen, "Florentine Tullio," 1–16.

12. I wish to acknowledge my gratitude to Dott. Ambrogio Piazzoni of the Biblioteca Apostolica Vaticana for arranging for me to consult MS Vat. Lat. 3793 in 2013. The MS is available in the facsimile series edited by Leonardi and online at https://digi.vatlib.it/mss/detail/Vat.lat.3793, fols. 141–59.

13. On Occitan exchanges in Italian manuscripts, see Travers, "Women in Medieval Italian Songbooks." On texts in Italian vernaculars, see Giunta, *Versi ad un destinatario*, 255–66; Steinberg, *Accounting for Dante*, 66–73, and "Compiuta Donzella," 1–31. Indicative texts include the *contrasto* "Rosa Fresca Aulentissima" [Fresh and most fragrant rose], attributed to Cielo d'Alcamo and Cecco Angiolieri's dialogue sonnets with Becchina.

14. Giunta, *Versi ad un destinatario*, 255–66; Steinberg, *Accounting for Dante*, 66–73, and "La Compiuta Donzella," 1–31.

15. Biblioteca Laurenziana, Florence, MS Laur Red 9 contains long sections preserving Guittone's letters and poetry. His verse is divided along the lines of his biography and its subject matter. His "preconversion" verse is attributed to "Guittone d'Arezzo" and is largely concerned with the erotic themes, though it includes *canzoni* on the contemporary politics of the Guelph-Ghibelline conflicts in Tuscany. The "postconversion" poetry is attributed to "Frate Guittone d'Arezzo," reflecting his entry into a lay brotherhood, the Ordo Militiae Beatae Virginis Mariae, commonly known as the Frati Gaudenti, and is engaged exclusively with moral and religious themes, preaching and praise. The exchanges with the lady comprise sonnets 37–49 and 81–86.

16. Guittone, *Canzoniere*, 243.

17. Ibid., 258.

18. Ibid., 257–59.

Vita nova XIX–XXIV [10.12–15.11]: A New and More Noble Theme

1. Donato Pirovano describes this episode as an "existential and poetic turning-point" (*Vita nuova*, Pirovano ed., 11). On aspects of "Donne ch'avete,"

the "matera nuova," and their response to the Cavalcantian *gabbo* chapters, see Barolini, *Dante's Poets*, 40–57 and 136–39; De Robertis, *Libro della "Vita Nuova,"* 71–156; Durling and Martinez, *Time and the Crystal*, 53–70; Harrison, *Body of Beatrice*, 31–46; Kay, *Dante's Lyric Redemption*, 112–17; Lombardi, *Wings of the Doves*, 128–29; Singleton, *Essay on the "Vita Nuova,"* 78–109; Steinberg, *Accounting for Dante*, 61–94 (focusing on the transmission of "Donne ch'avete"). The commentaries on the *Vita nova* and its lyrics by Barolini (*Rime giovanili / Dante's Lyric Poetry*), Foster and Boyde (*Dante's Lyric Poetry*), Gorni (*Vita Nova* [1996/ 2011]), Grimaldi (*Rime*), and Pirovano (*Vita nuova*) have all informed my understanding of this sequence of chapters.

2. On Dante's self-definition in *Purgatorio* 24, see, for example, Hollander, "Dante's 'Dolce Stil Novo'"; Kay, *Dante's Lyric Redemption*, 89–90; Martinez, "Pilgrim's Answer"; Mazzotta, *Poet of the Desert*, 204–10; Marchesi, *Dante and Augustine*, 144–53; Moevs, *Metaphysics*, 88–89; Pertile, "Penne e il volo," 124–25.

3. See Mazzotta, "Language of Poetry," 7: "The river, in a sense, explicates the process of creation, the easy flow from a source, a movement that transcends itself, and that is always the same by being always different."

4. See *Vita nuova*, Pirovano ed., 158.

5. See, for example, Gragnolati, "Trasformazioni e assenze."

6. *Dante's Lyric Poetry*, Barolini ed., 178.

7. See Kay, *Dante's Lyric Redemption*, 98–127.

8. On Dante's ideological opposition to Cavalcanti in the *Vita nova*, see, for example, Durling, "Guido Cavalcanti"; Gragnolati, "Trasformazioni e assenze"; Harrison, *Body of Beatrice*, 69–90. The question of whether Guido's "Donna me prega" pre- or postdates the *Vita nova* is a matter of debate. For two opposing views, see Malato, *Dante e Guido Cavalcanti*, and Marti, "Da 'Donna me prega.'" *Dante's Lyric Poetry*, Barolini ed., 179, notes that while the two poems share formal similarities, there is a notable tonal difference between the two *canzoni*, contrasting Dante's "warm, impassioned exuberance" here with Cavalcanti's "cold and rigorous logic."

9. On Guinizzelli in Dante, see, for example, Bowe, *Poetry in Dialogue*, 119–37; Cappello, "*Vita nova* tra Guinizzelli"; Carrai, "Presenza dei due Guidi"; Martinez, "Guinizzellian Protocols"; Moleta, *Guinizzelli in Dante*.

10. On the *tenzone*, see, for example, Borsa, "Foll'è chi crede"; Rea, "Avete fatto."

11. Cited from *Poeti del Duecento*, Contini ed., 2:481.

12. See Giunta, *Poesia italiana*.

13. See *Vita nuova*, Pirovano ed., 18–19.

14. Both the Italian and the translation are taken from *Poetry of Guido Guinizelli*, Edwards ed., 40–41.

15. "Passa per via adorna e sì gentile / ch'abassa orgoglio a cui dona salute, / e fa 'l di nostra fé se non la crede; / e non le pò apressare om che sia vile; / ancor ve dirò c'ha maggior vertute: / null'om pò mal pensar fin che la vede" [She passes through the streets so elegant and noble that she humbles pride in anyone she greets and converts all unbelievers to our faith. No base-thinking man can approach her, yet I'll tell you she has a power greater still: no man can ever think evil after he sees her].

16. "Dico, qual vuol gentil donna parere / vada con lei, ché quando va per via. / gitta nei cor villani Amore un gelo,/ per che onne lor pensero agghiaccia e père; / e qual soffrisse di starla a vedere / diverria nobil o si morria. . . . Ancor l'ha Dio per maggior grazia dato / che non pò mal fini chi l'ha parlato" [To look more noble all you have to do is be with her, in public by her side, while Love casts into vulgar hearts an ice that makes their thoughts drop dead from shocking cold. As for the one who manages to hold his gaze: he's either killed or dignified. . . . And God has granted her another grace: who talks to her can't finish in disgrace] ("Donne ch'avete," lines 31–36 and 41–42).

17. Cited from Cavalcanti, *Rime*, De Robertis ed.

18. For recent work on the relationship between Cavalcanti and Guinizzelli, see the eight essays compiled in *Chroniques italiennes* 32 (2017): 1–174, under the rubric "Les deux Guidi (Guinizzelli et Cavalcanti): Quelques prolongements"; also Grimaldi, "Sacro e profano."

19. Harrison, *Body of Beatrice*, 73.

20. *Vita Nuova*, De Robertis ed. [1984], 138–39, argues that some key terms from the Cavalcantian *gabbo* chapters (*tremar, smore, sospira*) are pointedly given a new meaning here in the context of a wholly different kind of love.

21. *Dante's Lyric Poetry*, Barolini ed., 184.

22. Gragnolati, "Authorship and Performance," 139.

23. *Dante's Lyric Poetry*, Barolini ed., 194–97, stresses the sociological interest of Dante's description of Florentine mourning customs here.

24. For chapter XXIII [14] and "Donna pietosa" as "gothic" in tone, see *Dante's Lyric Poetry*, Barolini ed., 206.

25. See Carrai, *Dante elegiaco*.

26. *Vita nuova*, Pirovano ed., 190. Pirovano argues that Dante's phrase "tanta miseria" (XXIII.3 [14.3]) [such great misery] evokes the twelfth-century *De contemptu mundi sive de miseria humanae conditionis*, by Lotario dei Conti di Segni (later Innocent III).

27. In his commentary on the Pseudo-Dionysius (c.xi, 1.1, 888), Pera ed., Aquinas states the sole "source of peace" (*principium pacis*) is God.

28. Lombardi, *Wings of the Doves*, 129.

29. See Barański, "Roots of Dante's Plurilingualism." See Lombardo, "Primi appunti," on the *libello* in the context of thirteenth-century prose writing.

30. For instance, Pirovano's recent commentary to *Vita nuova*, 157–207 passim, offers a richly documented account of Dante's biblical engagement in these chapters. On the model of the glossed medieval Psalter in the *Vita nova*, see Stillinger, *Song of Troilus*, 65–72.

31. Dante's act of joyfully storing the *canzone*'s *incipit* in his mind brings to mind several biblical *loci*. See *Vita Nova*, Gorni ed. [1996], 92.

32. See De Robertis, *Libro della "Vita Nuova,"* 154.

33. Tonelli, *Fisiologia della passione*, 125–34.

34. See Robiglio, "Dante e le *Auctoritates Aristotelis.*"

Vita nova XIX [10.12–10.33]

1. On the influence of scholastic commentaries on Dante's divisions, see Pio Raina, "Per le 'divisioni,'" 111–14; Rivers, "Dante at Dividing Sonnets," 290–95; Sandkühler, Frühen *Dantekommentare*, 41–42, and 50–53; and Cristaldi, "*Vita nuova,*" 5–54. De Robertis, *Libro della "Vita Nuova,"* 208–22, has argued for the influence of Brunetto Latini's *Retorica* on Dante's *divisioni*.

2. Most recently Lombardi, "Invenzione del lettore," 24.

3. Durling and Martinez, *Time and the Crystal*, 53–71 (56). For the thesis that Dante was writing for a select group of poets, see, among others, *Rime giovanili*, Barolini ed., 301–13, and *Vita nuova*, Pirovano ed., 170.

4. Lombardi (*Imagining the Woman Reader*, esp. 67–75) has recently argued in favor of the actual reality of the female audience of this *canzone*.

5. For an excellent history of the *divisio textus* in the Middle Ages, see Stillinger, *Song of Troilus*, chapter 3.

6. Steinberg, *Accounting for Dante*, 62. On Dante's reworking of the practice of attributing female gender to vernacular readers, see Ahern, "*New Life of the Book*," 1–16; and Cornish, *Vernacular Translation*, 5.

7. Steinberg, *Accounting for Dante*, 62.

8. The translation is in Musa, *Dante's "Vita Nuova,"* 32.

9. Spitzer, "Bemerkungen," 131–32.

10. As Durling and Martinez (*Time and the Crystal*, 58–59) note, dividing only the second of two members was not customary and would have looked unusual to anyone familiar with exegetical practice.

11. Durling and Martinez, *Time and the Crystal,* 56.

12. For a different interpretation, see Stillinger, *Song of Troilus,* esp. 94.

13. The same faith-based gnoseology is praised by Dante in *Par.* 24.64–65, where he quotes Hebrews 2:1 *ad verbatim*: "fede è sustanza di cose sperate / e argomento de le non parventi" (emphasis added) [faith is the substance of things hoped for and the evidence of the unseen].

14. On this tradition, see Tristan Kay's introduction to this section, 157–69. See also *Rime,* Grimaldi ed., 400–421, esp. 400–403.

15. See *Conv.* 1.9.5.

16. The term *ingegno* is used by Dante here with the sense of a "spontaneous ability," which can be acquired by birth or through experience. See Valente, "Ingegno."

17. Translation is mine and emphasis added.

18. Rivers ("Dividing Sonnets," 292) argues that the *ragioni* explains primarily the material and efficient causes leading up to the sonnet, whereas the *divisioni,* written after the fact, concentrate on formal and final causes, that is, primarily on the author's intention. For Botterill, "'Però che la divisione,'" the divisions provide narrative and contextual background, as well as the poems' paraphrases.

Vita nova XX [11]

I am grateful to Tristan Kay for his helpful comments on an earlier draft of this chapter.

1. The centrality of "Donne ch'avete" has become a critical commonplace in the major commentaries; see, for example, *Vita nuova,* Pirovano ed., 170–74. For further discussion, see at least Durling and Martinez, *Time and the Crystal,* 53–71; Kay, "Redefining the 'Matera Amorosa,'" 392–93, referring to it as the "poetic and ideological centrepiece"; Pirovano, "'Mia lingua . . .'"; Stillinger, *Song of Troilus,* 95–100. On Guinizzelli, see at least Ardizzone, "'Al cor gentil'"; Moleta, *Guinizzelli in Dante;* Sarteschi, "Guinizzelli nella prospettiva dantesca"; and see now the important and richly documented essay by Martinez, "Guinizellian Protocols." More particularly on the relations between Cavalcanti and Guinizzelli, see Barolini, *Dante's Poets,* 123–38; Picone, "I due Guidi." See now the important new study by Bowe, *Poetry in Dialogue.*

2. On *divulgare, Vita Nova,* Gorni ed. [2011], 915, cites Luke 1:65: "Et super omnia montana Iudeae divulgabantur omnia verba haec" [And the whole affair was talked about throughout the hill country of Judaea]; see also Luke 4:37: "Et divulgabatur fama de illo in omnem locum regionis" [And the news of him

traveled all through the surrounding countryside]. On the diffusion of "Donne ch'avete," see Steinberg, *Accounting for Dante*, 61–94.

3. The verb *tractare* has a technical force here. Of course, in patristic and scholastic Latin it is widely used to refer to the act of commentating on a text, above all biblical ones (e.g., Augustine, *Tractatus in Iohannem*). Notable too is the use of *tractare* in a technical sense in Andreas Capellanus's *De amore*; see 1.7.1, 1.7.3, "tractemus amore," and 1.11.1: "amore tractavimus." For other uses of the verb in the *Vita nova*, see "Donne ch'avete": tracterò," line 11; also XXI.1 [12.1].

4. For the "amico" as not being Cavalcanti, see *Vita Nova*, Gorni ed. [2011], 915–16.

5. On the medical tradition, see now the fine study by Tonelli, *Fisiologia della passione*. For Capellanus, see at least Malato, "Amor cortese," but the relationship with the *Vita nova* calls for further study.

6. There is an additional echo here—as is well known—of the opening line of Guinizzelli's "Omo ch'è saggio non corre leggiero" [A wise man does not run lightly [without reflection]].

7. There may be added suggestions from Guinizzelli's "Omo ch'è saggio non corre leggiero" and perhaps also from "Dolente, lasso, già non m'asecuro" [In pain, exhausted, I find no peace] with its reference to the generation of love in the eyes and through the heart at lines 10–13.

8. On the motif of the heart, see Bartoli, "Traccia scientifica e scritturale"; Borsa, "Immagine e immaginazione."

9. These points are echoed in the commentaries on this chapter by De Robertis (*Vita Nuova* [1980/1984], Gorni (*Vita Nova* [1996/2011], and Pirovano (*Vita nuova*), as well as in the accounts in Moleta, *Guinizzelli in Dante*, 39–48; *Dante's Lyric Poetry*, Foster and Boyde ed., 2:104–7; *Rime giovanili*, Barolini ed., 322–25.

10. *Rime giovanili*, Barolini ed., 324.

11. De Robertis, *Libro della "Vita Nuova,"* 139.

12. On such content and the prose, see the discussion and bibliography in Barański, "*Vita nova*"; on the prose, see also Lombardo, "Primi appunti." For a recent study of astronomy, see Chisena, "Astronomia di Dante."

13. For essential methodological background, see Barański, "On Dante's Trail." Among the best recent work with a stress on compendia and disputed questions in the Florentine milieu is Dell'Oso, "How Dante Became Dante," esp. 85–155. See also Robiglio, "Dante e le *Auctoritates Aristotelis*."

14. Averroës, *Compendia* 75–76, Shields ed.: "Dicitur enim quod sompnus est sensus in potentia, id est, rerum existentium. Dormiens enim videt, quasi co-

medat et potet et sentiat, per omnes quinque sensus. Vigilia autem est sensus in actu. Et ex hoc apparet quod sompnus est privatio viglie; quod enim est in potentia est privatio eius quod est in actu" [For it is said that sleep is sensation in potency, that is, pertaining to existing things. The sleeping person sees, and as it were eats and drinks and feels, by means of all five external senses. Thus, from this it appears that sleep is the privation of wakefulness, for what is in potency is a privation of that which is in act]. See also Albert the Great, *De somno* 2.1.1, Borgnet ed., 9:158: "Cuius est potentia, eius est actum," [The subject of potency is the same as that of act] and use of the term *subiectum*; Aquinas, *In Metaphisicorum* 12.8.2537, Cathala and Spiazzi ed., 594: "Delectatio maxime est in vigilia et sensu actuali, et intelligentia. Habent enim se intellectus et sensus in actu ad sensus ad intellectum in potentia, sicut vigilia ad somnum" [Pleasure is mostly fully found in wakefulness and in actual sensation, and intelligence. The relationship between the intellect and sensation in act to the intellect and sensation in potency is like that of wakefulness to sleep].

15. *Auctoritates Aristotelis,"* 201n70, drawing on the opening of the *De somnia et vigilia* (1.454a8): "cuius est potentia, eius est actum" [the subject of potency is the same as that of act]; see also 145n55: "forma dicitur magis natura quam materia" [form is said to be greater by nature than matter]. For "in subiectum," see 246. For this work and Dante, see now Robiglio, "Dante e le *Auctoritates Aristotelis*."

16. Geoffrey of Aspel, *Questiones super de somno et vigilia*, q. 1.1, Ebbesen ed., 269: "An sit verum quod somnum sit privatio vigiliae" [Whether it is true that sleep is the privation of wakefulness]; Geoffrey writes "Dicitur Commentator quod somnus est sensus in potentia et vigilia est sensus in actu; sed per Aristotelem quod est in potentia est privatio eius quod est in actu" [The Commentator (i.e., Averroës) said that sleep is sensation in potency and wakefulness is sensation in act; but for Aristotle what is in potency is the privation of the same thing that is in act]; see note 14.

17. Latini, *Tesoro* 6.8, Chabaille ed., 3:33–34. In a discussion of three kinds of good, moreover, Latini comments on beatitude as a *habitus* rather than a disposition that is in act and refers to the example of the sleeping person; see 6.5, 3:13: "Vedemo già che nelle cose naturali la Potenza va dinanzi all'atto; quando la beatitudine è nell'uomo in abito, e non in atto, allora si è virtuosa, come l'uomo che dorme" [We see manifestly in natural things that potency comes before act; when beatitude is in humans as a habitus and not as an act, then one is virtuous like someone who is sleeping]. Recent criticism has been particularly attentive to the role of Brunetto in the *Vita nova*; see Barański, "On Dante's Trail," 8.

Vita nova XXI [12]

1. Gurevich, "Popular and Scholarly Medieval Cultural Traditions," 74.
2. *Purgatorio*, Hollander ed., 201; Moore, *Studies in Dante*, 47–48.
3. Translations of the *Vita nova* in this paragraph are by Andrew Frisardi. All other translations in this chapter are my own.
4. *Vita nuova*, Pirovano ed., 175 and 177.
5. See *Rime giovanili*, Barolini ed., 334.
6. Bast, *Reformation of Faith*, 134.
7. See *Rime giovanili*, Barolini ed., 330.
8. Webb, *Medieval Heart*, 80.
9. *Rime*, De Robertis ed. [2005], 379; *Dante's Lyric Poetry*, Foster and Boyde ed., 108; Vallone, *Interpretazione della "Vita Nuova,"* 77.
10. *Rime*, De Robertis ed. [2005], 379.
11. Skoda, "Anger in *Inferno*," 125.
12. Ibid.
13. *Rime*, De Robertis ed. [2005], 379.
14. Took, "Dante, Pride," 88.

Vita nova XXII [13]

1. *Vita nuova-Rime*, Chiappelli ed., 47; translations from Italian scholars are my own.
2. See *Vita Nova*, Rossi ed., 106. See also *Vita nuova*, Pirovano ed., 178.
3. See *Vita Nova*, Rossi ed., 106.
4. *Vita nuova*, Pirovano ed., 178.
5. *Vita Nuova*, Colombo ed., 115.
6. Lancia, *Chiose alla "Commedia,"* Azzetta ed., 1:147.
7. Pietro Alighieri, *Comentum,* Alvino ed., 1:203; my translation.
8. See *Vita nuova*, Pirovano ed., 178.
9. See Santagata, *Io e il mondo*, 201. On the Florentine character of the *Vita nova*, see Barański, *"Vita nova,"* 108–13.
10. For further information on Folco's biography, see Zanoboni, "Portinari, Folco." On the social relations between Dante and the Portinari family, see Diacciati, "Dante," 251–53.
11. The three quotations are taken respectively from Boccaccio, *Trattatello (Toledano)*, 15, *Trattatello (Chigiano)*, 113, and *Esposizioni*, 114.

12. Diacciati, "Dante," 244.

13. See ibid., 252–53.

14. Other occurrences of the word *cittade* in the *Vita nova* are VI.2 [2.11] (referring to Beatrice); VII.1 [2.12] (the screen lady); VIII .1 [3.1] (Beatrice's deceased friend); IX.1 [4.1] (Beatrice's deceased friend); XIV.3 [7.3] (the marriage of a gracious lady); XIX. 3 [10.14] (Dante's return to Florence:); XXX.1 [19.8] (Beatrice's death); XLI.1 [30.1] (Beatrice); and XLI.3–4 [30.3–4] (the city grieving for Beatrice).

15. See *Vita nova*, Carrai ed., 102.

16. See *Rime*, Grimaldi ed., 449.

17. See *Vita nuova*, Pirovano ed., 180.

18. See Herczeg, *Saggi linguistici e stilistici*, 15.

19. See *Vita nuova*, Pirovano ed., 179.

20. See *Vita Nuova*, De Robertis ed. [1980], 143.

21. See *Vita nuova*, Pirovano ed., 179.

22. Castellani, *Trattato della dilezione*, 54.

23. Latini, *Tesoro*, ed. Chabaille, 276.

24. On the relationship between *Vita nova* and thirteenth-century Florentine prose, see Lombardo, "Primi appunti."

25. Andrea da Grosseto, *Trattati morali*, 239. See also Castellani, *Trattato della dilezione*, 119.

26. *Reggimento de' principi*, ed. Corazzini, 158.

27. See Giamboni, *Delle storie contra i pagani*, 148. See also Latini, *Tesoro*, ed. Chabaille, 142.

28. See Barański, "*Vita nova*," 89.

29. See Inglese, *Vita di Dante*, 52.

30. *Vita nuova*, Pirovano ed., 178.

31. *Rime*, Grimaldi ed., 445.

32. See ibid.

33. On markers of the elegiac style in the *libello*, see Carrai, *Dante elegiaco*, 22–36.

34. *Corona di casistica amorosa* 26.10, Maffia Scariati ed.

35. *Dante's Lyric Poetry*, Foster and Boyde ed., 119.

36. *Vita nova*, Carrai ed., 104.

37. Carrai, *Dante e il linguaggio*, 482.

38. *Vita Nuova*, De Robertis ed. [1980], 150.

39. *Vita nuova*, Pirovano ed., 183–84.

40. *Vita nova*, Carrai ed., 105. See also Giamboni, *Della miseria dell'uomo*, 3 and 8.

41. The form is standardized by Barbi, *Vita Nuova* [1932], but reinstated by Gorni, *Vita Nova* [1996].

42. See Carrai, *Dante e l'antico*, 12–14.

Vita nova XXIII [14]

1. See Carrai, "Segni premonitori."
2. Bonaventure, *Legenda Maior* 14.6.2.
3. Santagata, *Dante*, 83–84.
4. Bartolini, *Scultura gotica in Toscana*, 30–44.
5. Santagata, *Dante*, 84–85.
6. Angela da Foligno, *Libro dell'esperienza*, Pozzi ed., 108.
7. Schwarz, "Giottos Dante, Dantes Giotto."
8. Ibid.
9. See Borsa, "Immagine e immaginazione."
10. Karnes, *Imagination, Meditation and Cognition*.
11. Löhr, "Dantes Täfelchen."
12. K. Park, "Impressed Images," and Webb, *Medieval Heart*, 170–77.
13. *Petrarch's Lyric Poems*, ed. Durling, 264–67.
14. See C. Frugoni, "Playing with Clouds."

Vita nova XXIV [15]

During a time of general pandemic combined with an intercontinental move, the kindness of friends and colleagues must be acknowledged. Carolyn Muessig, Otfried Lieberknecht, and John Scott are first among equals, but I am grateful to all who helped me in their own way. Needless to say, I am the one responsible for all shortcomings.

1. Meo-Ehlert, *Leggere la "Vita Nuova."*
2. These words, as presented in Barbi's (*Vita Nuova* [1932]) edition, are not present in Sermartelli's (*Vita nuova* [1576]) edition; the rest of part XXIV [25] is on 42–43. Most English translations from the vernacular are based on *Vita nova*, trans. Frisardi (2012), but I have provided my own in places.
3. See, for instance, Russo, "Beatrice *beatitudinis non artifex*."
4. Singleton, *Essay on the "Vita Nuova,"* 79.
5. Boccaccio, *Trattatello in laude di Dante*, 577–78.
6. *Dante's Lyric Poetry*, Foster and Boyde ed., 80.

7. "Et nos cognovimus, et credidimus caritati, quam habet Deus in nobis. Deus caritas est: et qui manet in caritate, in Deo manet, et Deus in eo" [And we have known, and have believed the charity, which God hath to us. God is charity: and he that abideth in charity, abideth in God, and God in him].

8. Picone, *"Vita Nuova" e tradizione romanza*, 69–72.

9. Scott, *Perché Dante?*, 44.

10. See *Vita nova* II.1 [1.2]; V.2 [2.7]; V.4 [2.9]; XII.6 [5.13]; XIV.4 [7.4]; XXII.1 [13.1]; XXII.3 [13.3]; XXIII.3 [14.3]; XXIII.13 [14.13]; XXIII.13 [14.13]; XXI.3 [15.3]; XXIV.4 [15.4]; XXIV.5 [15.5]; XXIV.8 [15.8]; XXVIII.1 [19.1]; XXXIX.1 [28.1]; XXXIX.2 [28.2]; XL.10 [29.10]; XLI.13 [30.13]; and XLII.3 [31.3].

11. For the concept of "textual community" in medieval culture, see Stock, *Implications of Literacy*, 88–240.

12. See Freccero, "Dance of the Stars"; Lieberknecht, *Allegorese und Philologie*, 65–116; and Meyer and Suntrup, *Lexikon der mittelalterlichen Zahlenbedeutungen*, 620–45, 679–84.

13. The most complete survey is the brief *Enciclopedia dantesca* entry for "ridere" (Pasquini, "Ridere," 4:920–21).

14. *Vita nova*, Frisardi trans., 220–21.

15. *Vita nuova*, Cervigni and Vasta trans., 107.

16. Musa, *Dante's Vita Nuova*, 53.

17. *Vita Nuova*, Reynolds trans., 71.

18. P. Jones, "Humility and Humiliation"; Le Goff, "Enquête sur le rire."

19. Thomas Aquinas, *Summa theologiae* 2a2ae, q. 168, art. 4.

20. Julian of Norwich, *Shewings of Julian of Norwich* 1.13 (516–20), ed. Crampton, 56.

21. Meister Eckhart, *Meister Eckhart*, 245.

22. Hawkins, "All Smiles," 53.

Vita nova XXV–XXVII [16–18]: Literature as Truth

1. On the inconsistency and digressive mode of chapter XXV [16], see R. Harrison, *Body of Beatrice*, 62; Musa, "Essay," 108; Pinto, "Allegorismo dantesco," 109.

2. On the representation and conception of love in the Italian vernacular tradition, see Pirovano, *Dolce stil novo*, 158–254; Giunta, "Sullo stilnovo."

3. On the Christological character of the *Vita nova*, see Singleton, *Essay on the "Vita Nuova"*; Cristaldi, *"Vita Nuova,"* 165–203. Observations on the analogy

Beatrice-Christ are found throughout *Vita Nuova*, De Robertis ed. [1980], and *Vita Nova*, Gorni ed. [1996]. Studies that address the scriptural dimension of the *libello* also highlight its Christological elements: Martinez, "Mourning Beatrice"; Nasti, *Favole d'amore*, 43–85.

4. Gorni, *Lettera nome numero*, 73–85.

5. On Beatrice as beatitude, see Gorni, *Dante*, 110–22.

6. On chapter XXV [16], see Barański, "Roots of Dante's Plurilingualism," and "Dante *poeta* e *lector*"; Calenda, "Memoria e autobiografia"; Picone, "Teoria dell'*auctoritas*"; Tateo, "Aprire per prosa."

7. On *Vn* XII, see Singleton, "*Vita Nuova* XII."

8. On prosopopoeia, see Russo, *Saggi di filologia dantesca*, 53–69.

9. Beatrice, as an *analogia entis*, is a "mirror" of divine attributes according to Mazzoni, "'Trascendentale' dimenticato." According to Corti, *Percorsi dell'invenzione*, 58, Beatrice needs to be seen "as a form of knowledge of man as *imago Dei* and of God as a being beyond experience" (my translation).

10. On personification in medieval literature, see Copeland and Melville, "Allegory and Allegoresis," 159–87; Whitman, *Allegory*; Tambling, *Allegory*, 40–61. For general studies on personification, see Gombrich, "Personification," 247–57; Paxson, *Poetics of Personification*.

11. Augustine, *Sermones ad populum* 23.13 (col. 160), PL 38 (my translation).

12. On the complex definition of love as an accident, see Nardi, "Filosofia dell'amore."

13. The idea that the *Vita nova* preceded "Donna me prega" [A lady asks me] is based largely on Malato, *Dante e Guido Cavalcanti*, 22–49. *De vulgari eloquentia*, Tavoni ed., 1508, considers this view "solidly motivated." Challenging the hypothesis, Antonelli, "Cavalcanti o dell'interiorità," 12, believes codicological evidence supports the *Vita nova* having been written after "Donna me prega." Given the lack of reliable evidence, the chronology of Dante's and Cavalcanti's works remains a matter of dispute; see Inglese, "'. . . Illa Guidonis de Florentia,'" 209; Rea, "*Vita nuova.*" On Dante and Cavalcanti's philosophical views, see Falzone, "Dante e l'averroismo." Whether or not Dante wrote his *libello* before "Donna me prega," unlike the elitist Cavalcanti, Dante was keen to present himself as an expert in several fields to a wider audience; see Borsa, "Identità sociale."

14. On Dante's philosophical "identity," see Barański, "'Per similitudine.'"

15. Barański, "Classics," 112. On the notion of *auctoritas*, see also Picone, "Teoria dell'*auctoritas*."

16. Paxon, *Personification*, 21. See also Berisso, "Per una definizione"; Tomazzoli, "Linguaggio figurato di Dante," 15–52.

17. Tomazzoli, "Linguaggio figurato di Dante," 16, has noted Dante's focus on truthfulness in chapter XXV [16].

18. On Dante and rhetoric, particularly noteworthy are Buck, *Studi*; Battistini and Raimondi, *Figure della retorica*.

19. Camargo, "Pedagogy of the *Dictatores*," has argued that the *Poetria nova* was taught as part of grammar teaching at the preprofessional educational level. Manuscript evidence shows that *Poetria nova* was used also to teach *ars dictaminis* in Italy: Woods, "Using the *Poetria nova*."

20. The debate on the use of *progymnasmata* in medieval classrooms is ongoing. Lanham's claims in "Freshman Composition" continue to be challenged. However even a skeptic like Kraus, "Progymnasmata and Progymnasmatic Exercises," 189, concedes: "There can be little doubt that compositional exercises similar in character and complexity to their precursors . . . were widely practiced in the Middle Ages."

21. See Barański, "Dante *poeta* e *lector*."

22. *Vita Nuova*, De Robertis ed. [1980], 36. On Ovid in Dante, see Marcozzi, "Dal poeta dei *Remedia*"; Picone, "'Per Ovidio parla Amore.'" The bibliography on the medieval tradition of love poetry is vast; for assessments of its allegorical dimensions, see Allen, *Art of Love*; Minnis, *Magister Amoris*.

23. Barolini, "Dante and Cavalcanti," 97.

24. These are the false and lying gods decried by Virgil in *Inferno*: "dei falsi e bugiardi" (*Inf.* 1.72).

25. Picone was the first to note "qui non si tratta di abbellimenti esteriori al testo, bensì di manifestare la ricchezza semantica e ideologica interna al testo stesso. Dal piano retorico siamo cioè passati a quello ermeneutico. La 'vesta' serve a coprire una verità che si trova nascosta sotto di essa; verità che può essere fatta affiorare attraverso l'atto del 'denudare' o dello svelare. 'Vesta' corrisponde dunque alla *fictio*, al *sensus litteralis* o *historialis* della scrittura biblica e classica; mentre 'denudare' si riferisce all'operazione che porta al ritrovamento e all'evidenziamento da parte del commentatore del *sensus allegoricus*, della verità custodita dentro la finzione poetica." Picone, "Teoria dell'*auctoritas*," 186.

26. See Bernard Silvester's commentary on the *Aeneid* cited in Minnis, *Magister Amoris*, 15. For a discussion of "integument," see Akbari, *Seeing through the Veil*; Auerbach, "*Figura*."

27. For studies on different kinds of intended or real audiences in the *Vita nova*, see Azzetta, "Fece molte canzoni"; Steinberg, *Accounting for Dante*.

28. Jacobus de Voragine, *Liber Mariale*, *sermo* 41 and *sermo* 36; my translation.

29. See Tonelli, "Dante e la fisiologia"; Martinez, "Mourning Beatrice"; Cervigni, "Re-configuring the Self."

30. On lyric poetry and the Song of Songs, see Dronke, "Song of Songs." On the Canticle in the *Vita nova*, see Nasti, *Favole d'amore*, 43–85, and "Nozze e vedovanza."

31. Canticles 2:5; "Vulnerata caritate ego sum" and "amore langueo" are respectively the versions of line 2:5 in the Vetus Latina (the translations of the Bible predating Jerome's Vulgate) and in the Vulgate.

32. William of Saint Thierry, *Expositio super Cantica canticorum*, 405, lines 158–61; translation from DelCogliano, *Gregory the Great*, 197.

33. "Make haste, my beloved, / And be like a gazelle / Or a young stag / On the mountains of spices" (Canticles 8:14).

34. Muller, *Dictionary*, 283, defines *repletive* as "incapable of being judged or measured by circumscription or defined by physical limitations or spatial boundaries, but rather identified as filling space or acting upon space while at the same time transcending it."

35. Antonelli, "Morte di Beatrice."

Vita nova XXV [16]

1. Many critics have read chapter XXV [16] as a metapoetic exercise, including Lombardi, *Imagining the Woman Reader*, 103; R. Harrison, *Body of Beatrice*, 54–65; and Musa, *Dante's "Vita Nuova,"* 108–9. Barański, "Dante *poeta* e *lector*," 27, even suggests that "il capitolo 25 può essere letto come una *Poetria* in chiave minore."

2. Translations are my own with occasional reference being made to *Vita nova*, Frisardi trans.

3. On the critical debate over the chronology and potential relations of Cavalcanti's *canzone* and the *Vita nova*, see Gragnolati, "Authorship and Performance," 132n16.

4. See Barolini, *Undivine Comedy*, 53, on Ulysses as a "lightning rod Dante places in his poem to attract and diffuse his own consciousness of the presumption involved in anointing oneself God's scribe."

5. For indicative arguments see Singleton, *Essay on the "Vita Nuova,"* 74–75; and Musa, *Dante's "Vita Nuova,"* 107–27.

6. The sight of Beatrice inspires "una fiamma di caritade" [a flame of *caritas*] in Dante in chapter XI.1 [5.4], but the noun is immediately overshadowed by Dante's own first reported speech in the text, which, as the author's *primiloquium*, necessarily carries more symbolic weight: "E chi allora m'avesse domandato di cosa alcuna, la mia risponsione sarebbe stata solamente 'Amore'" (XI.2 [5.5])

[And if anyone had asked me anything at all in that moment my reply would have been only "Amore"].

7. See Kay, *Dante's Lyric Redemption*, Lombardi, "Pensiero linguistico," and Gragnolati, "(In)Corporeality," on how Dante integrates elements of the courtly erotic tradition with the drive toward Christianizing the discourse of love in the *Vita nova*.

8. See Barański, "Dante *poeta* e *lector*," "Dante's Plurilingualism," and "'Valentissimo poeta.'"

9. Ginsberg, "Dante's Ovids," 146.

10. See Lombardi, *Imagining the Woman Reader*, 87, on *Rhetorica ad Herennium* 4.53.66 and *Institutio oratoria* 9.2.29–37.

11. The sonnet is "Da più a uno face un sollegismo" (47) [[Deducing] from many things one thing produces a syllogism]. See Picone, "Ovidio di Dante," 110–11; Kay, *Dante's Lyric Redemption*, 103; and *Vita Nova*, Gorni ed. [2011], 972.

12. Kay, *Dante's Lyric Redemption*, 98–127.

13. On the circulation of this text, see Storey, "Following Instructions," 121.

14. See Storey, "Following Instructions."

15. Text cited from Capelli, *Del carnale amore*. Translations are my own.

16. See Lombardi, *Imagining the Woman Reader*, 80–103, on dressing and undressing as textual exegesis and, 102–3, specifically on chapter XXV.

Vita nova XXVI [17]

1. *Vita nova*, Frisardi trans., is the translation used unless otherwise stated.

2. Translation modified.

3. Translation by Lansing in *Dante's Lyric Poetry*, Lansing and Frisardi trans.

4. See De Robertis, *Libro della "Vita Nuova,"* 48.

5. On humility, see Contini, "Esercizio di interpretazione," 164; Cropp, *Vocabulaire courtois*, 172.

6. Text and translation from Andreas Capellanus, *On Love*, Walsh ed.

7. On Dante's lyric models, see Brugnolo, "'. . . Amor tenendo'"; Grimaldi, "Dante e la poesia romanza."

8. Translations of Guinizzelli are my own.

9. On the "autobiographical pact" that Dante establishes with his readers, see *Rime*, Grimaldi ed., 305–6.

10. Cavalcanti is quoted from *Poeti del dolce stil novo*, Pirovano ed.

11. Translations of Cavalcanti are taken from *Complete Poems*, Mortimer trans.

12. See Hunt, "*Song of Songs*"; Nasti, *Favole d'amore*; Grimaldi, "Sacro e profano."

13. See Paradisi, *Parola e l'amore*, 162, and, more generally, Rosenberg, "Incipit Citation."

14. See Paolazzi, *Maniera mutata*, 81.

15. See Leuker, "Sfoghi e sospiri," 124: Spitzer, "Osservazioni sulla *Vita Nuova*," 145: Giunta, "Sullo stilnovo," 14–15.

16. However, see Barański, "'nfiata labbia.'"

17. Rea, *Cavalcanti poeta*, 144.

18. Cino is quoted from *Poeti del dolce stil novo*, Pirovano ed.

19. On *onestà*, see Cherchi, "Dante e i trovatori," 29.

20. Bufano, "Parere," 297.

21. Contini, "Esercizio di interpretazione," 167–68.

22. See De Robertis, *Canzoniere escorialense* and "Sulla tradizione estravagante," and *Rime*, De Robertis ed. [2002], 2:879–926.

23. On sweetness, see Colombo, "Sonetto 'Tanto gentile.'"

24. On the importance of this hypothesis, see Malato, *Per una nuova edizione*, 23; Martelli, "Proposte per le *Rime*"; Grimaldi, "Anniversario di Beatrice."

25. See Azzetta, "Canto X," 323–33; *Rime*, Grimaldi ed., 481.

26. See *Rime*, De Robertis ed. [2005], 374; Martelli, "Proposte per le *Rime*," 282.

27. See Grimaldi, "Petrarca, il 'vario stile'" and "Varietà lirica."

28. See Carrai, *Dante elegiaco*, 43–75.

29. Aquinas, *Opera omnia S. Thomae*, Alarcon ed.

30. See Barolini, "Sociology of the *Brigata*."

Vita nova XXVII [18]

1. Translations are my own.

2. The length of the composition is identical to that of a sonnet, and the *fronte* could also be that of a sonnet in terms of rhyme scheme [ABBA ABBA]. The rhyme scheme of the *sirma* [(a)CDd CEE] would have been anomalous for a sonnet, however, as would the presence of the seven-syllable line 11.

3. See *Dante's Lyric Poetry*, Barolini ed., 240. See also *Vita nuova*, Pirovano ed., 225: "L'evento lirico è a tutti gli effetti evento narrativo" [The lyric event is to all intents and purposes a narrative event]. Both views seem indebted to De

Robertis's notion that the story of the *Vita nova* becomes increasingly the story of its poems. See De Robertis, *Libro della "Vita Nuova,"* 136–38 and 156, and *Vita Nuova*, De Robertis ed. [1980], 187.

4. On the nature of Dante's access to Aristotelian philosophy during and before the composition of the *Vita nova*, see Barański, "On Dante's Trail."

5. On the meaning of these terms across Dante's works, see Pazzaglia, "Disposizione" and "Disposto"; Mugnai, "Operazione"; Delhaye and Stabile, "Virtù"; and Bufano, "Adoperare" and "Operare."

6. *Vita Nuova*, De Robertis ed. [1980], 188.

7. Salsano, "Defettivamente"; *Vita Nova*, Gorni ed. [1996], 164.

8. *Vita nuova*, Pirovano ed., 225.

9. See De Robertis, *Libro della "Vita Nuova,"* 148n1. See also Musa, "Essay," 143–46.

10. This is the only instance in the *Vita nova* when Dante uses a term related to *disposizione*. Here he uses *disposto*, a passive past participle of the verb *disporre*, which is the root of the verbal noun *disposizione*.

11. See *Dante's Lyric Poetry*, Barolini ed., 239–42. See also *Vita Nuova*, De Robertis ed. [1980], 188–90; *Vita Nova*, Gorni ed. [1996], 164–65; and *Vita nuova*, Pirovano ed., 225–27.

12. *Dante's Lyric Poetry*, Barolini ed., 241–42.

13. See Agamben, *Stanzas*, 63–131, esp. 127–29.

14. Ibid., 129.

15. It is worth noting that the manuscripts read both "spiriti" and "sospiri" in line 13. The overlap between the two words was significant. Giosuè Carducci, among others, preferred "sospiri" to "spiriti" because it was more Dantesque; see *Vita Nuova*, Barbi ed. [1932], 75.

16. See Harrison, *Body of Beatrice*, 70–71.

17. Mazzotta, "Language of Poetry," 11.

Vita nova XXVIII–XXXIV [19–23]:
The Poetics of a New Affective Community

1. I have used Andrew Frisardi's translation in general, but have at times turned to Dino S. Cervigni and Edward Vasta's translation as well.

2. *Vita Nova*, Gorni ed. [1996], xxiv.

3. See, for example, John Freccero's accounts of the ways in which the *Comedy* revisits earlier works in a palinodic mode in his *Dante: Poetics of Conversion*.

4. R. Harrison, *Body of Beatrice.*

5. See Ibbett, "'When I Do,'" 245: "Affect [is] relational, but not a binary of action and passivity, since, as Brian Massumi puts it, in this case 'to be affected' is also a capacity."

6. See *Vita nuova*, Pirovano ed., 228; *Vita Nova*, Rossi ed., 153; Santagata, *Io e il mondo*, 27; Tavoni, "'Converebbe,'" following Grandgent, "Dante and St. Paul." *Dante's Lyric Poetry*, Barolini ed., 244, claims that "the death of Beatrice is not only announced but simultaneously classed as an Assumption."

7. *Vita nuova*, Pirovano ed., 229.

8. *Dante's Lyric Poetry*, Barolini ed., 244, has explored the parallels between "Donne ch'avete" and "Li occhi dolenti." See also *Vita Nuova*, De Robertis ed. [1980], 198–206.

9. On the "persona" as designating a specifically earthly body in this case, see Niccoli, "Persona," 436, and my *Dante's Persons.*

10. See Berlant, *Cruel Optimism*, 15: "affective atmospheres" are "shared, not solitary" and are lived through the body. On the link between *planctus* and *lode*, see *Dante's Lyric Poetry*, Foster and Boyde ed., 132, and *Dante's Lyric Poetry*, Barolini ed., 110–13, comments on Sordello's *planh* for Blacatz.

11. Carrai, *Dante elegiaco*, 22–27, quote at 27.

12. *Vita Nuova*, De Robertis ed. [1980], 198.

13. Gregg and Seigworth, *Affect Theory Reader*, 1–2.

14. *Vita Nuova*, Colombo ed., 151.

15. On the link between the Threni's incipit and the new placement of the divisions, see Vickers, "Widowed Words," 99–100.

16. Martinez, "Mourning Beatrice," 26. Martinez's translation of Durandus, 6.72.6: "Sic ergo istud officium, quod caret principio et fine, quasi mortuum et viduatum videtur, quia et patres nostri viduati post mortem Christi fuerunt."

17. See Moleta, "Oggi fa l'anno," 93–94.

18. Martinez, "Mourning Beatrice," 13, notes that "Venite a 'ntender" echoes Threni and links terms of mourning here to chapters XXVIII [19.1–3] and XXX [19.8–10].

19. *Dante's Lyric Poetry*, Barolini ed., 255.

20. See Santagata, *Io e il mondo*, 136; Carrai, *Dante elegiaco*, 67–68. On the concept of the "annovale" between social and religious acts of mourning and troubadouric anniversaries of encounter, see Grimaldi, "Anniversario di Beatrice."

21. *Vita Nova*, Gorni ed. [1996], 193. For further discussions, see Camilletti, "Dante Painting an Angel"; Ciccuto, "'Era venuta ne la mente mia' (*VN*, XXXIV.7)" and "'Era venuta ne la mente mia': Visione"; Cervigni, "'. . . Ricordandomi di lei'"; Pich, "Immagine."

22. *Dante's Lyric Poetry*, Barolini ed., 261.

23. Grimaldi, "Anniversario di Beatrice," 487–91.

24. Pich, "Immagine," 356.

25. *Vita Nova*, Gorni ed. [1996], 192.

Vita nova XXVIII [19.1–19.3]

1. Martinez, "Mourning Beatrice," 24–25.

2. *Ritus in ecclesia servandi* (Florence, Biblioteca Riccardiana, 3005, compiled between 1173 and 1205, very probably used throughout the thirteenth century), ed. Toker, *On Holy Ground*, 193 (lines 1288–96). Line numberings are those added by Toker to his edition. Translations from Latin texts are mine.

3. Brand, *Holy Treasure*, 149. Scholars are increasingly recognizing that medieval laypeople were not passive spectators of liturgy but rather participants in it and that participation in liturgy happened in many interrelated modes; for an overview, see Symes, "Liturgical Texts," 263–66.

4. See, for example, Durand, *Rationale divinorum officiorum* 4.15.3 (on listening to prayers) and 4.24.22–28, ed. Davril and Thibodeau; Sicard of Cremona, *Mitralis de officiis* 3.4 (102–255), ed. Sarbak and Weinrich (both on listening to the gospel); see Phillips-Robins, *Liturgical Song and Practice*, 229n85, for discussion of an anonymous guide to the Mass that includes instructions that laypeople should listen attentively.

5. Martinez, "Mourning Beatrice," 26.

6. Rushworth, *Discourses of Mourning*, 118.

7. Ford, *Self and Salvation*, 127. I also borrow the term *indwell* from Ford (127).

8. For Durand (*Rationale divinorum officiorum*), there is also a figural relationship between the deaths of Joshua and Christ mourned through these words.

9. On the many ways in which participation in liturgy shaped understandings and experiences of history, time, and one's own place in them, see Fassler, *Virgin of Chartres*, quotation from 61.

10. Glorying "under Mary's banner" (XXVIII.1 [19.1]) is an implicitly communal activity, as noted in the commentary of *Vita nuova*, Pirovano ed., 228: Beatrice glories "insieme alla schiera di anime radunate attorno al vessillo" [together with the crowd of souls gathered around the banner].

11. On the use of Marian names and titles in prayer, see Fulton Brown, *Mary*, 72–101. For examples of Marian *laude*, see *Florence Laudario*, Wilson and Barbieri ed.

12. "Virgo" also echoes the language of hagiography, as Niccoli, "Virgo," notes.

13. The others are Beatrice, Christ, Giovanna, John the Baptist, and, outside the narrative, the poets named in chapter XXV [16].

Vita nova XXIX [19.4–19.7]

I would like to thank Heather Webb, Helena Phillips-Robins, and Valentina Mele for their helpful comments on the earlier drafts of this chapter.

1. Gorni, *Lettera nome numero*, 75. All translations from Italian are mine unless indicated otherwise.

2. All translations of the *Vita nova* are from Andrew Frisardi's edition.

3. On the various meanings of *novo* in the early Italian lyric, see Carrieri, "Per una definizione."

4. The fact that Dante can juggle between various systems of measuring time with such ease demonstrates a certain degree of integration reached between Christian and Arabic astronomical culture, at least in Dante's mind. Although Dante does not indicate where his knowledge of Ptolemaic astronomy and different calendars comes from, it is likely that his source is al-Farghani's *Liber de aggregationibus scientiae stellarum et principiis coelestium motuum,* a summary of Ptolemy's astronomical *Almagestum*, which in turn is indebted to Aristotelian cosmology, especially *De caelo* and *De meteoris*. On Dante's astronomical knowledge and the computation of nines in various calendars, see Maraldi, "Stelle di Beatrice."

5. Mondschein and Casey, "Time and Timekeeping," 1666.

6. Added emphasis here and elsewhere in the chapter is mine.

7. On *plenitudo temporis* in *Vita nova* XXIX, see Sarolli, "Numero," 90.

8. *Vita nuova*, Pirovano ed., 230.

9. Dante's description of *arismetrica* in the *Convivio* (2.13.15–19) bears significant resemblance to Aristotelian and Pythagorean number theories, which were adapted for Christian exegesis through Origen. The Christian appropriation of Pythagoreanism was justified by Solomon's dictum in the Book of Wisdom: "Omnia mensura et numero et pondere disposuisti" (11:20) [But thou hast ordered all things in measure and number and weight]. In *De arithmetica* 1.2, Schilling and Oosthout ed., Boethius similarly praises number as "the principal exemplar in the mind of the creator," and Bonaventure suggests that number is "the principal vestige leading to Wisdom" (*Itinerarium mentis in Deum* 2.10, Quaracchi ed.). For more detailed discussions of the interpretation of numbers in

Christian philosophy, see Wedell, "Numbers"; Eckhardt, *Essays*; and Guzzardo, *Dante*.

10. Augustine, *De libero arbitrio* 2.16.171, Benjamin and Hackstaff trans.

11. Augustine, *De musica* 1.11.1, Jacobsson ed., quoting Romans 1:20.

12. Vecce, "Beatrice," 122–23.

13. Quoted in *Vita nuova*, Pirovano ed., 231–32.

14. Wedell, "Numbers," 1254.

15. *TLIO*: Tesoro della Lingua Italiana delle Origini, "sottile [2]," http://tlio.ovi.cnr.it/TLIO/.

16. In Moleta's interpretation of *Vita nova* XXIX [19.4–7], the discourse of subtlety in the chapter is of a Cavalcantian character: it is "a subtle gloss to which even his subtle former mentor could not take exception" (*Guinizzelli in Dante*, 174). The implied knowledge of Pythagorean lore and Chaldean astronomy contributes to the esoteric allure of Dante's explanation of Beatrice's "nineness," which would have appealed to Cavalcanti's "altezza d'ingegno" (*Inf.* 10.59). But the Cavalcantian influence is likely not the only one to shape Dante's understanding of *sottigliezza*, and in this chapter, I suggest that Dante's treatment of *sottile* in *Vita nova* XXIX [19.4–7] participates in the more general debate about intellectual discernment.

17. Quoted in Cornish, *Vernacular Translation*, 184.

18. On the meaning of subtlety in Latin and Latinate discourses and the early Italian lyric, see Bruni, "Semantica della sottigliezza."

19. Ibid., 111.

20. The symmetrical position of the syntagm "infallibile veritade" in relation to "cristiana veritade" has led Vecce to conclude that "più sottilmente" for Dante means reading the universe "coll'intervento della dottrina teologica" ("Beatrice," 130).

21. Translations of *Paradiso* are taken from Durling and Martinez ed.

22. Augustine, *De libero arbitrio* 2.12.34.

23. Petrarch, *Petrarch's Lyric Poems*, Durling ed. and trans., 211.

24. Vignuzzi, "Piacere."

Vita nova XXX [19.8–19.10]

1. All the translations of the *Vita nova* are taken from Frisardi ed.

2. According to the traditional division of the *Vita nova*, the *libello* is divided in two: one *in vita* (in life, chapters I–XXVII [1–18]) and one *in morte* (in death, chapters XXVIII–XLII [19–31]) of Beatrice. See *Vita Nova*, Gorni ed.

[1996], xxiv. In his recent commentary on the *Vita nova*, however, Donato Pirovano divides Dante's work into three parts: a first one (chapters I–XVI [1–9]), from the first encounter with Beatrice to the episode of the "gabbo" [ridicule], a second one (chapters XVII–XXVII [10–18]), in which Dante develops his idea of the "poesia della lode" [poetry of praise], and a third one (chapters XXVIII–XLII [19–31]), dedicated to the "nova materia" [new subject matter] after Beatrice's death. See *Vita nuova*, Pirovano ed., 14–15.

3. Santagata, *Io e il mondo*, 203–4. As for the stylistic form of this letter, *Vita Nova*, Gorni ed. [1996], 173, does not exclude the possibility of an epistolary poem. The majority of scholars, however, seem to prefer the idea of a letter written in prose; see *Vita nuova*, Pirovano ed., 223.

4. On the role of Jeremiah's Lamentations in the *Vita nova*, see, in particular, Martinez, "Mourning Beatrice," and Carrai, *Dante elegiaco*, 23–24. On the presence of Lamentations in thirteenth-century Florentine culture, see Pegoretti, "'Nelle scuole delli religiosi.'"

5. See, for example, the use of personifications, *sermocinatio*, and apostrophes. For an analysis of Dante's reuse of these tropes in the poems of the *Vita nova*, see Martinez, "Mourning Beatrice," 8–12.

6. See Vickers, "Widowed Words," 102; Martinez, "Mourning Beatrice," 24–25.

7. On the appeal for reader's engagement throughout the *Vita nova*, see also Carrai, *Dante elegiaco*, 22–27.

8. Martinez, "Mourning Beatrice," 4–5.

9. "Ancora lagrimando in questa desolata cittade, scrissi a li principi de la terra" (XXX.1 [19.8]) [I, still shedding tears in this desolate city, wrote to the rulers of the land]. Dante's behavior recalls the prologue of Lamentations: "Sedit Ieremias propheta flens, et planxit lamentatione hac in Ierusalem: et amaro animo suspirans et eiulans, dixit" [The prophet Jeremiah sat weeping, and he wailed this lamentation in Jerusalem: and sighing with a bitter soul, and mourning, he said]; see *Vita Nova*, Gorni ed. [1996], 172; *Vita nuova*, Pirovano ed., 233.

10. *Vita nuova*, Pirovano ed., 233.

11. See, for example, De Robertis, *Libro della "Vita Nuova,"* 166; Martinez, "Mourning Beatrice," 19; *Vita nuova*, Pirovano ed., 25–26.

12. *Vita nuova*, Pirovano ed., 20–22. See also Singleton, *An Essay on the "Vita Nuova,"* 55–77.

13. As scholars have noted, the name of the book itself, *Vita nova*, has strong religious and Christological connotations (see *Vita nuova*, Pirovano ed., 9; Casadei, "'Incipit vita nova'"). For an analysis of Dante's strategies in presenting

his book in the first chapters of the *Vita nova* (with a particular attention to Christological references) see Barański, "'Lascio cotale trattato,'" 16–23.

14. In this volume, Aistė Kiltinavičiūtė investigates the meaning of Beatrice's "nineness" and shows its relevance for the structure of the *Vita nova* and the universality of Dante's message. For further readings on Beatrice and the number nine, see Antonelli, "Morte di Beatrice"; Vecce, "'Ella era uno nove'" and "Beatrice e il numero amico."

15. Barański, "'Lascio cotale trattato,'" 1–7; 13.

16. For an analysis of this chapter in light of Dante's relationship with Latin language and literature, see Barański, "Roots of Dante's Pluringualism." For Dante's self-representation as an *auctor* through an implicit comparison with classical literature, see also Ascoli, *Dante and the Making*, 178–201.

17. As I noted above, both these passages are marked by the presence of a metapoetic language and, in particular, by the occurrence of the word *intendimento*.

18. In fact, Latin sentences are quite rare in the *Vita nova* and, in the text, are never spoken or written by Dante himself. In chapters II.4–6 [1.5–7], III.3–5 [1.14–16], and XII.3–4 [5.10–11], Dante reports the Latin sentences that the spirits or Love pronounce in his dreams. In chapter VII.7 [2.18], XXIV.4 [15.4], XXVIII.1 [19.1], and XXX.1 [19.8] he quotes from the Bible, in chapter XIII.4 [6.4] he uses a juridical expression, and in chapter XXV.9 [16.9] he cites passages from classical Latin texts. To this list, we should add the *Osanna* sung by angels at XXIII.7 [14.7] and the *libello*'s opening and closing formulas (I.1 [1.1]; [31.3]). For a consideration of how these Latin quotations contribute to the *Vita nova*'s plurilingualism, see Barański, "Roots of Dante's Pluringualism."

19. See Malato, "Introduzione," XXIV–XXXI.

20. Other references to Guido, always addressed as "primo amico" [best friend], are in III.14 [2.1], XXIV.3 [15.3], XXV.10 [16.10], and XXXII.1 [21.1].

21. For a synthetic overview on the correspondence between the two poets, see Malato, *Dante e Guido Cavalcanti*, 12.

22. For some scholars, the *Vita nova* still shows a community of purpose and ideas with the "primo amico" that will then be rejected by Guido, who will write his famous canzone, "Donna me prega" [A woman asks me], as a polemical response to Dante's concept of love (see, in particular, Tanturli, "Guido Cavalcanti contro Dante"; Malato, *Dante e Guido Cavalcanti*, 11–73). Other scholars point to the lack of philological evidence to support this hypothesis and are more inclined to believe that Guido's philosophical *canzone* predates the *Vita nova* (see, for example, Inglese, "'. . . illa Guidonis de Florentia'"; Barański, "Guido

Cavalcanti"). Following this more traditional chronological order, the *Vita nova* can be read as a subtle but firm refutation of the positions expressed by Guido in his poems (and in "Donna me prega" in particular). For additional bibliography on the relationship between Dante and Guido, see Contini, "Cavalcanti in Dante"; Fenzi, "Conflitto di idee"; Barolini, *Dante's Poets*, 123–53; Antonelli, "Cavalcanti e Dante."

23. See Barolini, "Dante and Cavalcanti," and Barański, "Guido Cavalcanti." See also Pasero, "Dante in Cavalcanti," who seems, however, to concur with the idea of "Donna me prega" as a polemical reaction to the *Vita nova.*

24. At III.14 [2.1–2], for example, Dante's "primo amico" appears incapable of interpreting Dante's dream, while in XXIV [15] Giovanna (Cavalcanti's beloved) is represented as subordinate to Beatrice (*Vita nuova*, Pirovano ed., 34). But, as Giorgio Inglese points out, these two sentiments can also coexist (Inglese, "'. . . illa Guidonis de Florentia,'" 182).

25. For the first reception of Cavalcanti and his status as *auctor*, see Barański, "Guido Cavalcanti."

Vita nova XXXI [20]

1. Contini, "Introduzione," 10. My translation.

2. Zygmunt Barański says that the preceding quotation "inaugurated the 'modern' interpretation of Dante": Barański, "Dante *poeta* e *lector*," 3, and "'Lascio cotale trattato,'" 1.

3. Cited in Ciociola, "Lava sotto la crosta," 534. My translation.

4. Cited from the first English edition, Maas, *Textual Criticism*, 40–41.

5. Carrai argued for a "trama sottile" [fine weave] of words conforming to a *stilus miserorum*, elegy, throughout the *Vita nova*. Of this *planctus*, "Li occhi dolenti" [The grieving eyes], Carrai writes: "Anche qui Dante poneva l'enfasi su questo gusto lacrimevole, studiandosi di congregare una serie di voci tematiche" [Dante here too placed the emphasis on this taste for the tearful, taking care to put together a series of thematic words]; *Dante elegiaco*, 29, 35.

6. Pirovano, "Per una nuova edizione," 277, 280, 285, 288, 294, 300–301, 307, 313.

7. Frisardi, in his edition of *Vita nova*, 84, gives three translations of the line "Poscia piangendo, sol nel mio lamento": "Then crying, alone in my lament, I call on Beatrice [or: crying, alone, in my lament; or: crying, in my lament I call only on Beatrice]." All further translations of the *Vita nova* are from Frisardi's edition.

8. Two foundational essays on the long tradition of female lament, "Dido's Lament: From Medieval Latin Lyric to Chaucer" and "Laments of the Maries: From the Beginnings to the Mystery Plays," are found in Dronke, *Intellectuals and Poets*, 431–89.

9. Cited from Dronke, *Intellectuals and Poets*, 477.

10. Chaucer, "Legend of Good Women," lines 1039–42.

11. Here I am adding a little bit more flesh to Dronke's note about these lines: "Who before Chaucer had evoked Dido by so daring a metaphysical conceit? If it has analogues, it is only in certain high-flying moments in Dante's early poetry and that of his friends, the 'stilnovisti.'" Dronke, *Medieval Poet*, 453.

12. *Vita Nuova*, De Robertis ed. [1980], 201, notes an earlier analogue to this idea in Geoffrey of Vinsauf's *Poetria nova*, where Geoffrey recommends it as an example of *amplificatio* in lament: "Mundus egebat eo. Sed eum magis eligis esse / tecum quam secum; mavis succurrere coelo / quam mundo" (lines 422–24) [The world lacked him. But you prefer him rather to be with you than with it; you prefer to come to the aid of heaven rather than the world].

13. *Vita Nuova*, De Robertis ed. [1980], 203.

14. *Vita Nuova*, De Robertis ed. [1980], 199, writes of line 13: "per la forma mediale cfr. *Tanto gentile*, 5, e in prosa III, 7" [for the middle form cfr. *Tanto gentile* [So noble], 5, and in prose III, 7 [1.18]]. He is recalling Contini's comment on that line in "Tanto gentile" in the latter's "Esercizio d'interpretazione": there Contini points to the "portata 'media' o 'deponente' di *si va*, azione riflessa sul soggetto, ormai smarrita nel fossile *se ne va*" [The "middle" or "deponent" bearing of *si va* [she [+ *si*] goes], an action reflected back on the subject, now lost in the fossil *se ne va* [one [+ *se ne*] goes]: Contini, *Varianti e altra linguistica*, 162.

15. "Il y a en effet, entre le parfait et le moyen grecs, diverses relations à la fois formelles et fonctionnelles, qui, héritées de l'indo-européen, ont formé un système complexe; par exemple une forme γέγονα, parfait actif, va de pair avec le présent moyen γίγνομαι" (Benveniste, *Problèmes de linguistique générale*, 69) [There are in fact many relationships, between the perfect and the middle voice in Greek, both formal and functional, which, inherited from Indo-European, formed a complex system; for instance the form *gegona*, active perfect, goes together with the middle present *gignomai*].

16. "Il est certain en tout cas que le parfait ne s'insère pas dans le système temporel du grec et reste à part, indiquant, selon le cas, un mode de la temporalité ou une manière d'être du sujet" (ibid., 69–70) [It is certain at any rate that the perfect does not belong to the tense system of Greek and remains distinct,

indicating, as the case may be, a mode of temporality or a manner of being of the subject].

17. Again in the poem at lines 18 and 42: "no la ci tolse" [did not take her from us] and "com'ella n'è tolta" [as she was taken].

18. Klopsch sees in earlier medieval reflections on this distinction an attitude of complete "Unentschiedenheit" [indifference] or "Vertauschbarkeit" [convertibility]. See Klopsch, *Einführung*, 71.

19. "The late medieval teacher with a particular concern for memory thus had two options: to versify, or to signal the *divisio* in whatever way seemed best to him." Dante does both. I am not sure that medieval Latin discussions of the relative value of verse and prose have yet entered discussions of the organization of the "libro de la mia memoria" (I.1 [1.1]) [the book of my memory]. In didactic contexts in particular, it was poetry's relative memorableness and conciseness in relation to prose that mattered. I cite here from Law, "Why Write a Verse Grammar?," 71.

20. A recent study of this phenomenon (in medieval Latin) emphasizes, following Klopsch, that the stated goal of many prose-verse versions was conciseness and memorability. See Piccone, *Dalla prosa ai versi*, 31.

21. On the reconfiguration of the traditional poetry-prose relationship in *Vita nova*, which sees it as a "homogenizing synthesis," see Barański, "'Lascio cotale trattato,'" 10.

22. *Vita Nuova*, De Robertis ed. [1980], 198, discusses the uncertainty of "pietà"—does it mean "compassione" [compassion] or "dolore" [suffering] in context? Proposed solutions "to*lgono* che quest'inizio sia particolarmente intricato" [do not take away the fact that this beginning is particularly intricate].

23. "Wie in Altfranzösischen (z. B. *il a la pucele veue*) konnte zwischen Hilfsverbum und Partizip ein Objekt (oder ein Satzteil) treten" (Rohlfs, *Historische Grammatik*, §985) [As in Old French (i.e., he saw the girl), an object (or a clause) can go between the auxiliary and the participle].

24. See ibid., §810.

25. The standard introduction to this topic is the first chapter in Minnis and Scott, *Medieval Literary Theory*, 12–36.

26. Contini, "Introduzione," 11.

Vita nova XXXII [21]

1. As De Robertis poignantly observed in his 2002 edition of the *Rime*, commenting on Dante's process of self-editing his lyrics in his *libello*: "Il caso non

fu, come per il *Convivio*, di assunzione di alcuni testi a una particolare funzione, di adibirli a una nuova letura, della proposta di un diverso senso, né, di fatto, secondo la natura dell'operazione, appunto di 'retractatio' . . .; piuttosto, di riconoscere ai testi, e alla propria ricerca, alla propria storia, il loro senso, e perciò di adattarveli" [The case was not, as for the *Convivio*, to assign a specific function to texts, to assign new readings to them by suggesting different interpretations, or to accomplish a "retractatio" . . .; rather, it was a matter of acknowledging the meaning of the lyrics, and to make them adhere to his own story and to his own research]. *Rime*, De Robertis ed. [2002], 2/2:879.

2. *Vita Nova*, Gorni ed. [1996], 4.

3. *Vita Nuova*, De Robertis ed. [1980], 28.

4. *Rime*, De Robertis ed. [2005], 392. See also *Rime*, Grimaldi ed., 502–3. For a discussion of the circulation of unpublished poems in the Middle Ages, see Berisso, "Sillogi e serie."

5. As De Robertis demonstrates, thirteen lyrics of the *Vita nova* circulated as independent texts before being incorporated into the *prosimetrum*—they had, in other words, a *tradizione estravagante*. For these poems we have a "prima redazione" [first draft], which De Robertis has printed in his 2002 critical edition of the *Rime*. The texts are "O voi che per la via d'Amor passate" (VII [2]); "Con l'altre donne mia vista gabbate" (XIV [7]); "Ciò che m'incontra ne la mente more" (XV [8]); "Negli occhi porta la mia donna Amore" (XXI [12]); "Tanto gentile e tanto onesta pare" (XXVI [17]; "Vede perfettamente onne salute" (XXVI [17]); "Venite a 'ntender li sospiri miei" (XXXII [21]); "Era venuta ne la mente mia" (XXXIV [23]); "Videro li occhi miei quanta pietate" (XXXV [24]); "Color d'amore e di pietà sembianti" (XXXVI [25]); "Lasso! per forza di molti sospiri" (XXXIX [28]); "Deh peregrini che pensosi andate" (XL [29]); and "Oltre la spera che più larga gira" (XLI [30]). For an assessment of the independent tradition of these texts, see De Robertis, "Sulla tradizione estravagante," in *Rime*, De Robertis ed. [2002], 2/2:879–926. For a philological discussion of the material witnesses and the variants of "Venite a 'ntender," see *Rime*, De Robertis ed. [2002], 3:403–5.

6. All quotations from the work of Guido Cavalcanti are taken from Cavalcanti, *Rime*, ed. Rea and Inglese.

7. On the relationship between the *libello*'s narrative and Dante's performative gesture of self-affirming his authorial identity, see Gragnolati, "Authorship and Performance."

8. As *Vita Nuova*, De Robertis ed. [1980], 207, observes, the commissioner is perhaps to be identified with "quel Manetto a cui è diretto un sonetto di Cavalcanti, *Guata, Manetto* appunto (che associerebbe in un unico testo i due primi amici di Dante) [the same Manetto to whom Cavalcanti's sonnet "Guata,

Manetto" is addressed (which would bring Dante's two closest friends together in one text)].

9. The definition is Stefano Carrai's, who uses it to refer to several passages of the *Vita nova*, inviting specific attention to the themes and lexis of the *libello*; Carrai, *Dante elegiaco*, 22–41. See also *Vita nuova*, Pirovano ed., 247.

10. Bertolini, "'Oi.'"

11. Dante, *Rime*, De Robertis ed. [2005], 393.

12. The bibliography on the medieval poet's reuse of philosophical and medical sources as connected to the physiology of love is extensive, and to discuss it would fall outside the scope of this study. For an insightful overview, with a diachronic perspective, of the permeation of some of these sources into early Italian poetry, see Borsa, "Immagine nel cuore."

13. *Vita Nova*, Gorni ed. [1996], 186.

14. Carrai, *Dante elegiaco*, 25. The parallelism is also emphasized by *Vita Nuova*, De Robertis ed. [1980], 207; and *Vita nuova*, Pirovano ed., 247.

15. Scholars have established that Lamentations plays a fundamental role in appreciating the language, style, and numerous calques that are present in the *libello*; see, in particular, Martinez, "Mourning Beatrice" and "Dante's Jeremiads"; Carrai, *Dante elegiaco*. More generally, Stefano Carrai has contextualized the numerous sources of Dante's *libello*, including Lamentations, proposing that one might read the work as if it were an elegiac *prosimetrum*.

16. The first substantial contribution on the presence of biblical intertexts in Cavalcanti's poetry is De Robertis's 1986 commentary on Cavalcanti's *Rime*. According to De Robertis, two verses from Lamentations (1:12 and 18), "percorrono tutto il dolente discorso cavalcantiano costituendo la prospettiva fissa della richiesta di attenzione e di partecipazione" [run through the entire sorrowful Cavalcantian discourse, constituting the model for the subject's request for attention]; De Robertis, "Caso di Cavalcanti," 343. As further emphasized by Martinez, in discussing the reuse of Lamentations in the wider context of thirteenth-century devotional literature, these passages "furnish a persisting leitmotif of Cavalcanti's verse, a key element in his fashioning of a lyric persona and voice"; Martinez, "Cavalcanti 'Man of Sorrows,'" 192. The reuse of these two passages has been recently discussed by Roberto Rea, who argues that Cavalcanti utilizes them to define the audience of his poetry—anticipating Dante's and Petrarch's similar operations in the *Vita nova* and in the *Rerum vulgarium fragmenta*; Rea, "Cavalcanti e l'invenzione." Rea's contribution is fundamental to understanding how Cavalcanti defines a new lyric addressee, reestablishing the missing element of the subject's love discourse. See also Rea, *Cavalcanti poeta*, 157–62. For other

insightful discussions of Cavalcanti's reuse of biblical sources, see Cavalcanti, *Rime*, Cassata ed.; De Robertis, "Un altro Cavalcanti?"

17. See, for example, Gragnolati's note in Dante, *Rime giovanili*, Barolini ed., 447; Dante, *Rime*, Grimaldi ed., 247.

18. Cavalcanti, *Rime*, De Robertis ed., 62–65; Cavalcanti, *Rime d'amore*, Rea ed., 117–21.

19. Rea, "Invenzione del lettore," 162–63.

20. Lamentations was a widely used and known text in the Middle Ages. Recently Anna Pegoretti has unearthed suggestive new evidence regarding the presence of Peter John Olivi's commentary on Lamentations in Santa Croce. The manuscript was written between 1287 and 1289 during Olivi's stay in the convent. It is not unlikely that Franciscan monks would have discussed Lamentations in public in their sermons and at quodlibetal debates; Pegoretti, "'Nelle scuole delli religiosi.'"

21. Gragnolati's note in Dante, *Rime giovanili*, Barolini ed., 447.

22. For a discussion of the manuscript tradition of the sonnet and its variants, see Dante, *Rime*, De Robertis ed. [2002], 403–5.

23. *Vita Nuova*, De Robertis ed. [1980], 208; *Vita Nova*, Gorni ed. [1996], 187; *Rime giovanili*, Barolini ed., 394; Barolini, *Dante's Lyric Poetry*, 448; *Vita nuova*, Pirovano ed., 247; Dante, *Rime*, Grimaldi ed., 505.

24. Personification and prosopopoeia are two of the *Rime*'s key rhetorical devices. See Favati, "Tecnica ed arte"; Corti, "Dualismo e immaginazione visiva"; Calenda, *Per altezza d'ingegno*.

25. Rea, *Cavalcanti poeta*, 287–89.

26. Gragnolati's note in Dante, *Rime giovanili*, Barolini ed., 448.

27. Note, however, that we still find "loco degno" in "Li occhi dolenti," line 31.

28. *Vita Nuova*, De Robertis ed. [1980], 207.

29. Moleta, "'Oggi fa l'anno,'" 84.

Vita nova XXXIII [22]

1. For my adaptations of Frisardi's translation to the more literal rendering sometimes useful in narratological analysis, I acknowledge a substantial debt to Cervigni and Vasta's translation and edition of the *Vita nova*.

2. For a brief outline of medieval reading practices, see Coleman, "Reading Practices."

3. *Dante's Lyric Poetry*, Barolini ed., 257.

4. Ibid.

Vita nova XXXIV [23]

1. For my adaptations of Frisardi's translation for the more literal rendering sometimes useful in narratological analysis, I acknowledge a substantial debt to Cervigni and Vasta's translation and edition of the *Vita nova*.

Vita nova XXXV–XXXIX [24–28]: The *Donna Gentile* Episode

1. The disputed quality of the episode is noted in all the major commentators. See also the incisive discussion in Stillinger, *Song of Troilus*, 100–107; Lombardi, *Imagining the Woman Reader*, 119–25.

2. See especially Cavalcanti, "L'anima mia vilment'è sbigotita" (*Rime* 7) [My spirit is dejectedly thrown into turmoil] and "Io non pensava che lo cor giammai" (*Rime* 9.34) [I never thought that my heart might ever]: "mi sbigottisce sì. . . ." I have consulted De Robertis's edition of Cavalcanti's *Rime* throughout. Particularly attentive to Cavalcanti's presence is *Dante's Lyric Poetry*, Barolini ed., 468. See also Kay, "Dante's Cavalcantian Relapse," 82–83, who speaks of a "failure to master the lesson of Beatrice's mortality" and a return to a "distinctively Cavalcantian phase of poetry."

3. For examples of the role of the window and its functions, see James-Raoul, "En guise de préface," and other contributions in the volume *Par la fenestre*. One major example is the encounter of Eneas and Lavine in *Roman de Enéas* 8047–50, ed. Petit: "Lavine fu an la tor sus, d'une fenestre garda jus, / vit Eneam qui fu desoz" [Lavine was high up on a tower and from a window looked down and saw Eneas who was below].

4. Ovid, *Met.* 14.752–54: "Et patulis iniit tectum sublime fenestri; / vixque bene impositum lecto prospexerat Iphim / deriguere oculi" [And she entered the high part of the house with its wide-open windows and scarcely had she taken a good look at the body of Iphis placed on the bier].

5. See esp. Wisdom 7:6: "De fenestra enim domus meae per cancellos prospexi et video parvulos considero vecordem iuvenem" [For at the window of my house I have looked through the lattice and I have seen amongst the young people a young man lacking sense]. See also Judges 5:28: "per fenestram respiciens" [looking through the window].

6. Lombardo, *Boezio in Dante*, 441–46, also suggests (444) a metaliterary interpretation of leaving behind vile poetry of pain.

7. The significance of the echo raises a set of complex interpretative questions; see the useful review in Pazzaglia, "I' vegno a te il giorno infinite volte."

8. Cavalcanti, "Veder poteste, quando v'inscontrai" (*Rime* 22) [You could see, when I met you], line 6: "lo dolente core" [the grieving heart] and line 8: "l'anima trista" [the sad spirit]; "Io prego voi che di dolor parlate" (*Rime* 19) [I implore you who speak pain], lines 4, 11, 18: "Lagrime ascendon de la mente mia" [Tears descend from my mind]; and "Deh, spiriti miei, quando mi vedete" (*Rime* 6) [Oh, my spirits, when you see me], line 13: "a l'alma trista, che parl'in dolore" [to my sad spirit, that speaks in pain].

9. References in order: Ovid, *Ars amatoria* 1.176, in *Heroides Amores*, Showerman ed.: "Palleat omnis amans; hic est color aptus amanti" [May every lover be pale: this is the appropriate color for lovers]; Propertius, *Elegies* 1.1.22; 1.5.21, 1.9.17, 1.13.7; cf. 1.6.6 and 1.15.39; Capellanus, *De amore* 2.5.6, Trojel ed., 400: "Mulier autem quae in sui coamantis aspectu pallescit in vero procul dubio consistit amore" [Without doubt love consists in a woman who in the presence of her lover becomes pallid]. For the earlier lyric tradition, see especially the *canzone* by Re Enzo in *Poeti della Scuola siciliana*, Antonelli, Di Girolamo, and Coluccia ed., "S'eo trovasse pietanza" (lines 49–50) [If I could find compassion]: "che 'l natural colore tutto perdo, / tanto il cor sbatte e lagna" [for I lose all my natural color so much does my heart beat and complain].

10. See Cavalcanti, "Vedete ch'i' son un che vo piangendo" (*Rime* 10) [See that I'm someone who goes weeping], line 14: "Questa pesanza ch'è nel cor discesa / ha certi spirite' già consumati" [This weight that has descended into my heart has already destroyed certain spirits], and "Io non pensava che lo cor giammai" (*Rime* 9) [I never thought that my heart might ever], lines 48–50: "li spiriti fuggiti del mio core, / che per soverchio de lo su' valore / eran distrutti" [the spirits that have fled from my heart which on account of the excess of her perfection were destroyed], where in both cases the role of the wounded, battle-weary heart is central. See also Cavalcanti, "A me stesso di me pietate vène" (*Rime* 16) [I feel compassion for myself], line 11: "sì feramente che distrugge 'l cor" [so savagely that she destroys my heart], and "Io vidi li occhi dove Amor si mise" (*Rime* 23) [I saw the eyes where Love had placed itself], line 4: "allora dico che 'l cor si divise" [and so I say that my heart split].

11. In addition to the commentaries by De Robertis (*Vita Nuova* [1980]), Gorni (*Vita Nova* [1996]), Carrai (*Vita nova*), and Pirovano (*Vita nuova*), see

Dante's Lyric Poetry, Barolini ed., 475–82, who notes the role of the woman as agent and the erotic charge of the sonnet.

12. The moral and spiritual dangers of sight are of course a rich and recurrent theme in the Bible; see John 5:28; Job 24:15; 2 Peter 2:14; Psalm 17:28; Isaiah 2:11; Ecclesiastes 14:8; Proverbs 27:20; Psalm 30:11.

13. *Dante's Lyric Poetry*, Barolini ed., 483–89.

14. Lombardo, *Boezio in Dante*, 443–44. See also Todorović, *Dante*, 33–34.

15. For the first two terms, see Psalm 139:10; 19.2; 21.12; 54.4. For *spiramento*, see 2 Esdras 16.63; Job 26.4.

16. While it is tempting to consider the possible imprint of major discussions such as Cicero, *De officiis* 1.28.101, the most recent findings on Florentine culture of the 1290s and our knowledge of the limited circulaton of Cicero there suggest that we should be careful about putting forward too readily any precise textual sources.

17. On time indications and biblical patterning, see Sbacchi, "Indicazioni orarie," 33–37.

18. Baldelli, "Visione immaginazione e fantasia"; Borsa, "Immagine e immaginazione"; Gubbini, "Immaginazione e malinconia"; Presti, "Dante's *forte immaginazione*"; Tavoni, "Visione interiore"; Tonelli, *Fisiologia della passione*, 125–34; Tonelli, "Tempi della poesia." More broadly, see Rea, "*Amor est passio*." On the role of the imagination in other visions, see *Vita nova* II.7 [1.8]; IX.3 [9.3]; XXIII.4 and 7 [14.4 and 7]. Still valuable is Hollander, "*Vita nuova*."

19. On the treatise (certainly known to Dante by the time of the *Convivio*), see Ricklin, "Albert le Grand"; Donati, "Dreams."

20. Albert the Great, *De somno et vigilia* 3.1.10, 192.

21. *De somno et vigilia* 3.1.9, 190: "Formae coelitus evectae ad nos, corpora nostra tangentis fortissime movent, et suas imprimunt virtutes, licet non sentiantur propter exteriorem tumultum: et ideo quando alienatio fit a sensibus, quocumque modo illud fiat, tunc percipiuntur motus sicut illud percipit motum passionis, licet non moveat ut passio, sed potius ut signum . . . anima autem imaginativa ad quam pervenit motus huiusmodi formae, recipit motum secundum modum possibilem sibi, et hoc est ad formas imaginationis" [Celestial forms are transmitted to us and make powerful contact with our bodies and imprint powers, although these are not sensed because of the tumult around us; but when we are removed from the senses, however this happens, then their movement is perceived and the person receiving that motion perceives it too, receiving this in the way that is possible to humans, and this is in imagined forms].

22. Especially notable is the imprint of "Se Mercé fosse amica a' miei disiri" (*Rime* 15) [If Mercy was a friend to my desires] and several of its rhyme words (*core, valore, miri, martiri*) that are closely echoed by Dante.

23. On the *donna gentile*, as well as the main commentaries, see the overviews in Cervigni, "*Donna Gentile*"; Petrocchi, "Donna gentile"; Took, "Lady Philosophy." See also Barolini, "Archeologia della donna gentile," "Case," and "Saggio di un commento"; and Dronke, *Dante's Second Love*. Barolini in particular has returned to the question of the second *rifacimento*, disputing strongly (and rightly in my opinion) the arguments of its most recent supporter, Maria Corti; see Corti, *Felicità mentale*, 146–56. For an earlier major refutation, see Marti, "Vita e morte."

24. On the chronology, see *Dante's Lyric Poetry*, Foster and Boyde ed., 2:341–62, and most recently Casadei, "Puntualizzare le puntualizzazioni."

25. See again the discussion in Barolini, "Archeologia della donna gentile," 100–104.

Vita nova XXXV [24]

1. Hirsh, "Prose Structure," 402.
2. Barolini, *Dante's Poets*, 16.
3. Barański, "Dante Alighieri," 568.
4. Barolini, *Dante's Poets*, 15.
5. Hogan, *Affective Narratology*, 36–37.
6. Ibid., 36.
7. Carrai, "Introduzione," 22 (translation mine).
8. Hogan, *Affective Narratology*, 5.
9. Chiarantini, "'Pricking of Memory,'" n.p.
10. Hogan, *Affective Narratology*, 34.
11. Pazzaglia, "Donne ch'avete intelletto d'amore"; my translation.
12. Hogan, *Affective Narratology*, 36.
13. Ibid., 18.
14. *Vita nuova*, Pirovano ed., 259.
15. My translation, adapted from *Vita nova*, trans. Frisardi, to retain double negation.
16. *Vita Nova*, Gorni ed. [2011], 1024.
17. Kay, *Dante's Lyric Redemption*, 124.
18. Pazzaglia, "Videro li occhi miei quanta pietate."
19. Minnis, *Medieval Theory of Authorship*, 10.

Vita nova XXXVI and XXXVII [25–26]

Michael Hofmann's epigraph is from *Poetry Book Society Bulletin* (Summer 1999), quoted in O'Driscoll, *Quote Poet Unquote*, 9.

1. All references to the *Commedia* are from *Commedia secondo l'antica vulgata*, ed. Petrocchi. See too Petrocchi's discussion of the variant *vanità, ad loc.* and 1:221, a variant reading endorsed by Fenzi, "'Costanzia de la ragione,'" 195–98. All translations are my own.

2. All reference to the *libello* are to *Vita Nuova*, Barbi ed. [1932], taking account of *Vita Nuova*, Barbi ed. [1907]; *Vita Nuova*, De Robertis ed. [1980], now in Alighieri, *Opere minori* [1984]; *Vita Nova*, Gorni ed. [1996], now in *Opere* [2011]; and *Vita nuova*, Pirovano ed.; for separate treatments of the two sonnets being discussed here, see *Rime*, Grimaldi ed., 567–73; see also *Rime della "Vita Nuova,"* Barbi and Maggini ed., 138–42; and *Dante's Lyric Poetry*, Foster and Boyde ed., 1:92–93 and 2:146–48. See also Pazzaglia, "Color d'amore" and "L'amaro lagrimar."

3. See Afribo, "Aspetti della metrica," 569.

4. See Solimena, *Repertorio metrico dello stil novo*, 53–56 (no. 91). The scheme does not occur in the Scuola Siciliana and occurs only once among the Siculo-Tuscans, for which see Solimena, *Repertorio metrico dei poeti siculo-toscani*, 131 (no. 172). Cfr. Biadene, *Morfologia del sonetto*, 39.

5. Pazzaglia, "Color d'amore," 63.

6. See *Poeti del dolce stil novo*, Pirovano ed., 523–24 (no. 94); and see *Poeti del dolce stil nuovo*, Marti ed., 644–45 (no. 94).

7. On the various techniques of connecting the *fronte* and the *sirma* in early Italian sonnets, see Menichetti, "Implicazioni retoriche," and Santagata, *Dal sonetto al canzoniere*, 57–113.

8. Texts will be cited from *CLPIO*, Avalle ed. The inclusion of the word *Donne* in V (Biblioteca Apostolica Vaticana, MS Vat. lat. 3793) renders the line hypermetric, though a (small) number of scholars have argued it constitutes a kind of anacrusis, not metrically counted; see Spampinato Beretta's note *ad loc.* in *Poeti della Scuola siciliana*, Antonelli et al. ed., 2:537.

9. See *CLPIO* V 646–V 669; see also Monte Andrea, *Rime*, Minetti ed., 168–85.

10. Another example of the noun *schianto* is found in the *canzone* "Donna senza pietanza" [Woman without pity], the only known work of an obscure figure Lapuccio Belfradelli, where the narrator begs the beloved to reveal what wrong (*fallare*) he has done her, which has her cause him suffering, "e poi mi· date schianto" (*CLPIO* V 296, line 26) [and then you give me suffering].

11. See Rapisarda, "Tommaso di Sasso."

12. Panvini felt that the reading "mi schianto" was "inappropriate to the sense" and emended the verb to "mi scantu" (I am frightened, or worried); see *Rime della Scuola siciliana*, Panvini ed., 1:70. However, Rapisarda (following Contini) sees such an emendation as unnecessarily audacious; see *Poeti della Scuola siciliana*, Antonelli et al. ed., 2:43–44 (note *ad loc.*).

13. Apart from the example in Cielo d'Alcamo already noted, see also the anonymous *canzone* "Del meo disio spietato" [Of my pitiless desire]: "Li schianti e lo sentore / mi· 'nfiamano d' uno volere, / ché mi· 'ngiengnano partire / di vostra 'namoranza' (*CLPIO* V 265, lines 13–16).

14. *CLPIO* V 309, lines 31–33; see *Corona di casistica amorosa*, Maffia Scariati ed., 239, and *Poeti del Duecento*, Contini ed., 2:706. The anonymous poet places *schianti* in rhyme with *davanti : manti : innanti : amanti*.

15. *Corona di casistica amorosa*, Maffia Scariati ed., xxxiv.

16. *Poeti del Duecento*, Contini ed., 2:696.

17. Citing Cavalcanti, *Rime*, De Robertis ed., 234–35 (Appendix no. 5).

18. Onesto da Bologna, *Rime*, Orlando ed., 54–55 (no. 11); and see *Poeti del dolce stil novo*, Pirovano ed., 604–5 (no. 132a), with *Poeti del dolce stil nuovo*, Marti ed., 748–49.

19. For sporadic other examples, see Panuccio del Bagno, "Raprezentando a chanoscensa vostra," in *Rime*, Panizza ed., 139–42 (no. 15); Meo de' Tolomei, "Io feci di me stesso un Ciampolino," in "Rime di Meo dei Tolomei," Bettarini Bruni ed., 67 (no. 17); and Antonio da Tempo, "Sempre si vuole aver con uomo pace," in Antonio da Tempo, *Summa artis rithmici vulgaris dictaminis*, Andrews ed., 26 (no. 12). On the form, see now Moccia, *Sonetto continuo*.

20. *Poeti del dolce stil nuovo*, Marti ed., 1033.

Vita nova XXXVIII and XXXIX [27–28]

1. Or, according to Simonelli, "'Donna pietosa,'" 147–49, the *donna pietosa*.

2. In this regard, see Maldina, "Salmi e l'autobiografismo."

3. Fenzi, "'Costanzia della Ragione,'" and Rea, "Amore e ragione," 187–91.

4. See the commentaries in *Vita Nova*, Gorni ed. [2011], 1037, and *Vita nuova*, Pirovano ed., 269.

5. On the role of Reason in Dante's *Vita nova*, see, more broadly, Rea, "Amore e ragione," according to which the infatuation for the *donna gentile* "thus involves a decentering: losing the intimate ideal of a rational love, and is com-

pleted in itself in order to venture forth again across the uncertain geometries of desire" (188).

6. See Carrai, *Dante elegiaco.*

7. See *Vita Nuova*, Ciccuto ed., 239.

8. See *Vita Nuova*, De Robertis ed. [1980], 237.

9. This is also because Matthew 24:29 offers the opening to a chapter in which "Dante finds again . . . his role as evangelist of the true love that Beatrice has represented and represents." *Vita nuova*, Pirovano ed., 277.

10. Fenzi, "'Costanzia della Ragione,'" 94, stresses, on the contrary, the importance of the model offered by Peter, who denies Jesus in Luke 22:50–56.

11. Ibid., 91: "[Dante] impulsively almost makes of her another Beatrice."

12. Martinez, "Mourning Beatrice."

13. See Dell'Oso, "Tra Bibbia e 'letteratura di costumanza.'"

14. On the importance of the notion of *vanitade*, see Fenzi, "'Contanzia della Ragione,'" 86–87.

15. Ibid., 89.

16. On the impossibility of the old and the new love coexisting, see ibid., 95.

17. On the importance of Cicero's treatise in this respect, see De Robertis, *Libro della "Vita Nuova"* [2nd ed., 1970], 159–60, and Fenzi, "Boezio," 136–38 (on *De amicitia* 27.102–4).

Vita nova XL–XLII [29–31]: A Portrait of the Artist as a Young Man

1. See Barański, "'Lascio cotale trattato.'"

2. For an authoritative review of the question of the numbering of the chapters and the title, see Pirovano, "Per una nuova edizione," 325: "La tradizione manoscritta non sostiene in nessun modo l'ipotesi di una paragrafatura originaria della *Vita nuova.*" Pirovano opts for the vernacular title because it is featured in a large part of the manuscript tradition and nearly all printed editions, while the form *Vita nova* appears "generalmente nel contesto di una formula incipitaria o esplicitaria in latino" (318) [generally speaking in the context of formulaic incipit or explicit in Latin].

3. Lansing, "Formal Structure," 92.

4. *Vita Nova*, Gorni ed. [1996], 275.

5. This aspect of the work made a deep impression on James Joyce. On the influence of the *Vita nova* on Joyce's *A Portrait*, see M. Reynolds, *Joyce and Dante*, 178–83, 194–99, 262.

6. Musa, "Essay," 168, affirms that the *Vita nova* ends "in failure and in the recognition of failure"; R. Harrison, *Body of Beatrice*, 12, writes that a "dramatic failure, an avowed authorial inadequacy, haunt the end of this work."

7. Levers, "Image of Authorship," 16.

8. See Steinberg, "Author," 4: "The roles of Dante-poet and Dante-character are not static in the *Commedia*: the poem tells the story of how its protagonist becomes its author. At the beginning of the poem, character and poet are at opposite ends of a temporal-spatial spectrum. . . . At the poem's end, these perspectives merge."

9. *Vita Nuova*, De Robertis ed. [1980], 245.

10. *Vita Nova*, Gorni ed. [1996], 278.

11. On the development of Dante's conception of the Empyrean, see most recently Pegoretti, "Empireo in Dante," but also Fioravanti, "Aristotele e l'Empireo"; Cristaldi, *Verso L'empireo*; Cachey, "Nota sugli angeli"; and especially Moevs, *Metaphysics of Dante's Comedy*, 15–35.

12. Chisena, "Astronomia di Dante."

13. See Fabian, "Cecco vs. Dante," 88–89.

14. See *Dante's Lyric Poetry*, Barolini ed., 177–87; *Dante's Lyric Poetry*, Foster and Boyde ed., 100; Durling and Martinez, *Time and the Crystal*, 53–70; Martinez, "Guinizellian Protocols."

15. The biblical resonances of the expression (Psalm 44:17, 148:11; Revelations 18:23) would appear to support De Robertis's interpretation (pace Gorni and Pirovano) of the phrase.

16. See *Purg.* 31.100–102 and *Par.* 31. 37–39, 43–48, and 103–11. See Cachey and Sbordoni, "'Ardüa sua opra.'"

17. Cachey, "Cosmology, Geography and Cartography," 230–31.

Vita nova XL [29]

1. The terms *figure* and *figural* are used here in the sense given to the word in medieval Christian exegesis; see Auerbach, *"Figura."*

2. See Picone, *"Peregrinus amoris"* and "Esilio e *peregrinatio."*

3. For an interpretation of Dante's work as cartographic writing, see Cachey, "Cartographic Dante," "Cosmographic Cartography," and "Cosmology, Geography and Cartography." See also Demaray, "Dante and the Book."

4. My translation.

5. The figure of St. James with reference to the pilgrimage to Galicia returns in *Par.* 25.17–18. For the legend of his miraculous burial place, see Iacopo da Varazze, "De sancto Iacobo apostolo."

6. *Vita Nuova*, De Robertis ed. [1980], 239, notes that *romei* were initially those who from Rome, or more generally from the West, went to the Holy Land; subsequently the word's meaning changed to indicate the pilgrims directed to Rome.

7. Ibid., 237.

8. For the link to Luke's Gospel, see Bolton Holloway, "*Vita Nuova*," which traces the presence of the paradigms of Exodus, Numbers, and Emmaus in the *libello*.

9. For the theme of vision in chapter XL [29], see Vettori, "Veronica"; for images and imagination, see Borsa, "Immagine e immaginazione."

10. Translations from the *Commedia* are taken from *Inferno; Purgatorio; Paradiso*, Hollander ed.

11. Rome in Dante's work has been the focus of many important studies. A still-essential starting point is Zingarelli, *Dante e Roma*; see also Basserman, *Orme di Dante*, 5–25; Muñoz, *Roma di Dante*; Ricci, *Roma nel pensiero di Dante*; Lenkeith, *Dante and the Legend*; Davis, *Dante and the Idea*; Fallani, "Idea di Roma"; Bracco, "Ricordo dei monumenti"; V. Frugoni, "Dante e la Roma"; Longo, *Papi, Roma e Dante*. For Rome as the destination of Dante-the-pilgrim and his journey, see Cachey and Sbordoni, "'Ardüa sua opra.'"

12. For the presence of elegy and elegiac models in the *Vita nova*, see Carrai, *Dante elegiaco*.

Vita nova XLI [30]

1. The English translations of *Vita nova* and *Convivio* are cited from Andrew Frisardi's editions. I have developed some of the ideas presented in this chapter in Dell'Oso, "Dante, Peter of Trabibus."

2. The relevance of the courtly tradition has been especially highlighted by Barbi, "Razionalismo e misticismo," 63; De Robertis, *Libro della "Vita Nuova"* [2nd ed., 1970], 121–24; *Vita Nuova*, De Robertis ed. [1980], 241–46, although he also observes that "è evidente sin d'ora l'adozione del linguaggio . . . dell'ascesi mistica" (243) [the adoption of the language of mystical asceticism is already evident]; and more recently in *Rime*, Grimaldi ed., 584–85. The presence of mystical elements was first highlighted by Marigo, *Mistica e scienza*, and Singleton, *Essay on the "Vita Nuova,"* 101–9; for more recent contributions, see Distefano, "Mistica della *Vita nova*," and Mocan, "'Intelletto d'amore.'"

3. *Vita nuova*, Pirovano ed., 286.

4. Leporatti, "Dolci rime d'amor," 107.

5. See especially Falzone, *Desiderio della scienza*, 257–77. The diffusion of this *sententia* is evident also in vernacular poetry. For instance, Guinizzelli mentions the image of the sun's impact on sight in his famous *canzone* "Al cor gentil" [The gentle heart], lines 41–42. The motif of the "sun shining before our eyes" is in fact used here as a simple term of comparison to emphasize how "God the creator shines before the angelic intelligence, the driving force of the sky" (*Poeti del Duecento*, Contini ed., 2:463; my translation). In addition, the motif of the relationship between God and the angelic intelligence is used exclusively to depict the lover's obedience to the woman (line 50). As we will see, Dante's use of the Aristotelian quotation is notably different.

6. On the *Vita nova*'s dating, see, most recently, Carrai, "Puntualizzazioni."

7. On Peter of Trabibus and Dante's intellectual formation, see Piron, "Poète et le théologien," and Nasti, "'Vocabuli d'autori.'"

8. Florence, Biblioteca Nazionale Centrale, *Conv. Soppr.* D.6.359, 109vb–110ra (q. 19): "Iuxta hoc quaeritur utrum per talem scientiam possit homo cognoscere de veritate fidei" [Immediately after this [*quaestio*], one wonders whether through this science [the science of humane letters] man can know a truth of faith]. In the *responsio,* Trabibus states that "naturalia scibilia per talem scientiam non sufficiunt ad iudicandum de fide" [the natural things known through the science of humane letters are not sufficient to make judgments on faith]. The *quaestio* remains unedited; however, Anna Pegoretti provided a transcription in a seminar given at the University of Notre Dame in 2014, entitled "Mendicant Schools and Philosophy in Dante's Florence." I was able usefully to compare her transcription with the one I later made in my PhD dissertation; Dell'Oso, "How Dante Became Dante." I thank Anna for sharing with me her transcription. The *quaestio* in which the "scientia litterarum humanarum" broadly refers to pagan poetry and philosophy is n. 18: "utrum scilicet scientia litterarum humanarum vel bonitas intellectus conferat ad sanctitatem animae" [whether the knowledge of humane letters or the goodness of the intellect contributes to the sanctity of the soul]. Here Trabibus stresses that "in philosophis et poetis est quaedam pulcritudo et sillabarum et dictionum conveniens proportio, et rationis deductio in philosophis" (109vb) [in the philosophers and poets there is a kind of beauty and an appropriate proportion of words and syllables, and a reason's deduction is in the philosophers]. This *quaestio* has been extensively studied by Piron, "Poète et le théologien." The manuscript BNC, Florence, *Conv. Soppr.* D.6.359, belonged to the ancient book collection of Santa Croce and is described in Giles of Rome, *Opera omnia*, 89–111, and in Albanese et al., *Dante e il suo tempo,* 2:600–604.

9. BNC, Florence, *Conv. Soppr.* D.6.359, 109vb: "Ratio in acquisitione scientiae fidei sequitur et movet motu non suo, sed *superinfuso* et *altiori* ad ea quae sibi divinitus revelata sunt" [In the acquisition of the science of faith, reason follows and moves, not by its own motion, but by a motion that is infused and is higher, toward those things that are revealed to itself by divine inspiration].

10. On Amore in "Oltre la spera," see Cristaldi, *Occasioni dantesche*, 227–38. According to Cristaldi, the "intelligenza nova" is not equivalent to divine inspiration, and Amore is still linked to an earthly perspective, even if it is on a "linea di confine," a borderline (233).

11. Peter's *quaestio* also recalls the movement "motu proprio" of the celestial spheres ("sperae") that, however, are moved by the movement of the firmament ("motu firmamenti"): "Sperae caelestes secuntur et moventur proprio motu contra orientem . . . sperae moventur motu firmamenti de oriente ad occidentem" [The celestial spheres follow and move with their own motion in the direction of the east, and the spheres are moved by the movement of the firmament from east to west]. This description of the movement of the "sperae" may have left some traces in Dante's description of the "pensero" that goes beyond the "spera che più larga gira," namely, the Primum mobile or the Crystalline sphere. On Dante's conception of the Empyrean, see Moevs, *Metaphysics of Dante's "Comedy,"* 15–35. On the Empyrean in the *Convivio*, see also Pegoretti, "Empireo in Dante."

12. Peter's criticism of poets and philosophers appears specifically in two *quaestiones* of his *Quodlibet* I (namely, numbers 18 and 19), but it can also be perceived in *quaestiones* 41 and 42. In the first *quaestio*, "utrum scilicet scientia litterarum humanarum vel bonitas intellectus conferat ad sanctitatem animae" [whether the knowledge of human letters or the goodness of the intellect contributes to the sanctity of the soul], Peter argues that humane letters (namely, pagan poetry and philosophy) can help achieve the sanctity of the soul, but they are useful only for young people who are not too dull-witted and who are suited for education (namely, for students). In *quaestio* 41, "utrum caelum absconderit vel impedimentum tale habuerit quod nullo modo lucem nobis praestiterit tempore mortis Christi" [whether heaven has hidden or had an obstacle such as not to offer us light in any way at the time of Christ's death], he criticizes pagan philosophers and poets who do not believe that an eclipse could have occurred at the time of Christ's death. In *quaestio* 42, "utrum scilicet, caelo quiescente, cessent omnes alii motus" [whether when the sky stops all other movements cease], the *lector* indicates the fallacy of philosophy by identifying an error of Aristotle's in the fourth book of *Physics*—"Non potest esse tempus sine motu, et motus sine tempore" [There cannot be time without movement, and movement

without time]—and maintains the superiority of the "sententia doctorum" to Aristotle's ideas.

13. For more on these issues, see Tavoni, *Qualche idea su Dante*, 295–334.

14. There are, of course, no firm grounds on which to argue that Peter and Dante were alluding to each other. However, one might reasonably suggest that Peter would not have approved of a *prosimetrum* like the *Vita nova*. Not only is Dante's work full of scriptural passages (some of them in Latin), but it also ends with a poem, "Oltre la spera," about a recently deceased woman who is treated as a celestial being. Dante's *libello* may have also elicited Peter's disapproval on account of its nontraditional soteriological purposes and its conclusion that directly appeals to God: "la quale gloriosamente mira ne la faccia di colui *qui est per omnia secula benedictus. Amen*" (XLII.3 [31.3]) [who gazes in glory into the face of him *qui est per omnia secula benedictus*]. On the salvific purpose of the *Vita nova*, see at least Singleton, *Essay on the "Vita Nuova"*; Cristaldi, *"Vita Nuova"*; Nasti, *Favole d'amore*, 43–85.

15. "Nè si dee chiamare vero filosofo colui che è amico di sapienza per utilitade, sì come sono li legisti, [li] medici e quasi tutti li religiosi, che non per sapere studiano ma per acquistare moneta o dignitade; e chi desse loro quello che acquistare intendono, non sovrastarebbero a lo studio" (*Conv.* 3.11.10) [Nor should one be called a true philosopher who is a friend of wisdom for utilitarian purposes, like judges and lawyers, doctors, and almost all the clerics, who study, not for the sake of knowledge, but to gain money or prestige; so that if anyone were to give them what they actually want, they would no longer persist in their devotion]. On Dante's criticism of the mendicants, see Montefusco, "'Sale o mura.'" On the criticism of the mendicants in vernacular literature between the thirteenth and fourteenth centuries, see Montefusco, "Maestri secolari." On antimendicant imagery, see Szittya, *Antifraternal Tradition*, and Geltner, *Making of Medieval Antifraternalism*.

16. Dell'Oso, "How Dante Became Dante." Elisa Brilli and Giuliano Milani (*Vite nuove*, 111–28) also convincingly present the *Vita nova* as a "committed" text.

17. On the *Vita nova*'s *fortuna*, see Azzetta, "'Fece molte canzoni,'" and Todorović, "Who Read the *Vita Nova*?"

Vita nova XLII [31]

1. Barański, "'Lascio cotale trattato,'" 13.
2. Ledda, *Guerra della lingua*, 63.

3. Ibid., 57. Translations of Ledda's book, and of all subsequent quotations from secondary texts in Italian, are mine.

4. Ibid., 62.

5. Ibid., 62. The English translations of the *Vita nova* are cited from Andrew Frisardi's edition.

6. Musa, *Dante's "Vita Nuova,"* 167–68; Harrison, *Body of Beatrice*, 11 and 30.

7. Barański, "'Lascio cotale trattato,'" 13; Ledda, *Guerra della lingua*, 62.

8. *Paradiso*, Hollander trans., in *Inferno; Purgatorio; Paradiso*.

9. *Vita Nova*, Gorni ed. [1996], xliii–xliv.

10. *Vita nuova*, Pirovano ed., 288.

11. Flamini, "Dante e lo 'stil novo,'" 230; see also E. Gilson, "Dalla *Vita Nuova* alla *Commedia*," 37.

12. Hardie, "Dante's 'mirabile visione,'" 135.

13. Barański, "'Lascio cotale trattato,'" 13.

14. *Vita Nova*, Gorni ed. [2011], 1061.

15. Ibid., 1063.

16. Singleton, *Essay on the "Vita Nuova,"* 7.

17. Ibid., 109.

18. Ibid., 8.

19. Levers, "Image of Authorship," 16.

20. Barański, "'Lascio cotale trattato,'" 12.

21. The translation is taken from *City of God*, trans. Sanford and Green.

22. Carrai, *Dante elegiaco*, 74–75.

23. In Boethius, *Theological Tractates*, Stewart, Rand, and Tester trans., Book 3, Chapter 12, lines 50–51 (310–11).

24. See Levers, "Image of Authorship"; E. Sanguineti, "Per una lettura."

25. Augustine, *Enarrationes in psalmos*, Psalm 39, toward the end of verse 9, PL 36; at the end of verse 8 and the beginning of verse 9 in *Expositions of the Psalms*, Boulding trans.

26. Pacioni, "*Auctoritas* poetica," 61.

27. Translation from *The Vulgate Bible*..

28. Dante, *Epistolae*, Toynbee trans. In the Toynbee translation, the letter to Can Grande is designated as Epistola X.

BIBLIOGRAPHY

Manuscript Sources

Florence, Biblioteca Nazionale Centrale, MS Magliabechiano VI 143.
Toledo, Archivo y Biblioteca Capitulares, MS Zelada 104.6.
Vatican, Biblioteca Apostolica Vaticana, MS Chigiano L V 176.
Vatican, Biblioteca Apostolica Vaticana, MS Chigiano L VIII 305.
Vatican, Biblioteca Apostolica Vaticana, MS Vat. Lat. 3793.

Primary Works

Albert the Great (Albertus Magnus). *De somno et vigilia.* Vol. 9 of *Opera omnia.* Edited by Auguste and Emile Borgnet. Paris: Vives, 1890.

Alighieri, Dante. *Commedia.* Edited by Anna Maria Chiavacci Leonardi. 3 vols. Milan: Mondadori, 1991–97.

———. *La Commedia secondo l'antica vulgata.* Edited by Giorgio Petrocchi. 4 vols. Milan: Mondadori, 1966; 2nd corrected reprinted ed., 4 vols. Florence: Le Lettere, 1994.

———. *Convivio.* Edited by Gianfranco Fioravanti. Canzoni edited by Claudio Giunta. In Dante Alighieri, *Opere,* 2:3–805. Milan: Mondadori, 2011–14.

———. *Convivio: A Dual-Language Critical Edition.* Edited and translated by Andrew Frisardi. Cambridge: Cambridge University Press, 2018.

———. *Il Convivio (The Banquet).* Translated by Richard H. Lansing. New York: Garland, 1990.

———. *Convivio.* Edited by Cesare Vasoli. Canzoni edited by Domenico De Robertis. Vol. 1, pt. 2 of *Opere minori.* Milan: Ricciardi, 1984.

———. *Dante's Lyric Poetry.* Edited and translated by Kenelm Foster and Patrick Boyde. 2 vols. Oxford: Clarendon Press, 1967.

———. *Dante's Lyric Poetry: Poems of Youth and of the "Vita nuova."* Edited by Teodolinda Barolini. Translated by Richard Lansing and Andrew Frisardi. Toronto: University of Toronto Press, 2014.

————. *De vulgari eloquentia.* Edited and translated by Steven Botterill. Cambridge: Cambridge University Press, 1996.

————. *De vulgari eloquentia.* Edited by Pier Vincenzo Mengaldo, vol. 2 of *Opere minori*, 1–237. Milan: Ricciardi, 1979.

————. *De vulgari eloquentia.* Edited by Mirko Tavoni. In Dante Alighieri, *Opere*, 1:1065–547. Milan: Mondadori, 2011.

————. *La Divina Commedia.* Edited by Natalino Sapegno. Florence: La Nuova Italia, 1968.

————. *Epistolae: The Letters of Dante.* Edited and translated by Paget Toynbee. 2nd ed. Oxford: Clarendon Press, 1966.

————. *Epistole.* Edited by Ermenegildo Pistelli. Florence: Società Dantesca Italiana, 1960. www.danteonline.it.

————. *Il Fiore e il Detto d'Amore attribuibili a Dante Alighieri.* Edited by Gianfranco Contini. Milan: Mondadori, 1984.

————. *The Inferno; Purgatorio; Paradiso.* Edited by Robert Hollander. 3 vols. New York: Anchor Books, 2000–2007.

————. *Opere minori.* 2 vols. Milan: Ricciardi, 1979–88.

————. *Paradiso.* Vol. 3 of *The Divine Comedy of Dante Alighieri.* Edited and translated by Robert M. Durling. Annotated by Ronald L. Martinez and Robert M. Durling. Oxford: Oxford University Press, 2011.

————. *Rime.* Edited by Gianfranco Contini. Turin: Einaudi, 1939; 2nd ed. 1946.

————. *Rime.* Edited by Domenico De Robertis. 5 vols. Florence: Le Lettere, 2002.

————. *Rime.* Edited and commented by Domenico De Robertis. Florence: SISMEL and Edizioni del Galluzzo, 2005.

————. *Rime.* Edited by Marco Grimaldi. In *Vita nuova; Rime*, edited by Donato Pirovano and Marco Grimaldi. Rome: Salerno Editrice, 2015.

————. *Rime della "Vita Nuova" e della giovinezza.* Edited by Michele Barbi and Francesco Maggini. Florence: Le Monnier, 1956.

————. *Rime giovanili e della "Vita Nuova."* Edited by Teodolinda Barolini. With notes by Manuele Gragnolati. Milan: Rizzoli, 2009.

————.*Vita nova.* Edited by Stefano Carrai. Milan: Rizzoli, 2009.

————. *Vita nova.* Translation, introduction, notes by Andrew Frisardi. Evanston, IL: Northwestern University Press, 2012.

————. *Vita Nova.* Edited by Guglielmo Gorni. Turin: Einaudi, 1996.

————. *Vita Nova.* Edited by Guglielmo Gorni. In Dante Alighieri, *Opere*, 1:745–1063. Milan: Mondadori, 2011.

————. *Vita Nova.* Edited by Luca Carlo Rossi. Milan: Mondadori, 1999.

———. *La Vita Nuova*. Edited by Michele Barbi. Milan: U. Hoepli, 1907.

———. *La Vita Nuova*. Edited by Michele Barbi. Rev. ed. Florence: Bemporad, 1932.

———. *Vita Nuova*. Edited by Marcello Ciccuto. Milan: Rizzoli, 1984.

———. *Vita Nuova*. Edited by Manuela Colombo. Milan: Feltrinelli, 2008.

———. *Vita Nuova*. Edited by Domenico De Robertis. Milan: Ricciardi, 1980.

———. *Vita Nuova*. Edited by Domenico De Robertis. Vol. 1, pt. 1 of *Opere minori*, 3–247. Milan: Ricciardi, 1984.

———. *La Vita Nuova: Con prefazione su Beatrice*. Edited by Aurelio Gotti. Florence: Civelli Editore, 1890.

———. *Vita nuova*. Edited by Donato Pirovano. In *Vita nuova; Rime*, edited by Donato Pirovano and Marco Grimaldi. Rome: Salerno Editrice, 2015.

———. *Vita Nuova*. Translated by Barbara Reynolds. Harmondsworth: Penguin, 1975.

———. *Vita nuova di Dante Alighieri: Con XV canzoni del medesimo e la Vita di esso Dante scritta da Giovanni Boccaccio*. Florence: Bartolomeo Sermartelli, 1576. Reprint, Rome: Edindustria, 1965.

———. *Vita nuova: Italian Text with Facing English Translation*. Edited by Dino S. Cervigni and Edward Vasta. Notre Dame, IN: University of Notre Dame Press, 1995.

———. *Vita nuova-Rime*. Edited by Fredi Chiappelli. Milan: Mursia, 1965.

Alighieri, Pietro. *Comentum. Redazione ashburnhamiano-barberiniana*. Edited by Giuseppe Alvino. 2 vols. Rome: Salerno Editrice, 2021.

———. *Il "Commentarium" di Pietro Alighieri nelle redazioni ashburnhamiana e ottoboniana*. Edited by Roberto Della Vedova and Maria Teresa Silvotti. Florence: Olschki, 1978.

Andrea da Grosseto. *Dei Trattati morali di Albertano da Brescia volgarizzamento inedito del 1268*. Edited by Francesco Selmi. Bologna: Romagnoli, 1873.

Andreas Capellanus. *De amore libri tres. Text und Übersetzung*. Edited by Emil Trojel and German translation by Fritz Peter Knapp. Berlin: De Gruyter, 2006.

———. *On Love*. Edited with an English translation by P. G. Walsh. London: Duckworth, 1982.

Angela da Foligno. *Il libro dell'esperienza*. Edited by Giovanni Pozzi. Milan: Adelphi, 1992.

Antonio da Tempo. *Summa artis rithimici vulgaris dictaminis*. Edited by Richard Andrews. Bologna: Commissione per i testi di lingua, 1977.

Aquinas, Thomas. *Commentaries on Aristotle's On Memory and Recollection*. In *Commentaries on Aristotle's On Sense and What Is Sensed and On Memory and*

Recollection. Translated with introductions and notes by K. White and E. M. Macierowski. Washington, DC: Catholic University of America Press, 2005.

———. *In duodecim libros metaphysicorum Aristotelis expositio*. Edited by M.-R. Cathala. Revised by Raimondo M. Spiazzi. Turin: Marietti, 1964.

———. *In librum beati Dionysii De divinis nominibus expositio*. Edited by Ceslas Pera. Turin: Marietti, 1950.

———. *Opera omnia S. Thomae*. Edited by Enrique Alarcón. Pamplona: Corpus Thomisticum, 2000–. www.corpusthomisticum.org/iopera.html.

———. *Quodlibetal Questions*. Translated and introduced by Turner Nevitt and Brian Davies. Oxford: Oxford University Press, 2020.

———. *Sancti Thomae de Aquino Summa theologiae*. Milan: Editiones Paulinae, 1988.

———. *Scriptum super Sententiis magistri Petri Lombardi*. Paris: Lethielleux, 1929.

———. *Summa contra gentiles*. Edited by Joseph Rickaby, Cyrille Michon, Vincent Aubin, and Denis Moreau. Turin: Marietti, 1946.

Les *"Auctoritates Aristotelis": Un florilège médiéval*. Edited by Jacqueline Hamesse. Paris: Vrin, 1974.

Augustine. *City of God. 5. Books 16–18.35*. Translated by Eva M. Sanford and William M. Green. Cambridge, MA: Harvard University Press, 1965.

———. *De civitate Dei contra paganos*. In *Opera omnia Augustini Hipponensis*. PL 41. Patrologia Latina database. http://pld.chadwyck.co.uk/.

———. *De doctrina christiana*. Edited by Josef Martin. Turnhout: Brepols, 1962.

———. *De doctrina christiana*. PL 34. https://tatooweb.unibo.it.

———. *De libero arbitrio* (*On Free Choice of the Will*). Translated by Anna S. Benjamin and L. H. Hackstaff. Indianapolis: Bobbs-Merrill, 1964.

———. *De musica*. Edited by Martin Jacobsson. Introduction by Martin Jacobsson and Lukas J. Dorfbauer. Berlin: De Gruyter, 2017.

———. *Enarrationes in psalmos*. PL 36.

———. *Epistula* 118. PL 33. https://tatooweb.unibo.it.

———. *Expositions of the Psalms 33–50*. In *The Works of Saint Augustine* (3rd release), vol. 3:16. Translated by Maria Boulding, edited by John E. Rotelle. New York: New City Press, 2000. http://www.nlx.com/home/.

———. *On Christian Teaching*. Translated by R. P. H. Green. Oxford: Oxford University Press, 2008.

———. *De vita beata*. In *Selected Writings*. New York: Paulist Press, 1984.

———. *Sermones ad populum*. PL 38.

Averroës (Ibn Rushd). *Compendia librorum Aristotelis qui Parva naturalia vocantur.* Edited by A. L Shields. Cambridge, MA: Mediaeval Academy of America, 1949.

Biblia Sacra Vulgata. Edited by Andreas Beriger, Widu-Wolfgang Ehlers, and Michael Fieger. 5 vols. Berlin: De Gruyter, 2018.

Boccaccio, Giovanni. *Decameron.* Edited by Vittore Branca. Milan: Mondadori, 1976.

——. *Esposizioni sopra la "Comedia" di Dante.* Edited by Giorgio Padoan. Milan: Mondadori, 1965.

——. *Trattatello in laude di Dante.* Edited by Pier Giorgio Ricci. In Giovanni Boccaccio, *Opere in versi. Corbaccio. Trattatello in laude di Dante. Prose latine. Epistole,* edited by Pier Giorgio Ricci, 587–650. Milan: Ricciardi, 1965.

——. *Trattatello in laude di Dante.* Edited by Pier Giorgio Ricci. Milan: Mondadori, 1974.

——. *Trattatello in laude di Dante (redaz. dell'autografo Chigiano: Secondo compendio).* In Giovanni Boccaccio, *Trattatello in laude di Dante,* edited by Pier Giorgio Ricci, 105–61. Alpignano: Tallone, 1969.

——. *Trattatello in laude di Dante (redaz. dell'autografo Toledano).* In Giovanni Boccaccio, *Trattatello in laude di Dante,* edited by Pier Giorgio Ricci, 3–101. Alpignano: Tallone, 1969.

Boethius. *De arithmetica.* Edited by Johannes Schilling and Henri Oosthout. Turnhout: Brepols, 1999.

——. *Theological Tractates. The Consolation of Philosophy.* Translated by H. F. Stewart, E. K. Rand, and S. J. Tester. Cambridge, MA: Harvard University Press, 1973.

Bonaventure of Bagnoregio. *Commentaria in quatuor libros Sententiarum.* In *S. Bonaventuarae opera omnia,* edited by Collegium S. Bonaventurae. 10 vols. Quaracchi: ex typographia Collegii s. Bonaventurae, 1882–1902.

——. *Itinerarium mentis in Deum.* In *S. Bonaventuarae opera omnia,* edited by Collegium S. Bonaventurae. 10 vols. Quaracchi: ex typographia Collegii s. Bonaventurae, 1882–1902.

——. *Legenda maior.* www.franciscantradition.org/early-sources-index.

I canzonieri della lirica italiana degli origini. Edited by Lino Leonardi. 4 vols. Florence: SISMEL and Edizioni del Galluzzo, 2001.

Cavalcanti, Guido. *The Complete Poems.* Translated by Marc A. Cirigliano. New York: Italica Press, 1992.

——. *Complete Poems: Dual Language.* Translated by Anthony Mortimer. London: Alma Books, 2012.

―――. *The Poetry of Guido Cavalcanti*. Translated by Lowry Nelson Jr. New York: Garland, 1986.

―――. *Rime, con le rime di Iacopo Cavalcanti*. Edited by Domenico De Robertis. Turin: Einaudi, 1986.

―――. *Rime*. Edited by Roberto Rea and Giorgio Inglese. Rome: Carocci, 2011.

―――. *Rime: Edizione critica, commento, concordanza*. Edited by Letterio Cassata. Anzio: De Rubeis, 1993.

Chaucer, Geoffrey. *The Legend of Good Women*. In *The Riverside Chaucer*, edited by Larry D. Benson, 587–630. 3rd ed. Oxford: Oxford University Press, 2008.

Cicero, *De amicitia*. Edited by R. Combès. Paris: Les Belles Lettres, 1971.

CLPIO [*Concordanze della lingua poetica italiana delle origini*]. Edited by d'Arco Silvio Avalle. Milan: Ricciardi, 1992–.

Commento alla "Divina Commedia" d'Anonimo fiorentino del secolo xiv, ora per la prima volta stampato. Edited by Pietro Fanfani. 3 vols. Bologna: Romagnoli, 1866–74.

La Corona di casistica amorosa e le canzoni del cosiddetto "Amico di Dante." Edited by Irene Maffia Scariati. Rome: Antenore, 2002.

Davanzati, Chiaro. *Rime*. Edited by Aldo Menichetti. Bologna: Commissione per i Testi di Lingua, 1965.

Douay-Rheims Bible and Latin Vulgate. https://drbo.org/drl/.

Durand, William. *Rationale divinorum officiorum*. Edited by Anselme Davril and Timothy M. Thibodeau. 3 vols. Turnhout: Brepols, 1995–2000.

Faidit, Gaucelm. *Les poèmes de Gaucelm Faidit, troubadour du XIIe siècle*. Edited by Jean Mouzat. Geneva: Slatkine, 1989.

The Florence Laudario: An Edition of Florence, Biblioteca Nazionale Centrale, Banco Rari 18. Edited by Blake McDowell Wilson and Nello Barbieri. Madison, WI: A-R Editions, 1995.

Geoffrey de Vinsauf. *Poetria nova*. In *Les arts poétiques du XIIe et du XIIIe siècle*, edited by Edmund Faral, 265–320. Paris: Champion, 1962.

Geoffrey of Aspel (Galfridus de Aspel). *Questiones super de somno et vigilia*. Edited by Sten Ebbesen. In *Cahiers de l'Institut du Moyen Âge grec et latin* 83 (2014).

Giamboni, Bono. *Della miseria dell'uomo, Giardino di consolazione, Introduzione alle virtù*. Edited by Francesco Tassi. Florence: Piatti, 1836.

―――. *Delle storie contra i pagani di Paolo Orosio libri VII, volgarizzamento di Bono Giamboni*. Edited by Francesco Tassi. Florence: Baracchi, 1849.

Gelli, Giovan Battista. *Commento edito e inedito sopra la "Divina Commedia."* Edited by Carlo Negroni. Florence: Bocca, 1887.

Giles of Rome. *Opera omnia. 1. Catalogo dei manoscritti (96–151)*. Edited by Francesco Del Punta and Concetta Luna. Vol. 6. Florence: Olschki, 1989.

Giraut de Borneil. *The Cansos and Sirventes of the Troubadour Giraut de Borneil: A Critical Edition*. Edited and translated by Ruth Verity Sharman. Cambridge: Cambridge University Press, 1989.

Gregory the Great. *Morals on the Book of Job*. Translated by Members of the English Church. 3 vols. Oxford: John Henry Parker; London: J. G. F. and J. Rivington, 1844–50.

———. *On the Song of Songs*. Translation and introduction by Mark DelCogliano. Collegeville, MN: Liturgical Press, 2012.

Guinizzelli, Guido. *The Poetry of Guido Guinizelli*. Edited and translated by Robert Edwards. New York: Garland, 1987.

———. *Rime*. Edited by Luciano Rossi. Turin: Einaudi, 2002.

Guittone d'Arezzo. *Canzoniere: I sonetti d'amore del Codice Laurenziano*. Edited by Lino Leonardi. Turin: Einaudi, 1994.

Iacopo da Varazze. "De sancto Iacobo apostolo." In *Legenda aurea: Con le miniature del codice ambrosiano C 240 inf.*, edited by Giovanni Paolo Maggioni, 2 vols, 1:726–39. Florence: SISMEL and Edizioni del Galluzzo, 2007.

Iacopone da Todi. *Laude*. Edited by Matteo Leonardi. Florence: Olschki, 2010.

Isidore of Seville. *Libri Etymologiarum sive Originum*. Edited by Wallace M. Lindsay. 2 vols. Oxford: Clarendon Press, 1911.

Jacobus de Voragine. *Liber Mariale*. http://sermones.net/thesaurus/list.php?coll=voragine%2Fmariale.

Joyce, James. *Portrait of the Artist as a Young Man*. Edited by Jeri Johnson. Oxford: Oxford University Press, 2000.

Julian of Norwich. *The Shewings of Julian of Norwich*. Edited by Georgia Ronan Crampton. Kalamazoo: Published for TEAMS in Association with the University of Rochester by Medieval Institute Publications, Western Michigan University, 1994.

Lancia, Andrea. *Chiose alla "Commedia."* Edited by Luca Azzetta. 2 vols. Rome: Salerno Editrice, 2012.

Latini, Brunetto. *La rettorica*. Edited by Francesco Maggini. Florence: Le Monnier, 1968.

———. *Il Tesoro di Brunetto Latini, volgarizzato da Bono Giamboni raffrontato con il testo autentico francese*. Edited by Pierre Chabaille. 4 vols. Bologna: Romagnoli, 1878–83.

Meister Eckhart. *Meister Eckhart: A Modern Translation*. Translation by Raymond Bernard Blakeny. New York: Harper, 1941.

Monte Andrea da Fiorenza. *Le rime.* Edited by Francesco Filippo Minetti. Florence: presso l'Accademia della Crusca, 1979.

Onesto da Bologna. *Le rime.* Edited by Sandro Orlando. Florence: Sansoni, 1974.

Ovid. *The Art of Love and Other Poems.* English and Latin edition. Edited and translated by Grant Showerman. Revised by George P. Goold. Cambridge, MA: Harvard University Press, 1979.

Panuccio dal Bagno. *Rime.* Edited by Nicola Panizza. Rome: Salerno Editrice, 2022.

Patrologiae cursus completes: Series Latina. Edited by Jacques Paul Migne. 221 vols. Paris: Migne, 1844–64.

Peter Lombard. *Sententiarum libri quatuor.* PL 191–92. Patrologia Latina database. https://tatooweb.unibo.it.

Petrarch, Francesco. *Petrarch's Lyric Poems: The "Rime Sparse" and Other Lyrics.* Translated and edited by Robert M. Durling. Cambridge, MA: Harvard University Press, 1976.

Poeti del dolce stil nuovo. Edited by Mario Marti. Florence: Le Monnier, 1969.

Poeti del dolce stil novo. Edited by Donato Pirovano. Rome: Salerno Editrice, 2012.

Poeti del Duecento. Edited by Gianfranco Contini. 2 vols. Milan: Ricciardi, 1960.

I Poeti della Scuola siciliana. Edited by Roberto Antonelli, Costanzo Di Girolamo, and Rosario Coluccia. 3 vols. Milan: Mondadori, 2008.

Pound, Ezra. *Cantos.* London: Faber and Faber, 1975.

Propertius. *Elegies.* Edited and translated by G. P. Goold. Cambridge, MA: Harvard University Press, 1990.

Reggimento de' principi di Egidio Romano (Del): Volgarizzamento trascritto nel MCCLXXXVIII. Edited by Francesco Corazzini. Florence: Le Monnier, 1858.

Le rime della Scuola siciliana. Edited by Bruno Panvini. 2 vols. Florence: Olschki, 1962–64.

Ritus in ecclesia servandi (Florence, Biblioteca Riccardiana, 3005). In Franklin Toker, *On Holy Ground: Liturgy, Architecture and Urbanism in the Cathedral and the Streets of Medieval Florence,* 157–264. Turnhout: Brepols, 2009.

Le roman d'Enéas. Edited by Aimé Petit. Paris: Livre de Poche, 1997.

Servasanto da Faenza. *Liber de virtutibus et vitiis.* In Antonio Del Castello, "La tradizione del *Liber de virtutibus et vitiis* di Servasanto da Faenza: Edizione critica delle *distinctiones* I–IV." PhD diss., University of Naples Federico II, 2013.

Sicard of Cremona. *Mitralis de officiis.* Edited by Gábor Sarbak and Lorenz Weinrich. Turnhout: Brepols, 2008.

The Troubadour Tensos and Partimens: A Critical Edition. Edited by Ruth Harvey, Linda M. Paterson, and Anna Radaelli. Cambridge: Brewer, 2010.

Virgil. *Aeneid: Books 7–12. Appendix Vergiliana.* Edited and translated by Henry Rushton Fairclough. Revised by George P. Goold. Cambridge, MA: Harvard University Press, 2000.

———. *Eclogues. Georgics. Aeneid: Books 1–6.* Edited and translated by Henry Rushton Fairclough. Revised by George P. Goold. Cambridge, MA: Harvard University Press, 2014.

The Vulgate Bible: Douay-Rheims Translation. Edited by Swift Edgar and Angela M. Kinney. 6 vols in 7. Cambridge, MA: Harvard University Press, 2010–13.

William of Saint Thierry. *Expositio super Cantica canticorum.* In *Guilelmi a Sancto Theodorico Expositio super Cantica canticorum, Brevis commentario, Excerpta de libris beati Ambrosii et Gregorii super Cantica canticorum,* edited by Paul Verdeyen. Turnhout: Brepols, 1997.

Secondary Sources

Afribo, Andrea. "Aspetti della metrica di Dante." In *Dante fra il settecentocinquantenario della nascita (2015) e il settecentenario della morte (2021),* edited by Enrico Malato and Andrea Mazzucchi, 2 vols., 2:559–75. Rome: Salerno Editrice, 2016.

Agamben, Giorgio. *Stanzas: Word and Phantasm in Western Culture.* Translated by Ronald L. Martinez. Minneapolis: University of Minnesota Press, 1993.

———. *Stanze: La parola e il fantasma nella cultura occidentale.* Turin: Einaudi, 1977.

Ahern, John. "Binding the Book: Hermeneutics and Manuscript Production in *Paradiso* 33." *PMLA* 97 (1982): 800–809.

———. "The New Life of the Book: The Implied Reader of the *Vita Nuova.*" *Dante Studies* 110 (1992): 1–16.

Akbari, Suzanne. *Seeing through the Veil: Optical Theory and Medieval Allegory.* Toronto: Toronto University Press, 2004.

Albanese, Gabriella, Sandro Bertelli, Sonia Gentili, Giorgio Inglese, and Paolo Pontari. *Dante e il suo tempo nelle biblioteche fiorentine.* 2 vols. Florence: Mandragora, 2021.

Allegretti, Paola. "L'autore." In Dante Alighieri, *Fiore. Detto d'Amore,* edited by Paola Allegretti, 183–230. Florence: Le Lettere, 2011.

Allen, Peter. *The Art of Love: Amatory Fiction from Ovid to the "Romance of the Rose."* University Park: University of Pennsylvania Press, 1992.

Ambrosini, Riccardo. "Dire." In *Enciclopedia dantesca*. Rome: Istituto della Enciclopedia Italiana, 1970–78. www.treccani.it/enciclopedia/dire_(Enciclopedia -Dantesca)/.

Amtower, Laurel. *Engaging Words: The Culture of Reading in the Later Middle Ages.* New York: Palgrave, 2000.

Antonelli, Roberto. "Cavalcanti e Dante: Al di qua del Paradiso." In *Dante: Da Firenze all'aldilà*, edited by Michelangelo Picone, 289–302. Florence: Cesati, 2001.

———. "Cavalcanti o dell'interiorità." In *Alle origini dell'Io lirico: Cavalcanti o dell'interiorità*, edited by Roberto Antonelli, 1–22. Rome: Viella, 2001.

———. "La morte di Beatrice e la struttura della storia." In *Beatrice nell'opera di Dante e nella memoria europea, 1290–1990*, edited by Maria Picchio Simonelli, 35–56. Naples: Cadmo, 1994.

Ardissino, Erminia. "*Vita nova*: Il libro delle 'transfigurazioni' d'amore." In *Vita nova. Fiore. Epistola XIII*, edited by Manuele Gragnolati, Luca Carlo Rossi, Paola Allegretti, Natascia Tonelli, and Alberto Casadei, 5–24. Florence: SISMEL and Edizioni del Galluzzo, 2018.

Ardizzone, Maria Luisa. "'Al cor gentil': A Notary in Search of Written Laws." *Modern Philology* 94, no. 4 (1997): 455–74.

Ascoli, Albert R. *Dante and the Making of a Modern Author.* Cambridge: Cambridge University Press, 2008.

Auerbach, Erich. "*Figura.*" In *Scenes from the Drama of European Literature*, 11–76. New York: Meridian Books, 1959.

———. "Figura." In *Studi su Dante*, 176–226. Milan: Feltrinelli, 1991.

Avalle, D'Arco Silvio, ed. *Concordanze della lingua poetica italiana delle origini (CLPIO).* Milan: Ricciardi, 1992.

———. *Le forme del canto: La poesia nella scuola tardoantica e altomedievale.* Edited by Maria Sofia Lannutti. Florence: Galluzzo, 2017.

Azzetta, Luca. "Canto X: Politica e poesia tra le arche degli eretici." In *Lectura Dantis Romana: Cento canti per cento anni*, vol. 1:1, *Inferno: Canti I–XVII*, edited by Enrico Malato and Andrea Mazzucchi, 311–42. Rome: Salerno Editrice, 2013.

———. "'Fece molte canzoni per lo suo amore et come pare a uno suo libreto cui ei pose nome la vita nova': Note sui primi lettori della *Vita Nova*." *Studj romanzi* 14 (2018): 57–91.

Bachelard, Gaston. *The Poetics of Space.* Boston: Beacon Press, 1994.

Baldelli, Ignazio. "Visione, immaginazione e fantasia nella *Vita Nuova*." In *I sogni nel Medioevo: Seminario internazionale, Roma, 2–4 ottobre 1983*, edited by Tullio Gregory, 1–10. Rome: Edizioni dell'Ateneo, 1985.

Banella, Laura. *La "Vita nuova" del Boccaccio: Fortuna e tradizione*. Rome: Antenore, 2017.

Barański, Zygmunt G. "The Classics." In *The Oxford Handbook of Dante*, edited by Manuele Gragnolati, Elena Lombardi, and Francesca Southerden, 111–26. Oxford: Oxford University Press, 2021.

———. "Dante Alighieri: Experimentation and (Self-)Exegesis." In *The Cambridge History of Literary Criticism*, vol. 2, *The Middle Ages*, edited by Alastair Minnis and Ian Johnson, 559–82. Cambridge: Cambridge University Press, 2005.

———. "Dante *poeta* e *lector*: 'Poesia' e 'riflessione tecnica' (con divagazioni sulla *Vita nova*)." *Critica del testo* 14, no. 1 (2011): 81–110.

———. "Guido Cavalcanti and His First Readers." In *Guido Cavalcanti tra i suoi lettori*, edited by Maria Luisa Ardizzone, 1–27. Florence: Cadmo, 2003.

———. "'Lascio cotale trattato ad altro chiosatore': Form, Literature, and Exegesis in Dante's *Vita nova*." In *Dantean Dialogues: Engaging with the Legacy of Amilcare Iannucci*, edited by Maggie Kilgour and Elena Lombardi, 1–40. Toronto: University of Toronto Press, 2013.

———. "''Nfiata labbia' and *dolce stil novo*: A Note on Dante, Ethics, and the Technical Vocabulary of Literature." In *Sotto il segno di Dante: Scritti in onore di Francesco Mazzoni*, edited by Leonella Coglievina and Domenico De Robertis, 17–35. Florence: Le Lettere, 1998.

———. "On Dante's Trail." *Italian Studies* 72, no. 1 (2017): 1–15.

———. "'Per similitudine di abito scientifico': Dante, Cavalcanti and the Sources of Medieval 'Philosophical' Poetry." In *Science and Literature in Italian Culture from Dante to Calvino*, edited by Pierpaolo Antonello and Simon A. Gilson, 14–52. Oxford: Legenda, 2004.

———. "The Roots of Dante's Plurilingualism: 'Hybridity' and Language in the *Vita nova*." In *Dante's Plurilingualism: Authority, Knowledge, Subjectivity*, edited by Sara Fortuna, Manuele Gragnolati, and Jürgen Trabant, 98–121. Oxford: Legenda, 2010.

———. "Sulla formazione intellettuale di Dante: Alcuni problemi di definizione." *Studi e problemi di critica testuale* 90, no. 1 (2015): 31–54.

———. "'Valentissimo poeta e correggitore de' poeti': A First Note on Horace and the *Vita nova*." In *Letteratura e filologia tra Svizzera e Italia: Miscellanea di studi in onore di Guglielmo Gorni*, edited by Maria Antonietta Terzoli, Alberto Asor Rosa, and Giorgio Inglese, 3 vols., 1:3–17. Rome: Edizioni di Storia a Letteratura, 2010.

———. "*Vita nova.*" In *Dante's "Other Works": Assessments and Interpretations*, edited by Zygmunt G. Barański and Theodore J. Cachey Jr., 71–124. Notre Dame, IN: University of Notre Dame Press, 2022.

Barański, Zygmunt G., Theodore J. Cachey Jr., and Luca Lombardo, eds. *Dante e la cultura fiorentina: Bono Giamboni, Brunetto Latini e la formazione intellettuale dei laici*. Rome: Salerno Editrice, 2019.

Barański, Zygmunt G., and Martin McLaughlin, eds. *Dante the Lyric and Ethical Poet*. Oxford: Legenda, 2010.

Barański, Zygmunt G., and Lino Pertile, eds. *Dante in Context*. Cambridge: Cambridge University Press, 2015.

Barbi, Michele. "Razionalismo e misticismo in Dante." In *Problemi di critica dantesca: Seconda serie (1920–1937)*, 1–86. Florence: Sansoni, 1975.

———. "Sulla 'fededegna persona' che rivelò al Boccaccio la Beatrice dantesca." In *Problemi di critica dantesca: Seconda serie (1920–1937)*, 415–20. Florence: Sansoni, 1941.

Barbour, Jennie. *The Story of Israel in the Book of Qohelet: Ecclesiastes as Cultural Memory*. Oxford: Oxford University Press, 2012.

Barolini, Teodolinda. "Archeologia della donna gentile." *Studj romanzi* 14 (2018): 93–124.

———. "The Case of the Lost Original Ending of Dante's *Vita Nuova*: More Notes toward a Critical Philology." *Medioevo letterario d'Italia* 11 (2014): 37–43.

———. "Cavalcando l'altr'ier per un cammino." In *Dante's Lyric Poetry: Poems of Youth and of the "Vita Nuova,"* edited by Teodolinda Barolini, 134–37. Toronto: University of Toronto Press, 2014.

———. "*Cominciandomi dal principio infino a la fine*: Forging Anti-narrative in the *Vita Nuova*." In *Dante and the Origins of Italian Literary Culture*, 175–92. New York: Fordham University Press, 2006.

———. "'Cominciandomi dal principio infino a la fine' (*V.N.*, XXIII, 15): Forging Anti-narrative in the *Vita Nuova*." In *"La gloriosa donna de la mente": A Commentary on the "Vita Nuova,"* edited by Vincent Moleta, 119–40. Florence: Olschki and University of Western Australia, 1994.

———. "Dante and Cavalcanti (on Making Distinctions in Matters of Love): *Inferno* V and Its Lyric and Autobiographical Context." *Dante Studies* 116 (1998): 31–63. Reprinted in *Dante and the Origins of Italian Literary Culture*, 70–101. New York: Fordham University Press, 2006.

———. "Dante and the Lyric Past." In *The Cambridge Companion to Dante*, edited by Rachel Jacoff, 14–33. Cambridge: Cambridge University Press, 1993.

———. *Dante's Poets: Textuality and Truth in the "Comedy."* Princeton, NJ: Princeton University Press, 1984.

———. "Editing Dante's *Rime* and Italian Cultural History: Dante, Boccaccio, Petrarca . . . Barbi, Contini, Foster-Boyde, De Robertis." In *Dante and the Origins of Italian Literary Culture*, 245–78. New York: Fordham University Press, 2006.

———. "Saggio di un commento alle *Rime* di Dante: I sonetti dell'episodio della donna gentile." In *Letteratura e filologia tra Svizzera e Italia: Studi in onore di Guglielmo Gorni*, edited by Maria Antonietta Terzoli, Alberto Asor Rosa, and Giorgio Inglese, 3 vols., 1:19–35. Rome: Edizioni di Storia a Letteratura, 2010.

———. "Sociology of the *Brigata*: Gendered Groups in Dante, Forese, Folgore, Boccaccio: From 'Guido, i' vorrei' to Griselda." *Italian Studies* 67, no. 1 (2012): 4–22.

———. *The Undivine Comedy: Detheologizing Dante*. Princeton, NJ: Princeton University Press, 1992.

Bartalini, Roberto. *Scultura gotica in Toscana: Maestri, monumenti, cantieri del Due e Trecento*. Milan: Silvana, 2005.

Bartoli, Vittorio. "Dante e la *pietosa* (*VN* 24–27): Le tre fasi della concupiscenza secondo Pietro Lombardo." *Studi danteschi* 75 (2010): 205–13.

———. "La traccia scientifica e scritturale della polisemia di 'cuore' nella *Vita Nova*." *Tenzone* 12 (2011): 11–42.

Basserman, Alfredo. *Orme di Dante in Italia*. Bologna: Zanichelli, 1902.

Bast, Robert, ed. *The Reformation of Faith in the Context of Late Medieval Theology and Piety: Essays by Berndt Hamm*. Leiden: Brill, 2004.

Battistini, Andrea, and Ezio Raimondi. *Le figure della retorica: Una storia letteraria italiana*. Turin: Einaudi, 1990.

Benjamin, Walter. "On the Concept of History." In *Selected Writings (1938–1940)*, edited by M. W. Jennings and H. Eiland. Cambridge, MA: Belknap Press, 2003.

Benveniste, Émile. *Problèmes de linguistique générale*. Paris: Gallimard, 1966.

Berisso, Marco. "'Per una definizione di prosopopea: Dante, *Convivio*, III, ix, 2." *Lingua e stile* 26, no. 1 (1991): 121–32.

———. "Sillogi e serie: Leggere la tradizione della poesia lirica tra Due e Trecento." In *La tradizione dei testi*, edited by Claudio Ciociola and Claudio Vela, 1–23. Florence: Società dei filologi della letteratura italiana, 2018.

Berlant, Lauren. *Cruel Optimism*. Durham, NC: Duke University Press, 2011.

Bertolini, Lucia. "'Oi': La 'voce' del pianto." *Lingua e stile* 39, no. 1 (2004): 149–56.

Bettarini Bruni, Anna, ed. "Le rime di Meo dei Tolomei e di Muscia da Siena." *Studi di filologia italiana* 32 (1974): 31–98.

Biadene, Leandro. *Morfologia del sonetto nei secoli XIII–XIV*. Florence: Le Lettere, 1977.

Bier, Miriam J. *"Perhaps There Is Hope": Reading Lamentations as a Polyphony of Pain, Penitence, and Protest*. London: Bloomsbury, 2016.

Black, Robert. *Humanism and Education in Medieval and Renaissance Italy: Tradition and Innovation in Latin Schools from the Twelfth to the Fifteenth Century*. Cambridge: Cambridge University Press, 2001.

———. "Teaching Techniques: The Evidence of Manuscript Schoolbooks Produced in Tuscany." In *The Classics in the Medieval and Renaissance Classroom*, edited by J. F. Ruys, John O. Ward, and Melanie Heyworth, 245–63. Turnhout: Brepols, 2013.

Boeckler, Albert. *Das Stuttgarter Passionale*. Augsburg: Dr Filser, 1923.

Bolton Holloway, Julia. "The *Vita Nuova*: Paradigms of Pilgrimage." *Dante Studies* 103 (1985): 103–24.

Borsa, Paolo. "'Foll'è chi crede sol veder lo vero': La tenzone tra Bonagiunta Orbicciani e Guido Guinizzelli." In *Da Guido Guinizzelli a Dante: Nuove prospettive sulla lirica del Duecento*, edited by Furio Brugnolo and Gianfelice Peron, 171–88. Padua: Il Poligrafo, 2004.

———. "Identità sociale e generi letterari: Nascita e morte del sodalizio stilnovista." *Reti medievali rivista* 18, no. 1 (2017): 271–303.

———. "Immagine e immaginazione: Una lettura della *Vita nova* di Dante." *Letteratura e arte* 16 (2018): 139–57.

———. "L'immagine nel cuore e l'immagine nella mente: Dal Notaro alla *Vita nuova* attraverso i due Guidi." In *Les deux Guidi: Guinizzelli et Cavalcanti: Mourir d'aimer et autres ruptures*, edited by Marina Gagliano, Philippe Guérin, and Raffaella Zanni, 75–92. Paris: Sorbonne Nouvelle Presses, 2016.

———. *La nuova poesia di Guido Guinizzelli*. Florence: Cadmo, 2007.

———. "Tra *Vita nova* e rime allegoriche: Nota sulla consolatoria di Cino da Pistoia per la morte di Beatrice." *Carte romanze* 2, no. 2 (2014): 301–12.

Botterill, Stephen. "'Però che la divisione non si fa se non per aprire la sentenzia della cosa divisa' (*V.N.* XIV, 13): The *Vita Nuova* as Commentary." In *"La gloriosa donna de la mente": A Commentary on the "Vita Nuova,"* edited by

Vincent Moleta, 61–76. Florence: Olschki and University of Western Australia, 1994.

Bowe, David. *Poetry in Dialogue in the Duecento and Dante.* Oxford: Oxford University Press, 2020.

Bracco, Vittorio. "Il ricordo dei monumenti di Roma e del mondo romano nella *Divina Commedia.*" *Studi romani* 13, no. 3 (1965): 281–95.

Branca, Vittore. "Poetica del rinnovamento e tradizione agiografica nella *Vita Nuova.*" In *Studi in onore di Italo Siciliano*, 2 vols., 1:123–48. Florence: Olschki, 1966.

Brand, Benjamin. *Holy Treasure and Sacred Song: Relic Cults and Their Liturgies in Medieval Tuscany.* New York: Oxford University Press, 2014.

Brilli, Elisa, and Giuliano Milani. *Vite nuove: Biografia e autobiografia di Dante.* Rome: Carocci, 2021.

Brugnolo, Furio. "'. . . Amor tenendo / meo core in mano . . .': Tre note sul primo sonetto della *Vita nuova.*" In *"Que ben devetz conoisser la plus fina": Per Margherita Spampinato*, edited by Mario Pagano, 140–56. Avellino: Sinestesie, 2018.

———. "Conservare per trasformare: Il *transfer* lirico in Dante (*Vita nuova* e dintorni)." In *Vita nova. Fiore. Epistola XIII*, edited by Manuele Gragnolati, Luca Carlo Rossi, Paola Allegretti, Natascia Tonelli, and Alberto Casadei, 25–65. Florence: SISMEL and Edizioni del Galluzzo, 2018.

———. "'Sovra la morta imagine avvenente': Commento a due sonetti di Dante (*Vita nuova*, VIII [3])." In *Charakterbilder: Zur Poetik des literarischen Porträts: Festschrift für Helmut Meter*, edited by Angela Fabris, 117–36. Göttingen: V & R Unipress, 2012.

Bruni, Francesco. "Semantica della sottigliezza." In *Testi e chierici del Medioevo*, 91–133. Genoa: Marietti, 1991.

Buck, August. "Gli studi sulla poetica e sulla retorica di Dante." In *Atti del Congresso internazionale di studi danteschi*, edited by Società Dantesca Italiana e l'Associazione internazionale per gli studi di lingua e letteratura italiana e sotto il patrocinio dei Comuni di Firenze, Verona e Ravenna, 2 vols., 1:225–47. Florence: Sansoni, 1965–66.

Bufano, Antonietta. "Adoperare." In *Enciclopedia dantesca*. Rome: Istituto della Enciclopedia Italiana, 1970–78. www.treccani.it/enciclopedia/adoperare _(Enciclopedia-Dantesca)/.

———. "Operare." In *Enciclopedia dantesca*. Rome: Istituto della Enciclopedia Italiana, 1970–78. www.treccani.it/enciclopedia/operare_(Enciclopedia -Dantesca)/.

———. "Parere." In *Enciclopedia dantesca*, 4:297–303. Rome: Istituto della Enciclopedia Italiana, 1973.

Cachey, Theodore J., Jr. "Cartographic Dante." *Italica* 87, no. 3 (2010): 325–54.

———. "Cosmographic Cartography of the Perfect Twenty-Eights." In *Vertical Readings in Dante's "Comedy,"* edited by George Corbett and Heather Webb, 3 vols., 3:111–38. Cambridge: Open Book, 2017.

———. "Cosmology, Geography and Cartography." In *Dante in Context*, edited by Zygmunt G. Barański and Lino Pertile, 221–40. Cambridge: Cambridge University Press, 2015.

———. "Una nota sugli angeli e l'Empireo." *Italianistica* 44, no. 2 (2015): 149–60.

Cachey, Theodore J., Jr., and Chiara Sbordoni. "'L'ardüa sua opra' (*Par.* 31.34): Architectural Aspects of Dante's Rome." *Opus Incertum* 7 (2021): 48–60.

Calenda, Corrado. *Appartenenze metriche ed esegesi: Dante, Cavalcanti, Guittone.* Naples: Bibliopolis, 1995.

———. "Memoria e autobiografia nella *Vita Nuova*." *Quaderni di retorica e poetica* 2, no. 1 (1986): 47–53.

———. *Per altezza d'ingegno: Saggio su Guido Cavalcanti.* Naples: Liguori, 1976.

Camargo, Martin. "The Pedagogy of the *Dictatores*." In *Papers on Rhetoric V: Atti del Convegno Internazionale Dictamen, Poetria and Cicero: Coherence and Diversification*, edited by Lucia Montefusco, 65–94. Rome: Herder, 2003.

Camilletti, Fabio. "Dante Painting an Angel: Image-Making, Double-Oriented Sonnets and Dissemblance in *Vita Nuova* XXXIV." In *Desire in Dante and the Middle Ages*, edited by Manuele Gragnolati, Tristan Kay, Elena Lombardi, and Francesca Southerden, 71–84. Oxford: Modern Humanities Research Association, 2012.

Candido, Igor. "Per una rilettura della *Vita Nova*: La prima *visio in somniis*." *Lettere italiane* 71, no. 1 (2019): 21–50.

Capelli, Roberta. *Del carnale amore: La corona di sonetti del codice Escorialense.* Rome: Carocci, 2007.

Cappello, Giovanni. "La *Vita nova* tra Guinizzelli e Cavalcanti." *Versants. Revue Suisse des Litteratures Romanes*, n.s., 13 (1988): 47–66. Reprinted in *La dimensione macrotestuale: Dante, Boccaccio, Petrarca*, 63–83. Ravenna: Longo, 1998.

Carrai, Stefano. *Dante e l'antico: L'emulazione dei classici nella "Commedia."* Florence: SISMEL and Edizioni del Galluzzo, 2012.

———. "Dante e il linguaggio dell'oltretomba: Schemi epigrafico-sepolcrali nella *Commedia*." *Giornale storico della letteratura italiana* 177 (2010): 481–510.

———. *Dante elegiaco: Una chiave di lettura per la "Vita nova."* Florence: Olschki, 2006.

———. "Introduzione." In Dante Alighieri, *Vita nova,* edited by Stefano Carrai, 5–23. Milan: Rizzoli, 2009.

———. "La presenza dei due Guidi nella *Vita nova*." *Chroniques italiennes* 32, no. 1 (2017): 145–55.

———. *Il primo libro di Dante: Un'idea della "Vita nova."* Pisa: Edizioni della Normale, 2020.

———. "Puntualizzazioni sulla datazione della *Vita nova*." *L'Alighieri* 52 (2018): 109–15.

———. "I segni premonitori della morte di Beatrice nella *Vita nova*." In *I sogni e la scienza nella letteratura italiana,* edited by Natascia Tonelli, 49–58. Pisa: Pacini, 2008.

Carrieri, Valeria. "Per una definizione del concetto di 'novità' nel lessico lirico dantesco e stilnovista." In *Stilnovo e dintorni,* edited by Marco Grimaldi and Federico Ruggiero, 31–77. Ariccia: Aracne, 2017.

Carruthers, Mary. *The Book of Memory: A Study of Memory in Medieval Culture.* 2nd ed. Cambridge: Cambridge University Press, 2008.

Casadei, Alberto. "'Incipit vita nova.'" *Dante Studies* 129 (2011): 179–86. Originally published in *Nuova rivista di letteratura italiana* 13 (2010): 11–18.

———. "Puntualizzare le puntualizzazioni: Ancora sui rapporti *Vita nova-Convivio*." *L'Alighieri* 60 (2019): 117–20.

Castellani, Arrigo. *Il Trattato della dilezione d'Albertano da Brescia nel codice II IV 111 della Biblioteca Nazionale Centrale di Firenze.* Edited by Pär Larson and Giovanna Frosini. Florence: Accademia della Crusca, 2012.

Cavarero, Adriana. *For More Than One Voice: Toward a Philosophy of Vocal Expression.* Translated by Paul A. Kottman. Stanford, CA: Stanford University Press, 2005.

Cervigni, Dino. "*Donna Gentile* of the *Vita Nuova*." In *The Dante Encyclopedia,* edited by Richard Lansing, 316–18. New York: Garland, 2000.

———. "Re-configuring the Self through Suffering, Violence, and Death in Dante's *Vita nuova* and *Comedy*." In *"Accessus ad auctores": Studies in Honor of Christopher Kleinhenz,* edited by Fabian Alfie and Andrea Dini, 115–35. Tempe: Arizona Center for Medieval and Renaissance Studies, 2011.

———. "'. . . Ricordandomi di lei, disegnava uno angelo sopra certe tavolette' (*VN*, 34. 1): Realtà, disegno, allegoria nella *Vita Nuova*." *Letture classensi* 35–36 (2007): 19–34.

———. "Segni paragrafali, maiuscole e grafia nella *Vita Nuova*: Dal libello manoscritto al libro a stampa." *Rivista di letteratura italiana* 13 (1995): 283–362.

Chaganti, Seeta. *Strange Footing: Poetic Form and Dance in the Late Middle Ages.* Chicago: University of Chicago Press, 2018.

Cherchi, Paolo. "Dante e i trovatori." In *Erudizione e leggerezza: Saggi di filologia comparativa*, edited by Giuliana Adamo, 23–34. Rome: Viella, 2012.

Chiarantini, Leonardo. "'The Pricking of Memory': Recollection as Punishment in Dante's *Inferno*." Paper presented at the International Medieval Congress, 2018, Leeds.

Chisena, Anna G. "L'astronomia di Dante prima dell'esilio: Gli anni della *Vita nova* (con un'appendice sul *Convivio*)." *L'Alighieri* 53 (2019): 25–52.

Ciacci, Otello. *Realismo della "Vita nuova."* Lanciano: Itinerari, 1974.

Ciccuto, Marcello. "'Era venuta ne la mente mia': Visione nella *Vita Nuova* e immagine nel pensiero di Dante." In *Icone della parola: Immagine e scrittura nella letteratura delle origini*, edited by Marcello Ciccuto, 95–111. Modena: Mucchi, 1995.

———. "'Era venuta ne la mente mia' (*VN* XXXIV.7): La visone nel libello e l'immagine in Dante." In *"La gloriosa donna de la mente": A Commentary on the "Vita Nuova,"* edited by Vincent Moleta, 181–93. Florence: Olschki and University of Western Australia, 1994.

Ciociola, Claudio. "La lava sotto la crosta: Per una storia delle *Rime* del '39." In *Il giovane Contini*, edited by Claudio Ciociola, 468–569. Pisa: Edizioni della Normale, 2014.

Coggeshall, Elizabeth. "Jousting with Verse: The Poetics of Friendship in Duecento *Comuni*." *Italian Culture* 38, no. 1 (2021): 99–118.

Cohen, Shaye J. D. "The Destruction: From Scripture to Midrash." *Prooftexts* 2 (1982): 18–39.

Coleman, Joyce. "Reading Practices." In *The Encyclopaedia of Medieval Literature in Britain*, edited by Sian Echard, Robert Rouse, Jacqueline Fay, Helen Fulton, and Geoff Rector, 4 vols., 4:1573–74. Oxford: Wiley, 2017.

Colombo, Michela. "Il sonetto 'Tanto gentile' e un passo apocalittico." In *Dai mistici a Dante: Il linguaggio dell'ineffabilità*, 73–89. Florence: La Nuova Italia, 1987.

Coluccia, Rosario. "Teorie e pratiche interpuntive nei volgari d'Italia dalle origini alla metà del Quattrocento." In *Storia della punteggiatura in Europa*, edited by Bice Mortara Garavelli, 65–98. Bari: Laterza, 2008.

Connor, Steven. *Dumbstruck: A Cultural History of Ventriloquism.* New York: Oxford University Press, 2000.

Contini, Gianfranco. "Cavalcanti in Dante." In *Un'idea di Dante: Saggi danteschi*, 143–57. Turin: Einaudi, 1976.

———. "Esercizio di interpretazione sopra un sonetto di Dante." In *Varianti e altra linguistica: Una raccolta di saggi (1938–1968)*, 161–68. Turin: Einaudi, 1970.

———. *Un'idea di Dante: Saggi danteschi*. Turin: Einaudi, 1970.

———. "Introduzione." In Dante Alighieri, *Rime*, 9–22. Turin: Einaudi, 1939.

———. *Varianti e altra linguistica: Una raccolta di saggi (1938–1968)*. Turin: Einaudi, 1970.

Cooper, Charlotte. "What Is a Medieval Paratext?" *Marginalia* 19 (2015): 37–50.

Copeland, Rita, and Stephen Melville. "Allegory and Allegoresis, Rhetoric and Hermeneutics." *Exemplaria* 3 (1991): 159–87.

Cornish, Alison. *Vernacular Translation in Dante's Italy: Illiterate Literature*. Cambridge: Cambridge University Press, 2011.

Corti, Maria. *Dante a un nuovo crocevia*. Florence: Libreria Commissionaria Sansoni, 1982.

———. "Dualismo e immaginazione visiva in Guido Cavalcanti." *Convivium* 5 (1951): 641–66.

———. *La felicità mentale: Nuove prospettive per Cavalcanti e Dante*. Turin: Einaudi, 1983.

———. *Percorsi dell'invenzione: Il linguaggio poetico e Dante*. Turin: Einaudi, 1993.

Crisafi, Nicolò. "The Master Narrative and Its Paradoxes." In *The Oxford Handbook of Dante*, edited by Manuele Gragnolati, Elena Lombardi, and Francesca Southerden, 513–28. Oxford: Oxford University Press, 2021.

Cristaldi, Sergio. *Occasioni dantesche*. Caltanissetta: Salvatore Sciascia Editore, 2004.

———. *La "Vita Nuova" e la restituzione del narrare*. Soveria Mannelli: Rubbettino, 1994.

———. *Verso l'empireo: Stazioni lungo la verticale dantesca*. Acireale: Bonanno, 2013.

Cropp, Glynnis M. *Le vocabulaire courtois des troubadours de l'époque classique*. Geneva: Droz, 1975.

Crudale, Alfred. "Love and *Civitas*: Dante's Ethical Journey in the *Vita Nuova*." PhD diss., University of Connecticut, 2013.

Curtius, Ernst Robert. *European Literature and the Latin Middle Ages*. Translated by Willard R. Trask. London: Routledge and Kegan Paul, 1953.

D'Addario, Arnaldo. "Portinari, Folco." In *Enciclopedia dantesca*, 4:608. Rome: Istituto della Enciclopedia Italiana, 1973.

Davis, Charles Till. *Dante and the Idea of Rome.* Oxford: Clarendon Pess, 1957.

Decaria, Alessio, and Claudio Lagomarsini, eds. *I confini della lirica: Tempi, luoghi, tradizione della poesia romanza.* Florence: SISMEL and Edizioni del Galluzzo, 2017.

DelCogliano, Mark. *Gregory the Great on the Song of Songs.* Collegeville, MN: Liturgical Press, 2012.

Delhaye, Philippe, and Giorgio Stabile. "Virtù." In *Enciclopedia dantesca.* Rome: Istituto della Enciclopedia Italiana, 1970–78. www.treccani.it/enciclopedia /virtu_(Enciclopedia-Dantesca)/.

De Libera, Alain. *La volonté et l'action.* Paris: Vrin, 2017.

Dell'Oso, Lorenzo. "Dante, Peter of Trabibus, and the 'Schools of the Religious Orders' in Florence." *Italian Studies* 77 (2022): 211–29.

———. "How Dante Became Dante: His Intellectual Formation in Florence between *Laici* and *Clerici* (1294–1296)." PhD diss., University of Notre Dame, 2020.

———. "Per la formazione intellettuale di Dante: I cataloghi librari, le tracce testuali, il *Trattatello* di Boccaccio." *Le tre corone* 4 (2017): 129–61.

———. "Tra Bibbia e 'letteratura di costumanza': Un'ipotesi su 'Ecce Deus fortior me' (*Vita nova*, 2.4)." In *Dante e la cultura fiorentina: Bono Giamboni, Brunetto Latini e la formazione intellettuale dei laici*, edited by Zygmunt Barański, Theodore J. Cachey Jr., and Luca Lombardo, 221–40. Rome: Salerno Editrice, 2019.

Demaray, John. "Dante and the Book of the Cosmos." *Transactions of the American Philosophical Society* 77, no. 5 (1987): 1–114.

De Robertis, Domenico. "Un altro Cavalcanti?" In *Guido Cavalcanti tra i suoi lettori*, edited by Maria Luisa Ardizzone, 13–27. Florence: Cadmo, 2003.

———. *Il canzoniere escorialense e la tradizione "veneziana" delle rime dello stil novo.* Turin: Loescher, 1954.

———. "Il caso di Cavalcanti." In *Dante e la Bibbia*, edited by Giovanni Barblan, 341–50. Florence: Olschki, 1988.

———. *Il libro della "Vita Nuova."* Florence: Sansoni, 1961. 2nd. ed., 1970.

———. "Sulla tradizione estravagante delle rime della *Vita Nuova.*" *Studi danteschi* 44 (1976): 5–84.

Diacciati, Silvia. "Dante: Relazioni sociali e vita pubblica." *Reti medievali rivista* 15, no. 2 (2014): 243–70.

Distefano, Santo. "La mistica della *Vita nova* secondo Riccardo di San Vittore." In *L'opera di Dante fra antichità, medioevo ed epoca moderna*, edited by Sergio Cristaldi and Carmelo Tramontana, 285–327. Catania: CUECM, 2008.

Dobbs-Allsop, F. W. *Lamentations.* Louisville, KY: John Knox Press, 2002.

Donati, Silvia. "Dreams and Divinatory Dreams in Albert the Great's *Liber de somno et vigilia.*" In *Contemplation and Philosophy: Scholastic and Mystical Modes of Medieval Philosophical Thought: A Tribute to Kent Emery, Jr.*, edited by Roberto Hofmeister Pich and Andreas Speer, 178–215. Leiden: Brill, 2018.

Dronke, Peter. *Dante's Second Love: The Originality and the Contexts of the "Convivio."* Leeds: Society for Italian Studies, 1997.

———. *Intellectuals and Poets in Medieval Europe*. Rome: Edizioni di Storia e Letteratura, 1992.

———. *The Medieval Poet and His World*. Rome: Edizioni di Storia e Letteratura, 1984.

———. "The Song of Songs and Medieval Love-Lyric." In *The Medieval Poet and His World*, 209–36. Rome: Edizioni di Storia e Letteratura, 1984.

———. *Verse with Prose from Petronius to Dante: The Art and Scope of the Mixed Form*. Cambridge, MA: Harvard University Press, 1994.

Durling, Robert. "Guido Cavalcanti in the *Vita nova.*" In *Guido Cavalcanti tra i suoi lettori*, edited by Maria Luisa Ardizzone, 176–86. Florence: Cadmo, 2003.

Durling, Robert M., and Ronald L. Martinez. *Time and the Crystal: Studies in Dante's "Rime petrose."* Berkeley: University of California Press, 1990.

Eckhardt, Caroline D., ed. *Essays in the Numerical Criticism of Medieval Literature*. Lewisburg, PA: Bucknell University Press, 1980.

Eisner, Martin. *Boccaccio and the Invention of Italian Literature: Dante, Petrarch, Cavalcanti and the Authority of the Vernacular*. Cambridge: Cambridge University Press, 2013.

———. "Dante's *Ballata:* The Personification of Poetry and the Authority of the Vernacular in the *Vita Nuova.*" *Mediaevalia* 39 (2018): 299–318.

Fabian, Seth. "Cecco vs. Dante: Correcting the *Comedy* with Applied Astronomy." PhD diss., Columbia University, 2014.

Faini, Enrico. "'Uno nuovo stato di felicitade': Bono Giamboni volgarizzatore di Orosio." In *Dante e la cultura fiorentina: Bono Giamboni, Brunetto Latini e la formazione intellettuale dei laici*, edited by Zygmunt G. Barański, Theodore J. Cachey Jr., and Luca Lombardo, 61–78. Rome: Salerno Editrice, 2019.

Fallani, Giovanni. "L'idea di Roma nel poema dantesco." *Studi romani* 10, no. 2 (1962): 136–43.

Falzone, Paolo. "Dante e l'averroismo di Cavalcanti: Un nodo storiografico da ripensare?" *Studi danteschi* 83 (2018): 267–306.

———. *Desiderio della scienza e desiderio di Dio nel "Convivio" di Dante*. Naples: Il Mulino, 2010.

Fassler, Margot E. *The Virgin of Chartres: Making History through Liturgy and the Arts*. New Haven, CT: Yale University Press, 2010.

Favati, Guido. "Tecnica ed arte nella poesia cavalcantiana." *Studi petrarcheschi* 3 (1950): 117–42.

Fenzi, Enrico. "Boezio e Jean de Meun, filosofia e ragione nelle rime allegoriche." In *Le canzoni di Dante: Interpretazioni e letture*, 111–74. Florence: Le Lettere, 2017.

———. "Conflitto di idee e implicazioni polemiche tra Dante e Cavalcanti." In *La canzone d'amore di Guido Cavalcanti e i suoi antichi commenti*, 9–70. Genoa: Il Melangolo, 1999.

———. "'Costanzia de la ragione' e 'malvagio desiderio' (*V.N.*, XXXIX, 2): Dante e la donna pietosa." In *"La gloriosa donna de la mente": A Commentary on the "Vita Nuova,"* edited by Vincent Moleta, 195–224. Florence: Olschki, 1994.

———. "'Costanzia della Ragione' e 'malvagio desiderio' (*Vn* 28, 2): Dante e la donna pietosa." In *Le canzoni di Dante: Interpretazioni e letture*, 83–10. Florence: Le Lettere, 2017.

Fioravanti, Gianfranco, "Aristotele e l'Empireo." In *Christian Readings of Aristotle from the Middle Ages to the Renaissance*, edited by Luca Bianchi, 25–36. Turnhout: Brepols, 2011.

Flamini, Francesco. "Dante e lo 'stil novo.'" *Rivista d'Italia* 2 (1900): 217–33.

Ford, David F. *Self and Salvation: Being Transformed*. Cambridge: Cambridge University Press, 1999.

Foucault, Michel . "Of Other Spaces." Translated by Jay Miskowiec. *Diacritics* 16 (1986): 22–27.

Freccero, John. "The Dance of the Stars: *Paradiso* X." In his *Dante: The Poetics of Conversion*, edited by Rachel Jacoff, 221–44, 309–14. Cambridge, MA: Harvard University Press, 1986.

———. *Dante: The Poetics of Conversion*. Cambridge, MA: Harvard University Press, 1986.

Frugoni, Chiara. "Playing with Clouds." *Burlington Magazine* 153, no. 1301 (2011): 518–20.

Frugoni, Vittorio. *Dante e la Roma del suo tempo*. Florence: Le Monnier, 1965.

Fulton Brown, Rachel. *Mary and the Art of Prayer: The Hours of the Virgin in Medieval Christian Life and Thought*. New York: Columbia University Press, 2017.

Gaimari, Giulia. "La letizia di Cristo nel *Purgatorio*: Un'ipotesi di lettura." *Studi danteschi* 81 (2016): 165–81.

Gardini, Nicola. *Lacuna: Saggio sul non detto*. Turin: Einaudi, 2014.

Gehl, Paul F. *A Moral Art: Grammar, Society, and Culture in Trecento Florence*. Ithaca, NY: Cornell University Press, 1993.

Geltner, Guy. *The Making of Medieval Antifraternalism: Polemic, Violence, Deviance, and Remembrance*. Oxford: Oxford University Press, 2012.

Genette, Gérard. *Paratexts: Thresholds of Interpretation*. Translated by Jane E. Lewin. Foreword by Richard Macksey. Cambridge: Cambridge University Press, 1997.

Gengaro, Maria Luisa, and Gemma Villa Guglielmetti. *Inventario dei codici decorati e miniati (secc. VII–XIII) della Biblioteca Ambrosiana*. Florence: Olschki, 1968.

Gilson, Étienne. "Dalla *Vita Nuova* alla *Commedia*." In *Dante e Beatrice: Saggi danteschi*, 29–45. Milan: Medusa, 2004.

Gilson, Simon. "Dante and the Science of 'Perspective': A Reappraisal." *Dante Studies* 115 (1997): 185–219.

———. "Visual Theory." In *The Oxford Handbook of Dante*, edited by Manuele Gragnolati, Elena Lombardi, and Francesca Southerden, 242–56. Oxford: Oxford University Press, 2021.

Ginsberg, Warren. "Dante's Ovids." In *Ovid in the Middle Ages*, edited by James G. Clark, Frank T. Coulson, and Kathryn L. McKinley, 143–59. Cambridge: Cambridge University Press, 2011.

Giunta, Claudio. *Due saggi sulla tenzone*. Rome: Antenore, 2002.

———. *La poesia italiana nell'età di Dante: La linea Bonagiunta-Guinizzelli*. Bologna: Il Mulino, 1998.

———. "Sullo stilnovo." In *Stilnovo e dintorni*, edited by Marco Grimaldi and Federico Ruggiero, 13–29. Rome: Aracne, 2017.

———. *Versi ad un destinatario*. Bologna: Il Mulino, 2002.

Giusti, Francesco. "Recitation: Lyric Time(s) I." In *Re-: An Errant Glossary*, edited by Christoph F. E. Holzhey and Arnd Wedemeyer, 35–47. Berlin: ICI Berlin, 2019.

Gombrich, Ernst H. "Personification." In *Classical Influences on European Culture, A.D. 500–1500*, edited by R. R. Bolgar, 247–57. Cambridge: University of Cambridge Press, 1971.

Gorni, Guglielmo. *Dante: Storia di un visionario*. Rome: Laterza, 2008.

———. "Le forme primarie del testo poetico." In *Letteratura italiana*, edited by Alberto Asor Rosa, 9 vols., 3.1:439–518. Turin: Einaudi, 1984.

———. *Guido Cavalcanti: Dante e il suo "primo amico."* Rome: Aracne, 2009.

———. *Lettera nome numero: L'ordine delle cose in Dante*. Bologna: Il Mulino, 1990.

———. "'Paragrafi' e titolo della *Vita Nova*." In *Dante prima della "Commedia,"* 111–32. Florence: Cadmo, 2001.

———. "Saggio di lettura, paragrafo per paragrafo." In Dante Alighieri, *Vita Nova*, edited by Guglielmo Gorni, 241–79. Turin: Einaudi, 1996.

———. "La *Vita Nova* dalla Donna Gentile a Beatrice, con un *excursus* sulla doppia redazione del libello." *Deutsches Dante-Jahrbuch* 81 (2006): 7–26.

Gosselin, Christine. "The Shape of Things to Come: Dante and the *donne* of the *Vita Nuova*." *The Italianist* 15 (1995): 5–28.

Grabowski, Stanislaus J. "St. Augustine and the Presence of God." *Theological Studies* 13, no. 3 (1952): 336–58.

Gragnolati, Manuele "Authorship and Performance in Dante's *Vita nuova*." In *Aspects of the Performative in Medieval Culture*, edited by Manuele Gragnolati and Almut Suerbaum, 125–41. Berlin: De Gruyter, 2010.

———. "(In-)Corporeality, Language, Performance in Dante's *Vita Nuova* and *Commedia*." In *Dante's Plurilingualism: Authority, Knowledge, Subjectivity*, edited by Sara Fortuna, Manuele Gragnolati, and Jürgen Trabant, 211–22. London: Legenda, 2010.

———. "Una performance senza gerarchia: La riscrittura bi-stabile della *Vita nova*." In *Vita nova. Fiore. Epistola XIII*, edited by Manuele Gragnolati, Luca Carlo Rossi, Paola Allegretti, Natascia Tonelli, and Alberto Casadei, 67–85. Florence: SISMEL and Edizioni del Galluzzo, 2018.

———. "Trasformazioni e assenze: La *performance* della *Vita nova* e le figure di Dante e Cavalcanti." In *Dante the Lyric and Ethical Poet*, edited by Zygmunt G. Barański and Martin McLaughlin, 74–91. Oxford: Legenda, 2010.

———. "Without Hierarchy: Diffraction, Performance, and Re-writing as Kippbild in Dante's *Vita nova*." In *Renaissance Rewritings*, edited by Helmut Pfeiffer, Irene Fantappiè, and Tobias Roth, 9–24. Berlin: De Gruyter, 2017.

Gragnolati, Manuele, and Elena Lombardi. "Autobiografia d'autore." *Dante Studies* 136 (2018): 143–60.

Gragnolati, Manuele, and Francesca Southerden. *Possibilities of Lyric: Reading Petrarch in Dialogue*. Berlin: ICI Berlin Press, 2020.

Grandgent, Charles Hall. "Dante and St. Paul." *Romania* 31 (1902): 14–27.

Green, Louis. "'Bono in alto grado' (*VN*, XXII, 2): Beatrice's Father, Nobility and the Nobility in Dante's Florence." In "*La gloriosa donna de la mente*": *A Commentary on the "Vita Nuova,"* edited by Vincent Moleta, 97–117. Florence: Olschki, 1997.

Gregg, Melissa, and Gregory J. Seigworth, eds. *The Affect Theory Reader*. Durham, NC: Duke University Press, 2010.

Grimaldi, Marco. "L'anniversario di Beatrice." In "*Per beneficio e concordia di studio": Studi danteschi offerti a Enrico Malato per i suoi ottant'anni*, edited by Andrea Mazzucchi, 479–91. Padua: Bertoncello, 2015.

———. "Dante e la poesia romanza." In *Per Enrico Fenzi: Saggi di allievi e amici per i suoi ottant'anni*, edited by Paolo Borsa, Paolo Falzone, Luca Fiorentini,

Sonia Gentili, Luca Marcozzi, Simona Stroppa, and Natascia Tonelli, 205–14. Florence: Le Lettere, 2020.

————. "Petrarca, il 'vario stile' e l'idea di lirica." *Carte romanze* 2, no. 1 (2014): 151–210.

————. "Sacro e profano in Guinizzelli e Cavalcanti." *P.R.I.S.M.I.: Révue d'études italienne* 16 (2019): 115–46.

————. "La varietà lirica dal Medioevo all'età moderna." In "La lirica del / nel Medioevo: Esperienze di filologi a confronto," edited by L. Spetia, M. León Gómez, and T. Nocita, special issue, *Spolia: Journal of Medieval Studies* (2019): 159–82.

Grossberg, Daniel. "Lamentations." In *The Jewish Study Bible*, edited by Adele Berlin and Marc Zvi Brettler, 1587–602. New York: Oxford University Press, 2004.

Gubbini, Gaia. "Immaginazione e malinconia, occhi *pieni di spiriti* e cuori insanguinati: Alcune tracce nella lirica italiana delle origini." In *La poesia in Italia prima di Dante*, edited by Franco Suitner, 29–39. Ravenna: Longo, 2017.

Gurevich, Aron. "Popular and Scholarly Medieval Cultural Traditions: Notes in the Margin of Jacques Le Goff's book." *Journal of Medieval History* 9 (1983): 71–90.

Guzzardo, John J. *Dante: Numerological Studies*. New York: Lang, 1987.

Hanna, Ralph, III. *Pursuing History: Middle English Manuscripts and Their Texts*. Stanford, CA: Stanford University Press, 1996.

Hardie, Colin. "Dante's 'mirabile visione' (*Vita Nuova* XLII)." In *The World of Dante: Essays on Dante and His Times*, edited by Cecil Grayson, 123–45. Oxford: Clarendon Press, 1980.

Harrison, Robert Pogue. *The Body of Beatrice*. Baltimore: Johns Hopkins University Press, 1988.

Hawkins, Peter. "All Smiles: Poetry and Theology in Dante's *Commedia*." In *Dante's "Commedia": Theology as Poetry*, edited by Vittorio Montemaggi and Matthew Treherne, 36–59. Notre Dame, IN: University of Notre Dame Press, 2010.

Herczeg, Giulio. *Saggi linguistici e stilistici*. Florence: Olschki, 1972.

Hirsh, John C. "The Prose Structure of the *Vita Nuova*." *Neophilolohus* 64 (1980): 402–4.

Hogan, Patrick C. *Affective Narratology: The Emotional Structure of Stories*. Lincoln: University of Nebraska Press, 2011.

Hollander, Robert. "Dante's 'Dolce Stil Novo' and the *Comedy*." In *Dante: Mito e poesia: Atti del secondo Seminario dantesco internazionale*, edited by Michelangelo Picone and Tatiana Crivelli, 263–81. Florence: Cesati, 1999.

———. "*Vita nuova*: Dante's Perceptions of Beatrice." *Dante Studies* 92 (1974): 1–18.

Holmes, Olivia. *Assembling the Lyric Self: Authorship from Troubadour Song to Italian Poetry Book.* Minneapolis: University of Minnesota Press, 2000.

———. "Dante's *Vita nova*." In *Assembling the Lyric Self: Authorship from Troubadour Song to Italian Poetry Book*, 120–44. Minneapolis: University of Minnesota Press, 2000.

Holton, Richard. "How Is Strength of Will Possible?" In *Weakness of Will and Practical Irrationality*, edited by Sarah Stroud and Christine Tappolet, 39–67. Oxford: Clarendon, 2003.

Hooper, Laurence E. "Exile and Rhetorical Order in the *Vita nova*." *L'Alighieri* 38 (2011): 5–27.

Hunt, Tony. "The *Song of Songs* and Courtly Literature." In *Court and Poet*, edited by Glyn S. Burgess, 189–96. Liverpool: Cairns, 1981.

Ibbett, Katherine. "'When I Do, I Call It Affect.'" *Paragraph* 40, no. 2 (2017): 244–53.

Inglese, Giorgio. "'. . . Illa Guidonis de Florentia *Donna me prega*' (tra Cavalcanti e Dante)." *Cultura neolatina* 55 (1995): 179–210.

———. *L'intelletto e l'amore: Studi sulla letteratura italiana del Due e Trecento.* Milan: La Nuova Italia, 2000.

———. *Vita di Dante: Una biografia possibile.* Rome: Carocci, 2015.

James-Raoul, Danièle. "En guise de préface: À la fenêtre: Approche d'un topos textuel dans les romans entre 1150 et 1250." In *Par la fenestre: Études de littérature et de civilisation médiévale*, edited by Chantal Connochie-Bourgne, 9–22. Aix-en-Provence: Presses Universitaires de Provence, 2013.

Jiménez, Alberto Corsín. "On Space as a Capacity." *Journal of the Royal Anthropological Institute* 9 (2003): 137–53.

Jones, Peter J. A. "Humility and Humiliation: The Transformation of Franciscan Humour, c.1210–1310." *Journal of Cultural and Social History* 18 (2018): 155–75.

Jones, William Powell. *The Pastourelle: A Study of the Origins and Traditions of a Lyric Type.* Cambridge, MA: Harvard University Press, 2013.

Joyce, Paul M. "Lamentations." In *The Oxford Bible Commentary*, edited by John Barton and John Muddiman, 528–33. Oxford: Oxford University Press, 2001.

Joyce, Paul M., and Diana Lipton. *Lamentations through the Centuries.* Chichester: John Wiley & Sons, 2013.

Karnes, Michelle. *Imagination, Meditation and Cognition in the Middle Ages.* Chicago: University of Chicago Press, 2011.

Kay, Tristan. "Dante's Cavalcantian Relapse: The *pargoletta* Sequence and the *Commedia*." *Dante Studies* 131 (2013): 73–97.

———. *Dante's Lyric Redemption: Eros, Salvation, Vernacular Tradition*. Oxford: Oxford University Press, 2016.

———. "Redefining the 'Matera Amorosa': Dante's *Vita nova* and Guittone's (Anti-)courtly 'Canzoniere.'" *The Italianist* 29, no. 3 (2009): 369–99.

Keen, Catherine. "A Florentine Tullio: Dual Authorship and the Politics of Translation in Brunetto Latini's *Rettorica*." In *The Afterlife of Cicero*, edited by Gesine Manuwald, 1–16. Bulletin of the Institute of Classical Studies Supplement 135. London: Institute of Classical Studies, 2016.

———. "New Lives of Dante's *Vita nova* Lyrics: Material Translations and Selections." Paper given at the Society for Italian Studies Biennial Conference, Oxford, September 2015.

———. "'Va', mia canzone': Textual Transmission and the *Congedo* in Medieval Exile Lyrics." *Italian Studies* 64, no. 2 (2009): 183–97.

Kempshall, Matthew S. "Dante's Lamentations: The History of Exile and the Politics of Restoration." In *Dante beyond Borders: Contexts and Reception*, edited by Nick Havely and Jonathan Katz with Richard Cooper, 47–60. Cambridge: Legenda, 2021.

Klein, Francesca, and Piero Marchi. "Archivio di Stato." In *Una volta nella vita: Tesori dagli archivi e dalle biblioteche di Firenze*, edited by Marco Ferri, 24–33. Florence: Soprintendenza Speciale per il Patrimonio Storico, Artistico ed Etnoantropologico e per il Polo Museale della città di Firenze-Sillabe, 2014.

Kleiner, John. "Finding the Center: Revelation and Reticence in the *Vita Nuova*." *Texas Studies in Literature and Language* 32, no. 1 (1990): 85–100.

Kleinhenz, Christopher. "Perspectives on Intertextuality in Dante's *Divina Commedia*." *Romance Quarterly* 54 (2007): 183–94.

Klopsch, Paul. *Einführung in die Dichtungslehren des lateinischen Mittelalters*. Darmstadt: Wissenschaftliche Buchgesellschaft, 1980.

Kraus, Manfred. "Progymnasmata and Progymnasmatic Exercises in the Medieval Classroom." In *The Classics in the Medieval and Renaissance Classroom: The Role of Ancient Texts in the Arts Curriculum as Revealed by Surviving Manuscripts and Early Printed Books*, edited by Juanita Feros Ruys, John O. Ward, and Melanie Heyworth, 175–97. Turnhout: Brepols, 2013.

Kruger, Steven F. *Dreaming in the Middle Ages*. Cambridge: Cambridge University Press, 1992.

Lanham, Carol Dana. "Freshman Composition in the Early Middle Ages: Epistolography and Rhetoric before the *Ars dictaminis*." *Viator* 23 (1992): 115–34.

Lansing, Richard. "The Formal Structure of the *Vita nuova*." In *"Accessus ad Auctores": Studies in Honor of Christopher Kleinhenz*, edited by Fabian Alfie and Andrea Dini, 77–92. Tempe: Arizona Center for Medieval and Renaissance Studies, 2011.

Larson, Pär. "A ciascun'alma presa, vv. 1–4." *Studi mediolatini e volgari* 46 (2000): 85–119.

Law, Vivien. "Why Write a Verse Grammar?" *Journal of Medieval Latin* 9 (1999): 46–76.

Ledda, Giuseppe. *La guerra della lingua: Ineffabilità, retorica e narrativa nella "Commedia" di Dante*. Ravenna: Longo, 2002.

———. "L'ineffabilità nella *Vita nova*." In *Vita nova. Fiore. Epistola XIII*, edited by Manuele Gragnolati, Luca Carlo Rossi, Paola Allegretti, Natascia Tonelli, and Alberto Casadei, 87–113. Florence: SISMEL and Edizioni del Galluzzo, 2018.

Lefebvre, Henri. *The Production of Space*. Oxford: Blackwell, 1991.

Le Goff, Jacques. "Une enquête sur le rire." *Annales. Histoire. Sciences Sociales* 52 (1997): 449–55.

Lenkeith, Nancy. *Dante and the Legend of Rome: An Essay*. London: Warburg Institute, 1952.

Leporatti, Roberto. "Le dolci rime d'amor ch'io solea." In *Dante Alighieri: Le quindici canzoni, I, 1–7: Lette da diversi*, 89–117. Lecce: Pensa Multimedia, 2009.

Leuker, Thomas. "Sfoghi e sospiri in Dante." *L'Alighieri* 20 (2002): 121–26.

Levers, Toby. "The Image of Authorship in the Final Chapter of the *Vita Nuova*." *Italian Studies* 57 (2003): 5–19.

Levitsky, Anne Adele. "Song Personified: The *Tornadas* of Raimon de Miraval." *Mediaevalia* 39 (2018): 17–57.

Lieberknecht, Otfried. *Allegorese und Philologie: Überlegungen zum Problem des mehrfachen Schriftsinns in Dantes "Commedia."* Stuttgart: Steiner, 1998.

Löhr, Wolf-Dietrich. "Dantes Täfelchen, Cenninis Zeichenkiste: 'ritratto,' 'disegno' und 'fantasia' als Instrumente der Bilderzeugung im Trecento." *Das Mittelalter* 13, no. 1 (2008): 148–79.

Lombardi, Elena. "Identità lirica e piacere linguistico: Una lettura di *Paradiso* XXVI." *Studi danteschi* 82 (2017): 51–80.

———. *Imagining the Woman Reader in the Age of Dante*. Oxford: Oxford University Press, 2018.

———. "L'*invenzione*' del lettore in Dante." In *C'è un lettore in questo testo? Rappresentazione della lettura nella letteratura italiana*, edited by Giovanna Rizzarelli and Cristina Savettieri, 23–41. Bologna: Il Mulino, 2016.

———. "Il pensiero linguistico nella *Vita nova.*" In *Vita nova. Fiore. Epistola XIII*, edited by Manuele Gragnolati, Luca Carlo Rossi, Paola Allegretti, Natascia Tonelli, and Alberto Casadei, 45–64. Florence: SISMEL and Edizioni del Galluzzo, 2018.

———. *The Syntax of Desire: Language and Love in Augustine, the Modistae, Dante.* Toronto: University of Toronto Press, 2007.

———. *The Wings of the Doves: Love and Desire in Dante and Medieval Culture.* Montreal: McGill-Queen's University Press, 2012.

Lombardo, Luca. *Boezio in Dante: La "Consolatio philosophiae" nello scrittoio del poeta.* Venice: Edizioni Ca' Foscari, 2013.

———. "'Ed imaginava lei fatta come una donna gentile': Boezio, Brunetto Latini e la prima formazione intellettuale di Dante." *Le tre corone* 5 (2018): 38–71.

———. "Primi appunti sulla *Vita nova* nel contesto della prosa del Duecento." *L'Alighieri* 60 (2019): 21–41.

Longo, Nicola. *I papi, Roma e Dante: Le idee e le immagini di Roma nella "Commedia" dantesca.* Rome: Bulzoni, 2004.

Low, Setha M., and Denise Lawrence-Zuniga, eds. *The Anthropology of Space and Place: Locating Culture.* Oxford: Blackwell, 2003.

Lucarella Agostino. "Il cittadino fiorentino Folco Portinari." *I Fochi della San Giovanni* 29, no. 1 (2003): 23.

Maas, Paul. *Textual Criticism.* Translated by Barbara Flower. Oxford: Clarendon Press, 1958.

Mainini, Lorenzo. "Schermi e specchi: Intorno a *Vita nova* 2, 6–9 e ad altre visioni dantesche." *Critica del testo* 14, no. 2 (2011): 147–78.

Malato, Enrico. "Amor cortese e amor cristiano da Andrea Cappellano a Dante." In *Lo fedele consiglio de la ragione: Studi e ricerche di letteratura italiana*, 126–227. Rome: Salerno Editrice, 1989.

———. "Cavalcanti nella *Commedia*: Il 'dialogo' ininterrotto fra Dante e Guido." *Rivista di studi danteschi* 6 (2006): 217–40.

———. *Dante e Guido Cavalcanti: Il dissidio per la "Vita nuova" e il "disdegno" di Guido.* 2nd ed. Rome: Salerno Editrice, 2004.

———. "Introduzione." In Dante Alighieri, *Vita nuova; Rime*, edited by Donato Pirovano and Marco Grimaldi, xix–xxxi. Rome: Salerno Editrice, 2015.

———. *Per una nuova edizione commentata delle opere di Dante.* Rome: Salerno Editrice, 2004.

Maldina, Nicolò. "A Classicising Friar in Dante's Florence." In *Ethics, Politics and Justice in Dante*, edited by Giulia Gaimari and Catherine Keen, 30–45. London: UCL Press, 2019.

———. "I Salmi e l'autobiografismo penitenziale di Dante." *Rivista di letteratura religiosa italiana* 3 (2020): 11–35.

Maraldi, Elisa. "Le stelle di Beatrice: Astronomia e astrologia nella *Vita nova*." PhD diss., Università di Bologna, 2015.

Marchesi, Simone. *Dante and Augustine: Linguistics, Poetics, Hermeneutics.* Toronto: University of Toronto Press, 2011.

Marcozzi, Luca. "Dal poeta dei *Remedia* al maestro della 'bella scola': L'evoluzione del percorso ovidiano di Dante tra *Vita Nova, Convivio* e *Commedia*." In *Miti figure metamorfosi: L'Ovidio di Dante*, edited by Carlotta Cattermole and Marcello Ciccuto, 67–79. Florence: Le Lettere, 2019.

Mariani, Andrea. "Trasfiguramento." In *Enciclopedia dantesca*, 5:698. Rome: Istituto della Enciclopedia Italiana, 1975.

———. "Trasfigurazione." In *Enciclopedia dantesca*, 5:698. Rome: Istituto della Enciclopedia Italiana, 1975.

Marigo, Aristide. *Mistica e scienza nella "Vita Nuova" di Dante: L'unità di pensiero e le fonti mistiche, filosofiche e bibliche.* Padua: Drucker, 1914.

Martelli, Mario. "Proposte per le *Rime* di Dante." *Studi danteschi* 69 (2004): 247–88.

Marti, Mario. "Da 'Donna me prega' a 'Donne ch'avete': Non viceversa." In *Da Dante a Croce: Proposte consensi dissensi*, 7–15. Galatina: Congedo, 2005.

———. "Vita e morte della presunta doppia redazione della *Vita nuova*." *Rivista di cultura classica e medievale* 7 (1965): 657–69.

Martinez, Ronald L. "Cavalcanti 'Man of Sorrows' and Dante." In *Guido Cavalcanti tra i suoi lettori*, edited by Maria Luisa Ardizzone, 187–212. Florence: Cadmo, 2003.

———. "Dante between Hope and Despair: The Tradition of Lamentations in the *Divine Comedy*." *Logos: A Journal of Catholic Thought and Culture* 5 (2002): 45–76.

———. "Dante's Jeremiads: The Fall of Jerusalem and the Burden of the New Pharisees, the Capetians, and Florence." In *Dante for the New Millennium*, edited by Teodolinda Barolini and H. Wayne Storey, 301–19. New York: Fordham University Press, 2003.

———. "Guinizellian Protocols: Angelic Hierarchies, Human Government, and Poetic Form in Dante." *Dante Studies* 134 (2016): 48–111.

———. "Lament and Lamentations in *Purgatorio* and the Case of Dante's Statius." *Dante Studies* 115 (1997): 45–88.

———. "Mourning Beatrice: The Rhetoric of Threnody in the *Vita nuova*." *MLN* 113, no. 1 (January 1998): 1–29.

———. "The Pilgrim's Answer to Bonagiunta and the Poetics of the Spirit." *Stanford Italian Review* 3 (1983): 37–63.

Massey, Doreen. *For Space*. Los Angeles: Sage Publications, 2005.

Mazzoni, Francesco. "Il 'trascendentale' dimenticato." In *Omaggio a Beatrice (1290–1990)*, edited by Rudi Abardo, 93–132. Florence: Le Lettere, 1997.

Mazzotta, Giuseppe. *Dante, Poet of the Desert: History and Allegory in the "Divine Comedy."* Princeton, NJ: Princeton University Press, 1979.

———. "The Language of Poetry in the *Vita Nuova*." *Rivista di studi italiani* 1, no. 1 (1983): 3–14.

Mazzucchi, Andrea. "Le glosse del Laurenziano Plut. 40.7 e la tradizione degli antichi commenti alla *Commedia*." In Dante Alighieri, *Commedia: Firenze, Biblioteca Medicea Laurenziana, Pluteo 40.7. I. Facsimile. II. Commentario*, edited by Sonia Chiodo, Teresa De Robertis, Gennaro Ferrante, and Andrea Mazzucchi, 123–87. Rome: Istituto della Enciclopedia Italiana, 2018.

McLain, Carin. "Screening the Past: Shifting Desire in the *Vita nuova*." *Italian Culture* 26, no. 1 (2008): 1–20.

Meneghetti, Maria Luisa. "Beatrice al chiar di luna: La prassi poetica delle visioni amorose con l'invito all'interpretazione dai Provenzali allo Stilnovo." In *Symposium in honorem prof. Martin de Riquer*, 239–55. Barcelona: Universitat de Barcelona, 1984.

Menichetti, Aldo, "Implicazioni retoriche nell'invenzione del sonetto." In *Saggi metrici*, edited by Paolo Gresti and Massimo Zenari, 109–39. Florence: Edizioni del Galluzzo per la Fondazione Ezio Franceschini, 2006.

Meo-Ehlert, Myrtha de. *Leggere la "Vita Nuova": Zur handschriftlichen Überlieferung und literarischen Rezeption der "Vita Nuova" von Dante Alighieri im Trecento*. Berlin: De Gruyter, 2020.

Meyer, Heinz, and Rudolf Suntrup. *Lexikon der mittelalterlichen Zahlenbedeutungen*. Munich: Fink, 1987.

Milani, Giuliano. "Dante politico fiorentino." *Reti medievali rivista* 18, no. 1 (2017): 1–53.

Minnis, Alastair. *Magister Amoris: The "Roman de la Rose" and Vernacular Hermeneutics*. Oxford: Oxford University Press, 2001.

———. *Medieval Theory of Authorship: Scholastic Literary Attitudes in the Later Middle Ages*. 2nd ed. Philadelphia: University of Pennsylvania Press, 2010.

Minnis, Alastair J., and A. B. Scott, eds. *Medieval Literary Theory and Criticism c.1100–c.1375: The Commentary Tradition*. Oxford: Clarendon Press, 1988.

Mocan, Mira. "'Intelletto d'amore': La mistica affettiva in Dante." In *Theologus Dantes: Tematiche ideologiche nelle opere e nei primi commenti*, edited by Luca

Lombardo, Diego Parisi, and Anna Pegoretti, 81–101. Venice: Edizioni Ca' Foscari, 2018.

Moccia, Sara. *Il sonetto continuo: Storia di un genere metrico da Giacomo da Lentini a Michele Mari*. Padua: CLEUP, 2020.

Moevs, Christian. *The Metaphysics of Dante's "Comedy."* Oxford: Oxford University Press, 2005.

———. "'Il punto che mi vinse': Incarnation, Revelation, and Self-Knowledge in Dante's *Commedia*." In *Dante's "Commedia": Theology as Poetry*, edited by Vittorio Montemaggi and Matthew Treherne, 267–85. Notre Dame, IN: University of Notre Dame Press, 2010.

Moleta, Vincent. *The Early Poetry of Guittone d'Arezzo*. London: Modern Humanities Research Association, 1976.

———, ed. *"La gloriosa donna de la mente": A Commentary on the "Vita Nuova."* Florence: Olschki, 1994.

———. *Guinizzelli in Dante*. Rome: Edizioni di Storia e Letteratura, 1980.

———. "'Oggi fa l'anno che nel ciel salisti': Una rilettura della *Vita Nuova* XXVII–XXXIV." *Giornale storico della letteratura italiana* 161, no. 513 (1984): 78–104.

———. "The *Vita Nuova* as a Lyric Narrative." *Forum Italicum* 12 (1978): 369–90.

Mondschein, Ken, and Denis Casey. "Time and Timekeeping." In *The Handbook of Medieval Culture*, edited by Albrecht Classen, 1657–79. Berlin: De Gruyter, 2015.

Montefusco, Antonio. "Maestri secolari, frati mendicanti e autori volgari: Immaginario antimendicante ed ecclesiologia in vernacolare, da Rutebeuf a Boccaccio." *Rivista di storia del Cristianesimo* 12, no. 2 (2015): 265–90.

———. "'Sale o mura, / de le limosine, alle genti strane' (CX.5–6): Esegesi di un passo 'antifrancescano' del *Fiore*." In *Virtute e canoscenza: Per le nozze d'oro di Luigi Scorrano con madonna Sapientia*, edited by Giuseppe Caramuscio, 141–50. Lecce: Grifo, 2014.

Moore, Edward. *Studies in Dante, Second Series: Miscellaneous Essays*. Oxford: Clarendon Press, 1899.

Mugnai, Paolo. "Operazione." In *Enciclopedia dantesca*. Rome: Istituto della Enciclopedia Italiana, 1970. www.treccani.it/enciclopedia/operazione_(Enciclopedia-Dantesca)/.

Muller, Richard A. *Dictionary of Latin and Greek Theological Terms: Drawn Principally from Protestant Scholastic Theology*. Grand Rapids, MI: Baker Academic, 1985.

Muñoz, Antonio. *Roma di Dante*. Rome: Casa Editrice d'Arte Bestetti e Tuminelli, 1921.

Musa, Mark. *Dante's "Vita Nuova": A Translation and an Essay*. Bloomington: Indiana University Press, 1973.

———. "An Essay on the *Vita Nuova*." In *Dante's "Vita Nuova": A Translation and an Essay*, 87–210. Bloomington: Indiana University Press, 1973.

Nardi, Bruno. "Dante e Guido Cavalcanti." In *Saggi e note di critica dantesca*, 191–219. Milan: Ricciardi, 1966.

———. "Filosofia dell'amore nei rimatori italiani del Duecento e in Dante." In *Dante e la cultura medievale*, 2nd ed., 9–79. Bari: Laterza, 1990.

———. "Il linguaggio." In *Dante e la cultura medievale*, 217–47. Bari: Laterza, 1949.

Nasti, Paola. *Favole d'amore e "saver profondo": La tradizione salomonica in Dante*. Longo: Ravenna, 2007.

———. "La memoria del *Canticum* e la *Vita nuova*: Una nota preliminare." *The Italianist* 18, no. 1 (1998): 14–27.

———. "Nozze e vedovanza: Dinamiche dell'appropriazione biblica in Dante e Cavalcanti." *Tenzone* 7 (2006): 71–110.

———. "'Vocabuli d'autori e di scienze e di libri' (*Conv.* II xii 5): Percorsi sapienziali di Dante." In *La Bibbia di Dante: Esperienza mistica, profezia e teologia biblica in Dante*, edited by Giuseppe Ledda, 121–78. Ravenna: Centro dantesco dei frati minori conventuali, 2011.

Niccoli, Alessandro. "Persona." In *Enciclopedia dantesca*, 4:436. Rome: Istituto della Enciclopedia Italiana, 1973.

———. "Virgo." In *Enciclopedia dantesca*. Rome: Istituto della Enciclopedia Italiana, 1970. www.treccani.it/enciclopedia/Virgo_(Enciclopedia-Dantesca)/.

O'Driscoll, Dennis. *Quote Poet Unquote*. Port Townsend, WA: Copper Canyon Press, 2008.

Pacioni, Marco. "L'*auctoritas* poetica e il personaggio Cavalcanti nella *Vita nova*." In "*Auctor / Actor*: Lo scrittore personaggio nella letteratura italiana," edited by Gilda Corabi and Barbara Gizzi, special issue, *Studi (e testi) italiani* 61, no. 17 (2006): 41–61.

———. "L'autobiografia nella *Vita nova* di Dante." *Diacritica* 6, no. 2 (2020): 19–46.

Paden, William. *Medieval Lyric: Genres in Historical Context*. Urbana: University of Illinois Press, 2000.

Palazzo, Éric. "Le rôle des *libelli* dans la pratique liturgique du haut Moyen Âge: Histoire et typologie." *Revue Mabillon* 62, no. 1 (1990): 9–36.

Paolazzi, Carlo. *La maniera mutata: Il "dolce stil novo" tra Scrittura e "Ars poetica."* Milan: Vita e Pensiero, 1998.

Paradisi, Gioia. *La parola e l'amore: Studi sul "Cantico dei Cantici" nella tradizione francese medievale.* Rome: Carocci, 2009.

Park, Arum. "Two Types of Ovidian Personification." *Classical Journal* 104, no. 3 (2009): 225–40.

Park, Katharine. "Impressed Images, Reproducing Wonders." In *Picturing Science, Producing Art,* edited by Caroline Jones and Peter Galison, 254–71. New York: Routledge, 1998.

Parkes, Malcolm B. *Pause and Effect: An Introduction to the History of Punctuation in the West.* Aldershot: Scolar Press, 1992.

Pasero, Nicolò. "Dante in Cavalcanti: Ancora sui rapporti fra *Vita Nuova* e *Donna me prega.*" *Medioevo romanzo* 22 (1998): 388–414.

Pasquini, Emilio. "Ridere." In *Enciclopedia dantesca.* Rome: Istituto della Enciclopedia Italiana, 1970. www.treccani.it/enciclopedia/ridere_(Enciclopedia-Dantesca)/.

Paxson, James J. *The Poetics of Personification.* Cambridge: Cambridge University Press, 1994.

Pazzaglia, Mario. "L'amaro lagrimar che voi faceste." In *Enciclopedia dantesca,* 2:556. Rome: Istituto della Enciclopedia Italiana, 1970.

———. "Color d'amore e di pietà sembianti." In *Enciclopedia dantesca,* 2:62–63. Rome: Istituto della Enciclopedia Italiana, 1970.

———. "Disposizione." In *Enciclopedia dantesca.* Rome: Istituto della Enciclopedia Italiana, 1970. www.treccani.it/enciclopedia/disposizione_(Enciclopedia-Dantesca)/.

———. "Disposto." In *Enciclopedia dantesca.* Rome: Istituto della Enciclopedia Italiana, 1970. www.treccani.it/enciclopedia/disposto_(Enciclopedia-Dantesca)/.

———. "Donne ch'avete intelletto d'amore." In *Enciclopedia dantesca,* 2:580–82. Rome: Istituto della Enciclopedia Italiana, 1970.

———. "I' vegno a te il giorno infinite volte." In *Enciclopedia dantesca,* 3:536–37. Rome: Istituto della Enciclopedia Italiana, 1971.

———. "Morte villana, di pietà nemica." In *Enciclopedia dantesca,* 3:1042. Rome: Istituto della Enciclopedia Italiana, 1971.

———. "Piangete, amanti, poi che piange Amore." In *Enciclopedia dantesca,* 4:477. Rome: Istituto della Enciclopedia Italiana, 1973.

———. "Videro li occhi miei quanta pietate." In *Enciclopedia dantesca.* Rome: Istituto della Enciclopedia Italiana, 1970. www.treccani.it/enciclopedia/ricerca/Videro-li-occhi-miei-/.

Pegoretti, Anna. "L'Empireo in Dante e la 'divina scienza' del *Convivio*." In *Theologus Dantes: Tematiche teologiche nelle opere e nei primi commenti*, edited by Luca Lombardo, Diego Parisi, and Anna Pegoretti, 161–88. Venice: Edizioni Ca' Foscari, 2018.

———. "Filosofanti." *Le tre corone* 2 (2015): 11–70.

———. "'Nelle scuole delli religiosi': Materiali per Santa Croce nell'età di Dante." *L'Alighieri* 50 (2017): 5–55.

Peraino, Judith. *Giving Voice to Love: Song and Self-Expression from the Troubadours to Guillaume de Machaut*. New York: Oxford University Press, 2011.

Pertile, Lino. "Le penne e il volo." In *La punta del disio: Semantica del desiderio nella "Commedia,"* 115–35. Florence: Cadmo, 2005.

———. "Works." In *Dante in Context*, edited by Zygmunt G. Barański and Lino Pertile, 475–508. Cambridge: Cambridge University Press, 2015.

Petrocchi, Giorgio. "Donna gentile." In *Enciclopedia dantesca*, 2:574–77. Rome: Istituto della Enciclopedia Italiana, 1970.

Petrucci, Armando. "Minute, Autograph, Author's Book." In *Writers and Readers in Medieval Italy: Studies in the History of Written Culture*, edited and translated by Charles M. Radding, 145–68. New Haven, CT: Yale University Press, 1995.

Phan, Chantal. "La tornada et l'envoi: Fonctions structurelles et poétiques." *Cahiers de civilisation médiévale (Xᵉ–XIIᵉ siècles)* 34, no. 1 (1991): 57–61.

Philippart, Guy. *Les Légendiers latins et autres manuscrits hagiographiques.* Turnhout: Brepols, 1977.

———. *Les Légendiers latins et autres manuscrits hagiographiques.* Updated ed. Turnhout: Brepols, 1985.

Phillips-Robins, Helena. *Liturgical Song and Practice in Dante's "Commedia."* Notre Dame, IN: University of Notre Dame Press, 2021.

Piccone, Carla. *Dalla prosa ai versi: Forme, usi, contesti della poesia didascalica grammaticale tra XII e XIII sec. Con l'editio princeps del "De voce" (Einsiedeln, Stiftsbibliothek Cod. 300).* Edited by Peter Stotz. Bern: Lang, 2014.

Pich, Federica. "L'immagine 'donna de la mente' dalle *Rime* alla *Vita nuova*." In *Le rime di Dante*, edited by Claudia Berra and Paolo Borsa, 345–76. Milan: Cisalpino, 2010.

Picone, Michelangelo. "Beatrice personaggio: Dalla *Vita Nova* alla *Commedia*." In *Scritti danteschi*, edited by Antonio Lanza, 111–28. Ravenna: Longo, 2017.

———. "Cino nella *Vita Nova*." In *Scritti danteschi*, edited by Antonio Lanza, 97–110. Ravenna: Longo, 2017.

———. "I due Guidi: Una tenzone virtuale." In *Guido Cavalcanti laico e le origini della poesia europea, nel 7° centenario della morte: Poesia, filosofia, scienza e ricezione,* edited by Rossend Arqués, 9–26. Alessandria: Edizioni dell'Orso, 2004.

———. "Esilio e *peregrinatio*: Dalla *Vita Nova* alla Canzone Montanina." *Italianistica* 36, no. 3 (2007): 11–24.

———. "Modelli e struttura della *Vita Nuova*: L'episodio del 'gabbo.'" *Pacific Coast Philology* 13 (1978): 71–77.

———. "L'Ovidio di Dante." In *Dante e la "bella scola" della poesia: Autorità e sfida poetica,* edited by Amilcare A. Iannucci, 107–44. Ravenna: Longo, 1993.

———. *Percorsi della lirica duecentesca: Dai Siciliani alla "Vita nova."* Fiesole: Cadmo, 2003.

———. "*Peregrinus amoris*: La metafora finale." In *"Vita Nuova" e tradizione romanza,* 129–92. Padua: Liviana, 1979.

———. "'Per Ovidio parla Amore . . .': Dante *auctor* della *Vita Nova.*" In *Studi in onore di Pier Vincenzo Mengaldo per i suoi settant'anni,* edited by Marco Praloran, 2 vols., 1:237–52. Florence: SISMEL and Edizioni del Galluzzo, 2007.

———. "Presenze romanzesche nella *Vita Nuova.*" *Vox romanica* 55 (1996): 1–15.

———. "La teoria dell'*auctoritas* nella *Vita Nova.*" *Tenzone* 6 (2005): 173–91.

———. "La *Vita Nova* come macrotesto." In Picone, *Percorsi della lirica duecentesca,* 219–35.

———. "La *Vita Nova* come *prosimetrum.*" In Picone, *Percorsi della lirica duecentesca,* 237–48.

———. "La *Vita Nova* come romanzo." In Picone, *Percorsi della lirica duecentesca,* 249–65.

———. *"Vita Nuova" e tradizione romanza.* Padua: Liviana, 1979.

———. "La *Vita Nuova* fra autobiografia e tipologia." In *Dante e le forme dell'allegoresi,* edited by Michelangelo Picone, 59–69. Ravenna: Longo, 1987.

Pinto, Raffaele. "L'allegorismo dantesco e l'orizzonte ermeneutico della modernità." In *Dante e le origini della cultura letteraria moderna,* 109–77. Paris: Champion, 1994.

Pipa, Arshi. "Personaggi della *Vita Nuova*: Dante, Cavalcanti e la famiglia Portinari." *Italica* 62, no. 2 (1985): 99–115.

Piron, Sylvain. "Le poète et le théologien: Une rencontre dans le *studium* de Santa Croce." In *Ut philosophia poesis: Questions philosophiques dans l'oeuvre de Dante, Pétrarque et Boccace,* edited by Joël Biard and Fosca Mariani Zini, 73–112. Paris: Vrin, 2008.

Pirovano, Donato. "'Chi è questa che vèn?' Guinizzelli, Cavalcanti e la figura femminile." In *Les deux Guidi Guinizzelli et Cavalcanti: Mourir d'aimer et autres ruptures*, edited by Marina Gagliano, Philippe Guérin, and Raffaella Zanni, 95–106. Paris: Presses Sorbonne Nouvelle, 2018.

———. *Il dolce stil novo*. Rome: Salerno Editrice, 2014.

———. "'La mia lingua parlò quasi come per se stesso mossa': Lettura di 'Donne ch'avete intelletto d'amore' (*VN* XIX 4–14)." In *Vita nova. Fiore. Epistola XIII*, edited by Manuele Gragnolati, Luca Carlo Rossi, Paola Allegretti, Natascia Tonelli, and Alberto Casadei, 135–52. Florence: SISMEL and Edizioni del Galluzzo, 2018.

———. "Nota al testo." In Dante Alighieri, *Vita nuova; Rime*, edited by Donato Pirovano and Marco Grimaldi, 37–75. Rome: Salerno Editrice, 2015.

———. "Nota introduttiva." In Dante Alighieri, *Vita nuova; Rime*, edited by Donato Pirovano and Marco Grimaldi, 3–36. Rome: Salerno Editrice, 2015.

———. "Per una nuova edizione della *Vita nuova*." *Rivista di studi danteschi* 12 (2012): 248–325.

Poulin, Joseph-Claude. "Les *libelli* dans l'édition hagiographique avant le XIIe siècle." In *Livrets, collections et textes: Études sur la tradition hagiographique latine*, edited by Martin Heinzelmann, 15–193. Ostfildern: Jan Thorbecke, 2006.

Presti Russell, Anthony. "Dante's *forte immaginazione* and Beatrice's *occulta virtù*: Lovesickness and the Supernatural in the *Vita Nuova*." *Mediaevalia* 22, no. 1 (1998): 1–33.

Raina, Pio. "Per le 'divisioni' della *Vita Nuova*." In *Strenna Dantesca I*, edited by Orazio Bacci and G. L. Passerini, 111–14. Florence: Lumachi, 1902.

Rapisarda, Stefano. "Tommaso di Sasso." In *Federico II: Enciclopedia fridericiana*, 2 vols., 2:844–46. Rome: Istituto della Enciclopedia Italiana, 2006–8.

Rea, Roberto. "Amore e ragione nella *Vita nuova*." *Studj romanzi* 14 (2018): 165–95.

———. "*Amor est passio virtutis ymaginative*: Immaginazione, immagine e *immaginare* nella lirica amorosa duecentesca." *Letteratura e arte* 16 (2018): 119–37.

———. "'Avete fatto como la Lumera' (sulla tenzone fra Bonagiunta e Guinizzelli)." *Critica del testo* 6, no. 3 (2003): 933–58.

———. "Cavalcanti e l'invenzione del lettore." In *Les deux Guidi: Guinizelli et Cavalcanti: Mourir d'aimer et autres ruptures*, edited by Marina Gagliano, Philippe Guérin, and Raffaella Zanni, 157–18. Paris: Sorbonne Nouvelle Presses, 2016.

———. "Cavalcanti nella *Vita nuova*: Una proposta di rilettura." In *Vita nova. Fiore. Epistola XIII*, edited by Manuele Gragnolati, Luca Carlo Rossi, Paola Allegretti, Natascia Tonelli, and Alberto Casadei, 153–72. Florence: SISMEL and Edizioni del Galluzzo, 2018.

————. *Cavalcanti poeta: Uno studio sul lessico lirico*. Rome: Edizioni Nuova Cultura, 2008.

————. "'Ego tanquam centrum circuli' (*VN* 5, 11)." In *La lirica romanza del Medioevo: Storia, tradizioni, interpretazioni*, edited by Furio Brugnolo and Francesca Gambino, 738–56. Padua: Unipress, 2009.

————. "La *Vita nuova* e le *Rime*: 'Unus philosophus alter poeta': Un'ipotesi per Cavalcanti e Dante." In *Dante: Fra il settecentocinquantenario della nascita (2015) e il settecentenario della morte (2021)*, edited by Enrico Malato and Andrea Mazzucchi, 2 vols., 2:351–38. Rome: Salerno Editrice, 2016.

"Redundare." In *Enciclopedia dantesca*. Rome: Istituto della Enciclopedia Italiana, 1970. www.treccani.it/enciclopedia/redundare_(Enciclopedia-Dantesca)/.

Reynolds, Barbara. "Introduction." In Dante Alighieri, *Vita Nuova*, translated by Barbara Reynolds, 11–25. Harmondsworth: Penguin, 1975.

Reynolds, Mary T. *Joyce and Dante: The Shaping Imagination*. Princeton, NJ: Princeton University Press, 1981.

Ricci, Corrado. *Roma nel pensiero di Dante*. Florence: Sansoni, 1921.

Ricklin, Thomas. "Albert le Grand, commentateur: L'exemple du *De somno et vigilia* III, 1." *Freiburger Zeitschrift für Philosophie* 45 (1998): 31–55.

Rivers, Elias L. "Dante at Dividing Sonnets." *Symposium* 11, no. 2 (1957): 290–95.

Robiglio, Andrea. "Dante e le *Auctoritates Aristotelis*." In *Les "Auctoritates Aristotelis," leur utilisation et leur influence chez les auteurs médiévaux: État de la question 40 ans après la publication*, edited by Jacqueline Hamesse and José Meirinhos, 187–202. Turnhout: Brepols, 2017.

Robinson, P. R. "The 'Booklet': A Self-Contained Unit in Composite Manuscripts." *Codicologica* 3 (1980): 46–69.

Roglieri, Maria Ann. "'Per Ovidio parla Amore, sì come se fosse persona umana' (*V.N.* XXV): The Case for Ovid's Figure of *Amore* in Dante's *Vita nuova*." *Carte italiane* 2, nos. 2–3 (2007): 1–22.

Rohlfs, Gerhard. *Historische Grammatik der italienischen Sprache und ihrer Mundarten: Syntax und Wortbildung*. Bern: Franke, 1954.

Rosenberg, Samuel N. "Incipit Citation in French Lyric Poetry of the Twelfth through Fourteenth Centuries." In *Courtly Arts and the Art of Courtliness*, edited by Keith Busby and Christopher Kleinhenz, 587–600. Cambridge: Brewer, 2006.

Rushworth, Jennifer. *Discourses of Mourning in Dante, Petrarch, and Proust*. Oxford: Oxford University Press, 2016.

Russo, Vittorio. "Beatrice *beatitudinis non artifex* nella *princeps* (1576) della *Vita Nuova*." In *Saggi di filologia dantesca*, 83–92. Naples: Bibliopolis, 2000.

————. *Saggi di filologia dantesca*. Naples: Bibliopolis, 2000.

Saarinen, Risto. *Weakness of the Will in Medieval Thought, from Augustine to Buridan.* Leiden: Brill, 1994.

Salsano, Fernando. "Defettivamente." In *Enciclopedia dantesca.* Rome: Istituto della Enciclopedia Italiana, 1970. www.treccani.it/enciclopedia/defettiva mente_(Enciclopedia-Dantesca)/.

Sandkühler, Bruno. *Die frühen Dantekommentare und ihr Verhaltnis zur mittelalterlichen Kommentartradition.* Munich: Hueber, 1967.

Sanguineti, Edoardo. "Per una lettura della *Vita nuova.*" In *Dante reazionario,* 3–33. Rome: Riuniti, 1992.

Sanguineti, Federico. "L'ombra di Miseno nella *Commedia.*" *Belfagor* 40, no. 4 (1985): 403–16.

Santagata, Marco. *Amate e amanti: Figure della lirica amorosa fra Dante e Petrarca.* Bologna: Il Mulino, 1999.

———. *Dal sonetto al canzoniere: Ricerche sulla preistoria e la costituzione di un genere.* Padua: Liviana, 1979.

———. *Dante: The Story of His Life.* Translated by Richard Dixon. Cambridge, MA: Belknap Press of Harvard University Press, 2016.

———. "Introduzione." In Dante Alighieri, *Opere,* 1:xi–cxxxii. Milan: Mondadori, 2015.

———. *L'io e il mondo: Un'interpretazione di Dante.* Bologna: Il Mulino, 2011.

———. "Il saluto di Beatrice." Festival del Medioevo (Gubbio, 25–29 September 2019). www.youtube.com/watch?v=HGiReLg4tVg.

Sarolli, Gian Roberto. "Il numero nelle opere di Dante." In *Enciclopedia dantesca,* 4:88–96. Rome: Istituto della Enciclopedia Italiana, 1973.

Sarteschi, Selene. "Guinizzelli nella prospettiva dantesca." In *Intorno a Guido Guinizzelli,* edited by Luciano Rossi and Sara Alloatti Boller, 137–53. Alessandria: Edizioni dell'Orso, 2002.

Sbacchi, Diego. "Le indicazioni orarie nella *Vita Nuova.*" *Lettere italiane* 67 (2015): 127–39.

———. "Sull'episodio del gabbo." *Rivista di letteratura italiana* 34, no. 3 (2016): 197–204.

Schwarz, Michael Viktor. "Giottos Dante, Dantes Giotto." In *Dante und die bildenden Künste,* edited by Maria Antonietta Terzoli and Sebastian Schütze, 163–84. Berlin: De Gruyter, 2016.

Scott, John. *Perché Dante?* 2nd ed. Rome: Aracne, 2017.

Sellgren, Rory. "Reading Dante's *Commedia* through Augustine's Hermeneutics of *Caritas.*" PhD diss., University of Leeds, 2019.

Simonelli, Maria. "'Donna pietosa' e 'Donna gentile' fra *Vita Nuova* e *Convivio.*" In *Atti del Convegno di studi su aspetti e problemi della critica dantesca,* 147–59. Rome: De Luca, 1967.

Singleton, Charles. *An Essay on the "Vita Nuova."* Cambridge, MA: Harvard University Press, 1958.

———. *"Vita Nuova* XII: Love's Obscure Words." *Romanic Review* 34 (1945): 89–102.

Skoda, Hannah. "Anger in *Inferno* and *Purgatorio.*" In *Dante and the Seven Deadly Sins,* edited by John C. Barnes and Daragh O'Connell, 125–50. Dublin: Four Courts Press, 2017.

Solimena, Adriana. *Repertorio metrico dei poeti siculo-toscani.* Palermo: Centro di studi filologici e linguistici siciliani, 2000.

———. *Repertorio metrico dello stil novo.* Rome: Presso la Società, 1980.

Southerden, Francesca. "The Lyric Mode." In *The Oxford Handbook of Dante,* edited by Manuele Gragnolati, Elena Lombardi, and Francesca Southerden, 546–62. Oxford: Oxford University Press, 2021.

Spitzer, Leo. "Bemerkungen zu Dantes *Vita Nuova.*" *Publications de la Faculté de lettres de l'Université d'Istanbul* 2, no. 1 (1937): 162–208.

———. "Osservazioni sulla *Vita Nuova* di Dante." In *Studi italiani,* edited by Claudio Scarpati, 95–146. Milan: Vita e pensiero, 1976.

Steinberg, Justin. *Accounting for Dante: Urban Readers and Writers in Late Medieval Italy.* Notre Dame, IN: University of Notre Dame Press, 2007.

———. "The Author." In *The Oxford Handbook of Dante,* edited by Manuele Gragnolati, Elena Lombardi, and Francesca Southerden, 3–16. Oxford: Oxford University Press, 2021.

———. "Brunetto Latini, *Rettorica,* ca. 1260: Introduction." In *Medieval Grammar and Rhetoric: Language and Literary Theory, AD 300–1475,* edited by Rita Copeland and Ineke Sluiter, 753–57. Oxford: Oxford University Press, 2009.

———. "La Compiuta Donzella e la voce femminile nel manoscritto Vat. Lat. 3793." *Giornale storico della letteratura italiana* 183 (2006): 1–31.

———. "Dante's First Dream between Reception and Allegory: The Response to Dante da Maiano in the *Vita nova.*" In *Dante the Lyric and Ethical Poet,* edited by Zygmunt G. Barański and Martin McLaughlin, 92–118. Oxford: Legenda, 2010.

Stillinger, Thomas C. *The Song of Troilus: Lyric Authority in the Medieval Book.* Philadelphia: University of Pennsylvania Press, 1992.

Stock, Brian. *The Implications of Literacy: Written Language and Models of Interpretation in the Eleventh and Twelfth Centuries.* Princeton, NJ: Princeton University Press, 1983.

Storey, H. Wayne. "Early Editorial Forms of Dante's Lyrics." In *Dante for the New Millennium,* edited by Teodolinda Barolini and H. Wayne Storey, 16–37. New York: Fordham University Press, 2003.

————. "Following Instructions: Remaking Dante's *Vita Nova* in the Fourteenth Century." In *Medieval Constructions in Gender and Identity: Essays in Honor of Joan M. Ferrante*, edited by Teodolinda Barolini, 117–32. Tempe: Arizona Center for Medieval and Renaissance Studies, 2005.

Symes, Carol. "Liturgical Texts and Performance Practices." In *Understanding Medieval Liturgy: Essays in Interpretation*, edited by Helen Gittos and Sarah Hamilton, 239–67. Farnham: Ashgate, 2016.

Szittya, Penn R. *The Antifraternal Tradition in Medieval Literature*. Princeton, NJ: Princeton University Press, 1986.

Tafuro, Antonio. "Bice di Folco Portinari." In *Beatrice donna di Dante: Amore dottrina estasi*, 142–69. Naples: Dante e Descartes, 2010.

Tambling, Jeremy. *Allegory*. London: Routledge, 2010.

————. "Thinking Melancholy: Allegory and the *Vita Nuova*." *Romanic Review* 96, no. 1 (2005): 85–105.

Tanturli, Giuliano. "Guido Cavalcanti contro Dante." In *Le tradizioni del testo*, edited by Franco Gavazzeni and Guglielmo Gorni, 3–13. Milan: Ricciardi, 1993.

Tateo, Francesco. "'Aprire per prosa.'" In *Questioni di poetica dantesca*, 51–75. Bari: Adriatica, 1972.

Tavoni, Mirko. "'Converebbe essere me laudatore di me medesimo': *Vita nova*, XXVIII.2." In *Studi in onore di Pier Vincenzo Mengaldo per i suoi settant'anni, a cura degli allievi padovani*, 2 vols., 1:253–61. Florence: SISMEL and Edizioni del Galluzzo, 2007.

————. *Qualche idea su Dante*. Bologna: Il Mulino, 2015.

————. "La visione interiore dalla *Vita nova* al *Convivio*." In *"Vedi il sol che 'n fronte ti riluce": La vista e i sensi in Dante e nella ricezione artistico-letteraria delle sue opere*, edited by Maria Maślanka-Soro, 43–66. Rome: Aracne, 2019.

Tisseron, Serge. "Intimité et extimité." *Communications* 88 (2011): 83–91.

Todorović, Jelena. *Dante and the Dynamics of Textual Exchange: Authorship, Manuscript Culture, and the Making of the "Vita Nova."* New York: Fordham University Press, 2016.

————. "Who Read the *Vita Nova* in the First Half of the Fourteenth Century?" *Dante Studies* 131 (2013): 197–217.

Tomazzoli, Gaia. "Il linguaggio figurato di Dante: Riflessioni teoriche e tipologie discursive." PhD diss., Università di Ca' Foscari, 2018.

Tonelli, Natascia. "Dante e la fisiologia dell'amore doloroso." In *Fisiologia della passione: Poesia d'amore e medicina da Cavalcanti a Boccaccio*, 71–124. Florence: SISMEL and Edizioni del Galluzzo, 2015.

———. *Fisiologia della passione: Poesia d'amore e medicina da Cavalcanti a Boccaccio*. Florence: SISMEL and Edizioni del Galluzzo, 2015.

———. "Medicine." In *The Oxford Handbook of Dante*, edited by Manuele Gragnolati, Elena Lombardi, and Francesca Southerden, 227–41. Oxford: Oxford University Press, 2021.

———. "I tempi della poesia, il tempo della prosa: A proposito di alcune visioni della *Vita nuova*." In *Vita nova. Fiore. Epistola XIII,* edited by Manuele Gragnolati, Luca Carlo Rossi, Paola Allegretti, Natascia Tonelli, and Alberto Casadei, 173–94. Florence: SISMEL and Edizioni del Galluzzo, 2018.

Took, John. "Dante and the *Confessions* of Augustine." *Annali d'Italianistica* 8 (1990): 360–82.

———. "Dante, Pride and the Gentle Dialectic of Love." In *Dante and the Seven Deadly Sins*, edited by John C. Barnes and Daragh O'Connell, 73–90. Dublin: Four Courts Press, 2017.

———. "Lady Philosophy." In *The Dante Encyclopedia*, edited by Richard Lansing, 551–53. New York: Garland, 2000.

Travers, Katherine. "Women in Medieval Italian Songbooks: From the *lenga d'oc* to the *lingua del sì*." PhD diss., New York University, 2021.

Turco, Jeffrey. "Restaging Sin in Medieval Florence: Augustine, Brunetto Latini, and the Streetscape of Dante's *Vita nuova*." *Italian Studies* 73, no. 1 (2018): 15–21.

Valency, Maurice. *In Praise of Love*. New York: Macmillan, 1961.

Valente, Vincenzo. "Ingegno." In *Enciclopedia dantesca*. Rome: Istituto della Enciclopedia Italiana, 1970. www.treccani.it/enciclopedia/ingegno_(Enciclopedia-Dantesca)/.

Vallone, Aldo. *Interpretazione della "Vita Nuova" di Dante*. Naples: Liguori, 1975.

———. *La prosa della "Vita Nuova."* Florence: Le Monnier, 1963.

Van Peteghem, Julie. *Italian Readers of Ovid from the Origins to Petrarch*. Leiden: Brill, 2020.

Vecce, Carlo. "Beatrice e il numero amico." In *Beatrice nell'opera di Dante e nella memoria europea, 1290–1990*, edited by Maria Picchio Simonelli, 101–35. Naples: Cadmo, 1994.

———. "'Ella era uno nove, cioè uno miracolo' (*VN* XXIX, 3): Il numero di Beatrice." In *"La gloriosa donna de la mente": A Commentary on the "Vita Nuova,"* edited by Vincent Moleta, 161–79. Florence: Olschki, 1997.

Vettori, Alessandro. "Veronica: Dante's Pilgrimage from Image to Vision." *Dante Studies* 121 (2003): 43–56.

Vickers, Nancy J. "Widowed Words: Dante, Petrarch, and the Metaphors of Mourning." In *Discourses of Authority in Medieval and Renaissance Literature*, edited by Kevin Brownlee and Walter Stephens, 97–108. Hanover, NH: University Press of New England, 1989.

Viegnes, Michel. "Space as Love in the *Vita nuova*." *Lectura Dantis* 4 (1989): 78–85.

Vignuzzi, Ugo. "Piacere." In *Enciclopedia dantesca*. Rome: Istituto della Enciclopedia Italiana, 1970. www.treccani.it/enciclopedia/piacere_(Enciclopedia -Dantesca)/.

Webb, Heather. *Dante's Persons: An Ethics of the Transhuman*. Oxford: Oxford University Press, 2016.

———. *The Medieval Heart*. New Haven, CT: Yale University Press, 2010.

Wedell, Moritz. "Numbers." In *The Handbook of Medieval Culture*, edited by Albrecht Classen, 1205–60. Berlin: De Gruyter, 2015.

Whitaker, William. *Words*. University of Notre Dame Archives. http://archives .nd.edu/words.html.

Whitman, Jon. *Allegory: The Dynamics of an Ancient and Medieval Technique*. Cambridge, MA: Harvard University Press, 1987.

Woods, Marjorie Currie. "Using the *Poetria nova* to Teach *Dictamen* in Italy and Central Europe." In *On Rhetoric V: Atti del Convegno Internazionale Dictamen, Poetria and Cicero: Coherence and Diversification*, edited by Lucia Calboli Montefusco, 261–79. Rome: Herder, 2003.

Zanoboni, Maria Paola. "Portinari, Folco." In *Dizionario Biografico degli Italiani*, 85:121–22. Rome: Istituto della Enciclopedia Italiana, 2016.

Zingarelli, Nicola. *Dante e Roma*. Rome: Loescher, 1895.

Zumthor, Paul. "The Text and the Voice." Translated by Marilyn C. Engelhardt. *New Literary History* 16, no. 1 (Autumn 1984): 67–92.

CONTRIBUTORS

Zygmunt G. Barański is Serena Professor of Italian Emeritus at the University of Cambridge and R. L. Canala Professor of Romance Languages and Literatures Emeritus at the University of Notre Dame.

David Bowe is an independent scholar and a member of the Centre for Dante Studies in Ireland.

Rebecca Bowen is postdoctoral research assistant at the University of Oxford on the Arts and Humanities Research Council project "Envisioning Dante."

Theodore J. Cachey Jr. is professor of Italian, Fabiano Collegiate Chair in Italian Studies, and Ravarino Family Director of Italian and Dante Studies at the University of Notre Dame.

Alessia Carrai is affiliated researcher in Italian at the University of Cambridge.

Ruth Chester is affiliated lecturer in Italian at the University of Cambridge.

K. P. Clarke is senior lecturer in medieval literature at the University of York.

Federica Coluzzi is Leverhulme Early Career Fellow at the University of Warwick.

Franco Costantini has recently completed a PhD in Italian at Sorbonne Université.

Nicolò Crisafi is teaching and research fellow in Italian and director of studies of Modern Languages at Pembroke College, Cambridge.

Lorenzo Dell'Oso is Alexander von Humboldt Postdoctoral Fellow at the University of Göttingen.

Peter Dent is senior lecturer in art history at the University of Bristol.

George Ferzoco is adjunct senior instructor in the Department of Classics and Religion in the University of Calgary, where he is also visiting fellow in the Calgary Institute for the Humanities.

Sophie V. Fuller is an independent scholar who completed her PhD on Dante and Statius at University College London in 2019.

Giulia Gaimari is postdoctoral fellow at the University of Toronto.

Filippo Gianferrari is assistant professor of literature at the University of California, Santa Cruz.

Simon Gilson is Agnelli-Serena Professor of Italian at the University of Oxford and fellow of Magdalen College.

Manuele Gragnolati is professor of Italian literature at Sorbonne Université, associate director of the ICI Berlin Institute for Cultural Inquiry, and senior research fellow at Somerville College, Oxford.

Marco Grimaldi is senior assistant professor of philology of Italian literature at the University of Rome "La Sapienza."

Claire E. Honess is visiting research fellow at the University of Leeds, where she was formerly professor of Italian studies.

Lachlan Hughes is a DPhil candidate at the University of Oxford and stipendiary lecturer in Italian at St Hilda's College, Oxford.

Tristan Kay is associate professor (reader) in Italian studies at the University of Bristol.

Catherine Keen is professor of Dante studies at University College London.

Aistė Kiltinavičiūtė is affiliated lecturer in Italian at the University of Cambridge.

Anne C. Leone is assistant professor of Italian studies at Syracuse University.

Rebekah Locke is an independent scholar who completed her PhD on the early reception of Dante's representation of Purgatory at the University of Bristol in 2020.

Elena Lombardi is professor of Italian literature at the University of Oxford and Paget Toynbee Fellow at Balliol College.

Luca Lombardo is senior assistant professor of philology of Italian literature at the University of Bergamo.

David G. Lummus is an independent scholar based in Rome.

Nicolò Maldina is senior assistant professor of Italian literature at the University of Bologna.

Valentina Mele is British Academy Postdoctoral Fellow at the University of Leeds.

Paola Nasti is associate professor of Italian at Northwestern University.

Daragh O'Connell is senior lecturer in Italian at University College Cork and director of the Centre for Dante Studies in Ireland.

Ryan Pepin is British Academy Postdoctoral Fellow at the University of York.

Helena Phillips-Robins is affiliated lecturer in Italian at the University of Cambridge.

Federica Pich is senior assistant professor of Italian literature at the University of Trento.

Katherine Powlesland is research associate on *Primo Levi: A Digital Commentary*, a project between the Universities of Cambridge and Notre Dame and King's College London.

Emily Kate Price is associate professor in French, Occitan, and Italian at Robinson College, University of Cambridge.

Brian Richardson is emeritus professor of Italian language at the University of Leeds.

Jennifer Rushworth is associate professor in French and comparative literature at University College London.

Chiara Sbordoni is adjunct professor of Italian at the University of Notre Dame Rome Global Gateway.

Francesca Southerden is associate professor of medieval Italian and tutorial fellow at Somerville College.

Matthew Treherne is professor of Italian literature at the University of Leeds.

Heather Webb is professor of Italian literature and culture at the University of Cambridge and fellow of Selwyn College.

INDEX